RESEARCH METHODS

IN COMMUNICATION

SECOND EDITION

RESEARCH METHODS
IN COMMUNICATION
SECOND EDITION

ISBN   978-1-885219-41-1

Vision Press
4195 Waldort Drive
P.O. Box 1106
Northport, AL 35476

Printed in the United States of America

RESEARCH METHODS

IN COMMUNICATION

SECOND EDITION

EDITORS

SHUHUA ZHOU & WM. DAVID SLOAN

University of Alabama

VISION V PRESS

ACKNOWLEDGMENTS

The authors and editors wish to thank the following individuals for their assistance in preparing this book:

Klaus Krippendorff for his comments on the draft of chapter 9 on content analysis

Edward J. Downes and Christiane M. Pagé for their comments on early drafts of chapter 22 on public relations research

Paula Quinn for her editorial guidance with chapter 23 on advertising research

Joanne Sloan and Cheryl Wray for reading the entire manuscript and making invaluable suggestions for improving its style and readability

CONTENTS

RESEARCH METHODS

IN COMMUNICATION

Fundamentals
of Research

Doing research is exciting, and the field of communication offers you a wide array of methods for doing it.

The methods range from those that employ elegant statistical formulas to those that rely on the creative thinking of the researcher. Some have been around for centuries while others have appeared in only the last few decades.

Whatever the method, though, all good research adheres to the same set of practices. Any research worth the name is *rigorous* and *systematic*, and the best researchers are *creative*. They understand how to use methods properly — and, from the information they gather, they are able to offer insight into important situations that we humans face and to advance our understanding of the world about us.

As you study the various methods explained in the chapters that follow, you may be tempted to think that communication methodology is just a hodgepodge of approaches, from legal research to opinion surveys and from historical research to experiments. Complicating the picture even more is the fact that each major method employs a variety of practices and strategies. But don't despair! Every method uses a logical structure and incorporates the same key steps.

So as you consider each method, it will help to keep the big picture in mind. It is this: Every good researcher is attempting to understand a situation, no matter the method employed, and does so by following these same steps:

1. Selecting a topic for investigation
2. Studying what other researchers have already learned
3. Gathering data
4. Analyzing the data
5. Providing an explanation of the findings

It's as simple as that!

To get you started, the six chapters in Part I will introduce you to the principles that are fundamental to all methods.

In Chapter 1, "The Nature and Purpose of Research," Prof. Shuhua Zhou of the University of Alabama begins by explaining what good research is — and what it isn't. The chapter will give you a primer on the various ways human beings acquire knowledge and explain how systematic research contributes to the way we know things. It will also explain the general categories of research and consider the differences and similarities between *quantitative* and *qualitative* methods.

In Chapter 2, "History of Research Methods," Prof. Dennis Davis of Pennsylvania State University provides an account of the development of methods and how they came into use in communication. The chapter will explain the nature of *empirical* methodology and show how it was a major breakthrough in the way humans acquire knowledge. The chapter will also trace how an important schism appeared a half-century ago in the ranks of communication researchers over the issue of quantitative versus qualitative methods. As Prof. Davis relates, however, that schism has begun to heal so that today's researchers have available a greater battery of methods than ever before.

In Chapter 3, "Research Ethics," Prof. Michael Ryan of the University of Houston explains why, even if a researcher has mastered the mechanics of methodology, research is legitimate only if "the process is fundamentally ethical and perceived as credible." The chapter will introduce you to the major ethics issues that confront communication research today. The bottom line is that researchers should not mistreat people or misuse research to advance or protect their own interests.

In Chapter 4, "The Library as a Research Source," Prof. Jim Pokrywczynski of Marquette University explains how to use the traditional "bricks and mortar" library along with the "library" that now goes by the name "Internet." The chapter covers the variety of important roles that libraries play in the research process. They are indispensable. This chapter will show you how to make the best use of them.

In Chapter 5, "Using Databases," Prof. Brian Parker of Florida State University focuses on the Internet and explains the types of material that databases contain and how to find the material you need in the most systematic and efficient manner. During a semester of study, time may be your most limited and valuable possession. The chapter will show you how to devise search strategies that will find what you want and need without clutter or waste.

In the final chapter in this first part of the book, "Bibliographies and Literature Reviews," Prof. David Davies of the University of Southern Mississippi explains the importance of knowing what other researchers have done before you try to do your own project. As he explains, the literature review "is a key element of your work." The chapter will take you step-by-step through the process of familiarizing yourself with other research that has been conducted on your topic. It will show you how to compile a bibliography with little wasted effort and then how to prepare a literature review for readers of your own research.

Anyone can do research. How well you do it is up to you. The chapters in Part I of this book will help you start thinking like a researcher. They will acquaint you with the basic knowledge you need as you begin that exciting, immensely satisfying endeavor called *research*.

1

The Nature and Purpose of Research

What is research?

The word *"research"* comes from the Middle French word "recherché," meaning to investigate carefully and thoroughly. Today, however, many people use the word to mean many different things. Your dad is proud to announce that his purchase of an iPad is the result of thorough research. Your nine-year-old brother claims he has researched Benjamin Franklin's life. Your roommate may tell you that she has done some "research" before she decides to take the research methods class.

What your roommate calls "research," of course, is nothing more than talking to people who have taken the methods class to ask if the subject is interesting (or boring), if the professor is a tough (or easy) grader, and if the course deals with math (or not). Your dad, on the other hand, has done some comparisons between the iPad and other tablet computers and decides that the slick design and light weight are worth the higher price tag. Your little brother has collected some information about Ben Franklin and knows that he was more than a politician.

Strictly speaking, these endeavors, as laudable as they are, are not research. Formal research is not the rummaging of information, nor should it be a catchword to get people's attention. For example, you may hear on TV that a cold medicine is the product of "years of research." Yet it functions exactly like *Tylenol Cold*. Pharmaceutical manufacturers make a lot of money because they know we trust research.

Real research is a *systematic process* to seek answers to questions and understanding of phenomena. Ultimately, research is a way to achieve certainty. Human beings love certainty. Businesses will make profits if they are certain that things are rosy and positive. Advertisers are willing to shell out $4 million for a 30-second spot in the Super Bowl telecast if they are certain that it will return a profit.

You may have heard that psychologists talk about *"psychological discomfort"* when we live in uncertainty (Galinsky, Stone & Cooper, 2000). This discom-

By Shuhua Zhou
University of Alabama

3

fort may occur at many levels. You will feel uncomfortable if you don't know whether you will pass a test or not. The whole country may be jittery about the unsettling economy. Planet Earth won't be at ease if we can't find solutions to global warming. Uncertainty arises with the lack of information.

Conversely, certainty comes with information. The better the quality of information, the more certainty it will afford. When information is fishy, little certainty may be warranted. Research, when conducted rigorously, provides verifiable information and, subsequently, certainty.

WAYS OF KNOWING

There are, of course, many ways to obtain information in addition to systematic research. These attempts to acquire knowledge are known as *ways of knowing* (Hatton & Plouffe, 1996). There are many ways to knowing, including *authority*, *personal experience*, *tenacity* (or *tradition*), *intuition* and the *scientific method*. Let's look at each one.

Knowing by Authority

Knowing through an *authority* is one of the most common ways to acquire knowledge. We go to school because there are teachers and professors, who are experts (hopefully) on particular subjects. We check the library for books written by authorities. We ask our accountants for tax tips. We call the plumber if our toilet gets stuck. When we are sick, we go to our doctors, who presumably know more than we do about certain diseases. Troubled stars, who have brushes with the law, resort to their attorneys with legal knowledge to cover their acts rather than betting on their star power to save them. In other words, the method of authority means learning through the assumed expertise of another person.

Often, the method of authority is a very efficient and quick way of finding answers. This method, however, is not without its pitfalls. Authorities may have areas in which they are usually correct, but they aren't infallible.

Authorities are human beings, and they can be biased. How many times have we seen "experts" disagree on television on matters ranging from constitutional law and economic policies, to dietary and fashion choices? Worse yet, even in criminal cases, expert witnesses on both sides often contradict each other regarding a particular set of evidence. Sometimes experts are not really offering their expertise. Rather, they are presenting their personal opinions. Some expert reviewers may rate a movie as a "thumbs up," others as a "thumbs down." Doctors asked to advertise a brand name drug may very well know that the generic version is just as effective, but they will recommend the brand name as part of their endorsement contract.

The problem with authorities stems from the assumption that, by virtue of their status as authorities, we can generalize their expertise to include the questions we ask. Athletes are featured in TV commercials selling shoes, soups, hamburgers and underwear. They have expertise in their own athletic fields, all right, but their knowledge of soups, hamburgers, underwear and even shoes may not be much better than our own. However, advertisers would like us to accept their recommendations based on their authority. People do accept the words of an authority without questioning them, especially when they seem to make sense.

Knowing by Personal Experience

Another valuable tool to acquire knowledge is through *personal experience*, which is learning through the five senses, particularly seeing, touching and hearing.

For example, a person may hold a much stronger opinion against drug abuse if she has seen friends or family members plagued by marijuana, alcohol or tobacco. She has witnessed first-hand how such irresponsible behaviors increase the cost for health care, create discord in the family and even ruin the lives of addicts.

Many Americans learn about other countries from the mass media. We may not realize that anytime an African country makes it to the media, it is probably because of an earthquake or a famine having struck the country. As such, our perception of Africa centers around skinny children, swarms of flies and devastated villages. However, those who personally visit the continent may leave with the images of the mighty Sahara, beautiful Ethiopia and happy Zimbabweans. Personal experience is direct knowledge. Sometimes there may be no substitute for this unmediated method of knowing.

However, personal experience is not without its bias. Because it is heavily dependent on our senses, it may lead to skewed perceptions or misconceptions. Our senses have limits.

For example, our hearing is different from that of other animals. We hear sounds of a limited range of frequency but miss others. Depending on their depth of knowledge, cultural orientation and experience, two people looking at the same object may come to different conclusions. After watching the same presidential debate, Republicans and Democrats often argue which candidate won. Also, humans have a strong, biased trust of personal experience. A Chinese proverb says that those who have been bitten by a snake once are afraid of a rope for ten years. My son refuses to eat a mango because when he was three he ate a mango and then got sick. He did not know that, at the time, he was actually coming down with a virus. He avoids the fruit now because the thought of eating it turns his stomach. Similarly, if you see that your neighbor's Lexus couldn't start the other day, you might believe that the Lexus is not a reliable car in spite of years of evidence to the contrary.

Knowing by Tenacity

The method of *tenacity* is in operation when people are comfortable with a belief that has been held for a long time. Knowledge passed down from generation to generation is a source of tenacious information. So the method of tenacity is sometimes called the method of *tradition*. Tradition in its most extreme form becomes the method of habits and superstitions. In other words, tenacity describes a willingness to accept something as true because it has been accepted for a long time. For many centuries, people believed the earth to be flat and that the sun revolved around it, until it was proven otherwise by Galileo. We also believe that eating carrots is good for our eyes. An apple a day keeps the doctor away, and breakfast is the most important meal of the day. These claims have been repeated again and again, and they have been accepted as true. You may often wonder why advertisers spend millions of dollars to repeat the same commercial. Well, it is their hope that enough repetition and exposure will lead consumers to believe the messages to be true.

Obviously, human beings have accumulated reservoirs of knowledge over the years. So the method of tenacity has a lot of validity. Much of the knowledge that our predecessors acquired has been tested and retested.

One problem with the method of tenacity, though, is that the information may not be accurate just because it's been believed for a long time. Take cultural perceptions of the moon. Traditionally, Americans imagine the figure of a man's face on the moon. The Chinese see a man watering flowers. In other words, different people can hold different, contradictory views. But they can't all be right. Recall the statements that eating carrots is good for our eyes, that an apple a day keeps the doctor away, and that breakfast is the most important meal of the day. All of them may be true to a degree. But the evidence to support them is not conclusive.

Knowing by Intuition

The method of *intuition*, on the other hand, is fast and quick. It relies on information accepted on the basis of a hunch or "gut" feeling. With this method, people are not using much logic. Rather they take information because it feels "right." Imagine you are going on a blind date. Upon the first sight of your date, you may tell yourself "this is it!" or "what a disappointment!" This is your intuition talking to you. In this method, people's behaviors may show a degree of consistency, or internal logic. In other words, years of learning and experience may have taught you something. You are using "psycho-logic" — that is, your behavior is determined by psychological factors, not strictly logical factors.

Obviously, the method of intuition is subjective, leaving itself vulnerable to chances of misconception and mistakes.

Knowing by the Scientific Method

Recognizing that personal experience, intuition and traditional and cultural beliefs influence both our perceptions and our interpretations of natural phenomena, researchers aim through the use of standard procedures and criteria to minimize those influences when acquiring knowledge and developing a theory. *Systematic research* attempts to minimize the influence of bias or prejudice of the researcher when testing a hypothesis or a theory.

There are many ways through which systematic research can be conducted. One of them is the traditional, social science approach, which will be covered extensively in the following paragraphs. Bear in mind, though, that not all communication researchers consider themselves "scientists," although their research is rigorous and systematic.

That being said, the *scientific method* embodies a systematic and objective set of techniques to investigate phenomena. In the process, new knowledge may be acquired. Old knowledge may be corrected. Or old knowledge may be integrated into new knowledge. The scientific method is the process by which researchers, collectively and over time, endeavor to construct an accurate representation of the world.

Although procedures vary from one field of inquiry to another, identifiable features distinguish scientific inquiry from other methodologies of knowledge. Scientific researchers propose hypotheses as explanations of phenomena and design studies to test these hypotheses. These steps must be repeatable, or replicable, in order to reliably predict any future results. If you don't believe a particular researcher, you can follow the same procedures and see for yourself whether the results are true or not. If the studies are conducted solidly, the conclusions ought to hold irrespective of the researcher's state of mind, religious belief or cultural background. A theory is not accepted based on its proponent's authoritative status. Rather, it is developed based upon the results and evidence obtained through repeated observations.

CHARACTERISTICS OF THE SCIENTIFIC METHOD

There are several *characteristics* that distinguish the scientific method. Let's look at each of them.

The Public Nature of Science

Science is *public*. The basic expectation for the scientific method is to document, archive and share all data and methodology so it is available for careful scrutiny by other scientists, thereby allowing other researchers the opportunity to verify results by attempting to reproduce them. You may ask why we need to reproduce, or *replicate*, a study. It sounds like a waste of resources. However, the goal of replication is to test the validity of the original study. When the results repeat themselves, they lend support to the original study. When the results do not duplicate, they cast doubt on the original study, or the current study, which calls for more repetitions.

Researchers make their observations public by publishing reports of their projects. In order to publish an article in a journal, an author has to submit a paper to the editor of a journal. The editor then selects two or more "judges," or established scholars who have conducted similar studies in the area of study, to review the article and to evaluate whether the study is conducted with rigor and whether the conclusions are warranted. In any typical paper, there is a method section in which the author specifies how the study was carried out, what procedures were followed, who was in the study, what instruments and apparatus were used and what kind of analytical tools were used. In sum, enough details should be given so others can repeat the study without difficulty.

The Objective Nature of Science

Science is also *objective*. As stated earlier, the scientific method attempts to minimize the influence of the scientist's bias and personal beliefs. That is, when conducting a study, such as testing a hypothesis or a theory, the scientist may have a preference for one outcome or another, and it is important that this preference not bias the results or the interpretation. You may have heard of the so-called hostile media, or the belief that the media are biased when they present information contradictory to your opinions. Apparently, whether the media are hostile or not partly depends on the person making the judgment. In a scientific study, we need to minimize perceptual bias, if there is no way to completely eliminate it. For example, if you are conducting a study on media bias, you need to design a measurement instrument so that anyone who uses the instrument, whether ideologically left or right, should come to the same conclusions. A solid inquiry must invariably be objective to reduce a biased interpretation of the results.

The Empirical Nature of Science

Science is *empirical*. The word "empirical" is easy to understand when it applies to the hard sciences such as physics, chemistry, biology and astronomy. When we say science is empirical, we mean that science studies natural phenomena that are observable and measurable, such as the speed of a Formula One race car, an atom or a rocket, or the patterns of planetary movement and the reaction of chemicals.

When applied to the so-called "soft sciences," it is a lot harder to understand. Communication and most other areas of social science, such as anthropology, psychology, political science and social work, involve the study of human social life. In these fields, "empirical" means that social scientists gather data using specialized tools in the social sciences to test hypotheses and theories. Data are the objective, empirical evidence or information we collect according to a set of rules and procedures. These data can be *quantitative*, such as heart rates to indicate attention, number of people voting Republican or Democrat in a presidential election, and the amount of clothing that a commercial model wears. Or data can be *qualitative*, such as the rhetoric of a political discourse, the expressiveness of a pictorial cartoon, and the manifestation of hegemony in a TV program. In other words, some of the phenomena can be observed directly, such as newscast format, layout of the newspaper or the use of minorities in a TV commercial. Other phenomena in social sciences may not be directly observable, such as cultural hegemony.

In other words, empirical evidence in social science is not limited to observations. We can also "observe" phenomena indirectly through direct observation of their impact on human and social institutions. At other times, when we encounter an abstract idea, we try to link it in the empirical world to something directly observable. Arousal, for example, is a concept that can be measured by self-reporting, by having judges make an assessment or by observing change in skin conductance.

That being said, science is not suitable to study supernatural phenomena such as mysteries, ghosts, spells and divination. For one thing, believers in the supernatural world and believers in the natural world do no share the same assumptions. Supernatural phenomena are believed to exist outside of the natural world and operate by a separate set of laws governing them. Some people look at the complexity and the mysteries of the universe and propose that a supernatural entity, or entities, are governing the universe. Naturalists, however, believe that humans cannot explain some events and happenings only because our knowledge is still limited, just as some of our ancestors did not understand thunder and lightning and ascribed them to supernatural forces. On the other hand, if there are indeed supernatural events, we ought not to be able to observe the cause behind them. When an event is observable, it ceases to be supernatural.

The Systematic Nature of Science

Science is *systematic*. Conducting research using the scientific method has to be systematic in all facets of the process. Conducting a study takes meticulous planning. Scientific research is not an excursion into happy expectation. Nor can we hope that results will eventually come our way. Instead, we need to carefully identify a worthy area of study that is interesting and important, thoroughly explicate the concepts in the study, define them conceptually and operationally, develop a solid method to collect data, use appropriate tests to analyze the data, isolate the variables of interests, control for other competing explanations and draw a conclusion based on the evidence.

Systematic research means studies are carried out according to certain rules. One such rule is to review the literature to see what has been done in the past on the particular topic under study so a researcher does not start from scratch. Based on that body of knowledge, a researcher designs a study that is explicit and logically sound. In other words, researchers build their study and plan their designs in a purposeful manner so the data collected address the questions at hand.

The Cumulative Nature of Science

Finally, science is *cumulative*. Only when results are replicated can we say that they have validity. When studies are replicable, different researchers working on the same problem can contribute knowledge to the area.

By cumulative, we also mean that scientific knowledge is gathered over long periods of time, involving various methods and means, by different people in the scientific community. Kuhn (1977) described science as puzzle-solving activities by a group according to agreed-upon rules in order to learn about natural phenomena. Different people may come up with different parts of the solution. Together the solutions help solve the puzzle. These solutions may be viewed as theories or models of the phenomena.

In order to solve a puzzle, we have to look at every piece, and when we have a solution, we need to test the solution to see if it works every time. To translate these processes into scientific terms: there is a process called *theory building*, and there is another called *theory testing*. When enough efforts are made in these processes, we build up our knowledge about the puzzle and about the validity of the solutions. Our knowledge increases, or accumulates.

FAIRNESS AND RIGOR

Even though many researchers in communication do not claim to use scientific methods, most employ practices that rely on solid evidence and that are intended to provide a clear, unbiased account.

It is true that some researchers — such as those in critical studies — make no bones about bringing their own views to their research. Most communication scholars, though, do attempt to be fair and judicious in their research. Legal researchers, for example, have not attempted to develop a "scientific" methodology simply because their subject does not lend itself to such methods. Yet, they use a systematic approach in collecting and analyzing evidence, with the purpose of providing an accurate account of the law.

In fact, all good researchers attempt to be rigorous, thorough and fair.

HOW RESEARCH CONTRIBUTES TO KNOWLEDGE

We stated that all methods of learning help us build confidence by acquiring knowledge and arriving at certain levels of certainty. People who study epistemology, however, will tell you that there are different kinds of knowledge. Namely, there are three main kinds: propositional knowledge, acquaintance knowledge and how-to knowledge (Lemos, 2007). Let's look briefly at each one.

Types of Knowledge

Propositional knowledge is a recognition that one has processed certain information before and that one is aware of that body of knowledge. *Acquaintance knowledge* is information acquired through actual contact, and *how-to knowledge* is procedural knowledge.

For example, when someone says "I know TV production," that person may mean that she has read a book about TV production and knows that it involves professional skills as well as a sense of aesthetics. But she may have never touched a camera. In this case, we say that she has propositional or "that" knowledge. The same person may also mean that she has been involved with a production company for ten years and has operated a camera and sat at the editing bay. In other words, she has propositional and acquaintance knowledge about production. After a couple of successful projects, she also learns how to direct a production and manage a crew. She is then entitled to claim that she has the how-to knowledge of production, which involves conceptualizing, directing, shooting and editing.

Here is another example. When I make the claim that "I know soccer," there are a lot of things that can be implied by this statement. I may mean that I have an encyclopedia knowledge of the game of soccer (proposition knowledge). I may also mean that, through repeated exposure to the game of soccer on TV, I know how the game of soccer is played, what formation is good for Argentina and how players such as Messi can be best utilized (acquaintance knowledge). But if I have never touched a soccer ball, I would still not have how-to knowledge.

As can be seen, knowledge is a complex and intricate matter. To relate this back to methods of inquiry, we can see that certain methods are good at acquiring certain types of knowledge. The method of tradition imparts a lot of propositional ("that") knowledge. The method of personal experience affords us good "acquaintance knowledge." The method of authority may offer reliable "that" and "how-to" knowledge. The method of intuition may provide a little bit of each. When we examine the scientific method, however, we can see that it does well on at least two if not so much on "how-to" knowledge. In doing a literature review, we learn what has been done before. In conducting a study, we come to know our subject matter and how to accumulate knowledge.

How a Research Course Helps You Build Knowledge

Given that systematic research is necessary as a way to acquire reliable knowledge, you still may want to know why you are taking a research methods class, other than the dubious reason that it's required. Indeed, many students take a course in methods because they have to. Some students choose to major in communication because they are afraid of math and hate to deal with numbers. They see courses such as research methods as an academic hurdle. But a course in research methods does not have to be difficult. Instead it should help you in many different ways.

First of all, communication is both an art and a science. You major in communication because you know how important it is to communicate effectively. Millions of dollars are spent for a 30-second commercial during the Super Bowl. You can bet that those footing the bills would like to know how to make an effective commercial. Governments would welcome research findings on persuasive communication strategies during a health crisis.

Communication scholars use systematic methods to study, gather and interpret communication information. A methods course will introduce you to these rigorous processes.

For example, in order to study media violence and its effects on viewers' aggression, researchers need to observe viewers, especially children, after exposure to media such as violent programs and violent video games. A researcher would need to decide exactly what characteristics to observe. Kicking, punching and hitting behaviors are sensible choices. But she can also observe verbal violence. Or she can measure children's attitudes toward violence. Are they being more callous after exposure? Are they endorsing the use of force to solve problems? She can also measure children's physiological response to violence to see if they are more excited and emotionally charged when they are watching violent scenes. In order to measure these responses, she would need to develop a system of objective and accurate observation and carefully plan a study to rule out other influences on aggression, such as personality or poverty, so that she could say whether media violence causes aggression in real life.

After you take this course and have a basic understanding of methods, it will be easier for you to appreciate what researchers have discovered about communication.

Secondly, for many students, who will be journalists, advertising professionals and other communication specialists, a grasp of research terminology and logic will allow you to understand research articles and research results. When a pharmaceutical company hands you, the local star reporter, a research report on a newly developed drug, the knowledge you will gain through a research course will allow you to read and critically evaluate the research findings. Similarly, if you are an advertising professional trying to decide whether to use an emotional or a rational approach to lure customers, you might review research articles that examine the effectiveness of different approaches for the kind of product you are trying to sell.

Finally, a research methods course will also add to your arsenal of critical thinking skills. Because methods are techniques people develop over the years to find answers, they are reliable ways of inquiry. A methods course will teach you to think systematically, define concepts, design a study, interpret results and discuss weaknesses. It is a thinking exercise that can only strengthen your reasoning ability, improve your analytical skills and help you make better decisions.

TYPES OF RESEARCH

As you leaf through journals and class readings, you may notice that there are very different research methodologies and approaches. There are different ways to categorize research: *exploratory* vs. *explanatory* research; *inductive* vs. *deductive* research; *basic* vs. *applied* research; and *qualitative* vs. *quantitative* research.

Exploratory Research

As the name implies, *exploratory* research usually takes place when the researcher first stumbles into an area where little previous research exists. The researcher has no way of knowing where the research leads and what she may find. Let's say the researcher is interested in finding out about the appeal and impact of secondlife.com (a website that allows users to assume an imagined and coveted role in virtual life). New technology today apparently allows us to venture into new, imagined domains in a way that was impossible before; and little research is available when you search for it via Google. In this case, the researcher is doing preliminary research. Years ago when people began to research the idea of "presence," or how big screen, high definition TV could transport viewers to be part of depicted scenes, they had to explicate the concept first (Lombard & Ditton, 1997). Thus, they analyzed how many dimensions that concept entails before they could study what "presence" could do to people. In other words, exploratory research is interested in addressing the "what" question. What is this concept of "presence" really about?

Exploratory studies are difficult to conduct because so little is known. But they can also be creative, open-minded, flexible and fun to carry out. In effect, exploratory studies try to present a description of a phenomenon and draw a picture of it. The more accurate the picture is, the more successful the studies are.

Explanatory Research

Once researchers have a picture of the phenomenon at hand, they may wonder why things are the way they are. *Explanatory* studies are interested in addressing the "why" question instead of the "what" question. They build on exploratory studies. Many studies, for example, have found that sex is used in television commercials. In attempting to understand why, an explanatory study may uncover that sex gets our attention. It may also discover that sex is a positive stimulus and that this positive feeling may transfer to the advertised product so that its image is enhanced. It may also find that using sexy models is just an easy way to create a commercial in the absence of more creative ideas (Reichert, 2003).

Inductive Research

We can also categorize research as inductive or deductive. Such categorizing is closely related to the research objective — whether it's conducted to build or to test theories. *Inductive research* is central to theory building, in which the researcher begins to observe and collect evidence. In this process, the researcher finds patterns and reaches a general conclusion based on specific cases. For example, suppose you try a tangerine and discover that it's sweet and juicy. A second tangerine is also sweet and juicy, and so is the third. You are then tempted to draw the conclusion that tangerines are sweet and juicy. Note that your inductive reasoning has reached a conclusion far beyond your observations of three tangerines to include all tangerines. If repeated observations yield the same conclusion, then a theory is in the works.

One of the better known inductive concepts in communication is the cultivation theory stating that people who watch a lot of TV tend to hold worldviews similar to those presented on television. Researchers, for example, find that many TV programs contain violence and that much of television focuses on the negative rather than the positive. They also show that, by the age of 18, most people will have witnessed about 20,000 murders on TV. Furthermore, the more a person is exposed to television, the more s/he tends to think the world is bad, resulting in the so-called "mean-world syndrome." Based on multiple observations of exposure effects, researchers reached inductive conclusions to propose the cultivation theory (Gerbner et. al. 1979).

Deductive Research

Based on cultivation theory, you can deduce that your roommate, who is glued to the box all the time, must have a pretty gloomy worldview. This thinking process is known as deductive reasoning. You begin with a universal statement and then make a specific prediction. To put it another way, in a *deductive approach*, you use a theory as the basis for reaching a conclusion about empirical data. Based on Newton's gravity theory, for example, you can predict that if an apple falls, it will fall to the ground, and that the same is true of an orange, a mango, a lichee or a durian, even though you may not have known or tasted these fruits.

Deductive research is complementary to inductive research. The two processes work together to refine our knowledge of the universe.

However, enough inductive research needs to be conducted so we can be sure that our conclusion is not aberrant. The worst thing that can happen in research is that you are observing a few very peculiar cases, but you think they are normal. If so, the conclusion you have is aberrant. It will not be sustainable in the long run. For example, just because you go out for a few consecutive nights and observe that there is no moon in the sky, you can't jump to the conclusion that the moon does not exist. It is very likely that the nights of your observation are really cloudy and that the thick, dark clouds prevent you from observing the moon.

Along a similar vein, enough deductive research has to be conducted to test a theory before the theory is said to be valid. Over the years, people have used Newton's gravity theory to predict the falling patterns of apples, durians, basketballs and every imaginable object in the earth's atmosphere. In all instances, the theory holds true. So the theory of gravity on planet earth is still sustainable. Similarly, to test the cultivation theory, you can use people of different demographics and exposure patterns to see if the prediction still holds true.

Inductive research and deductive research form the *circle of science*. Researchers often say that one study does not prove anything. Only when results replicate can we say that evidence supports a theory. This is the idea that we mentioned a few pages back: that science is cumulative. In the quest for knowledge, we begin with inductive research by looking at data, discovering patterns and reaching generalizations. We then use a generalization as a basis for predicting what data will be generated — that is, deducing an outcome based on a general rule. So the tests and retests go on. If everything goes fine, the theory receives support and is upheld. If evidence and data do not support the theory, more inductive and deductive research should be conducted either to refute or refine the theory, so that we can get closer to the truth.

Basic Research

From a practical perspective, we can also categorize research as *basic* or *applied*.

Basic research advances human knowledge about the universe we are living in. In communication research, it focuses on building or refuting theories that explain why communication works. It deals with such questions as what constitutes communication? What makes it happen? Why is communication necessary, and what role does it play in society and human life?

Many people fail to see the benefit of basic research. Because it does not solve specific, practical problems, they consider it a waste of time. In fact, it is usually ahead of its time. Basic research is akin to race cars. Manufacturers spend billions on refining their race cars, not only to win a race, but also to advance their knowledge and technology on the mechanics of car making so they will eventually build better, faster and more efficient cars for everyday use. Today's computer would have been impossible without the pure and basic research in mathematics conducted decades ago. Major scientific breakthroughs usually occur with basic research, because its significance is far-reaching and applicable in many domains.

Applied Research

Applied research, on the other hand, has immediate worldly implications. It is usually conducted because of a specific problem for a limited setting. Say, an Atlanta television station wants to increase the number of crawls, or running captions at the bottom of the screen, to maximize advertising exposure. It can hire a research firm to test if people are retaining any information from crawls, or are annoyed by them. While basic research is mostly theoretical, applied research can be both theoretical and descriptive. But it tends to be descriptive. The important distinction really is its practical use.

Qualitative and Quantitative Research

Although much of our discussion has focused on the scientific method, we must be aware that many researchers in communication use other methods. A perennial and hot debate centers on the advantages and disadvantages of *qualitative* and *quantitative* research. The difference between the two is that quantitative research uses numbers and qualitative research uses non-numbers.

We are all familiar with GPAs, used to measure academic performance. When we say Mr. Black is a 4.0 student, we are making a quantified statement about his scholastic achievement. Similarly, when we say Mr. Smith is a 2.0 student, we are also making a statement about his mediocre performance in school.

Note, however, that academic performance is not something inherently numerical. Qualitatively, we can say Black is a brilliant student and that Smith is an average student. But quantification does make our observation more concrete. University admission officers often use GPAs as a yardstick, along with other indicators, to make acceptance or rejection decisions. Departments also require students to maintain a certain GPA before they can enroll in high-level classes. Quantification makes university officials' job easier. In research, it makes summarizing data simple, and it opens up the data to other statistical analyses and models.

But quantification sometimes loses some nuances of the data. A GPA, for example, may not measure a student's creativity. It does not take into account how many jobs a student may have to juggle. Former President George W. Bush is famously quoted as saying that a C student can also be President. He may have a point. A 4.0 student is not the equivalent of a genius. Similarly, a C student may be bright, but have difficulty taking tests. By and large, however, the chance of a student with a perfect GPA being a dimwit is slim; and the probability of a C student being a genius is low.

In general, quantification does its job nicely. But it does not always capture the whole meaning. In painting, for example, it is the highly artistic painter who may use the fewest strokes to express the most, the so-called "less is more." Now try to quantify that! Imagine a hundred students with perfect GPA's. Some are sure to be brighter than others. Some may be stellar in arts, others in science. When we qualitatively say someone is smart, there is quite a bit of ambiguity there and the richness of meaning manifests itself exactly because of that ambiguity.

THE QUALITATIVE VS. QUANTITATIVE DEBATE

Given the differences in perspective and approaches between qualitative and quantitative research, the natural question is which one to choose: Qualitative or quantitative research?

Fortunately, we don't have to choose. Both methods are legitimate and useful in research. The two should be complementary, rather than competitive, as some would like you to think and believe. In fact, there is considerable ill will between some practitioners of both styles of research, with quantitative researchers insisting their standards be applied to qualitative research and qualitative researchers insisting theirs be applied to quantitative data. There are individuals on both sides who claim that the only legitimate methods are the ones they use. However, it is clear that finding fault with each other does not advance research or our knowledge.

Most of the misunderstanding can be attributed to a lack of knowledge of the other approach. Many people feel comfortable doing what they do, and they simply cease to venture into unfamiliar territories. Thus, it is a positive sign that more and more researchers are beginning to apply both approaches. However, the two approaches do have fundamentally different philosophical underpinnings and assumptions, and the methods they use are quite different.

How People Perceive Reality

Take the concept of reality, for example. Quantitative researchers assume that there is an objective, single reality.

Think about Stanford University. A quantitative researcher will describe it as a university that consistently ranks in the top five in the country, that is located about 40 miles from San Francisco, that has a highly competitive admission rate of around 10-15% and that has more graduate students than undergraduate students. Some qualitative researchers may take a different view and contend that that there is no single reality about Stanford that is alone correct, that each person socially constructs the reality of Stanford based on his/her knowledge and experience of the institution. Those who are graduates of Stanford, for instance, have a very different perception of the university than those who are not. The people who have gone through the "Full Moon in the Quad," a student party at Stanford's Main Quad where seniors exchange kisses with freshmen, have a much more dramatic story to tell about Stanford than those who are from elsewhere.

Positivism and Constructivism

These differing views of reality are closely tied to the perspectives of *positivism* and *constructivism*. A *positivist* believes in evidence gathered through the perception of our senses. A *constructivist* believes that humans actively make sense of what is happening around them. A positivist believes that reality is single and tangible. A constructivist believes there are multiple realities and that each person constructs his/her reality. You may often hear people ask "if a tree falls in the deep forest, does it make a sound?" To a positivist, there is no question that the tree made a sound because, when a tree falls, it makes a sound, and there is evidence that it did fall. A constructivist says the answer depends on whether there can be sound in the absence of ears to hear it.

A positivist tries to distance the researcher from observation, so that personal bias does not enter into the data collection process. The best positivist research should be value free. In fact, a study should be designed such that anyone who wants to replicate the study should be able to do so, regardless of such things as the person's religion, ideology or sexual orientation. A constructivist, on the other hand, maintains that all inquiries are value-bound because all interpretation and construction of meanings depend on the individual researcher. In that sense, the researcher, rather than questionnaires, scales and other measures, is the data collection instrument. No human beings, of course, can proceed without values.

Constructivists try to offer rich, contextual information so the interpretation of events can be more complete and accurate. One of the arguments of qualitative research is that human communication and behavior are significantly influenced by the setting in which they occur. Thus, one must study them in situations. A person communicates in a particular manner depending on such matters as the environment she is in, the group characteristics that are prominent at the time, the educational level of the audience and the political climate of the time. This complexity requires that the researcher document these situational variables as thoroughly as possible and take them into account in the process of interpretation. For better understanding of the situation, the researcher also takes an insider's perspective by immersing herself as part of the observation. This is believed to be ideal because the researcher can learn the most about a situation by participating in it.

On the other hand, the positivist tries to make sense of the world by classifying features, quantifying them and constructing statistical models based on probabilities in an attempt to explain what is observed. The positivist tries to use precise measurement to sort out complexities so that a meaningful, widely acceptable conclusion can be reached based on multiple observations. For objective reasons, the positivist takes an outsider's perspective by detaching herself from the observation, trying to avoid personal influence on the observation.

Qualitative and Quantitative Differences

Qualitative researchers can be both imaginative and rigorous. However, because of its exploratory nature, qualitative research tends to be inductive. It is often open-ended. Sometimes the researcher does not know where an inquiry will lead. Often, methods emerge as the project develops. The researcher may be more interested in the process than the outcome, which is open to interpretation anyway. It is the way people interpret meaning that is of most interest to the researcher.

On the other hand, quantitative research can be either inductive or deductive. But most quantitative research is deductive because its goal is to test and confirm hypotheses. Methods are pre-determined and carefully planned. The researcher knows exactly what she is looking for.

Table 1 summarizes the differences between qualitative and quantitative research in general. As you consider the list of characteristics, keep in mind that these are the characteristics that *generally* apply but that individual researchers using specific methods may be exceptions. For example, some scientific inquiry is based on the values of the researcher, and some researchers using qualitative methods attempt to remain objectively detached from their research.

RESEARCH STEPS

Regardless of the kind of research, whether qualitative or quantitative, good researchers follow certain steps to conduct their investiga-

Table 1. Comparison of Quantitative and Qualitative Characteristics

Quantitative Research	Qualitative Research
Assumptions: • One objective reality • Inquiry is value free • Quantifiable measurement	**Assumptions** • Multiple subjective realities • Inquiry is value-bound • Quality interpretation
Role of Researcher: • Objective observer • Objective description	**Role of Researcher:** • Participant • Empathic understanding
Goals: • Situation-free generalization • Prediction	**Goals:** • Contextualization • Situational Interpretation
Approaches: • Positivism • Induction and deduction • Objective instrument • Data reduced to numerical indices • Pre-planned design	**Approaches:** • Constructivism • Induction • Researcher as instrument • Uses non-numerical description • Emergent design

tion. Usually, the researcher (1) moves from a general idea to a narrower topic, (2) develops a methodology to approach the topic, (3) collects data or begins field work, (4) analyzes data or observations, (5) interprets results and (6) draws conclusions. In this process, the researcher is faced with a series of decisions about how to proceed. Here are the *basic steps of research*:

1. Identify a research topic
2. Conduct a literature review
3. Select a research design
4. Collect the data
5. Analyze data
6. Draw conclusions
7. Report results
8. Replicate the study

Let's look at each step.

Identifying a Research Topic

First, you need a research idea to begin with. Simply getting started is a problem for many researchers. Sometimes they don't know whether the research topic is feasible or not. Sometimes they get an idea, but they wonder if it is a valid one or if it has been researched thoroughly already.

To start this process, it is always a good idea to pick a topic that you are interested in. Research is a long and demanding process. If you don't have intrinsic interest in the topic, it can be a pain.

Research ideas can come from a variety of sources. They can come from practical problems in the field. For example, you wonder if crawls, or running captions, on the TV screen distract viewers from viewing the main program. You can conduct a study to compare a program with crawls to one without crawls.

Ideas can also come from your own reading. Many instructors, for example, use media violence to demonstrate media effects. One day after reading scores of articles on violence, you may notice that many point out that the effects of violence vary depending on whether it's the villain or the hero who commits the violence. You want to follow up on the idea that if a hero uses force to solve problems, it actually has far more detrimental effects than if the violence is committed by a villain. But then you wonder if such an idea can be applied in a comedy program. You may be thinking that the context has something to do with effects, that in a comical, light-hearted situation, violence is seen more as a technique to induce drama. So you might conduct a study in which you manipulate two variables — the violence perpetrator and the context — to investigate the influence of media violence on children's imitation behaviors.

Research ideas can also come from your own curiosity. By the time you take this course, you are probably a graduate student or are in your junior or senior year. You have observed that university professors have vastly different styles of teaching and communicating ideas and concepts. You are curious about which style of communication, a more personal approach versus a more formal approach, is more conducive to learning. You can interview professors to ask why they adopt one style over another and what are some of the motivations behind certain styles.

An effective approach to finding a research idea is to begin with a general topic and then let your background reading lead you to a specific idea. Most people are quite ambitious when they start research. The key is to narrow down your topic so it's manageable. It is good that you want to solve the world's problems. But we need to do it one at a time.

Conducting a Literature Review

After you develop a research idea, the next step is to do a systematic literature review. Research does not and should not exist in isolation. Each study should build on previous knowledge and try to expand that knowledge. Literature reviews and how to do them are explained in Chapter 6 of this book. In short, the goal in conducting a literature review is to locate relevant studies that define the current state of knowledge in a particular area and to identify a gap in the area that your study can fill.

Selecting a Research Design

The next step is to select a research strategy, or select a method. Choosing a research strategy means to decide on the general approach you will take to study your research question or approach your hypotheses. This is the focus of a research methods course.

There are many methods, or tools, from which to choose, as you will learn from the following chapters of this book. The choice of a method is usually determined by the type of question asked and other feasibility constraints such as time and budget.

If it's a question about causal effects, such as the imitation of violent behavior, you are better served by using the experimental method. If the research is about TV audience members' use of talk shows for political information, you will probably need to conduct a survey. If you are interested in how newsrooms make editorial decisions, you can use intensive interviews with editors.

The choices for methods are also limited by ethical and practical constraints. Some researchers, for example, would love to be able to test if long-time exposure to television is indeed causing today's children to have a short attention span. To test the idea, you might want to subject some children to long hours of television while subjecting others to limited exposure so you can measure their attention span. But it wouldn't be ethical to ask children to watch three hours of TV a day.

Collecting Data

Now that you have a design or a strategy, the next logical step is to conduct the study. At this point you should have decided on whom or what to study and what concepts and instruments to use, and how they are defined. If so, you are ready to make observations, or to collect data. Different methods have different observation techniques, and you should choose appropriate ones.

Regardless of the method, you will probably accumulate volumes of observations, which may not be immediately interpretable. You might spend six months in a CBS newsroom observing decision-making, and you may have dozens of field notes. A historical study may require months of collecting sources. In an experiment using physiological data to study people's reaction to media, you will have hours of data measuring viewers' skin conductance and heart rates. You may have conducted dozens of intensive interviews with community journalists to assess their ethics, and so forth. What you need at this point is to process the data and transform it for qualitative or quantitative analysis.

Analyzing Data and Drawing Conclusions

When the collected data are in a form suitable for interpretation, you are ready to analyze the data for the purpose of drawing conclusions about your research questions or hypotheses. There are many options available to analyze data, depending again on the method you use. Sometimes analysis may take just a few minutes. At other times it may take a few months if the study design is really complicated and the data requires massive transformation. Some results may not make sense. If so, it is prudent to step back and examine if there are peculiarities to the data. At this time, it is also a good idea to examine further whether your results are pertinent to the questions you are studying (internal validity) and whether they can be generalized to a larger setting (external validity).

As you attempt to draw conclusions from your analysis, you need to be judicious. Your creative juices should be flowing, but your conclusions must always be reasonable within the context of the data you have gathered and analyzed.

Reporting Results

When we discussed the characteristics of systematic research, we said that it is public, which means the results of your study should be written and shared with the scholarly community and/or the general public. This is usually accomplished in a research report or paper describing what has been studied, how it is studied and what is found, and how the findings are interpreted. Research results are reported so that they become part of the literature on that particular topic, expanding knowledge and enabling others to build on them to answer future questions and pose new research ideas.

Replicating the Study

In addition to contributing knowledge, reporting your study also enables others to replicate or refute your study by following your procedures. We can't stress enough that one study does not prove anything. It merely provides evidence to support a claim. Only when results consistently repeat themselves can we be more certain that we are arriving at some sort of truth. Replication therefore is the last, but not the least important step in a research phase. So the circle will continue, making the accumulation of knowledge possible.

TO LEARN MORE

Bauer, H. H. (1992). *Scientific literacy and the myth of the scientific method*. Champaign, IL: University of Illinois Press.

Becker, H. S. (1996). *The epistemology of qualitative research*. Chicago: The University of Chicago Press.

Hendricks, V. (2006). *Mainstream and formal epistemology*. New York: Cambridge University Press.

Holiday, A. R. (2007). *Doing and writing qualitative research*. London: Sage Publications.

Hughes, J. (1990). *The philosophy of social research*. White Plains, NY: Longman.

Lemos, N. (2007). *An introduction to the theory of knowledge*. New York: Cambridge University Press.

Peat, F. D. (2002). *From certainty to uncertainty: The story of science and ideas in the twentieth century*. Washington D.C.: National Academies Press.

REFERENCES

Galinsky, A. D., Stone, J. & Cooper, J. (2000). The reinstatement of dissonance and psychological discomfort following failed affirmation, *European Journal of Social Psychology*, 30 (1), 123-147.

Gerbner, G., Gross, L., Morgan, M., Signorielli, N., and Jackson-Beeck, M. (1979). The demonstration of power: Violence profile No. 10. *Journal of Communication*, 29, 177-196.

Hatton, J. & Plouffe, P. B. (1996). *Science and its ways of knowing*. NJ: Benjamin Cummings.

Kuhn, T. (1977). *The essential tension: Selective studies in scientific tradition and change*. Chicago: University of Chicago Press.

Lombard, M. & Ditton, T. (1997). At the heart of it all: The concept of presence. *Journal of Computer-Mediated Communication*, 3(2).

Reichert, T. (2003). *The erotic history of advertising*. Amherst, NY: Prometheus Books.

2

History of Research Methods

This chapter traces the development of empirical research methods and how they came to be used to study communication. It looks at the time period from 1820 to 1990 but focuses on the years from 1920 to 1960 when many research methods were developed.

There are two types of empirical methods: qualitative and quantitative. *Empirical methods* rely on data derived from observations. They are distinguishable from approaches that rely on reasoning, logic, or intuition only. *Quantitative methods* produce numerically based measurements of object attributes that can be subjected to numerical, statistical analysis. *Qualitative methods* produce data that can be organized and summarized in non-numerical ways.

These methods represent important breakthroughs in the history of research. They provide useful tools for observing the social world and assessing the role of communication in it. But each of these tools has important limitations that need to be balanced against its strengths. We can gain a better understanding of these methods by looking at how they were initially developed and applied.

Empirical methods were developed by researchers working in various disciplines. Communication researchers, for the most part, simply borrowed and adapted them. Historical and legal methods, for example, had long traditions before communication researchers began to use them. Psychologists developed most of the research designs and measurement tools used in experimental research, while sociologists led the way in creating survey research designs and questionnaires. Content analysis was pioneered by scholars from many different fields but especially by political scientists as part of their effort to understand political propaganda. The statistical techniques used to analyze data in communication research have been borrowed from researchers in many fields ranging from agriculture to education. In this chapter, we will consider the origin of a variety of methods — without trying to cover them all — but we will focus on how they came to be applied to the study of communication.

By Dennis K. Davis
Pennsylvania State University

THE METHODS SCHISM

Prior to 1920 most of the methods available to communication researchers were qualitative. In fact, qualitative methods were the most widely used ones in communication research until the 1950s. The earliest published study of mass communication in America was a historical account, Isaiah Thomas' *History of Printing in America*, published in 1810. A large body of such works followed it; and for more than a century, historical and similar qualitative studies dominated research. Thomas did a commendable job of collecting material such as newspapers and editors' personal papers to compile his history, although he was not a trained historian. In fact, it would not be until the middle decades of the 20th century that most researchers in communication received formal training in any type of methodology. From 1800 until around 1960, the majority of articles and books were descriptive studies that dealt with such matters as historical, legal or ethical aspects of communication. But then these descriptive studies gave way to research that used quantitative social science methods.

One of the reasons for the decline in the traditional historical and descriptive methods was that few journalism professors had been trained in their use. Even after colleges began to offer instruction in journalism early in the 20th century (the earliest field of professional communication to be taught in higher education), journalism research tended to be based on the descriptive methods used by journalists, such as the limited and convenient gathering of material as a reporter might do, rather than well-designed, systematic research done by academics trained in methodology. Hardly any journalism professors who researched, for example, the history of newspapers employed the rigorous methods used by historians. Thus, even though a few journalism historians produced some useful work, most of the studies that appeared in *Journalism Quarterly*, the main academic journal in the field of journalism education, did not meet standards set for professional historical research. The articles frequently were superficial in both their use of sources and their analysis. As a result, when other professors began to apply systematic methods to the study of questions in the social and behavioral aspects of communication, the work of professors using traditional methods appeared shallow and amateurish.

Despite the availability of methods for research in social and behavioral sciences, their use in communication research is comparatively recent. Studies of history, law, ethics, and professional practices predominated in journalism education books and journals until the middle of the 20th century. By the 1950s and into the 1960s, though, communication research increasingly used quantitative social science methods. A schism developed among communication researchers between those trained in social science and those who used traditional historical and descriptive methods. In 1957, Wilbur Schramm, one of the leading proponents of quantitative methods, assessed "progress" in 20 years of journalism research by looking at the amount of quantitative research being published in *Journalism Quarterly*. He found that in 5 years from 1937 to 1941 only 10% of the research published was quantitative. Just a decade later, 38% was quantitative; and 5 years after that it had risen to 48%.

During the era when quantitative methods were becoming the preferred way to conduct communication research, qualitative methods were often criticized as

Science, Statistics, and the Research Schism

The outlines of scientific methodology can be seen as early as 500 B.C. in Egypt and Greece. The modern reverence for it in the West, though, began with the writings of such people as Roger Bacon, an English philosopher and Franciscan friar, in the 1200s and the French philosopher René Descartes in the 1600s. They emphasized a systematic approach to observing and testing phenomena in the physical world. By the late 1800s, many people considered scientific methods to be the only reliable means of ascertaining a true picture of reality.

The reverence for the scientific method spilled over from the study of science into other fields, including social and behavioral science. The assumption in science is that nature operates according to physical laws that are predictable. Human behavior, though, the subject of social scientists, does not. So-

cial scientists thus faced the problem of how to determine regularity in human behavior.

The solution was found in *statistics*, which social scientists developed starting in the early 1800s to identify and quantitatively measure patterns of behavior. The purpose of statistics was thus to discover predictable underlying principles in human behavior – that is, behavioral and social "laws" equivalent to physical, scientific laws.

Starting around 1940, some journalism professors began to adapt social and behavioral science methods to communication. They believed such methods were better than qualitative and humanistic methods for developing useful ways of understanding the social world. By the 1960s, a schism existed between the advocates of the two approaches.

a less rigorous or scientific way to conduct research. Quantitative methods were said by proponents to provide more precise and objective ways of assessing the social world.

A key proponent for quantitative methods was Ralph Nafziger, a journalism professor at the universities of Minnesota and Wisconsin. When the University of Minnesota established the nation's first journalism research division in 1944, he was named director. With Marcus Wilkinson, he published the pioneering methodology book *An Introduction to Journalism Research* in 1949. Then in 1958, with co-editor David M. White, he published the book *Introduction to Mass Communication Research*. It eliminated chapters on historical and legal research, which his earlier book had contained. Delia labels it the leading research methods text and points out that it concentrated on quantitative methods and devoted only part of one chapter to field observations.[1] By the book's second edition in 1963, it was clear that the emphasis was solely on social science methods. "It was this orientation," Avery points out, "that led to the schism between traditional and social science methods found among communication scholars today."[2] Most subsequent textbooks on research methods in communication continued to emphasize social and behavioral science at the expense of other areas. That schism remained sharp until only recently.

THE ORIGIN OF EMPIRICAL METHODS

Empirical research methods were initially developed by physical scientists and used to gain an understanding of and control over the physical world. The development of such methods predates recorded

[1]Jesse. G. Delia, "Communication Research: A History," in C. R. Berger and S. H. Chaffee, eds., *Handbook of Communication Science* (Newbury Park, Calif.: Sage Publications, 1987), 20-98.

[2]Donald R. Avery, in Wm. David Sloan, ed., *Makers of the Media Mind: Journalism Educators and Their Ideas* (Hillsdale, N.J.: Lawrence Erlbaum Associates, 1990), 299.

human history and is found in most human cultures. Egyptian, Greek, Indian, and Chinese philosophers and scientists made important early contributions to the development of such methods. In Europe, the 16th century Renaissance revived interest in Greek conceptions of the physical world and renewed interest in systematic study of it. During the 17th century Enlightenment era, physical science became a well-established force within European society. Observation of physical phenomena and experimentation were combined with reason to create theories of the physical world that challenged traditional understandings grounded in metaphysical philosophy or religious doctrines.

The motivation to apply empirical methods in social research can be traced to the positivist revolution in philosophy that was sparked in the 1820s by Auguste Comte, a French philosopher.[3] *Positivism* is a doctrine that maintains that sense perceptions are the only admissible basis for knowledge of the social as well as the physical world. Comte advocated the development of sociology using the same empirical research designs and methods that the physical sciences had pioneered during the Enlightenment.

Though many of Comte's ideas proved controversial and were later rejected, his advocacy of the development of social sciences grounded in empirical research gained wide acceptance across Europe and in the United States. By the end of the 1800s early forms of empirical social science had become widely established in leading universities. The first experimental lab for psychology was established in 1879 by Wilheim Wundt at Leipzig University.[4] By 1900 the foundations had been laid for the development of empirical research in psychology, sociology, and anthropology.

In the early 1900s a group of Austrian philosophers known as the Vienna Circle developed a stricter and more carefully formulated version of positivism known as *logical positivism*.[5] This group argued that all forms of scientific theory and research should be firmly grounded in empirical observation. They urged that modern forms of logic be combined with empirical observation so that scientific research could be more systematic and objective. Their ideas were used to justify the use of empirical research methods and to design research.

POSITIVISM AND EMPIRICISM

All forms of positivism assert that the only useful way to develop theories of either the physical or the social world is to ground them in empirical observations. Theories need to be tested based on such observations, and if the observations support theories then theories are confirmed or verified. Theories that can't be confirmed are eliminated in favor of those that can be confirmed. Today most social theorists agree that theories should to some extent be grounded on observation of the social world. But they disagree about the way that empirical research should be conducted and used to ground, develop or test theory. Is it possible to begin our research without theories and then proceed inductively to develop theories based on observations? Or do we

[3]Auguste Comte and Gertrud Lenzer, *Auguste Comte and Positivism: The Essential Writings*, 1st Harper Torchbook ed. (New York: Harper & Row, 1975).

[4]K. Danziger and P.F. Ballantyne, "Psychological Experiments," 233-39 in W. Bringmann et al., eds., *Pictorial History of Psychology* (New York: Oxford University Press, 1997).

[5]Jonathon W. Moses and Torbjorn L. Knutsen, *Ways of Knowing: Competing Methodologies and Methods in Social and Political Research* (Basingstoke: Palgrave Macmillan, 2007).

need to create theories first and then proceed deductively to make observations that allow us to assess and develop theories? How should empirical observations be made? What rules or guidelines about making observations should researchers follow in order to assure that the observations are accurate, valid, or reliable? How structured and systematic do we need to be when we make observations? What do we do when the rules for making observations place too many limitations on observers or are too costly or impractical? As we will see in this book, these are questions that are very relevant today and are questions that you will need to answer for yourself as you decide which research methods are most useful and determine how they should be applied.

The basic arguments of positivism and empiricism are quite logical and consistent with common sense. In our daily lives we are constantly developing new ideas and refining them based on our personal experiences — our empirical observations. But relying on our observations doesn't always work well — especially if our observations are affected by our subjective expectations and feelings. We sometimes see what we want to see or expect to see rather than what actually takes place. In other words, we find it difficult to make *valid* observations that are *reliable*. For example, many people have strongly developed racial prejudices that make it difficult for them to accurately observe situations involving people of different races. Their observations may vary greatly depending on their emotions or the situations in which the observations take place.

A central objective of the people who developed empirical research designs and research methods was to overcome subjectivity. They sought ways to *structure* observations so that misperceptions induced by subjectivity could be avoided and valid observations could be made. They saw their work as a struggle to overcome the ideologies and prejudices that made it difficult to gather accurate data and reach useful conclusions about social problems. Although these motives were quite laudable, we now know that the early empirical researchers tended to exaggerate the usefulness of their methods and overlooked key limitations. Sometimes the structures they imposed on observations unintentionally produced biased observations. Researchers often debated the usefulness of imposing certain structures rather than others. For example, survey researchers debated the relative merits of quota sampling versus random sampling until 1945. Imposing structure on observations didn't guarantee objectivity. The value of each type of structure had to be demonstrated by its ability to improve the reliability and validity of observations.

This example illustrates one of the central limitations of empiricism: We often can't easily interpret what empirical observations really measure. One researcher may argue that a set of observations measures one thing, while another researcher can argue that it measures something entirely different. To deal with this problem, researchers have had to develop various ways of trying to demonstrate that observations actually measure what they are intended to measure. In other words, it's been necessary to establish that observations are valid indicators of the concepts they are intended to measure.

PRIVATE FOUNDATIONS AND EMPIRICISM

The development of empirical methods for social science research was aided greatly by research funding provided by private foundations.

Timeline of Major Events in Communication Research

1820 – Auguste Comte espouses positivism as a philosophical basis for the development of sociology.

1913 – Publication of "Psychology as the Behaviorist Views It" by J.B. Watson.

1918 – Publication of *Making Social Science Studies*, the first research methods textbook.

1922 – Vienna Circle is formed by philosophers at the University of Vienna to advance logical positivism as the foundation for all forms of science.

1932 – Publication of *A Technique for the Measurement of Attitudes* by Rensis Likert, a book describing how to use the attitude scaling technique that was named for him.

1933 – Publication of the Payne Fund Studies, a set of 8 books that presented findings from 12 studies of movies and their influence on children. This was the first large-scale empirical research focused on communication media.

1935 – Publication of *The Psychology of Radio* by Hadley Cantril and Gordon Allport.

1937 – Office of Radio Research established by Hadley Cantril at Princeton University with Paul F. Lazarsfeld as Director.

1940 – *The Invasion from Mars* published by Hadley Cantril, Hazel Gaudet and Herta Herzog, the first major research project that assessed the effects of a specific communication event.

1940 – Paul Lazarsfeld headed a research team that collected data from a large panel to assess how people decided to vote in a presidential election.

1949 – Publication of *An Introduction to Journalism Research*, by Nafziger and Wilkinson, the first journalism research methods textbook. It included essays on historical and legal research, statistical analysis, survey interviewing, content analysis and experimental methods.

1949 – Publication of *Experiments in Mass Communication*, an in-depth report by Carl Hovland of media experiments conducted during World War II.

1958 – Publication of *Introduction to Mass Communication Research*, by Nafziger and White. Omitting historical and legal methods, the book emphasized social science research methods and thus implied that those methods were more important.

The Rockefeller and Carnegie Foundations played a critical role in funding the development of empirical research methods in the United States. Calhoun reports that this funding began in the 1920s and was critical to fostering development of empirical research at major universities, including the University of Chicago, the University of North Carolina, and Columbia University.[6] He argues that this funding supported a trend toward what was then called *scientism* and was later referred to as *empiricism*. This trend encouraged development of strategies for conducting social research that mirrored work done in the physical sciences. Advocates of empiricism argued that it was possible to make objective statements of fact based on *systematic* empirical observations. These objective statements were held to be impartial and unaffected by the moral and political convictions of researchers. The possibility of being able to make objective statements concerning controversial social problems was particularly attractive in the 1930s when extreme political ideologies had gained widespread acceptance and threatened to dominate decision-making about social problems. The ability to make objective statements concerning the role and power of mass media became increasingly important during World War II and the Cold War that followed. In particular, it was considered essential to develop an objective understanding of the effects of mass-media-transmitted propaganda.

The rise of empiricism as an approach to doing research took place at the same time that empirical research on communication was first developed. Not surpris-

[6]Craig J. Calhoun, *Sociology in America: A History* (Chicago: University of Chicago Press, 2007), 234.

ingly, empiricism was embraced by many of the social scientists who pioneered the study of media. Research on communication was often controversial, and findings were likely to be challenged. Empirical findings were easier to defend since they were seen as being more objective and "scientific." In his history of communication research, Delia discusses the development of what he terms a "neopositivist" movement that strongly influenced early communication research. The movement was centered at Columbia University in the 1940s and was responsible for focusing research on the use of survey methods to study public opinion. Members of this movement also argued that many qualitative research methods were not sufficiently rigorous and therefore didn't permit objective conclusions to be reached.[7] As noted below, Paul Lazarsfeld played a central role in guiding this movement even though he recognized that qualitative methods were often quite useful. Glander has argued that the success of this movement had a profound impact on research in education. He traces how funding was directed away from education research and toward study of mass media. Within the field of communication, study of mass media became a dominant focus for empirical research.[8]

EARLY EMPIRICAL RESEARCH

The first use of empirical research methods to study communication occurred during a very troubled era — the 1920s and 1930s. During the 1920s, organized crime and juvenile delinquency were increasing in most U.S. cities. In the 1930s, economic depression was accompanied by the rise of numerous anti-democratic, extremist political movements that espoused right wing or left wing totalitarian and anti-democratic political ideologies. This was also a time period when there was rapid development of media technologies including radio, movies, and high-speed, better quality printing. By the end of the 1930s, radio networks spanned the United States and movie theaters could be found in most towns. Big cities had several competing newspapers. But this dramatic improvement in mass communication was accompanied by deepening social and political problems. Scholars and politicians speculated that media might somehow be causing or at least aggravating these problems. The possibility that mass media could be fostering extremist politics, delinquency, and crime was widely debated throughout the 1930s. According to Lowry and DeFleur, "Most intellectuals of the nineteenth century denounced them [mass media] at one time or another for their presumed destructive effects on the social order.... But these claims were just that — claims."[9] By the 1930s some of these claims had been well developed and were widely believed. It's not surprising that empirical research methods would first be used to assess whether media were causing social disorder.

The first large-scale and well-funded research on media was focused on movies. Beginning in 1928, the Payne Fund, a large philanthropic foundation, financed research that focused on how movies influenced children.[10] University re-

[7]Delia, "Communication Research: A History."

[8]Timothy R. Glander, *Origins of Mass Communications Research During the American Cold War: Educational Effects and Contemporary Implications, Sociocultural, Political, and Historical Studies in Education* (Mahwah, N.J.: Lawrence Erlbaum Associates, 2000).

[9]Shearon A. Lowery and Melvin L. DeFleur, *Milestones in Mass Communication Research* (New York: Longman, 1988), 17.

[10]Garth Jowett, I. C. Jarvie, and K. Fuller-Seeley, *Children and the Movies: Media Influence and the Payne Fund Controversy* (New York: Cambridge University Press, 1996).

searchers were identified and recruited by the Motion Picture Research Council (MPRC), a group that was especially concerned about the influence that movies might have on children. The MPRC was successful in recruiting some of the most talented social researchers from leading universities. These researchers used methods that were quite diverse and included early forms of qualitative and quantitative methods. Some researchers used empirical methods to assess whether movies had good or bad effects on children. The methods included survey questionnaires, case studies, experiments, and content analyses.[11] Overall, the research raised more questions about the influence of movies than it answered. The mixed findings did little to stem criticism of movies.

In their discussion of the Payne Fund research, Lowery and DeFleur pointed out that by the beginning of the 1920s statistical techniques were being increasingly applied in the social sciences. Several Payne Fund researchers used what were then quite innovative techniques to analyze data. One of the most important of these was Pearson's new procedure for calculating correlations between variables — the Pearson "product-moment coefficient of correlation." Other techniques included partial and multiple correlation, the analysis of variance, and nonparametric statistics.[12]

EARLY OPINION POLLING AND AUDIENCE RATINGS RESEARCH

Survey research methods had two quite important applications for media organizations beginning in the 1920s. Newspapers and magazines used survey research to conduct public opinion polls. These methods were also used to measure the size of audiences for radio programs. Straw polls of public opinion were found in newspapers in the 19th century. But until the 1920s, these polls were unscientific – there was no basis for determining whether the results provided a valid estimate of public opinion. Frankel and Frankel point out that currently used polling methods based on random sampling were not widely used until after the failure of most polls to predict that Truman would defeat Dewey in the 1948 election.[13] Prior to that, pollsters relied on quota sampling because it was cheaper and easier to use.

Fletcher reports that by the late 1920s advertising on radio had grown to the point where advertisers wanted information about audience sizes.[14] Broadcasters also wanted a way of measuring audience size so that they could charge more for advertising on popular programs. The first national radio audience survey was conducted in 1927 by the Archibald Crossley polling organization. By 1929 the Cooperative Analysis of Broadcasting (CAB), a regular program rating service, was established under the control of the Association of National Advertisers. The CAB conducted telephone interviews in 20 cities. Respondents were asked what radio programs they had listened to during the preceding 24 hours. A variety of different interviewing techniques and questions were used in early ratings research. Some researchers would only ask about programs being listened to when

---

[11]Kim A. Neuendorf, *The Content Analysis Guidebook* (Thousand Oaks, Calif: Sage Publications, 2002).

[12]Lowery and DeFleur, *Milestones in Mass Communication Research*, 20.

[13]Martin R. Frankel and Lester R. Frankel, "Fifty Years of Survey Sampling in the United States," *Public Opinion Quarterly* 51 (1987): Part 2 Supplement: S127-S38.

[14]James E. Fletcher, "Audience Research Methods" in C.H. Sterling, ed., *The Museum of Broadcast Communications Encyclopedia of Radio* (New York: Fitzroy Dearborn, 2004), 113-18.

the phone was answered. Other researchers went door to door and provided people with lists of radio stations and programs to aid respondent recall of what they had listened to.

Throughout the 1930s the methods for audience ratings research were improved in an effort to get more accurate measures. There were concerns that most audience surveys depended too much on the ability and willingness of audience members to accurately report their listening. In 1942, the A.C. Nielsen Company introduced a new ratings service called the Nielsen Radio Index that was based on information collected from audimeters placed in a "cross-section" of 1,000 households in nine Eastern and Central states.[15] The audimeter recorded each time a radio was turned on, the station it was tuned to, length of listening to each station, all changes in tuning, and when the radio was turned off. This method of collecting data completely avoided the problem of audience recall but had other limitations, including omission of rural audience members. Nevertheless, this method of data collection won the approval of advertisers and broadcasters and eventually led to the introduction of a device that would measure TV audiences. In 1949, the diary method of data collection was introduced. Initially, diaries were distributed door to door and respondents were asked to fill them in for a week. Only one person filled out the diary to report listening by all members of the household.

LAZARSFELD AND THE DEVELOPMENT OF COMMUNICATION RESEARCH

Paul Lazarsfeld was the single most important person responsible for the development of social science research in communication and a number of research methods. He has been credited with initiating the communication effects research tradition.[16] Rockefeller Foundation funding brought him to the United States from Austria in 1933. He was one of a number of Jewish social researchers who fled Europe as the Nazis consolidated their power. He was trained in mathematics, but early in his professional career he developed practical skills in survey research methods. He proved to be an innovative academic who excelled at applying what were then quite primitive empirical methods to solving practical research problems – especially problems faced by mass media and by marketers. One of the first articles that Lazarsfeld wrote after arriving in the United States explained how empirical research could be used to make advertising more effective.[17] During the 1940s and 1950s he became a strong and highly effective advocate for both positivism and empiricism in social research and the development and application of methods. From the start of his American career, he focused on mass communication topics including advertising effects, radio audience research, public opinion formation, propaganda effects, and voting research.

Most of Lazarsfeld's contributions were made though his direction of and involvement in the Institute for Applied Social Research at Columbia University (Rogers, 1994; Schramm, 1997).[18] This was one of the first successful applied social research institutes in the United States. It began in 1937 as the Office of Radio Re-

[15]Arthur C. Nielsen, "Two Years of Commercial Operation of the Audimeter and the Nielsen Radio Index," *Journal of Marketing* 9:3 (1945): 239-55.

[16]Everett M. Rogers, *A History of Communication Study: A Biographical Approach* (New York: The Free Press, 1994).

[17]Paul F. Lazarsfeld, "The Psychological Aspects of Market Research," *Harvard Business Review* 34 (1934): 54-71.

[18]Rogers, *A History of Communication Study*; and Wilbur Schramm, *The Beginnings of Communication Study in America: A Personal Memoir*, S.H. Chaffee and E.M. Rogers, eds. (Thousand Oaks, Calif.: Sage Publications, 1997).

search (ORR) located at Princeton University. It was founded by Hadley Cantril, and Lazarsfeld served as its director. In 1939, the ORR moved to Columbia University, and Lazarsfeld moved with it. During the 1940s, Lazarsfeld was able to obtain funding for landmark empirical research on the role and power of mass communication. The research included a series of studies of radio, radio station ownership, and radio audiences in the late 1930s and 1940s; studies of elections and voter decision-making in 1940, 1944, and 1948; and an innovative marketing survey conducted in 1945 of women in Decatur, Ill. The Decatur study led to the development of a theory of personal influence that has had extraordinary impact on mass communication theory and research.[19]

While he pioneered the development and application of various survey research and experimental methods, Lazarsfeld's most basic contribution to methodology involves his contribution to the language of social research. Much of the language that we use today to talk about empirical research methods and their application was developed by Lazarsfeld and his Columbia University colleagues.[20] One key area involved the conceptualization of communication effects so that they could be measured using survey methods and experiments.

During the 1940s and 1950s, Lazarsfeld worked directly with radio network executives and researchers. Several of the researchers went on to become broadcasting network executives. Lazarsfeld and Frank Stanton developed a method for measuring audience reactions to media programming that continues to be used. The technique is known as the Lazarsfeld Stanton Program Analyzer.[21] To do an analysis, 8 to 10 people were recruited and brought into a room. Each was handed a small box with a lever on top, a sort of crude joystick, that they could manipulate as they listened to radio program content. They were told to tilt the lever one direction when they heard content that they liked and to tilt it the other direction to show their dislike. If the lever wasn't tilted at all, it indicated a neutral view of the content. The likes and dislikes of a number of persons were recorded and aggregated electronically to create a graph that showed how overall audience likes and dislikes changed while they listened to the content. This technology allowed measurement of how people's feelings about content changed, but it couldn't assess *why* feelings changed. One of Lazarsfeld's colleagues, Robert Merton, developed a strategy for assessing why feelings changed. He waited until programs ended, and then he went into the room and asked the groups questions about their feelings. As a result, he developed what is now known as the focus group technique for doing research.[22] This example provides an illustration of how quantitative and qualitative methods can be combined to provide a better overall understanding of communication.

Lazarsfeld's first wife, Herta Herzog, is credited with originating the uses and gratifications approach to studying communication. One of the most popular

[19]Elihu Katz and Paul F. Lazarsfeld, *Personal Influence; the Part Played by People in the Flow of Mass Communications* (Glencoe, Ill.: Free Press, 1955); and Peter Simonson, "Introduction." *Annals of the American Academy of Political and Social Sciences* 608 (2006): 6-24.

[20]Paul F. Lazarsfeld and Morris Rosenberg, *The Language of Social Research: A Reader in the Methodology of Social Research* (Glencoe, Ill.: Free Press, 1955).

[21]Mark R. Levy, "The Lazarsfeld-Stanton Program Analyzer: An Historical Note," *Journal of Communication* 28 (1982): 30-38.

[22]Peter Simonson, "The Serendipity of Merton's Communication Research," *International Journal of Public Opinion Research* 17:3 (2005): 277-97.

types of radio programs during the 1940s was the soap opera. Herzog was interested in finding out why so many women tuned in to these programs. She used questionnaires and in-depth survey methods to question women about the programs. She found that the programs provided women with many different types of satisfaction.[23] This was the first time that media use was systematically linked to gratifications derived from it. Communication researchers, however, ignored the study of gratifications for several decades in favor of trying to measure and understand communication effects.

In 1949, Joseph Klapper, a Lazarsfeld protégé, published a monograph titled *The Effects of Mass Media*. He expanded and later republished it as *The Effects of Mass Communication* in 1960. It provides the most concise summary of the key findings that emerged from early research on media effects. Its primary conclusion was that media rarely bring about important changes in individuals or society. Instead, media tend to reinforce existing social trends and to reinforce what individuals already believe.

DEVELOPMENT OF EXPERIMENTS AND ATTITUDE MEASUREMENT

In 1879, psychological experiments were conducted in the first laboratory built for this purpose at the University of Leipzig in Germany under the direction of Wilhelm Wundt. Much of the research focused on physiological responses to various types of stimulation.[24] In the United States in the early 20th century, J. B. Watson pioneered both the development of experimental methods and the early stimulus response theories that were used to plan experiments and interpret their findings. He argued that all human behavior could be explained by the stimuli that people were exposed to. Experiments provided a means of establishing how stimuli could shape behavior.[25] Behaviorists like Watson rejected any effort to conceptualize or measure what went on in people's heads when they were exposed to stimuli. He argued that such thought processes merely rationalized behavior but didn't explain it.

Other psychologists rejected Watson's views and argued that it was possible to develop useful measures of thought processes. A number of concepts were proposed for studying thought processes, but the most successful involved the conceptualization of attitudes. W.I. Thomas is credited with introducing this concept in 1918. By 1935, Gordon Allport, a psychologist who pioneered attitude research, reported more than 16 definitions for attitude. Researchers often assume that it is possible to predict whether people have such predispositions to respond in a specific way to certain stimuli by asking them about their feelings or past actions. Communication researchers have focused on the way that communication can produce changes in attitudes. For example, advertising research assesses whether ads can influence attitudes toward products and whether changing attitudes can increase sales of products.

According to Converse, Emory Bogardus and L.L. Thurstone developed the most important attitude measurement methods. These men were responsible for

---

[23]Herta Herzog and Paul F. Lazarsfeld, *Daytime Serials: Their Audience and Their Effect on Buying* (New York: Bureau of Applied Social Research, Columbia University, 1942).

[24]Danziger and Ballantyne, "Psychological Experiments."

[25]John B. Watson, "Psychology as the Behaviorist Views It," *Psychological Review* 20 (1913): 158-77.

constructing the first "attitude scales," The scales consisted of sets of question-naire items that were designed to assess specific attitudes.[26] The measurement of attitudes became a focus of much early communication research. This research sought to measure effects of communication on a variety of different types of atti-tudes.

By the 1940s, attitude scales had become one of the primary ways of measuring responses to media messages. The use of attitude scales had certain advantages for researchers. These scales made it possible to explore message effects that went far beyond physiological reac-tions to messages. For example, propaganda researchers wanted to know if peo-ple had been persuaded by messages. But physiological reactions couldn't pro-vide direct evidence concerning persuasion. Researchers decided that the best way to assess persuasion was to measure changes in attitudes.

RESEARCH DURING WORLD WAR II

World War II provided empirical researchers with what many considered to be an ideal opportunity to conduct research on propaganda effects. These researchers were especially interested in whether various techniques for constructing propa-ganda could be shown to have a powerful influence on attitudes. In their view, if a scientific understanding of propaganda could be developed, then propaganda could be used to preserve rather than subvert democracy. Among other things, it might provide a means of mobilizing the nation behind the war effort, and it might motivate soldiers to fight more effectively. The man who led the efforts to study propaganda during the war was Carl Hovland, an experimental psycholo-gist from Yale whose research prior to the war focused on rats. In 1942, he was recruited by Samuel Stouffer to become the chief psychologist and head of the newly established experimental research unit in the Research Branch of the In-formation and Education Division of the War Department. Stouffer was a sociolo-gist with expertise in attitude measurement, and he wanted someone with strong experimental skills to design and conduct research on the power of propaganda to change attitudes.[27]

The experimental research that Hovland and his colleagues conducted during WWII was innovative both in terms of its conceptualization and the methods used.[28] Prior to Hovland's research there had been very little empirical research done on attitude change. Research centered on measuring attitudes and on how people differed in their attitudes. Only rarely was it concerned with change in atti-tudes.[29] Hovland recognized that one way to assess propaganda effects was to measure changes in attitudes. He set about developing experimental methods that would permit such effects to be measured.

Over the course of the war, Hovland designed field experiments that were increasingly sophisticated. He tried making some measurements days before sol-diers saw films, and he made other measures days after they saw films. He com-pared the effects of films that provided two-sided messages with films that were

[26]L. L. Thurstone and Ernest J. Chave, *The Measurement of Attitude: A Psychophysical Method and Some Experiments with a Scale for Measuring Attitude Toward the Church* (Chicago: University of Chicago Press, 1929).

[27]Rogers, *A History of Communication Study.*

[28]Carl I. Hovland, Arthur A. Lumsdaine, and Fred D. Sheffield, *Experiments on Mass Communication: Studies in Social Psychology in World War II* (Princeton, N.J.: Princeton University Press, 1949).

[29]Rogers, *A History of Communication Study.*

one-sided. He measured many different audience attributes to see if any of them helped explain effects. He brought in Lazarsfeld and Merton to assist with the research by using the Lazarsfeld Stanton Program Analyzer and focus group methods to try to assess what elements in the films could explain their effects. This was a pioneer effort to combine qualitative and quantitative empirical research methods to study propaganda effects. Throughout the war, Hovland engaged in a more or less systematic search to determine what factors were likely to increase the effectiveness of propaganda. This search was to continue for more than a decade after he left the military and returned to his professorship at Yale University. With hindsight, critics have raised fundamental questions concerning the usefulness of the line of attitude-change research that Hovland initiated. Hovland-style research on message effects dominated the communication research agenda throughout the 1950s and into the 1960s.

World War II also provided a focus for experimental research on group dynamics conducted by Kurt Lewin at the University of Iowa. His research laid the basis for the field of group communication and pioneered many of the experimental methods used to study social groups. He is known for his development of field theory, a perspective that challenged behaviorism and argued for the importance of communication in shaping the activity of groups.[30]

DEVELOPMENT OF CONTENT ANALYSIS

Krippendorf (2003) provides a useful introduction to the early use of content analysis. He traces the history of empirical content analysis back to the late 1600s when it was developed by the Catholic Church to assess the threat posed by printed materials and newspapers. The "first well-documented quantitative analyses of printed matter occurred in 18th-century Sweden." He points out that several early German sociologists, including Max Weber, conducted or proposed major analyses of newspaper content in the first decade of the 20th century. The first content analyses done in the United States were conducted to assess newspaper content. These studies measured the column inches that newspapers devoted to various topics and offered conclusions. One study argued than overwhelming space was "devoted to 'demoralizing,' 'unwholesome,' and 'trivial' matters as opposed to 'worthwhile' news items."[31]

Neuendorf provides a detailed description of an early study that used content analysis to assess the potential effects of movies. The research was supervised by Edgar Dale and was one of the studies paid for by the Payne Fund. The major themes of 1,500 movies released in 1920, 1925, and 1930 were classified into 10 categories. Most movies were found to fall into four categories: love, crime, sex, and comedy. Dale trained a team of content coders who were sent to theaters to classify movie content into nine major "social values" areas. The research concluded that the movies provided a misrepresentation of the social world with too much emphasis on life in the upper classes; problems of youth, love, sex and crime; motifs of escape and entertainment; and a focus on physical beauty.[32]

---

[30]Ibid.

[31]Klaus Krippendorff, *Content Analysis: An Introduction to Its* Methodology, 2nd ed. (Beverly Hills: Sage Publications, 2003), 4, 5.

[32]Kim A. Neuendorf, *The Content Analysis Guidebook* (Thousand Oaks, Calif.: Sage Publications, 2002).

Most of the content analysis research conducted during the 1930s focused on political communication and more specifically on propaganda. The person most identified with the development and popularization of content analysis methods in the United States is Harold D. Lasswell, a political scientist whose research interests ranged far beyond politics and often centered on mass media content. He began his academic career with a Ph.D. dissertation that focused on World War I propaganda and sought to draw lessons from it concerning the power of propaganda.[33] Most of the content analysis in this dissertation was qualitative rather than quantitative, but it served to illustrate the value of content analysis for assessing important forms of communication.[34] Later in his career, Lasswell became a strong advocate for quantitative content analysis. He continued to conduct content analysis research and to assess the usefulness of content analysis throughout his academic career. One of his last publications was a coauthored book that focused on propaganda.[35]

INSTITUTIONALIZATION OF COMMUNICATION RESEARCH

During the 1950s and 1960s, communication research became institutionalized within academic departments and research institutes in the United States. As noted above, the University of Minnesota established the first journalism research division in 1944 under the direction of Ralph Nafziger. Wilbur Schramm personally led the development of research institutes at the University of Illinois, Stanford University, and the University of Hawaii. A variety of academic departments placed increased emphasis on conducting communication research. These included speech, journalism and broadcasting departments. Delia argues that the separation of communication research into various departments and institutes served to compartmentalize communication scholarship. In particular, research on mass communication was typically conducted in isolation from interpersonal or group communication. Different professional associations were formed to support teaching and research done in journalism (Association for Education in Journalism and Mass Communication), speech (National Communication Association) and broadcasting (Broadcast Education Association).[36] The formation of communication departments in the 1960s brought together faculty doing different types of communication research but also saw the founding of yet another professional association (International Communication Association). Each of these professional associations supports academic journals that publish various types of communication research. Some of these journals mainly publish quantitative research, while others focus on qualitative work. The research published in these journals tends to use differing research designs and methods.

The increased emphasis on research in communication departments required specialized training of professors. More and more schools began to expect faculty members to conduct research, and the Ph.D. became an important consideration in hiring decisions. The first doctoral programs in communication were instituted in the late 1940s. Although students were able to study using a variety of meth-

---

[33]Harold D. Lasswell, *Propaganda Technique in the World War* (New York: A. A. Knopf, 1927).

[34]Krippendorff, *Content Analysis*....

[35]Harold D. Lasswell, Daniel Lerner, and Hans Speier, *Propaganda and Communication in World History* (Honolulu: University Press of Hawaii, 1979).

[36]Delia, "Communication Research: A History."

ods, by the 1960s most doctoral programs required research courses in quantitative methods. Many professors considered such methods the only legitimate ones. The traditional methods used in history, law, and ethics received declining attention. Beginning in the 1970s, qualitative and traditional methods regained importance. The reemergence of qualitative and traditional methods has taken place in part because there is a growing realization that quantitative methods have limitations that can be addressed or offset by using other methods.

THE RESURGENCE OF QUALITATIVE METHODS

Even though quantitative methods dominated communication research for many years, a renewed interest in qualitative methods came about in the 1970s. Delia traces it to a revival of Chicago School sociology along with a growing interest in critical cultural studies.[37] A number of European perspectives were advanced that challenged the dominant American focus on media effects research. These included political economy, the Frankfurt School, neomarxist sociology, and theories proposed by Habermas and Foucault. Revived interest in qualitative methods took place across the humanities and the social sciences. In the 1980s, James Carey became one of the leading advocates for cultural studies of media in the United States.[38] He challenged European approaches to cultural studies and advocated development of an American approach grounded in Chicago School sociology. In speech communication, Delia notes, Kenneth Burke had a profound impact on rhetorical scholarship and encouraged the use of qualitative research methods.

Communication professors who preferred traditional methods showed an increasing awareness of methodology. They made fuller use of available guidebooks, such as Pollack's *Fundamentals of Legal Research* (1956) and Vansina's *Oral Tradition As History* (1985). Others advanced those methods with a number of books devoted to their use in communication, such as Paul Smith's *The Historian and Film* (1976) and Startt and Sloan's *Historical Methods in Mass Communication* (1989). Also important were a variety of national scholarly organizations, such as the American Journalism Historians Association, devoted to specialized areas of research. The Law Division and the History Division of the Association for Education in Journalism and Mass Communication, for example, brought together communication professors of common interests. Also important were smaller regional organizations devoted to specialized areas of research. Through a variety of activities, particularly journals and annual research paper competitions, these organizations encouraged better use of methodology.

Not surprisingly, the period from 1970 to 1990 became a time when theories and research methods were widely debated.[39] During this era, quantitative researchers tended to staunchly defend their way of doing research, while qualitative researchers pointed out its limitations. Intense debates took place in which the strengths and weaknesses of various methods were exaggerated by proponents and critics. By 1990, some social researchers began to argue for the usefulness of mixed methodology, a strategy for combining qualitative and quantitative meth-

---

[37]Ibid.

[38]He made the case for a cultural approach in *Communication as Culture: Essays on Media and Society, Media and Popular Culture* (London and Boston: Unwin Hyman, 1989).

[39]"Ferment in the Field," *Journal of Communication* (Special Issue) (1983): 33.

ods. This argument has gradually gained adherents among communication researchers.

Despite many obvious advantages of using research designs that combine qualitative and quantitative methods, it's important to recognize that these methods are grounded in alternate worldviews or paradigms. Any combination of methods needs to be grounded in either a quantitative or a qualitative worldview. Willis argues that there are two quite different worldviews underlying qualitative methods that he labels as interpretivism and critical theory. He labels the quantitative worldview as postpositivist. He argues that these paradigms differ in many ways, including the nature of reality, reasons for doing research, usefulness of various methods, and ways of interpreting data.[40]

THE FUTURE OF RESEARCH METHODS

Over the 20th century, there was steady progress in the development and refinement of a large number of empirical research methods. In addition to specific techniques for making observations, overall research designs were established that allowed these techniques to be applied so that the validity and reliability of observations could be assessed and increased. A large and growing number of statistical techniques were developed for analyzing data so that it can be objectively and systematically summarized and interpreted. In combination, observation methods, research designs, and statistical techniques provide powerful ways of describing and interpreting the social world. They yield important insights into the role of communication in that world.

During the past 25 years, the rapid development of computers has greatly enhanced the power of many empirical research methods, making them more efficient to apply and improving their effectiveness. Later chapters in this textbook will bring you up to date on many of these innovations. New research designs have been made possible by the availability of computer-based data analysis. Experimental research methods have regained popularity as it has become easier to make observations in laboratories using data collection instruments that feed observations directly into computers for analysis. Computers have also greatly enhanced our ability to analyze the observations (data) produced by all types of methods. For example, analyses of survey data that once took weeks and rooms full of workers sitting at mechanical calculators can now be completed in seconds using statistical analysis program packages such as SPSS and SAS.

The field of communication will likely continue to support a diverse range of scholarship that uses a variety of research methods. As this textbook well illustrates, communication researchers now have a much larger and more refined set of tools for observing the social world. Communication researchers have an ever-enlarging set of research problems that they can address. Development of new forms of media has given rise to many new research questions. Young empirical researchers no longer need be concerned about breaking out of the limitations imposed by the communication effects tradition, and those working within this tradition are able to develop and evaluate much more complicated models of effects. They can choose to ground their work within either qualitative or quanti-

---

[40]Jerry Willis, *Foundations of Qualitative Research: Interpretive and Critical Approaches* (Thousand Oaks, Calif.: Sage Publications, 2007).

tative paradigms.

TO LEARN MORE Avery, Donald R. "The Methodologists," 289-329 in Wm. David Sloan, ed., *Makers of the Media Mind: Journalism Educators and Their Ideas*. Hillsdale, N.J.: Lawrence Erlbaum Associates, 1990.

Benoit, William L. and R. Lance Holbert. "Empirical Intersections in Communication Research: Replication, Multiple Quantitative Methods, and Bridging the Quantitative-Qualitative Divide." *Journal of Communication* 58 (2008): 615-628.

Bryant, Jennings, and R. Glenn Cummins. "Traditions of Mass Media Theory and Research," 1-13 in R. W. Preiss, et al., eds. *Mass Media Effects Research: Advances Through Meta-analysis*. Mahwah, N.J. : Lawrence Erlbaum Associates, 2007.

Delia, Jesse. G. "Communication Research: A History," 20-98 in C. R. Berger and S. H. Chaffee, eds., *Handbook of Communication Science*. Newbury Park, Calif.: Sage Publications, 2010.

Dennis, Everett E., and Ellen Wartella. *American Communication Research: The Remembered History*. Mahwah, N.J.: Lawrence Erlbaum Associates, 1996.

"Ferment in the Field." *Journal of Communication* (Special Issue) (1983): 33.

Glander, Timothy R. *Origins of Mass Communications Research During the American Cold War: Educational Effects and Contemporary Implications, Sociocultural, Political, and Historical Studies in Education*. Mahwah, N.J.: Lawrence Erlbaum Associates, 2000.

Lowery, Shearon A., and DeFleur, Melvin L. *Milestones in Mass Communication Research*. New York: Longman, 1988.

Packer, Jeremy, and Craig Robertson, eds. *Thinking with James Carey: Essays on Communications, Transportation, History*. New York: Peter Lang Publishing, 2006.

Pietila, Veikko. *On the Highway of Mass Communication Studies*. Cresskill, N.J.: Hampton Press, 2005.

Pooley, Jefferson. "The New History of Mass Communication Research," 43-65 in D. W. Park and J. Pooley, eds., *The History of Media and Communication Research: Contested Memories*. New York: Peter Lang Publishing, 2008.

Pooley, Jefferson. "Fifteen Pages that Shook the Field: Personal Influence, Edward Shils, and the Remembered History of Mass Communication Research." *The ANNALS of the American Academy of Political and Social Science* 608 (November 2006): 130-156.

Rogers, Everett M. *A History of Communication Study: A Biographical Approach*. New York: The Free Press, 1994.

Schramm, Wilbur. *The Beginnings of Communication Study in America: A Personal Memoir*, S.H. Chaffee and E.M. Rogers, eds. Thousand Oaks, Calif.: Sage Publications, 1997.

Simonson, Peter. *Refiguring Mass Communication: A History*. Champaign: University of Illinois Press, 2010.

3

Research Ethics

Research helps societies anticipate and solve problems — but only if the process is fundamentally ethical and perceived as credible. Credibility is undermined by researchers who behave unethically and by those who seek to advance or protect their own interests by making unwarranted and unethical attacks against legitimate research. Attacks can be motivated by both ideological and commercial self-interest. Such behavior undermines efforts to educate the public and hinders legitimate efforts to protect human health and safety and to improve human communication.

Researchers representing a wide array of disciplines, including communication in all its forms, frequently produce information that is critical in debates about society's most pressing problems. In extreme circumstances, these debates *must* produce practical solutions — or, as Pulitzer Prize-winning author Jared Diamond (2005) demonstrates, societies will fail. Societies "may make disastrous decisions," he argues, "for a whole sequence of reasons: failure to anticipate a problem, failure to perceive it once it has arisen, failure to attempt to solve it after it has been perceived, and failure to succeed in attempts to solve it" (p. 438).

Ethical behavior is mandatory if the process is to work.

This chapter will introduce you to (1) some of the ethical problems that can negate researchers' contributions to theory building and problem solving and (2) strategies for resolving ethical dilemmas. The first part describes two strategies for making ethical decisions and an objective approach to communication research. The following section defines ideological research and summarizes some of the problems of this approach. Next, the chapter describes professional obfuscators and the "research" techniques they use to undermine legitimate research. The fourth part explains the need to treat research participants with respect. Finally, the chapter explores ethics issues in collecting and analyzing data.

DECISION-MAKING STRATEGIES

To understand ethics issues related to communication research, we

By Michael Ryan
University of Houston

must first be familiar with the basic principles of ethics. Essentially, ethics deals with the issue of right and wrong. Moral philosophers have struggled for centuries with questions of right and wrong. Sometimes the issues are monumental, such as whether a planned war is "just." The theories of Saint Augustine (354-430), the first to outline conditions for a just war, were revisited in 2002-03 as Americans debated whether a pre-emptive military strike against Iraq would be just. Sometimes the issues are quite narrow, such as whether it is ethical for a journal referee to recommend rejection of an article because it attacks orthodox views in communication research and theory (Ryan & Martinson, 1999).[1]

Philosophers in many disciplines (e.g., religion, genetics, politics, journalism and communication, sociology, and education) have developed several strategies for making ethics decisions. *Deontology* and *teleology*, two widely used approaches, are the basis for many other approaches. A third, *objective* approach to conducting research also is integral to the systematic methods that communication researchers use as they make strategic and ethics decisions. They consider, for example, such matters as what research questions to ask and how to word them, what research methods or statistical tests to use, and how to sample from a population.

Deontology

A *deontological* approach to decision-making is defined most simply as evaluating potential actions in strict terms of right and wrong. Further, it declares that men and women must respect one another and treat one another with dignity. Deontologists such as Immanuel Kant (1724-1804), whose writings established much of the foundation for deontology, take absolute positions that focus on one's duty to a higher authority. Kant argued that any lie, even a "good" lie that protects someone or produces a good result, is unacceptable because it violates the source of law and therefore harms humanity. Kant's "*categorical imperative*" requires that human behavior, to be considered ethical, must be consistent with a higher law. That is, all people in similar circumstances should behave in the same way, thus creating a universal law that applies to that behavior in that circumstance regardless of time or geography.

Communication scholars sometimes seek universal laws through systematic research. For example, researchers who wanted to measure the ethical values of public relations professionals asked practitioners to respond to a hypothetical situation in which a research scientist must ensure that toxic wastes from medical experiments were disposed of properly. At the same time, the organization for which the scientist worked was asking the state for enough money to expand the research facility by 75 percent, an expansion that could make important medical discoveries possible. Just before the legislature acted, the research scientist learned that the disposal site was closing. A journalist heard the rumor and wanted to know if it was true. The organization decided to withhold the information. A sample of public relations practitioners was asked to indicate which of several possible responses to the journalist they perceived as most ethical (Ryan & Martinson, 1984). A deontologist would condemn the organization's decision on grounds that

[1] A referee advises a journal editor about the quality of an article submitted for potential publication. Editors typically rely on the judgments of at least two referees for each article. Referees are experts in the topics addressed in articles they review.

withholding information is a lie and that any lie violates higher law.

A difficulty with the deontological approach is that someone must decide what constitutes a higher law and what behavior is or is not consistent with that law (i.e., what behavior is "right"). Debates about whether journalists, for example, should use confidential sources show clearly that a broad consensus can be elusive.

Teleology

A *teleological*, or *utilitarian*, approach is defined most simply as predicting the consequences of ethics decisions and then doing what is best for the greatest number. The writings of John Stuart Mill (1806-1873), Jeremy Bentham (1748-1832), and Henry Sidgwick (1838-1900) helped establish the foundation for the view that consequences must be considered as one strives to make ethics decisions. Lying, for instance, might be perceived as ethical if the lie helps individuals avoid disaster.

A teleologist considering the toxic disposal problem might very well argue that (1) a public relations professional who withholds information is not really lying, particularly if the public, as represented by a journalist, has no legitimate right to that information, and that (2) more people would benefit by the expansion of the research facility than would be hurt by withholding the facts.

A problem with the teleological approach is that someone must predict, before s/he can know the consequences of a decision, what is best for the greatest number. Because each situation is different, those who follow the teleological approach have no real guidelines to follow as they make decisions, and they have no real qualifications for making judgments.

An Objective Approach

Critics sometimes argue that researchers cannot be objective as they make strategic decisions, and many communication researchers agree. But perfect personal objectivity is not required in research. Many researchers adopt an *objective approach*, which means they follow guidelines, such as the scientific method, that help to ensure that their personal attitudes and values are not unduly reflected in their work. Hence, they are convinced they can produce (or construct) a reasonably accurate description of some part of the world (Ryan, 2006). They do not claim their descriptions are accurate in every detail, that absolute objectivity is attainable,[2] or that they hold no opinions and values that could affect their work. They do claim they have used a systematic approach that permits them to produce more accurate descriptions of reality than any other approach allows.

Researchers who are committed to an objective approach are (1) scrupulous in following proven research procedures and in writing complete, clear reports so that everyone can see precisely what they have done; (2) willing to adopt promising new approaches when traditional procedures are inadequate; (3) truthful (to themselves and others) about their personal preferences, values, and idiosyncrasies; (4) vigilant about ensuring that personal feelings do not color their strategic research decisions; (5) unwilling to allow their research to serve any ideologi-

---

2 Many, in fact, reject the term "objectivity" because it implies that human beings can be objective, which of course they cannot. They prefer, instead, to talk in terms of an objective approach or procedure, which human beings can learn and follow.

cal, commercial, political, religious, cultural, or social interests; (6) skeptical of authority figures who may wish to influence the research process so that it will produce approved results; (7) receptive to alternative explanations and new ideas; and (8) willing to encourage those who criticize their work or procedures to suggest alternative approaches.[3]

A researcher who is committed to an objective approach must apply those principles not only to procedures (such as how many coders to use), but to all aspects of the research process (such as deciding what problems to study). For example, a communication researcher who wants to measure the sources (Internet, newspaper, television, or friends, for example) that people consult for information about global warming might use a survey technique (the method), but s/he might refuse to accept funding from an energy company that wants to place conditions on the way the researcher describes the results.

Some postmodernist, critical, and cultural studies scholars have criticized researchers who use an objective approach, arguing that individuals are influenced by social, political, religious, cultural, and economic attitudes, values, and assumptions. They claim that no researcher can construct a reasonably accurate representation of reality because nobody can transcend his or her values, attitudes, and perceptions, all of which are influenced by race, class, gender, and other personal, professional, environmental, and psychological factors (e.g., Berger & Luckman, 1967; Gergen, 2001). Many also attack the view that knowledge can be universal — that some research results are applicable across time and geography — a view that is held by many researchers who use an objective approach.

The postmodernist/critical/cultural critique has produced some positive change in the research process,[4] but the complete rejection of objective approaches and of the universality of some knowledge has not. According to communication theorist Robert McChesney (1993), "The argument that rejected the universality and neutrality of mainstream social science has evolved into a rejection of the very notions of truth, rationality, reason, science, logic, or evidence" (p. 101). The result is a rejection of the idea that "... all humans share the capacity to reason and that reason could be used to liberate the species" (p. 101; see also McChesney, 2000).

Dr. Evan Bowen — who works for a think tank in Washington, D.C. — is unhappy with media coverage of his preferred candidate, Donna Rose, for the Democratic nomination for president.[5] He thinks coverage of Rose is too critical and that coverage of Rose's opponents is too favorable. Bowen decides to use content analysis techniques to document what he sees as unequal coverage. He formulates a research question and uses procedures that will enable him to build the case he wants to make, rather than produce a reasonably accurate construction of reality.

The question guiding Bowen's research is this: How many more unfavorable

IDEOLOGICAL RESEARCH

---

[3] Journalists, public relations professionals, and other communication professionals who are committed to an objective approach also observe these principles, although they may state them somewhat differently.

[4] Many communication scholars, for example, have become sensitive to the ways in which mass media can convey a sexist ideology that supports a patriarchal society (Lont, 1993).

[5] "Bowen" is a fictional composite who represents a number of individuals and organizations who use ideological "research" as a propaganda technique.

stories do the news media publish and air about Rose than about her opponents?[6] The question reflects potential bias because it assumes before evidence is collected that the media do publish and air more unfavorable stories about Rose. Further, Bowen does not follow the prescribed procedures for content analysis research. He does not use multiple coders, opting instead to code all content himself. Nobody knows the reliability of the decisions because Bowen alone determines which stories go into which categories. He places each story about each candidate into one of two categories, critical or uncritical; and he does not supply the definitions for these important terms, as required in content analysis research.

Bowen's results — reported in one of the think tank's many publications and distributed to the news media — show that far more favorable stories are published and aired about Rose's opponents than about her. The media dutifully report the dubious results. Neither Bowen nor the news media have behaved ethically, for both have contributed to the distribution of information whose accuracy is questionable. Bowen's unexpressed goal is to "expose" media coverage of his candidate as unfair, so that subsequent coverage might be more to his liking. Ideological considerations, not systematic methodology, have driven his research.

Whereas the unethical nature of Bowen's conduct is readily evident, that of the media may be less obvious. However, just as the news media are ethically bound to refuse to publish verbal assertions they suspect are inaccurate, they should refuse to publish research results they suspect are inaccurate. The reality is that they often fail to bring the same ethical standards to bear on information that purports to be "scientific." Bowen, who recognized this and counted on the media to report his "research" results uncritically, also behaved unethically.

This hypothetical case occurs all too frequently in the real world, in which dueling ideologues typically produce very poor research. At best, such research does nothing to help societies identify and resolve their most pressing problems. At worst, it may inject so much misinformation and confusion into critical debates that nothing is resolved, or it may cause critical institutions to behave in unprofessional ways. The ideologue represented by Evan Bowen might actually succeed in changing media coverage of his preferred candidate, thus giving her an unfair edge in a party primary.

Although virtually everyone would condemn Bowen's research, not everyone condemns all ideological research. Some postmodernist, critical, and cultural studies scholars in communication have been in the vanguard of critics who argue that only ideologically progressive research is worthwhile and that personal experience must foreground any search for truth.[7]

Ideologically progressive research refers in this context to efforts by researchers to use their findings to redress perceived grievances; to advance cultural, religious, political, social, or other agendas; or to improve society or aspects of society along lines they define. "Progressive" can mean anything. The ideology is personal, but it can reflect conservative, reactionary, liberal, or radical views of larger groups or organizations. Finally, ideological research, as defined here,

[6] An ethical researcher would ask the question differently: What percentages of stories published about the Democratic presidential candidates are favorable, and what percentages are unfavorable?

[7] They reject the scientific method, for decades the dominant paradigm in communication studies, and the prevailing view that systematic data collection is essential if one is to explain increasingly complex phenomena.

means a researcher decides what his or her evidence will show before any evidence is collected.[8]

Postmodernist historians Ellen Somekawa and Elizabeth Smith (1988) argue that all interpretations of history are equally valid and assert that "we are all engaged in writing a kind of propaganda…. [R]ather than believe in the absolute truth of what we are writing, we must believe in the moral or political position we are taking with it" (p. 154). More fundamentally — communication scholars James Potter, Roger Cooper, and Michel Dupagne (1993) argue — an ideological approach "foregrounds its ideological perspective and analyzes texts or industry occurrences as evidence in support of that ideology" (p. 322).[9]

For some scholars, ideological considerations guide decisions about which questions they pose and how questions are framed. An ideological researcher, for example, might ask the question: How did the U.S. government's successful manipulation of the media and the public occur during the Persian Gulf War?[10] A communication researcher using an objective approach might ask, instead: Did the U.S. government try to manipulate the media and the public during the Gulf War? If so, did the government present a unified front (i.e., were dissenting voices stifled)? Was the manipulation, if any, successful? What other factors may have accounted for media and public actions, reactions, and attitudes?

Shortchanging Girls

A well-known study by the American Association of University Women (1991) is a classic example of how research can be used or interpreted to support ideological goals. The study was widely and uncritically reported by journalists who did not understand the methodological difficulties associated with ideological research. The report, *Shortchanging Girls, Shortchanging America: A Call to Action,* was a reaction to a study by psychologist Carol Gilligan (1982), in which she reported that the female culture of nurturing, accommodation, and caring was viewed by many girls as an important alternative to the dominant culture of competitive males and their abstract moral reasoning.

About the time they become teenagers, Gilligan said, girls discover that their unique knowledge, especially about human relations, is subversive to the patriarchal society; and they try to hide that knowledge to protect themselves. During her interviews of adolescent girls, Gilligan said, "I felt at times that I was entering an underground world, that I was led in by girls to caverns of knowledge, which then suddenly were covered over, as if nothing was known and nothing was happening" (Gilligan, 1990, p. 14).

The AAUW, alarmed by Gilligan's findings, commissioned a study, not to find out *whether* she was right, but to *prove* that she was. "We wanted to put some factual data behind our belief that girls are getting shortchanged in the classroom," AAUW President Sharon Schuster told *The New York Times* (Daley, 1991, p. B6). Gilligan was selected to help a polling firm develop a self-esteem questionnaire. "In effect, Gilligan cooperated in designing a study that was supposedly

---

[8] This critique of ideological research should not be interpreted as a generalized attack against critical theory, cultural studies, social science, or any other approach that can have a societal impact.

[9] This is not an argument against historians and others who render evaluations after careful analysis of the facts (see Vann, 2004) or against those who are critical of prevailing generalizations and conventional interpretations that have questionable support (see Hoffer, 2004).

[10] Douglas Kellner (1995) posed a similar question (in other terms) in his study of the Gulf War (p. 198).

offering independent confirmation of her claims" (Sommers, 1996, p. 374). The predictable results: Girls emerge from adolescence with less confidence than boys in their abilities, with poor self-images, and with relatively low expectations.

Later analyses, and even data within the AAUW report, suggested that the results and their interpretations were questionable. A *Science News* story reported that leading researchers were skeptical of the AAUW report. The director of the Center for the Study of Human Development at Brown University said the report was "as shaky as jello." The editor of the *Handbook on Adolescent Psychology* said the report was "awful" (Sommers, 1996, p. 375).

Consequences   One difficulty with ideological research, like all research, is that it can have an important, detrimental impact on public opinion and public policy, particularly when journalists assign to ideological research the same authority and credibility they assign to legitimate research. Because of the AAUW report, for example, "The public will soon be spending countless millions to address a fake self-esteem crisis" (Sommers, 1996, p. 378).

Another difficulty is the potential backlash by those who look with disfavor on ideological research. Biographer Fiona MacCarthy, for instance, rejects the view that a researcher's goal should be to find support for preconceived ideas. A result of this type of approach, MacCarthy writes, is that "the unprecedented growth of women's studies in the last twenty-five years has produced a great deal of very dull writing and — more dangerous — doubtful scholarship. Women's history has been vulnerable to the slipshodness of judgment and stridency of language that almost inevitably develop when an academic subject declines into a cause" (1997, p. 8).

Philosophy professor Susan Haack (1996) argues that an inquiry that makes a case for a proposition identified in advance is a sham and a fake. "So they [ideological researchers] are motivated," she reasons, "to avoid careful examination of any evidence that might impugn the proposition for which they are seeking to make a case, to play down or obfuscate the importance or relevance of such evidence, to contort themselves explaining it away" (p. 58).

Scholars who want to find support for approved positions — whether of the left or the right — pollute the scholarly literature by producing work that scholars outside (and sometimes inside) their own scholarly communities simply cannot trust. Scholarship is not trustworthy when the questions posed suggest quite clearly that one is not *seeking* truth but is, instead, trying to *construct* truth; when one does not use a systematic, carefully articulated method to decide which information should be included and which should be excluded; and when one generalizes broadly from one's own experiences and fails to validate those personal experiences by studying the experiences of others.

An ironic consequence of ideological research, and much of what that approach implies, is the loss of the very personal freedom for which many ideological scholars claim they struggle. Communication scholar Robert McChesney (1993) put the case quite well: "If we abandon the notion that all people share certain fundamental qualities and capacities and are capable of reason, we open the door to justifications for treating people fundamentally differently" (p. 101).

Cherry Applegate, a public relations professional who works for an organization that is a front for the tobacco industry, is paid by the industry to fight local efforts to ban smoking in public places.[11] Such bans, industry officials believe, could reduce their profits. Applegate, as part of her campaign to head off smoking bans, helps local people conduct "surveys" to show that local residents object to any smoking ban. Such "surveys" nearly always use non-random samples to generate results that may appear to be valid.

PROFESSIONAL OBFUSCATORS

One way to do this is to conduct a survey in a shopping mall and instruct survey takers to solicit the opinions of people who toss cigarettes as they enter the mall or who have the scent of smoke about them. These smokers are much more likely than non-smokers to oppose any smoking ban. Applegate could also skew the results by asking respondents a loaded question: Do you think it is right for a few elite civic leaders to demand that smokers give up their constitutional right to smoke?

Applegate is a communication specialist who uses bogus research results to confuse an issue to such an extent that no action is taken. She is not unlike Evan Bowen, who wants the media to give his preferred candidate favorable coverage. The difference is that Applegate, a professional obfuscator, seeks to protect commercial interests while Bowen seeks to advance ideological interests.

Professional obfuscators are hired to protect products and services from what they see as meddling do-gooders (consumer advocates, government regulators, progressive politicians, and the like). Professional obfuscators are paid by industrialists to stop efforts to regulate their industries, even if they have to behave unethically. They were hard at work in the lead industry in the 1920s, the chemical industry in the 1950s, the asbestos industry in the 1960s, the plastics and oil industries in the 1970s, the tobacco industry in the 1980s and 1990s, and the energy industry in the 1990s and 2000s ("The art," 2005, p. 30).

Research is an easy target for obfuscators because (1) the uncertainty built into the research process is easily and effectively exploited and (2) many people are easily swayed or confused by partisan attacks because they are not sufficiently literate about research to judge its merits.

It is easy for a partisan critic to raise enough questions to make virtually any systematic study seem weak. "By magnifying and exploiting these uncertainties," write two health researchers, "polluters and manufacturers of dangerous products have been remarkably successful in delaying, often for decades, regulations and other measures designed to protect the health and safety of individuals and communities" (Michaels & Monforton, 2005, p. S40).

Critics whose goal is to protect commercial interests often use two strategies: (1) Attack any research study that in any way threatens their commercial interests and (2) produce their own "research" to counter legitimate studies that report unacceptable findings (i.e., those that do not support commercial positions). While commercial interests come in for most of the criticism, we should also remember that special-interest groups (even scholarly and non-profit ones) can misuse research. The partisan research typically is misleading at best because sympathetic researchers are expected (and paid) to supply "data" that support partisan goals.

---

[11] "Applegate" is a fictional composite representing many people.

Professional obfuscators are firmly entrenched in many American industries and special-interest organizations. They frequently cherry-pick evidence that supports their position and discard evidence that does not.[12]

Tobacco and Sound Science　As an illustration of obfuscation, let's look at the tobacco industry. Over the last couple of decades, it used communication techniques successfully (and unethically) as it tried to deflect the regulation of its product, in part by discrediting scientific results documenting the harmful effects of cigarette smoke on smokers and non-smokers alike. An early tool was The Advancement of Sound Science Coalition (TASSC), a now-defunct front for its "sound science" campaign, which was intended to delay or to kill the Environmental Protection Agency's 1992 study reporting that approximately 3,000 non-smokers die of lung cancer every year because of secondhand smoke (Environmental Protection Agency, 1992). APCO Associates, a subsidiary of the huge GCI/Grey advertising and public relations firm, coordinated the campaign.

TASSC described itself as a "grassroots-based, not-for-profit watchdog group of scientists and representatives from universities, independent organizations and industry, that advocates the use of sound science in the public policy arena" (Advancement of Science, 1993, p. 3). The fierce attack against science included arguments against the EPA, which, TASSC charged, politicized science and made it conform to the political views of special interests.

One of TASSC's jobs was "to make the case that efforts to regulate tobacco were based on the same 'junk science' as efforts to regulate Alar, food additives, automobile emissions, and other industrial products that had not yet achieved tobacco's pariah status" (Rampton & Stauber, 2001, p. 239). The goal of the "junk science" campaign was to highlight or create uncertainty about research that could be used as a basis for regulation. This and similar campaigns by other industries are designed to discredit or ridicule cutting edge research and researchers who threaten powerful interests.

Partisans who attack research typically charge that studies (and systematic methods) used to justify new regulations are flawed, contradictory, or incomplete and that it is wrong or premature to impose new regulations or to compensate those who may have been harmed by a product (Michaels & Monforton, 2005, p. S40). The tobacco industry was comfortable with this approach, as a statement by one industry executive suggested: "Doubt is our product since it is the best means of competing with the 'body of fact' that exists in the mind of the general public. It is also the means of establishing a controversy" ("Smoking and Health," 1969, p. 4).

TREATING RESEARCH PARTICIPANTS WITH RESPECT　Ashley Brown shows up for her media and society class on Monday morning and discovers that her teacher, Jonathan Fredericks, wants the class to participate in a study of audience perceptions of violence on television.[13] He offers to add 10 points to the final exam grades of all who participate. This is a follow up, Fredericks

---

[12] It is not necessarily unethical to write an ideological treatise, to cherry-pick the facts, as long as the writer makes it clear that is what he or she is doing.

[13] "Fredericks" is a fictional composite representing many researchers and disciplines over many years.

says, to a questionnaire administered last Monday seeking students' opinions about violence in films. Fredericks has already divided names randomly into two groups, and he tells group A students to assemble at the back of the room and group B students to assemble at the front. He does not tell students the purpose of the research, and he does not give them a chance to opt out. Group A follows a graduate assistant to another room, and Group B stays with Fredericks.

Group B is shown an excerpt from each of 12 R-rated films. Six of the excerpts depict physical violence directed against women, and six depict violence directed against men. All of the violent characters are men. Characters are beaten with fists in four excerpts; they are shot in four; and characters are stabbed in four. Group A watches 12 excerpts from PG-rated films. Conflict, but no physical violence, is depicted in each excerpt. Students in both groups indicate their perceptions of each excerpt as it is shown and then complete the same questionnaire they filled out the previous Monday. They write their names and Social Security numbers on the questionnaires and leave at the end of the experiment. They hear no more about the study.

Fredericks' behavior would be criticized by many of his colleagues as unethical. Brown should not have been coerced into participating in this research, particularly since she might have been exposed in Group B to potentially disturbing violent episodes from films that she might never go see on her own. Fredericks should have explained the research, told students they could be exposed to violent scenes, allowed them to opt out of the experiment, and offered another way to earn the 10 extra points. To ensure students did not feel intimidated, Fredericks should have asked a colleague or graduate assistant to tell students they could opt out. Finally, Fredericks should have debriefed students at the end of the class or at the following class period. A complete explanation of the film clips, the method, and the guiding theory behind the research was required.

An important principle of ethical research is that a researcher must ensure s/he preserves a research participant's *autonomy*. Researchers must respect their participants' fundamental rights and decisions, the most important of which is the right not to participate. In an academic setting, this means student-participants must be given a realistic alternative to participation. A teacher who gives academic credit for participation in a research study must provide a comparable opportunity for students who do not wish to participate. The amount of credit must be the same, and the work required must be comparable. It would not be fair to have some students spend 90 minutes answering a survey while some must spend four hours writing a paper. The two tasks could in no way be considered comparable.

Since teachers wield significant power over their students, ethical researchers must seek ways to minimize the pressure on students to participate in research studies. One way is to arrange for others to administer questionnaires, collect extra-credit assignments, and award bonus points. Students should feel less pressure if they know teachers will not know whether they completed a survey or not.

A second important principle is that potential research participants have a right to sufficient information on which to base a decision about participating or not. Their consent must be *informed*. Consent cannot be considered to be informed until the following conditions are met:

• Potential research participants must be briefed as fully as possible about the research before data are collected. In general, this means researchers must not *conceal* information. They are obliged to give potential participants complete information about the proposed research. Unfortunately, researchers cannot always tell participants everything about the proposed research without ruining the study. For example, if researchers tell participants they want to measure the relationship of respondents' attitudes toward candidates for public office to media coverage of those candidates, respondents might change the ways they answer survey questions. They might try to give researchers the answers they think the researchers want, or they might try to hide their true attitudes. Concealment may be appropriate when (1) as little information as possible is concealed, (2) participants are told about the concealment during debriefing, (3) privacy is not invaded, (4) participants are not injured, and (5) names of those conducting or sponsoring the research are not concealed (see below).

• Potential participants must be informed about possible consequences of participation in the research. They must be told if there is a possibility that they might be physically injured or emotionally disturbed by images they might view during the research. Participants must be told ahead of time if the research design requires that they view violent scenes from films or magazines, for instance, or if they will be expected to play with other children following an experimental manipulation. In the case of children or older people who cannot make informed decisions, parents or guardians must be fully informed.

• Potential participants must be told how their privacy will be protected and who may see their responses. Will a teaching assistant, Dr. Fredericks, or someone else (in the hypothetical case discussed above) enter Ashley Brown's responses from her questionnaire into a database? Will the questionnaires be destroyed, or will they end up on Fredericks' bookshelves for years? Could students have access to her responses? Brown would have legitimate concerns about who might see her responses because her name and Social Security number are on the questionnaire and because the survey requested sensitive information. Ideally, Brown's name and number would not be on the survey, and questionnaires would be destroyed as soon as responses were entered into a database.

• Potential participants should be told the names of the researchers and the organization sponsoring the research. An individual who conducts research for a commercial purpose and who is sponsored by a corporation should not suggest that the research is sponsored or funded by an academic or government agency, both of which carry more credibility for many participants than a corporation, particularly a corporation that does not have a sound reputation.

A third important principle is to *avoid deception* — that is, to avoid intentionally giving participants false information. Many teleologists would argue that deception is acceptable when the potential benefit outweighs the potential harm, answers cannot be obtained without deception, harm to participants is temporary, participants can withdraw from the research at any moment, and participants are informed of the deception during debriefing (Elms, 1982). Researchers and others who endorse deontology for decision-making would reject these arguments as rationalizations. Deontologists would reject all deception as a violation of a universal law against lying.[14]

Research participants have suffered abuse in some instances. One of the most famous studies in which critics charge that participants were abused was conducted by Yale sociologist Stanley Milgram, who studied obedience among college students (Milgram, 1963). Although his research was not specifically about communication, it does provide an important lesson for communication researchers. The experiment was conducted in two rooms. In one was a "learner," someone who had to respond to questions from a "teacher" in another room. If the learner gave an incorrect response, the teacher — urged on by an "official" in a lab coat — punished him or her with an electrical shock. In fact, the teacher was the real subject of the research. The unseen learner was an actor who pleaded with each teacher not to shock him. No shocks were administered, but teachers did not know that. Milgram wanted to know how far a college student would go in punishing those who gave wrong responses. Sixty percent of the teachers obeyed orders to punish the learners by administering 450-volt shocks. No teacher stopped before administering 350 volts. Some of the teachers apparently were seriously disturbed by what they did, and Milgram was widely criticized (Baumrind, 1964; Clarke, 1999).[15]

Protecting Research Participants

Abuses have led to the creation in research institutes and universities of committees (or research ethics boards) to protect human participants. All research proposals must be submitted to the committees, which must determine whether participants are put at physical or psychological risk by proposed research. If the answer is yes, the research may not be allowed. Committees require researchers to inform potential participants about the title and purpose of the research, procedures, participation (that it is voluntary and anonymous and that one may withdraw at any time), potential risks and benefits, alternatives to participation, and potential publications. Institutions that do not have committees to protect human participants generally are ineligible to receive federal funding.

The job of a committee to protect human participants is not always as easy or straightforward as one might think, for attitudes and procedures can change over time. One example is Ellen Whiteman's experience in conducting a qualitative study in which she observed what adolescent girls did for fun on the Internet. Whiteman had consent from the adolescent girls and their parents and from the research ethics board at Whiteman's institution. "However," Whiteman wrote, "I did not consider whether I needed consent or assent from the people with whom my participants interacted as part of their demonstrations of how they played on the Internet" (Whiteman, 2007, p. 3).

Whiteman, who was criticized for her failure to get consent from the girls with whom her research participants played, argued that it would be impossible to get consent from all who participate in computer-mediated communication. If that is the standard, then research of this type might be impossible. Deontologists would not hesitate to stop such a study in its tracks, while teleologists would al-

---

[14] A fourth principle is that everyone, including those who participate in an initial study, must *share all benefits* derived from the research. This principle applies primarily to medical experiments.

[15] Some scholars argue that the criticism of the Milgram experiment was excessive and that critics may be too quick to stop research in which deception is proposed (Herrera, 2001).

low it to continue if the benefits seemed to outweigh the risks.

COLLECTING AND ANALYZING DATA

A *first principle* of data collection and analysis is that the *research process must be transparent*. That is, the exact wording of research questions and hypotheses and complete details about the method (e.g., wording of survey questions, points covered during debriefing, response rates, definitions, documents examined and excluded) must be reported. No data may be changed, invented, or thrown away. No information may be withheld from the public or research participants, even if they are not the results the researcher or sponsoring organization hopes for. Further, no information that would help the public evaluate the results may be withheld. Potential voters, for example, need to know that a poll showing candidate A with a 20-point lead was conducted before the media reported that candidate A beat her husband.

A *second principle* is that *researchers must be scrupulous in following stated procedures*. They must not cut corners. They must verify the accuracy of data entered from questionnaires into a statistical spreadsheet, and they must indicate clearly why some participants' responses are not used. They may, for instance, specify before data collection that a questionnaire will be discarded if a participant fails to supply at least 50 percent of the data requested or if there is strong evidence of response set (such as marking only "strongly agree" responses when that would make no sense). They also must use statistical techniques that are appropriate to the research questions and hypotheses. If an analysis of variance test assumes a normal distribution of data, it would not be appropriate to use that test if the sample were not randomly selected.

A *third principle* — which should be obvious, but sometimes is overlooked — is that *researchers must avoid errors*. It is not difficult to find published scholarly books and articles about communication that have errors. Fortunately, they have not been so critical as to create public controversy. That was not the case with Michael Bellesiles' book *Arming America*. It purported to show that gun ownership during the late 18th and early 19th centuries was less common than previously supposed, an argument that drew fire from gun advocates. It won praise and a major award. Then, however, a committee from Emery University, where Bellesiles worked, examined the evidence and found sloppy scholarship, misleading and unprofessional work, and evidence of data falsification, a charge he denied. Bellesiles eventually resigned his post (Meyerowitz, 2004, p. 1325). The principle that communication researchers should learn from the Bellesiles affair is that, regardless of the research method used, accuracy is essential.

A *fourth principle* is that *researchers must report appropriate conclusions and interpretations*. It is unethical to report conclusions that are not supported by the data or facts. A researcher, for example, might expect results that are consistent with his or her preconceptions or favored theory. When they are not consistent, a researcher might report the anticipated conclusions anyway. Or a researcher could violate ethics standards by generalizing beyond the data. Results of a study of college students' Internet usage habits, for example, might be generalized inappropriately to users of all ages.

A *fifth principle* is that *researchers must not plagiarize*. Plagiarism includes, among other lapses, using the work of other scholars without proper quotation marks and attribution. Two of America's best-known historians, Doris Kearns Goodwin and Stephen Ambrose, admitted they had used materials from other authors without proper documentation, a revelation that caused consternation among historians and the public and potentially undermined the credibility of the research process (Hoffer, 2004, ch. 6).

The peer review system ensures that manuscripts and grant proposals are vetted by a researcher's colleagues. Researchers' insistence on the replication of research also helps ensure that abuses (such as ideological research or cheating) ultimately are exposed. The scientific method and other systematic approaches, which establish the rules of the game, are intended to ensure that a researcher's work is transparent to other scholars and to the public and that the researcher follows procedures that have been validated in other studies. If procedures have not been validated in other studies, a researcher is obligated to explain why and how she or he developed a different research technique.

POLICING BAD RESEARCH

As with other aspects of the research process, corruption is inevitable. For example, blind review — meaning manuscript and grant proposal referees do not know authors' names or institutional affiliations — is intended to prevent abuses. Nevertheless, some referees behave unethically by rejecting any research or proposed research, regardless of quality, that casts doubt on the referee's favorite theory.

Some reject research because they dislike the author (for sometimes, although the name is not on a manuscript, it is possible to discover the author of a study or proposal). Further, some editors and grant administrators, who are the gatekeepers of scholar inquiry and who always know authors and institutions, occasionally reject research for less than ethical reasons. This unethical behavior can have a profound impact on the development of knowledge and practical solutions because some potentially useful research is never funded or published (Ryan, 1982).

TO LEARN MORE

Bentham, J. (1948). *An introduction to the principles of morals and legislation.* New York: Hafner.

Bloland, H. G. (2005). Whatever happened to postmodernism in higher education? No requiem in the new millennium. *The Journal of Higher Education, 76*(2), 121-150.

Christians, C., Fackler, M., Rotzoll, K., Mckee, K., Woods, R. (2005). *Media ethics: Cases and moral reasoning,* 7th ed. Upper Saddle River, N.J.: Allyn & Bacon.

Gergen, K. J. (2001). Psychological science in a postmodern context. *American Psychologist, 56*(10): 803-813.

Haack, S. (1996). Concern for truth: What it means, why it matters. In P.R. Gross, N. Levitt, & M. W. Lewis (Eds.), *The flight from science and reason* (pp. 57-63). New York: New York Academy of Sciences.

Kant, I. (1949). On a supposed right to lie from altruistic motives. In *Critique of practical reason and other writings in moral philosophy* (L. W. Beck, Ed. & Trans.) (pp. 346-350). Chicago: University of Chicago Press.

Knowlton, S., and Parsons, P. (1994). *The journalists' moral compass: Basic principles.* Westport, Conn.: Praeger.

Koertge, N. (Ed.). (1998). *A house built on sand: Exposing postmodernist myths about science.* New York: Oxford University Press.

Koertge, N. (1996). Wrestling with the social constructor. In P.R. Gross, N. Levitt, & M. W. Lewis (Eds.), *The flight from science and reason* (pp. 266-273). New York: New York Academy of Sciences.

Longino, H. E. (1990). *Science as social knowledge: Values and objectivity in scientific inquiry.* Princeton, N.J.: Princeton University Press.

Mill, J. S. (1998). *Utilitarianism* (R. Crisp, Ed.). Oxford: Oxford University Press.

Rampton, S., & Stauber, J. (2002). *Trust us, we're experts: How industry manipulates science and gambles with your future.* New York: Jeremy P. Tarcher/Putnam.

Sidgwick, H. (1893). *The methods of ethics*, 5th ed. London: Macmillan.

Sokal, A., & Bricmont, J. (1998). *Fashionable nonsense: Postmodern intellectuals' abuse of science.* New York: Picador USA.

Wagner, W. (2005). The perils of relying on interested parties to evaluate scientific quality. *American Journal of Public Health, 95*(Suppl. 1), S99-S106.

REFERENCES   The Advancement of Sound Science Coalition (1993, December 3). National watchdog organization launched to fight unsound science used for public policy comes to Texas, news release. Retrieved on October 10, 2005, at tobaccodocuments.org/pm/2046988980-8982.html.

American Association of University Women (1991). *Shortchanging girls, shortchanging America: A call to action.* Washington, D. C.: AAUW.

The art of obfuscation (2005, July 30). *St. Louis Post-Dispatch*, p. 30.

Baumrind, D. (1964). Some thoughts on ethics of research: After reading Milgram's "behavioral study of obedience." *American Psychologist, 19*(6), 421-423.

Berger, P. & Luckman, T. (1967). *The social construction of reality: A treatise in the sociology of knowledge.* London: Routledge and Keegan Paul.

Clarke, S. (1999). Justifying deception in social science research. *Journal of Applied Philosophy, 16*(2), 151-166.

Daley, S. (1991, January 9). Little girls lose their self-esteem on way to adolescence, study finds. *The New York Times*, p. B6.

Diamond, J. (2005). *Collapse: How societies choose to fail or succeed.* New York: Viking.

Elms, A. C. (1982). Keeping deception honest: Justifying conditions for social scientific research stratagems. In T. L. Beauchamp, R. R. Faden, R. J. Wallace, & L. Walters (Eds.), *Ethical issues in social science research* (pp. 232-245). Baltimore: Johns Hopkins University Press.

Environmental Protection Agency (1992). *Respiratory health effects of passive smoking: Lung cancer and other disorders.* Washington, D.C.: Office of Research and Development, Office of Health and Environmental Assessment.

Gergen, K. J. (2001). Psychological science in a postmodern context. *American Psychologist, 56*(10): 803-813.

Gilligan, C. (1982). *In a different voice: Psychological theory and women's development.* Cambridge, MA: Harvard University Press.

Gilligan, C. (1990). Preface: Teaching Shakespeare's sister: Notes from the underground of female adolescence. In C. Gilligan, N. P. Lyons, & T. J. Hanmer (Eds.), *Making connections: The relational worlds of adolescent girls at Emma Willard School* (pp. 6-29). Cambridge, MA: Harvard University Press.

Haack, S. (1996). Concern for truth: What it means, why it matters. In P. R. Gross, N. Levitt, & M. W. Lewis (Eds.), *The flight from science and reason* (pp. 57-63). New York: New York Academy of Sciences.

Herrera, C. D. (2001). Ethics, deception, and "those Milgram experiments." *Journal of Applied Philosophy, 18*(3), 245-256.

Hoffer, P. C. (2004). *Past imperfect: Facts, fictions, fraud — American history from Bancroft and*

54

Research Methods in Communication

Parkman to Ambrose, Bellesiles, Ellis, and Goodwin. New York: PublicAffairs.

Kellner, D. (1995). *Media culture: Cultural studies, identity and politics between the modern and the postmodern*. London: Routledge.

Lont, C. M. (1993). Feminist critique of mass communication research. In S. P. Bowen & N. Wyatt (Eds.), *Transforming visions: Feminist critiques in communication studies* (pp. 231-248). Cresskill, NJ: Hampton.

MacCarthy, F. (1997, February 6). How the other half lived. *The New York Review of Books*, pp. 4, 6, 8.

McChesney, R. W. (1993). Critical communication research at the crossroads. *Journal of Communication, 43*(4), 98-104.

McChesney, R. W. (2000). The political economy of communication and the future of the field. *Media, Culture & Society, 22*(1), 109-116.

Meyerowitz, J. (2004). History's ethical crisis: An introduction. *The Journal of American History, 90*(4), 1325-1326.

Michaels, D., & Monforton, C. (2005). Manufacturing uncertainty: Contested science and the protection of the public's health and environment. *American Journal of Public Health, 95*(Suppl. 1), S39-S48.

Milgram, S. (1963). Behavioral study of obedience. *Journal of Abnormal and Social Psychology, 67*(4), 371-378.

Potter, W. J., Cooper, R., & Dupagne, M. (1993). The three paradigms of mass media research in mainstream communication journals. *Communication Theory, 3*(4), 317-335.

Rampton, S., & Stauber, J. (2002). *Trust us, we're experts: How industry manipulates science and gambles with your future*. New York: Jeremy P. Tarcher/Putnam.

Ryan, M. (1982). Evaluating scholarly manuscripts in journalism and communications. *Journalism Quarterly, 59*(2), 273-285.

Ryan, M. (2006). Mainstream news media, an objective approach, and the march to war in Iraq. *Journal of Mass Media Ethics, 21*(1): 4-29.

Ryan, M., & Martinson, D. L. (1984). Ethical values, the flow of journalistic information and public relations persons. *Journalism Quarterly, 61*(1): 27-34.

Ryan, M., & Martinson, D. L. (1999). Perceived problems in evaluation of mass communication scholarship. *Journalism & Mass Communication Educator, 54*(1): 69-78.

Smoking and Health Proposal (1969). Internal Brown & Williamson memorandum, number 0000332506. Retrieved on October 10, 2005, at tobaccodocuments.org/bw/332506.html.

Somekawa, E., & Smith, E. A. (1988). Theorizing the writing of history or, "I can't think why it should be so dull, for a great deal of it must be invention." *Journal of Social History, 22*(1), 149-161.

Sommers, C. H. (1996). Pathological social science: Carol Gilligan and the incredible shrinking girl. In P. R. Gross, N. Levitt, & M. W. Lewis (Eds.), *The flight from science and reason* (pp. 369-382). New York: New York Academy of Sciences.

Vann, R. T. (2004). Historians and moral evaluations. *History and Theory, 43*(4), 3-30.

Whiteman, E. (2007). "Just chatting": Research ethics and cyberspace. *International Journal of Qualitative Methods, 6*(2), 1-9.

The Library as a Research Source

More than 6,500 scientific, technical, and medical articles are produced in the United States every day, 24,000 worldwide. That comes out to 1,000 each hour (Burckel, 2007). It is also estimated that information doubles every five years. That suggests that every time you go to research a topic, even if you conducted research on the same topic a year ago, there's 20 percent more information available and almost 2.4 million articles published since your last research, some of which will pertain to your topic.

The ease with which that information is accessible to you now through the Internet and with digital databases means the expectations are higher that each researcher has exhausted the range of information on the subject and has the latest data to work with. These are lofty heights to reach when tackling a research problem. The library becomes an even more important partner in this process.

With the Internet, the library's information monopoly has changed. Libraries still maintain a gate-keeping function, determining what information will be available on the shelves and what database access will be made available to visitors on site. But the amount of freely available information on the Internet is delivering satisfying results to millions of users. One must exercise caution, however, in using ease and speed as criteria for being "satisfied" with results. "Good enough" is becoming, for some researchers, unfortunately, a substitute for "best" sources of information (Burckel, 2007).

The library plays several important roles today in the process of research. One is to purchase published materials in a variety of formats and make them easily accessible to users. Another is to identify, preserve, and maintain unique collections and locally produced information. Most library experts believe there should be a 50-50 split in expenditures and that time should be devoted evenly to these two roles (Cochrane, 2007).

Libraries provide the gateway to accessing relevant, previously published literature on a subject to help build bibliographies and provide the content for thor-

By Jim Pokrywczynski
Marquette University

ough literature reviews. Bibliographies and literature reviews will be explained in Chapter 6 of this book. Once this first step is complete, libraries can also play a role in helping to determine whether secondary research using existing sources is adequate or whether primary research, which will involve gathering original data on your own, is the correct methodology to answer your research questions. Library staff can provide helpful advice on locating databases that may save a researcher from "reinventing the wheel" by collecting data via survey, experiment, observation or some other primary research method. If such databases exist, libraries can deliver that information and assist with use and interpretation.

These services typify the changing role of today's library. The library has evolved from primarily a depository of books and other materials to a service organization. "The library has moved from a place to get information to a place to gain knowledge," says David Martin, a leading designer of library buildings (Straight answers, 2006). Key people in the organization are *reference librarians*, who play the role of consultants familiar with database access and use, Interlibrary Loan services, and the variety of other resources available within the bricks and mortar library itself as well as elsewhere and online. For example, with Interlibrary Loan, any material categorized by the Library of Congress can be put in your hands in less than two weeks. Digital technology allows libraries to provide "immediate, simultaneous access to a vast amount of information formerly accessible only in certain buildings, at certain times, for a limited period" (Burckel, 2007). Technology allows users access at all hours of the day — in the comfort of their own home wearing pajamas and sipping a beverage of choice — to many things that are limited or forbidden in the library itself.

THE 'BRICKS & MORTAR' LIBRARY

Within the library system itself there is a treasure trove of materials available to help any researcher. Even though over the last several years huge volumes of material have been made available over the Internet, the Web still has large gaps, and it perhaps never — at least in the next several years — will have all the material that many researchers will need. So the library is necessary to much of the work that they do. Thus, understanding what material a library holds, how it organizes that material, and how you might find and make use of it is important. In this chapter we will not examine all the minute details of conducting research in a library. Perhaps you have never done research in your campus library. Don't let that bother you. When you are ready to begin, start by simply going to your campus library and walking through it. That will give you a feel for what types of material and facilities it has and where things are located. Your library may have a Website that provides directions on how to use it. You can find many universities' guides to doing research in their own libraries by doing a Google Internet search with the phrase "library research guide."

When you go to your campus library, reference materials, books, newspapers, magazines, and research articles in current issues or bound volumes of past work are among the resources that will greet you upon passing through the turnstile. Although you may be able to find some of the material digitized on the Internet, you will find much more at your fingertips in the library. Printed material at times will be easier to use for research than material on the Internet is. In the library,

"The Library, and Step on It"

Read. Brains get hungry too! – Hypatia's Library Tales, 2007

Medicine for the soul. – Inscription over the door of the Library at Thebes

"I left this CD in my car on a hot day and it warped, but I ironed it back into shape. Do I still have to pay for it?" – *Ashtabula* (Oh.) *Star Beacon*, 4/18/2007

Good as it is to inherit a library, it is better to collect one. – Augustine Birrell, English politician (1850-1933)

When a teacher recommends a library book to a stu-

dent, you can be certain that the teacher has checked out the only copy and has lent it to a friend in Peru. – IFLANET, 2007

I consume libraries. I wear out spines and ROM-drives. I do things like get in a taxi and say, "The library, and step on it." – David Foster Wallace, American novelist

You can be sure the student who has the most overdue books reads the least. – IFLANET, 2007

I have always imagined that Paradise would be a kind of library. – Jorge Luis Borges, Argentine writer (1899-1986)

related material is housed in close physical proximity; and you may find that, while looking for one specific item, you come upon many other items of interest. Once you have left your computer desk in your dorm room or apartment and gone to the library, you will probably discover that the time has been well spent.

The library of today, though, is so much more than a place to get resources. Today's libraries have become a destination for students to gather. A social meeting place. An area that supports new technology-driven learning and teaching. And still a place to find books as well as digital materials (Albanese, 2003). Turnstile counts at many libraries have been on the rise since about 2000, when the convenience of the Internet for accessing information appeared to bottom out attendance. According to the Association of Research Libraries, circulation of materials dropped an average of 12 percent from 1995 to 2004. Transactions at the reference desk declined 42 percent. However, use of reference services to help guide the search process are up significantly, whether that occurs through personal visits to the reference desk or email inquiries. Use of current periodicals and books has dropped, as more users consume such materials online or in some other digital form (Albanese, 2003).

Instead, users come to the library to access computers. They come to find a quiet place to read in the reference or reserves areas. They gather at the library to work on group projects. And they find the library a central place on campus to socialize, as more and more libraries accommodate patrons' wishes for food and beverage services (Whitmire, 2001).

For the purpose of research, though, let's look briefly as the most common types of material you will find in your campus library.

Reference Materials

Encyclopedias, yearbooks, handbooks, directories, and dictionaries are items a researcher usually cannot check out of the library and tend to be consulted for specific bits of information rather than read cover to cover. More and more reference books tend to be available online these days (not all — examples include *International Encyclopedia of Communication* and *World Communi-*

cation Report), although libraries vary in the size of budgets available to buy online versions.

Reference materials are, as two authorities explain "aids to research that provide basic information, an introduction to a subject, ... [or assistance with] definitions and descriptions.... [For the most part,] they should not be cited as bibliographic sources in a research paper."

The Library as a Reference Tool

Various items you may need in your studies can be found in your own university library. Answers to all the questions of a general informational sort (such as, for example, the identification of every person) that crop up as one does research can never be found. Yet, a great deal of such information can be located by an imaginative use of reference tools available in a university library.

The Reference Room of a library will become a familiar habitat for a researcher. It is a storehouse of information that enables one to find facts and to locate other information. In fact, the number and type of reference books can appear overwhelming. The Reference Room of any university library will be well stocked with contemporary and historical encyclopedias as well as a number of general surveys such as the New Cambridge Modern History. They represent, however, only a few of the reference works available for research. You also will discover lining the shelves of a Reference Room an array of almanacs, guidebooks, yearbooks, current and historical atlases and dictionaries, special subject encyclopedias, registers of events, and companion volumes to particular studies.

It is important for researchers to gain familiarity with key reference sources in the libraries they use most. What sources are available? How should they be used? The first question is easy to answer. Browse around a Reference Room and observe the sources held by the library. Take the time to make some notes on the sources that attract your particular attention. Make your own guide for these sources, taking care to include their location and potential use. The books mentioned earlier and the Online Catalog or the Card Catalog can help you designate specialized reference works (e.g., encyclopedias and source books for special subjects) that you may want to include in your guide. Regarding how these reference works should be used, it is important to study the Preface or Introduction for each work you select. Examine those sections for information on the work's arrangement, scope, and possible bias. Also, note the publication date of the work to see if it is up to date.

A few words of caution are in order about the use of reference works. These are, as the name implies, for "reference." They are aids to research that provide basic information, an introduction to a subject, or particular information regarding definition and description. Consequently, they should not be cited as bibliographic sources in a research paper. Reference works such as dictionaries, handbooks, and encyclopedias are tools to be used for research. They are not to be employed as substitutes for primary sources.

Adapted from *Historical Methods in Communication* by Wm. David Sloan and Michael Stamm

Book Collections

Libraries are resistant to devote all new acquisitions to digital versions of books because they have found users do not want to read longer pieces like books electronically. So for the foreseeable future at least, you can count on being able to check out your favorite book and take it to your favorite reading spot to engulf yourself in its contents.

Libraries arrange their book collections by subject matter. To identify where each book is, they use Library of Congress call numbers. The LoC number is a mixture of letters, representing subject areas, and numbers. Subject areas most relevant for communication researchers include H (Social sciences) HD and HF (Business), K (Law), D (History) and P and PN (Communication). To locate a book, first search for it through your library's online catalog or its physical card catalog. The catalog entry for the book will include its call number. As an illustration, let's say the book is *The Media in America*, whose call number is P92 U5 M425 2008. Your library will provide directions to the location where books whose call number begins with the letter "P" are found. All you have to do is go to the area and look at call numbers. The books will be arranged in numerical order according to their call numbers. That is, P1 will be followed by P2 and so on.

Special Collections

Almost every library has *special collections* of materials with limited public access on a particular subject. For example, at Duke University, the John W. Hartman Center for Sales, Advertising, and Marketing History offers online access (http://scriptorium.lib.duke.edu/adaccess/) to more than 7,000 print ads as well as the archives of the Outdoor Advertising Association of America and other ad collections. The print ads — ranging in date from 1911 to 1957 and categorized by products (Beauty and Hygiene, Radios, Televisions, Transportation and ads supporting government efforts such as bond sales during World War II) — were created by the J. Walter Thompson ad agency. At the University of Illinois at Urbana, a collection of more than two million print advertisements covering a span of about 100 years created by another nationally renowned ad agency, D'Arcy Masius Benton and Bowles, is available for study. However, this collection is not available online, requiring a site visit and review of microfilm copies. Vanderbilt University holds an extensive archive of television evening news programs from ABC, CBS, NBC, Fox, and CNN, with only CNN's programs available online since 1999. Orders for others can be delivered on DVD or VHS. Radio and television political ads for all levels of political office dating back to 1936, 90,000 spots in all, are available by order from the University of Oklahoma Political Communication Center.

Newspapers and Magazines

Periodicals can be very valuable for many research projects. Most libraries subscribe to a variety of national and international newspapers. Libraries remain the best resource for archived local newspapers. That remains true even though subscription funding is going the way of the dinosaur as more people read online versions. Online, readers can select the topics on which they want news updates, while ignoring the rest. The question with online is how much of a historical record will be kept of these digital editions.

Archived newspapers can be found in one of two forms at libraries — bound or microfilm/fiche. If you've ever experienced the struggle of loading a film reel onto a special reader, spinning the wheel in the proper direction to find the issue and page of your reference, only to find the story hard to read or jumped in the middle to another page that was not recorded, you understand the inconvenience of microfilm. Despite this inconvenience, microfilm/fiche provides stable reproduction quality compared to bound volumes since newspapers usually print on low quality paper stock that wasn't intended to last beyond the end of the day when it was used to line the garbage can or cat litter box. Some companies are now scanning older volumes of daily newspapers and providing online access (e.g., ProQuest offers the *New York Times* online back to 1857). However, these are very expensive; so few libraries can afford them.

Magazines are most likely found archived as bound volumes on the library shelves. Hard copies of these publications are very useful when research requires intense analysis of content, whether that be editorial writing, photographs, or advertising. Often, key variables in studies of how news is covered, how people are depicted, and how products are displayed make it important to review content in its actual size, in color, and in the actual position it was found in the original issue.

Arguably the most objective, credible, and widely accessible sources **Research Articles** for reliable research information on which to base a position paper, critical analysis or subsequent research manuscript are *research articles*, also known as scholarly journal articles. (See Figure 1 for a list of major journals in communication.) There are three primary suppliers to provide researchers with access to these works: aggregators, libraries, and publishers. Aggregators, like ProQuest and EBSCO, provide a wide range of sources for current research articles, with access primarily through electronic links from a library's Website. More on how to use these aggregators for article search appears later in this chapter. Libraries also provide a similar array of sources; but along with providing electronic access to current articles, they also house numerous bound volumes of older materials on their shelves.

Figure 1: Leading Communication Journals

American Behavioral Scientist	*Journal of Consumer Research*
American Journal of Psychology	*Journal of Current Issues & Research in Advertising*
American Journalism	*Journal of Media Law and Practice*
American Political Science Review	*Journal of Radio Studies*
Canadian Journal of Communication	*Journalism & Mass Communication Quarterly*
Communication	*Journalism History*
Communication and *Journalism Monographs*	*Journals of Marketing* and *Marketing Research*
Communication Education	*Mass Comm Review*
Communication Quarterly	*Media, Culture and Society*
Communication Research	*Newspaper Research Journal*
Communication Studies	*Political Communication and Persuasion*
Communications and the Law	*Public Culture*
Critical Studies in Mass Communication	*Public Opinion Quarterly*
Human Communications Research	*Public Relations Journal*
InterMedia	*Quarterly Journal of Speech*
Journal of Advertising	*Signs: Journal of Women in Culture and Society*
Journal of Advertising Research	*Southern Communication Journal*
Journal of Applied Communication Research	*Telecommunication Journal*
Journal of Broadcasting and Electronic Media	*Theory and Society*
Journal of Communication	*Visual Communication Quarterly*
Journal of Communication Inquiry	*Western Journal of Communication*

A third source that has grown in popularity in the last few years is publishers that produce a variety of scholarly journals. One such publisher, Sage, produces 37 communication-related journals, ranging by title from *Animation* to *Written Communication*, that are accessible in electronic form. Although the range of sources is limited to those from one publisher, the advantage is it includes less popular journals, yet ones that provide valuable research in very narrow subject areas. Two examples of such journals in the Sage family are *Animation* and *British Journalism Review*. Another source, Haworth Press, publishes business related journals with such focused titles as *Journal of Promotion Management* and *Journal of Hospital Marketing*.

A helpful tool for researchers to stay on top of the latest scholarly research provides notifications personalized to a researcher's interests. One service, IngentaConnect's InTouch, provides researchers the opportunity to be notified when articles of interest appear across a spectrum of publications. Tables of Contents from journals selected by individual researchers are sent with each new edition of a journal. Although access through IngentaConnect to the full text is available only for a fee per article, copying the citation to your library's indexes will usually produce the access you need. A similar service is provided by Google Scholar, accessed off the Google homepage. Google Scholar provides a free, advanced search of articles accessible somewhere on the Internet. Access through Google to the actual articles requires a fee per article.

STEPS IN CONDUCTING LIBRARY RESEARCH

In conducting library research — whether it is to be done in your campus' physical library or on the Internet — organizing your search for information is an important first step. Actually, a good search strategy involves a series of steps. Don't assume the process is linear. As you get immersed in the process you may find you follow a more circular route, discovering citations, examining bibliographies, and reviewing materials that lead you in different directions than originally planned.

Select, adjust, and eventually narrow your topic to make it fit the parameters of your assignment. Obviously a ten page paper will need to have a more focused topic in order to address all sides of the issue compared to a doctoral dissertation of several hundred pages that can investigate a few more nuances to the topic. Still, no matter the size of the project, narrow is always better for researching a subject thoroughly.

Identifying Types of Sources Needed

A researcher needs to determine early on the types of sources most relevant for each study. This determination can be influenced by the topic, the level of knowledge the researcher has about the subject already, and the audience for the research. A current events topic may need to rely more heavily on articles published in the popular press, like daily newspapers or weekly magazines, since more extensive scholarly research may not be published on the subject yet. Research reported to an academic audience is more likely to need sources from scholarly journals to make a case grounded on sound theoretical and controlled experimental evidence, while research directed toward communication professionals in the industry may benefit from citing trade publications relevant to the subject of study. This being said, most research studies need to access a variety of sources to thoroughly review and understand the topic.

The determination of appropriate sources affects the selection of article indexes that your library makes available. *Indexes* combine articles published by dozens of different sources into a list that can be sorted by author, subject, topic keyword, time period, and a host of other variables. Most libraries make multiple indexes available to users. More general indexes that cover a variety of popular press, trade press, and scholarly publications from aggregators such as ProQuest and EBSCO are often supplemented with more specialized indexes focusing on articles in a specific subject area. For example, ABI-Inform Global (from ProQuest) and Business Source Elite (from EBSCO) focus on articles dealing with business, management, and economics in both trade and scholarly publications. Communication Abstracts focuses on scholarly literature in communication. PsycInfo, which covers articles dating back to 1872, focuses on, you guessed it, psychology.

It is important to understand the range of sources indexed and time period covered. Rarely are studies done only in the past five years the most valuable and useful to your topic. Good research stands the test of time, meaning that studies as far back as the middle of the twentieth century on media effects, for example, are essential to consider in any media-effects research at present. Try several indexes to be sure you're covering all the materials that may be relevant to your research. Always investigate limit functions for these indexes to help narrow your search if you seek only research studies, or only qualitative or quantitative studies, or specific methods such as content analysis or experiments. For example, ABI-Inform has an advanced search function that uses classification codes to sort documents into subcategories based on subject area, industry or market, geographical area, article type, or the method that a researcher used. In the pull-down menus, the code 9130, for example, narrows a search to reports of research studies that have collected data through surveys, experiments, focus groups, observations, or a variety of other quantitative and qualitative methods.

USING THE INTERNET AS A LIBRARY

For much of today's work, the researcher will use a combination of the physical library and the Internet. Although you have probably used the Internet for a variety of purposes, when you use it for research, it is important to be systematic and organized. To get started, *keywords* are a key.

People growing up in the age of Internet search engines are likely to know the power of selecting appropriate keywords to generate the most relevant choices for information. The same concepts apply to successful use of such items as databases and article indexes. With a world of information accessible at our fingertips, there is nothing more frustrating than receiving search results that indicate "over 1,000 matches have resulted from your search."

Instead, some careful thinking in advance of a list of specific words related to your research subject will help narrow your search to the most relevant 20 to 30 sources that will require a fraction of the time to review that would be otherwise necessary to review 1,000 matches.

Let's say, for example, we are interested in studying something about advertising. This ubiquitous marketing activity is the subject of many people's thoughts and words. A search using the keyword "advertising" on ABI-Inform Global would likely generate a list of more than 305,000 matches! But congratulations are not in order because this activity is not bowling, where high score wins. It's more like golf. So your next step is to determine what type of advertising to research. One way to narrow would be based on target audience, let's say "youth." Now an ABI-Inform Global search is likely to generate a list of more than 37,000 matches.

Only slightly more manageable. Narrowing further to "advertising to youth/children" knocks that list down to about 500 matches. Further limiting the search to only primary research studies would result in 85 matches. A doable task, and one that is likely to make the focus of the rest of your research that much stronger.

Libraries on the Internet The Internet Public Library (www.ipl.org) is a virtual library set up to mimic the real thing — with Reference Room, Reading Room, and other areas — and provides a convenient starting point to understand the range of materials available on a given subject. The "Ask a Question" service provides near real time answers from reference librarians. One of its most useful features is its series of links to other Websites containing the texts of such items as books, encyclopedia, and magazines. One of the most useful sites is the Library of Congress (www.loc.gov). It provides arguably the most complete listing of published books in the world. Other unique services include detailed studies of more than 70 countries, a digital library of historical photos and documents, the official listing of copyright owners for U.S. produced materials, and records describing more than 13,000 research organizations willing to share information with anyone on any subject. WorldCat (www.worldcat.org), a national union catalog, lists more than one billion items in more than 10,000 libraries worldwide.

Databases Internet Sleuth (www.islueth.com) gives searchable access to more than 1,500 business, science, and job directories and a directory of more than 5,000 regularly published newsletters. Websites that provide access to a treasure trove of data on populations, trends, spending habits, consumption patterns, and other important information come from three primary sources: the government, trade associations/publications, and syndicated sources. For the United States population, www.census.gov and http://factfinder.census.gov provide quick access to mountains of information that before the Internet required long hours of sorting through huge printed volumes to find the page that showed data appropriately displayed the way you wanted it. Now, with a basic understanding of how spreadsheets work, you can input variables that you'd like cross-tabulated with the census dataset, and the page quickly appears. But the Census Bureau is not the only government entity that collects and posts large amounts of valuable data. Government agencies concerned with issues of housing, food and drugs, and the economy gather huge mounds of data and make most of it available on their Websites.

Internationally, industry trade associations and publications focusing on those industries collect and share valuable data. For example, in the advertising industry, *Advertising Age*, a leading, weekly publication on the latest activities in advertising across the world, shares trend data on consumers, advertising practices, and other related topics by clicking on "Data Center" at www.adage.com.

Syndicated sources sell the data they collect. Fees are usually substantial and unaffordable for an individual user. However, two leading syndicated data sources of interest to communicators (Mediamark Research and Simmons) provide reduced subscription access through libraries for data on U.S. consumption habits, lifestyles, and media habits. The one catch for these discounted offers is that the data is usually a few years old. For class projects or instruction, though, slightly aged data may be acceptable. Your instructor will normally give you guidelines. (See Figure 2 for a list of relevant Websites for communication related research information.) Information on how to navigate databases can be found in Chapter 5 of this book.

Figure 2: Useful Internet Addresses

http://www.amazon.com (bookstore)

http://www.barnesandnoble.com (bookstore)

http://www.cios.org (Communication Institute for Online Scholarship - CIOS)

http://www.ecola.com (periodical indexes)

http://www.ipl.org (Internet Public Library)

http://www.isleuth.com (people finder)

http://www.iTools.com/research-it (research source)

http://www.library.uiuc.edu/cmx (Communications Library, University of Illinois)

http://www.loc.gov (Library of Congress)

http://www.moviedatabase.com (movie database)

http://www.acronymfinder.com (the meanings of acronyms)

http://www.nytimes.com (*New York Times*)

http://www.nara.gov (National Archives & Records Administration)

http://www.netlibrary.com (2,000 books, periodicals, journals, and articles)

http://www.onelook.com (dictionaries)

http://www.uky.edu/~drlane/links.html (communication links)

http://www.worldcat.org (library catalogues)

http://www.wsj.com (*Wall Street Journal)*

http://www.wsu.edu:8080/~brians/errors/ (common errors in English)

http://www.Yahoo.com/Reference (research source)

Media on the Web

Who has the money to subscribe to the top newspapers of the world, such as the *New York Times*, the *Wall Street Journal*, or the *London Times*? Or the time to read them? Ditto for television news programs. Yet, the media provide great leads to interesting research questions, and the Internet has made searching for an elusive article or program so much easier.

A number of Internet sites include links to large numbers of individual periodical publications. Electronic Newsstand (www.enews.com) provides access to hundreds of consumer magazines. It includes the actual articles, not links that take you away from a Website never to be found again. Ecola Newsstand (www.ecola.com) provides separate indexes for newspapers, magazines, and computer publications. Editor & Publisher Interactive Online Newspaper Database (www.mediainfo.com/ephome/npaper/nphtm/online) is the most comprehensive list of 1,500 online newspapers. Similarly, the Internet Public Library newspaper list (http://www.ipl.org/div/news/) provides links to most daily newspapers in all 50 states and many from around the world.

Major U.S. television news networks — including ABC, CBS, NBC, Fox, and CNN — as well as international news networks, such as BBC and Al Jazeera, the Arabic news channel of the Middle East — have a significant Web presence for current news and allow access to archived stories as well.

Government Information on the Web

Bureaucratic and legislative information, guidelines and applications for grants, and consumer publications related to social and economic development — including the environment, education, and health care — are among the research studies and information available online. Links to the Congressional Record, the official record of proceedings in the

U.S. Congress, also provide full text newspapers articles related to current bills.

The Google Challenge

Libraries face a monumental challenge in the coming years to provide service at a level capable of overcoming the following scenario:

• Students start their search with a visit to Google. A student types in "communication on drug abuse" in the keyword search and gets a list of Web-sites with relevant information — the good, bad, and inadequate. Using the Google Scholar search function found on a page — which also shows ads and an option to use Google's shopping service (Froogle) — the student gets a list of journal articles and monographs in order, based not on content quality, but popularity of being cited. Even with the Advanced Search feature, the best a student will get is author, publication, and an approximate date of the material's publication: no vocabulary lists or subject headings that provide clues of details covered by an article. Since search engine data show that few people ever go much beyond the 20th listing on a search, it is likely this research effort will not produce much depth. Combined with the frustration of clicking on one listing, a link to a government document, only to find the document is no longer accessible online, the shallowness of the material causes the student to give up and go back to the Google homepage to do some shopping for badly needed jewelry.

A recent survey (Head, 2007) says a search engine is the starting point for research for only 20 percent of college students. But the convenience of search engine access is likely to increase this percentage in the future. It is a problem some libraries are actively addressing by taking reference questions by email, instant messaging, and using computer software to help direct more efficient information searches. And, with a Pew Institute study (Estabrook, Witt, Rainie, 2007) showing young adults 18-30 are the biggest users of public libraries, staying on the cutting edge of technology will deliver services to keep the library at the top of the list as an important research source.

Library research — in both the physical and the online libraries — can be immensely rewarding. A wealth of material exists in each one. If you are familiar with both of them before you start a specific research project, your job will be both much easier and more productive. So at the outset, get to know your way around them.

TO LEARN MORE

Beasley, David. *Beasley's Guide to Library Research*. Toronto: University of Toronto Press, 2000.

George, Mary. *The Elements of Library Research: What Every Student Needs To Know*. Princeton, N.J.: Princeton University Press, 2008.

Mann, Thomas. *Library Research Models: A Guide to Classification*. Oxford, N.Y.: Oxford University Press, 1993.

Mann, Thomas. *The Oxford Guide to Library Research*. Oxford, N.Y.: Oxford University Press, 2005.

Rodrigues, Dawn, and Raymond J. Rodrigues. *The Research Paper: A Guide to Library and Internet Research*, 3d ed. Upper Saddle River, N.J.: Prentice Hall, 2003.

Ruger, Stefan. *Multimedia Information Retrieval*. San Rafael, Calif.: Morgan & Claypool, 2010.

REFERENCES

Albanese, Andrew. "Deserted no more." *Library Journal*, volume 128, April 15, 2003, 34-36.

Burckel, Nicholas. "Libraries: Stability and Change." *Marquette Lawyer,* Spring (2007); 54-59.

Cochrane, Lynn. "If the academic library ceased to exist, would we have to invent it?" *Educause Review,* (2007, Jan/Feb), 6-7.

Estabrook, Leigh, Evans Witt, and Lee Rainie. "Information searches that solve problems." Pew Institute report, December 30, 2007. www.pewInternet.org/pdfs/Pew_UI_LibrariesReport.

Head, Alison. "Beyond Google: How do students conduct academic research?" *First Monday,* volume 12, number 8 (August 2007). http://firstmonday.org/issues/issue12_8/head/index.html.

Hypatia's Library Tales. www.geocities.com/Athens/Parthenon/2776/quotes.html, accessed 12/28/2007.

IFLANET-Library Humour. www.ifla.org/I/humour/humour.htm, accessed 12/28/2007.

McGuire, M., L. Stillborne, M. McAdams and L. Hyatt. Libraries, Databases, Media and Government (Chp. 5) in *The Internet Handbook for Writers, Researchers and Journalists.* New York: Guilford Press, 2001.

Sloan, Wm. David, and Michael Stamm. *Historical Methods in Communication,* 3rd ed. Northport, Ala.: Vision Press, 2010.

Straight answers. *American Library,* volume 37, number 4, April 2006, 21.

Whitmire, Ethelene. "A longitudinal study of undergraduates' academic library experiences." *Journal of Academic Librarianship,* volume 27, number 5, September 2001, 379-385.

5

Using Databases

Future generations progress by improving on information others have learned and passed on. The same is true in science — scientific progress usually depends on researchers building on the work of past researchers, thereby contributing to the general body of knowledge. Humans have always preserved information for others to use, evident in ancient cave drawings, clay tablets, papyrus text, and even song and dance. For hundreds of years, information has been stored in written form, accessible in journals and books primarily through libraries and other collections, particularly those held in university and college systems. Today, a substantial amount of human knowledge is stored in electronic databases, accessible at the click of a mouse on the information superhighway.

A *database* is something that stores information and provides a logical system for data retrieval and management. This textbook, for example, is a database, because it stores information that is easily retrievable, using both an index and a table of contents. Likewise, an *electronic database* stores digitized information organized for ease of use and rapid retrieval via a computer. Computer technologies make possible a multiplicity of databases, including collections of music and sounds, videos and images, and text of all kinds, from abstracts to full-text publications.

Access to a database once required the user to be in the presence of the storage device, usually a computer or CD-ROM. With the advent of the Internet, access to electronic databases has changed the way we conduct research and gather information. Online databases provide quick access to comprehensive information sources that researchers can download, print, and e-mail from the convenience of their own computers, personal digital assistants (PDA), or smart phones.

This chapter presents a general explanation of electronic database systems and advanced search techniques to help enhance your chance of finding relevant and quality information. Devising a search strategy based on components of a research topic is suggested as a means to better control search queries, retrieve rele-

By Brian Parker
Florida State University

vant records, and organize a process that tracks information gathered, keywords searched, and sources used. The chapter concludes with an overview of select databases used by communication and mass media scholars, students, and educators.

DATABASES IN COMMUNICATION RESEARCH

Databases are research tools that facilitate all areas of communication scholarship by expediting information gathering and increasing the breadth of available information. A database search is frequently the first step in research, used to bring clarity to preliminary topics and build the theoretical foundation for hypotheses. Online databases have diminished the need to roam musty libraries to locate journal articles for literature reviews, search aging micro-film for news stories, or browse large indexed volumes of consumer and market data for advertising insights.

Some researchers exploit more rigorous applications of electronic databases. For example, investigative journalists utilize databases for *computer-assisted reporting* (CAR) to craft original stories. Information embedded in databases has become an important source of untold stories on many topics and social institutions. CBS pioneered CAR techniques in the newsroom to predict the 1952 presidential race with a rudimentary computer and early return data (Cox, 2000). Building on basic reporting and critical thinking skills, CAR is now a regular practice in newsrooms.

In a similar manner, advertising researchers use data mining techniques to explore untapped information in data archives. *Data mining* is a research technique that utilizes statistics and proprietary software programs designed to discover hidden patterns in a database. Discoveries are used to create audience profiles, fine tune communication strategies, and help increase the overall efficiency of tactical communication executions.

No matter the purpose, when used to their fullest potential, databases help uncover quality information that gives one an edge. However, finding the best available information requires mastering advanced search techniques. Database search skills are easy to learn and do not differ much from techniques commonly used with online search engines like Google. Even though the appearance of databases and system software varies, there are search techniques and information retrieval systems common to most.

DATA STRUCTURE AND RETRIEVAL

The manner in which an electronic database structures and retrieves information depends on the model used. A number of data structure models exist across the variety of databases available. The *relational data model* is the structure of most database systems today, primarily because of its flexibility for retrieving data and low operating cost on computer systems (Date, 2000).

Relational databases organize information using a combination of *fields*, *records*, and *files* (Codd, 1970). According to size, they are in the following order:

A *field* represents a single piece of information (e.g., "author" or "year of publication").

A *record* is a complete set of single fields.

A *file*, also called a *table*, is a complete set of records. *Relational tables* arrange data fields in columns and records in rows.

Relational databases contain multiple tables, each with a unique dataset that enables users to sort information based on any field and cross reference fields in other data tables. Large relational databases have thousands of tables that cross reference each other, allowing many different information requests.

The central concept of data retrieval is that of requesting information from a database using a *query*. Database queries use different computer languages and algorithms to retrieve specific records. The query language used most often with relational databases is *Structured Query Language*. SQL queries search any combination of fields and records using relational operators (i.e., computer commands) that provide a filter mechanism by selecting database records that contain requested field values. SQL queries typically generate results in terms of relevancy to search criteria.

Database queries are often initiated by entering a single word or simple phrase into a search engine interface. Such a query is known as a *keyword search*. SQL relational database systems examine the fields in each stored record for queried keywords and return all records that match. Basic keyword searches often generate numerous results, possibly thousands in large databases, many irrelevant. It is at this point that advanced search skills and a search strategy will tap the full potential of an electronic database.

DATABASE SEARCH STRATEGIES

There is no single optimal way to initiate the database research process. Ultimately, how one starts a search is a function of the researcher's knowledge of the library and resources, knowledge of the research topic, work habits, and effort expended. However, organization and a search strategy will enhance efficiency and the chance of locating relevant, high quality information.

As part of a search strategy, it is important to develop procedures for tracking keywords and other searched information, as well as databases used. It is easy to branch out in many directions while searching and lose important citations and other pieces of critical information. Figure 1 illustrates a six-step process for turning a research topic into a workable keyword search strategy that documents search criteria and resources used as a search expands. Let's examine each step.

Figure 1: Database Search Strategy

Step 1: Separate Concepts

Step 2: List Keywords

Step 3: Identify Keyword Relationships

Step 4: Identify Databases

Step 5: Conduct Search

Step 6: Evaluate Information

Before starting a database search, divide the research topic into its principal concepts. Topic component concepts are the main words and/or phrases that comprise a research topic. They should be the **Step 1: Separate Concepts** first items queried and provide the structure used to plan strategies intended to limit or expand a search. For example, given the research topic to compare "television and online news coverage of the 2008 U.S. presidential debates," the principal concepts are "television news coverage," "online news coverage," and "2008 U.S. Presidential debates."

Principal concepts provide the basis for refining search strategies and tracking words searched. For example, the concept "online news coverage" is divisible into two concepts: "online" and "news coverage." You can expand a search strategy — that is, locate a larger range of records — by using alternate but similar concepts (e.g., "internet" and "online" or "media coverage" and "news coverage"). Each additional spelling relates to a principal concept, making it easy to keep track of words searched.

After separating a research topic into concepts, next develop a short list of keywords for each topic concept. Use single and multiple key- **Step 2: List Keywords** words to represent concepts. Short, specific words and phrases achieve the best search precision, while broad keywords increase search range. Unless it is your intention to search for a particular phrase, avoid long descriptive phrases, which tend to severely limit search results to records that only contain the phrase.

Include related terms, synonyms, and alternative spelling forms for each primary concept. At this point, a keyword list may include known authors, publication titles, and dates. From the example above, the keyword short list for each topic component follows:

- Television news coverage: television news stories, television media coverage, television press coverage
- Online news coverage: online news stories, online media coverage, online press coverage
- U.S. Presidential debates: United States Presidential debates, American Presidential debates, national Presidential debates, Democratic Presidential debates, Republican Presidential debates

At the beginning of a database research project, you should start with a few keywords and phrases, typically the primary topic concepts, and gradually expand the search strategy using the alternative concept keywords. The original list will produce the majority of search results. Also, the search process itself reveals new keywords, articles, and other items that add precision to the search strategy. Throughout the search process the keyword list serves as a checklist of searched terms.

To increase the chance of retrieving relevant information, it is important to establish relationships between keywords. Discussed in step 5, **Step 3: Identify Keyword Relationships** most database search systems use procedural operator commands (e.g., AND, OR, etc.) that instruct the computer how to treat each keyword or phrase (e.g., "television news coverage" AND "U.S. Presidential debates") in a database query. Certain relationships will help constrain search results, while others will have the opposite effect and will increase record retrieval. Therefore, keyword relationships are central to the development of an effective search strategy.

Step 4: Identify Databases

There are thousands of databases and hundreds of data providers, including sites for news, historical resources, media literacy, communication law and theory, freedom of the press, and legal issues. For the novice researcher, finding databases best suited for a particular topic can be a daunting task. With experience, one becomes familiar with the premier databases available for specific topics. To get you started, the last section of this chapter reviews a selection of major databases used across communication disciplines.

Step 5: Conduct Search

Database system programs accept queries and communicate with the host computer to display query results. To conduct a search of a database, enter keywords or phrases into the provided interface using the keyword list, starting with the topic components. Depending on your query parameters, the system computer displays results in a predetermined order, often indicating the number of records retrieved.

Common problems experienced by novice searchers include retrieving too many records, too few records, and irrelevant records. Controlling the amount of relevant information presents the central challenge to the user. To enhance search precision, use specific time periods and ranges, choose databases most appropriate to the search subject, and use specific search terms. Database systems also have built-in mechanisms for limiting search results. They include the following:

Title field searching is used to restrict a query to specific records in a database. Database systems use different fields; but common options are searching by topic, within text, by author(s), by journal title, and by year of publication. For example, searching "by author" using Sigmund Freud as the keyword will retrieve articles by Freud, whereas searching "by subject" using Sigmund Freud will retrieve articles with Freud as the topic. Using title fields limits information retrieval at times to the exact items desired.

The most common technique for controlling how a search system interprets queries is *Boolean logic* commands (Bell, 2007). Developed by George Boole in the 1800s, Boolean algebra is a symbolic logic system of operators that act like floodgates, allowing and inhibiting record retrieval in a database search. Operators serve to connect keywords and phrases, instructing the computer how to treat each. The operators most often used to connect keywords are AND, OR, and NOT.

Table 1 on the next page displays these search commands and the function of each one in controlling keyword queries. AND logic instructs a database system to retrieve records if and only if all keywords are present. The OR operator tells the computer to retrieve records if any keyword is present. NOT logic instructs the computer to retrieve records that contain certain keywords and not others. It is important to note that, if operators are not used, most database systems construe space between words to mean AND.

To limit search results, it is useful to combine Boolean operators with phras-

Table 1: Boolean Operator Functions

Operator	Function
AND (+)	The AND operator searches for all records that contain both keywords. Limits results (generates fewer hits) because all keywords must appear in a record for retrieval. The "+" sign often represents AND.
OR	OR operator links terms so a database will locate documents in which any of the keywords appear. Expands search (generates more hits) by locating all records containing either keyword.
NOT (-)	Finds records containing the keyword before NOT, but not the terms after. Limits a search by excluding all records containing the keyword after the operator. The "-" sign often represents NOT.

es created with keywords. Create phrases using keywords related to the information of most importance in a research topic. Quotation marks should surround a phrase that contains more than two words. For example, a search for the phrase "television news coverage" AND "U.S. Presidential debates" AND "2008" should retrieve mainly records that reference television news coverage and Presidential debates in 2008.

Use *proximity operator* commands in search queries to find keywords with distance thresholds in a record. In other words, depending on the operator, specific keywords must appear within a certain number of words of another keyword, or within the same sentence or paragraph, for a document to be retrieved. Database systems use different symbols for proximity operations. Common commands are near (N) and within (W), often tied with "#" to specify the number of words or distance constraints for record retrieval. For example, "presidential W/10 debate" retrieves records where the searched keywords are within ten words apart, either before or after each other in a document. The near (N) search command performs a similar operation by instructing a database system to produce documents that have specified keywords near each other. With both commands, you alter the number to control how far apart the keywords must appear in a record to be included in search results.

To expand search results, use *truncation* techniques to find multiple terms related to a single prefix. Truncation utilizes special symbols such as an asterisk (*) to command a database to retrieve all variants of a word. For example, using the truncation symbol with the keyword stem creat* will retrieve all records containing words such as creation, create, creating, creator, and creature. Truncation symbols vary across database systems. Use overview help screens to learn the symbols used by each.

Using search results. Database system technologies provide different options for using and displaying search results. Results of an electronic database query are usually displayed as a list or set of records retrieved. A hyperlinked record title is often the first available option that allows users to view document information such as an abstract, author(s), title, and publication name. Databases that offer full-text options allow users to *read, print,* and *save* copies of entire documents. Different formats are available for viewing documents. Most common are PDF,

HTML, and rich-text format.

Depending on query parameters, the number of *hits* (i.e., records retrieved) ranges anywhere from zero to thousands. It is common that database systems enable the user to *sort* results by date, author, publication, etc. By default, records are often sorted by relevance to query information, often indicated by level of relevance to keywords. This is called *relevancy sorting* and is a critical database system feature, particularly as the volume of information continues to multiply.

Users tend to browse hits looking for records of interest. Database systems provide options to *mark* records of interest for future retrieval. The database system will temporarily keep track of marked records while the user continues to browse other records from a search query. Generally, marked records are available until the researcher initiates a new query.

Premium databases often provide *suggested topics* related to query information. For example, results for the keyword search "advertising" may include links for records that include the topics "advertising and market strategy" and "television advertising." Suggested topics are clickable hyperlink titles that produce a new query and set of records when selected.

Individual results from a query search often include the publication title as a hyperlink. Selecting the link allows the user to browse the publication. This option is helpful because publications often release articles with related topics, potentially revealing important and highly relevant documents not originally located.

Step 6: Evaluate Information

The goal of systematic searching is to increase the chance of finding relevant, quality information. Source credibility is a strong indicator of quality information. The Internet does not have gatekeepers that substantiate information accuracy. There is a large risk of finding inaccurate information online. It is best to use databases from trusted and objective sources that contain information obtained from an original source. A general rule with database information is that the chance of inaccurate information increases the farther data moves from the original source.

The degree to which information is relevant is a function of informational needs and characteristics of the retrieved records. Relevancy increases when there is a match between the topic of investigation and the subject matter of a retrieved document. Relevancy also increases with current information. Dated information often has less value. Ultimately, it is up to researcher scrutiny to determine the usefulness of database information.

If gathered information is insufficient, the search strategy needs refinement, indicated by the dotted arrow in Figure 1. Often there is a need to expand the amount of information, find different information, or locate more specific information. To expand the amount of information, either (1) use new keywords related to each topic component or (2) develop new topic components based on information gathered in the original search, develop new relationships between keywords, and select new databases.

A highly relevant and heavily cited article is very useful when fine-tuning a search strategy. Major, heavily cited articles in a field of study typically include references to other significant research articles and information sources. Locating such a source in turn leads to other related articles, and so on. Search and refinement should continue until you are satisfied with your research or until you have exhausted the data sources and information.

There are hundreds of databases useful to communication students, educators, and researchers. This section provides a brief overview of select electronic databases that appear often in communication collections, are the highest quality available, and are considered the first option for most research initiatives. The majority of these databases are fee-based and available online to members of subscribing institutions. Check your institution's library reference for availability and help connecting remotely to each. For convenience of use, the databases are divided into four categories based on the type of information accessible: general academic, mass communication general, journalism/news media, and advertising/PR.

COMMUNICATION AND MASS MEDIA DATABASES

General Academic Databases

Academic Index is a multi-disciplinary database of both academic and general-interest periodicals. It contains more than 14 million articles. Many of them are full-text journal, magazine, and news articles. It provides more than 20 years of backfile coverage that adds depth to information searches.

Academic OneFile database delivers peer-reviewed, full-text articles from references and research journals worldwide. It provides access to more than 11,000 journals and millions of full-text articles in the social and physical sciences, technology, medicine, and a range of other major topics.

General OneFile is one of the most comprehensive periodical databases available and provides access to indexed and full-text records from an extensive range of periodical and news sources that includes both general research journals and specialized trade journals. It provides access to hundreds of newspapers worldwide.

JSTOR is a collection of back runs of core scholarly journals across a wide spectrum of disciplines. It is primarily an archival database, not a current-issue database, which contains full-text of select periodicals dating back to their earliest issues. Records are scanned images of original journal pages in terms of design and illustrations.

LexisNexis Academic is one of the largest providers of information, covering a variety of topics and is used by professionals from legal, corporate, government, academic, and law enforcement communities. It provides access to over 30,000 information sources and at least 5 billion documents, the vast majority full-text.

Project MUSE is a collection of 100% full-text, top-tier journals in history and the humanities, social sciences, and the arts. It provides the highest quality scholarship from the most respected, peer-reviewed journals. Complete content of every issue from over 300 journals is online and available in most formats.

ProQuest is an extensive database collection and the first choice of many academic researchers. It provides a wide spectrum of scholarship from more than 125 billion pages of information and more than 9,000 periodical titles that date back 500 years (Proquest, 2007). In addition, it contains the preeminent dissertation collection and the largest digital newspaper collection.

Wilson OmniFile Full Text, Mega Edition. OmniFile is an expansive periodical resource with access to full texts of articles, page images, abstracts, and citations from thousands of sources. Users have access to information on virtually every subject. Coverage dates back to as early as 1982.

Mass Communication General Databases

ComAbstracts, provided by the Communication Institute for Online Scholarship (CIOS), is dedicated to literature in the communication disciplines and includes records from over 100 journals related to mass communication, new media, rhetoric, journalism, and communication law.

Communication and Mass Media Complete provides the most extensive collection of content in areas related to communication and mass media study with references from over 500 titles. It is an invaluable resource for all students, educators, and researchers with an interest in any aspect of communication.

Communication Studies: A SAGE Full-Text Collection includes full-text access to 19 journals published by SAGE, some dating back to 1982. Coverage includes journalism, mass communication, political communication, media studies, television, film, and other communication studies. Every record links to a complete full-text PDF file.

Journalism/News Media Databases

AccuNet/AP Multimedia Archive is a leading multimedia database that contains more than 750,000 news photographs, 500,000 audio sound bites, and 800,000 news articles covering more than 160 years of historical documentation by the Associated Press (AccuNet/AP, 2007; Machovec, 2001). It is updated daily with new photos and audio from around the globe.

Factiva, provided by the Dow Jones company, is a leader in the areas of financial, industry, and company information. It is a comprehensive online database for tracking business news and information from nearly 8,000 sources and 118 countries (Factiva, 2007).

NewsBank NewsFile Collection provides news articles from national newspapers, wire services, and broadcast transcripts from both U.S. and Canadian sources. News articles are both historical and current and cover a wide spectrum of topics. The database includes full-text and is updated daily.

Advertising/PR Databases

ABI/Inform is a combination of four databases that provide an extensive collection of advertising, business, and marketing journals. Information is available on national, regional, and local businesses, including profiles on company personnel. It provides access to the latest news from most major U.S. industries.

*Ad*Access* is a comprehensive online database that contains a selection of more than 7,000 historical advertisements from U.S. and Canadian magazines and newspapers. The collection comes from the J. Walter Thompson Competitive Advertisement Collection at Duke University.

AdForum is a database of advertisements from the largest ad markets worldwide. It draws on information from over 20,000 ad agencies and contains more than 70,000 television, print, and interactive ads.

Gales Research Inc. "Market Share Reporter" contains over 2,000 product/service categories in nearly all industries. The primary data reports shares (i.e., percentage of sales in a given market) for each brand in a product category. You can search by four primary information types: company, brand, region, and product. Market Share Reporter covers companies from the United States, Canada, and Mexico.

Standard & Poor's NetAdvantage provides financial and operating information on publicly traded U.S. and international companies in over 30 markets worldwide, including balance sheets, listings of company personnel, recent news, and Securities and Exchange Commission (SEC) reports.

STAT-USA/Internet is a government database sponsored by the Department of Commerce that provides access to business and trade information from multiple federal government agencies containing current and historical economic data, international market research, and other analyses.

TO LEARN MORE

Date, C.J. (2000). *An introduction to database systems* (7th ed.). Reading, Mass.: Addison-Wesley.

Larose, D.T. (2005). *Discovering knowledge in data: An introduction to data mining.* Hoboken, N.J.: John Wiley & Sons, Inc.

Lescher, J.F. (1995). *Online market research: Cost-effective searching of the internet and online databases.* Reading, Mass.: Addison-Wesley Professional.

REFERENCES

Bell, S. (2007). Tools every searcher should know and use. *Online, 31(5),* 22-27.

Codd, E.F. (1970). A relational model of data for large shared data banks. *Communications of the ACM, 13(6),* 377-387.

Cox, M. (2000). The Development of computer-assisted reporting. A paper presented to the *Newspaper Division, Association for Education and Mass Communication, Southeast Colloquium, March 17-18, 2000.* University of North Carolina, Chapel Hill.

Date, C.J. (2000). *An introduction to database systems* (7th ed.). Reading, Mass.: Addison-Wesley.

Machovec, G.S. (2001). Accuent/AP multimedia database now available. Information Intelligence Online Libraries and Microcomputers, 19(5), 8.

AccuNet/AP. (2007). *User Guide.* Retrieved August 15, 2007, from http://ap. accuweather. com/apphoto/userguide_guide.htm#about

6

Bibliographies and Literature Reviews

If you're like many scholars, when you're diving into a new research project your urge is to cut immediately to the chase. You want to start collecting data to answer the research question (or questions) you originally set out to illuminate. Compared to this exciting work, the literature review seems an unappetizing detour from the informative work ahead.

But in fact, the literature review for any research project, often culminating in a bibliography attached to your finished research project, is a key element of your work. Done well and compiled early on in your project, it can provide the background and lay the foundation for your research and make your conclusions more meaningful. Simply put, you must understand what other scholars have written about your topic, and the literature review is the beginning of your path to understanding.

This chapter will first underscore the importance of literature reviews by explaining their place in the overall research process. Then it will offer you tips in compiling bibliographies and creating reviews from them. The hope is that by understanding why literature reviews matter you'll be more inclined to give them the attention they deserve. By appreciating literature reviews and how they inform your understanding of your research, you will be better able to produce nuanced, informed projects that add to the very literature you're citing.

WHY LITERATURE REVIEWS MATTER

Before we tackle the how, let's first take on the what and the why of the literature review. Let's define our terms first. In its simplest meaning, a *bibliography* is a list of the printed materials — the books and articles — on a topic or subject area. A *literature review* is a summary and interpretation of that material. While some literature reviews are written as stand-alone research articles, researchers more commonly include them as one section in a larger research project. To appreciate them requires an understanding of the research process as a whole, which we'll cover in the briefest of outlines.

By David R. Davies
University of Southern Mississippi

When a scholar takes on a new research project, s/he typically has one of several goals in mind. Often the researcher is simply responding to curiosity about a subject. Sometimes s/he may be responding to the assignment from a book editor to conduct an investigation of a particular topic. For their part, students may be researching a topic assigned by an instructor.

Whatever the reason for beginning the project, any scholar hopes that upon its completion the work will add to the body of knowledge. In communication study, as in other disciplines, the hopeful scholar aspires to fill a niche in a particular area. Sometimes, but certainly not always, this means that the scholar is conducting research into an area that has never before been investigated. Other times the scholar is investigating — and perhaps hoping to add to, or even to contradict — a particular stream of established research in a given topic area. But in every case the scholar aims, at the end of the research project, to have arrived at research findings that are significant, that is, that are important in one area or another of the literature. After all, we all hope, by the end of the day, to do something important in our work. The literature review, as it turns out, is key to demonstrating the significance of your work.

To explicate this just a little further, let's consider the question of significance with regard to a specific research project, one of several research projects to which we'll refer occasionally in this chapter to illustrate the place of the literature review. Let's take the example of a research project into the editorial influence of a Mississippi editor, J. Oliver Emmerich of the *Enterprise-Journal* in small McComb, in southwest Mississippi. Emmerich was a civic-minded business leader whose steady editorial leadership is widely credited with restoring calm to his community in the violent summer of 1964, when McComb was coming to terms with heightened civil rights activities locally and all across the state.

In beginning a research project on this important figure in civil rights journalism, a researcher would need to understand the complexities of small-town McComb, the civil rights movement, the intersection of the news media and civil rights, and Mississippi's special place in the overall movement. (In fact, this author undertook just such a study and worried about these very questions.) The questions are important because they explain the context for Emmerich's journalism as well as the context for the research project that will attempt to explain it.

History, and indeed any question in communication research, is all about context, which can only be gained through a thorough literature review. To understand Emmerich we need to understand his time and place (1950s and 1960s Mississippi) and the political milieu in which he published his award-winning newspaper.

That's a pretty obvious point, but there's still more that we need to understand. If we're to appreciate Emmerich's importance, we need to understand how other scholars have written about the media and the civil rights movement so that we can gauge our own contribution to the scholarship. Consider these historiographical points, which we can only understand through the literature review:

• Emmerich was typical of many Southern editors of his day, in that he believed in fair treatment of all citizens at the same time as he held on to segregationist views typical of successful Mississippi businessmen of his generation. So, his strong stance in favor of restoring calm to the strife-torn town of McComb during the height of the civil rights movement, while heroic given the upheaval in his hometown, at the same time was typical of other Southern editors who were moved to support gradual desegregation in the interest of restoring calm to their towns and to their business communities. Many other scholars have written about heroic editors who took brave stands, many of them for reasons similar to Emmerich's.

• While Emmerich's stand was by no means unique, it was indeed heroic given the tenor of the times. Southwest Mississippi was long considered "the ninth circle of hell" by civil rights workers because of the level of violence they faced there. The area was home to a large contingent of Ku Klux Klansmen, who sometimes operated with the approval of local police. Over the years, numerous scholars have painted the broad canvas of the civil rights movement in Mississippi. John Dittmer, Charles Payne, and other scholars have explained the Mississippi civil rights movement in the context of the social, political, and cultural environment of 1950s and 1960s America and of the American South. Without an understanding of that movement, it's difficult to make sense of just what Emmerich was facing in his local community from the time of the U.S. Supreme Court's 1954 school desegregation decision in *Brown v. Board of Education* through the Voting Rights Act of 1965.[1]

• A study of Emmerich would need to take into account what other historians have written about the interaction of the press and the civil rights movement. For years, historians tended to treat editors in the civil rights era as either heroes or villains, defenders of the segregated status quo in the South or of the civil rights activists who challenged it. This rendering was, literally speaking, divided into black and white, pitting good editors against bad editors, with little understanding of the historical forces that differed in community after community. More recently, scholarship has become more nuanced, reflecting community-based studies in civil rights that have focused more on the individual circumstances of different cities. These studies view local editors in terms of their local communities, those communities' politics, and the unique local culture confronted by each newspaper.

In other words, we would not be able to adequately understand Emmerich and what he did in his times without an understanding of the contextual issues outlined above. A researcher comes to an understanding of these issues through a thorough literature review.

In sum, the literature review gives us two things. *First*, it gives us an understanding of the background to the issue under study, so that as we delve into primary research we can make greater sense of the topic under study. *Second*, the literature review affords us an understanding of what other researchers have found out about the topic, in particular their interpretations of the scholarly issues that have arisen. Thus, the literature review gives us a nuanced understanding of previous scholarship so that we understand the contribution our research is making to the world of knowledge.

---

[1]See John Dittmer, *Local People: The Struggle for Civil Rights in Mississippi* (Chicago: University of Illinois Press, 1994).

The best literature review is thorough, having surveyed the breadth of available articles and books about a subject and appropriately categorizing them so that one's current research project makes better sense by being placed in its context. Getting that result is possible with a methodical approach to exploring the literature.

GETTING STARTED

As you jump into the literature review, you must first determine the outlines of the literature topics you'll be exploring. Usually, the literature will fit into two categories:

(1) the broader category of the general subject into which your more narrow research project fits and

(2) the narrower topic that you are exploring.

Let's consider this categorization with regard to the Emmerich project we discussed above. In this project the broad category is the civil rights movement as a whole; the narrow literature review topic is the question of the press and the civil rights movement. As it happens, both areas have a rich literature. Scholars have delved into numerous aspects of the civil rights movement, and a subset of media scholars has considered the intersection of the civil rights movement and the press. In this case, the two general areas that the literature review should cover are fairly clear.

That's not always the case, however. You'll need to do some thinking to make certain you're covering your bases here, and the best way to do so is to think of broad subject areas into which your subject fits. Let's say, for example, that you're doing a study of Illinois newspapers' characterization of the yellow fever epidemic of 1878. As you consider how to categorize the literature for such a study, remember to think in the broadest possible terms. At first blush, you might think that your literature review should explore the coverage of yellow fever over time. Well, maybe, but doing so would probably result in a fairly narrow source base. It would be better to broaden your exploration to include the broadest search area. So, you'd want to explore the literature of press coverage of communicable diseases or of pandemics and epidemics. After all, you're not writing about yellow fever only; you're writing about a disease, and to place press coverage into its proper context you'd want to consider the broader area. Moreover, you'd want to consider scholarship associated with yellow fever generally, i.e., not just press coverage of the disease but scholarly work about the disease itself. Considering a broader area will give you more of a context into which to place your study, therefore returning a richer harvest of articles and books in the literature review.

Let's take another example, this time of a quantitative study of the portrayal of couples in modern American advertising, specifically in magazine advertising. To compile the literature review for such a study — to repeat the point we made earlier — you would want to look for scholarly work both through the narrow lens of your specific topic and the broader research category into which your topic fits. Let's say that your initial foray into the literature finds that there are virtually no studies of your narrow topic — the portrayal of couples. Therefore you would turn to a broader topic, i.e., the portrayal of gender.

To justify your own approach to the topic, you would delve into the literature to get an idea of how scholars have studied the portrayal of men and women in American advertising and how researchers have established the importance of their research in terms of the literature. This would tell you how your own research will add to what other scholars have written.

Moreover, in a quantitative study such as this one, the literature review would also provide you with research models that you might want to imitate. You could learn, for example, ways that other scholars have measured gender portrayals in magazines, measurements that you might want to replicate.

SEARCHING FOR MATERIALS

Conceptualizing the literature review as you begin will ensure that you find a good range of sources. But, more importantly, it will lead to a literature review that will provide you the context you need to place your findings in the proper perspective. Once you've conceptualized the topics you want to explore, now you must consider how to find the sources you'll need. We're assuming for the purposes of this chapter that you have a good familiarity with the library and the sources it offers. So we'll avoid turning this section into a primer on the basics of library use. Instead, we'll cover some basic ways to get started in finding a range of materials on a particular topic and go from there. If you need a refresher on using the library, you may wish to reread Chapter 4 in this book.

First, let's cover a few things *not* to do. As Internet-dependent as much of the world has become, this writer included, you must avoid the pitfall of over-relying on the Internet in compiling a literature review. Simply put, Googling your topic is no substitute for the hard work of delving into the literature. It's an obvious point that the Internet is only a starting point, but too often students — even an occasional graduate student, sad to say — rely upon it as the be-all and end-all of searching the literature. But Google is simply no substitute for the sources we'll mention below. As thorough as Google can be to search the contents of the Internet, it is not nearly so reliable in finding scholarly literature. For example, a Google search of "press reporting of race" indeed returns a hit on Gene Roberts' and Hank Klibanoff's excellent *The Race Beat* (2006),[2] which would be terrific background reading for anyone delving into a study of Emmerich or of other civil-rights-era editors. But it doesn't record any of the dozens of other books you'd need to consult, and it won't return scholarly articles at all.

One additional warning: Avoid the freshman mistake of posting to listservs to say "I'm doing a paper on so-and-so topic" and plead for help with important books on the topic. You'll come off as amateurish to your colleagues or future colleagues in the scholarly community. More importantly, you'll appear as if you're avoiding the time-consuming task of doing the literature review spadework yourself. This rule is broken much more than you might imagine. On the other hand, it's perfectly acceptable to spread the word among your close colleagues about your research topic generally and what you are investigating specifically. You'll be amazed at how many people come forward with terrific suggestions of books and articles they've run across that might be valuable to you.

With those two gentle warnings out of the way, let's get started. The first thing to do is to compile a bibliography.

---

[2]Gene Roberts & Hank Klibanoff, *The Race Beat: The Press, the Civil Rights Struggle, and the Awakening of a Nation* (New York: Knopf, 2006).

The absolute best way to get underway is to survey the standard text-books in your field. If you're doing a media history topic, for example, head straight to the library and delve into every media history **Survey the Standard Textbooks** text you can find, though obviously more recent textbooks are likely to be of greater value to you. Check the textbook for background on the broad topic into which you are delving (civil rights and journalism, say, or press coverage of pandemics). But also check the chapter covering the time period of your topic. It may be that your topic gets only the briefest mention, but the bibliography may still prove useful.

If the bibliography is annotated, that is, if it includes a brief summary of the contents of the listed article or book, so much the better. The standard text in the field of mass communication history, for example, is Wm. David Sloan's *The Media in America*, which has the added advantage that its chapter bibliographies are annotated. Textbooks on a given topic, be it communication history or another area, are usually grouped together in university libraries. Look up the call number for one, find it on the shelf, and then explore nearby textbooks on the shelf as well.

Like so much of your work in compiling bibliographies, your perusal of the textbooks is simply giving you another place to look for other materials. Once the textbooks take you to citations for books and articles in the topic area you're studying, go find those materials. As you find them, read as you go to get a sense of context for your topic as well as the range of arguments, but also look at the footnotes in each reading to search for other materials. Obviously you're searching for articles that touch most directly upon your subject. Also useful would be articles that offer a literature review in your specific field or in a related one, which would help you by showing how other scholars have parsed the literature in your area.

Specialized bibliographies that break down the literature in a given **Examine Specialized** field will prove especially beneficial as well. For example, Richard **Bibliographies** Schwarzlose's *Newspapers, A Reference Guide* and Wm. David Sloan's *American Journalism History: An Annotated Bibliography* break down media history topics into subtopics and provide an index that breaks down subject areas into many additional subtopics. While both of these books were published more than a decade ago, they nonetheless are useful by giving you a place to start. Both are particularly helpful because they are annotated, giving you a brief overview of the contents of the article, chapter, dissertation, or other publication.[3]

An obvious — but often overlooked — source for useful materials is **Search Journal** the journal index. Most academic journals compile a yearly index of **Indexes** their contents, and some compile more comprehensive indexes every five or ten years, resources that you can peruse for references to your topic. Often these indexes are broken down by subject, making your job even easier. Sometimes, particularly with smaller journals, there is no compilation of indexes; and your only option is to peruse the table of contents for each issue of the journal. As tedious as this might sound, such a search can be unusually fruitful, as you may

---

[3]See Wm. David Sloan, *American Journalism History: An Annotated Bibliography* (New York: Greenwood, 1989) and Richard A. Schwarzlose, *Newspapers, A Reference Guide* (New York: Greenwood, 1987).

find articles that benefit your literature review that might not have turned up in a keyword search of an index.

Search Online Databases

Online databases available through your university library are incredibly helpful to your research. These include general databases (covering all kinds of topics) as well as more specialized ones by topic. Communication scholars often explore JSTOR, a large database of communication journals and publications, as well as other more specialized databases. General databases include EBSCOhost, which includes articles from a wide variety of scholarly articles and can be tweaked so that your more specialized databases broken down by topic area are searched. For more information on using databases, see Chapter 5 in this book. Some databases have links to the full texts of articles your search returns, while others will require you to find the articles on library shelves or on microfilm or microfiche.

It's tempting, for beginners at least, to over-rely upon those full-text citations since they fell into your lap with so little work, but it's important to use your legs and physically look up all of the articles your research returns. Millions of articles that are important to research are not available in full-text, and your research should be as comprehensive as possible.

Find Theses and Dissertations

Search the wide variety of databases that might relate to your topic, and also search the most general databases as well. WorldCat, a database that literally searches the library catalogs of universities all across the globe, can prove particularly useful in finding master's theses and doctoral dissertations. These specialized works can offer you numerous leads, as each usually includes its own literature review that could help you determine if you've covered all your bases. Because theses and dissertations tend to be more specialized, you're more likely to find full-length works that deal in great detail with an aspect of your topic.

While these works are often housed in remote libraries, usually in the library of the university from which the author graduated, don't let this discourage you. The interlibrary loan department of your university should be able to borrow the item on your behalf, or you may be able to buy a copy of the dissertation outright if it appears especially valuable. In either case you'll have to wait a few weeks for the thesis or dissertation to arrive the old-fashioned way in the postal mail. Therefore, you will want to do a search for theses or dissertations early on in your research process to give yourself enough lead time. The wait will usually pay off if the thesis or dissertation relates directly to your topic.

Use Keywords Creatively

Navigating the online databases is fairly intuitive. The main difficulty is narrowing the keywords of your research in such a way as to retrieve articles and other citations that match your research topic. Mix and match your keywords to come up with as wide a variety of search results as you can, as it will take some tweaking to get the search engine in the database to narrow the topic to the level you require.

If you have absolutely no luck in narrowing down your search, don't hesitate to visit the library personally and ask a seasoned research librarian to help you navigate the ins and outs of the more esoteric databases. But do so only after you've done some experimenting on your own. Too often beginning researchers give up on the search process and seek help after only the most cursory search of databases.

Be careful as you compile materials, however, to delineate between scholarly and non-scholarly articles. Many beginning researchers, particularly undergraduates, don't differentiate between the two; and their literature reviews are weaker as a result. To return to a point we stressed earlier, literature reviews cover what other *scholars* have written, meaning that you are exploring what other academics have concluded in a scholarly, methodical investigation of your topic. While you no doubt will find voluminous materials related to your topic in a wide range of periodicals in the popular press (newspapers and magazines), they're not suitable for your literature reviews. This isn't to say they don't have value. Rather, their approach and method generally do not reflect a systematic review that equals the rigor and depth demanded of a scholarly work. For example, a database search of materials related to the press and the civil rights movement might include a large Mississippi newspaper's retrospective on the changing nature of press coverage of race since the 1950s. While this might catch your eye if you're compiling a literature review of that topic, most of the time such articles will not inform your review. They might cover the nuts and bolts of changing press practices, but more than likely they are not going to shed light into how scholars have investigated this topic.

Scholarly vs. Non-scholarly Articles

As you compile your listing of articles, you'll need to keep several things in mind. The first is to *take notes about the articles as you go along.* You may be tempted to postpone going through the articles in your enthusiasm for finding ever more articles, books, and other publications. In fact, it's critically important for you to read the scholarship that you collect as you copy or print them. Your understanding of the literature will widen as you read each piece of work in your steadily expanding collection. Just as importantly, a careful reading of the articles, and the footnotes or citations they contain, will likely lead you to more articles sooner than you would otherwise have found them. Your understanding of your topic will deepen and become more nuanced as you read, and this may lead you to consider new questions — and new literature — associated with your topic. Read as you go along, and you will find more information sooner in the research process. If you wait until the last minute to review the literature, you will miss some important citations until too late in the research process.

Take Notes as You Read

Secondly, you'll want to *watch for common threads* among the various articles that you find. If you classify articles into categories as you go along, the composition of the literature review will be that much easier later on. This process is not nearly so daunting a task as it might first appear. First and foremost, remember this: Classify, classify, classify. Separate the various elements of the literature into their most obvious categories. What are the predominant strains of argument in favor of and against the primary findings that

Watch for Common Threads

you might advance in your piece? If you decide on categories of classification in this stage of the research process, it will make the actual writing of the literature review that much easier when the time comes.

WRITING THE LITERATURE REVIEW

Writing the literature review should be a straightforward process if you've been systematic in collecting materials, have been reading your materials closely as you collect them, and have given considerable thought to how the literature could logically be classified. Just keep in mind the purposes of the literature review as you sit down to write. Again, the literature review should do two things:

(1) provide the contextual background for your study, and

(2) explain where your study fits into the broader literature.

A word of caution about one pitfall to avoid. A common mistake of beginning researchers is to treat the literature review as simply a list of what other scholars have written. Such literature reviews might go on for pages and pages, explaining important contributions to the literature one by one. Even if such a list is exhaustive in its compilation of sources, a simple list falls far short of the job that a literature review must do. It's tedious, for one thing, but that's the least of your worries. If the literature review doesn't do the tough job of classifying the literature under review and further explaining where your research fits, then it has fallen short of your larger goals.

Before you begin writing, ask yourself this: Have I compiled the sources necessary to complete an adequate literature review? In other words, do I have enough? Students often ask this question of their professors. There are several ways to tell if your list of background sources is exhaustive. First, after a thorough search, you should find yourself in the happy position of finding little new information in any additional articles you locate. That is, you are no longer finding articles that advance major themes unknown to you. Sure, there will always be articles on the periphery of your topic that you didn't cover in any detail, and that's perfectly acceptable. But you should have the sense before you begin writing that you've read the major articles, books, and other publications that touch upon your topic. In reviewing even the most recent literature, you'll probably get the sense that you're not finding anything new.

Structure of the Literature Review

If that's the case, then you're ready to begin writing the literature review. The structure of the literature review is going to be similar to other forms of writing that you do. You'll start with an introduction that provides an overview of the focus you are bringing to the literature review, work your way through the body of the review, and then offer conclusions. Like any piece of writing, the body of the review can be organized in one of two primary ways — chronologically or thematically. In the case of a literature review, a chronological presentation would arrange the important literature by publication date. The thematic presentation would organize the literature by argument, findings, or topic. The conclusion, in addition to summarizing the thrust of your theme in the review, might also cover suggested areas for research.

The key to the writing process is the classification work that you have been (or should have been) doing all along. Below is a possible outline of how you might proceed:

1. State the two or three (or three or four, whatever the case may be) broad themes of the literature in your topic. What you're doing here is explaining *the major approaches that scholars have taken in explaining this topic*. Some scholars will have explained the topic in terms of X, and others will have looked at it in terms of Y. Some will have considered that A is the first and foremost concern, and others will have determined that B is most important.

2. Explain, if you can, why these various schools of thought have developed. You may not always be able to explain this, but it's possible. Were the varying perspectives reflective of the era in which they were espoused? (Many times they are.) Can the schools of thought be broken down by, for example, theoretical perspective, geography, profession, philosophical school of thought, or other means?

3. After laying out the schools of thought, now you get to the crux of the literature review: *Where do your findings fit into the literature?* That is, which of the perspectives above match your approach, your argument, your results? How do your conclusions add to this mix of perspectives either by contradicting it or by building upon it? If you are building upon the established literature, how are you doing so? What parts of the previously unanswered questions are you answering?

The third element above is absolutely crucial, and it's the heart and soul of what the literature review is all about. You should be able to state, in a nutshell, the importance of your research. It's the literature review that enables you to do that. The importance of a piece of research is always established by how it compares to or contrasts with what has already been written about the research area.

Formats of the Literature Review

The format of a literature review — its length and its position within the finished written product — will vary according to the research discipline. In communication history, for example, the literature review, while no less important than in any other research discipline, can be quite brief. It's often possible to state in just a few short paragraphs early in your paper your topic's significance and its fit within the overall literature. Usually this section will follow or precede your statement of theme for the overall paper. You may choose to cite milestones in the literature that are important examples of the various subthemes in your topic, but you shouldn't feel compelled to list them all. The footnotes (or endnotes, if you prefer) of the literature review are another matter, however. The footnotes should hit the high points in the literature of the various subthemes and should be as detailed as possible.

If, on the other hand, you're writing an article in the social sciences, your literature review likely will be considerably longer. In writing up the results of a survey or of a content analysis (or of any other social science method), you will cover one by one the major articles or books or other research studies, and your literature review could go on for pages and pages. You will be going into considerably more detail, listing more articles and then explaining more about their significance within the context of the research.

In sum, a good literature review can help assure a high-quality research project.

Time spent compiling background and context helps the researcher reach sound conclusions. As much as you might be tempted to rush into the primary research, don't. A good literature review will nearly always pay off in a stronger, better-researched project.

TO LEARN MORE

Cooper, H. M. *Integrating Research: A Guide for Literature Reviews*, 2nd ed. New-bury Park, Calif.: Sage Publications, 1989.

Cooper, H. *Synthesizing Research: A Guide for Literature Reviews*. Thousand Oaks, Calif.: Sage Publications, 1998.

Galvan, J.L. *Writing Literature Reviews*, 3rd ed. Los Angeles: Pyrczak Publishing, 2005.

Harmon, Robert B. *Elements of Bibliography: A Simplified Approach*. Metuchen, N.J.: Scarecrow Press, 1989.

Harner, James L. *On Compiling an Annotated Bibliography*. New York: Modern Language Association of America, 2000.

Krummel, Donald William. *Bibliographies, Their Aims and Methods*. New York and London: Mansell Publishing, 1984.

Macauley, P. *The Literature Review*. Geelong, Victoria, Australia: Deakin University, 2001.

Machi, Lawrence A., and Brenda T. McEvoy. *The Literature Review: Six Steps to Success*. Thousand Oaks, Calif.: Corwin, 2008.

Social and Behavioral Sciences

The fundamentals in the previous section lay the groundwork for the discussions in the rest of the book. Now that you have a picture of the different kinds of research and the basic tools to find answers to questions, you may be itching to get your feet wet and to embark on the exciting journey called *research*.

In Section II, you will be introduced to a number of well-established techniques for doing research and for finding out something new and original about the communication world. To do the job competently, researchers need to think logically, follow rules, and repeat steps over and over. Because different research questions require different methods, we have assembled a set of tools that are the pillars of social and behavioral approaches in this section.

The methods in this section are empirical in nature, based on observations and evidence. They all share the positivist outlook. Researchers in this school believe that there is an observable, objective reality that can be categorized, studied, and theorized.

The process for scientific inquiry begins first by defining and measuring concepts. It also requires selecting a subset of the population to study, coming up with a study design, and using statistical means to test hypotheses. This procedure is common to all social scientific methods. Section II will introduce you to the details of the process and will explain the three most frequently used social science methods in communication: content analysis, survey, and experiment.

In Chapter 7, "Measurement," Prof. Ken Doyle of the University of Minnesota first explains that the goal of measurement is to make good decisions. He shows that we can often measure some concepts rigorously, but those concepts tend to be trivial and boring. The concepts that we struggle to measure are the most interesting. That is why the rest of the chapter focuses on *concept explication*, that is, what the concept really entails and how many facets it has. He then identifies areas that can go wrong in the measurement process. He uses two seemingly simple concepts, "good teacher" and "effective online banner ad," to illustrate the many pitfalls that one may encounter in the measurement process.

In Chapter 8, "Sampling," Prof. Kate Peirce and Prof. Gilbert Martinez of Texas State University explain why it is possible to draw accurate conclusions about an entire population based on a sample — if rigorous sampling techniques are used. The logic of sampling is simple: It is often not feasible to study an entire population. The authors cover the pros and cons of different samples and the procedures and potential errors that may come with them, from probability samples — such as a simple random sample, systematic random sample, and multi-stage cluster sample — to non-probability samples — such as a convenience sample, purposive sample, and snowball sample.

In Chapter 9, "Content Analysis," Prof. Natalie Jomini Stroud of the University of Texas and Prof. Vanessa de Macedo Higgins of Southern Methodist University explain how to analyze media content quantitatively. They first examine what content analysis can accomplish, other than the obvious function of examining content. They then lay down the steps in content analysis, from defining the population of messages, deciding on a coding unit, creating a codebook, training coders, and calculating inter-coder reliability to analyzing the data. The chapter also discusses challenges and opportunities with the advances of computer technology.

In Chapter 10, "Survey," Prof. Catherine Luther of the University of Tennessee elucidates the processes of doing a competent survey. Much of the chapter focuses on how to ask the right questions — because what you ask is what you get. A survey researcher has to be aware of questionnaire bias. Prof. Luther also explains different kinds of survey techniques, from telephone survey, personal interview, and group-administered survey to online survey. The chapter concludes with pointers on how to improve survey results.

In Chapter 11, "Experiment," Prof. Sam Bradley of Texas Tech University explains what an experiment can or can't do and how to control for extraneous variables. He describes various designs with concrete examples and explains the advantages and disadvantages that come with each design. The chapter also focuses on important issues associated with stimulus manipulation and experimental bias.

In Chapter 12, "Hypothesis Testing," Prof. Meghan Sanders of Louisiana State University explains what hypothesis testing is, the rationale behind it, and the types of errors associated with it. She describes ways to balance Type I and Type II errors and the criteria to decide on significance levels. She also points the reader to the appropriate tests under different circumstances.

In Chapter 13, "Statistics," Prof. George Watson of Arizona State University uses a couple of small data sets to explain clearly what various statistics really mean, from descriptive to inferential statistics. A common belief about communication students is that they are afraid of math. Prof. Watson's chapter will probably make a lot of students feel better about their "math" capability.

As you can see, Section II includes a collection of methods people can reliably use to produce knowledge in a systematic manner. Mastery of such techniques will not only help your research endeavors, but also make you a more logical and critical thinker.

7

Measurement

Sometimes I wish I were a physicist or chemist — because my job would be so much easier. Imagine how simple it would be to measure physical properties like density, specific gravity, mass, and velocity. What a piece of cake, compared to social and psychological measurement!

But in communication, social and psychological measurement is our fate. So let's make the best of it. Let's begin at the beginning.

WHY MEASURE? We measure in order to make decisions. Often, in order to make good, solid, dependable decisions, we need to collect and evaluate data. That's what measurement is all about.

Measurement helps us decide how much we can trust the data that people are going to use to make decisions — sometimes, in communications, multi-million dollar decisions. The principles of measurement can also help us improve our data from the start, before it's too late. They might even keep us from making mistakes that could cost us our jobs. And that's a nice thing.

But measurement specialists often fall into the trap of measuring for the sake of measuring. We get hyper about every little aspect of the problem. We get tangled up in statistics and put all our energy into the pursuit of the perfect test or questionnaire. Sometimes we even try to impress our colleagues with our statistical prowess, even if there's no earthly value to what we're doing.

With Cronbach and Gleser (1965, p. 1), I think the better goal is to help people learn enough about measurement principles that they can arrive at good decisions on the basis of a whole range of quantitative and qualitative data. I'm not advocating tender-minded or — heaven help us — "critical" measurement theory. I'm advocating practicality.

MEASURE WHAT? Epicurus (long before Voltaire) warned us to define our terms. So let's.

By Kenneth O. Doyle
University of Minnesota

I'll try to make this as painless as possible.

Concept. A concept is a purely abstract idea clear enough that you can point out what's like it and what's not like it. "Dog" is a concept (when you're thinking of "dog-ness," not a particular dog). So is "happiness." So is "hunk" (hunkness). For that matter, so are "Creative Director" and "Compelling Ad," maybe even "Budweiser Campaign." Each of these is pretty abstract, and for each of them you can say what fits under the concept and what doesn't. But the minute they stop being abstract, they stop being a concept.

Construct. A construct — a hypothetical construct — is like a concept except that a construct has more connotations, more implications, more meaning. Its relations to other concepts and constructs are more fully spelled out. The difference between a concept and a construct is just a matter of degree of articulation, or spell-outed-ness. For convenience, in this chapter I'll generally talk about constructs rather than "concepts and/or constructs," although what I'll say will apply to both.

Some constructs are "uni-dimensional" (one facet, like height), and some are "multi-dimensional" (more than one facet, as with self-esteem or effectiveness).

Every dimension of a construct can be a variable. A *variable* is something that — Are you ready? — varies. Creative Director Effectiveness can be a variable, as in a study of what makes creative directors effective or who's the best creative director in town. The Budweiser frogs can be variables, each of them or all three together (Bud, Weis, and Er). So can any attribute of any of the frogs: cute, witty, gross, edible, or whatever.

Attach numbers to variables (according to any consistent rule), and they become quantitative variables. Talk about them without numbers, and they're qualitative variables. Good research can focus on quantitative and/or qualitative variables. Often the best research involves both.

Some variables are *discrete* (which means unconnected), as distinguished from *continuous* (which means connected or flowing). Don't confuse "discrete" with "discreet" (which means cautious). Sex is a discrete variable (about which one ought usually to be discreet). Intelligence is a continuous variable (about which some people ought to be especially discreet). Clarity, importance, and effectiveness are continuous. Republican, Democrat, Green, and Independent are probably discrete, although you could make an argument that they're all just points on the same continuum, hence continuous.

To do anything interesting with variables, you have to measure them. To measure them, you have to create a measure. What's a *measure*? It's a quantifier, something that lets you assign numbers to constructs so you can analyze and understand them. Questionnaires and, more broadly, focus groups are among the most popular measures in communications, along with plain old observation. Also very popular are the rating scales that often appear in questionnaires — sequences of words like Poor, Fair, Good, Very Good, Excellent, or Rarely, Seldom, Sometimes, Frequently, Nearly Always, usually with numbers attached.

Often, measures are also called *instruments*. Occasionally they're called *indicators*, which is a pretty good term because it reminds us that, with interesting variables, usually the best we can do is point toward their meanings. Rarely can we hit the bull's-eye.

Objectivity means "distanced from the mind," that is, without the ambiguities and uncertainties that come from subjectivity. In social science, it's often very difficult to stay objective because many of our variables are themselves subjective (e.g., empathy, inspiration, hypochondria).

Standardization means doing everything the same way for all people and conditions in the research, i.e., maintaining an even playing field. Standardization is what social scientists often do in lieu of objectivity.

Sampling governs how far you can generalize your results, to just the people (or circumstances) at hand, to people in the adjacent state, across the country, in the Principality of Monaco, or in the Night Market in Chang Mai, Thailand. Sampling is important enough that there's a whole separate discussion on it in chapter 8 of this book by Prof. Peirce and Prof. Martinez.

Here endeth our vocabulary lesson. Now, on to syntax.

FROM ABSTRACT TO CONCRETE

One of the challenges in any kind of research is to get from your (abstract) construct to the (concrete) instrument that measures it. The way you do this is by turning your conceptual definition to an operational definition. A *conceptual definition* is very abstract, e.g., "'Reputation' is what people think of you." An *operational definition* is very concrete and always describes a process ("operation") through which the conceptual definition is measured: "'Reputation' is the average score on a particular measure that indicates what a particular group of people thinks about particular qualities of a particular person or organization at a particular point in time." Whew. But that's how it works. Your research can be no better than your operational definition.

THE FIDELITY / BANDWIDTH DILEMMA

What makes a person especially crazy in reference to social and psychological measurement is that the things you can measure rigorously are generally pretty boring, even trivial, while the things that are really interesting and important are so tough to measure that you can rarely do the job as well as you want. It's easy to measure the length of my desk or the temperature of my office — but who cares? What's difficult to measure are high-level abstractions like "worthiness," "soulfulness," or "effectiveness."

This is what Professor Cronbach called the *fidelity/bandwidth dilemma*: What's really worth measuring can generally be measured only roughly; what can be measured with great accuracy may not be worth the effort.

RANDOM AND SYSTEMATIC ERROR

The reason it's so much easier to measure desks than effectiveness is that there's much less "error" associated with the concrete world than with the abstract world.

I don't mean error like not knowing the answer to a test question or even forgetting to put your name on your paper. It's far more subtle than that. *Error* is anything and everything that interferes with our true understanding of reality. In all of measurement, one of the biggest problems is to identify and control error.

When it comes to measuring the length of my desk, the nature and extent of error is pretty limited. Maybe I bought a cheap tape measure, and the gradations are a little off. Maybe the tape is stretchy. Or maybe I'm distracted when I lay the tape along the edge of the desk or sloppy when I go to read the markings. Maybe I'm even a touch dyslexic. This is why good carpenters always "measure twice, cut once."

Even in this brief and simple description, you should notice two broad kinds of error, *Random Error* and *Systematic Error*. ***Random Error*** is error that pops up unpredictably, like momentary distractions in one person or another. ***Systematic error*** is error that's steady across a person, like somebody's tendency to be careless, or across a group of people, like a team's good spirits because they just got some great news from the coach. You've got to be extra careful about systematic error because it's sometimes really hard to distinguish it from the reality — the "true variance" or "valid variance" — you're hoping to understand (Brown, 1976, p. 63).

MAXIMUM VS. TYPICAL PERFORMANCE

Measuring devices can be divided into *Measures of Maximum Performance* and *Measures of Typical Performance*.

Measures of maximum performance involve right and wrong answers, and they assume people will try to get as many right answers as they can. The SAT, the ACT, and the typical course exam are measures of maximum performance.

Measures of typical performance assess opinions, attitudes, values, personality traits, and the like, where there are no right or wrong answers and where the questions ask about how things usually are.

Both kinds of measures use open-ended items (like short-answer items) or closed-ended items (like multiple-choice items, ratings, and rankings). In communications research, measures of typical performance are much more common than measures of maximum performance.

The Fidelity/Bandwidth Dilemma applies importantly here. Closed-end tests and questionnaires tend to be higher on fidelity and lower on bandwidth. That is, what they measure they measure well, but it's often — not always — of limited depth and interest. Open-ended tests, questionnaires, and interviews (as well as oral tests) are generally of lower fidelity — they contain more error — but higher bandwidth. They measure more important things, but not as well. In my view, improved bandwidth is usually worth the lowered fidelity.

LEVELS OF DATA

Bear with me now. Because all measurement books include them, I have to mention what I think are the most over-emphasized concepts in all of social and psychological research: Levels of Measurement.

Levels of measurement refer to different categories of data in terms of whether or not they permit particular statistical operations. At the same time, they give some guidance in phrasing test and questionnaire items.

There are four (or five, depending on whom you talk to) levels of data. Let's look at each one.

1. *Nominal Data*, also called *categorical*, like eye color or race or hometown. Nominal data just name something. Statistically, all you can do is count them up and make a frequency distribution: How many men in the group? How many women? How many were born in Chicago? Atlanta? Timbuktu?

On the nominal level, the measure of central tendency is the *mode*. The measure of variability is the *range*. For heaven's sake, don't calculate a mean. It just wouldn't make sense. Neither would a median.

Don't panic if at this point you don't understand statistical terms. You will get an introduction to them in chapter 13 of this book. You can also find them in the glossary at the back of the book.

2. *Ordinal Data*, like year in school. Ordinal data name something and rank it. *Rankings* are scales that order stimuli relative to one another: She's best, he's next best, his sister is next best, and so forth. The ranking can be on just about any dimension you can think of.

When you're ranking something, it's important to tell people whether a high position or a low position is better. In American usage, we can describe the best in either of two ways: "We're Number One!" or "She's a 10!"

In ranking, it's also important to know that the difference between first place and second place isn't necessarily the same as the difference between any other pair of adjacent places. That is, the *intervals* between the ranks aren't equal.

Notice that levels of data form a taxonomy: Each level can do its own statistical thing (like rank something), as well as the statistical things of every lower level (like create a frequency distribution). Statistically on the ordinal level, you can do ranking as well as create the frequency distributions you can also do on nominal data. On the ordinal level, the measure of central tendency is the *median*; the measure of variation — nobody ever uses this, not since Moses — is the inter-quartile range and its variations, such as the semi-interquartile range. You still can't legitimately do a mean or standard deviation.

3. *Interval Data* are data in which the distances, or intervals, from one unit to the next are all the same, like Fahrenheit temperature. That is, the distance from 98 to 99 degrees is the same as the distance from 41 to 42 degrees. Because the distances are all the same, you can use your favorite statistics, like the *mean* (for central tendency) and the *standard deviation* (for variation), as well as all the lesser statistics (e.g., median, mode).

However, just because something can be numbered does not mean the intervals will necessarily be the same. For example, in a talent contest with scoring possibilities of 0 to 10, the difference in talent between two contestants who get scores of 9 and 10 may not be the same as the difference between two others who get scores of 7 and 8. As you can imagine, a talent of 10 may be one of a kind, whereas the distance between 7 and 8 may mean little difference.

4. *Ratio Data*, like weight and height, do have zero points — zero pounds, zero inches. When you have ratio data, you can use rare statistics like the geometric mean and the coefficient of variation — and what a treat that would be!

It's worth a moment's pause to consider the difference between ordinal and interval data. Think about this: If your data are only ordinal, you shouldn't, as I've been harping about, be computing means and standard deviations. Your results just won't make sense. You should stick with medians and inter-quartile ranges, which are much less sensitive than means and standard deviation, and much clumsier to use, especially the hemi-semi-demi-interquartile range.

So, what do you do with widely used measures like rating scales, that is, ad-verbial, adjectival, or Likert agree-disagree scales? Can you compute means and standard deviations on agree/disagree (or similar) responses, or must you stick with clumsy and insensitive ordinal-level statistics?

The answer is to try, when you first build your agree/disagree scale (or other measure), to do your best to make the intervals as consistent as possible. For instance:

[Ordinal]	Poor	Inadequate	Good	Excellent	Fabulous
[Interval]	Poor	Fair	Good	Very Good	Excellent

The psychological distance from Inadequate to Good on the upper line is certainly not the same as the distance from Excellent to Fabulous; and the other intervals are, at best, confusing. But all the intervals on the lower line seem pretty much the same. The descriptive words may not be true interval data, but they're better than pure ordinal data. Many researchers now call these "quasi-interval data" and agree that it's OK to use our beloved means, standard deviations, analyses of variance, and so forth. I agree with them.

The bottom line is this: Don't do dumb things like averaging ordinal (or nominal) data. But you knew that. And don't do equally dumb things like computing a mean among steps on a rating scale the intervals of which, to a sensible observer, seem too different from one another. And do write items that come as close to interval data as you can.

With all that out of the way, let's get down to the business of controlling error and building meaning. This is, as I've insisted, what measurement is all about.

CONTROLLING ERROR

Let's try to get a little better handle on what error means and where it lives.

Errors in Measures of Maximum Performance

Measures of Maximum Performance and Measures of Typical Performance both involve random error and systematic error associated with the main parts of the measurement situation. In any measure of maximum performance, there are three main parts: the test, the test-taker, and the circumstances of testing. Let's just touch on these, because, as I mentioned above, measures of maximum performance aren't all that common in communication research. For an example of a more detailed analysis, see Stanley (1971).

1. *Error in the Test*. Errors in the test are pretty much always errors in the instructions or in the wording of the test items. The instructions or layout could be confusing. Any item or type of item could be ambiguous. Most important, the collection of items as a whole may not measure what's important. For the most part, these kinds of errors are systematic. That is, they're consistent across the group of people. However, if a scattering of individuals simply misread one or another item or instruction, that's random error.

2. *Error in the Test-Taker*. You're likely to find a greater variety of error types in the test-taker simply because that's where the human contribution is most intense and complicated. Random error in test-takers includes the individual moods of members of the group. It also includes some kinds of distractions, like one person flashing forward to a tasty lunch and another flashing back to a particularly pleasant or unpleasant experience last night. The distinction is that, as random

error, the flash-forwards or flash-backs aren't patterned in the group. If the whole group is brought down by a communal hangover, or distracted by a passing train or comely classmate, it's systematic error.

3. *Error in the Circumstances*. Some people get extra prep time (make-up tests) or testing time (doctor's orders). Some people are more sensitive to the physical environment than others, a room too hot or too noisy. Some people whee-dle hints out of the instructor or TA or proctor. Some people exhibit response sets, like choosing response alternative "B" whenever they're not sure of the answer. It's all error, though generally not really serious; and it all interferes to some degree with our understanding of the piece of reality we're interested in.

Errors in Measures of Typical Performance

Besides not having right or wrong answers, measures of typical performance are different from measures of maximum performance in that the former have four components, not just three. This important difference led me once upon a time (Doyle, 1981) to propose an "error-analysis" approach to reliability and generalizability.

1. *Error in the Rater*. The rater might have a tough time coordinating the rating question with the ratee's "typical performance." He (or she) might be trying to harass the ratee, or connect with her, or reward her for something pleasant. The rater might be especially subject to response styles: Leniency/Stringency, Leveling/Sharpening, Halo/Discrepancy Effect, Contrast Effect, Implicit Theories, and Social Desirability.

Let's look more closely at these response styles, also known as *Rater Error* (Guilford, 1954, Ch. 7), because they're particularly important kinds of error in measures of typical performance:

The *Leniency/Stringency* response style reminds us that some people tend to be generous in their ratings, other people harsh. Sometimes this tendency is a response to circumstances (e.g., you don't want to endanger the ratee's job, or you want to get even for something). Sometimes it's a personality characteristic of the rater (tough guy or bleeding heart).

Leveling/Sharpening (also called *Central Tendency Error*) reminds us that some people shy away from the extremes of opinion while others like to empha-size differences. The former crowd their ratings (and their emotions) into the mid-dle of the scale. The latter flock to the extreme points.

Halo/Discrepancy Effect tells us that some people over-emphasize general impressions of people while other people over-emphasize people's disparate parts. For some, their feelings toward some ratee (often a political figure) are so strong that they're blinded to her or his good qualities. (Did you just say Hillary? Or was it Newt?) Others see only the specific attributes. They can't find the forest for the trees.

The *Contrast Effect* reminds us that some ratees remind raters of important figures in their lives whom they particularly like or dislike. A ratee may, on a con-scious level or not, remind a particular rater of the rater's imperious father or pusillanimous mother and provoke a strong negative reaction. It's like psychoan-alytic "transference."

Implicit Theories (once called *Logical Error*) remind us that many people ex-pect certain behaviors to occur together in certain kinds of people: Fat people are jolly, Blondes are ditzy, Democrats are big spenders, and Republicans are mean-spirited. Implicit theories are a specialized kind of stereotyping that can influence how we evaluate people.

Social Desirability is closely related to Political Correctness. It's the inclination to rate highly those things that the people in a social circle consider good and proper and downgrade everything else, whatever offends or disagrees with the predominant group. This kind of error seems to be becoming a bigger problem every year, at least on campus.

2. *Error in the Ratee*. The ratee could try to influence the rater, like a teacher who might try to kiss up to students just before the course evaluation by passing out candy in an effort to sweeten the ratings. Some ratees simply ask for leniency — Americans, especially young Americans, love to support people who claim to be oppressed — or hint that good things will happen to the raters if the ratings are favorable, bad things if they aren't.

3. *Error in the Rating Instrument*. As with measures of maximum performance, ambiguity in the directions or in the phrasing of any item is a common kind of error in rating instruments. But the greater potential for error has to do with the content of the test questions and questionnaire items themselves. Although many researchers don't seem to recognize it, a test or questionnaire presents a theory of whatever it's trying to measure, whether it's Good Teaching or Good CEO or Good Banner Ad. So, if a questionnaire isn't really well thought out, it may present a lousy theory and gather equally lousy data.

4. *Failure to ask the right questions*, all the right questions, and nothing but the right questions is the most important kind of error in any measuring device. The right questions are what validity is all about. Failure to ask those questions clearly and in language your respondents can fully understand is the essence of reliability.[1]

RELIABILITY AND VALIDITY

Finally, the very core of measurement: How much can we trust the data at hand (reliability), and how do we assure ourselves about what those data really mean (validity)? These considerations apply with equal force to quantitative and qualitative data and, for that matter, in every social and natural science. The details may differ, and how you apply the concepts may vary, but the essence remains the same.

What Is Reliability, and How Do You Assess It?

The traditional way to define and assess the kinds of error we've been talking about is by calculating a reliability coefficient. A *reliability coefficient* is simply a correlation. It measures *consistency*, or pattern, in a set of data. Reliability coefficients are undeniably convenient, but, as we shall see shortly, they don't tell us as much as we'd like them to. Sometimes they even mislead us.

Early measurement people decided that there were two straightforward ways to see if there was enough pattern in their data. The first they called *test-retest reliability*. They gave the same test or questionnaire to the same people twice, just a few minutes apart. Because the measurements were taken so close together in

[1]Campbell and Stanley (1963) described errors found in research studies. They classified the errors into those affecting Internal Validity, or the quality of the study, and External Validity, the generalizability of the study.

time, the researchers argued, any difference between the initial and subsequent sets of data must be due to some kind of error in the test, test-taker, or circumstances of measurement. If the correlation were high, the same pattern must exist in both sets of data. So, high test-retest correlations meant high reliability.

Careful, though: There can be several explanations for data that change from Time 1 to Time 2. First, maybe, as the theoreticians opined, the respondents just threw up their hands in confusion and marked whatever occurred to them at the moment. If that were the case, the low test-retest correlation would be a decent indicator of some kind of error in the respondent. But maybe the variable the researcher was measuring was a fleeting state, like cheerfulness, rather than a relatively steady trait, like gregariousness. Or maybe the respondents were annoyed at, or just playing with, the researcher and intentionally changed their answers. The reliability coefficient doesn't tell us very much about the source or cause of any inconsistency, only the amount.

Because it was inconvenient (and seemed a little silly) to give the same test or questionnaire two times in a row, the early specialists found ways to measure consistency in a single administration of the test or questionnaire. One such approach involved splitting the test or questionnaire in half and correlating the first half with the second half. They called this method "Split-Half Reliability." When the test or questionnaire was split in half on the basis of odd vs. even item numbers, they called the technique "Odd-Even Reliability." You just can't beat statisticians for verbal wit.

Over the years, significant refinements were made upon these early ideas. Reliability coefficients that measure consistency across test questions or questionnaire items came to be called *internal consistency reliability* coefficients. What the ideas have in common is consistency over content: Do the questions together describe a loud-and-clear theme, or do some questions measure one thing, others another? The most thorough, sophisticated, and widely used of the modern techniques is Cronbach's *Coefficient Alpha* — Yep, Cronbach again — the average correlation among all pairs of items.

Just as you can measure consistency over time ("test-retest") and consistency over content ("internal consistency"), you can measure consistency over people ("generalizability"). High reliability coefficients mean high consistency of whichever sort. Low coefficients mean low consistency. After Cattell (1964), *test-retest reliability* is often called *stability*, *internal consistency reliability* is often called *homogeneity*, and *transferability* is just a step or two short of what's commonly called *generalizability*.

Again, be careful. Whatever kind of consistency you measure, it's only good to find high coefficients if you should have high consistency. That is, if you're measuring a state rather than a trait, you should expect to see less consistency because states fluctuate a lot. If it's a trait, you should insist on greater consistency. If you're measuring the opinions of a diverse group of people, you should expect to see some degree of inconsistency, reflecting different points of view. If the people are relatively similar, you should require high consistency. And if you're measuring something multi-dimensional, you should expect to see reduced consistency; if uni-dimensional, increased. Statistical techniques with names like "factor analysis" and "cluster analysis" can help you arrange your people, items, and even points in time into consistent groupings. Backing off and thinking about what you should find will go a long way toward making your reliability analysis more meaningful.

Here's a final and even more important caution: Sometimes high reliability coefficients are bad! The coefficients we've been talking about all measure consistency, and consistency can come either from clear instructions, well phrased questions, and plenty of rater familiarity with what's being rated — good stuff — or it can come from bad stuff like Leniency/Stringency, Halo Effect, and the other Rater Errors. So we're stuck. We can't tell for sure if the consistency comes from good or bad sources. Kind of annoying for a statistic that's been in use for more than fifty years! That's why some of us, a small but handsome minority, prefer the error-analysis approach.

The bottom line is that you can't just calculate and report reliability coefficients without thinking about them, even though lots and lots of people do!

Generalizability Theory

In about 1972, Professor Cronbach and associates devised a general statement of reliability, which they called *Generalizability Theory*. Generalizability Theory lays out, for the researcher's consideration, all possible dimensions along which data can be patterned, including but far from limited to the dimensions we've already mentioned. Generalizability Theory makes researchers think about how much consistency of what kinds should, and shouldn't, exist in their data, and about what research designs are needed to evaluate that consistency. It goes far beyond the mechanical application of statistical formulas, and it forces researchers to think about what patterns should appear where. My 1981 approach to error analysis parallels Cronbach's theory: You should do error analysis on each and every one of his facets, or dimensions of consistency. My cautions about the misleading effects of rater error apply here, too.

VALIDITY: BUILDING MEANING

What is validity? Validity is what results from validation, the *attribution of meaning to data*. Validity is the outcome; validation is the process that gets us there. Validity is meaning. It's your measure's reflection of reality.

Remember what I said previously: You can't have validity unless you have reliability. You can't attach meaning to random data. You can't paint a picture of reality without patterns. Or, as the theorists put it, reliability sets the upper limit for validity.

So, how does one go about attaching meaning to (reliable) data? Generally, measurement specialists talk about three kinds of validity, three tools or techniques of validation: Content Validity, Criterion-oriented Validity, and Construct Validity.

Always the problem child, I say there's only one kind of validation — Construct Validation — and that Content Validation and Criterion-oriented Validation are just two of a number of approaches to Construct Validation. Maybe sometimes they're all we want, as in a simple predictive study. But they're certainly not on the same level of importance as Construct Validation.

Again, not everybody agrees with me. But they have a right to be wrong.

OK, here we go.

Content Validation is the attribution of meaning in terms of the questions on a test or items on a questionnaire, the content. It asks: Are these the right questions — the most important items — to ask? Content Validation answers that question solely in terms of subjective judgment. A common way to appraise content validity is through "Expert Judgment": You simply ask some experts — poets, priests, professors; whoever — either to help you select the questions to ask or to evaluate the collection of questions you've put together. Hopefully, the help they give you will be based on their knowledge of research, theory, and practical application. The quality of your content validation is exclusively a function of the ability and motivation of your experts.

Some researchers play fast and loose with Content Validation. Some say, "These questions look relevant. So they must be valid." That's "Face Validity," the weakest form of validity mankind has yet devised. Others say, "I'm the expert, and I say my questions are the best possible ones to ask." Arrogance aside, this argument certainly doesn't lead to scientific reproducibility.

Criterion-oriented Validation is the attribution of meaning through correlations with other measures. In its simplest form, your test ought to correlate with a test that's trying to measure pretty much the same thing. Why would you want to write a test that measures pretty much the same thing as an existing test? Maybe yours is cheaper or shorter or more up-to-date. In any event, for basic Criterion-oriented Validation you just get the same people to take both tests and correlate their scores. If the correlation is high enough, you can say you've added to the meaning of your test or questionnaire by showing something that it correlates with.

Some people distinguish two kinds of Criterion-oriented Validity, predictive and concurrent. *Predictive Validity* predicts: Does the student's performance on the SAT predict her undergraduate grade-point average? *Concurrent Validity* is everything else. It just means that the tests are administered at the same time.

More sophisticated researchers ask the same people also to take a second test that shouldn't correlate with the first one. In other words, you can add even more meaning by saying, "Here's something that my test should correlate with and does, as well as something it shouldn't correlate with, and doesn't." If you're trying to construct a test of creativity, for example, it should probably correlate with other tests of creativity more highly than with tests of math skill or even verbal fluency.

Professors Campbell and Fiske (1959) were following this line of thought when they devised their "multitrait-multimethod matrix," a statistical table that presents the correlations of a variety of tests and a variety of methods (multiple-choice, ratings, essay) in a format that lets you tell if there are high correlations where there should be, medium correlations where they should be, and low correlations where they should be. Campbell and Fiske called this the study of "convergent" and "discriminant" validity.

Uh Oh! Do you see what we're doing? We're waxing philosophical. We've just stepped into the highly philosophical domain of Construct Validation. For that matter, we just demonstrated that Content Validity and Criterion Validity are subsets of Construct Validity.

Let's dig more deeply into Construct Validation.

Construct validation — better, the validation of constructs — is one of the most important, and one of the most poorly understood, processes in all of social and psychological research, including communication research. Here I'd like to help you understand what it really means to define and validate a construct, how challenging a task it is, how valuable, and how humbling.

CONSTRUCT VALIDATION: ROUND I

What, again, is a *construct*? It's simply a conception we have about something, an abstract mental image, a blurry picture (Cronbach & Meehl, 1955). More articulated than a mere concept, it's an idea about which we already know something but need to know more. As an example, let's use a construct with which we're all at least somewhat familiar: Good Teacher. Even after all these years of study and discussion, the Good Teacher construct has still got components we're guessing at. That's OK. Part of every construct always remains hypothetical.

So, a hypothetical construct is a concept we have that we want to understand better. We understand it better first by trying to agree on a definition and then by comparing and contrasting it to other constructs or to intervening variables. This is the process of construct validation.

You wouldn't think it would be all that difficult to define "Good Teacher." Right off the bat, we've all got some ideas. But, as we're about to see, every definition has some problems. We aren't anywhere near scientific consensus as to what constitutes Good Teacher. Here are some ideas:

Defining the Construct

1. Good Teacher is someone who causes students to learn.
2. Good Teacher is someone who creates the opportunity for students to learn.
3. Good Teacher is someone who exhibits certain characteristics, namely the ones we see on course-evaluation forms.

Let's look more closely at each of these.

The strength of the first definition, of course, is that it goes straight to the fundamental goal of teaching: student learning. The main problem I have with this definition is that learning itself is so hard to define. What is learning, and how do you measure it? Do you really think the tests you take are good measures of "True Learning"? What do we really know about instructor traits and behaviors that influence student learning for most if not all students?

Finding a good measure against which to evaluate the possible definitions of our construct — Criterion-oriented Validity — is called the *criterion problem*. It's vexing.

In my mind, True Learning is itself a construct, and at least as hard to define as Good Teacher.

The second problem I have with this definition — "causes student learning" — is that it makes the teacher wholly responsible for what his or her students do or don't do. Isn't learning at least as much the responsibility of the student?

The strength of the second definition — "creates the opportunity to learn" — is that it shifts a good dose of the responsibility for learning from the instructor to the students. The main problem is that it's too abstract. We don't really know what's involved in "giving students the opportunity to learn." That's where the third definition comes in.

The third definition — "exhibits certain characteristics" — contains both promise and problems. Its strength is that it's more concrete, more specific than the other definitions, better at telling teachers how to behave. In addition, it's easy to come up with a list of characteristics — "face validity" — that seem as though they describe a Good Teacher, characteristics like "organized," "approachable," "engages students," "gives feedback promptly, " "grades fairly," and "uses visual aids effectively." It's hard to know, though, whether or not they are related to student learning, and, if so, how.

This is important: The main problem with lists of fine-sounding teacher characteristics is that there's little if any research that says that any of these characteristics has anything to do with any kind of learning, especially what I just called True Learning. Who says students learn more from clear presentations than from unclear ones? Who says that the clearer the presentation is, the more or better the students learn? Who says students learn more from nice guys than from jerks? (See an article about likeability and teaching: Uranowitz & Doyle [1978].) Who says the more promptly the instructor gives feedback, the more her students learn? Or the "fairer" the instructor is, the better his students learn. Prompt feedback, fair grading, effective use of visual aids may each make a contribution; but I'd be reluctant to say there's a significant linear correlation between them and any measure of student learning.

Who says students learn more or better from teachers who engage than from teachers who don't? Actually, I do! I think there's good reason to say Good Teachers are those who really engage their students, although, realistically, engagement is probably a two-way street: The student has to be willing to be engaged. But I have a hard time justifying the inclusion of fair grading and visual aids on this list. (See an article about academic motivation: Doyle & Moen [1978]).

It's not all that hard to improve on the usual practice to come up with a list of characteristics that's more tightly tied to Definition 1: Causes Learning, or Definition 2: Creates the Opportunity to Learn. Characteristics that define the Instructor's Effectiveness at Giving Students an Opportunity to Learn might include terms like "Was clear enough that students could understand him," "Was cordial enough that her interpersonal style didn't interfere with student learning," and "Engaged Students."

Notice that the first two characteristics are binary yes/no questions. That's because I don't want my definition to say there's a direct linear relationship between instructor clarity and student learning. The instructor just has to be clear enough. Same with likability. She just has to be likable enough. The third item — "engages students" — might be linearly connected with learning: The more effectively the instructor engages students, the more they learn. Maybe.

This isn't just a list of questions that some professor or committee of professors thought sounded good. It's different because there's a miniature theory of Good Teaching behind the set of characteristics that I selected: The Good Teacher is the one who gives students the opportunity to learn. The Excellent Teacher is the one who gives students the opportunity to learn and engages or motivates them to take advantage of that opportunity. There's research behind each item on the list, and at least a little theory about how the items relate to one another.

In other words, we have at least a somewhat advanced construct of Good Teacher. But we're still far from consensus as to the definition of this hypothetical construct.

Can you, gentle reader, come up with a definition of Good Teacher? Try it. Take a break and think about it.[2]

The process of validating hypothetical constructs requires, in addition to the best definition we can agree on, a well planned collection of research studies that incrementally add to our understanding of the construct. Let's continue to use Good Teacher as our example for a few more minutes.

ADDING MEANING TO A CONSTRUCT

Cronbach and Meehl (1955) list different kinds of research studies that can help advance the meaning of a construct. For present purposes, the most important dimensions or a construct are *Group Differences* and *Patterns of Relationships with Other Measures*.

Group Differences

Let's make some predictions about which group differences might help us understand Good Teacher as one who gives students the opportunity to learn by being clear enough and likable enough, and the Great Teacher as one who really engages students, drawing out the best in them. Here are some possibilities:

Gather two groups of students. In one group, the members all scored above their predicted midterms. In the other, they all scored below. Ask students in each group to say who were their favorite teachers and why. See what similarities and differences in clarity, likeability, and engagement you can find between the two lists of teachers and the two sets of explanations.

Gather two groups of teachers. In the first group, all the members got high student ratings on "gave opportunity to learn"; in the second group, low ratings. Ask members of each group to list and describe learning opportunities they provided. See if the first group's lists aren't longer and more interesting than the second group's.

Following up on the first study — two groups of students — ask the students in both groups to list the best teachers and richest learning opportunities they saw in their classes. See if the Great Teachers' students don't prepare the longest lists, the Good Teachers' student the next longest, and the lesser teachers' students the shortest lists.

Patterns of Correlations

If we were to build a Good Teacher test or questionnaire, with which measures should it correlate, and with which ones should it not correlate?

The Good Teacher test or questionnaire should correlate more highly with Engages Students than with Nice Guy or Organized.

It should correlate with tests of student learning.

It should correlate higher with tests of high-level students learning than with

[2]In our Good Teacher scenario, we started with a rather weak measure – some classroom tests – against which to validate questionnaire items. Subsequent study will refine that measure and make for more meaningful relationships. Cronbach and Meehl (1955) called this phenomenon the "Bootstraps Effect," as in "lifting oneself by one's own bootstraps."

tests of mere memorization.

It should correlate with student ratings of overall teacher effectiveness.

There are many other studies researchers can do to add meaning to their construct. The key is that the study is always designed to search out similarities and differences and that the results are always in the predicted direction. Even a little bit of adverse information can derail the entire train.

So you see how a planned series of studies helps add meaning to the construct. The interconnection among these hypotheses (and the data) is called the *"nomological network,"* the interlocking array of behavioral *"laws,"* (*nomos*) surrounding the construct. The more intricate and deeper a network you come up with, the more meaning you have attributed to your construct.

But don't fall into the trap that many researchers do. These good citizens do any old study that might somehow relate to the construct and then say, "This contributes to the construct validity" of whatever construct they might be studying. No, it probably doesn't. Unless the researcher explicitly refers to the construct from the beginning and shows where there's a gap in our understanding of the construct, and then proceeds to fill that gap, he's just running numbers. Construct validation is an extremely thoughtful and rigorous procedure. If it ain't thought out, it just don't count.

CONSTRUCT VALIDATION: ROUND II

OK. We've now gotten our feet wet by trying to validate the construct Good Teacher. We chose Good Teacher to practice with because everybody who's reading this chapter has experience with teaching and surely has some opinions about it. Now let's do another round, this time focusing on a mass communication construct: Effective On-Line Banner Ad. We could have chosen Good Creative Director, Ideal Client, Sweet Spot (Fortini-Campbell), or any of dozens of other communication constructs.

Defining the Construct

What on Earth is an Effective On-Line Banner Ad?

There are at least three ways to come up with a definition.

First, you could do exactly as we did with the Good Teacher construct. Go straight to the heart of the matter:

Definition 1: An Effective On-Line Banner Ad is one that causes people to buy the product.

Second, recognizing that it's pretty hard to tie increases and decreases in sales to an individual ad, you could use a "proxy," a substitute, for actual purchasing. The most popular proxy for actual purchasing is "next-day recall."

Definition 2: An Effective Banner Ad is one that causes people to recall the message the day after they see it.

The strength of this definition is that it's realistic. While you can't easily measure sales or connect your ad to the ebbs and flows of your client's sales, you can fairly easily use focus groups or telephone surveys to measure second-day recall. This is pretty much the definition that ad practitioners are using these days, although it's entirely based on the dubious assumption that people who recall a brand or message are going to purchase the product.

Third, because just talking in terms of desirable outcome doesn't tell us very much about how to create or recognize an Effective Banner Ad, you could try to come up with a list of attributes of such an ad. As I'm sure you recognized instantly, this is parallel to what we did with our Good Teacher construct.

There are at least two ways to try to come up with such a list. Both cases come under the heading of Content Validation. The first is the "armchair method." It's considered the weaker, but it's not necessarily a bad way to start. You, maybe with the help of a few professional colleagues, could try to list as many attributes as possible of what you think is an Effective Banner Ad. You could just dig around in your own imagination, but you'd probably do better if you asked advertising practitioners and professors for their advice and if you dug into the research literature. Eventually you could tidy the list into a collection of "exhaustive" and "mutually exclusive" categories (Q-sort). But what you have would still be just a tidy list of people's best guesses as to what makes for an Effective Banner Ad.

Arguably a better way is Flanagan's (1954) Critical Incidents Technique. You could get a bunch of people who are familiar with banner ads — a "representative sample" of some relevant population — and ask them to tell you true stories, maybe 100 words long, about banner ads that worked with them and ads that didn't — banners that led them to buy or to remember the product, turned them off, drove them to a competitor, and so forth. From their stories you could dig out the qualities that, according to your respondents, distinguish Effective Banner Ads from Ineffective Banner Ads. Once you feel you've collected as many "incidents" as you're going to get, once you start hearing the same stories over and over again, you can tidy them up just the way you tidied up the armchair collection.

The main difference between armchair attributes and critical incidents is that the critical incidents tend to sound a little more realistic. But armchair attributes collected from the research literature and with the help of experienced practitioners can compete well with critical incidents.

Either way, what you'll have is a collection of characteristics with probably pretty good content validity, but, at this point, only that.

Definition 3: An Effective Banner Ad is one that exhibits certain characteristics, like "funny," "sexy," "informative," "simple," "focused," and/or "timely."

Here's an Opportunity to Learn: If you'd pause a bit and write out what you think differentiates Effective and Ineffective Banner Ads, you'll probably get more out of this discussion than if you simply read it. Why not take a few minutes and do that? Feel free to talk about it with other people.

[Pause to reflect.]

To me, the first definition sounds good — after all, what's advertising for? — but it's unrealistic. Like Good Learning, Effectiveness-as-Sales-Increases is hard to measure. It's even harder to make a causal connection between an ad and real-world sales. While increases or decreases in sales certainly affect the relationship between a company and its ad agency, the connection generally isn't strong enough or clear enough for scientific purposes.

The second definition — "second-day recall" — is what advertising researchers generally use. Its strength is that it's easy to study. You can simply convene some focus groups and ask. You can even do it by telephone survey. Its weakness is that it's based on the supposition that people who remember a TV ad the day after they see it are more likely to buy the product in the future.

The third definition is appealing, but only to the extent we know that each of the characteristics on the list works, that is, influences people to buy products (or promotes second-day recall). It's a lot like Good Teacher. We like ads that are funny, but there's precious little data to show that funny ads are more effective. We say we like ads that are informative, but if those are effective it's probably only when we're actively looking for the product. Also like teaching, it's probable that different kinds of ads are effective with different kinds of people, maybe even different kinds of products. (Here, we're dealing with Trait/Treatment Interactions: "Different strokes for different folks.")

ADDING MEANING TO A CONSTRUCT (AGAIN)

As with Good Teacher, if we're going to expand on the construct we have to get at descriptive variables, like those alluded to in the third definition:

Funny — For the right kind of product/audience combination, "funny" grabs attention and creates a positive atmosphere. It reduces anxiety and threat. It may leave you with positive feelings toward the product and its maker.

Informative — At the right point in time, when the target is interested in this product, "informative" satisfies a practical need.

Sexy — Arguably more for optically sensitive males, a touch of the erotic not only holds attention but enhances the product itself, even if it's a truck tire promoted by a sexy model. Although this observation will annoy some readers, sexiness — eroticism — in advertising is different for males and females.

Simple — Easy to follow, even with only a part of one's attention.

Timely — Happens to appear when the prospect is looking for that kind of information.

Again, the patterns always have to be as predicted, or it's back to the drawing boards. A little bit of negative information is more important than a large amount of positive information, because negative results can tell you you're heading in the wrong direction.

Group Differences

Let's devise some studies based on predictions of how our construct is taking shape:

Create two groups of people: one that's looking to buy a product like the one you're advertising, and the other that's not. Expose them to the ad. Next day ask if they're more likely to buy your product. Ask later if they (a) bought your product or a competitor's or (b) at least thought more about your product than your competitor's.

Use eye-tracking devices to measure how long people's glance lingers on your ad, even parts of your ad. Create two groups: brief glance and longer glance. Ask and observe if the members of one group say they're more likely to buy the product and, later, if they actually bought the product.

What other group-difference studies can you come up with? How about males versus females? First-time buyers versus experienced buyers?

Patterns of Correlations

Use the preceding designs with correlations, as well as group-difference statistics, to dig more information out of your data.

Systematically vary your ad as to "funny," "informative," "sexy," and so forth. See if the different ads affect people's stated intent to purchase as well as their physiological responses like galvanic skin response. Do these analyses cross geographic, demographic, and psychographic types, e.g., VALS-II?

Remember, the more intricate and deeper your nomological network becomes, the more shape your construct will take, because you will have attached more and more meaning to your construct.

To my way of thinking, the validation of hypothetical constructs is the most important and most difficult activity in all of social and psychological measurement — important because it focuses on making good decisions, including very important decisions, and difficult because it makes us look for truth in reality. In addition, I find construct validation humbling, because there's nothing like trying to lay out a nomological network to remind us how little we actually know.

As Amos — "Mr. Cellophane" — said in *Chicago*, "I hope I haven't taken up too much of your time."

TO LEARN MORE

American Educational Research Association, American Psychological Association and National Council on Measurement in Education (1985). *Standards for Educational and Psychological Testing*. Washington, DC.

Cureton, E. E. (1950). Validity, Reliability, and Baloney. *Educational and Psychological Measurement, 10,* 94-96.

Likert, Rensis A. (1932). A Technique for the Measurement of Attitudes. *Archives of Psychology*, No. 140.

Meehl, Paul E. (1954). *Clinical versus Statistical Prediction*. Minneapolis: University of Minnesota Press.

Nunnally, Jum C. (1994). *Psychometric Theory*. New York: McGraw-Hill.

Thurstone, L. L., and E. J. Chave (1929). *The Measurement of Attitude*. Chicago: University of Chicago Press.

Torgerson, W. S. (1958). *Theory and Methods of Scaling*. New York: Wiley.

REFERENCES

Brown, F. G. (1976). (2nd ed.) *Principles of Educational and Psychological Testing*. New York: Holt, Rineheart, Winston.

Campbell, D. T., and Fiske, D. W. (1959). Convergent and Discriminant Validation by the Multi-Trait Multi-Method Matrix. *Psychological Bulletin, 56,* 81-105.

Campbell, D. T., and Stanley, J. C. (1963). Experimental and Quasi-experimental Designs for Research on Teaching. In N. L. Gage (Ed.) *Handbook of Research on Teaching*. Skokie, IL: Rand McNally.

Cattell, R. B. (1964). Validity and Reliability: A Proposed More Basic Set of Concepts. *Journal of Educational Psychology, 55,* 1-22.

Cronbach, Lee J., and Gleser, G. C. (1965) (2nd ed.) *Psychological Tests and Personnel Decisions*. Urbana, IL: University of Illinois Press.

Cronbach,, L. J., Gleser, G. C., Nanda, H., & Rajaratnam, N. (1972). *The Dependability of Behavioral Measurements: Theory of Generalizability for Scores and Profiles*. New York: Wiley, 1972.

Cronbach, L. J., and Meehl, Paul E. (1955). Construct Validity in Psychological Tests. *Psychological Bulletin, 52,* 281-301.

Doyle, K. O. (1981). *Evaluating Teaching*. Lexington, MA: Lexington Books.

Doyle, K. O. (1999). *The Social Meanings of Money and Property: In Search of a Talisman*. Thousand Oaks, CA: Sage.

Doyle, K. O., and Moen, R. E. (1978). Toward the Definition of a Domain of Academic Motivation. *Journal of Educational Psychology,* 70(2), 231-236.

Flanagan, J. C. (1954). The Critical Incident Technique. *Psychological Bulletin,* 51, 327-358.

Guilford, J. P. (1954). *Psychometric Methods.* New York: McGraw-Hill.

Helmstadter, G. C. (1964). *Principles of Psychological Measurement.* New York: Appleton.

Stanley, J. C. (1971). Reliability. In R.L. Thorndike (Ed.), *Educational Measurement* (2nd ed.). Washington, DC: American Council On Education.

Thorndike, R. L., (1951). Reliability. In E. F. Lindquist (Ed.), *Educational Measurement.* New York: American Council on Education.

Uranowitz, S., and Doyle, K. O. (1978). Being Liked and Teaching: The Bases and Effects of Personal Likeability in College Instruction. *Research in Higher Education,* 9.

8

Sampling

An old saying goes, "One rotten apple spoils the barrel." It might be true that one bad apple means that the rest in the barrel are bad, but a skeptical observer might note that one apple represents too small a sample size to generalize to the entire bunch.

With sampling, the goal of the researcher is (1) to identify a population, (2) to survey a small selection of that population and (3) to draw accurate conclusions about the entire population based on the small selection.

To understand sampling, a researcher first needs to consider a population. A *population* is an entire group of people, a whole collection of objects or, in the world of media, something such as every television program currently showing or all newspaper stories on a particular issue.

One way to learn about a population is to poll or take a *census* of the entire population, meaning that every person or item in the population is surveyed or examined. The U.S. government takes a census every 10 years (but probably misses more than a few citizens in its attempt to count them all) in order to describe the nation's population. A census, time consuming and expensive, is not something most researchers choose to do to find out about a population. Furthermore, it is not statistically necessary to do one in order to draw conclusions about a population.

Instead, researchers randomly select a *sample*, or a small portion, of the population to represent that population. *Random selection* means that each member of the population has an equal chance of being selected for the sample. In other situations, researchers are not concerned with representing a population and, therefore, choose their samples in less scientific ways.

The following definitions are useful to know before we begin our discussion of sampling techniques.

Population: Everyone or everything that can be studied — for example, all residents of the United States or all newspaper articles relating to a specific sub-

By Kate Peirce and Gilbert D. Martinez
Texas State University

ject. The concept of population is most often discussed in theoretical terms, for studying a total population is usually too time consuming and cost prohibitive.

Sample: A small portion of the population. It may be selected from the population randomly or nonrandomly, depending on the purpose of the study.

Elements: The individual members of the population. These are the units from which researchers actually sample, such as all students from one university, not all students in all universities nationwide or globally.

Sampling frame: A list of all elements in the population. The registrar at a university, for example, might part with a list of all registered students. From it the researcher will choose the sample.

TYPES OF SAMPLING

Sampling consists of two major types: *probability* and *nonprobability*, also known as *random* and *nonrandom* sampling.

Probability sampling involves the random selection of a sample. All members of the population must have the same opportunity to be selected for the sample. The sample is then selected by one of five major types of probability sampling: (1) simple random sampling, (2) systematic random sampling, (3) stratified random sampling, (4) cluster random sampling and (5) multistage cluster random sampling.

Nonprobability sampling, which does not involve random selection, includes (1) convenience or available sampling, (2) purposive sampling, (3) quota sampling and (4) snowball sampling.

Researchers consider the following four main points in deciding whether to use probability or nonprobablity sampling:

1. *Purpose.* If the purpose of the study is to reach general conclusions about a population, a researcher will choose probability sampling. If, instead, the researcher is not interested in generalizing results to the whole population, nonprobability sampling may be more appropriate.

2. *Cost.* Researchers must consider the cost of studying a sample. If the cost to select a random population is too high, using a nonprobability sample might be an appropriate choice.

3. *Time.* Time constraints may force a researcher to abandon probability sampling, which can be time consuming, for nonprobability sampling, which often takes less time.

4. *Acceptable error*. The amount of error that a researcher considers acceptable may determine whether to use probability sampling, where sampling error can be several percentage points, or nonprobability sampling, where sampling error cannot be determined. For example, a researcher conducting a pilot study, where sampling error is not the prime concern, might consider nonprobability sampling appropriate.

PROBABILITY (RANDOM) SAMPLING
Simple Random Sampling

There are several methods for selecting a random sample. *Simple random sampling* involves selecting subjects based on the premise that each subject in the population has an equal chance of being selected. The selection process is *random*, meaning that subjects are selected without a pattern.

If the population is small enough, the researcher could simply write the name of each member on a piece of paper, place all the names in a basket and then, without looking at the names, draw out as many as needed for the sample. A *table of random numbers* may also be used to select the sample. In this approach, each participant is assigned a number. Random numbers are selected or generated and then matched to the participants who correspond to the selected numbers.

Random Digit Dialing

Another approach is *random digit dialing*. It is a simple random sampling method in which the computer generates random telephone numbers of respondents. To randomly select telephone numbers, including active area codes and exchanges, the first six numbers of a phone number are identified and then the last four numbers are randomly selected through a computer program designed for this purpose. In San Marcos, Texas, for example, the area code is 512, and two of the possible exchanges are 396 and 754. The researcher chooses this area code and these exchanges and lets the computer choose the last four digits for as many numbers as the researcher deems necessary.

Not all the numbers generated will be real numbers, and some will belong to businesses or pay phones. Thus, it is important to generate a list of more numbers than the sample size needed.

There are several methods for generating numbers that reduce the inefficiency of unrestricted random selection. One of these methods involves selecting actual numbers from telephone directories and replacing the last one or two numbers with fixed numbers.

Because the first step in random digit dialing is to randomly select telephone numbers rather than actual people to interview, the second step is to randomly select the person at each of those numbers to be interviewed. Various methodologies have been developed for this step, too. For example, the interviewer might be instructed to ask for the person with the most recent birthday.

An example of random digit dialing to select a sample is provided by a study that Weaver and Drew (1995) conducted to find out whether traditional or nontraditional media had more impact for voters in the 1992 presidential election. They used a method of random digit dialing that allows for unpublished and newly listed numbers to be included in the sample. They then used a mathematical procedure for randomly selecting participants at each number.

Pros and Cons

The primary advantage of simple random sampling is that it is generally the easiest and quickest way to choose a sample when the researcher has a complete sampling frame, that is, a list of the population. Disadvantages include not always having a complete sampling frame or having to create such a list, which can be time consuming and/or costly. Finally, if there are subgroups that the researcher wants to include, a simple random sample is not the best way to include them.

One example of simple random sampling can be seen in a study about the depiction of juvenile offenders by race on television news in the Los Angeles area (Dixon and Azocar, 2006). The researchers analyzed a random selection of television programming over a two-year period after identifying their population of news programs from Los Angeles-based television stations. They used a method of sampling that allowed them to randomly select channels, program types, time-of-day sampling times and time-of-year sampling periods. Based on this random selection method, the researchers assembled two seven-day composite weeks of news programming to analyze for their study.

Systematic Random Sampling

Systematic random sampling is a variant of simple random sampling that requires a list of the population. It involves the numbering of every subject and then using a mathematical process to select participants. We might, for example, select every *nth* person from the registrar's list of all students in a university for our study — after a random start, that is. To do this, we must know how many students are on the list and how many we want for our sample. If there are 10,000 names and we want 1,000 in our sample, we will need to divide 10,000 by 1,000, which equals 10, which means we will take every 10th name. To determine our random start, we put the numbers 1-10 in a basket and select one. If we draw out 4, for example, we start at the top of the registrar's list and count to 4. This is the first name in our sample. With name number 5, we start over with our counting and choose every 10th name until our sample is selected.

Stratified Random Sampling

Stratified random sampling requires that the population be divided into homogenous subgroups, from which several simple random samples are conducted to determine participants for the study. We must have the sampling frame, or list of the population, for each subgroup. Then we randomly select from each group by drawing as many names out of a box as we need or matching numbers to participants (as discussed earlier under simple random sampling).

Such sampling is useful to make sure that each subgroup has equal representation. A sample of university students, for example, could be selected by randomly choosing from the entire population. The sample would probably include a variety of freshmen, sophomores, juniors and seniors. But if it were important to be absolutely certain that the sample contained representatives from each class, we might choose an equal number from each class.

Proportionate Stratified Sampling

A variation on stratified sampling is *proportionate stratified sampling*. In this case, we choose numbers from subgroups that are equal to their numbers in the population. If, for example, freshmen are 30% of a university population and seniors are 20%, we would choose a sample that is 30% freshmen and 20% seniors.

But what if we believe seniors know more than freshmen and we want more seniors in our sample than freshmen? We could choose to oversample seniors and undersample freshmen. This would result in a *disproportionate stratified sample*, also a variation of the stratified sample.

The primary advantage of stratified sampling is that we can be sure all subgroups are represented as we wish them to be in the sample. The disadvantage is finding or creating the sampling frame.

Kelly (1995) used stratified sampling to find out how various charitable organizations practice fundraising differently. She sampled fundraising practitioners from six major types of charitable organizations. Because she wanted to make sure she had equal numbers from the six types of organizations, she decided a stratified sample was the best method for her purposes. She used a membership list compiled by the National Society of Fund Raising Executives (NSFRE) and, using NSFRE's computer, randomly selected the sample. The computer was instructed to start at a random location within each of the organizational types and recycle through the names, stopping at intervals specified for each subpopulation, until the sample was selected.

Cluster Random Sampling

Cluster random sampling calls for dividing the population into distinct clusters, usually geographic locations, and then randomly selecting one cluster and surveying everyone in the cluster for the study. On a university campus, for example, dormitories might serve as clusters. One dormitory could be randomly selected, and all students living in that dorm would serve as the sample.

Multi-stage Cluster Sampling

Multi-stage cluster sampling is similar to cluster sampling, but the researcher chooses a sample at various stages. It involves, for example, randomly selecting a dorm, then randomly selecting a floor in the dorm and finally selecting a person on that floor to include in the sample. The researcher starts with inanimate objects but eventually ends up with human beings in the sample.

Advantages of cluster sampling are that we do not need to have a list of the entire population in order to choose a sample. We do not, in fact, need a list at all. We could sample from the entire United States using geographic locations — a region, a state in the region, a city in the state, a block in the city and a house on the block — until we eventually end up with a person in the house to survey. The primary disadvantage of such a method is that the many steps in the sampling process increase the chance that the sample is less likely to represent the population than would a sample representing a smaller and less diverse population.

An example of such sampling is a study about adolescents and their values. The authors wanted to know how compassionate and materialistic adolescents are and how they find meaning for their lives. They first randomly selected public and private schools — the first stage — and then randomly selected students in those schools to be in the sample (Beutel and Marini, 1995).

THE THEORY BEHIND PROBABILITY SAMPLING

While the goal of a study conducted using a probability sample is to represent the population in the findings, it is the rare sample that perfectly matches the population. Let's think in terms of a pot of vegetable soup from which several bowls are poured. Each bowl of soup will be similar, containing some carrots and some peas.

We can come to conclusions about our population based on our sample — even though it is just one small part of the population. We do not have to use more than one bowl of soup as our sample to describe our population.

The Central Limit Theorem

Our justification for being able to do this? The *Central Limit Theorem*. The theorem is based on the *normal curve*, which works this way: The more samples that are taken from the population and placed on a grid, the more the grid will resemble a normal curve with most of the samples in the middle of the curve. If our pot of soup is 50% peas, then most of the bowls of soup will be somewhere near 50% as well. One or two might be at 75%, and another one or two might be at 25% — but the majority will be in the middle of the grid, closer to 50%, and not at the outer edges.

We can be more specific mathematically. According to the Central Limit Theorem, 68% of all samples will end up within plus or minus one *standard deviation* from the population, 95% will be within plus or minus two standard deviations and 99% of all samples will be within plus or minus three standard deviations from the population. (See Figure 1.) We'll discuss standard deviation in just a moment.

Figure 1. Areas Under the Normal Curve

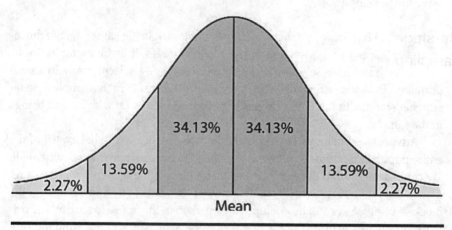

Of course, each bowl will not have the exact same number of vegetables. One might have more carrots than peas, and another more peas than carrots. But most will resemble the pot from which they came. The difference between the contents of the bowls and of the pot is *sampling error*. **Sampling Error**

There can be several causes for such error. Let's look at them.

One cause of error is *chance*. Strictly by chance, our sample bowl of soup contains 75% peas while our pot of soup is 50% peas. The best way to overcome this type of error is to choose a large enough sample.

Poor sampling techniques can also cause error. If our ladle is large enough only to hold peas, we will no doubt have fewer carrots in our sample than we would with a better method of sampling.

Nonsampling error, caused by the measuring instrument or the participants themselves, can also contribute to discrepancies between our sample and the population. We will discuss this type of error later in this chapter.

A *standard deviation* is a unit of distance in a sampling distribution **Calculating** and indicates the amount of *sampling error*. We can calculate error **Sampling Error** with a formula, or we can look it up on a chart. (See Table 1.) Sampling error is based on sample size and responses given.

As an illustration, let's take a popular pastime during election years: public opinion polling. We want to know whether people are planning to vote for the Republican or the Democrat. We survey 1,000 people and find that 48% plan to vote for the Republican and 52% plan to vote for the Democrat. Before proclaiming that the Democrat will win, we must determine the amount of error possible in our survey.

We turn to Table 1. The figures are based on two standard deviations, or a 95% confidence level, meaning that 95% of the time sampling error will not be larger than the figures listed. In the "percentages near" column, we look at 50% — since our polls says the Republican will get 48% and the Democrat 52% of the vote — and match it with our sample size of 1,000. According to the chart, sampling error with these particular answers and the particular sample size is 3. With this figure we can compute the confidence intervals in which the population percentages should be found. For the Republican, the interval is 45-51% (48 plus or minus 3 percentage points) of the vote; and for the Democrat, it is 49-55% (52 plus or minus 3 percentage points). The election is, of course, too close to call.

Table 1. Percentage of Error at 95% Confidence Level

Percentage near	Sample Size				
	1000	750	500	250	100
10%	2	2	3	4	6
20%	3	3	4	5	9
30%	3	4	4	6	10
40%	3	4	5	7	10
50%	3	4	5	7	11
60%	3	4	5	7	10
70%	3	4	4	6	10
80%	3	3	4	5	9
90%	2	2	3	4	6

Source: Gallup Poll: Public Opinion 2004

The beauty of sampling theory is that we do not need more than one sample in order to estimate population parameters — even if our estimations simply tell us that the election is too close to call.

Most statisticians agree that using a 95% confidence level is confident enough and do not recommend increasing to three standard deviations, a 99% confidence level, which would make us more confident but would increase the amount of error possible. Similarly, if we used a 68% confidence level, our confidence intervals would be smaller, but we would not be very confident about our findings (32% of the time the population figures would be outside the error figures computed).

The best way to reduce sampling error is to increase sample size. If our election poll had had only 100 respondents, the error at nearly 50% would have been 11% percentage points rather than 3. Clearly, a sample of 1,000 is better than a sample of 100. However, a sample of 3,000 is not necessarily three times better than a sample of 1,000. In fact, when a sample size reaches a certain threshold, the ability of larger sample size to reduce error decreases dramatically. So, the small reduction in error may not justify the time and money spent to increase the sample.

NONPROBABILITY SAMPLING

With nonprobability sampling, we can make no claims about the population as a whole. But there are times when it isn't possible or practical to use a probability sample. In those instances, nonprobability sampling is used. Nonprobability samples include the (1) available or convenience sample, (2) snowball sample, (3) purposive sample, (4) quota sample, and (5) volunteer sample. Let's examine each one.

Available Sample

An *available or convenience sample* is one in which participants are chosen for inclusion in a study because they are a captive audience and/or are willing to participate. When, for example, students are given extra credit to participate in a research project during class, they have not been randomly selected for participation. When a researcher wants to survey elementary school students, the school principal is likely to tell the researcher which students she may survey. The students are not randomly selected by anyone.

The advantage of an available sample is that it is easy to find. We can survey our friends or our students/classmates and not have to take the time to assemble a random sample. The main disadvantage, however, is that, when we talk about results, we can only talk about our sample. We can make no claim that the sample represents the population when our sample has not been selected randomly.

Snowball Sample

Because Internet surveys are becoming more and more popular and there is no sampling frame of Internet users, researchers are using nonrandom sampling methods with more frequency. For example, Cindy Royal, a faculty member at Texas State University, used an available sample to examine users' activities on social networking sites on the Internet. Because there is no listing of such users, she invited all users of Myspace, Facebook and Youtube to talk about how they use the sites. She also used a nonrandom technique called *snowball sampling* by asking respondents to forward the survey to their friends and family.

Another Texas State teacher, Dara Quackenbush, chose a similar sampling technique. She was interested in finding out characteristics of people who read weblogs, or *blogs*, on the Internet. She posted participation requests on various blogs, Internet discussion groups and forums and email lists. She then asked people who received the survey to forward the request to others.

One of the authors of this chapter wanted to interview transgendered individuals. As there is no registry of such people and no easy way to randomly select such a sample, she chose to use snowball sampling. One transgendered person named another who might be willing to be interviewed. That person named another and so on until the sample contained an adequate number of interviewees. We cannot generalize to the population as a whole with snowball sampling or with any other nonrandom sampling method, but generalizing to the population is not always the goal of research. For example, the transgendered participants do not necessarily represent all transgendered people, but they can provide information about transgenders' experiences.

Purposive Sample

Sometimes we want a sample that contains a particular characteristic or does a specific activity, such as watching *The Sopranos*. We do not care what people who do not watch *The Sopranos* think. So we choose a ***purposive sample*** of *Sopranos* viewers. A purposive sample means the sample has been chosen because each member contains the characteristic we are interested in. A random sample would no doubt include some *Sopranos* viewers but would also include those who do not watch and who would not add information to the study.

In another example of using a purposive sample, Trammel and Keshelashvili (2005) wanted to examine different characteristics in blogs. In particular, they wanted to see how the writers of the most popular blogs presented themselves on their blogs. They identified the top single-authored blogs through a ranking site called Popdex and, through it, obtained a sample of 209 blogs.

An advantage of a purposive sample is that we do not have to search our sample to find those we are interested in. A disadvantage, as with all nonrandom samples, is that we cannot generalize to the population at large with our findings.

Quota Sample

A ***quota sample*** sounds similar to a stratified random sample: We need to interview 20 freshmen and 20 sophomores, for example; and when we have done so, we stop interviewing. The difference between a quota sample and a stratified sample is this: The participants in a stratified sample are randomly selected, but those in a quota sample are not.

Many of us have been accosted by marketing representatives at the mall who want to ask questions. We have not been randomly selected. The marketing representatives have instead been told to interview *n* number of men and *n* number of women or *n* number of people of various ages. We end up in the sample because we happened to be at the mall that day and other people did not. Even if we consider the population to be all the people at the mall, our marketing representative still does not have a random sample because he chose the people to be interviewed. He would have had to assign each person a number and then randomly select numbers for the sample to be random. Few if any marketing representatives at malls do this. They simply choose whoever is walking by and whoever will agree to be interviewed.

An advantage of a quota sample is that it is an easy way to find a sample. If the research is such that representing the population is not necessary, it is a good way to achieve a sample quickly. If representing the population is important, a quota sample, like other nonrandom samples, is not the best type to choose.

Volunteer Sample

A ***volunteer sample*** relies on participants to select themselves for a research project. A student, for example, might volunteer after seeing a notice on a campus bulletin board, especially if the notice indicated a monetary reward for participating. A radio station might ask listeners to call in with an opinion on a subject. While voting for an *American Idol* contestant is not exactly scholarly research, the method for collecting the information is similar to collecting information from a volunteer sample for a scholarly project.

A disadvantage of a volunteer sample is that the people volunteering may be very different from those who do not volunteer. Therefore, the results of a study may be skewed.

SOURCES OF ERROR IN RANDOM SAMPLING

We have already discussed sampling error associated with random samples as the amount of error possible simply because a sample is not the entire population. Other sources of error can come from a survey itself, question wording, and/or question and interviewer bias. We must also be concerned with how different those who agree to take a survey or answer a poll are from those who do not agree. Do people with caller ID and who never answer the phone differ from those without it who do answer the phone? For a discussion of such issues, you may wish to read Chapter 10 on survey research in this book.

Two other sources of error, though, are of primary importance in a discussion of sampling. They are (1) errors in sampling procedures and (2) errors in reporting.

Errors in Sampling Procedures

Sample selection can skew the results of a survey or poll. One of the most famous failures in opinion polling is the *Literary Digest* poll in 1936 that found overwhelming support for Republican presidential candidate Alf Landon over the Democratic candidate, Franklin Roosevelt. As we have never had a President Landon, it is clear that the poll, based on 2 million returned postcards, was wrong. What happened? The magazine sent the postcards to people whose names they had gotten from automobile registrations and telephone books. Those sources, though, excluded a large percentage of the population in 1936, in particular lower-income people who were more likely to vote for Roosevelt (Neuman, 2004).

At the same time, George Gallup correctly predicted Roosevelt's win by using quota sampling. People were selected for the sample based on percentages of characteristics in the population. Thus there were genders, income levels and ages in the sample that matched their percentages in the population. Quota sampling, though, can only work when the sample figures really do match the population figures (Babbie, 1998). Thus, Gallup, too, had his embarrassing moment in 1948 when he predicted that New York Governor Thomas Dewey would defeat incumbent Harry Truman for the presidency. His samples did not represent the population for at least two reasons: (1) His pollsters stopped polling too early despite a shift toward Truman in the last days of the campaign and (2) more of the undecided voters ended up supporting Truman.

A more recent example also shows the limits of drawing conclusions from a random sample. During the selection process for the 2008 Democratic presidential candidate, Barack Obama was riding a wave of momentum after a strong Iowa caucus win over front-runner Hillary Clinton. Early polls pointed to an Obama win in New Hampshire, and political pundits seemed eager to portray the Clinton campaign in disarray. Yet, when results started to pour in after the polls closed, some political analysts were shocked at the narrow Clinton victory. One even called it "one of the greatest political upsets in American political history" (Bauder, 2008). In the days following the New Hampshire primary, analysts tackled the "what happened?" question. Similar to the Truman-Dewey race, most surveys were done while Obama was basking in the glow of the Iowa win, surmised a senior vice president with CBS News. While the polls might have been accurate at that time, it appeared that the voters' sentiments changed in the day or so before the election.

Several factors contributed to the difficulty in predicting the primary. They included the following: (1) enough undecided voters who didn't decide whom to vote for until election day; (2) New Hampshire primary rules that allow independent voters to wait until the last minute to decide whether to vote in the Democratic or Republican primaries, thereby making it difficult for pollsters to predict elections; and (3) a tendency among New Hampshire voters to buck conventional wisdom (Bauder, 2008).

In pondering how the polls got Clinton's demise so wrong that night, one frustrated cable news analyst lamented that the media "should just stay home" rather than cover the election. Longtime news anchor Tom Brokaw responded, "No, no, we don't stay home.... [W]e don't have to get in the business of making judgments before the polls have closed, and trying to stampede and affect the process." Indeed, Brokaw said one of the lessons learned by the media was that the late decisions by voters in New Hampshire exposed one of the drawbacks of random sampling and led to a discussion about the role of the news media in electoral politics.

Even randomized clinical trials can have drawbacks, as one review of medical trials concluded (Bakalar, 2007). Researchers examined 29 clinical trials of 13,991 patients who had surgical procedures involving different types of cancer. The study found that there were disparities in the study that overrepresented some populations, such as Caucasian participants, and underrepresented others, such as African-American patients. Women were less likely to be in some of the clinical trials. These problems undermined the conclusions that were drawn from the studies. "Our ability to generalize the findings of surgical trials is directly dependent on having equitable participation in trials by underrepresented groups," said lead author Dr. John H. Stewart IV, an assistant professor of surgery at Wake Forest University.

Errors in Reporting   Finally, how a survey and its sampling methods and sample error are discussed can skew impressions of the findings. For example, Burns (2006) analyzed the reporting of pre-election polls in the 2004 presidential election by *USA Today*, looking at 165 statements in the newspaper that dealt with the differences between candidates according to various polls. She found that while the newspaper reported the numbers accurately, 45 of the statements about the findings were not accurate. When there was no statistically significant difference between the candidates, the newspaper used such phrases as "is ahead" or "leading." Sixty-two percent of the 45 statements favored George Bush. She found one instance in which a reporter suggested that John Kerry's lead was not significant despite the fact that he was ahead by 13 percentage points.

Despite the problems that have arisen with sampling, if the method of sampling is chosen based on the goals of the research, the techniques discussed in this chapter are effective. If the goal of research is for the sample to make predictions about a population, then a random sample must be used. If representing the population is not an issue, then one of the nonrandom techniques may make more sense. In any case, few researchers are able to survey or analyze the population as a whole. With proper sampling procedures, it is not necessary to do so.

TO LEARN MORE

Auster, C. (2000). Probability sampling and inferential statistics: An interactive exercise using M & M's. *Teaching Sociology, 28*(4), 379-385.

Central Limit Theorem, The — How to tame wild populations. http://www.intuitor.com/statistics.CentralLim.html

Evans, W. D. & Ulasevich, A. (2005). News media tracking of tobacco control: A review of sampling methodologies. *Journal of Health Communication, 10,* 403-417.

Probability Sampling. http://www.socialresearchmethodsl.netl/kb/sampprob.php

Rushing, B. & Warfield, I. (1999). Learning about sampling and measurement by doing content analysis of personal advertisements. *Teaching Sociology, 27*(2), 159-166.

Sampling in Research. http://www.socialresearchmethods.net/tutorial

Taylor, H. Myth and reality in reporting sampling error: How the media confuse and mislead readers and viewers. http://www.pollingreport.com/sampling.htm

Trochim, W. M. The Research Methods Knowledge Base, 2nd Edition. Internet WWW page, at URL: http://www.socialresearchmethods.net/kb/ (version current as of October 20, 2006).

REFERENCES

Babbie, E. (1998). *The Practice of Social Research.* Belmont, CA: Wadsworth.

Bakalar, N. (Dec. 25, 2007) Insights: Clinical Trials May Not Represent Population. *NY Times.* Retrieved Jan. 20, 2008, from http://www.NYTimes.com.

Bauder, D. (2008). "New Hampshire a Surprise for Media, Jan. 9, 2008. Associated Press. Retrieved Jan. 20, 2008, from http://sfisonline.com

Beutel, A. & Marini, M. (2005). Gender and values. *American Sociological Review, 60,* 436-448.

Burns, K. (2006). Problems found in reporting USA Today pre-election polls. *Newspaper Research Journal, 27*(4), 38-51.

Dixon, T. & Azocar, C. (2006). The representation of juvenile offenders by race on Los Angeles area television news. *Howard Journal of Communications, 17*(2), 143-161.

Kelly, K. S. (1995). Utilizing public relations theory to conceptualize and test models of fund raising. *Journalism and Mass Communication Quarterly, 72*(1), 106-127.

Neuman, W. L. (2004). *Basics of Social Research.* Boston: Allyn and Bacon.

Trammel, K.D. & Keshelashvili, A. (2005). Examining the new influences: A self-presentation study of A-list blogs. *Journalism and Mass Communication Quarterly, 82*(4), 968-982.

Weaver, D. & Drew, D. (1995). Voter learning in the 1992 presidential election: did the "nontraditional" media and debates matter? *Journalism and Mass Communication Quarterly, 72*(1), 7-17.

9

Content Analysis

Have you ever wondered which television programs attract the most fast food advertisements? How about the frequency with which people use the term "like" in conversation? Or how about how favorably the news media cover your favorite political candidate?

Questions like these can be investigated using content analysis.

Content analysis is a *method of quantitatively analyzing communication messages*. By communication messages, we mean any type of communication: texts, visuals, sounds, anything. This method is quantitative because it involves using numbers to describe communication messages.

When you use this method, you want to learn about the meanings contained within communication messages, whether the messages are newspaper articles, transcripts, movies, or other items. For example, if you wanted to know how frequently men and women are quoted in the newspaper, you would look at the newspaper and add up how many quotations are from men and how many are from women. This would be a type of content analysis!

A number of formal *definitions* have been proposed for content analysis. Berelson (1952), for example, defined content analysis as "a research technique for the objective, systematic, and quantitative description" of communication messages (p. 18). Krippendorff (2004a) defines content analysis as "a research technique for making replicable and valid inferences from texts (and other meaningful matter) to the contexts of their use" (p. 18). These two definitions highlight the most important feature of content analysis: This methodology is focused on analyzing communication messages so that if future researchers want to conduct the same study, they will reach the same conclusions.

HISTORY   Although content analysis was not formalized and popularized until the 1930s and '40s, the idea of systematically analyzing communication messages has long existed. In the early 18th century, for example,

By Natalie Jomini Stroud and Vanessa de Macedo Higgins
University of Texas at Austin

the State Church of Sweden believed that a collection of hymns had undesirable effects on its followers. Intellectuals at the time began investigating the contentious religious documents — what was it about these hymns that seemed to lead people away from the State Church? One orthodox clergyman decided to count references to various religious symbols in the hymns. He found that the hymns placed more emphasis on Jesus and less emphasis on other symbols referring to the Trinity in comparison to the religious teachings of the State Church. He concluded that the hymns differed from the traditional Christian themes of the State Church, posing a threat to the established religious tradition. Although this early study was not conducted with the rigor of today's content analyses, the information it provided was used to support the Church's concerns about the hymns (Dovring, 1954-1955).

More systematic analyses of communication messages were conducted in the early 1900s. Walter Lippmann, for example, carried out an early content analysis of *New York Times* coverage of the Russian Revolution in the 1920s and concluded that the coverage had an "anti-Bolshevik bias" (Rogers, 2004, p. 4). Harold Lasswell is often credited with developing the quantitative aspects of content analysis, having elaborated on methods of coder training, testing, and reliability assessment (Neuendorf, 2002). Among his early projects using content analysis, Lasswell and his team content analyzed propaganda messages presented in the media during World War II (Rogers, 2004).

One of the most famous and long-lasting content analysis studies is the Cultural Indicators Project. Led by George Gerbner, it involved the systematic content analysis of television programming, with special attention to television violence. In their examination of over three decades of television messages, Gerbner and his colleagues found that television, regardless of genre, presented an image of a violent world: At least half of the characters were involved in violence each week (Gerbner, Gross, Morgan, Signorielli, & Shanahan, 2002).

Content analysis is a useful method for addressing the following types of research issues:

QUESTIONS THAT CONTENT ANALYSIS CAN ANSWER

• First, as a stand-alone method, it can be used to examine communication messages and attributes. It also can be used to compare media depictions to reality. That is, is the world as shown in the media similar to reality?

• Second, it can be used commercially to assess corporate or personal images as presented in the media.

• Third, it can be used to make inferences about message producers, audiences, or effects when it is used in conjunction with other data.

Many content analysis projects aim to investigate *attributes of communication messages*. Researchers can investigate the *substance* of a message, such as the information that can be obtained from the message, or they can analyze the *form* of a message, such as the size of a headline. Descriptive content analysis projects like these can be used to evaluate communication messages at a single point in time (e.g., the frequency with which minorities are portrayed as criminals in prime time dramas) or over time (e.g., whether the percentage of minorities portrayed as criminals in prime time dramas has increased or decreased over the past decade).

Content analysis also can be used to *evaluate a single source* (e.g., advertisements shown during Saturday morning cartoons) or to *compare multiple sources* (e.g., advertising during Saturday morning cartoons compared to advertising during prime time programming). Tuggle and Owen (1999), for example, evaluated the substance of media coverage at a single point in time from a single source. They conducted a descriptive content analysis to evaluate the amount of coverage devoted to female athletes and events during the 1996 Summer Olympics. They found that coverage of female athletes focused more on individual sports than team events. Other researchers have used content analysis to compare the world as depicted in the media to reality. For example, younger people are over-represented on television in comparison to the percentage of younger people in reality (Signorielli, 2004).

Although content analysis is a method used by academics, it is used in the business world as well. Many of us probably have heard the phrase "image is everything," and content analysis is a good method to use to assess image. Research companies use this method to inform clients about how they are being portrayed in the media and to build strategies to improve client images. Clients can range from individuals, such as politicians and CEOs, to groups, such as governmental institutions, non-governmental organizations, and private companies. Research firms conducting content analyses focus on the messages and the issues presented in the media relating to their clients and competitors, as well as the source of the messages.

Content analysis also can be used to evaluate whether public relations firms are successful in presenting a desired image. For example, if a company hires a new public relations firm, it should be able to see positive and increasing coverage over time if the public relations firm is successful. The systematic and objective analysis of communication messages has been adopted by a number of firms, including Media Tenor, Echo Research, and Carma International.

Researchers also can use content analysis to answer questions about message producers, message audiences, and effects of message exposure by integrating information about the context or the audience with the content analysis data (Neuendorf, 2002). Many agenda-setting studies, for example, use both content analyses and surveys to evaluate how the news media influence audiences. These studies find that the news media inform the public about which issues are most important (McCombs, 2004; McCombs & Shaw, 1972).

Using a combination of content analysis and other methods is helpful in the development of mass communication theory (Riffe, Lacy & Fico, 1998). Using multiple methods is not very common, however. In a review of published articles using content analysis, Riffe and Freitag (1997) found that only 10 percent of the studies integrated content analysis with other methods.

WHAT YOU CAN CONTENT ANALYZE The short answer to the question of what you can content analyze is this: any message to which people bring meaning.

The long answer is this: You can conduct a content analysis of print or visuals or audio, of newspapers or cartoons or diaries or interpersonal conversations or nonverbals or television or websites — the possibilities are endless. Here are some examples of how content analysis has been used in communication research:

• In mass communication, researchers have used content analysis to evaluate the amount of violence in video games. They have found that the amount of violence in video games differs depending on the game rating (e.g., "E" for Everyone, "T" for Teen, etc.; Smith, Lachlan, & Tamborini, 2003).

• In political communication, researchers have examined how late night jokes characterize political figures. Young (2004) found that late night jokes typically focus on candidates' personalities, not their issue stances.

• In health communication, researchers have evaluated the content of direct-to-consumer prescription drug advertisements. In particular, researchers have been interested in whether pharmaceutical companies are providing adequate information about the risks associated with taking various drugs (Kaphingst, Dejong, Rudd, & Daltroy, 2004).

Each of these studies used a content analysis in order to draw conclusions about the information contained within communication messages.

STRENGTHS AND CHALLENGES

Like all research methods, there are strengths of using content analysis and challenges that researchers can encounter. Let's look at some of them.

Strengths

There are several advantages to using content analysis. Consider the following:

• First, content analysis methods are helpful in summarizing large bodies of communication messages. If you wanted to know, for example, how frequently an issue was discussed in the newspaper this past year, content analysis would be an appropriate method.

• Second, content analysis is an unobtrusive technique, for there is no need to interact with human subjects to use this methodology.

• Third, content analysis enables people to systematically study historical moments and over-time differences. For example, it is not possible to interview George Washington, but one could conduct a content analysis of his writings. Furthermore, one can examine how communication messages have changed over time.

Challenges

Here are some challenges you may encounter in conducting a content analysis:

• Like any research method, content analysis cannot be used to investigate all of the questions that researchers may have. For some research questions, it is relatively easy to create reliable data such that each person who evaluates the communication message will come to the same conclusion. Other times, however, it is more challenging.

When researchers are looking to analyze something relatively easy to see (e.g., the number of males and females in leading roles in the movies), it is possible to create reliable data. When researchers are looking to evaluate something more *complex* in a communication message — where, for example, different people might substantially disagree about the meaning of the message — content analysis is not well-suited to address the issue because it is difficult to generate reliable data. For example, content analysis is unlikely to be a useful technique in uncovering cultural values in the media. It would be difficult to get several people to agree on the cultural values contained within a communication message without dramatically simplifying this complex concept.

• A second difficulty in using content analysis is that it does not provide insight into the *effects* of communication messages. For example, if you found that media coverage of presidential campaigns frequently discusses the candidates' personalities, you would not know whether such coverage causes people to vote on the basis of personality. It is possible that, because of this coverage, people increasingly would vote based on candidates' personalities rather than candidates' issue positions; but a content analysis alone would not allow you to draw this conclusion. The only information you have from a content analysis is about the message. If you wanted to investigate the effects of media messages, you would need to use another method in addition to content analysis such as survey research or experiments. Those two methods will be covered in Chapter 10 and Chapter 11 in this book.

• Similarly, content analysis by itself cannot explain *why* the message is as it is. Since content analysis *describes* what is contained in the content of a message, it cannot tell us, for example, what the motive of the content's creator was.

CREATING A SAMPLE FOR ANALYSIS

Once you have determined that content analysis is the appropriate tool for your research question or hypothesis, you must decide on three important details:

1. The population to be examined
2. The sampling unit
3. The coding unit

Let's look at each one in some detail.

Population To Be Examined

First, you will want to determine the *population of messages* that is relevant for your study. If, for example, you are conducting a content analysis of how the *Los Angeles Times* covered terrorism over the past year, the population of messages would consist of every article the *Los Angeles Times* printed about terrorism over the past year. You'll want to think carefully through the population of interest: Are editorials and opinion pieces relevant to your hypotheses or research questions? Are articles that were picked up from the Associated Press newswire relevant? Are you interested in *all* articles about terrorism in the *Los Angeles Times* or only those articles that discuss a more specific issue, such as terrorism and the United States?

Sampling Unit

After determining your population, your next task is to locate available sampling units. *Sampling units* are the communication messages that you will gather for inclusion in your content analysis (Krippendorff, 2004a). For a study about prime time advertisements, for example, your sampling units may be individual advertisements. In order to obtain these ads, you may record a month of prime time television. As another example, if you are looking at *Washington Times* articles over the past year, you might use an online database such as Factiva or Lexis Nexis to search for articles that appeared in the newspaper. Here, your sampling unit would be an article.

When obtaining sampling units from databases like Lexis Nexis and Factiva, it is important to make sure that they include the population of messages in which you are interested. For example, are stories from the Associated Press Newswire included in the database? There also are methods to evaluate whether your method for searching (your search string) is capturing the relevant communication messages (Stryker, Wray, Hornik, & Yanovitzky, 2006). You want to make sure that your search string does not leave out an important subset of communication messages. For example, if you search for newspaper articles about "kids," but fail to include "children" in your search string, you may have left out an important set of articles. For a discussion of how to conduct database searches, see Chapter 5 in this book.

Previous research can be a good guide for selecting your coding unit and gathering a relevant population of messages. For a discussion of how to identify the work that already has been done related to your topic, you may wish to reread Prof. Davies' Chapter 6 on literature reviews in this book. You also will find Chapter 4 on libraries and Chapter 5 on databases helpful.

For some research questions and hypotheses, previous research may lead you to choose different messages to content analyze. For example, the Vanderbilt Television News Archive provides abstracts for its collection of news programs. For some projects, researchers may be able to content analyze these abstracts as opposed to the actual broadcasts (Althaus, Edy, & Phalen, 2002). Furthermore, it may be possible to use the New York Times Index as opposed to the *New York Times* for some research questions and hypotheses (Althaus, Edy, & Phalen, 2001). Although using indices and abstracts can be a valuable time-saving strategy, it is not always appropriate. Consulting books and research articles that address the issue can help you to figure out an appropriate sampling unit.

Coding Unit

In addition to determining your sampling unit, you also must decide on your *coding unit*. A coding unit is the communication message chosen to be categorized individually for your content analysis (Krippendorff, 2004a).

Your coding unit and sampling unit may be the same. For example, if you are interested in racial and ethnic diversity in a specific soap opera, your coding and sampling units might be each soap opera episode. Here, you would analyze each episode. Once you have finished gathering your data, you would then be able to report on the percentage of episodes that included African Americans, Hispanics, etc.

Although sometimes your coding unit will be identical to your sampling unit, this is not always the case. Your coding unit can be different from your sampling unit because the sampling unit is the type of communication message that you gather for your analysis (e.g., newspaper articles), while the coding unit is the type of communication message that you actually evaluate in your analysis (e.g., sentences in newspaper articles). For example, if you are interested in the number of times that men versus women are quoted in the newspaper, you might select newspaper articles as your sampling unit and quotations as your coding unit. Here, at the close of your study, you can report the percentage of quotations from women and the percentage of quotations from men. In this example, the coding unit (quotations) will be different from the sampling unit (newspaper articles).

How Many Items To Use? After figuring out your sampling and coding units, you have two options. First, you may decide to use all of the sampling and coding units that you gathered for your study. For example, if you gathered newspaper articles about car accidents in your local newspaper over the past ten years, you might include all of the available articles in your study.

Second, you may decide to include only a subset of the coding or sampling units in your study. If there were thousands of articles about traffic accidents in your local newspaper over the past year, for example, you may elect to analyze only a subset of these articles. This happens frequently in practice. For example, when Barnhurst and Mutz (1997) wanted to evaluate news coverage between 1894 and 1994, they sampled news stories; they noted, "Our total sample of news stories comprised six independent random samples drawn at 20-year intervals...." (p. 30)

CODES AND CODEBOOKS After determining your sampling and coding units, the next task is to decide what to evaluate in each coding unit in order to answer your research questions and hypotheses. Ask yourself: What do I want to know about these communication messages? This is the first step to developing *codes*, or standard instructions that provide details about how a coder should evaluate each coding unit. For some research questions and hypotheses, previous researchers already may have developed codes. Thus, it is well worth your while to do a literature search to see if this is the case.

If codes have not been established, you will need to develop your own. If, for example, you wanted to know how often Israel is mentioned, you might have a code saying "If the sentence mentions Israel, code 1. If the sentence does not mention Israel, code 0." Here, the *coding categories* are 0 (does not mention Israel) and 1 (mentions Israel). Given the following two sentences, a coder would code a 1 for Sentence #1 and a 0 for Sentence #2:

Sentence #1: Today, Congress discussed the situation in Israel.
Sentence #2: Several members also had a spirited debate about immigration policy.

The codes generally correspond to a spreadsheet or form on which coders note their coding decisions. Table 1 gives an example.

As shown in Table 1, each *row* of data corresponds to a single coding unit. Each *column* represents a different variable. The first row of data, for example, corresponds to the first sentence, where Israel was mentioned (noted with a 1). For the second sentence, Israel was not mentioned.

One important detail to notice is that the coding units are *numbered* (e.g., Sentence 1, Sen-

Table 1: Coding Spreadsheet

Sentence #	Israel
1	1
2	0

tence 2, etc.). Giving each coding unit a unique number is a helpful practice for several reasons. First, when you are analyzing whether coders reach the same conclusions about a coding unit, you have to match each person's coding to all other coders. Second, if there ever is a question about how someone coded a coding unit — perhaps, for example, a coder coded a 0 when the only available codes were 1 or 2 — then you can return to the exact coding unit to check the coding.

When creating codes for a content analysis, you need to keep in mind the following five principles:

Principles for Writing Codes

1. You should endeavor to create codes that are *applicable to all coding units*. Coders should be able to read the code and clearly apply the instructions with little guessing. When you write your codes, think through different types of coding units that a coder may encounter and try to clarify these in the codebook. Continuing with the previous example, if coders encounter a sentence mentioning the political leadership of Israel, but not the country by name, would you want them to code the sentence as mentioning Israel or not?

2. The coding categories should be *exhaustive*. This means that no matter what type of coding unit is encountered, there should be a corresponding coding category. No coding unit should be left uncodable.

3. Coding categories should be *mutually exclusive*. This means that each coding unit should be associated with one and only one coding category for each code.

4. Think carefully about the *number of categories* for each code. Although one could conceive of a code with many categories, it is advisable to keep the number of categories to a *minimum* so that it is manageable for the coders (Stempel, 1981).

5. On the other hand, you do not want to have too few categories so that you are unable to answer your research questions and hypotheses (Holsti, 1969).

By keeping these principles in mind, you will be able to create more readily understandable and reliable content analysis codes.

To understand how to apply these principles, let's contrast an example of a not-so-good code with an example of an improved code.

How To Improve Codes

First, take a look at the "Not-So-Good Code" shown in Figure 1. What problems do you see with this code?

Figure 1. Not-So-Good Code

---

(1) **Topics Mentioned.** If the sentence mentions the economy, code 1; healthcare, code 2; the environment, code 3; prescription drugs, code 4.

Using the coding instructions in Figure 1, think about how coders *could* code "Topics Mentioned" in the following sentence:

Sentence #1: "The presidential hopefuls addressed a number of issues in last night's debate, including the environment and prescription drug benefits."

Employing the coding instructions from Figure 1, coders could encounter significant problems in figuring out what to code. Consider these problems:

First, the sentence definitely mentions the environment (3) and prescription drugs (4), but do prescription drug benefits count as healthcare (2)? From the instructions in Figure 1, it isn't clear what the coder should do.

Second, the coding categories here are not mutually exclusive. Each coding unit should have a single coding category associated with it. But here, the sentence has three possible codes associated with it: 2, 3, and 4.

Third, the coding categories are not exhaustive. If you had a sentence that read "The presidential hopefuls discussed education policy" — how would you code it? There is no matching coding category.

Now think about how you might improve the code from Figure 1. One way is shown in Figure 2. Here, each topic is treated as a separate code, the categories are mutually exclusive and exhaustive, and the coding instructions clarify that related terms should be counted as a mention of each of the topics.

Figure 2. Improved Code

(1) Does the sentence mention the **economy**? (include related terms, such as taxes, budget, inflation, etc.)

    0 – Not mentioned

    1 – Mentioned

(2) Does the sentence mention **healthcare**? (include related terms, such as Medicare, Medicaid, prescription drugs, etc.)

    0 – Not mentioned

    1 – Mentioned

(3) Does the sentence mention the **environment**? (include related terms, such as global warming, deforestation, etc.)

    0 – Not mentioned

    1 – Mentioned

Now go back to sentence 1 ("The presidential hopefuls addressed a number of issues in last night's debate, including the environment and prescription drug benefits.") and think about how you would code it using the updated coding instructions in Figure 2. Easier, right? Here, we would choose category 0 for the first code (economy), 1 for the second code (healthcare), and 1 for the third code (environment).

Writing codes takes practice, and you should expect to make some revisions before getting the process right. The goal is to make the coding instructions understandable and easy to apply given the diversity of coding units that you are interested in analyzing.

The codes for all of the research questions and hypotheses you hope to address in your content analysis are typically included in a codebook. A *codebook* is a document with formally written instructions for the coders. The codes shown in Figure 2 would be a very short codebook. If other researchers wanted to replicate your content analysis, they should be able, using the instructions in your code-book, to analyze the same communication messages and reach the same conclusions.

TRAINING CODERS

Once you have developed a codebook, the next task is to obtain qualified coders and train them. Typically, content analysis studies using human coding *employ more than one coder*. The purpose is to allow you to measure agreement between the coders, which can be taken as an indicator of the reliability of the data generated by coding.

For some projects, you will need coders who already have some background knowledge. For example, if you are coding Spanish-language transcripts, you will need coders who can read Spanish. For other projects, you may need students who are well-versed in politics so that they can adequately identify different political figures.

Once you have coders with adequate background for your study, an essential step is training them. During training sessions, researchers introduce the coders to the specific characteristics of the content analysis process, from the material that will be content-analyzed to the codebook and the recording process. If coders are not familiar with the method, a brief explanation of content analysis also is in order. Coders should be given an opportunity to practice coding in order to ensure that they understand the codes and coding instructions.

Once coders are briefed on the project and familiar with the codebook, each coder should be given an identical sample of coding units to code individually. The coders' answers then can be compared in order to discover any codes causing confusion. Coder training is directly related to the development of the codebook (Neuendorf, 2002), and codes can be revised to increase clarity during the training process.

Training is necessary to make sure that coders can draw on a similar and consistent understanding of the coding instructions in reaching decisions about how to code each coding unit. When training is consistently done and disagreements are discussed in a directed way, training can increase levels of agreement between the coders (Holsti, 1969).

Importance of the Codebook

It is important to note, however, that training is not a substitute for clear instructions found in the codebook. Hak and Bernts (1996) have warned that informal decision rules can develop during coder training. Such informality can lead to biased data and invalid conclusions despite increased agreement between the coders. Whatever happens during the training process must remain replicable at another location, using a different set of coders categorizing the same set of coding units. If informal rules established during training are not incorporated into the codebook, they can hinder the replicability of the study. A precise and detailed explication of the coding instructions and codes can help researchers to avoid subjective and biased coding (Kolbe & Burnett, 1991).

RELIABILITY

In conducting a content analysis, researchers go to great efforts to ensure that their results are replicable and to test the reliability of their data. *Reliability* is the principle that if other researchers replicated the content analysis, they would arrive at the same conclusions. The main potential problem in establishing reliability is that coders can vary in how they interpret communication messages.

Conducting a Reliability Analysis

After creating the codebook and training coders, the next step is to assess the reliability of the codes. In assessing reliability, researchers evaluate the extent to which coders agree with each other when coding communication messages in accordance with the instructions provided in the codebook.

To conduct a reliability analysis, different coders *working independently* code the *same* set of coding units (Krippendorff, 2004a). The coders must work independently so that their coding can be compared. If they worked together, the reliability analysis would not provide any information about whether other researchers would obtain the same results if they replicated the study. The coders also must evaluate an identical set of coding units so that it is possible to evaluate whether they agree or disagree with each others' coding decisions.

Generally, given time and budget constraints, it is not feasible to have all of the coders code all of the available communication messages for a reliability analysis. Nor is it necessary, for a sample of the coding units can provide an adequate representation of the reliability of the codes (Krippendorff, 2004a). The number of coding units required for conducting a reliability analysis will vary depending on the frequency with which the coding categories appear in the coding units and the minimum level of reliability that is acceptable for the project. If, for example, very few newspaper articles mention Africa and one of your codes asks about mentions of Africa, you'll need more articles in your reliability analysis. Further, the higher your reliability standards, the more articles required to assess reliability. The coding units included in the reliability analysis should be roughly representative of the variety of coding units that are possible in the population of communication messages you are analyzing. In the reliability analysis, efforts also should be made to select coding units that include all of the coding categories of the codes to be tested.

Measuring Reliability

How do researchers know when their content analysis is producing reliable data? To answer that question, researchers must compute a measure of intercoder reliability. An *intercoder reliability statistic* measures the extent to which coders, working independently to code the same messages, reach the same conclusions.

One statistic that is sometimes used, but has been subject to numerous critiques, is *percentage agreement*. This statistic measures how many times coders reach the same conclusions about coding units. It theoretically ranges from 1, where the coders are in perfect agreement, to 0, where the coders are in perfect disagreement. The following examples illustrate how this statistic is computed.

Let's say that you have two coders coding 10 newspaper articles for whether or not each article mentions the economy. If the two coders agree that 5 of the articles mention the economy and that the otjer 5 do not, then they agree 100 percent of the time. This level of agreement is illustrated in Table 2 on the next page.

Table 2. 100 Percent Coder Agreement

	Article 1	Article 2	Article 3	Article 4	Article 5	Article 6	Article 7	Article 8	Article 9	Article 10
Coder 1	1	1	1	1	1	0	0	0	0	0
Coder 2	1	1	1	1	1	0	0	0	0	0

If, however, they disagree on two articles — with one coder thinking that Articles 5 and 6 mention the economy and the other coder thinking that they do not — then the percent agreement would fall to (8/10) = 80 percent. This level of agreement is illustrated in Table 3.

Table 3. 80 Percent Coder Agreement

	Article 1	Article 2	Article 3	Article 4	Article 5	Article 6	Article 7	Article 8	Article 9	Article 10
Coder 1	1	1	1	1	1	1	0	0	0	0
Coder 2	1	1	1	1	0	0	0	0	0	0

Percentage agreement as a measure of reliability has been critiqued, however, for the following reasons:

First, the measure is limited to only two coders.

Second, codes with more categories are less likely to achieve reliability using percentage agreement (Hayes & Krippendorff, 2007).

Third, percentage agreement does not take into account agreement that would occur merely by chance. Continuing our earlier example, let's say that you are interested in how frequently the economy is mentioned in newspaper articles. Imagine that you have two rebellious coders working on your project who decide not to look at the articles at all. Rather, each coder flips a coin in order to decide whether to code the article as mentioning the economy. When the coin lands on heads, the coder codes that economy is in the article; and when the coin lands on tails, the coder codes that economy is not in the article. Here, we would expect that the two coders would agree 50 percent of the time simply by chance.

Other statistics, including Scott's *pi* (Scott, 1955) and Krippendorff's *alpha* (Krippendorff, 2004a), have been proposed as ways to measure intercoder reliability that remedy the critiques of percentage agreement. Although these statistics can be computed by hand, computer programs have been created to automate the process. Krippendorff (2004a) includes formulas for computing the statistics by hand, and Hayes and Krippendorff (2007) discuss computer programs for doing the work.

After you compute a reliability statistic, how do you know whether your code is reliable? The answer is that, in general, codes that yield reliability statistics of between 0.8 and 1.0 are considered to be reliable. Codes with intercoder reliability between 0.67 and 0.8 are considered adequate for exploratory studies (Krippendorff, 2004b; Neuendorf, 2002). Intercoder reliabilities below these levels are generally not considered to be reliable. Note that for the coding results displayed in Table 3, the percentage agreement statistic would indicate that the coding is reliable (0.80). For the same data, however, Krippendorff's *alpha* is 0.62, indicating that the code is not reliable.

Causes of Unreliability

When researchers conduct a content analysis, sometimes codes will not be reliable and the intercoder reliability statistics will dip below desired levels. Typically, unreliability is a result either of the coders or of the codes (Holsti, 1969).

Problems with Coders

Coders can be a source of unreliability when they are inadequately trained or when they are not being diligent in working on the coding. When coders have not received adequate training, they may be incorrectly or inconsistently applying the coding instructions. To detect this problem, a researcher can meet with the coders after the reliability test and ask them why they coded the coding units certain ways. Such a discussion often is a valuable way to clear up ambiguity. And spending additional time training coders is often helpful in improving reliability. As Hak and Bernts (1996) remind us, however, researchers must be careful that increases in reliability do not occur because of systematic biases brought about by the development of informal decision rules among the coders.

Coders also may not have adequate background to complete the coding task. However, reliability generally improves over time (Stempel, 1981). Practice is especially important when working with coders who are new to content analysis. Beyond a lack of familiarity with the method of content analysis, coders may not have adequate background to understand the codes. If, for example, you ask coders to evaluate whether a newspaper article has an issue or a strategy frame, but the coders have little background in what strategy and issue frames are, they are unlikely to produce reliable data. Depending on the extent of the coders' lack of background, researchers can either spend additional time training or can hire new coders who already possess the necessary background.

Unreliability also can result when coders are not being careful enough in their work. When coders are not in perfect agreement when the content of a message is clear, it is an indication that the coders are not exercising enough care. To improve this issue, researchers may consider changing *where* their coders are working. For example, having coders work in an office setting may improve reliability compared to having coders work wherever they like.

Problems with Codes

Codes also can be a source of unreliability. When they are not clear enough or do not provide enough information for coders to reliably judge content, they can cause unreliability. In coding, for example, whether or not a fast food advertisement shows a child, suppose coders encounter a cartoon child. For some coders, a cartoon child may count as a child. For others, it may not. Adjusting the coding instructions to say "cartoon children should be coded as children" (or "cartoon children should not be coded as children" depending on your hypothesis) will clear up any ambiguity.

Problems with Samples

Although the coders and the codes are the most common sources of unreliability, there are other possibilities.

Specifically, the reliability sample also can cause problems. Suppose, for example, that you are asking coders to evaluate whether people use text abbreviations (e.g., LOL, BRB) in their speech and you took a sample of previously recorded conversations between friends. Let's further suppose that text abbreviations are used infrequently in speech. When a coding category occurs infrequently, a single disagreement can have a devastating effect on reliability statistics, particularly when using the more complicated reliability formulas. If an infrequent code is unreliable, you may conduct another round of reliability analysis where you purposefully select conversations that contain that code. In doing so, however, you must make a special effort to ensure that you are equally likely to include more and less tricky instances of the code.

Strategies for Improving Reliability

After identifying and remedying causes of unreliability, researchers should check for intercoder reliability by giving coders a fresh sample of coding units to categorize and then by analyzing the new data. Tests for reliability sometimes are conducted several times and adjustments made until acceptable reliability is reached. The process can be a long one, requiring multiple revisions to the codebook in order to ensure that the project produces reliable data.

Reliability and Validity

It is important to recognize that a *reliable* code is not necessarily a *valid* code. Recall from Chapter 7 on measurement that *validity* refers to the extent to which you are measuring what you actually want to measure. *Reliability*, in contrast, refers to the extent to which the results are replicable.

Since reliability tests only assess agreement about what to code, systematically incorrect coding would yield high reliability and low validity. For example, assume that a researcher is interested in looking at how often Iraq is discussed in the newspaper. Coders evaluate every time Iraq is mentioned, and they achieve a reliability of 0.85 using Krippendorff's *alpha*. However, if the coders did not code Iraq*i* or Iraq*is* or Baghdad or Saddam Hussein, the researcher may not have a valid code. As this example shows, just because a code is reliable does not mean that it is valid.

To assess whether codes are valid, researchers may use techniques for establishing measurement validity for the codes. For example, they may attempt to establish *convergent validity* by documenting that their results for one code are related to the results for another similar code. Even if researchers do not formally test the validity of their codes, they should take special care to think through whether or not their codes are measuring what they would like to measure.

ANALYZING THE DATA

Once you have established that your codes are reliable, each coder can code a different set of communication messages. This is because by establishing reliability, you confirm that the coders are nearly indistinguishable from one another and that their coding decisions will be approximately the same.

After you have coded all of your coding units, your next challenge is analyzing the results. Since your data is quantified, you now can use many different types of statistical methods to analyze your data. (Such methods will be covered in Chapter 12 on hypothesis testing and Chapter 13 on statistics).

Some content analysis projects will run descriptive statistics to evaluate their results. For example, you may be interested in the number of news stories that include quotations only from women vs. the number of news stories that include quotations only from men. Based on your dataset, you could add up the number of stories that quoted only women and compare that to the number of stories that quoted only men.

Other studies may compare two types of messages. For example, did CNN cover an issue differently than Fox News did? Here, you could compare the tone of articles from the two news organizations. (For an example of such a study, see Aday, Livingston, & Hebert, 2005.)

Furthermore, you might compare the data you obtain from the content analysis to survey or experimental data to investigate the effects of communication messages. Cultivation researchers, for example, find that heavy television viewers adopt impressions of reality in keeping with the world as depicted on television. Thus, heavy television viewers are more likely to believe that they could be a victim of a crime, a finding that coincides with content analyses of television programming showing that the frequency of crime on television far exceeds the frequency of crime in reality (Gerbner, Gross, Morgan, Signorielli, & Shanahan, 2002).

COMPUTERIZED CONTENT ANALYSIS

Computers can be used at different stages of a content analysis, from helping researchers access communication messages to analyzing the collected data with statistical analysis programs such as SPSS or Microsoft Excel. Computers can minimize the *time* spent in data collection, coding, and analysis. They also can minimize the *cost* of the research project if a researcher uses a computer instead of humans to code the data. The importance of computers cannot be underestimated, and their use is growing (Riffe & Freitag, 1997).

Computers can be especially useful in helping researchers to code data because they can handle *large amounts of data* quickly and can minimize the *subjectivity* that arises from using multiple coders (Miller, 1997).

There are a number of *software programs* available for this purpose. Several content analysis textbooks describe available computer content analysis programs, with an explanation of their purposes (Krippendorff, 2004a; Neuendorf, 2002). Neuendorf (2002) also provides links to several programs in the online support for her book. The sophistication of these programs varies from simple word counts to artificial intelligence programs (Riffe, Lacy, & Fico, 1998).

One relatively simple way to use computers to assist with coding data is to use the "find" command to search for specific words within text-based communication messages. Researchers can quickly count the number of times that the words "liberal" and "conservative," for example, are mentioned in a sample of communication messages. Search engines such as Google and online databases such as Lexis Nexis and Factiva also can be used to identify the frequency with which various words and phrases are used.

Researchers also can use computer programs to identify instances in which words and phrases *co-occur*. For example, researchers can evaluate how frequently newspaper articles mention both Google and Yahoo.

Another widely used type of computer content analysis is *readability*, which measures how easy a text is to read. This type of analysis can be done with widely available word processing programs (Riffe, Lacy, & Fico, 1998).

Other programs categorize communication messages into pre-defined categories. For example, the DICTION program categorizes messages into a number of categories, such as the level of optimism contained within the message (Hart, 1985). The Linguistic Inquiry and Word Count programs categorize by types of emotions conveyed in a message. The program is described at www.liwc.net.

Limitations of Computer Analysis

Not all studies lend themselves to the use of computer content analysis, however, and researchers should carefully consider whether to use computer coding or human coding. The following two considerations can help you to determine whether a computer content analysis is appropriate.

First, the type of communication messages that you are analyzing can dictate whether a computer content analysis is possible, for it is not possible to conduct a computer content analysis on all types of communication messages at this time. Although evolving technology is making computer content analyses of visuals and sounds more possible, most of the studies that employ computers for coding data are analyzing written texts, such as newspaper articles and broadcast transcripts (Riffe, Lacy, & Fico, 1998).

Second, your research questions and hypotheses may make human coding a superior option compared to computer coding. Several studies have compared human coding to computer coding with mixed results. Rosenberg, Schnurr, and Oxman (1990), for example, found that computer content analysis was a superior method compared to human coding when using transcripts of interviews to diagnose patients. Nacos et al. (1991) and Royal (2002), however, found mixed evidence for the promise of computer coding over human coding when looking at newspaper coverage. These researchers found that while computerized content analysis programs are very efficient at coding explicit, easily identified attributes of communication messages, more subtle uses of language are more difficult to capture using a computer program.

In sum, computers can be useful for content analysis and are commonly used during the process of gathering sampling units, recording coding decisions, assessing reliability, and analyzing results. In some instances, they also can be used, instead of humans, as a tool to code the data. The success of such research depends on the researcher's careful consideration of whether computerized content analysis is appropriate. In general, researchers should consider using both humans and computers to assist at various stages of a content analysis.

CONTENT ANALYSIS ON THE INTERNET

The Internet has changed the way people look for and send information, socialize, use the news — in other words, how they communicate.

In the communication discipline, scholars have begun to use content analysis to analyze online communication messages. They've addressed such questions as these:

What audiences do U.S. Congressional Representatives target with their websites (Jarvis & Wilkerson, 2005)?

How do members of Fortune 100 use their company's websites (Perry & Bodkin, 2000)?

What is the nature of blogs (Herring, Scheidt, Bonus, & Wright, 2004; Trammell, Williams, Postelnicu, & Landreville, 2006)?

Do left-leaning websites cover the news differently than right-leaning websites (Baum & Groeling, 2008)?

Do extremist websites link to other extremist websites (Gerstenfeld, Grant and Chiang, 2003)?

Challenges in Conducting Online Content Analysis

The procedures for conducting a content analysis of online communication messages are similar to those used for analyzing traditional media. However, it is necessary to adapt some of the procedures to fit the distinct nature of the web. Interactivity, hypertextuality, and multimediality characterize the Internet; and these elements require researchers to develop new ways of content analyzing online communication messages. Let's look at three challenges that researchers are facing.

• One challenge lies in *identifying the population* of relevant communication messages. For instance, let's assume that a researcher is interested in studying certain characteristics of blogs. How could you list all available blogs? How could you even know exactly how many active blogs there are? New blogs are created on a daily basis, and old ones may cease to be used without being removed from the web. This situation complicates the identification of the population and makes it impossible to draw random samples (Herring, 2010). Even when using an electronic database of communication messages, researchers must investigate how comprehensive it is (Stryker, Wray, Hornik, & Yanovitzky, 2006).

Most studies of the Internet, therefore, tend to use *purposive samples* instead of probability or random samples. As you will recall from Chapter 8 on sampling, purposive samples of online communication messages could include websites or blogs that are easy to access or well known. Purposive samples cannot be generalized to the entire population. Just looking at well-known blogs tells us nothing about lesser-known blogs. However, they still provide us with information about the blogs that were included in the study. Researchers also can use tools such as web crawlers, also known as spiders and robots, to identify relevant communication messages. These tools, however, are not able to provide researchers with a complete and definite population of online communication messages — at least not yet.

• The *temporality* of web messages also presents a challenge for ensuring that your study is replicable (Foot, 2006). If other researchers were to replicate your study, would they be able to analyze the exact same messages that you did? For example, the ways in which news organizations present information online have changed dramatically over the past several years. If you wanted to replicate a content analysis of news websites conducted in 2000, you certainly would arrive at different conclusions today.

Ensuring that the online messages you analyzed can be accessed at a later point without having changed is one of the precautions that a researcher conducting a web content analysis needs to take. Web archives are one of the technological advancements that can assure the maintenance of a stable dataset. IMorth, for example, is one tool that preserves copies of a web page over a certain time period. Another precaution needed is to ensure that all coders are using the same browser, monitor, and Internet connection, as these may change what a user can access from the web (Weare & Lin, 2000).

• A third challenge is *determining the coding unit* (McMillan, 2000). In off-line newspapers, for example, coding units traditionally are articles, paragraphs, or sentences. In conducting an analysis of online messages, however, there are few conventions about which coding units are most appropriate. If the researcher considers only the homepage in the analysis, for example, important messages might be embedded in later pages and the study would miss important information. For some studies, however, the homepage may be an adequate coding unit because it arguably is the page on some websites that most users encounter (Herring, 2004).

Coding an entire website, on the other hand, could be an extremely time-consuming project. If you consider, for example, that a website may link to many other websites, researchers must decide the boundaries of their study and to what extent linked pages are part of the same communication message.

Furthermore, websites can incorporate text, sound, and video — and the researcher must decide which of these aspects should be coded. Whatever the logic for the coding unit, the researcher should justify it and point to potential shortcomings and advantages of that selection.

There is a lot of work ahead to develop strategies for using content analysis to quantify online communication. Researchers in this area, however, have the advantage of pioneering the application of content analysis to the web and of building theory applicable to this new communication medium.

Whether one is dealing with the Internet or with traditional media, we can conclude that content analysis is particularly important to communication researchers because it allows us to systematically and reliably evaluate communication messages. When you first begin working on a content analysis project, it can be challenging to write reliable codes. Different people approach communication messages differently, and so there is plenty of opportunity for disagreement when people code communication messages. Once you have worked through your codebook and developed reliable codes, however, you and your coders can consistently code concepts of interest. You then can examine important characteristics of communication messages, trends in communication messages, and relationships between communication messages and people's beliefs, attitudes, and behaviors.

TO LEARN MORE

Althaus, S. L., Edy, J. A., & Phalen, P. F. (2001). Using substitutes for full-text news stories in content analysis: Which text is best? *American Journal of Political Science, 45*(3), 707-723.

Berelson, B. (1952). *Content analysis in communication research.* Glencoe, IL: Free Press.

Dovring, K. (1954-1955). Quantitative semantics in 18th century Sweden. *The Public Opinion Quarterly, 18*(4), 389-394.

Fico, F. G., Lacy, S., & Riffe, D. (2008). A content analysis guide for media economics scholars. *Journal of Media Economics*, 21(2), 114-130.

Hak, T., & Bernts, T. (1996). Coder training: Theoretical training or practical socialization? *Qualitative Sociology*, 19(2), 235-257.

Hayes, A. F., & Krippendorff, K. (2007). Answering the call for a standard reliability measure for coding data. *Communication Methods and Measures*, 1(1), 77-89.

Herring, S. (2004). Content analysis for new media: Rethinking the paradigm. *New Research for New Media: Innovative Research Methodologies Symposium Working Papers and Reading* (pp. 47-66). Available online at: http://ella.slis.indiana.edu/~herring/newmedia.pdf.

Herring, S. (2010) Web content analysis: Expanding the paradigm. In J. Hunsinger, M. Allen, & L. Klastrup (Eds.), *The international handbook of internet research* (pp. 233-249). New York: Springer.

Holsti, O. R. (1969). *Content analysis for the social sciences and humanities*. Reading, MA: Addison-Wesley.

Krippendorff, K. (2004a). *Content analysis: An introduction to its methodology* (2nd ed.). Thousand Oaks: Sage.

Krippendorff, K. (2004b). Reliability in content analysis: Some common misconceptions and recommendations. *Human Communication Research*, 30(3), 411-433.

Krippendorff, K., & Bock, M. A. (2009). *The content analysis reader*. Sage: Thousand Oaks, CA.

McMillan, S. (2000). The microscope and the moving target: The challenge of applying content analysis to the World Wide Web. *Journalism and Mass Communication Quarterly*, 77(1), 80-98.

Neuendorf, K. A. (2002). *The content analysis guidebook*. Thousand Oaks, CA: Sage.

Riffe, D., & Freitag, A. (1997). A content analysis of content analyses: Twenty-five years of Journalism Quarterly. *Journalism & Mass Communication Quarterly*, 74(4), 873-882.

Riffe, D., Lacy, S., & Fico, F. G. (1998). *Analyzing media messages: Using quantitative content analysis in research*. Mahwah, NJ: Lawrence Erlbaum Associates.

Stryker, J. E., Wray, R. J., Hornik, R. C., & Yanovitzky, I. (2006). Validation of database search terms for content analysis. *Journalism & Mass Communication Quarterly*, 83(2), 413-430.

REFERENCES

Aday, S., Livingston, S., & Hebert, M. (2005). Embedding the truth: A cross-cultural analysis of objectivity and television coverage of the Iraq War. *The Harvard International Journal of Press/Politics*, 10(1), 3-21.

Althaus, S. L., Edy, J. A., & Phalen, P. F. (2001). Using substitutes for full-text news stories in content analysis: Which text is best? *American Journal of Political Science*, 45(3), 707-723.

Althaus, S. L., Edy, J. A., & Phalen, P. F. (2002). Using the Vanderbilt Television Abstracts to track broadcast news content: Possibilities and pitfalls. *Journal of Broadcasting & Electronic Media*, 46(3), 473-492.

Alves, R. C., & Weiss, A. S. (2004). Many newspaper sites still cling to once-a-day publish cycle. *Online Journalism Review*. Available online at: http://ojr.org/ojr/workplace/1090395903.php.

Barnhurst, K. G., & Mutz, D. (1997). American journalism and the decline in event-centered reporting. *Journal of Communication*, 47(4), 27-53.

Baum, M. A., & Groeling, T. (2008). New media and the polarization of American political discourse. *Political Communication*, 25(4), 345-365.

Berelson, B. (1952). *Content analysis in communication research*. Glencoe, IL: Free Press.

Dovring, K. (1954-1955). Quantitative semantics in 18th century Sweden. *The Public Opinion Quarterly*, 18(4), 389-394.

Foot, K. A. (2006). Web sphere analysis and cybercultural studies. In D. Silver & A. Massanari (Eds.), *Critical cyberculture studies* (pp. 88-96). New York: New York University.

Gerbner, G., Gross, L., Morgan, M., Signorielli, N., & Shanahan, J. (2002). Growing up with television: Cultivation processes. In J. Bryant & D. Zillmann. (Eds). *Media effects: Advances in theory and research* (2nd ed., pp. 43-67). Mahwah, NJ: Lawrence Erlbaum Associates.

Gerstenfeld, P. B., Grant, D. R., & Chiang, C. (2003). Hate online: A content analysis of extremist Internet sites. *Analyses of Social Issues and Public Policy, 3*(1), 29-44.

Hak, T., & Bernts, T. (1996). Coder training: Theoretical training or practical socialization? *Qualitative Sociology, 19*(2), 235-257.

Hart, R. P. (1985). Systematic analysis of political discourse: The developments of DICTION. In K. R. Sanders, L. L. Kaid, & D. Nimmo. (Eds.), *Political communication yearbook 1984* (pp. 97-134). Carbondale: Southern Illinois University Press.

Hayes, A. F., & Krippendorff, K. (2007). Answering the call for a standard reliability measure for coding data. *Communication Methods and Measures, 1*(1), 77-89.

Herring, S. (2010) Web content analysis: Expanding the paradigm. In J. Hunsinger, M. Allen, & L. Klastrup (Eds.), *The international handbook of internet research* (pp. 233-249). New York: Springer.

Herring, S. C., Scheidt, L. A., Bonus, S., & Wright, E. (2004). Bridging the gap: A genre analysis of weblogs. Proceedings of the 37th Hawaii International Conference on System Sciences.

Holsti, O. R. (1969). *Content analysis for the social sciences and humanities.* Reading, MA: Addison-Wesley.

Jarvis, S., & Wilkerson, K. (2005). Congress on the Internet: Messages on the homepages of the U.S. House of Representatives, 1996 and 2001. *Journal of Computer-Mediated Communication, 10*(2), Article 9.

Kaphingst, K. A., Dejong, W., Rudd, R. E., & Daltroy, L. H. (2004). A content analysis of direct-to-consumer television prescription drug advertisements. *Journal of Health Communication, 9*(6), 515-528.

Kolbe, R. H., & Burnett, M. S. (1991). Content-analysis research: An examination of applications with directives for improving research reliability and objectivity. *The Journal of Consumer Research, 18*(2), 243-250.

Krippendorff, K. (2004a). *Content analysis: An introduction to its methodology* (2nd ed.). Thousand Oaks: Sage.

Krippendorff, K. (2004b). Reliability in content analysis: Some common misconceptions and recommendations. *Human Communication Research, 30*(3), 411-433.

McCombs, M. (2004). *Setting the agenda: The mass media and public opinion.* Cambridge: Polity Press.

McCombs, M. E., & Shaw, D. L. (1972). The agenda-setting function of mass media. *Public Opinion Quarterly, 36*(2), 176-187.

McMillan, S. (2000). The microscope and the moving target: The challenge of applying content analysis to the World Wide Web. *Journalism and Mass Communication Quarterly, 77*(1), 80-98.

Miller, M. M. (1997). Frame mapping and analysis of news coverage of contentious issues. *Social Science Computer Review, 15*(4), 367-378.

Nacos, B. L, Shapiro, R. Y., Young, J. T., Fan, D. P., Kjellstrand, T., & McCaa, C. (1991). Content analysis of news reports: Comparing human coding and a computer-assisted method. *Communication, 12.* 111-128.

Neuendorf, K. A. (2002). *The content analysis guidebook.* Thousand Oaks, CA: Sage.

Perry, M., & Bodkin, C. (2000). Content analysis of Fortune 100 company websites. *Corporate Communications: An International Journal, 5*(2), 87-96.

Riffe, D., & Freitag, A. (1997). A content analysis of content analyses: Twenty-five years of Journalism Quarterly. *Journalism & Mass Communication Quarterly, 74*(4), 873-882.

Riffe, D., Lacy, S., & Fico, F. G. (1998). *Analyzing media messages: Using quantitative content analysis in research*. Mahwah, NJ: Lawrence Erlbaum Associates.

Rogers, E. M. (2004). Theoretical diversity in political communication. In L. L. Kaid (Ed.), *Handbook of political communication research* (pp. 3-16). Mahwah, NJ: Lawrence Erlbaum Associates.

Rosenberg, S. D., Schnurr, P. P., & Oxman, T. E. (1990). Content analysis: A comparison of manual and computerized systems. *Journal of Personality Assessment, 54*(1&2). 298-310.

Royal, C. (2002, November). Comparison of computerized and traditional content analysis techniques: A case study of the Texas democratic gubernatorial primary. Paper presented at the Southwest Council for Education in Journalism and Mass Communication Symposium.

Scott, W. A. (1955). Reliability of content analysis: The case of nominal scale coding. *Public Opinion Quarterly, 19*(3), 321-325.

Signorielli, N. (2004). Aging on television: Messages relating to gender, race, and occupation in prime time. *Journal of Broadcasting & Electronic Media, 48*(2), 279-301.

Smith, S. L., Lachlan, K., & Tamborini, R. (2003). Popular video games: Quantifying the presentation of violence and its context. *Journal of Broadcasting & Electronic Media, 47*(1), 58-76.

Stempel III, G. H. (1981). Content analysis. In G. H. Stempel III & B. H. Westley (Eds.), *Research Methods in Mass Communication* (pp. 119-131). Englewood Cliffs, NJ: Prentice-Hall.

Stryker, J. E., Wray, R. J., Hornik, R. C., & Yanovitzky, I. (2006). Validation of database search terms for content analysis. *Journalism & Mass Communication Quarterly, 83*(2), 413-430.

Trammell, K.D., Williams, A.P., Postelnicu, M., & Landreville, K.D. (2006). Evolution of online campaigning: Increasing interactivity in candidate Web sites and blogs through text and technical features. *Mass Communication & Society, 9*(1), 21-44.

Tuggle, C. A., & Owen, A. (1999). A descriptive analysis of NBC's coverage of the centennial Olympics: The "Games of the Woman"? *Journal of Sport and Social Issues, 23*, 171-182.

Weare, C., & Lin, W. (2000). Content analysis of the World Wide Web: Opportunities and challenges. *Social Science Computer Review, 18*(3). 272-292.

Young, D. G. (2004). Late-night comedy in election 2000: Its influence on candidate trait ratings and the moderating effects of political knowledge and partisanship. *Journal of Broadcasting & Electronic Media, 48*(1), 1-22.

10

Survey

Did you know? ...

• According to the 2000 U.S. Census, the average family size in the United States is 3.14 persons, and the median family income is $50,046 (U.S. Census Bureau, 2000).

• An opinion poll regarding the importance of privacy taken by MSNBC.COM found that 60% of those who responded reported feeling that their privacy was slowly slipping away and that it bothered them (MSNBC.COM, 2006).

• In a study among college students, exposure to thin television female actresses was found to predict eating disorder symptoms among adolescent females (Harrison, 2000).

The above information was gathered in some way, shape, or form through a survey method. With the growth of news media outlets and the drive to gather information for news purposes, the number of surveys conducted has increased over the years. Whereas earlier ones were often conducted for governmental, business, or academic data gathering purposes, surveys are now frequently used to gain tidbits of interesting information to relay to the general public. It is hard to go through one day of broadcast news without an anchor or a reporter mentioning some piece of information that was obtained through a survey.

Of course, not all surveys are scientific in nature, as will be discussed later — and it is important not only for individuals who are conducting surveys, but also for individuals who are exposed to surveys, to understand the different kinds of surveys that exist. They also need to understand the degree of *reliability* and *validity* each survey holds. **Reliability** deals with the consistency in the administration and interpretation of the questions. **Validity** is the degree to which what the researcher is attempting to measure is what the survey actually measures.

Broadly speaking, survey research involves any procedure that is used to ask questions of respondents. Surveys, like other forms of research methods, can fall into the categories of either **descriptive** or **analytical**. The surveys from which the

By Catherine A. Luther
University of Tennessee

first two examples presented at the beginning of this chapter were derived would fall under the descriptive category. The third survey concerning television viewing behavior and eating disorder symptoms among adolescent females would come under the analytical category. So, what exactly are the differences between descriptive surveys and analytical surveys? The following section explains.

KINDS OF SURVEYS

There are two kinds of surveys: (1) descriptive ones and (2) analytical ones. Let's briefly examine each one.

Descriptive Surveys

The primary purpose of a descriptive survey is to describe current situations, opinions, or beliefs. A descriptive survey focuses on the characteristics of certain individuals or groups that are of particular interest. It is exploratory in nature and concentrates on creating profiles. With descriptive surveys, prior assumptions are not usually made about the population that is of interest to the researcher. The objective is not to explain, but rather to simply describe or make estimates.

Analytical Surveys

Unlike descriptive surveys, the main objective of analytical surveys is to explain.

Analytical surveys not only describe situations, opinions, and beliefs but also attempt to understand why they exist. Through an analytical survey, efforts are made to decipher what types of factors might serve as explanations or predictors of certain viewpoints or a particular phenomenon. Prior assumptions are made about the population of interest, and speculations are made about why members of the population have certain characteristics.

ESTABLISHING OBJECTIVES

Regardless of whether the proposed survey will be analytical or descriptive, the first step that needs to be taken in the development and execution of any survey is to establish the exact objectives of the survey. Is the purpose to survey news station managers about the racial or ethnic distribution of their staff members? Is the goal to examine the association between college students' viewing of reality television programs and their views on interpersonal relationships? Is the main purpose to estimate the proportion of people who like a particular presidential candidate and his campaign methods? Thinking about the overarching survey objectives will help the researcher draft the specific research questions and possible hypotheses that will be explored in the survey.

Research Questions and Hypotheses

Research questions are basically statements that express the core exploratory interests of the survey. The questions should succinctly relay the issues, events, or phenomena that the researcher hopes to study through the survey. They should identify the key concepts that are of particular interest. In order to come up with good research questions, the researcher should be familiar with the subject matter. S/he should review pertinent literature and understand those questions that have been left unanswered by prior work.

A *hypothesis* is a tentative explanation of a particular phenomenon or a supposition about relationships that might exist between two or more concepts (Baran & Davis, 2005). A well-formulated hypothesis for a survey should allow the researcher to make predictions about how one *variable* (i.e., an entity that varies or changes) is related to another variable and to test the relationship through a survey method. A hypothesis is often presented in the form of "if A, then B." Here is an example of a hypothesis that could be simply tested through a survey: "The higher the number of hours a child spends on the Internet, the lower the number of hours that child spends interacting with other children during non-school hours." For each proposed hypothesis, a solid rationale should be provided.

Narrowing the research to specific questions and/or hypotheses will help the researcher design a survey that is concise and to the point. Novices at survey research often make their surveys too long because they jump right into drafting questionnaire items without considering the reasoning behind and the need for the various items. Surveys that are too long frequently lead to participant fatigue or refusal. Potential respondents might take a look at the length of the survey and decide not to take the survey, or they might begin to take the survey but discontinue midway through because of its length.

Formulating research questions and hypotheses will allow the researcher to further pinpoint the population that s/he wants to study. Is the researcher interested in television station managers across the United States? Is the researcher interested in college students attending public universities? Is the researcher only interested in a particular demographic group?

In considering the population, the researcher can then begin thinking about the sample that will be targeted for the survey.

SURVEY SAMPLE

A *sample* is basically a subset of a population. As you will recall from chapter 8 on sampling, two types of samples exist: a probability sample and a nonprobability sample.

With a *probability sample*, a systematic method is used to come up with a sample that will represent the general population. Probability sampling, also known as random sampling, should give every member of a particular population a chance to be included in the sample. Identifying a *sampling frame* provides the researcher with a basis for drawing a probability sample. A sampling frame is a resource that provides information regarding the general population (Biemer & Lyberg, 2003). It should list all who are eligible to be included in the sample. Common resources relied upon as a sampling frame are telephone directories and official listings of registered voters. If the resource is comprehensive and a sample is drawn from that source in a systematic manner, the results from the survey can be safely generalized to the population.

In order to draw the sample in a systematic manner, three sampling techniques are frequently relied upon. They are *simple random sampling, stratified sampling*, and *cluster sampling*. Let's consider each one of them.

In **simple random sampling**, for each member of a sampling frame to get an equal chance of being included, a sampling interval is first chosen (e.g., every 20th name listed). Then a random sample starting point is selected (e.g., the seventh name listed). Beginning with the starting point, each member falling on the chosen interval is included in the sample.

Stratified sampling is more complicated and is used when the researcher is interested in examining certain groups of people. In stratified sampling, individuals within a particular sampling frame who have similar characteristics (e.g., females, males, juniors, freshmen, etc.) are grouped together. From each group, a systematic random sample is then chosen. By doing so, the researcher can be assured that the characteristics of interest are included in the sample.

Cluster sampling involves dividing or clustering a population into groups that share similar features. The clusters are then analyzed. For example, if a researcher is interested in examining the employment policies of public relations firms, s/he can cluster public relations firms according to the size of their work force. Those clusters are then randomly chosen for analysis. The sample of clusters should ideally reflect the population as a whole.

With a *nonprobability sample*, members of a particular population are drawn because those members are readily available or can be easily contacted. Included in nonprobability samples are a *convenience sample* and a *snowball sample*.

A *convenience sample* consists of individuals who are used as survey participants because they are easily accessible to the researcher. An example would be a sample consisting of students taking communications courses at a college.

A *snowball sample* is made up of individuals who are used in a survey through introductions. Each participant, beginning with the first, introduces the researcher to another potential participant. That individual is recruited for the survey; and s/he, in turn, introduces an additional participant. The pool of participants, in essence, grows like a snowball; and the sample size depends on the number of people who can be introduced and reached. Snowball samples are often used when individuals with certain characteristics of interest are hard to locate. For example, if a researcher were interested in surveying the homeless, a snowball sample would be an option.

Nonprobability samples, such as the snowball sample or convenience sample, can reveal important information; but it should always be kept in mind that any information that is gathered cannot be generalized to the larger population.

After the researcher identifies the type of sample s/he is interested in acquiring and the overarching research questions and hypotheses that will be explored via the survey, the design of the questionnaire can then be initiated.

QUESTIONNAIRE DESIGN

Questions included in a survey should get at the heart of a study's objectives. It may be tempting for a researcher to include additional questions that are tangentially related to the purpose of the survey for exploratory purposes, but this will lead to a lengthy survey and might interfere with the quality of the responses for the core questions.

When developing a survey, it is a good idea to first think about the organization of the survey. To help in this process, an organizational chart could be created with each research question and/or hypothesis written at the top. Under each research question and/or hypothesis, the researcher then lists the potential survey items that will aid in answering or testing the proposed overarching questions and/or hypotheses. A preliminary plan can be made in the ordering of the items and the sections in which they will appear in the survey. After the organizational chart is created, the researcher should then revisit the potential survey items to decide on their exact form and wording.

Open-ended vs. Closed-ended Questions

In designing survey questions, a researcher should decide whether they will be open-ended, closed-ended, or both. *Open-ended questions* require that the respondent fill in an answer after each question. *Closed-ended questions* require that the respondent choose an answer from a listed selection of responses.

An advantage to open-ended questions is that respondents can freely respond using their own words. The responses might provide unique insights that were not considered by the researcher.

Here are some examples of open-ended questions:

- "What type of music do you like to listen to over the radio?"
- "What are your favorite magazines to read?"
- "Why do you shop at the New World Mall?"

The major disadvantage of open-ended questions is that it takes longer for respondents to answer them than closed-ended ones. Another disadvantage is that it might be difficult for the researcher to read the respondent's handwriting or to interpret the responses given. A response might make sense to the person writing it, but it might come across as convoluted to the researcher.

A main advantage of closed-ended questions is that it will take less time for the survey participant to respond to the questions since the response categories are specified and the participant usually only needs to choose one category. Another advantage is that it will take less time for the researcher to analyze the responses since numbers are assigned to each category and the researcher can easily tabulate the numbers for analysis.

Response categories for closed-ended questions that are frequently used in surveys are based on the *Likert scale*. With a Likert scale, respondents provide their level of agreement to a question. An example of a question using a Likert scale for its response categories is the following:

- The viewing of pornography makes men more aggressive toward women.
1 - strongly disagree
2 - disagree
3 - neither agree nor disagree
4 - agree
5 - strongly agree

Another frequently used response format only provides labeled end points of a scale. An example of a question using such a format is the following:

- On a scale of 1 to 9, with 1 meaning "not at all satisfied" and 9 meaning "extremely satisfied," how satisfied are you with the School of Communication's new program?

Not at All Satisfied   Extremely Satisfied

1   2   3   4   5   6   7   8   9

Other common response categories for closed-ended questions include those that get at level of knowledge (e.g., very familiar, somewhat familiar, not too familiar, not at all familiar), frequency of behaviors (e.g., always, frequently, seldom, never), and ratings (e.g., excellent, good, fair, poor) (Czaja & Blair, 2005; Sudman & Bradburn, 1982).

A disadvantage of closed-ended questions is that they do not allow room for respondents to answer using their own words. The response categories, in essence, contain the possible answers that can be given. Another significant disadvantage is that the response categories chosen by the researcher might be too limiting. It is often difficult to decide on the type and number of responses that are most suitable for a particular question. Furthermore, the respondents might not agree on the meanings of the words used in the responses. For example, the word "excellent" might hold a different meaning for one respondent than for another.

The advantages and disadvantages of closed-ended and open-ended questions must be carefully considered in designing a questionnaire, and the final choice of question type should ultimately be based on the purposes of the study and the degree of in-depth responses the researcher requires from the respondents. See Figure 1 for a summary of the advantages and disadvantages of the two types of questions.

Figure 1. Advantages and Disadvantages of Open- and Closed-ended Questions

	Advantages	Disadvantages
Open-ended questions	• Respondents can freely respond in unique manner • Responses might reveal unexpected insights	• Takes longer to answer questions • Responses might not be legible
Closed-ended questions	• Respondents can answer questions quickly • Responses can be tabulated quickly	• Respondents are limited in their responses • Respondents might not agree on meaning of response categories

Quality of Survey Questions

In addition to determining the type of questions that will be used in the survey, the researcher must also take into account the quality of the questions.

Most importantly, questions should be easy to comprehend. The rule of thumb is the shorter, the better. Short questions allow respondents to read the questions quickly and should cut down on the degree of ambiguity that might be involved with the questions. The wording should also be simple and should take into consideration the target respondent. Specialized jargon (e.g., legal words, technical words, etc.) should be avoided if possible.

The inclusion of *double-barreled questions* is often a problem that novice survey researchers encounter. A **double-barreled question** is one that is actually asking more than one question. An example of a double-barreled question is the following: "Do you think the major television networks are doing a good job of providing educational and entertaining programs for preschoolers?" A respondent might believe that the television networks are doing a good job of providing entertaining programs but not educational programs for preschoolers. Each question should be scrutinized to ensure that it does not contain more than one question. If such a question is found, the parts of the question should be separated into different questions.

Another problem researchers new to survey construction often experience is the use of **double negatives**. Double negatives can confuse those taking the survey. This is especially the case when the respondent is required to express agreement or disagreement with a statement. For example, consider the following statement, "I am not uncomfortable expressing how I feel while chatting with others over the Internet." Would a respondent clearly know whether to disagree or agree with this statement? Complexity in sentence structures should be avoided in surveys. Survey items should provide respondents with an opportunity to clearly express their thoughts about a topic.

Survey researchers should also stay away from questions that are highly personal in nature. If a respondent comes across a question that is viewed as touching on intimate details, s/he might be turned off by the question and refuse to take the rest of the survey. Asking such questions might be necessary depending on the purpose of the survey, but references to private information such as a person's sexual behavior or illegal activities should generally be avoided.

When designing the specific survey items, the researcher should also keep in mind that certain questions can lead to biased answers. Detection of questionnaire bias can be challenging. Bias can be embedded within a question and can be subtle. Recognizing such bias entails a careful reading of each question and thinking about all of the ways a respondent might possibly react to the question.

Questionnaire Bias   Those who have studied questionnaire design have long recognized that an individual's response to a particular question can depend on the wording of the question. Questions that lead individuals to respond in a particular manner or suggest an expected response are considered biased. They are **leading questions** that should be avoided in surveys. An example of a leading question is the following: "Since PBS has helped to bring about better television programming for children, do you think the government should provide it with more funding?" With the question implying that PBS has been doing a good job, it would be difficult for a respondent to express disagreement with more funding. Care should be taken to avoid wording that suggests a certain position that the researcher is seeking.

Another **biasing effect** can occur with a question when a well-known individual or institution is mentioned in the question. Perhaps a question describes a new program that a mayor would like to implement for his city. The respondent is asked if s/he would be in favor of the program. The respondent might be in favor of the program based on its description, but because the respondent dislikes the mayor and an association is made between the mayor and the program, the respondent answers that s/he is not in favor of the program. Personal feelings toward a prominent individual or institution can create a biased reaction. If usage of a well-known personality or institution is not really needed in the question, it should be avoided.

Using *loaded words* in a question can also produce a biasing effect. Words such as "bureaucracy," "capitalistic," "radical," or "welfare" can produce unintended reactions from individuals because of the connotations associated with them. If a word is viewed as potentially creating a biasing effect, efforts should be made to express the same idea using words that are less provocative. See Figure 2 for a summary of general tips on writing survey questions.

Figure 2. General Tips on Writing Survey Questions

- Questions should be concise and comprehensible
- Avoid specialized jargon
- Do not ask double-barreled questions
- Do not use double negatives
- Avoid biased or leading questions
- Avoid words that can produce a biasing effect
- Avoid sensitive questions if not directly related to the purpose of the research

Questionnaire Order

After taking into account the quality of the questions and the organizational chart that was created at the outset of the survey design, the actual survey instrument can then be constructed. At the very beginning of a survey, an introduction should also be provided. It should at the very least include information about the general purpose of the survey, the primary individual or institution that is responsible for conducting the survey, and the general length of time required to participate in the survey. It is best to keep the introduction short and simple. Keep in mind, however, that certain institutions such as universities or colleges require that certain information be included in the introduction in order to meet the requirements of Human Subject committees. For example, a statement regarding who should be contacted if the respondent has questions regarding his/her rights as a survey participant might be required to be included in the introduction.

In terms of the flow of the survey, questions that pertain to the same topic should be grouped together into sections, and brief statements should be provided before each section to identify the topic and act as a transition device. Questions that are least sensitive should be provided first, followed by the more sensitive questions. Likewise, general questions should also precede more specific questions. Questions regarding demographics are usually left to the end, although some survey methodologists recommend placing questions pertaining to basic demographic information such as age and gender at the beginning. The reason is that if a respondent chooses not to complete the entire survey, the researcher still has the basic demographic information and some of the completed questionnaire items to use for analysis.

In considering questionnaire order, the researcher should keep in mind that the order in which the questions are presented can produce biased responses. The ordering of questions on a related topic can sway respondents to answer in a certain way for questions that come later in the survey. Let us say that a researcher has asked a series of questions regarding how television news has covered terrorism. A question later on in the survey is open-ended and asks respondents to write down three problems that they view as important ones facing the nation. Discussion of terrorism in the previous questions might very well sway the respondent to answer that terrorism is one of the important problems facing the nation. In other words, the earlier questions might have biased the answer to this later question. Placing the open-ended question regarding the problems facing the nation before the series of questions regarding news coverage of terrorism would help alleviate this problem.

PRETEST Following the construction of the survey instrument, the researcher should analyze whether the instrument is indeed appropriately designed. This can be done through a pretest of the instrument.

All survey instruments should be pretested before initiating the actual survey. Doing so will help the researcher identify any questions that are unclear to the respondent and any problems with the organizational structure of the survey instrument. In the end, the pretest will help the researcher avoid wasting time and expenses on administering a poorly designed survey.

A *pretest* is an initial testing of the instrument among a small group of respondents who are similar to the larger sample that the researcher hopes to target with the survey. After the respondents in the pretest take the survey, the researcher should openly discuss the survey with the participants to gain feedback on the clarity of the survey instrument and ways to improve it. Various methods exist in carrying out pretests, including asking respondents to describe how they went about answering the questions and asking them to paraphrase questions to acquire an idea about question comprehension (Collins, 2003). Based on the pretest, the survey instrument should be revised and additional pretests conducted until the researcher is satisfied that s/he has developed a sound survey instrument. The pretesting phase of a survey can take from a few weeks to several months.

A pretest should be conducted in the same manner in which the actual test will be conducted. For example, if the survey will be administered by telephone, the pretest should be done via telephone as well. In other words, the form of the pretest will depend on the form in which the final survey data will actually be gathered.

ADMINISTRATION The method used to collect data should be driven by the primary objectives of the study. What method would be most appropriate for providing the type of information that the researcher is seeking? Among the several survey approaches are mail survey, telephone survey, personal interview survey, group-administered survey, and online survey.

Mail Survey In a mail survey, respondents are sent the questionnaire in the mail with a detailed cover letter explaining the purpose of the survey, the individual or institution conducting the survey, confidentiality, and a timeline for returning the survey. A return envelope should also be included. It is crucial that the questionnaire and the instructions for completion for mail surveys are easy to understand (Dillman, 1978; Dillman, 2007). If not, respondents might be tempted to throw away the survey or skip the items that are unclear.

With mail surveys, the researcher must keep track of which individuals responded and which did not. If the budget permits, a second or even a third mailing should be sent to those who did not respond. They also could be contacted by a separate postcard or by telephone to request participation.

Mail surveys offer several advantages. One is the cost. They are usually less costly than telephone or personal interviews. With mail surveys, respondents also have more time to contemplate each question in a survey. They are able to consult with certain personal records that might help them respond in a more concise manner. Since an interviewer is not present, the respondent might feel less inhibited in responding to sensitive questions (Tourangeu, Rips, & Rasinski, 2000).

One of the major disadvantages of mail surveys is the low response rate (i.e., the number of surveys actually completed divided by the total number of members in a sample) that is usually attained. Respondents who receive surveys in the mail are not often motivated to take the survey. Although monetary or other incentives such as small gifts are sometimes included with mail surveys, studies have shown that such incentives are not particularly effective in increasing the response rate (Church, 1993; Czaja & Blair, 2005). A type of response bias might also occur in mail surveys. People with certain characteristics might be more willing to complete and send back mail surveys than others. Level of education and interest level in the topic are two factors that have been identified as potentially leading to a response bias.

With mail surveys, since the researcher must also rely on respondents to return the surveys in a timely fashion, delays can be experienced in receiving the completed surveys. If urgency is involved in collecting completed surveys, the telephone survey is one option that can be considered.

Telephone Survey

Telephone surveys require the training of interviewers who will conduct the actual surveys over the phone. In addition to the questionnaire, the researcher must prepare a guidebook for the interviewers with specific instructions on how to contact the respondents and how to conduct the interview. Each interviewer is provided a list of phone numbers that have been derived from such techniques as randomly selecting phone numbers from a phone book or through Random Digit Dialing (RDD), a method that generates phone numbers through a random process. Interviewers must be consistent in their asking of questions and should avoid prompting answers from the respondents in any way. It is best if all the surveys can be conducted at a single location where telephone equipment is available and where the researcher can monitor the quality of the interviews.

A widely used method for collecting data, telephone surveys have several advantages. One is that the response rate is usually good if repeated callbacks are made to those respondents who were initially unavailable. Although the costs involved are higher than for mail surveys, the higher response rate tends to justify the cost, and data can be collected in a much more time-efficient manner (Mangione, 1998). Another advantage is that with well-trained interviewers, in cases in which the responses are muddled, the interviewer can probe the respondent for clarification. An additional advantage is that, because an interviewer is involved, respondents can be convinced of the importance to participate in the survey and complete the survey in its entirety.

A major drawback to telephone surveys is related to technology. Options such as caller ID, call blocking, and answering machines have made it more challenging to reach survey members. Even with repeated callbacks, it is at times difficult to overcome these problems. The number of unlisted telephone numbers also poses a problem, but RDD has helped to resolve this by allowing researchers to rely on random digits generated within preferred area codes. The only remaining problem here is that Federal Communication Commission regulation specifies that RDD cannot be used to contact cellular telephones.

Another disadvantage of telephone surveys is that the length of the survey questions must be short. Although it is generally best to have simple sentences in all forms of surveys, simplicity becomes particularly important in telephone surveys due to the fact that respondents are listening to the questions being read to them. With complex and lengthy sentences, respondents might not remember the question, resulting in the interviewer having to repeat the question.

Telephone surveys also do not allow the use of visuals. Perhaps a researcher is interested in examining recall of advertising logos. A telephone survey would make it difficult for interviewers to ask about the respondent's recall of specific logos. A survey method that would allow such an examination would be the personal interview.

Personal Interview Survey

In the personal interview survey method, interviews are held face-to-face with the respondent. They can be conducted at the respondent's home or at a location designated by the researcher or respondent.

Before any interview is conducted, though, a sample needs to be identified first. Then an interviewer instruction guidebook must be prepared, and those recruited by the researcher to conduct the actual interviews must be trained. Specific instructions are given on how to conduct the interview. Some interview surveys require that the interviewer follow the predetermined flow of the interview, while others allow the interviewer to veer off into different directions and ask additional questions if it is deemed useful to do so (Berry, 2002). During the actual interviews, the interviewers either write down the responses and/or record the responses on audio or video. Following the collection of data, spot checks should be made with a sub-sample of the interviews to verify the responses given during the interviews.

Personal interviews have several advantages, including response rate. Since it is often difficult to refuse or terminate an interview when face-to-face, the percentages of completed surveys tend to be higher than in mail or telephone surveys. The interviewer also has the opportunity to build a rapport with the respondent and might be able to elicit more detailed responses or gather additional information from the respondents. The interviewer also has the option of using visuals or audio during the interview.

The major disadvantages of the personal interview method are the costs and time that are involved. It requires that interviewers travel to the place of each interview and hold each interview separately.

A form of response bias might also pose a potential problem with personal interviews because respondents might be more prone toward providing socially desirable responses. With a fear of being embarrassed in a face-to-face interview, respondents might be less likely to express their true opinions, especially regarding sensitive topics.

Even with such drawbacks, personal interviews are often chosen as a method in cases in which the researcher is attempting to access individuals living in areas with inadequate telephone or mail services. For a detailed explanation of intensive interviews, you may wish to read Chapter 18 in this book. Group-administered surveys are also used in such cases as well.

Group-administered Survey

In group-administered surveys, respondents are recruited to take a survey together at a central location. Surveys that are administered to students in classroom settings are considered group-administered surveys. Surveys that are conducted following a test screening of a film or television program are also viewed as group-administered surveys. The researcher or his/her research team member usually introduces the purpose and sponsor of the survey and then administers the questionnaire to the group of respondents.

The group-administered survey method has two main advantages. The first is the good response rate that is usually acquired. Since respondents have been recruited specifically for the purpose of taking the survey, they are more apt to complete the surveys as requested. Another advantage is that if questions arise concerning the questionnaire during the administration of the survey, a research team member is on-hand to answer the questions.

The group-administered survey method has two main disadvantages. The first that, because respondents are taking the survey together, the potential exists for interactions among the respondents. They might make comments while taking the survey and influence the responses of other participants. Where a potential for such problems exists, it is up to the research team member who is administering the survey to make sure that comments are not made during the taking of the survey. Another possible disadvantage is the costs that might be involved. Although group-administered surveys can be easily executed, depending on the survey design, several group-administered sessions might be needed; and travel expenses might be incurred. With the availability of the Internet and the cost-effective manner in which surveys can be conducted via the Internet, some researchers have opted to go with online-surveys instead.

Online Survey

Online surveys have become increasingly popular over the last several years, with some speculating that the method will eventually replace all survey data collection methods (Couper, 2000).

Several approaches exist in online surveys. Although non-scientific in nature, an approach that is frequently used is the placement of a survey link on popular Web sites or portals with an invitation to users to participate in the survey. For example, a researcher who is interested in learning about the music preferences of youngsters might post a link on Facebook or on YouTube's Web site inviting users to participate in the survey. A more scientific approach involves acquiring a list of e-mail addresses (i.e., a sampling frame) and then inviting a random sample of those listed to participate in the survey. An e-mail message is often sent with a URL included for accessing the survey site. Access can be limited to only those who are invited to participate in the survey by providing unique user IDs and passwords. An example of this approach would be a researcher obtaining a comprehensive list of student e-mail addresses at a particular university and then sending e-mail solicitations to a randomly selected sample of those addresses.

One of the reasons why online surveys have become so popular is the potential to access a large number of respondents at one time at much lower costs than with other survey data collection methods (Huang, 2006). The data from the online surveys can also be automatically entered into a software program for analysis, saving the labor costs involved in data entry. In addition, visuals or audio can be utilized as part of the survey.

Online surveys have three main disadvantages. The key one is related to the fact that a large number of individuals still do not have access to or do not use the Internet. For researchers who are interested in carrying out probability-based surveys, coverage error (i.e., the sample is not representative of the population of interest) can be a major problem. Response bias can also be a problem. People with lower levels of education or those who are less computer savvy have been found to be less likely to respond to online surveys (Dillman, 2007). Another drawback is that the online approach requires that the survey be fairly short in length (Couper, Traugott, & Lamias, 2001). If the survey is too long, respondents might be tempted to exit the site mid-way through the survey.

See Figure 3 on the next page for a summary of the advantages and disadvantages of survey approaches.

DATA ANALYSIS After survey data are collected, several software programs are available for data analysis. For the closed-ended questions that have numerals assigned to each response category, if the researcher is simply interested in conducting descriptive analyses such as generating frequency figures and distributions of responses, Microsoft's Excel program might suffice. For carrying out more sophisticated statistical analyses, however, the researcher is better off using such programs as SPSS, SAS, or SUDAAN.

SPSS, developed by the SPSS Corporation, is a frequently used program that allows a large number of statistical analyses and can produce various graphics, including pie charts and bar graphs. For example, a researcher can take a few variables and examine how they are correlated or associated with other variables. The researcher can see if respondents who were more likely to respond in one direction (e.g., express agreement) with one question are more likely to respond in another direction (e.g., express disagreement) with another question. The researcher can also analyze the extent to which certain variables (e.g., level of income, gender, ideological views, etc.) can serve as predictors of another variable (e.g., likelihood of supporting a controversial measure to censor certain programming content).

SAS, from the SAS Institute, can perform all of the statistical analyses that

Figure 3: Advantages and Disadvantages of Survey Data Collection Methods

	Advantages	Disadvantages
Mail Survey	• Less costly than telephone or personal interview • Respondents have more time to contemplate questions • Respondents might feel less inhibited since interviewer is not present	• Low response rate • Low motivation to take survey • Response bias (e.g., More educated might be more likely to take survey) • Delays in survey returns
Telephone Survey	• Good response rate • Data are collected in time-efficient manner • Interviewer can probe respondents • Interviewer can urge respondents to participate	• Technology-related difficulties in reaching respondents • Length of questions must be short • Does not allow usage of visuals
Personal Interview	• Good response rate • Interviewer can build rapport with respondent • Allows usage of visuals and audio	• High costs • Consumes time • Response bias (e.g., respondents might provide socially desirable responses)
Group-administered Survey	• Good response rate • Researcher available to answer questions from respondents	• Potential interaction between respondents • Potential high costs
Online Survey	• Can access large number of respondents at one time • Low costs in data collection • Data can be automatically entered into program for analysis • Allows usage of visuals and audio	• Not all potential respondents have Internet access or use the Internet • Response bias (e.g., people who are not computer savvy might not respond) • Survey length must be short

SPSS can perform and even more. It is a powerful statistical program that allows researchers to handle more sophisticated data analysis than SPSS can. Any data that are entered into SPSS can be easily transferred into the SAS program.

SUDAAN, developed by RTI International, can also deal with esoteric statistical analysis. It is particularly deft at handling samples drawn from complex survey designs such as cluster samples and stratified samples.

In the case of open-ended questions, both SPSS and SAS provide programs that allow the researcher to conduct a text analysis. The *SPSS Text Analysis for Surveys* can categorize open-ended survey responses based on wording and whether or not the responses are negative or positive. *SAS Text Miner* assists the researcher in conducting a semantic analysis by uncovering certain themes in the open-ended survey responses, clustering the themes into categories, and then finding relationships among the themes.

Other useful programs are WordStat and NVivo. *WordStat,* produced by Provalis Research, allows text analysis of open-ended responses. With it, the research-er can create a predetermined list of categories (i.e., a dictionary of words and phrases) and search for those categories within the responses. Like WordStat, *NVivo*, created by QSR International, can classify and sort responses to open-ended questions. It also permits the researcher to look for associations between certain words or phrases.

IMPROVING SURVEY RESULTS

Strategies for conducting survey research and techniques for data analysis are continually improving. Ways to accentuate the advan-tages and overcome the disadvantages of each survey approach are always being discussed and devised.

If time and budget permit, in order to overcome some of the pres-ent disadvantages associated with certain survey methods, it is advisable to try to combine survey methods (Dillman, 1978; Dillman, 2007; Fowler, 2002). For exam-ple, because of the ease and low costs involved in collecting data through online surveys, some researchers might want to consider combining this method with another method such as the telephone method. As mentioned earlier, not all indi-viduals choose to use the Internet. By also using a telephone approach, the re-searcher could contact members of the population sample who did not respond to an online survey request.

Regardless of the methods used or the scope of the survey design, what should always remain constant is the care that is taken to ensure that each stage of a survey is conducted in the most appropriate way possible to result in useful information. The initial focus should be on the exact objectives of the survey, and then the following phases of the survey process should reflect those objectives. Even if technology advances to the point where the administration of surveys is even easier than it is presently, researchers should always strive to create substan-tive surveys that are designed to provide illumination on public knowledge or be-havior.

TO LEARN MORE

www.aapor.org/resources

Biember, P.P., & Lyberg, L.E. (2003). *Introduction to survey quality*. New York: John Wiley & Sons.

Conrad, F.G., & Schober, M.F. (2000). Clarifying question meaning in a household tele-phone survey. *Public Opinion Quarterly, 64*(1), 1-28.

Couper, M.P. (1997). Survey introductions and data quality. *Public Opinion Quarterly, 61*(2), 317-338.

Couper, M.P. (2008). Web survey methods. *Public Opinion Quarterly, 72*(5), 831-835.

Delva, J., Allen-Meares, P., & Momper, S.L. (2010). *Cross-cultural research*. New York: Oxford University Press.

Lavine, D., & Maynard, D.W. (2001). Standardization vs. rapport: Respondent laughter and interviewer reaction during telephone surveys. *American Sociological Review, 66*(3), 453-479.

Schrum, L.J. (2007). The implications of survey method for measuring cultivation effects. *Human Communication Research, 33*, 64-80.

Smith, T.W. (2003). Developing comparable questions in cross-national surveys. In J.A. Harkness, F.JR. Van de Vijver, & P.H. Mohler (Eds.), *Cross-cultural survey methods* (69-91). Hoboken, NJ: John Wiley & Sons, Inc.

van Kammen, W.B., & Stouthamer-Loeber, M. (1998). Mail surveys. In L. Bickman, & D.J. Rog (Eds.), *Handbook of applied social research methods* (399-428). Thousand Oaks, CA: Sage Publications.

Wilson, D.C. (2010). Perceptions about the amount of interracial prejudice depend on racial group membership and question order. *Public Opinion Quarterly*, 74(20), 344-356.

REFERENCES

Baran, S.J., & Davis, D.K. (2005). *Mass communication theory* (4th ed.). Belmont, CA: Wadsworth/Thomson.

Berry, J.M. (2002). Validity and reliability issues in elite interviewing. *P.S.: Political Science and Politics*, 35(4), 679-682.

Biemer, P.P., & Lyberg, LE. (2003). *Introduction to survey quality*. New York: John Wiley & Sons.

Church, A.H. (1993). Incentives in mail surveys: A meta-analysis. *Public Opinion Quarterly*, 57(1), 62-79.

Collins, D. (2003). Pretesting survey instruments: An overview of cognitive methods. *Quality of Life Research*, 12(3), 229-238.

Couper, M.P. (2000). Web survey: A review of methods and approaches. *Public Opinion Quarterly*, 64(4), 464-494.

Couper, M.P., Traugott, M.W., & Lamias, M.J. (2001). Web survey design and administration. *Public Opinion Quarterly*, 65(2), 230-253.

Czaja, R., & Blair, J. (2005). *Designing surveys: A guide to decisions and procedures* (2nd ed.). Thousand Oaks, CA: Pine Forge Press.

Dillman, D.A. (1978). *Mail and telephone surveys: The total design method*. New York: John Wiley & Sons.

Dillman, D.A. (2007). *Mail and internet surveys: The tailored design method* (2nd ed.). New York: John Wiley & Sons.

Fowler, F.J. (2002). *Survey Research Methods* (3rd ed.). Thousand Oaks, CA: Sage.

Harrison, K. (2000). The body electric: Thin-ideal media and eating disorders in adolescents. *Journal of Communication*, 50(3), 119-143.

Huang, H.M. (2006). Do print and web surveys provide the same results? *Computers in Human Behavior*, 22, 334-350.

Mangione, T.W. (1998). Methods for sampling and interviewing in telephone surveys. In L. Bickman, & D.J. Rog (Eds.), *Handbook of applied social research methods* (429-472). Thousand Oaks, CA: Sage Publications.

MSNBC.COM (2006). *Is your privacy important? Are you losing it?* Retrieved on September 7, 2007, from www.msnbc.com/id/14850268

Sudman, S., & Bradburn, N.M. (1982). *Asking questions: A practical guide to questionnaire design*. San Francisco, CA: Jossey-Bass Publishers.

Tourangeau, R., Rips, L., & Rasinski, K. (2000). *The psychology of survey response*. New York: Cambridge University Press.

U.S. Census Bureau (2006). *Census 2000 demographic profile highlights*. Retrieved on September 7, 2007, from http://factfinder.census.gov

11

Experiment

Every research method benefits from certain strengths and suffers from certain limitations. Thus, the choice of methodology for a given project should be guided by which methodological strengths are most valuable to the study.

In terms of experimentation, its greatest strengths are control and causation. Ideally, an experiment allows a researcher to control every possible variable and measure only the effects of the independent variable being studied. By controlling outside influences and systematically manipulating variables of interest, experiments allow researchers to make inferences about causation. That is, a researcher can feel confident that her manipulations caused any changes observed in the dependent variable because every other possible cause was controlled.

When we do research about how people communicate, we want to know how they realistically use communications in their daily lives. Therefore, measuring behavior in actual homes with actual consumers clearly tells us the most about how people communicate, watch television, surf the Web, and read the newspaper. When we do research in these natural settings, the studies tell us a great deal about the outside, or external, world.

Thus we say that these types of research projects possess a great deal of *external validity*. That is, they generalize to the real world.

Unfortunately for the communications researcher, the real world is a moving target. Consider a multi-million dollar national television advertising campaign. Months of planning precede any advertising campaign. After the research results are in, advertisements are written, directors and actors are hired, commercials are filmed, television time is purchased to air the ads, and finally the ads are shown on national television. This is a long process. A lot can — and usually does — happen between idea and execution. Along the way, advertising campaigns succeed and fail for a host of reasons. Some of those reasons have to do with the advertisements, but some of the reasons have nothing to do with the ads. Instead some third variable, or *confounding variable*, may have doomed the campaign, and this

By Samuel D. Bradley
Texas Tech University

confounding variable may have had nothing to do with the ads themselves.

Consider the case of Old Milwaukee's Swedish Bikini Team advertising campaign in 1991. The campaign was a textbook example of using sexual appeals to sell beer, a common appeal in this product category. Although the amount of sex portrayed in beer advertisements has varied over the years, scantily clad women are a common theme in marketing beer (Chambers, 2006). These sexual portrayals draw a good deal of criticism, but there was no reason to suspect that the Swedish Bikini Team ads would have caused a stir. Unfortunately for Old Milwaukee and its advertising agency, the campaign came as America was mired in controversy surrounding attorney Anita Hill's sexual harassment allegations against U.S. Supreme Court nominee Clarence Thomas. The risqué ads likely would have been brushed aside in any other year, but they came just as the country closely contemplated its sexual morality (Chambers, 2006). Overall, the campaign failed to achieve the desired success.

But what did we learn? Did we learn something about sexual portrayals in beer advertisements, or did we learn something about sexual portrayals in beer advertisements *released while a country contemplates its morality*? The truth is that we will never know. There were too many variables at work and not enough control.

CONTROL

A primary benefit of experimental design is that you can *control* almost everything. A major detriment is that you *have* to control everything. For researchers with relatively "well behaved" subjects — such as chemistry and geology — it is comparatively easy to control actions. The combination of two chemicals under similar conditions in Boise, Idaho, should easily replicate in Athens, Georgia. With communication phenomena, however, all other things beyond your main manipulations are almost never equal.

Consider a study of broadcast journalism where researchers want to know whether visual imagery overpowers the text of the news story read by the news anchor (Bucy & Bradley, 2004). If news anchors read a largely negatively toned story while the background images show a smiling politician — which is incongruent with the story — it is possible that viewers' cognitive processing of the story will be impaired. Consider for a moment how you might go about designing an experiment to test this idea. Let's assume that it is not possible to find a videotape of every type of newscast that you hope to show. Broadcast journalists are in the business of delivering the news, not creating a variety of types of newscasts. So in this case, you would have to edit existing news broadcasts to match the design of the experiment. For example, you could combine footage from one news anchor introducing the story with background video from a different news story. However, the editing could make the resulting material look unauthentic. This editing would introduce an element of artificiality; but it also would allow you to have precise control over the *stimulus material*, that is, the material shown to participants as the experimental treatment.

THE POWER OF THE STIMULUS

For any media-related study, stimulus materials are crucial. Many communications researchers want to examine something about actual media messages. They are interested in Web pages, news releases,

many cases, participants will try to deduce the "correct" answer and supply it when asked. If the purpose of the experiment is obvious, then it is easy for participants to guess the answer the researchers are seeking. Transparent experiments will then tend to produce the desired result not because the experiment is successful but because the participants were trying to be helpful and provided the desired response.

The Importance of Experimental Design

Many methods exist to control for experimental demand. However, the best one is clever, thorough experimental design. Returning to the example of sexual portrayals in advertisements, we can assume that many participants will quickly discern the purpose of the study if it involves viewing 30 advertisements — 15 of which feature graphic portrayals of sex, 15 of which feature no sexual references whatsoever — and if each ad is followed by questions about the participants' attitudes toward women. Indeed, it would be a rare participant who failed to uncover the purpose of this experiment.

A better experimental design would involve asking several questions after each advertisement so that sex-related questions were intermixed with questions not related to sex.

An even better design would make the dichotomy between heavy sexual portrayals and no sexual portrayals less obvious. Along these lines some studies include ads with sexual innuendo and multiple levels of sexual content. Another possibility is to embed the advertisements within an hour-long television drama so that the experience is more like real television viewing and less likely to focus 100% of the participants' attention on the advertising.

The point here is not to make recommendations about the perfect experiment to study sexual portrayals in advertisements. Indeed, no such study exists. Rather the point is to illustrate that experimental design involves a long series of choices. Each choice can strengthen the experiment in one way, but that choice is also likely to make the experiment vulnerable to other criticisms. This is one reason that research questions are often answered through a *series* of related experiments.

Using Deception

Another way to control for experimental demand is through the use of *deception*, which is especially common in psychology. In experiments employing deception, the true purpose of the experiment is hidden from the participants, who are instead told a cover story about the experiment's purpose. Deception generally is used when researchers believe that there is no way to conduct the experiment if the participants are aware of the genuine purpose of the study. Concealing the purpose of the study is important in social psychological studies because awareness would dramatically alter the outcome. One would not expect, for example, to be able to successfully conduct a study on whether participants mimic behavior of attractive people but not unattractive people if the participants were told the purpose at the outset. Instead, participants might be told that they are participating in a mock interview, and no mention would be made of attractiveness or mimicry. (See, for example, Casa de Calvo, 2007.)

One potential problem can be one participant telling another about the experiment. When participants are drawn from a large population, such as a metropolitan area, and have little chance to interact with one another, information sharing is not a problem. In settings where participants are likely to know one another — as is the case with much university research — there is a danger of one participant revealing the purpose to a future participant before she or he has the chance to participate.

Concealment

In addition to deception, experiments sometimes employ *conceal-ment*, where the genuine purpose of the experiment is concealed, but the participants are not told a lie. In such instances, researchers do not feel the need to mask the actual purpose of the study, but there also is a worry that explicitly drawing attention to the purpose of the study might bias results. In this case, the true purpose of the experiment is concealed until after data are collected, at which time the participants are *debriefed*, or told the actual purpose of the experiment.

Some studies on selective exposure have attempted to obscure the true purpose of the study through concealment. In these types of studies, participants are led into a room made to resemble a typical living room. A couch and a coffee table covered with magazines are often present. A television is present, and participants are told that they may watch if they so choose. Because these studies often involve college students, participants are sometimes told that they may do homework if they choose. The dependent variable usually involves the participants' media choices (such as television or magazines) or which television content they select. By providing magazines and newspapers and mentioning homework, the researcher hopes to conceal a focus on television viewing.

Deception and concealment are frequently used in communications research when attitudes or sensitive subject matters, such as racism or media bias, are involved. For example, one study was designed to determine whether the race of people shown in news photographs affected participants' perceptions (Gibson & Zillmann, 2000). The researchers wrote a fictitious news story about a disease spread by ticks. Although victim ethnicity was not mentioned in the news story, the accompanying photographs varied the number of white victims and black victims shown. Participants then estimated the risk of the disease to various minority and nonminority populations. Following the experiment, "Respondents were debriefed about the deception entailed in the ... news report. It was explained that it was imperative to cover an issue that is novel and about which respondents cannot have pre-existing beliefs" (Gibson & Zillmann, 2000, p. 359). The study revealed that showing a greater number of minority victims in photographs made participants report that minorities were more at risk, even though there was no mention of race or ethnicity in the story. It is extremely unlikely that this result would have been obtained if participants had been told the purpose of the study in advance.

ETHICAL CONCERNS

The difficulty of obtaining data without deception or concealment does not excuse researchers from ethical considerations, nor does it provide blanket permission to employ deception or concealment. Research in most academic institutions is governed by an institutional review board (IRB) tasked with protecting human participants. The process of obtaining approval to conduct research typically involves many bureaucratic hurdles. They are in place to prevent the repetition of previous abuses of the rights of human participants that have happened in the name of science.

The Milgram Experiment

One of the most cited potential abuses of participants' rights occurred in the laboratory of former Yale psychologist Stanley Milgram. In part due to the Nazi Holocaust, Milgram wondered why seemingly ordinary people would commit atrocious acts in the name of obedience to authority. To study this phenomenon, Milgram (1965) designed an experiment wherein participants would be required to administer an electric shock as part of a learning test. Participants were told that they were randomly assigned to be either a "teacher" or a "learner," when in fact the participants were always the teacher and a *confederate*, or associate of the researcher pretending not to be affiliated, always assumed the role of learner. Participants were seated in front of a machine labeled "shock generator," and the confederate was placed in an "electric chair" in another room not visible to the participant. The participants then engaged in a prescripted series of questions and answers. The confederate was not connected to any machine, and his standardized answers were played back via audiotape. This allowed each participant to hear the exact same responses.

As the experiment unfolded, a research assistant wearing a lab coat and appearing very official stood over the participant. The entire point was to determine how far the participants could be pushed. Mistakes by the learner — which were scripted — were punished by what seemed to be an electric shock. The voltage on the fake shock generator ranged from 15 volts to 450 volts and bore descriptions ranging from "Slight Shock" to "Danger: Severe Shock." In the scripted responses, the learner demanded to quit at 150 volts. He physically cried out and said he could not stand the pain at 180 volts. The verbal responses ceased at 300 volts, and each subsequent shock was met with nothing but a shriek of pain. Yet the participants were ordered to proceed. In most cases, they asked to stop. In each case, the all-male participants were told "You have no other choice, you must go on!" In the original study, 65% of participants continued all the way to the maximum shock, 450 volts.

Participants were debriefed after the study, but the psychological harm that they endured can never be known. Milgram reported that follow-up questionnaires revealed that 83.7% of participants said they were "glad" that they participated. Given the demand characteristics and social desirability of that answer, one cannot know the true figure. When the experiment ended, 65% of the participants knew something new about themselves: that an authority figure could bully them into committing an atrocity. They were willing to deliver dangerous and potentially fatal shocks to a seemingly unconscious man simply because they were instructed to do so. This is likely something that most people would prefer not to know about themselves.

Sex, Violence, and Ethics

Milgram's shock generator and research lab may, at first, seem largely irrelevant to the communication researcher; but this is not the case. Many of the landmark pornography studies of the 1970s and 1980s would draw much greater scrutiny if conducted today. Several of them took ordinary college sophomores and exposed them to hours and hours of pornography.

Sometimes the pornography was relatively tame by industry standards, but sometimes it included fetish acts, such as bestiality. If these studies were proposed in a university setting today, they probably would not be permitted because of the potential harms of viewing large doses of extreme pornography. The same is true of studies of media violence.

Many researchers want to study the effects of sex and violence because they believe that the effects might indeed be harmful. However, such experiments create an ethical dilemma for researchers. If you believe that there are harmful effects from viewing violence and pornography, then how can you in good conscience design studies that require participants to view such material? The researcher is knowingly and purposively subjecting the experimental participants to what is believed to be harmful. In these cases, the institutional review board often requires researchers to take steps to minimize the risk to participants. In the private sector, there usually is no such protection for research participants.

CLASSIC EXPERIMENTAL DESIGNS

You are now aware of the most common potential problems when designing an experiment. For any given project, some concerns will be more worrisome than others. Because the combination of concerns is unique to each project, there is no single ideal experimental design. Instead the research team makes decisions about design based on the factors most interesting to the study.

The most authoritative source on how to conduct experiments is Campbell and Stanley's (1963) *Experimental and quasi-experimental designs for research*. Although the subject matter of experiments has changed dramatically since they wrote that book, the ways in which to conduct an experiment have remained the same.

Campbell and Stanley outlined three pre-experimental and three experimental designs. We'll use the following notations to illustrate each of the six designs. In keeping with standard experimental design notation, the *experimental treatment* or *independent variable* is denoted as X. An *observation* — or measurement of the *dependent variable* — is denoted as O. Finally, random assignment to a treatment condition is denoted at R. The names of the designs that follow are taken from Campbell and Stanley (1963).

Pre-Experimental Designs
One-Shot Case Study

One-Shot Case Study. Consider the case where a small daily newspaper begins publishing a Saturday edition when it had previously published only 6 days a week. Six months after the introduction of the Saturday paper, the publisher looks at sales data of single copy sales. The relationship can be diagrammed in the following manner:

$$X \quad O$$

The introduction of the Saturday edition is shown as X, and the observation of sales six months later is the O. The important question is whether any inferences can be drawn about the relationship between the two. In truth, very little can be determined because we have no frame of reference to which we can compare the Saturday sales figures. Thus, at best we can attempt to make a comparison between sales data now and six months ago. We might also compare Saturday sales to those of other newspapers or to previous sales on Friday or Monday. Most comparisons available to the one-shot case study are unsatisfying. Campbell and Stanley (1963) call this design a "minimum reference point." Unfortunately, many communication research projects involve just such a simplistic design.

One-Group Pretest-Post-test   Although the *one-group pretest-post-test design* is still not a true experiment, we can add a little complexity by measuring a variable before and after some event. In the restaurant business, for example, same-store sales are often measured before and after an advertising campaign. Such a study is not truly an experiment since all consumers might or might not have been exposed to the advertisements. So comparisons are limited. With national advertising campaigns, not much more is possible. The design for such a study can be diagrammed as follows:

$$O_1 \quad X \quad O_2$$

Any difference in sales between the observation at Time 1, O_1, and the observation at Time 2, O_2, may have been due to the advertising campaign, X — but it also might have been due to a host of other factors. There might have been a mad cow scare. There may have been new studies released about the negative effects of cholesterol. Or the competition might have launched a better advertising campaign. These are all problems of *history*, and they cannot be controlled here. In addition to the independent variable of interest, the history of the consumers changed between Time 1 and Time 2. In this design, none of the rival hypotheses can be ruled out.

Another problem inherent in this design is the possibility of *testing effects*. This is not a problem in determining same-store sales, but it might be a problem if the study involved attitudes about the restaurant before and after the advertising campaign. In the case of attitudes, the pretest, O_1, would have introduced participants to the questions. When the researcher returned to ask about their attitudes for the post-test, O_2, after the campaign, the questions would not be new. Participants would have experience with the questions. They may have been thinking about the questions during the campaign whereas there was no opportunity to think about the questions before the campaign. The questions also might have closely focused the participants on the purpose of the experiment.

Participants also may have changed in other ways during the experiment. They may have grown tired of the questions or have been bored by them during the post-test. These are problems of *maturation*. The participants have somehow matured or changed over the course of the study. By design, participants will be older during the post-test. But they also may have changed in other ways. And it is difficult to know whether any results obtained are due to the independent variable or due to maturation.

Static-Group Comparison   Now consider the case where we want to compare two groups and a given independent variable (the X) is true for only one of the groups. We could use a *static-group comparison design*. Let's say that scientists have invented a pill that will supposedly increase people's IQ. To test whether the pill indeed will work such wonders, an experiment can be designed in which we gather a pool of participants and give one group of them the pill but nothing to the other group (the comparison or control group). After the first group takes the pill, we will give both groups an intelligence test to compare their scores. This gives us the following design:

$$X \quad O_1$$
$$O_2$$

In this instance, the X represents the IQ pill, or the treatment, and the Os represent IQ measurements of the two groups. Notice that a pretest, or pre-measurement, is not included in this design.

In this design, we are mostly interested in determining whether the two groups are different after the treatment, in this case, after the first group takes the IQ pill. Typically, we measure the differences by comparing the group means. Let's say that the study shows that, before the first group takes the pill, the mean for the group is 107, whereas it is 105 for the second group. It is tempting to say that the IQ pill works, because the mean for the first group is bigger than for the second. There are, however, many potential *confounds*, or factors other than the independent variable (the IQ pill in this case), that may affect the scores. For example, the two groups may be different to begin with. Because there is no pre-test, we don't know if the first group is smarter or, actually, dumber. It could be that the true average in the first group is 102 and that the IQ pill really does work — boosting everyone's IQ by 5. It could also be that the average in the first group is 115 to begin with and that the IQ pill dramatically *reduces* people's IQ by 8 on average, making them dumber. We cannot be certain.

Genuine Experimental Designs

Along with the pre-experimental designs described above, there are a number of what we might call "genuine" designs. Let's look at several of them.

Randomization and Control Groups

Many of the problems with the above designs can be solved with *randomization* and a *control group*.

It is worth taking a moment to consider the difference between random and arbitrary assignment. In a true *random* assignment, every member of the population has an equal chance of being selected (or being assigned to an experimental condition), and there are no biases. Random is not the same as *arbitrary*, which involves assignment with no apparent pattern or system. Humans are incapable of random assignment without the help of some external device, such as a fair coin, a pair of dice, a computer, or a random number table.

An experiment must involve true random assignment. If the experimenter looks at a participant when s/he walks through the door and selects an experimental condition, then the experiment is not random at all. The experimenter may be selecting based on some unconscious — and unknowable — predisposition toward hair color, eye color, or some other factor. This type of arbitrary assignment introduces an unknown bias and contradicts the intention of random assignment.

If participants are truly randomly assigned to groups, then differences with demographic variables, preexisting attitudes, and other individual difference variables will tend to equalize between groups. Sample size is especially relevant. For a discussion of sampling, you may wish to reread Profs. Peirce and Martinez's Chapter 8 in this book. As samples become larger, the researcher can be more confident that individual difference variables will be equal between groups.

Let's see how randomization and control groups are used in experimental design.

Pretest-Post-test with Control Group Consider a study on media violence. Suppose a researcher wants to know whether watching media violence makes teenagers more aggressive. The researcher decides to use a *pretest-post-test with control group design.* S/he recruits a group of 100 teens to watch TV programs. Upon arrival, half are randomly assigned to watch a violent program, and the other half are randomly assigned to watch nothing. In order to ensure that the groups do not differ in aggression before the viewing session, each participant fills out an aggression questionnaire before viewing. We can denote this experimental design in the following way (with R indicating random assignment of participants):

$$R \quad O_1 \quad X \quad O_2$$
$$R \quad O_3 \quad \quad O_4$$

Here one group (R) is randomly assigned to watch the media violence, the X, and the control group (R) watches nothing. Pre-existing differences in aggression can be assessed by comparing the two groups' pretest scores, O_1 and O_3. With 50 participants in each group and true random assignment, one would not expect to see a difference in pretest aggression. Following the viewing period, differences in aggression can be measured by comparing the pretest and post-test scores — O_1 and O_2 — for the experimental treatment group. If there is a difference between these aggression scores, it is likely due to the violent television content. However, without the control group, one cannot rule out history effects. Recall that there is sometimes a problem when asking the same questions twice. Perhaps there was no effect of violent television on aggression, but having to fill out the same questions a second time angered the participants, which made them aggressive.

This is a classic history effect that can be checked with the control group. If the increase in aggression were due to having to fill out the questions twice, then the control group should also show a difference between pretest and post-test scores. If there is no difference between O_3 and O_4, then the researcher has strong evidence that observed differences in the experimental group are indeed due to the effect of violent television, X.

With true communication research variables, however, there is rarely such a thing as a genuine control group. Ask yourself what would actually serve as a control group to watching violent television. In the example above, the control group watched nothing. This is boring, and participants would have grown restless staring at a blank wall. This restlessness might even have angered the participants, which may have made them aggressive. So in addition to a true control group, this design might have included a condition that involved watching a calming nature program about flowers. Here television viewing is controlled, but the violent nature of the television *content* is manipulated. For these reasons, communications research is a challenging enterprise, and different researchers may choose very different experimental designs to shed light on the same hypotheses.

The pretest-post-test design with a control group has one serious limitation: the pretest. Although the presence of a pretest allows for meaningful comparisons, it adds its own problem of history. This design controls for history since both the treatment and control groups were asked questions during the pretest and the post-test. However, controlling the history effect does not eliminate it. In order to ensure that observed differences are not due to history effects, one needs an equal number of groups that were not subject to a pretest.

The **Solomon Four-Group Design** replicates the pretest-post-test design with control group design and includes an additional treatment group and control group that are not exposed to the pretest.

Solomon Four-Group Design

$$R \quad O_1 \quad X \quad O_2$$
$$R \quad O_3 \quad \quad O_4$$
$$R \quad \quad X \quad O_5$$
$$R \quad \quad \quad O_6$$

Although this diagram of the Solomon (1949) four-group design can be intimidating, the design is extremely powerful because it allows the researcher to make confident statements about which factors caused any observed differences.

All of the comparisons described in the previous section are still applicable in the Solomon design. However, history effects can be compared two ways. If answering the questions twice produces an effect, there should be a difference between O_4 and O_6. If there is no difference between these measurements, it does not appear as if there is an effect of history by itself.

However, the experimental condition might combine with a history effect to alter results. In this case, perhaps violent television alone is not enough to make these adolescents aggressive. Likewise, answering the questions twice might not be enough to make the participants aggressive.

However, watching violent television *and* filling out the questions twice might have been enough to push our participants over the edge. In this case, there should be a difference between groups O_2 and O_5. This is called an *interaction effect* because two independent variables interact in their effect upon the dependent variable.

This ability to examine several possible confounding variables is a particular strength of the Solomon design. This strength comes with a cost, however. If the pretest-post-test with control group design in the previous section required 100 participants, the Solomon design would require 200 participants. If the researchers are paying participants, then this cost is doubled. Experimental facilities will be tied up for twice as much time, and twice as many hours of staffing time will be required to conduct the experiment.

Despite the fact that Solomon wrote about this design more than six decades ago, it is conspicuously absent from communications research. Its absence is especially curious given that Solomon specifically recommended the design for "experiments on induced changes in existing attitudes" (p. 137). Although there is no way to know for certain, it may be the comparatively high burden on resources that prevents the Solomon design from being employed as often as it should be in communications research.

Post-test-Only Control Group The final experimental design outlined by Campbell and Stanley (1963) addressed the problem of the pretest leading to history effects by eliminating the pretest. In this sense, the *post-test-only control group design* represents only the final two groups of the Solomon four-group design and is denoted as follows:

$$R \quad X \quad O_1$$
$$R \quad \quad \quad O_2$$

This type of design — or a variant of it — is common in communications research. It solves the problem of the pretest cluing participants to the purpose of the study. This is important both when repeated questions will fatigue the participants and when repetition may cause participants to focus unduly on the manipulations of the independent variable. For example, a study of first-person shooter video games asked participants during the post-test to report their emotions while hunting for an opponent, upon encountering an opponent, while fighting an opponent, and after killing the opponent (Lang & Schneider, 2001). It may have been difficult for participants to answer these questions during a pretest — especially if they had never played such a game. The greater concern was that a pretest might have caused participants to focus their attention on their emotions while playing the game instead of playing naturally.

The limitation of this design is that it provides no check for preexisting differences between the experimental and control groups. When sample sizes are large, this concern is somewhat lessened because differences between the two groups diminsh. Without an actual pretest, though, there is no way to ensure that observed post-test differences were not, in fact, due to preexisting differences.

MULTIPLE TREATMENT LEVELS AND FACTORIAL DESIGNS

If you were to head to the university library with a list of communication journals, it would take some time to locate an exact example of each of these designs. In part this is due to the complicated nature of communication stimuli. Communication, at its core, is about messages (Shannon, 1948), and these messages are neither simple nor straightforward. Researchers in some fields — psychologists, for example — can often reduce a stimulus down to its most elemental form (e.g., a single word presented on a screen), but such simplicity is impossible for communication researchers. Because most of them want to draw conclusions about actual human communication, they tend to study actual messages in the ways that actual humans interact with them. This is a complicated enterprise.

Multiple Levels of Independent Variables

In order to study communication, we often look at varying (and multiple) levels of the independent variable. Returning to our example of pornography, we see a subject matter that drew much interest in the

1970s and 1980s and is drawing increased interest today due to the Internet. Many people probably watch no pornography whatsoever. Some people may have had very limited exposure to pornography, whereas some people are massive consumers of it. In order to design an experiment to study this controversial topic, the researcher must determine how much pornography should be shown in the experimental condition? Should participants be shown a single scene, 30 minutes, 2 hours, or 40 hours of adult films in order to make a meaningful comparison to the control group? The futility of this decision is obvious. A study that uses any one of those durations is not a study simply about pornography but a study about exposure to a very specific amount of pornography.

Thus, experiments often turn to multiple levels of an independent variable so that the researchers can vary the levels. Zillmann and Bryant (1984), for example, used multiple levels to examine how exposure to pornography affected physiological and attitudinal responses a week later. All participants came to 6 one-hour viewing sessions in consecutive weeks. The first group saw an "innocuous" film during each session, and this group served as the control. The second group saw pornography during half of the sessions and innocuous films during the other half of the sessions. The final group saw pornography during all six sessions. The two pornography-viewing groups were dubbed "intermediate" and "massive exposure," respectively; and the design allowed the researchers to examine differences attributable to levels of pornography viewing. As expected, the massive exposure condition exhibited greater effects than the intermediate exposure condition. This study is arguably an extension of the post-test-only control group design. However, it is questionable whether watching innocuous films is indeed a control condition as outlined above.

Multiple Independent Variables

In addition to multiple levels of a single independent variable, researchers often want to study multiple independent variables simultaneously. Experiments that use multiple independent variables — or multiple factors — are called *factorial designs*. These designs allow researchers to examine whether any one factor affects the dependent variable, or whether two or more factors interact to affect the dependent variable. The classic factorial design involves two levels of two independent variables and is called the 2 x 2 (i.e., "two by two"). Countless graduate theses in communications research have employed the 2 x 2.

In order to illustrate the 2 x 2, consider a photojournalism study designed to investigate the effects of color photography and the presence of blood in photographs from combat zones on attitudes toward a war. In such a study, a publisher might want to know how newspaper coverage influences public opinions. If we have two types, usually called *levels*, of photography (color vs. black-and-white) and two types of blood presence (present and absent), we have the classic 2 x 2 and four possible photographs, as diagrammed in the figure on the next page.

Conducting an experiment that compares these four types of photographs would allow researchers to determine whether photography or the visible presence of blood affects attitudes or whether the two factors interacted to affect attitudes. That is, it is possible that the presence of blood is shocking only when it is in color.

		Blood Presence	
		Present	Absent
Photography	Black & White	Black & White Blood Present	Black & White Blood Absent
	Color	Color Blood Present	Color Blood Absent

The 2 x 2 is the basic factorial design; but the levels of factors can be increased, and the number of factors can be increased. A word of caution is merited here: Analysis has shown that increasing complexity of the experimental design increases the odds that the statistical analysis will find differences that are not real (i.e., Type I error) and fail to find differences that are real (i.e., Type II error) (Smith, Levine, Lachlan, & Fediuk, 2002). Prof. Sanders discusses such errors in Chapter 12 of this book.

REPEATED-MEASURES DESIGNS

Much of the logic of control groups depends upon random assignment. Experimental researchers hope that with relatively large sample sizes, individual differences will balance out between the treatment group and the control group.

However, if we don't have the luxury of large sample sizes, yet we want to control for individual differences, we can use *repeated-measures* experimental designs. Such designs allow researchers to take multiple measurements from the same participants. This type of design is sometimes called a *within-subjects* design because the independent variable varies within each subject, or participant.

In the strictest sense, both the pretest-post-test control group and the Solomon four-group designs are repeated-measures designs because they make multiple observations of the same participants. However, the use of repeated-measures designs allows for more interesting designs.

In some situations, it would be unrealistic to use a repeated-measure design. In medical studies, for example, one group often gets the treatment while another group receives a placebo, or a fake treatment, because giving the same participants both the treatment and the placebo would not work. However, this is not true of media messages. It is possible for the same participants to watch advertisements with sexual portrayals and advertisements without such portrayals — and we can still measure their reaction to both. In the medical example, on the other hand, if a participant were given both the treatment and a placebo, the researcher could not be certain about what the cause was of any particular effect.

A recent study of political advertising used this type of design. Each participant saw negative political ads, positive political ads, and ads that were neither negative nor positive (Bradley, Angelini, & Lee, 2007). The researchers were able to compare each participant's memory for negative ads with that participant's memory for positive ads. These data revealed that the negative ads were better remembered. This finding seems more plausible since all of the participants saw all the types of ads. If some participants had seen negative ads and some participants had seen positive ads, any observed differences could have been attributed to in-dividual differences between the groups.

Repeated-measures designs are common in studies when it makes sense to look at various levels of a stimulus. One study investigated the emotional re-sponses of college-age women as they watched televised sporting events with male and female athletes participating in masculine and feminine sports (Ange-lini, 2008). Here it made sense for participants to watch each type of sporting event. Had the study predicted that viewing female sporting events would cause young women to enroll in extracurricular sporting activities at a greater rate than if they had watched male sporting events, a repeated-measures design might have been ill-advised. By the end of the study, participants would have seen both types of sporting events (hopefully in equal numbers). So it would have been impossi-ble to attribute post-test differences in sports participation to a single type of por-trayal. For this type of research question, a design such as the no exposure/inter-mediate exposure/massive exposure used by Zillmann and Bryant (1984) would have been preferable.

Using Multiple Messages

Repeated-measure designs allow researchers to handle another im-portant concern to media studies that often is overlooked: using mul-tiple messages to represent one level of the independent variable. Let's look at an example. If you turn on your television, it will not take long to find an advertisement that features a minority actor. Likewise, it will not take long to find an advertisement that does not feature a minority actor. You could easily re-cord these two commercials and show them to two randomly assigned groups of participants. After each group viewed its commercial, you could have them fill out a questionnaire asking about attitudes toward minorities. Presume for a moment that you found differences in attitudes between the two groups. Can you then at-tribute these differences between portrayals to the presence or absence of minori-ties in the ads?

Many researchers believe that you would be unable to conclude anything from such a study. Although the two ads do indeed differ in terms of minorities portrayed, they are confounded on just about every other dimension that one could imagine. From the lighting of the set to the type of product advertised, these two advertisements are likely to represent the proverbial apple and orange. Any difference between viewers for the two types of ads is just as easily attributable to something such as differences in the number of trees included in the ads.

The simple — and far too seldom utilized — remedy is to include multiple messages representing each treatment condition (Reeves & Geiger, 1994). If you have a half dozen advertisements with minorities and six with no minorities, it is far less likely that the two groups of ads will systematically differ in other ways. That is, it is unlikely that all of the minority-present ads, for example, will have more trees than minority-absent ads. How many ads would you need? As with most factors in experimental design, the question is best answered by balancing what needs to be done with what can be done. In every case, however, the answer is "More than one" (Reeves & Geiger, 1994, p. 167).

Limitations of Repeated Measures

Repeated-measures studies are not without limitations. Perhaps the most serious limitation is that of testing effects, which was described earlier. By their very nature, repeated-measures studies require experimenters to take the same measurement at multiple different times. If you are a dietician weighing your participants, this is not a problem. Learning how the scale works does not change a participant's weight. But for the communications researcher, the problem is more serious. If I show you a print advertisement and then ask your attitudes about it, you are unlikely to view the second ad (i.e, the repeated measure) the same way. In fact, you might view that second ad and immediately ask yourself how it makes you feel. This was not the case for the first ad.

In addition, practical matters sometimes restrict the use of repeated-measures designs. Consider a study investigating the effects of negative political ads. Some people believe that negative ads make voters more likely to stay home on election day. To study this issue, you might design a study involving viewing negative ads and positive ads and then ask about voting intentions. However, it would not make sense to show all people both positive and negative ads. If you genuinely suspect that negative ads drive down voting intentions, then if you show everybody negative ads, voting intentions would be lowered for everyone — you would have no comparison to make. Instead, you would be better off to randomly assign some participants to see negative ads, some to see positive ads, and some to see no ads. With a large enough sample size, you could examine whether the negative ads actually lower voting intentions.

QUASI-EXPERIMENTAL DESIGNS

The best experiment is clearly one in which the researcher can control as many variables as possible. Although this is the ideal, many circumstances prevent complete control. For instance, the researcher may be unable to randomly assign participants to treatment conditions, or the researcher may not be able to precisely control the timing of the experimental treatment. Do such difficulties mean that the experimental method should be abandoned altogether? Simply put, no. Campbell and Stanley (1963) outlined several instances of *quasi-experimental designs*, where researchers can employ something similar to an experimental design without having complete control.

Time-Series Experiments

There are situations where researchers have a series of measurements before and after some experimental condition. These measurements stretch across time and can be depicted this way:

$$O_1 \quad O_2 \quad O_3 \quad O_4 \quad X \quad O_5 \quad O_6 \quad O_7 \quad O_8$$

Researchers can look at these observations over time to determine whether a significant difference occurs as a function of X. For example, a study of television news investigated the cognitive processing of news stories before and after a channel change (Lang et al., 2005). The investigators wanted to know whether attention drifts before a channel change and then re-engages after the change. They hypothesized that participants grow bored, leading them to change channels. To test this hypothesis, the researchers wrote questions testing memory for information contained in the news stories and then administered the questions at intervals. Then they recorded the times of channel changes. But they did not control *when* the participants would change channels. In order to test their hypothesis, the researchers had to examine the performance on the memory test before and after the channel changes. Results of this study suggest that attention was indeed waning in the time leading up to the channel change, and attention was re-engaged after the change. If the researchers had forced the participants to change channels at particular times, the study would not have provided insight into the cognitive processes that underlie channel changing because the changes would not have occurred at natural times. This quasi-experimental design allowed the researchers to examine the phenomenon in a more natural, free-choice environment.

Nonequivalent Control Group

In market research, companies often want to test differences in a product or a local advertising campaign. For example, two similar cities might be chosen, and one of the cities might receive a new product. This city is known as the test market. Obviously residents of the two cities were not randomly assigned. And although the cities are often selected to be similar, the participants selected are not exactly equivalent. Using a *nonequivalent control group design*, the study can be depicted as follows:

$$O_1 \quad X \quad O_2$$
$$O_3 \qquad\;\; O_4$$

This design differs from the Pretest-Post-test Design with Control Group primarily in that there is no random assignment here. Any given participant who walks into a restaurant, for example, cannot be randomly assigned to one of the two cities. Residents live where they live.

So this design allows one to test an X in the real world but removes some of the limitations seen in the one group pretest-post-test design, but it is not a true experimental design. This quasi-experimental design allows, for example, a major fast food company to test market a new sandwich in two — or more — similar markets. If sales increase in the market(s) with the new sandwich, the X, but sales remain steady or decrease in the markets without the new sandwich, the restaurant chain has some evidence that the new sandwich does indeed drive sales. However, the causal link is much weaker than if a true experimental design had been employed. Given the nature of the restaurant business, it would be impossible to administer a true experimental design in the real world. Thus, the nonequivalent control group design is much preferable to no study whatsoever.

In sum, we can conclude that experimental methodology provides researchers the opportunity to have great control over confounding variables and to make strong statements about the nature of causation. However, to use the methodology effectively, researchers must understand several key points. We can summarize them as follows:

1. Experiments require researchers to make difficult decisions about the relative importance of internal and external validity. Often, experimentalists are not so much interested in external validity as they are in establishing causal effects. Experiments conducted in the laboratory allow for a great degree of control and

thus allow researchers the opportunity to maximize internal validity. However, for most communications research, laboratory experiments are extremely artificial.

2. Conversely, field experiments allow for a more natural communications environment, which increases external validity. However, the lack of control in the field might lead to confounding variables affecting results.

3. For every study, researchers must balance the relative strengths of one design versus its relative weaknesses. Sometimes these choices are straightforward, but often there is no clear preferred alternative. When participants are randomly assigned experimental conditions and a control group is used, experiments can rule out confounding variables.

4. Usually, the more complex the design, the more participants are required and the greater the cost of the experiment.

5. Although repeated-measures designs can help reduce the number of participants required, these studies are more complicated to design and introduce their own limitations.

6. When investigating communications phenomena, the quality of the messages — or stimuli — is usually crucial to the success of the experiment.

7. Because any two messages are likely to vary on a number of dimensions, using multiple messages to represent a given experimental condition is key to the success of an experiment.

TO LEARN MORE

Basil, M. D. (1996). The use of student samples in communications research. *Journal of Broadcasting & Electronic Media, 40*, 431-440.

Bradac, J. J. (1983). On generalizing cabbages, messages, kings, and several other things: The virtues of multiplicity. *Human Communication Research, 9*, 181-187.

Campbell, D. T., & Stanley, J. C. (1963). *Experimental and quasi-experimental designs for research.* Boston: Houghton Mifflin.

Greenwald, A. G. (1976). Within-subjects designs: To use or not to use? *Psychological Bulletin, 83*, 314-320.

Lang, A. (1996). The logic of using inferential statistics with experimental data from nonprobability samples: Inspired by Cooper, Dupagne, Potter, and Sparks. *Journal of Broadcasting & Electronic Media, 40*, 422-430.

Lang, A., Bradley, S. D., Chung, Y., & Lee, S. (2003). Where the mind meets the message: Reflections on ten years of measuring psychological responses to media. *Journal of Broadcasting & Electronic Media, 47*, 650-655.

Maxwell, S. E., & Delaney, H. D. (2000). *Designing experiments and analyzing data: A model comparison perspective.* Mahwah, NJ: Erlbaum.

Reeves, B., & Thorson, E. (1986). Watching television: Experiments on the viewing process. *Communication Research, 13*, 343-361.

REFERENCES

Angelini, J. R. (2008). How did the sport make you feel? Looking at the three dimensions of emotion through a gendered lens. *Sex Roles, 58*, 127-135.

Bradley, S. D., Angelini, J. R., & Lee, S. (2007). Psychophysiological and memory effects of negative political ads: Aversive, arousing and well remembered. *Journal of Advertising, 36*(4), 115-127.

Bucy, E. P., & Bradley, S. D. (2004). Presidential expression and viewer emotion: Counterempathic responses to televised leader displays. *Social Science Information, 43*, 59-94.

Campbell, D. T., & Stanley, J. C. (1963). *Experimental and quasi-experimental designs for re-*

search. Boston: Houghton Mifflin.

Casa de Calvo, M. P. (2007). The dark side of mimicry: The relationship between nonconscious behavioral mimicry and behavioral confirmation (Doctoral dissertation, Texas Tech University).

Chambers, J. (2006). Taste matters: Bikinis, twins, and catfights in sexually oriented beer advertising. In T. Reichert & J. Lambiase (Eds.), *Sex in consumer culture: The erotic content of media and marketing* (pp. 159-177). Mahwah, NJ: Erlbaum.

Crowne, D. P., & Marlowe, D. (1960). A new scale of social desirability independent of psychopathology. *Journal of Consulting Psychology, 24,* 349-354.

Gibson, R., & Zillmann, D. (2000). Reading between the photographs: The influence of incidental pictorial information on issue perception. *Journalism & Mass Communication Quarterly, 77,* 355-366.

Lang, A., & Schneider, E. (2001). Physiologic and emotional responses to first-person shooter video games. *Psychophysiology, 38,* S60.

Lang, A., Shin, M., Bradley, S. D., Wang, Z., Lee, S., & Potter, D. (2005). Wait! Don't turn that dial! More excitement to come! The effects of story length and production pacing in local television news on channel changing behavior and information processing in a free-choice environment. *Journal of Broadcasting & Electronic Media, 49,* 3-22.

Milgram, S. (1965). Some conditions of obedience and disobedience to authority. *Human Relations, 18,* 57-76.

Orne, M. T. (1969). Demand characteristics and the concept of quasi-controls. In R. Rosenthal & R. L. Rosnow (Eds.), *Artifact in behavioral research* (pp. 143-179). New York: Academic Press.

Reeves, B., & Geiger, S. (1994). Designing experiments that assess psychological responses. In A. Lang (Ed.), *Measuring psychological responses to media* (pp. 165-180). Hillsdale, NJ: Erlbaum.

Shannon, C. E. (1948). A mathematical theory of communication. *The Bell System Technical Journal, 27,* 379-423, 623-656.

Smith, R. A., Levine, T. R., Lachlan, K. A., & Fediuk, T. A. (2002). The high cost of complexity in experimental design and data analysis: Type I and Type II error rates in multiway ANOVA. *Human Communication Research, 28,* 515-530.

Solomon, R. L. (1949). An extension of control group design. *Psychological Bulletin, 46,* 137-150.

Zillmann, D., & Bryant, J. (1984). Effects of massive exposure to pornography. In M. Malamuth & E. Donnerstein (Eds.), *Pornography and sexual aggression* (pp. 115-138). Orlando, FL: Academic Press.

12

Hypothesis Testing

Okay, you've completed your literature review, developed your research questions and hypotheses, designed your study, and collected your data. Now, what do you do? An important part of the research process is analyzing and interpreting your data.

But how does one do this ... without getting a migraine in addition to your results? The answer is hypothesis testing.

In this chapter, you'll learn about hypothesis testing (which is also called *data analysis*) and how to interpret results using a variety of techniques.

WHAT IS HYPOTHESIS TESTING?

Hypothesis testing is the statistical procedure designed to test a claim. You may recall from previous chapters that *hypotheses are explicitly stated relationships between variables*. These statements are ones based on your background research and can involve either categorical variables, numerical variables, or a combination of the two. For a refresher on levels of measurement, you may wish to reread Prof. Doyle's Chapter 7 on measurement in this book.

With hypothesis testing, you are actually considering twice as many hypotheses as you originally stated. Confused? Well, there are two types of hypotheses with which you are working: the *null hypothesis* and the *alternative hypothesis*. *The goal of hypothesis testing is to reject one hypothesis and accept the other.*

Null Hypothesis

The *null hypothesis* is the one that states *no difference or change*. For studies that deal with differences between groups or categories, the null hypothesis alludes to no difference between the two entities. For studies interested in relationships between interval and ratio-level variables, it implies that there is no relationship between your independent and dependent variables. This hypothesis is represented by the symbol H_0. The null hypothesis is never explicitly stated in research reports, although it is always implied.

By Meghan S. Sanders
Louisiana State University

Why do we need a null hypothesis, then? It is always possible that two variables are not related or that groups will not differ along a given dependent variable. Yet, it makes no sense to state it. It does not further research to initially pose a null finding/effect, but the possibility of its existence is still there.

Alternative Hypothesis

The *alternative hypothesis* is your statement of prediction, the expected difference or relationship. This hypothesis is what we typically see stated in research reports. It is your educated guess as to what may occur if the null hypothesis is incorrect.

The alternative hypothesis, denoted as H_a, can take a number of forms. It can state simply that two groups may differ from one another on some dependent variable, without describing what that difference looks like (e.g., Group A will be different from Group B). This is a *non-directional/two-tailed hypothesis*.

On the other hand, the alternative hypothesis can state what the difference looks like (e.g., Group A will be higher than Group B) or state what a relationship between two variables looks like (e.g., as ratings on Variable A increase, so will ratings on Variable B). These are *directional/two-tailed hypotheses*.

In simple terms, you might think of the alternative hypothesis as the *actual research hypothesis*. The researcher believes that the effect that the alternative hypothesis proposes is genuine. The null hypothesis, on the other hand, is the possibility that the effect is a result merely of chance.

The Goal of Hypothesis Testing

The ultimate goal of hypothesis testing is either to reject your null hypothesis in favor of your alternative one or to accept your null hypothesis and reject your alternative hypothesis. The burden of proof, however, falls on the alternative hypothesis. Your null hypothesis, although not explicitly stated, is considered correct until evidence is presented to the contrary. Let's take what we have discussed so far and put it in a relatable context.

Imagine this scenario. Donovan is a college student who loves music. He receives an email from the university telling him that downloading music from certain websites without paying for it is illegal and should not be done, especially using university Internet access. The letter adds that there is evidence that music downloading took place using Donovan's access account, which is tied to the IP address of his personal computer. As a result, he is going to be brought before the university student disciplinary committee. The committee, made up of faculty members and students, will decide if Donovan is indeed guilty and what the consequences for his actions will be. Donovan contends, however, that he did not download any music. Rather, his roommate has access to his computer as well as his login information; and Donovan's cousin, another university student, has witnessed the roommate's use of both.

You have been selected to serve on the disciplinary committee to determine whether Donovan is guilty of committing the infraction. Since neither you nor any of the other members of the committee were present at the time of the downloading, you will need to consider and rely on the evidence presented by both sides when making your decision.

As in a jury trial, initially one presumes that Donovan is innocent. To judge him guilty, there must be sufficient evidence to remove reasonable doubt. In making your decision (innocence or guilt), you will need to examine and weigh the evidence presented to warrant rejecting the presumption — or *hypothesis* — of innocence in favor of the belief of guilt.

The presumption of innocence can be thought of as the null hypothesis. You will either reject this notion or not reject it (keeping it as your decision), based on the evidence presented during the hearing. If you reject the null hypothesis (innocence), then you have concluded that there is adequate support for the alternative decision/hypothesis of guilt. Using this example, we would write our hypotheses as follows:

H_0= Donovan is innocent — i.e., no change from innocence to guilt.
H_a= Donovan is guilty.

STATISTICAL SIGNIFICANCE

Deciding when to reject or accept the null hypothesis is tantamount to determining if your results, your evidence, is convincing enough — or *statistically significant*. When rejecting the null hypothesis, you're saying there are significant differences between groups or a significant relationship between variables. Thus, statistical significance refers to an effect or result that is *unlikely to have occurred merely by chance*.

A number of software packages are available for computing statistical significance, including SPSS, JMP, and SAS. Regardless of the software you use, the same information regarding significance will be available for use. Among the key pieces of information are the following: (1) the p-value, or significance level, (2) the effect size value, (3) the test statistic, and (4) the degree(s) of freedom.

Significance Levels

As a researcher, you want to select a significance level that is sufficiently low. Why low? Think of *significance level* as being *the probability that you are incorrect when rejecting the null hypothesis*. Another way to think of it is the probability that your results reflect only random chance. The significance level that a researcher selects is an arbitrary decision. In communication, however, researchers typically select p<.05. What this means is that we are willing to take only a 5% chance in being wrong. If our obtained *p-value* (that is, the significance level), based on our data, is less than .05, then there is less than a 5% chance that we are incorrect in rejecting the null hypothesis AND there is a less than 5% chance that our results happened purely by chance.

Let's pretend that we have conducted a study to examine gender differences in the enjoyment of psychological thrillers (Oliver & Sanders, 2005). We hypothesize that females will report a greater interest in viewing psychological thrillers than will males. Formally, our *alternative hypothesis* is this:

H_a: Females will report a greater interest in viewing psychological thrillers than will males.

That leaves our *null hypothesis* to be one of no difference, that is:

H_0: Males and females will not differ in their interest in viewing psychological thrillers.

From our data analysis, we see that the achieved p-value for the gender effect is equal to .002. Really, what this tells is that males and females do enjoy the films at different levels, and there is only a 2 out of 1000 chance that we're wrong in drawing this conclusion. We can reject the null hypothesis of no difference between men and women. Do we at this point have sufficient evidence to accept our alternative hypothesis? Not quite.

We would have enough evidence to accept a non-directional hypothesis, one that specifies a difference but not the nature of it. Our hypothesis, though, is a directional one. When posing *directional hypotheses* — that is, ones that state that the difference or relationship will occur in a specific way — it is important also to look at whether or not our data is consistent with the direction we originally proposed. Our data should show that females do indeed show a greater level of interest in this film genre, and not the other way around. If our data are consistent with our predictions AND the obtained p-value is less than the accepted significance level, then we can accept the alternative hypothesis. That is, we can say that the data support it.

Recall that the selection of a significance level can be up to the researcher. If you want to be absolutely sure that you reject the null hypothesis when your alternative hypothesis is very likely to be correct, should you choose a large or a small significance level? Before answering this question, think about this. If you have a significance level of .5, you are saying that you may be wrong 50% of the time! If you have a significance level of .01, you may be wrong 1% of the time. This may not seem like too big a deal, but think about medical testing. Would you rather take a medicine or undergo a procedure that has been shown not to work effectively 50% of the time, 1% of the time, or even less than 1% of the time? To minimize your chance of being wrong in rejecting the null, you want to select a smaller significance level. We will discuss this point again a little later in this chapter.

Imagine two researchers who gathered data in the exact same way, using the same number of participants and collected data that looked exactly alike. Researcher A selects a significance level of .05, while researcher B selects one of .01. Who is more likely to reject the null?

	Researcher A	Researcher B
# Participants	78	78
Test Results	10.79	10.79
Accepted Significance level	.05	.01

Researcher A is willing to take more of a risk of being wrong. So it will be easier for him to reject the null. His accepted significance level is larger than Researcher B's.

A lot of our previous discussion has been on the probability of being wrong. Note that in that discussion, the idea of 100% confidence was never broached. That's because we can never be 100% sure of our results. Keep in mind that the data we collect is from a sample of the general population. Since we're working with only a sample, there is going to be some variation between what occurs in our sample and what exists in the population as a whole. You never expect your data to be exactly the same as the population, but you should expect it to be pretty darn representative. And even if we find statistical significance, we can still be wrong in our conclusions.

We have been talking about the *probability* of being wrong — but in real life there are real consequences for being wrong. When making a decision either to reject or to accept the null hypothesis, you must also be able to live with the consequences. If you conclude that a claim isn't true, but in reality it is, will that result in a lawsuit, adverse health or psychological effects, or unnecessary changes in an advertisement? If you conclude that a claim is true, when it isn't, will you continue to use ineffective marketing techniques, or lobby for banning *all* use of video games because you found that they are detrimental even in educational settings? This is why researchers do the tests in the first place: because the results of tests will have an impact.

And because results do have an impact, it is important to interpret them correctly and to be on the lookout for errors. Our conclusions should reflect what exists in reality. Table 1 illustrates when decisions are made correctly and incorrectly.

Table 1. Hypothesis Testing Decision and Implications

	What Exists in Reality (What the researcher should do)	
What Researcher Does (based on Sample Data)	H_0 is false Reject the Null	H_0 is true Not Reject the Null
Reject the Null	Correct	Type I Error (alpha error)
Not Reject the Null	Type II Error (Beta error)	Correct

Errors of Analysis As can be seen from Table 1, there are two primary ways in which we, as researchers, can be wrong in saying our results mirror reality: (1) by committing a Type I error and (2) by committing a Type II error. Let's look at each type.

Type I Error *Type I error* refers to *being wrong when rejecting the null hypothesis* when we really should have accepted it. Some refer to the error as a *false positive* because it gives the illusion of support for the alternative hypothesis. Here's an example.

Suppose that a study aid is advertised as being guaranteed to improve test scores. A consumer group tests this claim. The hypotheses are as follows:

H_0: The study aid does not improve test scores.
H_a: The study aid improves test scores.

After testing the study aid with a sample of college students, the group stands by the alternative hypothesis that the study aid does provide the improvement it promises. This is actually a big deal, especially for the students who have bought or are considering buying the materials. If the group can stand by its claim, then it has served its purpose. But what if the group is wrong? And it is possible the group is wrong because its conclusions are based on a sample of college students and not the entire population. It could be that the sample, while collected at random, just happens to be an atypical one whose results are actually quite different from the rest of the population. H_0 could be correct, but the results have led the group to a different conclusion. It has rejected the null hypothesis when it should not have done so. The test results do not coincide with what exists in reality. Yet, the group has encouraged students to buy the study aid.

So what is one to do? The significance level was set to .05, the study was well designed, and the data collected and analyzed appropriately. Well, it's not that the group did anything wrong, per se. Remember that significance level refers to the probability that your results occurred by chance. The group rejected the null hypothesis because it found that chance to be less than 5%. But a chance is still a chance. The chances of committing a Type I error are equal to the significance level. This is why Type I error is also known as *alpha* error because α is the Greek symbol used to represent significance level. If your α is .05, there is a 5% chance of committing Type I. At .01, there is a 1% chance. This means that, as a researcher, you actually have quite a bit of control over your chance of making this kind of error. The group could have minimized the possibility of error by selecting a lower significance level, such as .01. In this case, it would have had a less than 1% chance of incorrectly rejecting the null hypothesis. It is prudent to set a conservative significance level in research areas such as medicine where precision is important.

A *Type II error*, also known as a *beta* error, is the second type of mistake researchers can make. It is the opposite of a Type I error. It occurs *when a researcher does NOT reject the null hypothesis when s/he should have.* In other words, the researcher *should have accepted the alternative hypothesis.* Imagine that a man has really committed a crime — but because the evidence is nebulous, the jury renders a verdict of innocence. The jury committed a Type II error. It should have sent him to jail. Type II error is known as a *beta* error because β is the Greek symbol used to represent the rate of false negatives in statistics, or the likelihood of a researcher to report positive results as negative ones.

Type II Error

Type II errors occur because the study fails to detect a small difference. Suppose Mary Beth and Ed invented an IQ pill that would enhance people's IQs by an average of 2 points. That is a small number when you are talking about the average IQ being 100. In order to detect small differences, you have to zoom in on them — that is, increase power. Greater power is a function of statistical significance level, sample size, and effect size.

Recall that the statistical significance level is within your control. You can set a more conservative significance level, such as .001, to reduce the probability of incorrectly keeping the null hypothesis. An increased sample size is another way to detect situations where the null hypothesis is false and to avoid Type II errors. If Mary Beth and Ed recruit only 50 participants in the IQ study, for example, and there are two real dimwits there who pull down the average IQ score, they are unlikely to find that the pill improves the average IQ score. But if the sample size is 1,000, it is likely that people with extremely high or low IQs will cancel each other out, and that the difference due to the effect of the pill will show. Another way to avoid Type II errors is to increase effect size. If the IQ pill makes people 10 points smarter instead of just 2 points, it is certainly easier to detect that difference. We will discuss effect sizes more a little later.

Think of power like a magnifying glass. The more power you have or the stronger the glass, the more likely you are to detect significant results when they exist, even if they are small.

Now, increased power through sample size and significance levels has its pros and cons. The more people in your sample, the more likely you are to find differences (because large samples can magnify a small effect) and to reject the null hypothesis, even in cases when you should not. While increased power can decrease the likelihood of committing Type II error, the chance is now increased for a Type I error. Conversely, setting a very low significance level dramatically decreases the odds of committing a Type I error but increases the odds of a Type II error. By establishing a more stringent threshold for your level of significance, you are in essence making it more difficult for your data to achieve the burden of proof for rejecting the null hypothesis. So the two types of error have an inverse relationship, kind of like a seesaw.

Balancing Type I and Type II Errors

There is no easy way to balance the two error types, but there is a way to deal with the issue and establish a risk for Type II errors.

First, parametric statistics are generally more statistically powerful than are nonparametric statistics. *Parametric statistics* make more assumptions about your data — for example, that you are using probability-based sampling methods, that your data have a normal distribution, and that you have interval or ratio-level dependent variables. (For a discussion of parametric statistics, you may wish to jump ahead and read Chapter 13 on statistics in this book by Prof. Watson. For a book-length discussion, see Tabachnik & Fidell, 2007.)

Second, statistics can be more powerful when the hypotheses tested are *directional* ones as opposed to *non-directional* ones. Directional hypotheses are more powerful because they allow you to use what are called *one-tailed statistical tests*. One-tailed tests are more stringent because they predict that the results will fall in only one direction. Researchers can also look at both the obtained statistical significance levels and effect sizes.

Effect Size

The *effect size* is the degree to which variables are interdependent. New researchers tend to confuse what statistical significance, or p-value, does with what the effect size is designed to tell us. *Significance tests*, or p-values, can help to illustrate group differences and associations between variables, telling us how much confidence we can place in the association uncovered — but they don't tell us the degree to which our variables are related to one another, that is, *how much* association there is. Effect sizes do. *Effect sizes* reflect the proportion of variance in the dependent variable that is associated with levels of an independent variable. In other words, the effect size tells us the amount of change, or variance, that happens to the dependent variable because of the variations in the independent variables. It tells us whether or not the difference we see is one that really matters. Figure 1a illustrates the relationship.

Figure 1a. Effect Size and Interdependence of Variables

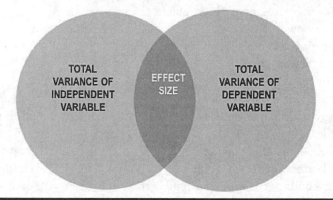

Two variables can be tested at the .05 or even the .001 significance level, but this doesn't necessarily mean that the two are strongly related to one another. A lower obtained p-value doesn't necessarily mean a bigger or stronger effect, as sample size can affect whether or not something is statistically significant. Again, this is one of the dangers of an increase in sample size leading to Type I error. The larger the sample, the more likely the researchers are to find significance, but the effect sizes will not change with the sample.

For example, let's say you decide to conduct an experiment to test the effects of different study methods. For the treatment group of 150 students, you play classical music as they study for two hours. For the control group of 150 students, no music is played; the room is silent. You then test both groups and find that the music group achieved a significantly higher score (A+ range as opposed to A-range), significant at the .03 level (meaning that there is a 3% chance this result occurred by chance). You accept the alternative hypothesis that presence of music during studying has an important effect on test scores. But it's possible that this effect is only one small explanation for the higher scores, as illustrated in Figure 1b.

What could be allowing this difference to appear as statistically significant could be the large sample size of 300 participants. In this situation, you may still be correct in concluding that the presence of classical music during studying has some effect on test performance. It's just not as large as, say, the type of study strategy a student uses. (See Figure 1c).

In other situations, inferring such a conclusion could be wrong. Let's assume that we conduct a study that concludes that diet does not have an effect on weight because we found no statistical significance or p >.05. We know that in reality diet actually does have a large effect. However, for some reason it wasn't statistically significant in our study.

So it's important to look at both the obtained significance values and the effect size values in order to have more faith in our results. A small effect size is easy

Figure 1b. Effect Size and Interdependence of Variables

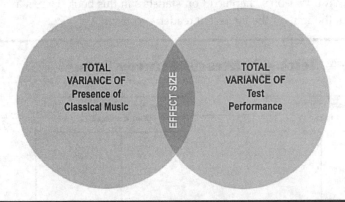

Figure 1c. Effect Size and Interdependence of Variables

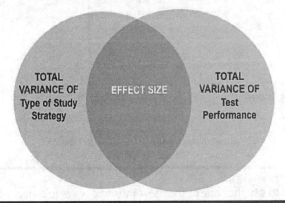

to see if you use a strong enough magnifying glass or, in our case, people. A larger effect is easier to see even if you don't have a lot of people in your study.

Effect size can range in value from 0 to 1, with 0 indicating no effects and 1 signifying perfect association. Many researchers follow Cohen's (1988; 1992) rule of thumb: Small effect size=.1; medium effect size=.3; large effect size=.5.

STATISTICS IN HYPOTHESIS TESTING Now that we have a sense of how hypothesis testing works, and some of the pitfalls to watch for, we can move on to talk about some of the statistical tests that allow us to determine the level of support for our findings. While the tests researchers use can vary, the main ideas (i.e., p-values, rejecting the null hypothesis, test statistic, etc.) are the same.

There are generally four steps to analyzing your data using statistics. They are the following:

1. Decide on a statistical test
2. Compute a test statistic
3. Determine if results are statistically significant (rejecting or accepting the null hypothesis)
4. Interpret results

There are different ways to determine which statistical test is the most appropriate for your study. For a more complete discussion, please refer to Prof. Watson's chapter 13 on statistics in this book. Here's a diagram, though, for the interested reader to consult:

Step 1. Decide on a Statistical Test

Figure 2. Testing Differences Between Groups

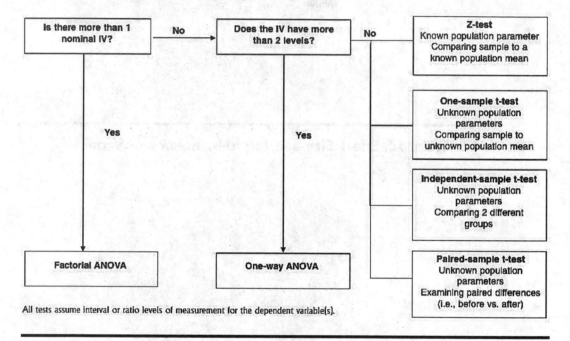

All tests assume interval or ratio levels of measurement for the dependent variable(s).

Suffice it to say that one of the most intuitive ways to determine the right test is to refer back to your variables and the levels of measurement each one attains. Examine your hypotheses, identifying the levels of measurement for the independent variable(s) and the dependent variable(s). You will then be able to determine what kind of statistical analysis to run.

A *test statistic* is a value that represents the relationship between your variables of interest and how they are expected or presumed to be in reality. The form it takes depends on the test being used. There are at least four ways to calculate a test statistic. You can do so by hand, use a statistical calculator online, use a spreadsheet program such Microsoft Excel or Quattro Pro, or use a statistical program such as SPSS. Calculating test statistics by hand can be tedious, especially when dealing with a large dataset. With the widespread use of electronic methods of calculation, we recognize that using the hand calculation method is the least likely to occur. However, we will discuss a few formulas and simple examples to explain the different numbers used by the statistical tests.

Step 2. Compute a Test Statistic

To determine if your results are statistically significant — that is, seeing if you have enough evidence to support your alternative hypoth-

Step 3. Determine If Results Are Statistically Significant

esis and reject your null — you must determine if your test statistic exceeds a *critical value* or a threshold number that represents the point at which a relationship between variables becomes statistically important. You have two available options of determining statistical significance. The first is to compare your calculated test statistic to a value provided in a critical values table, or a standardized table showing the critical points a study has to achieve before it can be declared statistically significant under specified conditions. An excerpt of the critical t-test table is provided in Figure 3. (For a complete t-Table, please refer to http://www.statsoft.com/textbook/sttable.html)

Figure 3. T-Table of Critical Values

df\p	0.40	0.25	0.10	0.05	0.025	0.01	0.005	0.0005
1	0.324920	1.000000	3.077684	6.313752	12.70620	31.82052	63.65674	636.6192
2	0.288675	0.816497	1.885618	2.919986	4.30265	6.96456	9.92484	31.5991
3	0.276671	0.764892	1.637744	2.353363	3.18245	4.54070	5.84091	12.9240
4	0.270722	0.740697	1.533206	2.131847	2.77645	3.74695	4.60409	8.6103
5	0.267181	0.726687	1.475884	2.015048	2.57058	3.36493	4.03214	6.8688

To use this table, you must know two things: the probability or significance level, which you have already determined by this point; and the degrees of freedom (df). *Degrees of freedom* is a term that represents the number of scores in a statistical test that are free to vary in their value. Imagine an empty table, much like the one illustrated below. The numbers at the end of each row represent a sum, as do the numbers at the bottom of each column.

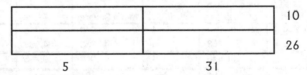

Knowing these sums, can you fill in the missing values?

No? Well, how about if you know that the value that belongs in the first cell is a 5? Can you complete the table now? Yes!

5	5	10
0	26	26
5	31	

You can now determine that the second cell number is 5, the third is 0 and the last is 26. And you only had to begin by knowing one number. This is one way to think of degrees of freedom, the possibility for variation within a statistical model, or rather: How many numbers must be provided to us (or how many fixed numbers must there be) in order for us to fill in the rest of the missing numbers? In the previous example, the degree of freedom is 1. The amount of variation depends on the sample size and the number of groups being compared. Each statistical test has its own set of degrees of freedom. How to calculate them will be explained in the discussion of each test.

Knowing the degrees of freedom now allows you to fully use the critical values table. Let's say we have conducted a study for which the degrees of freedom is equal to 3, and we have a test statistic of 3.01. To determine if this value exceeds the critical value threshold at the $p<.05$ level, we locate the row representing 3 degrees of freedom and the column representing $p<.05$. We next find where the row meets the column. Since our test statistic of 3.01 is greater than the listed critical value of 2.35, we can reject the null hypothesis and conclude that our result is statistically significant at the .05 level. If we decide on a more stringent test, $p<.01$, then we would go to the column representing $p<.01$. We see here that the critical value is 4.54. Because our test statistic is less than the listed critical value, we cannot reject the null hypothesis at the $p<.01$ level.

The second option for determining statistical significance takes the finger walking out of the picture. It simply requires looking at the statistical output provided by software or a spreadsheet program. An example of output from SPSS is shown in Figure 4. What is of interest in this case is the significance column. Your independent variable has its own row. Let's say your independent variable of interest is the gender of each participant represented by the variable name "sex." If we look at the significance value for the "sex" variable, we see that it is .002, less than .05. We can conclude that there is a statistically significant difference between men and women on the dependent variable, which in this case is hours spent watching television.

Figure 4. Tests of Between-Subjects Effects

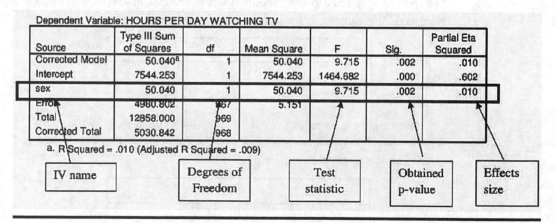

Dependent Variable: HOURS PER DAY WATCHING TV

Source	Type III Sum of Squares	df	Mean Square	F	Sig.	Partial Eta Squared
Corrected Model	50.040a	1	50.040	9.715	.002	.010
Intercept	7544.253	1	7544.253	1464.682	.000	.602
sex	50.040	1	50.040	9.715	.002	.010
Error	4980.802	967	5.151			
Total	12858.000	969				
Corrected Total	5030.842	968				

a. R Squared = .010 (Adjusted R Squared = .009)

IV name	Degrees of Freedom	Test statistic	Obtained p-value	Effects size

Recall that supporting the alternative hypothesis requires more than simply looking at the obtained p-value from your data. If you have posed a directional hypothesis, it is important to look at additional information to determine whether or not you can truly accept the alternative hypothesis. Let's say that we are conducting a study on television viewing habits. We

Step 4. Interpret Results

have reason to believe that men and women differ in not only the kinds of television they watch but also in the amount of television they watch. So we pose the simple hypothesis:

H_a: Men watch more television than do women.

Using the data in Figure 4, we can conclude that there is a statistically significant difference between men and women on the amount of television they watch. Not only is the obtained p-value less than .05, but it is less than .01. So there is a less than 1% chance that this difference occurred by chance. But before accepting the alternative hypothesis, we also have to make sure that men actually did report watching more television than what women reported.

For this information, we must look at the average ratings associated with each group. (See Figure 5.) According to our data, women on average actually reported viewing more hours of television (Women $M=3.04$; Men $M=2.58$). These numbers contradict our original hypothesis of men viewing more television. So, can we reject our null hypothesis? Yes, we can because the null is a statement of no difference between the two groups (that is, that men and women watch the same amount of TV). However, we cannot say that our evidence supported our alternative hypothesis because the means were in the opposite direction.

We must also be careful in our interpretation of the strength of this effect. Looking at the effects size (.01) in Figure 4, we see that gender does not account for a large portion of the variance. So in rejecting the null, what we could actually be seeing is an influence, or in statistical terms, an *artifact* of sample size (N=969) magnifying a very small effect.

Figure 5. Estimates

Dependent Variable: HOURS PER DAY WATCHING TV

RESPONDENTS SEX			95% Confidence Interval	
	Mean	Std. Error	Lower Bound	Upper Bound
MALE	2.584	.110	2.367	2.800
FEMALE	3.042	.097	2.852	3.233

Average rating for each group

Interpreting the results may seem difficult; but it isn't … if you know what you're looking for.

Many researchers are good about reporting their results carefully, pointing out the limitations and explaining the results with caution when necessary. But others take a lot more liberty with their conclusions, reporting only half of the story. In reporting, you should err on the side of caution — and when all else fails, fall back on what we were all taught in our first journalism class: Report the facts and tell the whole story.

The following sections illustrate the above steps within the context of three often used inferential statistics that test differences between groups: z-test, t-test, and Analysis of Variance (ANOVA). *Inferential statistics* are used to make generalizations from a data sample to a population.

TESTING DIFFERENCES BETWEEN GROUPS

In the next chapter, on statistics, you will learn about means, standard deviations, and z-scores. These numbers work primarily with individual scores. Based on individual scores, we can get the average rating on a given variable for our sample, how far on average each person in the sample deviates from this mean, and the distribution of the individual scores.

Z-test

However, to test differences between groups we have to look at the groups as a whole rather than at the individual members. Rather than working with standard deviation, inferential statistics like z-tests require you to work with standard errors (SE), represented by the symbol σ. *Standard error* is very similar to *standard deviation*. The **standard deviation** is how much scores vary within a distribution. **Standard error** is how much we expect the means drawn from a distribution of means to vary. It is the standard deviation of means.

When you want to know how much your sample differs from the general population or if some factor — such as a study aid, for example — has caused your sample to be different from the general population, then you would use the z-test to see if your sample group mean is different from the population mean. In this case, we would use the following formula to perform a z-test.

$$z = \left(\frac{\overline{X} - \mu}{\sigma} \right)$$

The z-test score is determined by the sample mean ($\overline{X}$) and the population mean, represented by the symbol μ, and the standard error (σ).

What this means is that in the case of z-tests, you have to know what the population mean value actually is. Using the z-table, you can determine if your sample is statistically different from the population.

Let's use an example. The average grade in Professor Crawford's mass communication research class is 82%, with a standard error of 1.65. In an effort to improve understanding and student grades, Professor Crawford has developed a series of exercises and notes designed to better engage the students and explain the information in a simpler and more practical way. The average grade of a subset of students who used these materials was 86%. Did the students who used the materials differ significantly from the entire population of students who have taken her course? In this case, the hypotheses are the following:

H_0: The average grade of students who used the new materials is equivalent or similar to the average grade of all students in Professor Crawford's class.

H_a: The average grade of students who used the new materials differs from the average grade of all students in Professor Crawford's class.

Plugging in the above information, we get this equation:

$$z = \left(\frac{86 - 82}{1.65} \right) \qquad z = 2.42$$

We get a calculated z-value of 2.42. From our critical values table (see http://www.statsoft.com/textbook/sttable.html), we know that a z-test statistic is significant at the $p<.05$ level if it exceeds ± 1.96 (Note: the alternative hypothesis was two-tailed. The critical value for one-tailed is 1.64 at the $p<.05$ level.)

Typically, when you don't know whether the independent variable — in this case, the study aids — can increase or decrease the dependent variable, you use a two-tailed test, meaning it can go either direction. However, when you are certain that the IV is going to move the DV in one direction only, you use a one-tailed test. Our calculated value does exceed the critical value. So we can reject the null hypothesis. The students who used the new material differed significantly from the total population of students in the class.

T-tests   More often than not, we don't know what the actual population looks like. We can only guess, based on the information provided by our sample. This being the case, z-tests are not appropriate statistical measures because they require that we know the population mean. When we are left to our estimations, rather than concrete information, we have to rely on a t-test, an extension of the z-test, to do the statistical job for us. The primary difference is in a substitution in the original z-test formula where s represents the estimated standard error:

$$z = \left(\frac{\overline{X} - \mu}{\sigma} \right) \qquad t = \left(\frac{\overline{X} - \mu}{s} \right)$$

Say, for example, Professor Crawford does not know the average grade of her students but can estimate that the typical student earns an 82%. The t-statistic, the test statistic for a t-test, would be 2.42. Rather than using the z-table, we can use the t-table of critical values. For this statistical test, we must know the degrees of freedom. In the case of the t-test, degrees of freedom is equal to (N-1), where N is the size of our sample. Assuming that Professor Crawford has 35 students, the degrees of freedom in this case would be equal to 34. According to the t-table of critical values at 34 degrees of freedom, the calculated value would need to exceed 2.03 for a two-tailed hypothesis. (See http://www.statsoft.com/textbook/sttable.html.) We can thus reject the null hypothesis and conclude that there is a significant difference between the sample of the students and the wider population of Professor Crawford's students.

We can also use t-tests to test differences between two groups when there is an independent variable with only two levels (i.e., gender, presence vs. absence of a treatment, etc.). This is called an *independent sample t-test.* For this test, degrees of freedom is calculated by using the following formula:

$$DF = (N1 + N2 - 2)$$

where "N1" represents the number of people in the first sample, and "N2" the number of people in the second sample. Suppose that Derrick, a student at University A, and Harriet, a student at University B, want to examine the political knowledge of college students. Derrick believes that University A students will exhibit higher levels of political knowledge, while Harriet believes that University B students will.

Figure 6. Independent Sample T-Test

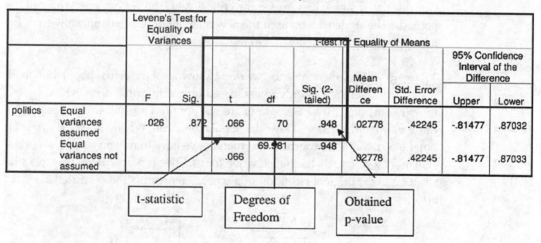

Group Statistics

	school	N	Mean	Std. Deviation	Std. Error Mean
politics	A	36	7.6389	1.80717	.30120
	B	36	7.6111	1.77728	.29621

Independent Samples Test

		Levene's Test for Equality of Variances		t-test for Equality of Means					95% Confidence Interval of the Difference	
		F	Sig.	t	df	Sig. (2-tailed)	Mean Difference	Std. Error Difference	Upper	Lower
politics	Equal variances assumed	.026	.872	.066	70	.948	.02778	.42245	-.81477	.87032
	Equal variances not assumed			.066	69.981	.948	.02778	.42245	-.81477	.87033

t-statistic	Degrees of Freedom	Obtained p-value

According to their study's results, shown in Figure 6, there is no significant difference between the two schools in regard to political knowledge. We cannot reject the null hypothesis of no difference, for the obtained *p*-value is greater than .05. Looking at the mean values for the two schools, we see that they are very close (A: *M*=7.64; B: *M*=7.61). Both Derrick's and Harriet's directional/one-tailed hypotheses are rejected.

There are also those instances when we want to know "Which one is better?" For example, a taste test could ask, "Which soda is better: A or B?" Or a pre-posttest design assesses some measure, exposes participants to something (i.e., a treatment), and then assesses the measure again to see if the exposure had an effect. These situations call for a *paired sample t-test*. Let's take one more example.

Pat is an elementary school teacher who is interested in seeing whether teaching students math with a video game gives better results than teaching math with a more traditional method. A recent article in the *Journal of Communication* leads her to believe that video games may be more effective. She randomly selects 30 students and puts them into 15 pairs in which one student learns math using the video game and the other learns math through the traditional method of teaching.

She assesses each student's math competency. What she is truly interested in is the difference in math competency scores. The null hypothesis would say that the difference in scores would be equal to 0 (that is, the scores would be equal), while the alternative one-tailed hypothesis would show a difference greater than 0, since her argument is that video games are better than the traditional method. (A two-tailed alternative hypothesis would simply state that there is going to be a difference.)

Figure 7. Paired-Sample T-test

Paired Samples Statistics

		Mean	N	Std. Deviation	Std. Error Mean
Pair 1	computer	57.6389	72	30.37294	3.57949
	traditional	76.2500	72	17.79678	2.09737

Paired Samples Test

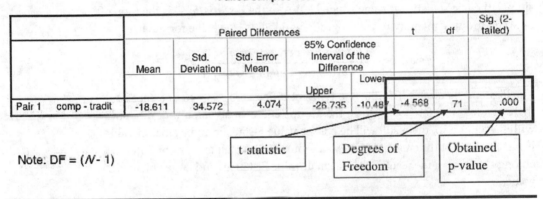

		Paired Differences					t	df	Sig. (2-tailed)
		Mean	Std. Deviation	Std. Error Mean	95% Confidence Interval of the Difference				
					Upper	Lower			
Pair 1	comp - tradit	-18.611	34.572	4.074	-26.735	-10.48	-4.568	71	.000

Note: DF = (N - 1)

| t statistic | Degrees of Freedom | Obtained p-value |

The results for Pat's study are shown in Figure 7. According to the results, there is a significant difference in math competency scores at the $p<.001$ level. Pat can reject the null hypothesis. However, she cannot accept her alternative hypothesis. Why? If we look at the means, students who learned math through traditional methods had higher math competency scores ($M=76.25$) than did the students who learned math using video games ($M=57.64$), contrary to her prediction. This is also why the t-statistic is negative in value. The method thought to result in lower scores is subtracted from the one thought to result in higher scores. Since in reality the second option resulted in higher scores than did the first option, the t-test value has a negative sign.

Analysis of Variance Sometimes you are going to compare more than two groups of people to one another on some dependent variable. Rather than conducting multiple t-tests (group 1 versus group 2, group 2 versus group 3, and group 1 versus group 3), you can instead use another statistical test to look at differences among all groups simultaneously.

Suppose we have data from an experiment in which we have three types of anti-smoking advertisements: (1) ads that show a young person smoking, (2) ads that show a middle-aged person smoking, and (3) ads that show an older person smoking. We are interested in determining which type of ad is the most persuasive. So we randomly assign participants to one of the ad type conditions, meaning each person sees only one kind of ad. We then assess persuasiveness, by asking the participants to answer a series of questions on a 7-point Likert-type scale where "1" represents no persuasiveness and "7" represents strong persuasiveness. Our goal is to determine if the three groups differ on their perceptions of ad persuasiveness, beyond what we would expect by chance. A *one-way ANOVA* helps us to achieve this goal.

With this statistical test, we're interested in differences among groups in addition to how much variation exists within each group. Within each advertisement group, individuals' responses are going to vary. They may vary a little, which we call *small within-group variability*, or they may vary a lot (*large within-group variability*). The same can be said for differences among the three groups. They can differ quite a bit from one another (*large between-group variability*) or only by a small amount (*small between-group variability*).

There is quite a bit of math involved in the actual calculation; but put quite simply, the test statistic for a one-way ANOVA — the *F-statistic* — is the ratio of between-group variability to within-group variability. Here's the formula:

$$F\text{-statistic} = \left(\frac{Variability\ between\ groups}{Variability\ within\ groups} \right)$$

Figure 8 illustrates how the two types of differences relate to one another. If there is a lot of difference between the groups and a small amount of difference within each group, the result will be a large value F-statistic and a small p-value. If there is a lot of difference within each group and a small amount of difference among the groups, the result will be a small value F-statistic and large obtained p-value.

The F-statistic is called an *omnibus test* because it tells us whether or not significant differences are somewhere in the results. An example is provided in Figure 9. As in other tests, we want to look for the degrees of freedom, the test statistic (which is F), and the obtained p-value.

Figure 8. Between-Group Variability

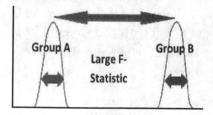

Large between-group variability; small within-group variability. The people in Group A are very different from those in Group B. The people in Group A are very similar to one another, while the people in Group B are very similar to one another. The F-statistic will be large.

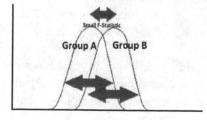

Small between-group variability; large within-group variability. The people in Group A are very similar to those in Group B. The people within Group A are very dissimilar, and the people within Group B are very dissimilar. The F-statistic will be small.

Figure 9. F-statistic Tests for Significant Differences

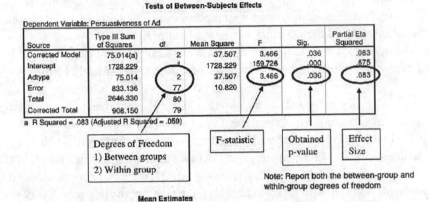

Tests of Between-Subjects Effects

Dependent Variable: Persuasiveness of Ad

Source	Type III Sum of Squares	df	Mean Square	F	Sig.	Partial Eta Squared
Corrected Model	75.014(a)	2	37.507	3.466	.036	.083
Intercept	1728.229	1	1728.229	159.726	.000	.675
Adtype	75.014	2	37.507	3.466	.036	.083
Error	833.136	77	10.820			
Total	2646.330	80				
Corrected Total	908.150	79				

a R Squared = .083 (Adjusted R Squared = .059)

Degrees of Freedom
1) Between groups
2) Within group

F-statistic

Obtained p-value

Effect Size

Note: Report both the between-group and within-group degrees of freedom

Mean Estimates

Dependent Variable: Memory

Primary Residence	Mean	Std. Error	95% Confidence Interval	
			Lower Bound	Upper Bound
Young	5.956	.633	4.695	7.216
Middle-aged	4.352	.633	3.091	5.612
Old	3.638	.645	2.354	4.923

Means for each group

Multiple Comparisons

Dependent Variable: Persuasiveness of Ad
Bonferroni

(I) Primary Residence	(J) Primary Residence	Mean Difference (I-J)	Std. Error	Sig.	95% Confidence Interval	
					Upper Bound	Lower Bound
Young	Middle-aged	1.6037	.89525	.232	-.5873	3.7947
	Old	2.3171(*)	.90382	.037	.1051	4.5291
Middle-aged	Young	-1.6037	.89525	.232	-3.7947	.5873
	Old	.7134	.90382	1.000	-1.4986	2.9254
Old	Young	-2.3171(*)	.90382	.037	-4.5291	-.1051
	Middle-aged	-.7134	.90382	1.000	-2.9254	1.4986

Based on observed means.

Reading across each row: Comparing the Young Smoker condition to the Middle-aged Smoker condition, the difference between the two groups obtains a p-value of .232. Comparing the Young Smoker condition to the Old Smoker condition, the difference obtains a p-value of .037. Comparing the Middle-aged Smoker condition to the Old Smoker condition (the fourth row), the difference obtains a p-value of 1.00.

From the statistical output in Figure 9, we see that the type of ad had a significant impact on persuasiveness. The difference is significant at the $p<.05$ level, and there is a small effect size.

While we see that there is statistical significance, the omnibus test alone does not tell us what is driving these differences. It could be that all three groups are different from one another or that only two of them are different.

In interpreting the difference, we must turn to the averages/means calculated for each group and use a follow-up procedure called *post hoc comparisons*. There are many options in regard to post hoc comparisons (Tukey, Holm's Sequential Bonferroni, LSD, etc.). For this example, we used one of the most popular, Bonferroni. Looking at the bottom of Figure 9, we can see that differences in persuasiveness (between those who viewed ads with young people smoking and ads with old people smoking) are what is driving the statistical significance. Specifically, those people who saw a young person smoking thought the ad was more persuasive (M=5.96) than those who saw an old person (M=3.64).

Interpreting data for a one-way ANOVA is similar to that of a t-test. The only difference is that you're comparing three or more groups instead of two.

Factorial ANOVA

In Chapter 11 you read about the different kinds of experiments that researchers can conduct. Among them were experiments that involve more than one independent variable. When you are conducting these kinds of experiments, or are simply interested in the individual and combined effects of two or more independent variables, a one-way ANOVA will not cut the mustard. A *factorial ANOVA* is best. This test builds on the logic of the one-way ANOVA, except there will be multiple F-ratios and multiple follow-up tests to determine where any significant differences may lie.

Suppose Tyson and Al wanted to know the effects of different kinds of promotions for television shows. They have noticed that advertisements for shows frequently appear at the bottom corners of television screens while another program is airing. A little bit of research told them that these promotions are called "snipes." They notice that when snipes appear on the screen, not only do they notice them, but the snipes distract them from the programs they are trying to watch. So Tyson and Al decide to conduct an experiment to determine whether the presence of snipes diminishes the enjoyment of television viewing. They take it one step further and also examine whether the effect is stronger when watching dramas or comedies. Hence they have two independent variables: the presence of snipes (present or absent) and genre of television program (comedy or drama). Their dependent variable is level of enjoyment.

They conduct a 2x2 factorial experiment in which participants are randomly assigned to one of the four conditions. All participants are given the enjoyment measure which ranges from a low of "1" to a high of "5." From their experiment, they obtain the results shown in Figure 10.

Notice that there are three F-ratios: one representing the effect of snipe presence, one representing the effect of television genre (these are called *main effects*) and another representing the interaction between snipe presence and television genre (*interaction effect*). As Figure 10 shows, both main effects are statistically significant beyond the .05 level. So we can reject null hypotheses of no differences. Participants who viewed a program without a snipe enjoyed the program significantly more (M=3.64) than did those who viewed a program with a snipe (M= 1.54). This was actually a medium-sized effect, as the effect size is .45. Additionally, those who viewed a comedy reported more enjoyment (M=2.94) than did those who saw a drama (M=2.23). This effect was not as large as the snipe effect. There was no significant combined or interaction effect between snipe presence and television genre. The obtained significance value was greater than .05.

Examining the post hoc results for the main effects was unnecessary as there were only two levels for each independent variable. However, if you are working with a larger number of groups for each IV, post hoc comparisons would be nec-

Figure 10. 2x2 Factorial Experiment Results

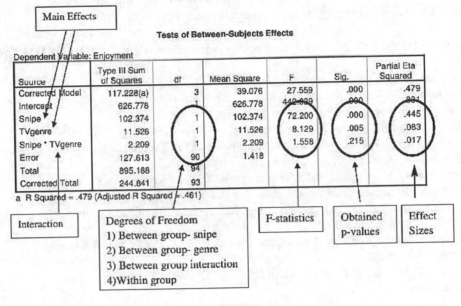

Main Effects

Tests of Between-Subjects Effects

Dependent Variable: Enjoyment

Source	Type III Sum of Squares	df	Mean Square	F	Sig.	Partial Eta Squared
Corrected Model	117.228(a)	3	39.076	27.559	.000	.479
Intercept	626.778	1	626.778	442.039	.000	.831
Snipe	102.374	1	102.374	72.200	.000	.445
TVgenre	11.526	1	11.526	8.129	.005	.083
Snipe * TVgenre	2.209	1	2.209	1.558	.215	.017
Error	127.613	90	1.418			
Total	895.188	94				
Corrected Total	244.841	93				

a R Squared = .479 (Adjusted R Squared = .461)

Interaction

Degrees of Freedom
1) Between group- snipe
2) Between group- genre
3) Between group interaction
4) Within group

F-statistics

Obtained p-values

Effect Sizes

Estimates

Dependent Variable: Enjoyment

Snipe	Mean	Std. Error	95% Confidence Interval	
			Lower Bound	Upper Bound
Absent	3.635	.172	3.293	3.977
Present	1.543	.176	1.192	1.893

Estimates

Dependent Variable: Enjoyment

TVgenre	Mean	Std. Error	95% Confidence Interval	
			Lower Bound	Upper Bound
Comedy	2.940	.168	2.605	3.275
Drama	2.238	.180	1.881	2.595

Snipe*TVgenre

Dependent Variable: Enjoyment

Snipe	TVgenre	Mean	Std. Error	95% Confidence Interval	
				Lower Bound	Upper Bound
Absent	Comedy	4.140	.238	3.667	4.613
	Drama	3.130	.248	2.637	3.624
Present	Comedy	1.740	.238	1.267	2.213
	Drama	1.345	.260	.829	1.861

essary to help determine where the significant differences actually exist. For a more detailed explanation on how to examine post hoc comparisons in a factorial ANOVA, you should refer to Tabachnik and Fidell (2007).

THE IMPORTANCE OF HYPOTHESIS TESTING

Developing hypotheses and testing them doesn't have to be a complicated process. Yet it is one that is integral to better understanding the media world around us. Knowing which hypothesis is applicable, and which one is not, informs our decisions. But we also have to be aware of possible errors and understand that statistical significance does necessarily mean positive results. Finally, we should remember that, even though researchers tend to be disappointed with non-significant findings, such findings can be just as informative and important as a significant one.

TO LEARN MORE

Cohen, Jacob (1988). *Statistical Power Analysis for the Behavioral Sciences*. New York: Academic Press.

Cohen, Jacob (1992). A power primer. *Psychological Bulletin, 112,* 155-159.

Grisson, Robert J., & Kim, John J. (2005). *Effect Sizes for Research: A Broad Practical Approach.* Mahwah, NJ: Lawrence Erlbaum.

Langley, Russell (1970). *Practical Statistics Simply Explained.* New York: Dover Publications.

Miller, Jane E. (2004). *The Chicago Guide to Writing About Numbers: The Effective Presentation of Quantitative Information.* Chicago: University of Chicago Press.

Morgan, Susan E., Tom Reichert, and Tyler R. Harrison (2002). *From Numbers to Words: Reporting Statistical Results for the Social Sciences.* Boston: Allyn and Bacon.

Oliver, Mary Beth. *The Story of Hypothesis Testing.* http://www.lsu.edu/faculty/msand/oliver/hypothesistesting.pdf

Siegel, Sidney, and N. John Castellan Jr. (1988). *Nonparametric Statistics for the Behavioral Sciences.* New York: McGraw-Hill.

Tabachnick, Barbara. G., and Linda S. Fidell (2007). *Using Multivariate Statistics,* 5th ed. Boston: Pearson.

REFERENCES

Cohen, Jacob (1988). *Statistical Power Analysis for the Behavioral Sciences*. New York: Academic Press.

Cohen, Jacob (1992). A power primer. *Psychological Bulletin, 112,* 155-159.

Oliver, Mary Beth, & Meghan S. Sanders (2005). *The Enjoyment of Psychological Thrillers.* Paper presented at the annual meeting of the National Communication Association, Boston, MA.

StatSoft Electronic Textbook. http://www.statsoft.com/textbook/stathome.html

Tabachnick, Barbara. G., and Linda S. Fidell (2007). *Using Multivariate Statistics,* 5th ed. Boston: Pearson.

13

Statistics

The chapters in this book provide introductions to their topics. To gain a well-developed knowledge of any single topic, you would need to read at least one complete book — and perhaps several.

The same is true with statistics. This chapter can give you only an introduction. To be able to really use statistics, you will need to supplement the material in this chapter with resources on the Web or the Help options on a statistical software package or, better yet, a companion statistics text. This chapter will introduce you to what communication professionals and, for that matter, any educated person should know about statistical analysis.

We use statistical procedures to help us describe, explain, and predict phenomena. Statistical applications vary by whether the focus is on a single variable, two variables, or more than two variables. The matrix in Table 1 on the next page illustrates how to apply particular statistical methods appropriately, once you know what data you have and what it is you wish to do.

There's no substitute for working with actual data when doing statistics. We shall provide a very small data set within this chapter to illustrate many of the fundamentals of statistics. See the bibliography at the end of the chapter for referral to larger datasets that you can access and work with.

Table 2 on page 205 presents a small data set belonging to a single college student. If rows in a computer spreadsheet typically represent the *unit of analysis*, then you may observe that we have gathered data on classes that this student has taken. The columns identify the properties (*variables*) of the classes, including which semester the class was taken, how many hours of credit were given to the class, the student's grade, the conversion of that letter grade to a number, and the size of the class. By identifying the class by subject and course-level, the left-most column also provides property information. POS100, for example, is both a political science class and a 100-level class.

There are, as you can see, 23 cases in this data set, a *case* being one of what-

By George Watson
Arizona State University

Table 1. An Organization for Statistical Analysis

	Describe	Explain	Predict
One Variable	arrays frequency distributions relative frequencies central tendency variation		central tendency variation
Two Variables	contingency tables correlations statistical tests	contingency tables correlations statistical tests	contingency tables regressions statistical tests
Three + Variables	contingency tables partial correlations	contingency tables partial/multiple correlations	contingency tables partial/multiple regressions

ever the unit of analysis is, in this example a particular class. Each of the variables possesses a set of *attributes*. For "semester," the scores of 1, 2, 3, and 4 represent the first four semesters of the student's work. When attributes, such as grades, are not represented as numbers, statisticians typically assign numbers to them to facilitate statistical analysis. We have done that here, assigning a score of 4 for an A, 3 for a B, and so on.

STATISTICAL ANALYSIS OF A SINGLE VARIABLE

Analysis of a single variable is the most common treatment of data, in large part because it is the simplest use of data. Analysis of a single variable is almost always descriptive in nature, although certain descriptions may also be used to predict. For example, while writing this chapter I heard a news report of an upcoming football game predicting a high scoring contest, based on the high scoring averages of the two teams involved. That constitutes a simplistic prediction, but it's not without reason to think that what might happen in the future will be similar to what typically has happened in the past.

Please note, though, that while simple descriptions and predictions can occur with a single variable, no explanation can be provided for the manner in which a single variable is distributed without introducing a second variable as a causal impetus for that distribution. If, for example, we want to know why someone gets Cs in certain classes and As in others — in other words, to explain why one's grades are distributed in the manner they are — we would look at certain explanatory variables, such as class size, type of course, etc.

Arrays, Frequency Distributions, and Relative Frequencies

Describing a single variable takes many forms.

The simplest description is a listing of the variable attribute for each case in the data set. Such a listing is an *array*. Arrays are useful, especially when the purpose is to display each case's attribute on a variable, as when instructors post grades so students can see their individual scores on an exam. Such an array is informative, but it does

Arrays

Table 2. Dataset for Student Classes in First Four Semesters

Class	Semester	Hours	Grade	Grade Pts.	Class Size
POS100	1	3	B	3	237
ENG101	1	3	A	4	25
MAT136	1	3	B	3	19
BIO112	1	4	C	2	133
GER100	1	5	A	4	30
POS120	2	3	B	3	66
ENG121	2	3	B	3	19
MAT212	2	2	C	2	31
GER101	2	5	A	4	32
CHM101	2	4	D	1	80
PED215	2	1	B	3	17
GER201	3	4	B	3	29
JRN101	3	3	A	4	97
MCO100	3	3	B	3	124
PSY112	3	3	C	2	77
PED221	3	1	B	3	23
SOC130	3	3	C	3	90
GER202	4	4	C	2	27
JRN201	4	3	A	4	55
MCO200	4	3	B	3	83
PED250	4	1	B	3	22
STA200	4	3	A	4	40
MUS215	4	2	B	3	103

not facilitate analysis of the information because the array is usually ordered by names or ID numbers. If, however, you arrayed a list of scores from the highest to lowest scores, a visual inspection would easily identify, for example, the highest and lowest scores, whether the scores overall were high or low, how much they were dispersed, and where you fit into this distribution.

Frequency Distributions   More common than an array for descriptive purposes is a *frequency distribution*, in which each unique attribute of a variable is listed, along with a count of the frequency with which it occurs. For example, if we wanted to know quickly how many As, Bs, Cs, and Ds our student in Table 2 had in the first two years of college, we would list the grades, along with how often they occur, as in Table 3 on the next page.

Frequency distribution tables have titles and include headings. Each column is labeled, the attribute column with its label and the frequency column with an *f*. The frequencies are totaled in the bottom row, typically presented in parentheses

Table 3. Frequency Distribution of Grades

Grade	f
A	6
B	11
C	5
D	1
(N)	(23)

Table 4. Grouped Frequency Distribution for Class Size

Class Size	f
100+	4
50-99	7
25-49	7
0-24	5
(N)	(23)

with an (N) in the attribute column, which stands for the number of cases. A lower-case *n* is used if the cases represent a sample from a larger population of cases. An upper-case *N* is used if the cases presented constitute the entire population of cases. Because grade has orderable attributes, these grades are listed in order, typically from the highest score to the lowest. With a frequency distribution, we may glean quite quickly information about this student's grades.

To simplify data display, you may also collapse numbers to form groups. For example, from Table 2 create a frequency distribution for class size. While it is useful to see the class sizes ordered from high to low, it is also helpful to group classes of similar sizes. Let's say we decide to group classes having 100 or more students as one category, those having 50-99 as another, 25-49 as another, and those having 24 or fewer students as our last category. Thus, variables having quantitative attributes are displayed as *grouped frequency distributions*. The grouping scheme is arbitrary, but the goal is to make the table succinct, yet informative, while not distorting the underlying distribution of the scores.

Table 4 provides an example. There can be different rationales for creating the groups of a grouped frequency distribution. In Table 4, for example, we could have opted for only three categories (such as small, medium, and large). However, a couple of basic conventions are (1) to avoid overlapping categories (0-24 and 25-49, not 0-25 and 25-50) and (2) to have no fewer than three and no more than seven groupings.

While frequency distributions are useful for displaying information, their utility is quite limited, especially when the number of cases is large. Frequencies have meaning only in context. The four classes of 100+ in Table 4 acquire meaning only in the context of the 23 classes and in comparison to the frequencies of the other categories.

When the number of cases gets larger, the difficulty of making quick sense of them increases. One can process pretty quickly that 4 out of 23 classes were large or that the student had twice as many classes between 25 to 49 as 100 or over. Such observations come less easily in Table 5, which lists class sizes for a university rather than an individual student.

With larger numbers (1000s, 100,000s and millions) statisticians con-   *Relative Frequencies*

Table 5. Class Sizes for a University	
Class Size	**f**
100+	313
50-99	582
25-49	640
0-24	566
(N)	(2101)

Table 6. Percentages of Class Sizes for a University	
Class Size	**%**
101+	14.90
50-99	27.70
25-49	30.46
0-24	26.94
(N)	(2101)

vert frequencies to *relative frequencies*. The most common is the *percentage*. Literally "per 100," a percentage is simply a *proportion* (f/n) multiplied by 100. Thus, the proportion of large classes in Table 5 is 313/2101, or .1490. Multiplying by 100 gives a percentage of 14.90%. Completing the conversion of frequencies to percentages produces Table 6.

It is especially important in a percentaged table to report the number of cases on which the percentages are based. With this number known, you may convert a percentage back to a frequency by reversing the process. Divide the percentage by 100 and multiply the resulting proportion by the number of cases. Thus, 14.90% of 2101 is 313 [(14.90/100) x 2101]. Note that rounding off percentages (e.g., 14.90% to 15%) introduces some error in reproducing the original frequency [(15/100) x 2101 = 315].

Retaining the proper level of accuracy requires computing the original proportion to the same number of digits contained in the number of cases. Thus, in Table 4, converting 5 of 23 classes to a percentage requires only two places [5/23 = .22 or 22%]. Because accuracy to the units place (that is, the location of the decimal point) becomes less important as numbers increase, calculating proportions beyond four digits and, thus, percentages beyond two places to the right of the decimal is rare.

Percentages permit comparisons of attributes across different cases because they convert the world to 100 cases and compare variable distributions, large and small, to the same base of 100. For example, 22% of the student's classes (5/23) in Table 2 were small, while about 27% of the university's classes (566/2101) were that size. In other words, for the university, 27 out of every 100 classes were of size 25 or smaller.

Rates   Frequencies may be converted to a base other than 100. A *rate* is a proportion converted to a whole number, usually one, two, or three digits on a base of some multiple of 1,000, 10,000, 100,000, or 1 million. Rates are particularly useful when proportions are too small to visualize.

For example, in one recent year Alaska had 36 murders in its population of 670,053 people. We could simply note what percentage of its population was murdered, namely, 36/670,053 = .0000537 or .00537%.

Such a number, however, defies visualization. A major goal of statistical description is to make data comprehensible. Rather than produce a percentage, moving the decimal place farther to the right sufficient to make a number greater than 1 permits us to visualize what the data tell us. In the case of Alaska, moving the decimal place over five places produces the number 5.37. Moving the decimal place to the right is equivalent to multiplying the number by exponents of 10. Simply put down a 0 for every place you move the decimal point and put a 1 in front of the zeroes. Moving the decimal point five places to the right in the proportion .0000537 is the same as multiplying that number by 100,000. Consequently, Alaska had a murder rate of 5.37 murders per 100,000 population. Now we can compare murder in Alaska to murder in any other state. If New York had 921 murders that same year with its population of 18,306,183, which state had more murders relative to its population? It appears New York was actually somewhat safer with 5.03 murders per 100,000 population.

A *ratio* compares the size of two numbers by placing them in a fraction.   Ratios

For example, in Table 3, the ratio of A and B grades to C and D grades is [(6+11)/(5+1)=17/6]. It is customary to convert the ratio to a base of 1 by simply performing the division designated by the fraction (17/6 = 2.83/1), reporting that ratio as 2.83 to 1 — or, because of the small numbers involved here, you might simply say the ratio of As and Bs to Cs and Ds is about 3 to 1. You may also report the ratio by referring to the base of 1 first. For every C and D grade the student received, she earned about 3 As and Bs.

A Bureau of Justice Statistics report used ratios to compare the victimization of women compared to men. In one year of the report, women were more than 5 times as likely as men to have been victims of violence at the hands of someone intimately known to them (900,000/167,000 = 5.39/1). In other words, for every man victimized by an intimate, there were 5.39 such victimizations of women.

Percentage change generates a percentage to reveal the relative   Percentage Change
amount of change over time. By dividing the amount of change over
time for a given variable or attribute with its initial value or score and then multiplying by 100, you have the percentage by which something has changed. For example, an increase in tuition and fees from $13,000 to $14,000 is an increase of $1,000. An increase of 1,000 over a base of 13,000 [(14,000-13,000)/13,000 x 100] is a 7.7% increase in intuition and fees. If you like formulas, then

$$\text{percentage change} = \left(\frac{X_2 - X_1}{X_1}\right) \times 100$$

where X_1 is the initial value and X_2 is the more recent value. Pay attention to the direction of change. There can be percentage decreases as well as increases. Tuition and fees may never decline, but if the cost of a computer drops from $1,099 to $949, then the percentage change is [(949-1099)/1099 x 100] or -13.6%.

Standardizing frequencies to a common base is only one set of ways   Central Tendency
to describe and analyze the distribution of a variable. Another is to

summarize the distribution with regard to its central tendency. *Central tendency* is a construct that refers to the score or attribute of a variable that is most typical or representative of the variable distribution. As a construct, it requires *operationalization*, a specification of instructions (operations) by which these measures of central tendency (generically called *averages*) will be produced.

Mode   The *mode* defines what is most typical or representative as the attribute or score in a variable distribution that occurs most frequently. By that definition, you can see that the modal grade in Table 3 is a B. Be sure to remember that the mode is the score or attribute of a variable that occurs most frequently, not the frequency itself. Thus, the mode in Table 3 is B, not 11.

Distributions can have more than one mode. Indeed, bimodal distributions, having two modes, are very important because they identify two central tendencies in the distribution. The frequency count for two modes need not be the same; the mode is more impressionistic. If there were 10 Ds in that distribution along with the 11 Bs, the distribution would be considered bimodal.

It may also be the case that the mode may not be very typical. The modal class size in the Table 2 data set is 19, but only two of the 23 cases are that size, while 20 of the 23 are classes larger than 19 students.

Median   The *median* is the score or attribute of the case that is in the middle. To have a middle, a variable must be at least *ordinal* in nature. A *nominal* variable has no middle because it possesses no underlying order among the attributes.

As an example, look at the data in Table 2. There is no median class subject because there is no middle, no above or below in a set of course subjects. There is a median class size, however. You may ask the computer to find the median for class size, or you may arrange the class sizes in order, ranging from the lowest score of 17 to the highest score of 237, and then note the score of the case in the middle. Since there are 23 cases, the middle case is the 12th one — 11 cases have scores above the 40 class size of the middle case and 11 cases have smaller class sizes than 40. If a variable has an even number of cases, split the difference between the scores of the two middle cases.

Arithmetic Mean   The *arithmetic mean* defines the most typical or representative score as a distribution's arithmetic balance point. (It is the same as the common mathematical average.) This balance point is easily determined. Simply add the scores of all the cases on a particular variable and divide that sum by the number of cases. As a formula, we would say:

$$\overline{X} = \frac{\Sigma X_i}{n}$$

where $\overline{X}$ = arithmetic mean, Σ = the sum of, X_i = scores of the individual cases, and n = number of cases

This arithmetic mean is a balance point by virtue of the fact that the sum of the deviations from the mean for those cases above the mean is equal to the sum of the deviations from the mean for those cases with scores below the mean. A *deviation* is the difference between a score and the mean. From Table 2, for example, the sum of all class sizes is 1459. Divide by 23, the number of cases, and you have 63.4, the arithmetic mean. You can verify that 63.4 is the arithmetic balance point by summing the differences between the mean and each case's score in the distribution. Since the sum of those deviations for the scores higher than 63.4 will equal the sum of those deviations for the scores lower than 63.4, the sum of all deviations from the mean will equal 0.

The *weighted arithmetic mean* assigns weights to the value of each case's score on a variable.

Weighted Arithmetic Mean

For example, calculating the grade point average (mean) for the student in Table 2 cannot be done simply by summing the grade points assigned for each grade (A=4, B=3, etc.) because hours of credit for the course vary. Thus, for example, the grade in the one-hour PED215 course does not weigh the same as the grade in the five-hour GER101 course. Instead of $\sum X$ to sum up the case scores, you must do $\sum wX$, namely, sum the product of the weight and the score. So, POS100 multiplies the 3-hour weight value times the 3 grade points for a B to get 9. ENG101 adds 12 to the sum (that is, 3 hours times 4 grade points for the A). The result across all 23 cases is a sum of 208. Rather than divide by n, the number of cases, you must divide by the sum of the weights, $\sum w$, the total number of hours, namely, 69. The result is a grade point average of 3.0.

We now have various measures by which to report the central tendency of a variable's distribution. Which one is best to use depends on the characteristics of the distribution and the purpose of the description.

Choosing the Best Measure

In the instance of class size for the student as shown in Table 2, the mode is 19, the median is 40, and the mean is 63. Which one do you think better typifies the distribution? The following conventions exist for making choices:

1. Use the mode for a nominal variable.
2. Report the modes for bimodal distributions, even if you also report a median or mean.
3. Report the arithmetic mean for distributions for quantitative (interval and ratio) variables in which the median and arithmetic mean are relatively close together. These are symmetrical distributions, and the arithmetic mean has greater utility than the median.
4. Report the median for distributions in which the arithmetic mean and the median are not very close together. These are skewed distributions in which the arithmetic mean is unduly influenced by so-called *outliers*, extreme scores at one end of the distribution.
5. Continue to use the commonly accepted measure of central tendency for a particular variable. Average income in demographic data, for example, is conventionally reported as median family income. So, even if the income distribution is not skewed, continue to use the median anyway.

Returning to the class size variable in Table 2, I would argue that the mean size of 63 is not a typical size of this student's classes. Furthermore, only two of the 23 classes were 19, which otherwise are the second and third smallest classes.

I would opt for the median of 40 as the best choice. By definition, it is the most central score, and the mode and mean offer no compelling reasons for selecting them.

Variation   Does it seem somehow wrong to you to use a single point in a distribution of a variable to represent that distribution? Consider three students, each of whom has a grade point average of 3.0. Does that make them equivalent in terms of their academic performance? The first student achieved that score by securing a B in every class he took. The second divided her grades evenly by having an A in one-third of her hours, a B in one-third, and a C in one-third. A third student attained a 3.0 by virtue of having half As and half Cs. Three students, three very different grade distributions — yet all painted as the same B-student with their 3.0 gpas.

From such examples, we can see that averages can be very misleading depending in large part on how much variation there is among the attributes or scores of the individual cases that comprise a variable distribution. Consider your friends and fellow students. To the extent that there is little variation among you, you might be characterized as being alike, homogenous, equal, similar, common, in agreement, and exhibiting consensus. The more variation there is among you, the more you are unalike, heterogeneous, unequal, dissimilar, uncommon, in disagreement, and characterized by dissensus. Modes, medians, and means best capture what is typical or representative where there is little variation. They don't do well, and in fact can misload, in instances where there is considerable variation.

That's why scholars almost always report some measure of *variation* when they report measures of central tendency. Understanding variation is every bit as important as understanding central tendency. Just as central tendency is key to description and prediction, variation is used to assess the quality of central tendency measures and plays a significant role in statistical contributions to explanation.

Variation Ratio   Each measure of central tendency has corresponding measures of variation that help to evaluate how representative the central tendency measure is in characterizing a variable distribution. The *variation ratio* is simply the proportion of cases that fall outside the *mode* in a variable distribution. The mode for class size in Table 2 is 19. But the mode contains only two cases. Fully 21/23 of the cases, which is .91 or 91%, fall outside the mode. This tells us that the mode of 19 is not a very representative indicator of class size.

Range   The worth of the *median* as a measure of central tendency is dependent on how narrowly scores are dispersed in the distribution. The *range* is the difference between the highest and lowest scores of a distribution. In the Table 2 dataset, the range in class sizes is 237-17=220. As you can see, any extreme score in a distribution, commonly referred to as an *outlier*, will greatly affect the range. That much sensitivity is not desirable.

Inter-ranges   A more stable set of measures, called *inter-ranges*, drop off a specified highest and lowest percentage of the cases. The most popular are the *inter-decile range, inter-quintile range, and inter-quartile range*. Deciles are tenths, quintiles are fifths, and quartiles are fourths. These inter-ranges drop off the highest and lowest 10%, 20% and 25% of the cases, respectively, and then calculate the range of the remaining cases.

For example, the inter-quartile range for class size in our small dataset would drop off the highest one-fourth and lowest one-fourth of the 23 cases. It's not an even number (23/4=5.75), but we'll round up and drop off the top six (237, 133, 124, 103, 97, 90) and bottom six cases (17, 19, 19, 22, 23, 25). Of the remaining scores, the range is 56 (83-27). It is proper to say, then, that the range of the middle 50% of the cases is 56. The median, of course, remains at the center of these middle 50% of the cases, giving some indication on how tightly the middle 50% of the cases are clustered about the median.

The mean deviation, variance, and standard deviation are three measures based upon how much the scores in a variable distribution deviate from the *arithmetic mean*. These measures must work around the fact that the sum of all deviations from the mean is zero. The *mean deviation* does so by summing the absolute deviations, that is, without regard to whether the deviation is positive or negative. It then divides that sum by the number of cases, producing an average deviation of scores from the mean. The *variance* squares each deviation from the mean, sums those squared deviations, and then divides by the number of cases to produce the average squared deviation. The *standard deviation* is the square root of the variance.

Deviation from the Mean

Table 7 illustrates the calculations of two measures (the *deviation from the mean* for each case and the *squared deviations* — to make them positive so as to sum them later on) from the Table 2 dataset. For simplicity, we are only doing the first two semesters of work. The mean class size for those 11 classes is 62.6. The largest class deviation from that mean is 237-62.6 = 174.4. The smallest class deviates from the mean by 17-62.6 = -45.6. While the sum of deviations from the mean will always be zero, the absolute deviations sum to 530.8, and the mean deviation is 530.8/11 = 48.3, the average amount by which a case deviates from the mean. The squared deviations sum to 45,978.6, which makes the variance 45,798.6/11 = 4179.9, and the standard deviation 64.7. Any spreadsheet or statistical package will calculate these three measures.

While the mean deviation has the most intuitive interpretation, the squared deviations approach of the variance and standard deviation is preferred because of its utility in more complex statistical operations.

Prediction with Single Variable Distributions

Prediction in statistical work refers to guessing the unknown, not necessarily predicting the future. Archeologists and astronomers, among others, typically guess the age of things past and may use statistical techniques we would classify as predictive in nature. For example, if an archeologist discovered that the ages of most skulls in a tomb seemed to deviate from 40, with some younger and others older, he may conclude that the average age of people buried in that tomb was 40 when they died.

By their very nature of identifying the most typical or representative attribute or score in a variable distribution, central tendency measures can be used to predict (guess). As an example, let's make a guess about our student in Table 2. She

Table 7. Deviations from Class Size Means for Semesters 1 and 2

Class Size	Deviation from Mean	Squared Deviations
237	174.4	30415.36
133	70.4	4956.16
80	17.4	302.76
66	3.4	11.56
32	−30.6	936.36
31	−31.6	998.56
30	−32.6	1062.76
25	−37.6	1413.76
19	−43.6	1900.96
19	−43.6	1900.96
17	−45.6	2079.36
Sum	0.0	45978.56
Sum Absolute Values	530.8	

has a 3.0 gpa, and her modal grade is a B, having almost as many Bs as all other grades combined. What would you guess her grade in her next class will be? In the absence of any other information, your best guess is B. But what about a student with a 3.0 gpa for whom a modal grade is C, specifically 30 hours of A, 7 hours of B, and 32 hours of C? Your best guess in terms of being either right or wrong is a C, but the variation ratio tells us the likelihood of being wrong is 37/69, which is .54 or 54%.

STATISTICAL ANALYSIS OF BIVARIATE DISTRIBUTIONS Analysis of a single variable at a time is neither very useful nor particularly interesting. Only by examining the various statistical descriptions of a single variable across the attributes of a second variable do we gain meaning and insight regarding the distribution of that initial variable. A gpa of 3.0 offers meaning only in context. Among those competing for academic scholarships, a 3.0 may be considered low. Among those who entered the university on academic probation, a 3.0 may be considered high. The average income for professors may seem high compared to the average income for all workers, but low compared to the average income of attorneys or doctors. Within the university itself, the average income of faculty will vary considerably by professorial rank, the discipline of the faculty member, and perhaps by gender or length of service.

Introducing a *second variable* across which to analyze some initial variable of interest provides context that gives meaning to descriptions, a basis for providing explanations, and a refined way to make better predictions.

The staple of bivariate analysis is the *contingency table*, also known as the crosstabulation or *crosstabs table*, in which the occurrences of attributes on one variable are tabulated across, or are said to be *contingent on*, the attributes of a second variable. Suppose we wish to analyze the student's grades from Table 2 by the class size. Simply create a table of rows and columns for the category scheme you wish to use. Let's use the groupings from Table 4 for class size. Notice that Table 8 has a title identifying the variables (grades and class size), that the columns and rows are both labeled with the attributes for the variables, and that the total column and row, which are called *marginals*, provide the frequency distribution for each of the two variables respectively.

When a table has few cases, such that most cells have only single digit fre-

Table 8. Grades by Class Size

	0-24	25-49	50-99	100+	Total
A	0	4	2	0	6
B	5	1	2	3	11
C	0	2	2	1	5
D	0	0	1	0	1
Total	5	7	7	4	23

Table 9. Test Result and Cancer Status

	Cancer	No Cancer	Total
Positive	108	312	420
Negative	12	4368	4380
Total	120	4680	4800

quencies, there is little need to convert the frequencies to percentages. As the number of cases increases, the interpretation of the data is facilitated by converting the frequencies to percentages. Let's consider the issues involved in calculating percentages by examining Table 9 and Table 10.

Table 9 cross-tabulates the positive and negative results from a cancer-screening test with whether or not the individual was determined to actually have cancer. The task of converting the frequencies to percentages is confounded by the fact that there are three different ways in which these frequencies can be percentaged: dividing each cell frequency (1) by the total number of cases in the table, (2) by the total number of cases in the column for that cell, and (3) by the total number of cases in the row for that cell.

The manner in which the table should be percentaged depends on the purpose of the analysis, be it description, explanation, or prediction. To divide a cell by the total number of cases is inherently descriptive. Each cell is treated as if it were an attribute of a single variable. The combination of these two dichotomous variables in Table 9 could be viewed as creating a single four-attribute variable, namely the validity of a particular cancer-screening test, containing four categories that classify the test results as (1) true positive (tested positive and does have cancer), (2) true negative (tested negative and does not have cancer), (3) false positive (tested positive but does not have cancer), and (4) false negative (tested

Table 10. Test Result and Cancer Status

	Cancer	No Cancer	Total
Positive	2.25% (true positive)	6.50% (false positive)	(420)
Negative	0.25% (false negative)	91.00% (true negative)	(4380)
Total	(120)	(4680)	(4800)

negative but does have cancer). Table 10 shows the results of the percentaging using the total number of cases as the base number.

Explanation and prediction, as well as comparative description, involve percentaging a table by dividing cell frequencies by either their column totals or their row totals. In these instances, it is necessary to classify each of the two variables according to function. It is helpful to label them as Y and X variables — illustrated by the scheme in Table 11.

After determining the type of analysis in which you are engaged, percentage the distribution of the Y variable within each of the X attributes. Explanation, for example, establishes independent and dependent variables, roughly equivalent to cause and effect. A cause must precede its effect in time. Consequently, whether or

Table 11. Distinguishing Variables in a Bivariate Distribution by Purpose of Analysis

	Description	Explanation	Prediction
Y-variable	Variable being described	Dependent (effect) variable	Variable to be predicted
X-variable	Comparison variable	Independent (cause) variable	Predictor variable

Table 12. Test Result by Cancer Status

	Cancer	No Cancer	Total
Positive	90.00%	6.67%	8.75%
Negative	10.00	93.33	91.25
(n)	(120)	(4680)	(4800)

Table 13. Cancer Status by Test Result

	Cancer	No Cancer	Total
Positive	25.71%	74.29	(420)
Negative	0.27%	99.73	(4380)
Total	2.50%	97.50	(4800)

not one actually has cancer precedes the test results from the screening, making the former the *independent* (X) variable and the test results the *dependent* (Y) variable. Percentaging the distribution of test results (positive/negative) means dividing a cell frequency by its column total (108/120=.900, see Table 9). The resulting percentages tell us what percentage of cases with the X attribute possess the Y attribute. Ninety percent of those with cancer tested positive. See Table 12 for the full table percentaged down the columns.

When predicting, either variable may be used to predict the other, and the resulting percentages serve as probabilities. Since the purpose of a screening test is to predict the disease, Table 13 establishes the test result as the *predictor* (X) variable and whether or not one actually has cancer as the variable to be *predicted* (Y). The result is a table that is percentaged across the rows, dividing each cell frequency by its row total, producing percentaged distributions of cancer/no cancer within each attribute of the test result (positive and negative). The result is striking. Whereas 90.0% of those with cancer test positive (see Table

12), only 25.7% of those testing positive actually had cancer (108/420). Whereas only 6.5% (312/4800) of those being screened produced false positive results (see Table 10), 74.3% (312/420) of those testing positive were in fact false positives (Table 13). The direction in which a table is percentaged makes a considerable difference, and it is critical to understand the purpose of the analysis in order to percentage the table correctly.

When interpreting tables that are already percentaged, establish how the percentages have been calculated. If the percentages down the column total 100%, then the X variable attributes are the columns. If the percentages total 100% across the rows, then the row categories are the X variable attributes. If all cell percentages total 100%, then there is no X or Y variable. Rather, the two variables are being treated as a single variable, and each cell represents an attribute of the combined variables. If column totals or row totals exceed 100%, either multiple responses for a case have been permitted or multiple Y variables have been included in a single table. Remember that in any percentaged table with identifiable Y and X variables, the percentage represents the percentage of cases within the X-variable attribute that possess the Y-variable attribute.

Scatterplots, Regression, and Correlation

Contingency tables work well for variables that are nominal or ordinal or with grouped frequency distributions of interval and ratio level variables. More sophisticated analyses for both prediction and explanation are available, however, when analyzing continuous variables that utilize interval and ratio level numeric scales.

Visually, such data may be arrayed in a *scatterplot*, in which the X variable is aligned along the horizontal axis and the Y variable along the vertical axis. Figure 1 examines a fairly persistent feature of American politics, the tendency since 1950 of the president's political party to lose seats in the U. S. House of Representatives during the mid-term election. A causal factor in these elections and a potential predictor of how many seats the president's party might lose is the president's approval rating in the couple of months preceding the election. Approval rating is treated as the X variable in Figure 1.

Each dot represents a case and provides its scores on the X and Y variables. The left-most dot, for example, represents President Bush's approval rating in 2006 of around 38% and the Republican loss of 31 seats (see Table 14). Interestingly, President Bush is also the lowest dot in the chart at a -8, which actually represents a seat gain for the Republicans when his approval rate hovered around 63% in 2002. The horizontal line extending from the Y-axis at about 22 is the mean seat loss in the mid-term elections without regard to presidential approval. Even though the mean is the arithmetic balance point of seat loss, observe how far from that mean line most of the dots are, indicating considerable variation and how poorly the mean would serve as a predictor of seat loss.

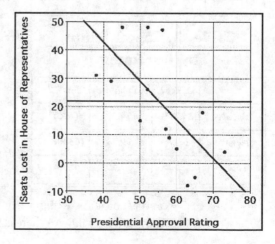

Figure 1. Seat Loss in House by Presidential Approval Rating

Table 14. Seat Loss in House of Representatives and Presidential Approval Rating in Mid-Term Elections

Year	1950	1954	1958	1962	1966	1970	1974	1978	1982	1986	1990	1994	1998	2002	2006
Seat Loss	29	18	48	4	47	12	48	15	26	5	9	54	-5	-8	31
Pres. Rating	42	67	52	73	56	57	45	50	52	60	58	45	65	63	38

Regression   Introducing presidential approval scores exhibits a distinct connection (relationship) with seat loss. As approval ratings increase, seat loss values decrease. Using a technique called *simple linear regression*, we can calculate a straight line that serves as a moving average for the Y variable, seat loss in this example, given any value of X, presidential approval rating in this example.

We need not rely on the visual of the line. A very simple formula locates any Y point (Yp) on the line for any given value of X: $Yp = a + bX$, where a is the Y-intercept, the value of Y when X=0, and b (the *regression coefficient*) is the slope of the line, the average change in Y when X increases one unit. Any spreadsheet or statistical package will produce these calculations. In the seat loss data of Figure 1, a=97.4 and b= -1.4. What seat loss, then, would you predict in a mid-term election in which the president had an approval rating of 50%? $Yp = 97.4 + (-1.4 \times 50) = 27.4$. The president's party should lose somewhere in the vicinity of 27 seats.

Correlation   While the regression line itself facilitates prediction, analysis of the variation around the line in comparison with how much variation existed in the variable prior to its regression on the X variable provides a statistical component of explanation, measuring the impact one variable has on another.

The logic goes like this. Why is there variation in seat loss in mid-term elections? What accounts for high seat loss in one year, a medium amount in another year, and even a small gain in another? We see with the regression line that presidential approval rating, when associated with seat loss, exhibits a pattern in which a regression line drawn through the bivariate distribution considerably reduces the variation in seat loss. The variance around the mean of seat loss is 381.5. The variance around the regression line is 209.8. The result is a reduction in variation of 171.7. Dividing that reduction by the original variance of 381.5 produces a proportion by which the original variation in the Y variable (seat loss) has been reduced when associated with the X variable (presidential approval rating), namely, 0.45 or 45%.

This proportional reduction in variation is used as the basis for measuring association between two variables: ([original variation in Y — variation remaining in Y when associated with X] divided by the original variation in Y).

The most famous of these measures is *Pearson's correlation coefficient* (r), which possesses the attributes desired in a good measure of association. It ranges from .00 to a ±1.00, with .00 indicating two variables are not associated (do not covary) in any statistical way and ±1 .00 indicating perfect association, signifying zero variance around the regression line. A positive association indicates that those cases with higher scores on the X variable also have higher scores on the Y variable (and cases with lower X scores also have lower Y scores). A negative association indicates that cases with higher scores on the X variable tend to have lower scores on the Y variable (and lower Xs are associated with having higher Ys). In the case of Pearson's r, squaring the r is necessary to obtain the interpretation of proportional reduction in Y brought about by its association with X.

There are many other measures of association. Some use different measures of variation, appropriate to the level of measurement of the Y and X variables. Others simply emulate the Pearson's r formula, which involves measuring the co-variation between the Y and X variables. Some emulate the regression coefficient, measuring the amount of change in Y with a unit change in X. Still others provide for a reduction in error used with other prediction techniques. Table 15 summarizes some of these measures, which will typically appear as options in statistical packages when running contingency tables or asking for correlation options.

A Significant Divergence: Statistical Tests

You have already been introduced to hypotheses in Chapter 1 and to the testing of hypotheses in Chapter 12. Research involves the specification and testing of hypotheses, statements of conjecture typically about the relationship between two or more variables. Science proceeds not only by testing whether data support the alternative hypothesis (that is, the research hypothesis), but whether the null hypothesis might be rejected. (To refresh your memory about alternative and null hypotheses, you may wish to re-read pages 181-182 in Prof. Sanders's Chapter 12 in this book.)

A research hypothesis usually asserts the existence of some relationship between variables. For example, a study of salary differences between male and female professors might assert that there is a salary difference, a nondirectional hypothesis that does not speculate about the nature of that relationship. Given the historical differences between the sexes and income earnings, one might speculate with a directional hypothesis that male professors have higher salaries than female professors. All nondirectional and directional hypothesis have a null/random chance alternative, namely, that there is no relationship between the variables and that any observed relationship is due to chance. In a sample, that chance factor certainly involves random sampling error, even assuming an unbiased, representative sample. It also involves, even in a population dataset, the fact that random processes can produce chance appearances of a relationship where none truly exists.

Calculating Relationships

Statistically, we can compare models of no relationship with what we actually observe in the data and calculate a probability of being wrong if we reject that null/random chance hypothesis. We have statistical tests for virtually all of the statistical calculations that we produce.

Goodness-of-fit tests evaluate an observed univariate, bivariate, or multivariate distribution against a given model, often but not always of non-association, to assess whether random variations in the data could account for observed deviations from the model.

The most famous of these tests uses a probability distribution called *chi-*

Table 15. Measures of Association

	Coefficient	Level of Measurement	Interpretation
1	Pearson's r	quantitative	r^2=% reduction in variation (variance)
2	Lambda	nominal	% reduction in variation (variation ratio); % reduction in error
3	Goodman & Kruskal's tau	nominal	% reduction in variation (index of qualitative variation)
4	eta	Y = quantitative X = nominal	eta^2=% reduction in variation (variance)
5	phi	dichotomies	Pearson's r analog
6	Spearman's rho	ordinal (no ties)	Pearson's r analog
7	Kendall's tau-a	ordinal (no ties)	Pearson's r analog
8	Kendall's tau-b	ordinal (tied ranks)	Pearson's r analog
9	Percentage difference	dichotomies	slope (regression coefficient) analog
10	Somer's d	ordinal (tied ranks)	slope (regression coefficient) analog
11	gamma	ordinal (tied ranks)	% reduction in error

square (X^2) and produces a probability value (P or p).

Most measures of association, including the slope (regression coefficient), can be tested against the null hypothesis that the association coefficient is only a random deviation from .00 (no association), with the result also being a given probability value.

There are tests for differences between or among proportions and between or among means of different groups, as well as other statistics. Again, the null hypothesis tested is that there is no difference between or among those observed proportions or means, any observed difference being due to chance. And while these tests use different probability distributions (the t-distribution, the F-distribution, the binomial distribution, the normal distribution, among others), all produce a probability value for evaluating the status of the null/random chance hypothesis.

We use the probability value to decide whether or not to reject the null/random chance hypothesis. Rejecting the null/random chance hypothesis eliminates a significant statistical alternative to the research hypothesis, permitting one to declare that the statistical measure being evaluated is statistically significant. The decision not to reject the null/random chance hypothesis means that it remains as a viable alternative to the research hypothesis. The conventional probability value used to reject the null/random chance hypothesis and declare the statistical measure statistically significant is $p \leq .05$. Other levels may be used by researchers, but the .05 level is conventional. This p value is the likelihood of being in error when rejecting the null hypothesis.

Table 16 is a complex table designed to demonstrate a number of the statistical applications that have been presented in this chapter. It presents salary data for a university's faculty, looking at the mean differences between men and women, between Anglos and non-Anglos, and among the three different professorial ranks of assistant professor, associate professor, and professor.

Examples

Table 16. Salary by Sex, Ethnicity, and Professional Rank, Respectively

	Male	Female		Anglo	Nonanglo		Asst.Prof.	Assc.Prof	Prof.
Mean Salary	80,322	64,045		76,056	75,266		58,383	63,797	89,901
ANOVA	p < .001			p = .662			p < .001		
eta-squared	$\varepsilon^2=.09$			$\varepsilon^2=.00$			$\varepsilon^2=.33$		
slope	b=16277; p <.001			b = 790; p = .662			b = 17379; p < .001		
Pearson's r	r=.30, $r^2=.09$			r=.01; $r^2=.00$			r=.54; $r^2=.29$		

The row below the mean salaries labeled ANOVA refers to a statistical test of the differences in means between groups, called *analysis of variance*. The ultimate output of the test is a probability value that evaluates the null hypothesis of an ANOVA, namely, that there is no difference in the means of the different variable groups — that any observed difference is simply due to chance. If p ≤ .05, we reject that null hypothesis and declare the difference is statistically significant. As you can see, the $16,277 difference between men and women is statistically significant, as are the differences in professorial rank, both with p-values of less than .001. The $790 difference between Anglos and non-Anglos is not statistically significant, having a p-value of .662, which is substantially above the threshold of ≤ .05.

An appropriate measure of association for these three bivariate distributions is *eta*, the fourth measure listed in Table 15. Specifically, ε^2 tells us how much the original variation in salary has been reduced when associated with some X variable. Sex provides a 9% reduction, professorial rank produces a 33% reduction, but the ethnicity variable has no relationship with salary as shown by its inability to reduce the variation in salary. When the X variable is a dichotomy, Pearson's r and eta are equivalent, and the slope (regression coefficient) in a linear regression is equivalent to the difference in Y means between the two X variable categories. While linear regression and, thus, Pearson's r, is not recommended for an ordinal X variable like professorial rank, such limitations are sometimes relaxed. The results in Table 16 for professorial rank reveal statistically significant results (p < .001 for b and, while not shown, for Pearson's r). Considering such a variety of measures, you can begin to appreciate that it's either time to learn more about statistics or to consult a statistician.

Salary differences among the professors of different ranks are expected. After all, promotion through the ranks is accompanied by pay raises, and a common percentage increase will produce a higher increase for those with higher pay. More disconcerting is a substantial difference of more than $16,000 in salaries between men and women. One might be tempted to bang the drum about pay inequities between men and women. But one should be careful. Let's consider why.

STATISTICAL ANALYSIS OF THREE OR MORE VARIABLE DISTRIBUTIONS

Multivariate statistical analysis is often little more than an extension of bivariate techniques. The use of multivariate analysis, however, is critical. Using bivariate distributions to make causal inferences and predictions can produce erroneous results. Let's follow up on this supposed salary difference between male and female professors.

Rank affects salary in an accepted and expected manner, increasing as one moves from the lowest (assistant) to the highest (professor) rank. Perhaps one reason the average salary for men is higher than that for women is that there are more men at the highest rank compared to the lowest. After all, rank is partly a matter of time. Those most likely to be professors have been around quite a while. Women have come to the professoriate in larger numbers more recently than men. So we might expect more of them at the lower ranks. Table 17 presents a crosstabs (contingency) table of gender by rank — and it does indeed show that while men and women are in the assistant professor rank in nearly equal proportions, men outnumber women by more than two to one at the professor rank.

The appropriate statistical test to evaluate the null/random chance hypothesis that there is no difference among the ranks with respect to the proportions of men and women is a *chi square test*. It's p value is <.001, suggesting that the null hypothesis be rejected, that the differences across ranks in the distribution of men and women are statistically significant.

Table 17. Sex by Professorial Rank

	Asst. Prof.	Assc. Prof.	Prof.	Total
Male	50.6%	64.3%	81.3%	69.9%
Female	49.4	35.7	18.7	30.1
(N)	(235)	(387)	(587)	(1209)

Chi-square (X^2) = 83.12; p < .001

Does this fact have any impact on salary differences between men and women? Table 18 suggests that it does. This multivariable table examines mean salaries for men and women within the different ranks. Rank is considered a control variable, its effect on salary held constant while looking at the difference between men and women. Observe that the difference between men and women among assistant professors is about $10,430. For associate professors, the difference is $6,637;

Table 18. Salary by Sex and Professorial Rank

	Assistant Professor		Associate Professor		Professor		Total
	Male	Female	Male	Female	Male	Female	
Mean Salary	63,531	53,101	66,164	59,527	91,902	81,221	75,418
(N)	(119)	(116)	(249)	(138)	(477)	(110)	(1209)

and for professors, the difference is $10,681. It appears, then, that about a third of the original $16,000 difference between men and women was due to rank, not to gender.

We could also apply a regression model using *multiple linear regression*. In Table 19, observe that Model 1 simply looks at the impact of gender on salary and finds a difference between men and women of $16,277, the slope for a dichotomy being the same as the mean difference observed between men and women in Table 16. Model 2 adds professorial rank into the equation, in a linear regression equivalent to the crosstabs created by Table 18. It says that the difference in mean salaries of men and women has dropped to $9,273, an amount that remains statistically significant.

Table 19. Multiple Regression Models for Salaries

	Model 1	Model 2	Model 3
Sex	b = 16277 p < .001	b = 9273 p < .001	b = 2645 p = .008
Professorial Rank		b = 15936 p < .001	b = 16495 p < .001
College (Mean Salary)			b = .958 p < .001

Extending the process, it makes sense to ask what other variables might produce differences in salaries between men and women. You may not know this, but salaries in universities vary considerably by college. Generally, faculty in business, law, and engineering have higher salaries than faculty in liberal arts and education, who in turn make more than faculty in nursing and the fine arts. It's also true that women are more likely to be found among the faculty in nursing, the fine arts, and education than in business, law, and engineering. While that is becoming less so, it was very much true throughout the 20th century. Fitting college, a nominal variable, into a linear regression is a tricky business. One could create dichotomies (called dummy variables) out of the colleges (e.g., liberal arts v. not liberal arts). In Model 3 of Table 19, we introduced college by using the mean college salary as a surrogate value for the college, providing a metric that accurately applied the salary differences of the colleges.

Observe, in Model 3, what now happens to the gender difference. While still statistically significant, the difference between men and women, controlling for the effects of rank and college, is now $2,645, quite a far cry from the $16,000+ difference first observed in the bivariate distribution. There are still other variables that could be introduced — for example, number of years in the professoriate, number of years in rank, and specific departments within colleges, as well as more intricate measures called *interaction effects* in which the combined effects of two variables together exceed their separate effects.

The point to understand is this: the world is complex. Explaining or predicting some phenomenon as a function of one other factor is almost inevitably an oversimplification. Multivariate analysis is an essential step to understand correctly the statistical relationships among different variables.

This chapter may be one of the most condensed presentations on the basics of statistics you will ever see. Among important aspects of statistics not discussed are the visual presentation of statistics through charts and graphs (see Tufte), nonlinear models of relationships be-

BEYOND THIS CHAPTER

tween and among variables, and alternatives to the multiple linear regression model, among other things.

Just as with the methods explained in the other chapters in this book, a single chapter cannot adequately provide you with the skills needed to perform statistics or give you the understanding necessary to apply and interpret statistics. The bibliography refers you to texts that can be helpful. You can also use the Internet to find good information on specific statistical applications. Acquire and learn to use a statistical software package, which remains at the moment far preferable to working with a spreadsheet package.

Always remember, though, that statistical analysis can only be as good as the data you use. The valid and reliable measurement and acquisition of data are essential to the productive use of statistics.

Statistical Software. Considerable statistical software is available across a wide price range. The more expensive programs are more comprehensive, not only with the statistics themselves but with the capacity to manipulate the data in very useful ways to facilitate its analysis. Many of the better packages have relatively inexpensive student versions. One of the better lists of such software is in *Wikipedia*, under the entry "Comparison of Statistical Packages." Three of the more common packages that are comprehensive and may be at your university's computing sites or available through student versions are SPSS (Statistical Package for the Social Sciences) at <www.spss.com>; SAS (Statistical Analysis System) at <www.sas.com>; and Minitab at <www.minitab.com>.

TO LEARN MORE

Cohen, Sarah. (2001). *Numbers in the Newsroom: Using Math and Statistics in News*. Columbia, MO: Investigative Reporters and Editors.

Coolidge, Francis L. (2006). *Statistics; A Gentle Introduction*. Thousand Oaks, CA: Sage Publications.

Tufte, Edward. (2001). *The Visual Display of Quantitative Information*. Cheshire, CT: Graphics Press.

Utts, Jessica M. (2004). *Seeing Through Statistics*. Pacific Grove, CA: Duxbury Press.

Weiss, Neil A. (2007). *Introductory Statistics*. Reading, MA: Addison-Wesley.

Datasets for Public Use

http://factfinder.census.gov/
Census Bureau's data release page

http://people-press.org/dataarchive/
Pew Research Center for the People and Press survey data

http://www.cdc.gov/nchs/surveys.htm
Centers for Disease Control surveys and data systems

III Humanities and Professional Studies

The methods discussed in the last several chapters are usually identified with quantification and with the social and behavioral sciences in communication. The chapters that follow in Part III turn toward methods that tend to rely less on statistics. They also usually are identified with studies in the humanities or with the practical aspects of professional communication.

Even though in Part III we will see a change in the outward characteristics of the methods, don't let that change fool you into thinking that the underlying purpose or essential requirements are different. The methods in Part III will use different tools than the methods in Part II, but their purpose is the same: to help us answer questions and understand situations. And, just as with the methods used in social and behavioral sciences, remember that the methods in the humanities and professional studies are intended to be systematic and rigorous. If a researcher ever employs any of them in a shoddy manner, the problem is not with the methods but with the researcher.

In Chapter 14, "Legal Methods," Prof. Larry Burriss of Middle Tennessee State University explains the processes for studying issues in American law. As he points out, "the law is the most organized and documented area of human endeavor." Researchers have available to them a mass of material, and the key is knowing how to find and understand it. The chapter emphasizes that, as Prof. Burriss notes, "despite all of the material available, and despite all of the high-tech tools you can use, the basic tools of the legal researcher are the same as for any other researcher: curiosity, persistence and flexibility."

In Chapter 15, "Historical Methods," Prof. David Sloan of the University of Alabama covers the procedures that researchers may use to come to an understanding of the past. The chapter explains such essential matters as the use of primary sources and how they differ from secondary ones, how to locate sources, how to determine if sources are authentic and credible, and the practices that historical research uses to guard against bias and other errors. Historical methods, the chapter points out, "are not difficult to understand," but they do require specific procedures and rigorous standards.

In Chapter 16, "Field Observations and Case Studies," Prof. Tracy Tuten of

East Carolina University explains the methods researchers employ in observing behavior in natural settings (*field observation*) and in collecting extensive information about a particular situation (*case study*). The chapter will walk you through the very specific steps and practices that are required for either method to be done properly.

In Chapter 17, "Oral History," Prof. Anthony Hatcher of Elon University explains the techniques involved in getting first-hand information — in the form of memories and personal stories — through interviewing. The process involves planning, preparation, systematic interviewing, recording, cataloguing, and transcribing. When done properly, oral history can contribute significantly to the human record.

In Chapter 18, "Focus Groups and Intensive Interviews," Prof. Tuten explains two methods that are related to those she covered in Chapter 16. As she points out, focus groups and intensive interviews are the "workhorses" of much qualitative data collection. The former involves groups of individuals in the same setting, while intensive interviews focus on only one person at a time. Both methods involve structured questions and procedures.

In Chapter 19, "Cultural and Critical Studies," Prof. Sean Baker of Central Michigan University explains the variety of analytical approaches that scholars use to investigate the dominant social values presented in the media. Many of the scholars are critical of the existing order, and, as Prof. Baker points out, the field is based on a number of ideological assumptions. Thus, this area of research is more prone to researcher bias than the others in communication are. Yet, the techniques for analysis of communication content offer an avenue for investigation of a broad range of social issues.

14

Legal Methods

Some 2,300 years ago the philosopher Aristotle said, "The law is reason free from passion." For the lawyer preparing a case, that is certainly true: attorneys must deal with the law as it exists, not as they would like it to be. For attorneys, legal research means finding laws that support their position: look at the problem and find a law to deal with it.

For the legal researcher, however, the focus is different: the law is both reason and passion. Thus, the researcher must ask such questions as these: How should a particular law be applied? What are the trends in the law? How has the law changed? What is the connection between the law and, for our purposes, anything having to do with media?

On the surface, legal research appears so easy. After all, the law is the most organized and documented area of human endeavor. To start a research project, just go to your media law textbook and find a subject that appeals to you. Then just pick one case, any case — and if you know the right tools, finding aids and the appropriate rules, and if you can find the right index, then you will find your case, every case your case cited, every case that cited your case, and dozens of commentaries about each of these cases. Plus, almost all of this material is available online and, in many cases, is cross-linked.

But despite all of the material available, and despite all of the high-tech tools you can use, the basic tools of the legal researcher are the same as for any other researcher: curiosity, persistence and flexibility. Christina L. Kunz et al., *The Process of Legal Research* xxvi (6th ed. 2004).

It's been said that "curiosity killed the cat." But most people leave off the second part: "But satisfaction that he found what he wanted brought him back to life." The researcher has to have an insatiable curiosity about the how and why of the human experience.

Persistence has to be combined with that curiosity. The preacher in Ecclesiastes (1:9) said, "There is nothing new under the sun." As for legal research, he

---

By Larry L. Burriss
Middle Tennessee State University

may have been right. I can't think of any topic that hasn't been addressed in some form in some legal forum. So is there anything new to be discovered in the area of mass communication law? Yes, but you sometimes have to keep looking and digging until you find the information you need.

Which leads us to flexibility. No, maybe your very particular, very narrow, very specific legal topic hasn't yet been addressed; but you need to be flexible enough to recognize that you may need to take a step back from your particular topic and see the larger issue. For example, almost any mass media topic is related to the larger issues of freedom of expression and the First Amendment. Or you may have to use analogies, similarities and even differences to see how to relate one concept to another, seemingly totally different concept. Flexibility is the key.

As this chapter will demonstrate, the intersection of mass communication and the law can be frustrating, demoralizing and downright difficult. But if you follow the legal research methods outlined in this chapter, the rewards will be new insights into this most important of our freedoms.

A BRIEF TOUR OF LEGAL RESEARCH

Legal research. What could be easier? The law books are in the library or online. Hundreds, if not thousands of law reviews are there to provide background. No pesky Institutional Review Boards as required when conducting research on human subjects. No one hanging up when you try to do a telephone survey. You're not doing a questionnaire — so there are no layout or design problems. No sifting through dusty old newspapers. No audio tape, video tape or DVD problems.

And the topics! Just combine any media issue with any other idea, and there you go: instant topic. Libel and the horse (libel cases dealing with racing). Deceptive advertising and the airplane (court cases or legal periodicals addressing advertising by airlines or airports). Copyright and trees (books, television programs, photographs or movies that have dealt in any way imaginable with trees).

What, you can't think of any existing cases about your favorite topic? Then make something up. If you can't find a court case that is, in legal parlance, "on point," then speculate on how you think the court would rule or ought to rule in a particular situation.

And the Internet makes it all so easy! A search of < "New York Times" Sullivan libel > brought up 116,000 entries on Google. A more sophisticated search through federal and state cases on the popular electronic database LexisNexis yielded more than 1,000 court cases. A search through the LexisNexis law review database found more than 1,000 law review articles.

How much easier could it get?

The reality is, of course, much different.

Of all areas of media research, none is so well documented and analyzed as the law. The researcher's basic data source, the law itself, is readily available, generally at the touch of a button. Legal encyclopedias, treatises, annotations and law reviews all analyze the law to find patterns and meanings. In addition, most of this information is cross referenced and cross indexed using standard notations. A case will have references to other cases as well as to law reviews. Law reviews (periodicals that provide in-depth articles about particular cases or issues) will contain detailed references to cases and to other reviews. In both instances there will be standardized notations as to where the original sources can be found.

But this plethora of information and sources can quickly swamp the researcher. Wrong interpretations and misunderstandings can quickly lead the researcher into a seemingly inescapable morass of conflicting laws and incompatible rulings.

Legal Language

One of the enduring myths about researching legal topics is that there is some kind of arcane legal language that is impenetrable to all but the most highly trained minds. In the past that might have been true, but over the last few years the language of the law has been simplified, as practitioners came to realize that dense legalese was hard on everyone, lay reader and practitioner alike. True, some phrases and words may, at first, be hard to understand, but keeping a small law dictionary handy will solve most, if not all of these problems.

In fact, there are probably only four terms you really must know:

1. *Plaintiff* — The person bringing the lawsuit
2. *Defendant* — The person who is sued
3. *Injunction/Restraining order* — A court order telling someone to do (or not do) something
4 *Summary judgment* — A court order issued without a trial

So a typical court case might simply read:

"Plaintiff Jones sued Defendant Smith for running a deceptive advertisement. At the outset the court issued an injunction stopping Smith from running the ad. After a further hearing the court issued a summary judgment saying the ad was not deceptive. Case dismissed."

A Legal Roadmap

Of course, in a real court case Jones will have to show why she thinks the ad is deceptive. She will have to *cite court decisions* to show why the ad should be stopped. Smith will *present evidence and cases* to show why he believes the ad is not deceptive and should be allowed to run.

Following this give-and-take, the court will render a *decision* and tell us why an injunction was initially proper. Then both sides will be given an opportunity to explain why they feel the injunction was proper (or improper). And finally the court will tell us why the case was dismissed.

All of these actions and decisions will be supported by *precedent*. That is, all sides (the plaintiff, the defendant and the court) will rely on laws and past court decisions to support their own positions.

Then, following the final court decision, *law reviews* will analyze the case from any number of perspectives. The various *indexes* and *finding aids* will list the case under a number of different headings (advertising, commercial speech, freedom of expression, summary judgment) and may even give a sentence or two explaining what the court did.

Then other sources will *list this case* (*Jones v. Smith*) and tell us what cases this *case cited* (perhaps, for example, Jones or Smith used *Brown v. Black* to support their legal position). Still other indices will show us which *later cases* used *Jones v. Smith* as support for their own cases (that is, for example, one of the parties in *Scarlet v. Gray* used *Jones v. Smith* to support its position).

Other sources will *evaluate the importance* of *Jones v. Smith* in the overall scheme of media law.

And still other, *later sources* will tell you if *Jones v. Smith* is still good law, or if courts at either the federal and state level have criticized the case or looked on it favorably.

So the amount of documentation readily available is phenomenal, and most of it is accessible in both hard copy and electronic form. But as we mentioned before, the sheer volume of information available can be daunting at best and downright dangerous at worst.

Sorting Through the Legal Sources

So how do you sort though all of these sources to find what you really need? That's what this chapter will help you do: Separate the wheat from the chaff, and in the process help you find just what you need to analyze the law for almost any kind of media law research project with which you are involved.

So let's jump right in.

Well, on second thought, maybe we can't just jump right in. Doing research involving the law requires two interlocking skills:

1. An understanding of the legal citation system and how legal material is organized and

2. An understanding of available source material, and the difference between the law itself (primary material) and supporting material (secondary sources).

The problem is that you have to learn both at the same time. On the one hand, it's hard to begin a topic if you don't know how the legal system works. On the other hand (lawyers are very good at using both hands), it's hard to know how the legal system works if you don't know how to read a court case. So this chapter is going to jump around a bit, appear to go off on tangents and move back and forth between the law, the citation system and source materials.

Perhaps the easiest part of the legal research process is understanding *legal notation*, also known as *citations*. Fortunately there is a standard format. So if you can understand a reference to, for example, a case, then you can figure out a reference to a law journal or a statute.

LEGAL CITATION FORMS

First, let's look at how to read a legal citation. Here are some examples of source material and their citations:

New York Times v. United States, 403 U.S. 713, 91 S. Ct. 2140, 29 L. Ed. 2d 822 (1971).

Doe I v. Gonzales, 449 F.3d 415 (2d Cir. 2006).

Burriss v. Central Intelligence Agency, 524 F. Supp. 448 (M.D. Tenn, 1981).

Candidates for Public Office, 47 U.S.C. § 315 (2006).

Matthew Silverman, *National Security and the First Amendment: A Judicial Role in Maximizing Public Access to Information*, 78 Ind. L.J. 1101 (2003).

Let's look in detail at the citation in the first case above, *New York Times v. United States*.

The citation begins with the *names of the parties* involved in the case: *The New York Times* and the United States. (This case, by the way, is known popularly as the *Pentagon Papers* case.) The name of the party bringing the suit or appealing a decision always appears first. So we know the action is being brought by the newspaper. But wait, why is the newspaper suing the government? It's time for a slight detour into the intricacies of the American judicial system.

The federal court system has three levels:

1. District court
2. Appellate court and
3. United States Supreme Court.

Cases start at the district court level. In the *Pentagon Papers* case the government was trying to stop the newspaper from publishing. So the suit was first filed in federal district court. At that point the citation for the case was *United States v. New York Times*, 328 F. Supp. 324 (S.D.N.Y. 1971). The S.D.N.Y in the citation indicates that the court hearing the case was the federal district court for the southern district of New York (the state, not the city).

Without going into too much detail, suffice to say the newspaper won at the district court level.

So the United States then "went up" to the Court of Appeals for the Second Circuit, and the case was styled *United States v. New York Times*, 444 F.2d 544 (2d Cir. 1971). Here the Second Circuit Court of Appeals ruled against the newspaper and in favor of the government.

Then, because the newspaper was appealing the appellate court decision against it, when the case went to the Supreme Court it became known as *New York Times* [the party bringing the action] *v. United States*.

Reporters   But what are all of those numbers and abbreviations? They tell us where the case can actually be found, where it is recorded.

Cases are reported in bound volumes called, appropriately enough, *reporters*. The format for naming the reporters is the same: volume number, abbreviation for the name of the reporter, and page where the decision starts. The *Pentagon Papers* citation names three reporters (called a "parallel citation"), although in most citations only one is used.

403 U.S. 713 — This is the official version as published in *United States Reports* by the Supreme Court. The decision is found in volume 403 and begins on page 713. This is the reporter that is always used when citing cases. The following two reporters are optional.

91 S. Ct. 2140 — This is an unofficial version, *Supreme Court Reporter*, issued by West Publishing. In this reporter, the decision is found in volume 91 and begins on page 2140.

29 L. Ed. 2d 822 — This is another unofficial version, *Lawyers Edition*, published by LexisNexis. Here the decision is found in volume 29 of the second series of reports, beginning on page 822.

All three reporters contain the official, word-for-word opinion of the Court. Where they differ slightly is in their explanatory material (discussed later in this chapter). The reporters are almost identical, but you should always use, at minimum, the official *U.S. Reports* for citations.

Appellate and district court decisions follow the same general format, although the names of the reporters are slightly different.

Decisions of the courts of appeal are found in the *Federal Reporter* and include the circuit in which the decision was rendered. In the example above, *Doe I v. Gonzales*, 449 F.3d 415 (2d Cir. 2006) indicates the decision, as rendered by the 2nd Circuit Court of Appeals, is found in volume 449 of *Federal Reporter* third series, beginning on page 415.

By the way, the citation is read "Doe One," indicating there is more than one case involving Doe and Gonzales. There is also a Doe II (Doe Two).

District court decisions are found in the *Federal Supplement*. Thus *Burriss v. Central Intelligence Agency*, 524 F. Supp. 448 (M.D. Tenn, 1981) was decided by the Federal District Court for the Middle District of Tennessee in 1981 and is found in volume 524 of *Federal Supplement*, starting on page 448.

Note that there may be another number following the page number. If this is the case, then the second number refers to the page on which a quotation is found. Thus the citation *New York Times v. United States*, 403 U.S. 713, 720 (1971) indicates a quotation is found on page 720.

Be aware that there are literally hundreds of jurisdictions (and abbreviations). Consult the latest version of Harvard Law Review *The Blue Book: A Uniform System of Citation* (18th ed., 2005) for details of the different citation formats.

For federal court cases, remember that U.S. Supreme Court cases are always found in *U.S. Reports*, appellate court decisions are in *Federal Reporter*, and district court decisions are in *Federal Supplement*.

The fourth citation above — Candidates for Public Office, 47 U.S.C. § 315 (2006) — is to a *statute* in the United States Code, Title 47, Section 315. A *title* is simply a subdivision of the entire U.S. Code. For the communication researcher, particularly relevant sections of the code are the following:

Title 5 — Government Organization (including the Freedom of Information Act)

Title 15 — Commerce and Trade

Title 17 — Copyright

Title 47 — Telegraphs, Telephones, and Radiotelegraphs

The fifth citation above — Matthew Silverman, *National Security and the First Amendment: A Judicial Role in Maximizing Public Access to Information*, 78 Ind. L.J. 1101 (2003) — is to an article in a *law review*, *Indiana* (University) *Law Journal*. This particular article begins on page 1101 of volume 78.

REFERENCE STYLES

At this point let's take a very short digression to discuss how you refer to legal materials in your class project. Law reviews generally use endnote style (numbers in the text referring to notes at the end of the paper). Legal documents (briefs, court opinions, etc.) use in-line or in-text style (sometimes called "sentence style"). So the "correct" style will be what your law teacher wants you to use. If you are preparing a legal brief or a court opinion, use the in-text style. That is the style used in this chapter. If your instructor wants you to do a project simulating a law review article, then the endnote style will be appropriate. In either case, the format of the citation is the same.

The authoritative style guide for legal material is *The Bluebook: A Uniform System of Citation*, published by the *Harvard Law Review*. However, each jurisdiction (local, state and federal) may have what are called "local rules" for how citations should be prepared.

GOING TO THE LIBRARY VS. GOING ONLINE

All of the sources we are discussing are available online, all are available in a law library, and many may be available in your general university library. There are advantages (and disadvantages) to each.

Admittedly, online sources generally provide the fastest way of gathering information. In the two major electronic sources, Westlaw and LexisNexis, you simply type in your search terms; and dozens, hundreds or even thousands of cases, articles and statutes will appear. Both systems are very intuitive, at least for simple searches.

Be aware, however, that this ease comes with a price: too much information. Many beginning researchers assume that if they locate a hundred or more sources they have done a good search. Nothing could be further from the truth! Ask yourself if you are *really* going to read through the 50 cases (totaling perhaps 1,000 pages), 134 law review articles (totaling perhaps 5,000 pages) and 15 statutes (let's assume they are small statutes and that they total only 150 pages) your search turned up. No, you aren't. A good electronic search is one that turns up maybe a dozen or so sources.

Doing an online search is much like shining a flashlight in a crowded room: It only illuminates a few people at a time. What happens if you want to look at two people on different sides of the room? This is where the library comes in.

Benefits of Using a Real Library

Using a brick-and-mortar library gives you the opportunity to scan multiple sources at the same time to see what kind of material may be helpful. Sometimes you may want to just run your finger down a table of contents or through an index to see if you can find relevant material. Such "fuzzy logic" doesn't work well for online sources but is easy sitting at a table in the reserve room in the library.

But can't you open a couple of windows on your computer so you can compare two sources? Yes, you can. But ask yourself this: How many windows can you comfortably open at one time on your computer so you can compare sources with each other? Two? Three? Maybe four? Now, let's go back to that table in the reserve room: You can have a couple of law reviews open, three or four cases, a statute or two plus a couple of magazines, all open at the same time; and you can easily flip between them to compare and contrast what they are saying. Finally, on a personal note, I'll mention that I have never had a library come crashing down around my ears. I can't say the same about my computer!

Using a Law Library

Now, what about law libraries? At some universities you may need to be enrolled in a law class to use the law library. Others have an open-door policy. For schools that have a closed library policy, you may be able to obtain temporary permission to use the law library.

Major law libraries will have court decisions from every federal and state court in the country. They will have cases from foreign countries. They will have hundreds of law reviews. You will be able to find laws and regulations from every state and many foreign jurisdictions.

Finally, and perhaps most persuasively, printed sources are considered the "gold standard" for accuracy and completeness — and these paper copies are found in the library. The situation may be changing as online services convert to image-based documents (PDF images of the actual page); but for the moment, paper copies are considered the ultimate credible source.

PRIMARY SOURCES: CASE LAW

One of the hardest concepts for beginning legal researchers to grasp is the notion that in the law there are some absolute absolutes. Those absolutes are called *primary sources*. They are documents that tell us what the law actually is: Constitutions, statutes, administrative regulations, city ordinances. They form a good portion of the law, and they can be found in law books and online.

But in the United States, there is another source of law, known as *common law*. The term "common law" can refer to laws that developed out of customs and tradition. It has a second definition, though, which is the one that concerns us here. "Common law" can also refer to laws as laid down by judges in court decisions. In that sense "common law" is sometimes referred to as *case law* (or *caselaw* or *case-law*).

How Case Law Originates

As an example of such case law, let's take the famous libel case *New York Times v. Sullivan*, 376 U.S. 254 (1964). In the early 1960s *The New York Times* ran an advertisement that Montgomery, Alabama, city commissioner L.B. Sullivan said defamed him. Alabama had a law that said if a public official was defamed, the newspaper had to give him reply space.

But now we need to backtrack a bit and briefly discuss libel law. In order for Sullivan to show libel, he had to prove three elements: publication, identification and defamation. Finding those elements was easy: the story was obviously published, Sullivan was obviously identified and the ad contained an obvious false statement about him. All three elements — publication, identification, defamation — were there. *The New York Times* had obviously violated Alabama law.

So Sullivan asked for reply space, and the newspaper refused. Sullivan sued, and the case eventually ended up in the United States Supreme Court, which ruled the Alabama law was unconstitutional. The court further said, among other things, that if a public official wants to recover damages from a false story, he has to show, not only publication, identification and defamation, but also "actual malice": that the newspaper knew the information was false.

So the court created a new legal standard, a new law. Later, using that precedent, it ruled (created new laws) that not only public officials, but also public figures, *Curtis Publishing v. Butts* and *Associated Press v. Walker*, 388 U.S. 130 (1967), and those involved in matters of public importance, *Rosenbloom v. Metromedia*, 403 U.S. 29 (1971), have to show actual malice in order to win a libel judgment. And that is a very high standard indeed.

But wait. We need to backtrack again.

The Law Is the Law

Let's ask ourselves: Are those court rulings about public officials and public figures the right thing to do? Shouldn't public officials and public figures have some kind of protection against defamatory statements? Where is the morality here?

At this point we need to take a deep breath and recognize that in dealing with the law and court cases we can't — if we want to understand the law —get involved in morality, and statements such as "should" and "should not" are often irrelevant. *The law is the law*. We may disagree with the law; we may want the law changed; we may think the law is wrong. But the law is the law. And that is a fundamental principle of the American legal system. We have to start with what the law actually says — not with what we want the law to say; not with what the law ought to say; not with what the law should say. We start with what the law actually says. Period.

But this conflict between what the law should do and what the law actually does can provide a fertile ground for legal research. How do we square the law, as codified or enacted, with what is right, moral or proper?

HOW TO BEGIN   So at this point we need to begin discussing the actual process of doing legal research and the resources available to the researcher.

Recall that earlier chapters of this book have discussed various research methodologies in some detail. The rules that apply to surveys, experiments, and other methods also apply to legal research and work the same way.

The first step is to *define your problem*: What are you interested in knowing about? What is your problem statement? Then you have to conduct a literature review: What has already been written or discovered about your topic?

However, at this point legal research becomes a bit different, because all of the information (data) you need already exists. You may certainly have your own thoughts and ideas about the law, but the law itself is already there, as are discussions and interpretations. Remember, the law generally consists of statutes and court cases (plus Constitutions, treaties, ordinances, administrative rules, etc.). That material is already available in printed or online form. And every law, rule, ruling, etc., is already backed up with explanation, history and interpretation.

Let's say you want to do a research project about cameras in the courtroom and the implications for the accused. But you don't want to write a 20-page paper simply regurgitating what those cases say. You're much better than that. So you decide to relate cameras in the courtroom to privacy concerns of the accused. Is there a connection — you think there is — and how should that connection be manifested in the law?

There are two ways of approaching this problem: one is to find appropriate cases and then find explanatory material. The other is to look first at explanatory material and then go to the law (cases, statutes, etc.).

PRIMARY SOURCES   *Primary sources* are the heart and soul of legal research. They are what the law actually says, not someone's interpretation or explanation of the law.

There is, of course, much philosophical debate over what "the law" actually is. Are laws created by legislators and judges? Or do laws somehow existentially exist and are then discovered? Are we under a moral obligation to obey bad laws? If not, then can there even be such a thing as a bad law?

These questions, and a myriad of others, are all the stuff of legal research. However, at some point the courts, and your research paper, must always come back to one central question: What does the law say? Rarely will even the justices of the United States Supreme Court rely on a moral argument for deciding a case.

In almost every instance they will ask, "What does the Constitution [a primary source] have to say about this particular topic?" True, the justices are sometimes more than willing to interpret what laws and previous decisions mean, but in almost every instance they will give at least a nod to the Constitution.

Although your classroom project may seem like a long way from the Supreme Court, in terms of your legal reasoning, like the justices you must always go back to primary sources: what does the law actually say?

Thus it is that laws, in their various forms, are primary sources for deciding court cases and for conducting legal research. So, what are these sources? The list is actually quite short. It includes the following:

1. Constitutions
2. Statutes and ordinances
3. Treaties
4. Administrative rules
5. Court decisions

At this point we need to take a little excursion "around the edges" to make sure we understand how all of these sources are related and what they actually do.

Constitutions are the supreme law in a jurisdiction, generally a country or state. However, they are often written in broad strokes and are thus sometimes vague on certain points and open to interpretation. Constitutions are also notoriously difficult to change.

Statutes and ordinances are developed by legislative bodies ranging from Congress to the smallest city council. They are more specific than constitutions. Depending on the nature of the statutes and ordinances, they may or may not deal with specific issues and problems. Although easier than constitutions to change, the process for changing statutes and ordinances is still cumbersome.

A *treaty* is an agreement between two countries that, for the United States at least, is made by the President with the advice and consent of the Senate. A treaty is considered to have the full force of law.

Administrative rules are similar to statutes, except they are promulgated by administrative agencies. Some of the agencies the communication researcher is likely to encounter include the Federal Communications Commission (which deals with rules concerning broadcasting, including the so-called "Equal Time" provisions), the Securities and Exchange Commission (which deals with rules regulating the advertising of stocks), and the Federal Trade Commission (which deals with advertising rules).

Of course, communication research can involve any and all government agencies. For example, just plug the name of any federal, state or local agency into this topic: "Media Control as Exercised by the (name of agency): An Historical Review." Or try this one: "(Advertising / Public Relations / Television / Radio / Newspapers) and the (name of agency): Legality and Morality." See, instant research paper topics.

Court Decisions

It is the court system, however, that is at the heart of legal topics in media research. There are two main reasons for this state of affairs:

1. Courts have the final authority to determine what the law is,

Marbury v. Madison, 5 U.S. 137 (1803).

2. The courts can deal with immediate problems in settling disputes.

Finding court material for a legal research project is simplicity itself: go to any number of online sources, type in your topic, and there will be hundreds, thousands, maybe even millions of hits. For the beginner, this looks like a dream come true. But stop and think for a moment about something we already said: are you really going to be able to use a million sources? Absolutely not. As noted earlier, the great search is not the one that finds the most hits. It is the one that finds the least; the one that finds the single case that is right on point. That's a successful search!

Thus the real trick, for the beginning student researcher as well as for the professional scholar, is to *find just the right case* and then *understand just how the court ruled* in that case. So let's look at what you are going to find in a court opinion and what it all means.

A typical opinion consists of just a few parts:

1. The citation
2. A syllabus
3. The opinion
4. The concurring and dissenting opinions.

None of these is particularly difficult to understand.

The **citation**, as we mentioned earlier, is merely the title and reference to the case. For the *Pentagon Papers*, the full citation is *New York Times v. United States*, 403 U.S. 713, 91 S. Ct. 2140, 29 L. Ed. 2d 822 (1971).

Following the citation there are a number of other elements that may be present, depending on whether or not an online or hard-copy source is used and, if online, which particular database or reporter the researcher is accessing.

For *U.S. Reports*, the most common resource, the researcher should next go to the **syllabus**. This is a brief summary of the court's decision prepared by the Reporter of Decisions and is invaluable in understanding how the justices ruled. But be careful here: The *syllabus is not part of the official decision* and should absolutely *never be cited or used as a reference*. Only the part after the words "Justice Thomas delivered the opinion of the court" or something similar is what the court actually said.

If you are using LexisNexis, the citation will be followed by a series of **headnotes** (H1, H2, etc.) keyed to specific sections in the opinion. These headnotes explain what a particular section in the actual decision means.

In Westlaw there will be a series of **KeyCites**. This is an extensive and complex series of links between cases and concepts. For example, in *44 Liquormart v. Rhode Island*, 517 U.S. 484 (1996), some of the KeyCites include

92 — Constitutional law.

92k3851 — The First Amendment applies to the states.

92k1540 — The First Amendment does not protect commercial speech about unlawful activities.

Clicking on these links will bring up other cases dealing with those particular concepts. Clicking on other parts of the KeyCite will take you to the appropriate section of the case.

Once you have read the preliminary material, you need to read and understand the court's *opinion*. This is what the court says the law actually means. In all of your research you need to be referring to the law (statutory, administrative and case) as it currently exists.

But did you catch that last phrase, "as it currently exists"? How do you know if the law is still applicable? You cannot simply rely on the date and assume old law has been overturned. A case we mentioned before, *Marbury v. Madison*, an 1803 case, is still good law.

Fortunately, the electronic versions of LexisNexis and Westlaw will tell you if the case you are dealing with has been overturned or is still good law. For example, in the *Liquormart* case cited above, the two online databases show there are more than 1,100 instances where the case has been cited. This list will tell you if the case has been overturned, if the case was discussed in other cases, if the case was used in *concurring* or *dissenting* opinions (opinions by judges who agree and disagree with the majority court opinion), and how the case was differentiated from other cases; and it will give citations listed by district courts and appellate courts.

In LexisNexis, this case analysis is called *Shepardizing* and is based on Shepard's Citations Service. It will tell you if a case is still good law. Westlaw uses a series of flags (red and yellow) and green stars to indicate a case's history and treatment.

Statutes

The federal laws of the United States are in the United States Code (U.S.C.), which is divided into 50 sections called *Titles*, each dealing with a broad topic area.[*]

The United States Code uses the same general notation scheme as court cases. For example, regulations dealing with political candidates who buy advertising time on television are covered in 47 U.S.C. § 315. That is, Title 47 (Telegraphs, Telephones, and Radiotelegraphs) and Section 315 (Candidates for Public Office). There may also be sub-parts — such as 47 U.S.C. § 315(a)(1) (which exempts bona fide newscasts from the overall requirements of the section) and 47 U.S.C. § 315(b)(2)(C)(ii) (which deals with statements by the candidate that he or she approves the ad being shown).

As with case law, the two main unofficial sources for the codes are produced by LexisNexis and Westlaw. The two versions are U.S.C.A. (*United States Code Annotated*, produced by Westlaw) and the U.S.C.S. (*United States Code Service*, produced by LexisNexis). Both of these services provide annotations, explanatory material, legislative history, etc., that will help you better understand the law.

Administrative Rules and Regulations

Administrative agencies have sometimes been called the fourth branch of government. The fact that they have some of the functions of the three official branches of government (legislative, executive and judicial) makes them powerful forces within our society. Yet at the same time their power is so diffused they sometimes seem powerless to take any action at all.

Administrative agencies are created by the legislative branch, their members

---

[*] By the way, don't try to find the *PATRIOT Act* in the United States Code; it isn't there. The *PATRIOT Act* (Public Law 107-56) is not a stand-alone act. Rather, it amended numerous other laws that can be found in the United States Code.

are chosen by the executive branch, and all of their decisions can be reviewed by the judicial branch. Yet the agencies are empowered to create rules (a legislative function), enforce those rules (an executive function) and adjudicate those rules (a judicial function).

Agencies themselves do not pass laws. Rather, they create rules and regulations that have the force of law. These agency actions are found in the *Code of Federal Regulations* (C.F.R.). The citation scheme for the rules and regulations generally follows the same pattern as that for court cases and laws. Thus the Supreme Court case dealing with union pickets, *Hudgens v. National Labor Relations Board*, 424 U.S. 507 (1976), dealt with an NLRB decision, 205 N.L.R.B 628, concerning the *National Labor Relations Act*, 29 U.S.C. § 151.

As with other sources, agency rules and regulations are covered by both LexisNexis and Westlaw and use the same type of annotations and research aids.

SECONDARY SOURCES

Let's reiterate an important point: *secondary sources* are not the law. They are *descriptive*, not *prescriptive*. They are explanations of what the law says (or doesn't say). They help explain the law or the reasoning behind it. They are not authoritative in the sense of what the law actually is. Thus, they have no relevance in determining what the law really says. In preparing briefs or arguments before the court, attorneys never rely on secondary sources to make their case or arguments. But they can help attorneys understand the law and how the law applies to a particular set of facts.

Likewise you must never rely on secondary sources to make your point or argument. You can use a secondary source to provide explanation for a case or law, but never as if it is a primary source itself.

Law Textbooks

A good place to find a research topic is with a secondary source right at your fingertips: your media law textbook. And don't forget, you can combine concepts. So suppose you are interested in how issues of cameras in the courtroom impact a defendant's privacy rights. Simply go to the chapters on cameras in the courtroom and on privacy, and there they are: perhaps a dozen cases or more tracing the history of cameras in the courtroom and the development of privacy law.

Although your textbook will have a few cases that are on point, the explanations may be no more than capsule summaries. You will still need more background information. So your next step may be to use any of a number of other, more detailed, secondary sources. But before you run off to the library and start pulling books from the shelves, or before you start punching your keyboard to access an online source, you need a plan. So, let's look at some secondary sources that can give you the necessary background to do your research.

Legal Encyclopedias

Another good place to start your research is with a legal encyclopedia such as *Corpus Juris Secundum* (C.J.S.) and the second edition of *American Jurisprudence* (Am. Jur. 2d). The reason is that just like the *Encyclopedia Britannica* or *World Book*, a legal encyclopedia gives overviews on hundreds of topics. In addition, legal encyclopedias provide lists of cases, both state and federal, that support the statements made. In fact, as is typical of all legal writing, almost every sentence in the encyclopedia has a footnote linking it to a particular case.

A question that often arises at this point is this: Which is better, the print or the online edition of an encyclopedia? Both major electronic databases, Westlaw and LexisNexis, have electronic versions of Am. Jur. and C.J.S. Simply go to the appropriate database and type in the name of the subject in which you are interested. You will be taken to the appropriate sections.

However, there are advantages to the print versions. Both Westlaw and LexisNexis are well-organized and have excellent finding aids, but it is easier to browse the print versions.

Perhaps you have noticed we have used the words "finding aids" several times in this chapter. Recall that we also said earlier that legal materials have extensive cross referencing and indexing. How are these helpful?

Go back to your law course textbook. It probably has a list of every case cited in the book. So, if you know the name of a case, which will also tell you the reporter, you can go to the appropriate page in the reporter to find the court's decision. Encyclopedias have the same kind of information, plus a great deal more. The encyclopedias will not only have a list of every case cited in the entire set, but they will also have a list of every law and statute cited. There will also be an index of all of the topics covered.

Law Reviews

For a more in-depth treatment of a legal topic, you need to go to a law review. There are several hundred law reviews produced in the United States, most of which are published quarterly. Most fall into two major categories: those that deal with a wide variety of topics (such as *Harvard Law Review* and *Vanderbilt Law Review*) and those that focus on a specific topic (such as *Intellectual Property Law, First Amendment Law Review* and *Media Law and Policy*).

As with encyclopedias, there are both paper and online copies. LexisNexis and Westlaw have extensive databases of legal periodicals, although a particular journal may not be covered all the way back to the first issue. At least one online service, Hein-on-Line, does provide coverage from the first issue of many law journals. However, Hein-on-Line is a subscription service, unlike the free services that may be offered through your college or university library.

What is a law review article like? It may be an historical overview, tracing the development of a particular area of the law. It may be a lengthy (10,000 words or more) treatment of a very narrow topic. It may be a proposal for changes in common law or legislation. In any case the article will have hundreds of references that will include cases, statutes, other law review articles and even non-legal sources such as newspaper and magazine articles. For an example of a "lengthy" article, see David M. Rabban, *The Emergence of Modern First Amendment Doctrine*, 50 U. Chi. L. Rev. 1207 (Fall 1983). The article is 76,274 words long, contains 923 footnotes and covers nearly 150 pages of text. That is approximately 300 pages of typescript. So let's not hear any complaints about your 15-20 page term paper! A search of the LexisNexis law journal database recently found 19 articles of more than 50,000 words and five with more than 60,000.

Although law reviews are secondary sources, and thus have no precedential value, they have, on occasion, led to changes in the law. For example, our current privacy laws are based on a law review article written in 1890 (Samuel D. Warren

& Louis D. Brandeis, *The Right to Privacy*, 4 Harvard Law Rev. 5 [1890]).

Other Secondary Sources

There are a number of other secondary sources that may be appropriate for more advanced research projects (graduate-level papers, theses, dissertations, etc.), but that are probably not necessary for the typical undergraduate law paper. Nevertheless the undergraduate researcher should at least recognize these materials, since they may be cited in other sources the beginner will probably use.

Treatises

A legal *treatise* is an in-depth discussion of a particular topic. The topic may be broad and cover an entire area of the law (contracts, torts, etc.), or it may focus on a very narrow area (a single statute, for example). Treatises are book-length, and many are multi-volume. Two examples of treatises that may be of particular use to the communication student are *Law and the Information Highway* by Henry H. Perritt, Jr., and *Treatise on Constitutional Law: Substance and Procedure* by Ronald D. Rotunda and John E. Nowak. For an extensive list of treatises, visit the Harvard University Law School Library web site at http://www.law.harvard.edu/library/services/research/guides/united_states/basics/legal_treatises_subject.php

The utility of a treatise for a beginning researcher is open to debate. If you don't know anything at all about a topic, then a treatise may be a good place to start. The treatise will explain what the law is and various rules related to the law. The treatise will thus describe what the law actually is ("black letter law") as well as provide analysis.

However, going through a treatise for the first time can be a daunting experience.

A.L.R. Annotations

As the name implies, A.L.R. (*American Law Reports*) ***Annotations*** provide two kinds of information: reports and annotations.

The reports portion consists of the leading case on a particular topic. But of course, the leading case can be found in any number of other sources. The real value to A.L.R. is in the annotations, which are descriptions (rather than interpretations) from various jurisdictions around the country. Thus A.L.R. will allow you to see how different courts have applied the law to a particular set of facts.

As with most other legal sources, A.L.R. also provides cross references to other secondary sources.

Restatements

In 1923 the American Law Institute began a series of publications designed to provide ***restatements*** (that is, *interpretations* and *explanations*) of court rulings. In contrast to most other secondary sources, which are often written by one author, restatements go through a lengthy vetting process by both individuals and committees, probably making them the most authoritative secondary source.

For the legal researcher in communication issues, however, the restatements may be of limited use. There are only about a dozen topics covered by the restatements, and while all of them may tangentially touch on media issues, only one, torts, has direct relevance to mass media. (Libel and invasion of privacy are torts.)

The *legislative history* of a law is another important secondary
source. This history, which may consist of committee hearings, Congressional debates and so forth, is not the law; but it is invaluable in helping
judges determine what the law really means and why a law is worded the way it
is. Westlaw and LexisNexis both provide bill tracking, legislative histories and
committee reports.

Legislative History

Here are some of the legislative history materials that may prove useful to the
researcher:

• *Bills*. These are pieces of proposed legislation as originally reported or introduced.

• *Congressional Record*. As the term implies, the *Congressional Record* is a
record of the debates in the Senate and House of Representatives. Be aware that
although the *Congressional Record* is the official version of Congressional activities,
it is not necessarily the most accurate version. Members are allowed to "revise and
extend" their remarks. Thus items that appear in the *Congressional Record* may not
have actually occurred on the chamber floor.

It is also interesting to note that *videotapes* of the proceedings of Congress are
available to the public through C-SPAN. These tapes show what actually happens
in each chamber, but it is the *Congressional Record* version that is considered authoritative.

• *Committee documents*. The multitude of congressional committees all issue
hearing transcripts (also available through C-SPAN), reports and other documents.

ONLINE SOURCES

Throughout this chapter we have made frequent reference to Lexis-
Nexis and Westlaw. Both of these services are professional-level and
are used by practicing attorneys who have to research legal materials.
These databases have access to literally billions of documents. Pricing schemes for
their services are based on complex formulae that include such factors as number
of users, level of searching, number of databases in the subscription package, etc.,
but can easily run to thousands of dollars a month. The services also offer "pay-
as-you-go" plans, and abbreviated versions of these services may be available
through your university library.

There are, however, numerous other online sources that can provide access to
court cases, legislative materials, etc. For example, every government agency has
a web site that provides access to agency rules and regulations and, in many instances, access to court cases relevant to that particular agency. And no, we're not
going to give you a list of government web sites. If you can't figure out how to
find, for example, the Federal Communications Commission or the Central Intelligence Agency or the House of Representatives, you probably shouldn't be attempting legal research anyway!

There are, in addition to agency web sites, government sites devoted strictly
to providing research resources. Two of the most popular are

• http://www.fedworld.gov/ — A portal for government information ranging from jobs to passports. The site claims to have access to more than 30 million
web pages.

• http://thomas.loc.gov/ — Legislative information. Bill tracking. Votes. Debates.

There are also numerous non-government web sites that provide a wide range of information. But be aware that these portals tend to have a great deal of circularity. Site ABC will link to DEF, which will link back to ABC. Both ABC and DEF link to EFG, which in turn goes back to the first two sources. So in using these sources you should probably use the search function to find what you are specifically looking for, rather than going from portal to portal. Some of the more useful sites are the following:

- http://www.findlaw.com — This site is a good place to start your non-government-hosted search. This is one of the most trafficked sites and provides a wealth of information about cases, legislative material, etc.
- http://www.lawguru.com — This site has a search engine plus a large question-and-answer section devoted to a number of specialized law topics.
- http://fatty.law.cornell.edu/ — This site is maintained by the Cornell University Law School. Note that most law school web sites provide some kind of search engine to access legal materials.
- http://www.law.cornell.edu/statutes.html — Another site at Cornell University provides links to numerous constitutions, the United States Code, etc.
- http://www.phillipsnizer.com/internetlib.htm — This site is maintained by a law firm as a public service. A nice, clean site, it provides a somewhat limited drop-down list of topics, some of which are related to communication. The site provides a link to subscribe to a free internet law newsletter.

Finally, there are numerous general online sites and search engines that can provide access to legal information. But be careful. The quality of these sites can vary tremendously, and some are notoriously inaccurate.

In sum, we may say that in many ways conducting legal research is much like any other research using available data: develop a subject, review the literature, gather the data, analyze the data, interpret the data. However, legal research also requires the practitioner to understand areas that are unique to the field: the nature of law, the nature of the legal system and the nature of citations.

Unless the researcher is specifically analyzing secondary sources, that is, the project is actually about secondary sources, then the law itself is, in content analysis terms, the unit of analysis. And the researcher must be very careful never to mix up primary and secondary sources — never to confuse the law with the interpretation of the law.

TO LEARN MORE   Adamson, L. Kurt. *European Union Legal Research: A Guide to Print and Electronic Sources*, 6 Computer Law Review & Technology Journal 67 (2001).

Bast, Carol M. and Margie A. Hawkins. *Foundations of Legal Research and Writing* (3rd ed. 2005).

Cordon, Matthew C. *Beyond Mere Competency: Advanced Legal Research in a Practice-Oriented Curriculum*, 55 Baylor Law Review 1 (2003).

Elias, Stephen, and Susan Levinkind. *Legal Research: How to Find and Understand the Law* (13th ed. 2005).

Foster, Lynn, and Bruce Kennedy. *The Evolution of Research: Technological Developments in Legal Research*, 2 Journal of Appellate Practice and Process 275 (2000).

Gallacher, Ian. *Forty-Two: The Hitchhiker's Guide to Teaching Legal Research to the Google Gen-*

eration, 39 Akron Law Review 39 (2006).

Harrington, William G. *A Brief History of Computer-Assisted Legal Research*, 77 Law Library Journal 543 (1985).

Harvard Law Review. *The Bluebook: A Uniform System of Citation* (18th ed. 2005).

Hilyerd, William A. *Using the Law Library: A Guide for Educators Part I: Untangling the Legal System*, 33 Journal of Law & Education 213 (2004).

Hilyerd, William A. *Using the Law Library: A Guide for Educators Part II: Deciphering Citations and Other Ways of Locating Court Opinions*, 33 Journal of Law & Education 365 (2004).

Hilyerd, William A. *Using the Law Library: A Guide for Educators Part III: Oh, Statute (or Regulation), Where Art Thou?* 34 Journal of Law & Education 101 (2005).

Hilyerd, William A. *Using the Law Library: A Guide for Educators Part IV: Secondary Sources to the Rescue*, 34 Journal of Law & Education 273 (2005).

Hilyerd, William A. *Using the Law Library: A Guide for Educators Part V: Finding Legal Materials by Topic*, 34 Journal of Law & Education 533 (2005).

Hilyerd, William A. *Using the Law Library: A Guide for Educators Part VI: Working with Judicial Opinions and Other Primary Sources*, 35 Journal of Law & Education 67 (2006).

Jacobstein, J. Myron, et al. *Fundamentals of Legal Research* (7th ed. 1998).

Kunz, Christina L., et al. *The Process of Legal Research* (6th ed. 2004).

Long, Judy A. *Computer Aided Legal Research* (2002).

Putman, William H. *Legal Research* (2005).

15

Historical Methods

The purpose of historical methods is easy to grasp. It is this: to help us understand the past.

Any research tool that can help us study the past can be used in historical research. Therefore, historical methods may include a variety of methods used in other fields. Some historians, for example, use content analysis to examine old newspapers. Others apply statistics to help make sense of the data they collect. All such methods may, when the topic under investigation is appropriate, be used with success.

Most historians, though, mainly use traditional methods. Those methods were applied as long ago as 2,500 years, and over the centuries they have been enlarged and refined — so that today historical methodology provides a systematic, rigorous tool for helping us understand the past.

Some individuals have taken up the study of history because they thought other methods of research in communication are too demanding — and that history would allow them to sit back and take it easy. They were wrong. As with any other methods, one can do historical research poorly. But proper historical research is systematic and rigorous. If you have any notions that historical research is cushy, soft like Jell-o, forget them now.

On the other hand, historical methods are not difficult to understand. Many of the practices are a matter of common sense. The challenge of doing historical research may seem daunting to you at first, but it can be mastered. Doing it well is a matter of applying yourself to the task. When you do it right, you will find it very satisfying.

We normally credit the Greeks with inventing the study of history. In a sense, historians today still work under the timeless shadow of Herodotus and Thucydides, those two Greek writers who gave birth to history as a literary form. What do these two founders have to do with communication history today? The answer is: quite a bit. Herodotus, "the Father of History," opened *The Persian Wars*

By Wm. David Sloan
University of Alabama

by explaining that he was publishing his "researches ... in the hope of ... preserving from decay the remembrance of what men have done...." Few historians have written better or conveyed more of a sense of humanity than he. Curious about the Persians as well as the Greeks, he conducted a careful inquiry into the people and cultures involved in the famous war of which he wrote. Thucydides seems even more modern. He did an exhaustive examination of written *records* for his classic study *The Peloponnesian War*. As he tells us, he measured the accuracy of his evidence against the "most severe and detailed tests possible." Both he and Herodotus sought to produce an account of a singular event worthy, they thought, of contemplation then and in the future. Thus, they tell us quite a bit about the nature of historical research.

Since then, innumerable people have taken up the study of history, and hundreds of books have been written about the methods historians use. Thus, historiography is a highly developed field.

With all the material that is available, this chapter nevertheless will focus on methods as they are used specifically in communication — and it will emphasize means available to you as a student. If you had plenty of money — to travel to any repository of records in the world — and plenty of time to conduct research — rather than only one semester — you would do much more than you can in a few months. But the methods you would use would be essentially the same as you can use this semester. A short, semester research project will go a long way in helping you start to master historical methods.

SELECTING A TOPIC

Most of historical methodology deals with sources: how to find them and how to evaluate them. We will spend most of this chapter dealing with those two points. Let's begin, though, at the beginning. Every historical project must begin with a topic. As you consider selecting the topic, keep four questions in mind:

1. *Is it interesting to you?*

Within the requirements of the research assignment you may have, pick a topic that actually appeals to you. Being interested in the topic will go a long way in helping you "connect" with the research and get excited about it.

2. *How significant is it?*

Whenever you consider a topic for investigation, you have the choice between an important and an insignificant one. Doing the research for each one may take the same amount of time. So why not choose an important one? Here are two questions to answer as you try to determine the importance of a topic. Does it relate in an explainable way to things considered consequential in the past? Does it relate to matters that are important for society or for the field of communication today?

3. *Is it manageable?*

Researchers must have the skills necessary for the investigation they're considering. If they don't, they must be willing to acquire them. One would have to have knowledge of the Russian language, for instance, to investigate the Soviet press during Lenin's time. Communication history can involve so many aspects of life and society that the range of expertise regarding language, economics, politics, religion, and many other things related to it is great. Without the expertise that will allow you to understand the topic in its historical setting, you would have to do an enormous amount of work to become familiar with it. Otherwise, your research will suffer. If you don't have the expertise to understand a topic, or you can't acquire the expertise, you should select another.

4. *Finally, is the topic workable in terms of availability of sources?*

History depends on evidence, and that evidence must exist in sufficient quantity to provide answers for significant questions you will ask. Moreover, some topics, however fascinating they might be, are unknowable. For instance, what was the source of the sense of humor that President Lincoln displayed so often in his dealings with reporters? Can it be known beyond doubt? In short, selection involves establishing the feasibility of investigating a topic.

Limiting the Topic

With those four questions answered, a topic must be delineated or restricted in terms of time, space, and content. You can accomplish this task by considering the who, what, where, and when of the topic.

1. *Who*. Decide who or what groups or people will be included in the investigation.

2. *What*. Determine what aspect of communication (the issue, one might say) the study will examine. What are the important questions about the subject that have confronted previous historians? Does the topic have unity of its own? Every topic is related to others in close proximity to it. Yet the successful topic should lend itself to individual treatment. That is, it must be self-contained. If it cannot be explained without a lengthy examination of other, related topics, then researching it will be a time-consuming task.

3. *Where*. Define the precise geographical area of the topic.

4. *When*. Determine a particular span of time to cover. Be sure it has a logical beginning and end.

WORKING WITH BIBLIOGRAPHIES

Once you have your topic, the next thing to do is to find out what other historians have already told us about it. To do that, you need to compile a *bibliography*. Prof. Davies discussed that task in Chapter 6 of this book. So we will deal only briefly with it here as it relates to historical research. Compiling a bibliography is a step that beginners sometimes want to skip. It seems like a waste of good time. However, it is probably the most valuable use of any time that you will spend while doing historical research.

To compile your bibliography, the first thing you need to know is how to find books and articles that historians have written on your topic. You could go to the library and start browsing through the shelves, or you could locate the volumes of a relevant research journal, such as, for example, *American Journalism*. At some point you *might* need to do that, but that approach is not an efficient use of your time. Instead, you should try to find a book or article — that is, a bibliography — that lists histories written about your topic. To do that, first find a book that lists bibliographies. You could begin with a broad work, such as *Bibliographic Index*. Published since 1937, it appears three times a year and examines about 2,800 periodical sources, in addition to books. It includes bibliographies published either separately or as parts of books and articles.

Or you could begin with a bibliography dealing more narrowly with communication history. Here, for example, are three standard bibliographies in the field:

Pallay, Richard W. *Information Sources in Advertising History*. Westport, Conn.: Greenwood, 1979.

Sloan, Wm. David. *American Journalism History: An Annotated Bibliography*. Westport, Conn.: Greenwood, 1989.

Sterling, Christopher. *Broadcasting and Mass Media: A Survey Bibliography*. Philadelphia: Temple University, 1974.

It would take a separate book of considerable length to describe all the bibliographic sources that one might use. For a list of such sources of particular value to communication historians, consult chapter 5, "Searching for Historical Materials," in the book *Historical Methods in Communication* (2010), by Wm. David Sloan and Michael Stamm. Leads to additional standard sources can be found in Francis Paul Prucha's *Handbook for Research in American History: A Guide to Bibliographies and Other Reference Works* (2nd ed., 1994). M. Gilbert Dunn and Douglas W. Cooper's *Journalism Monograph*, No. 74, "A Guide to Mass Communication Sources" (November 1981), contains numerous listings of bibliographies and sources of historical material. Although now dated, it is an invaluable guide for communication historians. You should not, however, expect to find leads to material of interest to you only in sources designated as "Communication Sources." Many general historical bibliographic sources are rich in references to materials that are useful, indeed indispensable, in communication history.

Compiling a good bibliography will achieve the following three important goals: ### The Benefits of Bibliographies

1. With only a small investment of time, it will help you get a good overview of the history of your topic. You need to know at least the general landscape of that history before you begin your own original research. Historians have spent years researching in areas related to your topic. You should take advantage of their time and expertise. A bibliography will lead you to histories they have written. Start with a general history of your field, such as a textbook. Then find books and articles that have focused more narrowly on your topic. Familiarity with the general history of your topic will save you time and help you avoid errors.

2. A bibliography will make you aware of the questions about your topic that are of most historical interest. When you read a book or article, focus more deeply than on just its topic. See what the historian's point of view is. Pay particular attention to the *theme* — that is, the conclusion or the main point of the work. What explanation does the historian give about the topic? For example, you might find that historians have been particularly interested in knowing whether the First Amendment was intended at the time it was adopted to guarantee a broad or a limited freedom of expression. Once you know what the issues are that have most concerned historians, you will be able to focus your own research more sharply in an effort to address those important issues.

3. A bibliography will point you to sources that you can use in your own research. All good histories are based on *primary* sources. We'll discuss those in a moment. As you read the history books and articles for your bibliography, look at their footnotes. Those footnotes cite the sources that the historians used. Track

down those sources yourself, if possible. They may include material you can use in your own research project.

As you approach the task of building a bibliography, don't short-change yourself. Before trying to begin your own research, you will find that the time you spend compiling a bibliography will more than repay itself.

THE ROLE OF EVIDENCE

Assuming you are now actually doing a historical research project, at this stage you have done two things: (1) selected a good topic and (2) found out what other historians have said about it. It is even possible that, after reading those historians, you have revised or fine-tuned your topic. You are now ready to begin your quest to understand the topic on your own — and to provide an account of it that is interesting and meaningful to others. That means that you must find *evidence*.

That is the key word: *evidence*, for *without evidence, one does not have history!* Those unfamiliar with historical research sometimes make the mistake of thinking that history is simply a matter of one's opinion. They believe that historical accounts come mainly from the writer's imagination and that history thus is merely subjective. Evidence, though — not opinion — is the grist of history, and research involves finding it, evaluating it, and reconstructing a part of the past based upon it. When historians speak of producing a well-researched study, they mean one that rests upon hard facts, on evidence — and that *evidence must exist in sufficient quantity to provide answers for significant questions that the researcher and readers will ask of it.*

PRIMARY VS. SECONDARY SOURCES

When historians speak of sources, they divide them into two categories: primary and secondary. Historians give pre-eminence to primary sources as the raw materials, the foundation, of history. They employ secondary sources only with discretion as the circumstances merit. Here is how each is defined:

Primary sources are contemporaneous records, or records in close proximity to some past occurrence. They are records (e. g., newspapers, periodicals, letters, diaries, government documents, etc.) created during the historical time being studied. Ideally, they are records left by eyewitnesses.

Secondary sources may be based on primary sources, but usually they are not contemporaneous with the subject under study. Most of them are published later. Books and articles that historians write about the past are typical examples of secondary sources.

To help make the distinction clear, consider the following comparison. The record books titled "Publishers of the U. S. Laws, 1820-70" found in the National Archives contain State Department appointments of various newspapers that were designated to publish the laws. They are hand written and represent a *primary* source of State Department newspaper patronage. On the other hand, Culver H. Smith's book *The Press, Politics, and Patronage: The American Government's Use of Newspapers 1789-1875* (1977), which uses those records as a source, is a *secondary* source.

The distinction between primary and secondary sources, unfortunately, is not always so clear cut, and historians must ask some probing questions. Reporters, for example, may produce pure primary records when they cover events; and, if the records survive in their original form, historians classify them as primary. But suppose the original records have been destroyed and all we have is an edited, published account. Is that primary? Suppose a reporter did not witness an accident and based his report on the testimony of people who did. Would the report be a primary record? Or imagine that the only record remaining of that accident was an account of a conversation about it several days later. Would such a record be primary?

Most historians would accept the above examples as worthy of "primary" classification, although obviously one record might not be considered as ideal as another. To say that historians only recognize an eyewitness account immediately recorded as primary is misleading. In practice, they deal with degrees to which a record is primary. They tend to use a flexible definition of "primary" and extend it to include evidence recorded in "nearness" to an event, and they allow reasonable judgment to guide them in determining the time and space requirements needed to establish "nearness."

There is still the matter of the historian's *object* or purpose to consider in determining primary evidence. Imagine that the accident referred to in the previous passage was mentioned in a letter written years after it occurred. That letter may be of only tangential importance if the historian's object were to describe the accident. On the other hand, it would be of great value and considered as primary evidence if the object to probe into the thought of the person who wrote the letter. Thus, a clearly defined secondary source in one instance might become a primary source in another. For example, a published work by a nineteenth-century historian that would be identified as secondary in most cases might become primary in a study about American thought in the 1800s.

The Preeminence of Primary Sources

Why do historians give preeminence to primary sources? To answer that question, let's remember what the purpose of history is: *to understand the past*. To illustrate the importance of primary sources to understanding the past, consider this analogy.

Imagine that, rather than wanting to understand the past, you wanted to come to a full knowledge of a place you have never been, a far country. It *might* help to read what someone who has never been to that country has written about it — but the best way for you to get a true understanding would be to go there and spend time getting to know the country and its people. If you were unable to travel there, the next best thing would be to talk by telephone to the people, read letters from them, watch television programs they have produced about themselves, read their magazines and newspapers, and examine any other material or records that they have created. Such items would be, in historical terminology, primary sources.

If you wanted to understand the past in its truest sense, you would do the same thing. Obviously, you could not physically travel to the past — but you could examine the records that people have left. You could attempt to find out all that is possible to know about life at a specific time and place in the past. You could try to become so thoroughly familiar with that time and place that you might have the sense that you had actually lived then and there. If you did that, you would be doing what historians do.

THE VARIETY OF PRIMARY SOURCES

Students beginning their first historical research sometimes bemoan what appears to be a scarcity of primary sources. Primary sources, though, come in all forms; and a variety of them usually can be found on any major topic.

The problem with a shortage of sources sometimes is the result of researchers having a restricted view of what types of sources they should be looking for. It is not unusual, for example, for journalism historians to think of research only into newspaper content. Thus, the same publications — such as the *New York Times* — show up as the usual, one might say monotonous, sources. When researchers think in such narrow terms, the temptation is to think there are few primary sources to use. However, they come in a wide variety; and the more one has a vision for that variety, the more quickly one recognizes the wealth of potential sources.

Before beginning the task of finding primary sources, imagine the variety of types of sources — both published and unpublished — to hunt. Most fall into the following categories:

A. Unpublished collections of personal papers (such as diaries, letters, and autobiographies)

B. Published collections of personal papers

C. Confidential records (such as military dispatches and business documents)

D. Public records (such as government documents)

E. Media content (such as newspapers, magazines, broadcasts, films, pamphlets, and contemporaneous literature)

For purposes of illustration, here are some samples of *published* primary sources readily available in most university libraries for two typical topics of student research papers:

Topic: The Press and the American Civil War

Autobiographies: Franc Wilkie, *Pen and Powder*; Henry Villard, *Memoirs of Henry Villard*; Charles T. Congdon, *Reminiscences of a Journalist*

Government documents: *The War of the Rebellion, A Compilation of the Official Records....*

Newspaper content: Charles T. Congdon, *Tribune Essays: Leading Articles Contributed to the New York Tribune from 1857 to 1863*; Howard Perkins, ed., *Northern Editorials on Secession*; Dwight Dumond, ed., *Southern Editorials on Secession*

Topic: American Advertising, 1870-1920

Autobiographies and other works by advertising professionals: George P. Rowell, *Forty Years an Advertising Agent, 1865-1905*; Claude Hopkins, *My Life in Advertising...*; Walter D. Scott, *The Psychology of Advertising*; George Creel, *How We Advertised America*

Advertisements (originals and collections): *Cosmopolitan, Harper's*, and other magazines of the era; Frank Rowsome, Jr., *They Laughed When I Sat Down*

Periodicals: *Printer's Ink* (professional journal)

As you search for primary sources, keep in mind these two basic principles:

1. *Find as many primary sources as possible.* With only a handful of sources, you

will be able to get only a superficial understanding of your topic. The more sources you get, the fuller and better understanding you will have. Good historians often have at least one primary source for every sentence in the account they write — because they want to be certain that every statement they make is accurate. Although in a short semester project you may not have enough time to be that thorough, at a minimum you need at least one primary source for every substantive point you make. Although counting sources can be an artificial way to determine the adequacy of research, you do need a reasonable number of primary sources in your own research. As you gather material, keep in mind the goal of achieving a deep understanding of the topic.

2. *Use a wide variety of types of primary sources.* The greater the variety, the more complete the understanding you will have of your topic. Keep in mind that life is not one-dimensional. That is just as true of the past as it is of today. If you rely on only one type of primary source — such as, to repeat an earlier example, the *New York Times* — you will end up with a one-dimensional picture. As you consider the types of sources you might use, think along lines such as the following: not just one newspaper but several newspapers; not just newspapers but other types of publications (such as magazines and books); not just public media but other types of published documents (such as government records); not just public material but items that were intended to be private when originally written (such as letters and diaries). A good idea before you begin your search is to list the categories of primary sources — that is, unpublished personal papers, published personal papers, confidential records, public records, and media content — and then create a "wish list" of items in each category. From that list, determine which items will be available to you. Then try to examine them all.

HOW TO FIND PRIMARY SOURCES

One quickly recognizes that primary sources exist in abundance. The challenge is locating them. Should the historian have all the time in the world — and money — finding them would present no problem. The practical, real-world task, though, is to locate them with an efficient use of one's time.

It is possible to find historical materials almost anywhere. However, when one speaks of historical materials, it is usually collected, organized, or classified materials that one has in mind. Although some may be held privately, the researcher will find materials of this sort most often in a library or some other institution that involves itself in organizing and preserving sources of history.

In most cases, academic libraries will have collections of magazines, an archives, a rare-book collection, or other such primary material. Accordingly, researchers can sometimes find materials in their own institutions. In other cases, however, they may have to travel to a library that has specific manuscripts or to an institution that holds significant archival materials. Historians might have to spend time working in an archives such as the National Archives in Washington, D. C., or the American Antiquarian Society in Worcester, Mass. Visits to state and local historical societies may be in order. Some material is in private possession, and researchers may need to locate and use it, too. Even in the case of books and other published materials, historians have to learn which ones their own library holds and which ones have to be ordered. Some documents are available in digitized form on the Internet, but they make up only a fraction of the total body of primary material that exists.

The search for historical materials can be an involved process, but numerous tools are available in a university library and on the Internet to help conduct it. For a comprehensive discussion of how to locate materials in your own and other libraries, consult Thomas Mann's *The Oxford Guide to Library Research* (3d ed., 2005). If you need, go back and reread Prof. Pokrywczynski's Chapter 4 in this book on using the library as a source. In the discussion that follows, we'll treat the wide range of sources that professional historians use and suggest ways that you, as a student, can find primary materials within the limitations you may have on your time and money.

Since communication historians often deal with the content of the mass media, they should know how to find items such as newspaper and magazine files and broadcast transcripts and tapes. There are a vast number of collections of such material, many more than we can discuss here, and of indexes to the material. Dunn and Cooper's "A Guide to Mass Communication Sources," mentioned earlier, will prove invaluable in your search for indexes and media files. Indexes to the media and their contents are available in most good university libraries. For guides to indexes and material available online, see Chapter 6, "Historical Research on the Internet," in the book *Historical Methods in Communication*, by Sloan and Stamm, mentioned earlier.

Primary sources come in two forms: unpublished and published. The former are usually found in repositories called *archives*, and the latter, in libraries. As we discuss these sites, bear in mind that many libraries have archival collections along with published sources. In the last several years, the Internet has also become a place where one may find primary sources. Let's look at each of these types of sites: libraries, archives, and the Internet. The quest for research materials usually begins at an academic or large public library. So let's begin our discussion there.

Libraries   Researchers may need to visit a major research library such as the Library of Congress in Washington, D. C., or the Newberry Library in Chicago. Both of these national libraries hold large amounts of material, but you will find that your own university library contains many materials. Not only books but also documents, newspapers, periodicals, etc., are to be found there. So your first job is to become familiar with how your library operates.

It is possible that you will find materials in your library that are completely unexpected, and you probably will discover that your library has much more primary material than you imagine at the beginning. Your search may seem to begin slowly — but as you continue, you will find that the number of items will multiply quickly. The most common primary items you will find in a library are of the following four types:

1. Books   As we consider books, remember that we are looking for *primary* items, not works by historians. Most books are secondary sources, but your library may have a number of books that are primary on any topic. The key factor in determining whether a book is a primary source is either of the following: (a) it was published during the time period you are researching, or (b) its author had first-hand knowledge of the topic.

Here are the quickest ways to locate such books:

a. Do a *key-word* search of your library's card catalogue, including as one of the key words the years your research topic covers. Let us imagine that your topic is advertising design in the 1930s. Do a search for a combination of words such as "advertising design" and "1930." The importance of including the year is that on-line catalogue searches use publication dates as key words. Thus, such a search will find books on your topic published in 1930. Then do a second search using the words "advertising design" and "1931." Continue searches until you have exhausted all the years your topic covers.

b. Do an *author* search by the name of each individual who was involved with your topic. Such a search may identify autobiographies or monographs related to your topic. Such books can be a gold mine of material. Identify as many individuals as you can, including even those who may have had just a tangential connection to your topic. It may be that some of them included references to your topic.

2. Magazine Articles

Magazines can be an excellent source of material for almost any research topic you choose. Most university libraries hold large collections of bound volumes of magazines that offer a wealth of material. Magazines have been published in America since the 1740s and have printed millions of articles covering almost every topic of any importance. Any article published at the time of your topic will probably be a primary source, and many eyewitnesses to topics wrote articles about them. The magazines themselves can be a primary source if you are researching some feature of magazine history — such as, for example, the nature of magazine design — and for topics in advertising history, they are a repository of millions of items (advertisements) that are primary sources.

Trade journals such as *Editor and Publisher* (1901-), *Advertising Age* (1947-), *Broadcasting* (1931-), *Moving Picture World* (1907-1927), and *Variety* (1905-) also offer many articles written by historical figures in the mass media and other material based on primary research.

Magazines are convenient to research because several indexes to their contents exist. The indexes will help you locate relevant articles with hardly any trouble. Indexes of magazine content may be found in such reference works as *American Periodicals, 1741-1900; an Index to the Microfilm Collections* (1979), *Poole's Index to Periodical Literature, 1802-1906* (1882-1908), *Nineteenth Century Readers' Guide to Periodical Literature, 1890-1899, with Supplementary Indexing, 1900-1922* (1944), *The Readers' Guide to Periodical Literature* (1900-), and *Popular Periodicals Index* (1973-1990). These published guides list article titles, topics, and authors in alphabetical order. Some — such as *Readers' Guide* — were published on an annual basis. So narrowing your search to your time period is an easy matter. Making finding relevant articles even easier is the fact that databases of some of the indexes allow key-word searches.

3. Newspapers and Other Media Content

As with magazines, newspapers themselves may serve as primary sources for research on such topics as, for example, newspaper design and headline writing. With as many issues of thousands of different newspapers as have been published in America for more than three centuries, articles can be found on virtually any topic the historian can imagine.

Copies of newspapers can be found almost anywhere. No library, though, surpasses the Library of Congress. The American Antiquarian Society's collection is the largest for early American newspapers, including some 2,000 published between 1690 and 1872 in most states east of the Mississippi River and in Louisiana, Arkansas, Texas, and Missouri. They are reproduced in a set of 70,000 microcards. The set is available in many libraries. The Wisconsin State Historical Society and Harvard University libraries also have substantial national collections. State, regional, and special newspaper collections can be found in various libraries. The United States Newspaper Program has located, catalogued, and preserved on microfilm newspapers published from the eighteenth century to the present. Directories to individual state projects are available online at http://www.neh.gov /projects/usnp.html. *Newspapers on Microfilm* (1967) and *Newspapers in Microform* (1978) catalog all American newspapers that were available in microform at the time those guides were written.

Unfortunately, once the researcher locates a newspaper, considerable effort remains to locate content relevant to the topic under study. Fortunately, many databases have been compiled of numerous newspapers, and most university libraries subscribe to many of them. They usually are word-searchable. Furthermore, printed indexes to the contents of a number of papers are available. Unfortunately, most have begun only recently and do not include early newspaper issues. Indexing of the *Wall Street Journal*, for example, began in 1959 and of the *Christian Science Monitor* in 1960. The contents of some newspapers, however, have been indexed for long periods. The best known and most used index is that of the *New York Times*, dating from 1851. Thomas W. Jodziewicz's *Birth of America: the Year in Review, 1763-1783: A Chronological Guide and Index to the Contemporary Colonial Press* indexes fifty-two newspapers. A number of major newspaper indexes are available online. Indexes are also available in most libraries or through the inter-library loan system in either print or microprint. (Anita C. Milner's three-volume work *Newspaper Indexes: A Location and Subject Guide for Researchers* provides a helpful guide.) Bear in mind, however, that most newspapers have not been indexed, and research in their pages will require considerable time searching for particular types of material.

In addition to the media content that may be found in files, much primary media material is available in books. Anthologies of journalistic writing, editorial cartoons, newspaper front pages, magazine art, photographs, advertisements, and various other items have been published in large numbers. Works such as Louis Snyder and Richard Morris' *A Treasury of Great Reporting* (1962) and Allan Nevins' *Newspaper Press Opinion, Washington to Coolidge* (1928), for example, contain numerous articles as they originally appeared in newspapers. Most anthologies contain works in one genre (such as Sloan, Wray, and Sloan, *Great Editorials* [1992] and Sloan and Wray, *Masterpieces of Reporting* [1997]) or works by a single author or publication.

Similarly, for other communication sources, material is available in abundance, but the historian must know how to find it. Pamphlets, for example, may be found in various libraries and collections. You will find valuable such biblio-

Research Methods in Communication

graphical sources as Charles Evans, comp., *American Bibliography: A Chronological Dictionary of All Books, Pamphlets and Periodicals Printed in the United States of America* (1639-1800) (a fourteen-volume work published between 1903 and 1959) and Bernard Bailyn's *Pamphlets of the American Revolution* (1956).

Finding historical material on film, radio, and television is more difficult. Much of the content of broadcasting was never recorded, and the high costs of recording and using broadcast material discourage preservation. Many silent films were photographed on combustible nitrate stock — and entire archival collections have exploded, with the loss of numerous films. There have been efforts to transfer motion pictures to other types of film stock; but they come too little and too late, and much material has been lost permanently. Thus archives and library holdings for broadcasting and film are not as large as for print. Copyright regulations also have discouraged the duplication of material. The high costs of storing recordings sometimes have led to decisions by their owners to destroy them.

Despite the problems, substantial amounts of programming material may be found. Union lists provide guides to locating programs. Among the more thorough are *History in Sound: A Descriptive Listing of the KIRO-CBS Collection of the World War II Years and After* (1963), Alex McNeil's *Total Television: A Comprehensive Guide to Programming from 1948 to the Present* (1996), and Tim Brooks and Earle Marsh's *The Complete Directory of Prime Time Network Television, 1946-Present* (1995). Similar guides to motion picture films are also available.

Some indexing of broadcast programming has been done, but it is not as voluminous as indexing for the print media. Vanderbilt University's Television News Archive has published *Television News Index and Abstracts* since 1972 covering evening news broadcasts on the national networks. Since 1975 the Microfilming Corporation of America has published *CBS News Indexing*. As the permanent value of broadcast programming has gained heightened recognition in the last few years, such services have increased; and today broadcast and film historians have at their disposal a considerable store of guides.

4. Primary Material in Secondary Sources

Along with the standard forms of primary sources, you should also be alert to finding primary material in secondary works. Historians with plenty of time to do research usually rely on books and articles by other historians to point them to sources of primary material. Then they locate those original primary sources. Students who have less time to research may find it acceptable to gather primary material directly from such books and articles. In that way, you may find it easy to amass a large collection of primary items. Your instructor should give you instructions on whether you may do that.

If you may, then still you should not be satisfied with using the material simply as you find it. Instead, determine if the original source is available. For example, a book may quote from another, earlier book written by someone who was an eyewitness. Rather than simply using the quotation from the secondary source, determine if your library has that original book. If it does, then examine it for material. Furthermore, if you are allowed to gather primary material from secondary sources, you should use as wide a variety of secondary sources as possible. Historians sometimes are selective in using material from primary sources, and it could be that, if you use only one historian's work, s/he will give you a distorted selection. Be sure to compare that material with what you find in other sources. Finally, if you do get primary material from a secondary source, you must indicate your secondary source in your notes when you write your paper.

Archives   *Archives* are repositories of unpublished primary sources and other records. They are especially important because archival and manuscript material is of prime interest to professional historians. The foundation of their research rests on these types of resources more than on anything else.

In considering archival collections, it is useful to contrast the terms "original" and "primary" sources. We know from our earlier discussion that *primary* sources are essentially records that were made contemporaneously with the events they recorded or that were made later by individuals who were eyewitnesses. Many primary sources have now been published. *Original* sources are defined the same way — except that they are *unpublished*. Thus, for example, a handwritten letter would be an original source, while that same letter later reprinted in published form (although still a primary source) would not be an original source. Original material is almost synonymous with archives.

Libraries and archives have some similar features, but they are also distinct from one another. Like an archives, a library may hold collections of unpublished matter, but its archival material tends to be uneven and individualized; and items may not have been kept with preservation in mind. For an archives, though, it is not the chance collection of records that dictates inclusion, but rather how those records fit into the materials of an individual or organization or perhaps a special type of preserved historical record. An archives receives the records of individuals, organizations, agencies, and so forth, and it arranges that material according to its origin (that is, by organization or agency, etc.). Such materials are then cataloged in a systematic way and described in guides, inventories, and lists.

Archival materials are found in many places. They may be in one of the presidential libraries, in state libraries and historical societies, in academic libraries, and in a variety of other repositories. The National Archives and the Manuscript Division of the Library of Congress are the most important repositories in this country. Along with the National Archives, federal records are dispersed among various regional federal archives and record centers. Many state and local organizations maintain archives. There are, in addition, a variety of other archives available to researchers. Of particular interest to communication historians are Vanderbilt University's Television News Archives; the data Archive of the Inter-university Consortium for Political and Social Research in Ann Arbor, Michigan; the American Newspaper Publishers' Association Foundation in Washington, D. C.; and the Wisconsin State Historical Society Library, to name only a few. Special collections can be found in many other libraries. Perhaps your own university library holds some. Before using archival materials, you should consult Philip C. Brooks' *Research in Archives: The Use of Unpublished Primary Sources* (1982), which provides a useful introduction.

Because archival materials are dispersed so widely, the problem of identifying the materials you need from the multitude of those existing is formidable. Where and how do historians find all the items to examine in their inquiries? A library provides numerous tools to assist in this task. They include published guides, catalogs, bibliographies, indexes, abstracts, and many other such items. Various guides — such as the *Directory of Archives and Manuscript Repositories in the United States* (1988) and Philip M. Hamer's *A Guide to Archives and Manuscripts in the United States* (rev. ed., 1965) — prove invaluable. Most libraries have databases for many of these sources, particularly for the most used indexes. However, each library selects the databases it wishes to put online according to its own needs. To see which databases a library has online, go to its computerized Home Page and then to its Database Page.

The Internet

Since the early 1990s, the most dramatic change in the research process has been the proliferation of information on the Internet. Today, there are more than a triillion Web pages on more than 170 million Websites. For the last few years, the number of pages has been increasing at a breakneck pace.

The Internet offers several benefits for historical research, but it also has many limitations. Historians should take advantage of the benefits while exercising a critical mind about the limitations.

Benefits of the Internet

The most obvious benefit for students is that the Internet can give them access to material that they otherwise probably could not get without traveling. It probably will never provide files of all the primary or even secondary material that historians require. However, much material is now available on the Internet that at one time could only be found in archives. Archival material is so essential that professional historians invest large amounts of time and money to examine it. Travel is still required for most archival material, but the Internet has reduced the amount of travel historians have to do. That is of particular importance to students, who usually have to complete a research project in the course of one semester and have neither the time nor the money to travel to distant archives.

On most topics in communication history, the Internet will not be the fullest source for primary material, but a growing body of primary documents is now available there. Some sites are devoted to specific topics, and they sometimes provide large numbers of documents. Others provide registers (finding aids) for manuscript collections. Unfortunately, there are few such sites dedicated to the field of communication history, and most of those offer only a small portion of the primary material that might be relevant to one's investigation.

An immense advantage the Internet has over most archives is that much of its textual material is searchable by individual words. Paper documents in archives typically are only categorized. The benefits of searchable text are readily evident. For example, the University of Michigan's "Making of America" Collection — which has more than 4,000,000 items digitized — includes approximately 300,000 pages from American magazines in the 1800s, and the entire collection is searchable. Thus, if, for example, an historian were looking for references to the editor Sarah Josepha Hale in any of those articles, they could be found almost instantaneously. Prior to the Internet, such a search might have taken months.

The Internet can also help with locating secondary sources and conducting bibliographical searches. A variety of Web pages contain secondary accounts of historical topics, and many of them provide bibliographies or links to other sites with bibliographies. Chat groups also can provide a source of ideas on topics, and often members of the groups will help inquirers identify history articles and books on specific topics. In the field of communication history, for example, the "Jhistory" site furnishes a forum for historians to exchange information. Its URL is http://www.h-net.msu.edu/~jhistory. Of course, many statements that are posted on such sites are not authoritative, but often members of the group are able to provide useful references to both primary and secondary sources.

Limitations *of the Internet* Despite the attractive features of the Internet, it does present a number of limitations. The greatest shortcoming is that most of the primary material that exists in some form today has not been digitized and placed on the Internet. Despite the fact that some well publicized projects have put the contents of a number of publications on the Internet, the fact remains that most magazines, newspapers, and other forms of mass communication are not available there. The same is true of most other forms of primary material, from private diaries to public reports. For example, the Manuscript Division of the Library of Congress houses more than 11,000 separate manuscript collections containing more than 50,000,000 items, and only a fraction of them are on the Internet. A thorough historical research project will require primary sources, and the only place most of them may be found is in physical archives.

Furthermore, a substantial amount of Internet material is on sites that require an access fee. In the field of communication history, for example, "HarpWeek" has digitized the contents of *Harper's Weekly* magazine from 1857 to 1912, but a subscription to just the first twenty years costs $35,000. Several fee-based bibliographic databases also provide access to the contents of secondary sources. Through those services, researchers can access searchable full texts of a wide range of journal articles. Some major vendors are EBSCO, First Search, ProQuest, and the Gale Group. Subscription fees are so expensive as to be prohibitive for individuals, but many libraries subscribe to the services and make them available to patrons.

Another problem the researcher should be aware of is that errors, fabrications, incompleteness of the text, and related shortcomings are more likely to appear in Internet documents than in paper documents. Printed books usually have gone through an editing and proofreading process before being published. Virtually anyone, however, can put a text on the Internet without following rigorous safeguards. Errors can be made in the scanning or keyboarding process required in digitizing a text. Parts of a text may be omitted or altered for any variety of reasons. Texts may even be fictionalized. For example, a document called the "Willie Lynch speech of 1712" can be found on hundreds of Websites without any indication that it was created in the twentieth century. The speech purports to be the remarks of a slave owner about how to control American slaves. Several groups have taken the text off the Internet, apparently accepted it at face value, and used it to support their political agendas.

The superficiality of much of the secondary material on the Internet deserves particular attention. It is often of an introductory nature and lacks the depth needed for serious research. You might compare it to how a textbook or an encyclopedia covers your topic, and often it is inferior even to those broad treatments. Similarly, you should be wary of material that members sometimes share on chat groups. Frequently, it is not based on evidence, is biased, is superficial, or suffers from other shortcomings.

The easy accessibility of Internet material poses another trap for students. If you have used a number of Internet sources for a research project, what indication is there that they were the best sources? To address this problem, some professors limit the percentage of sources that may be taken from the Internet. For example, if a research project uses ten sources from the Internet, then forty more might have to be taken from print sources. Others require students to compare their Internet sources with traditional ones found in the library. Surfing the Web and quickly locating sources for a paper does not guarantee its quality.

Clearly, historians using the Internet must bring the same critical faculties to evaluating sources found there as one would with traditional sources.

Primary Documents on the Internet

The ideal world for historical research might be one in which every record ever created existed in digitized, searchable form on the Internet. We are light years from such a situation, but a large body of primary material does exist on the Internet. Your library probably subscribes to a number of databases containing the texts of many, many periodicals and other published documents. You should familiarize yourself with the holdings. The greatest amount of material on the Internet is about general history, not specifically communication history. However, communication historians often will find that research into a wide variety of materials will give a fuller perspective on communication topics than communication research alone will do. Thus, many collections that are not specifically about communication contain some pertinent documents that will help to shed light on the communication topic.

One site in particular deserves special mention. It is "American Memory" (subtitled "Historical Collections for the National Digital Library"). It contains "collections of American culture and history, mostly derived from Library of Congress special collections. Photographic panoramas, sound files, movies, photos and documents can be found in abundance." It offers several million digitized items from more than 100 historical collections. The texts are searchable by individual words. There is no fee for access.

Two other excellent sites are the University of Michigan's and Cornell University Library's "Making of America" (MOA) Collections, a part of the "American Memory" project. Each provides a "searchable digital library of primary sources in American social history from the antebellum period through Reconstruction, [and is] particularly strong in the subject areas of education, psychology, American history, sociology, religion, and science and technology."

A number of sites also have digitized texts and images that are specific to communication history. They run the gamut from advertising to magazines to newspapers to broadcasting. A few, especially those that are part of the "American Memory" project, contain substantial collections. Most, however, have only a small portion of the extant primary material on their topics, but even those can provide sources to serve as a starting point for a research project.

EVALUATING PRIMARY SOURCES

Whenever one finds a primary source, s/he may be tempted to shout for joy. For the student, the find may be an occasion of excitement over acquiring a really good piece of material or relief at finding just anything. Unfortunately, not every primary source is necessarily a good one. In order to use primary sources in the most careful way, historians employ several types of analysis. So you should be critical in dealing with sources. Don't let your excitement at having found a source mislead you into thinking that it is surely a credible one. To help you in making judicious decisions about the quality of the sources you find, let's look briefly at tests that historians apply in evaluating primary sources.

The methods fit into two categories of "criticism": *external* and *internal*. These two forms of criticism are central to the work of historians in dealing with primary records. ***External criticism*** is aimed at determining the *authenticity* of a record. ***Internal criticism*** is aimed at determining its *credibility*.

External Criticism

Testing for authenticity is mainly the work of specialists in linguistics, genealogy, and so forth. Its purpose is to *determine whether a document is what it appears to be*. It asks questions such as "Who was the author? Is the text of the document, if it is a copy, accurate? Is the document a fraud?" A recent example of such issues was the episode during the 2004 U.S. presidential election when the CBS program *60 Minutes Wednesday* broadcast a segment based on photocopied memos claiming that George W. Bush had performed improperly while serving in the Air National Guard in the 1970s. Immediately after the program aired, experts questioned the authenticity of the memos. They pointed out, for example, that the typeface used in the memos was not available on typewriters in the 1970s. An investigation later found that CBS had rushed the segment onto the air without adequate checking, and it raised questions about whether partisan bias was the root cause of the problem. In this instance, failure to perform a procedure that historians consider an elementary one resulted in both controversy and embarrassment for CBS. Its longtime news anchor, Dan Rather, retired; and CBS fired the segment's producer and asked three other employees to resign.

Fortunately, most documents that historians deal with have already been examined by experts to determine their authenticity. Editors of book collections of documents, for example, and curators at archives have already decided that works are authentic before they include them. Nevertheless, familiarity with the basic process is helpful to historians. The elements of evaluation include the following:

1. Examining such elements as handwriting, paper, language, and document formats to determine whether documents are fraudulent
2. Determining the authorship of a document and its date of production
3. Comparing texts to determine if they have suffered by being copied

Internal Criticism

Although external criticism is mainly the realm of the specialist, the case of internal criticism is different. It should be a concern for all historians and a consideration with every source. It involves *questioning records to determine if they are trustworthy and convincing*. As with external criticism, the processes used in internal criticism involve several types of tests. They relate specifically to these issues: (a) the meaning of the text, (b) whether the record can be corroborated by other evidence, (c) the *ability* of the source to tell the truth, and (d) the *willingness* of the source to tell the truth.

The main elements of evaluation are the following:

Documents may be complicated by archaic, colloquial, technical, and diplomatic terms and language. Furthermore, the meaning of some words (e.g., imperialism, gay, etc.) changes from time to time. Sometimes expressions are made ironically, allegorically, or humorously. The historian must recognize and understand all such variations and must grasp the real meaning.

1. "Real" vs. "Literary" Meaning of Words

As you attempt to understand people and their actions, or the meanings of words and documents, keep uppermost in your mind the error of *present-mindedness*. That is the error of *judging the past by views of the present*. Remember that not only words but many ideas, values, practices, and so forth were different in the past than they are today. Present-mindedness is always a danger. Be on your guard against falling prey to it. To help, continually ask yourself if you are understanding any records or other details of the past by the mindset of today.

In trying to "confirm" a text, historians deal with particular aspects of the document. They ask such questions as these: (a) Can this particular point be corroborated by other evidence? (b) Does the validity of this particular point meet the canons of common sense?

2. Confirmation of the Text

The value of all "literary evidence" involves a personal factor. For an adequate evaluation of a document, the historian must consider certain characteristics about the author. Essentially they fall into two categories: (a) How *able* was the author to tell the truth? (b) How *willing* was the author to tell the truth?

3. Credibility of the Author

Judgments about the author's *ability* involve these factors:

(a) *Nearness* to the event recorded, in terms of both space and time. For example, did the author of the record actually see the event, or did s/he simply hear about it from someone else? If s/he just heard about it, how much time had passed after the event before s/he heard about it? Even if s/he were an eyewitness, how much time passed before s/he wrote a record? Historians always study time lapse. In some cases, the passage of time might impair the validity of the document. One of the essential principles to keep in mind in assessing records is that memory fades or changes with time. Personal memoirs written in old age, for instance, can be untrustworthy sources despite the fact that they record details about which the author had personal knowledge. Thus, all other factors being equal, more credibility is given to a record made immediately after an event than one made later.

(b) The *availability of material*. Did the author have access, for example, to events, conversations, and so forth to allow her to provide a reliable report?

(c) The author's *competency*. How able was the author to understand? This aspect of evaluation can include such matters as the author's expertise on a particular topic, his cultural and social perceptions, and his attention to or interest in the subject or event.

Judgments about the author's *willingness* to tell the truth involve these factors:

(a) The author's *bias*. Was s/he biased on political, social, cultural, economic, or other matters? If so, did that bias influence the report? Is it probable that the report was slanted to please an employer or the public or some other interest? For the historian, being aware of the nature and degree of the author's possible bias on the subject of a record is essential. Simply because someone wrote something in the past does not mean that it was necessarily an objective, unbiased account. Everyone has biases — and keep in mind that that principle also applies to you. Examine your own perspectives. Be careful not to let them unfairly influence the way you understand or judge people's views and actions in the past.

(b) The author's *purpose* in composing the document. Was it to propagandize, to publicize, to persuade, to praise, to promote, for example — or was it merely to provide a factual record? The general principle is that if the author's intent was merely to record fact, then the record is more likely to be credible.

(c) The *confidential nature* of the report. The basic principle is that, *everything else being equal, the fewer eyes for which a report was intended, the more credible it is likely to be.* Thus, for example, a diary entry is likely to be more forthcoming and honest than an account of the same detail if the same author were writing an autobiography for publication.

How Much Research Is Enough?

Finally, as you attempt to evaluate sources, you must ask yourself, "How much research is enough?" When do you get to stop collecting sources? In class projects, instructors sometimes give students a numerical answer to that question. A requirement in your class might be, for example, using a minimum of thirty primary sources or some other such number. Such a requirement is normal in semester projects, but in real-life historical research the answer is never a matter of numbers. Professional historians continue researching until they have exhausted all the sources necessary for a full understanding of their subject. That is the key: understanding fully enough that the historian feels as if s/he knows the people, their thoughts and actions, issues, and other matters as completely as s/he would if s/he had lived in the time past.

DRAWING CONCLUSIONS AND PROVIDING EXPLANATION

After gathering and evaluating all the primary sources available, historians finally have to ask, "What does it all mean?" They are not satisfied with simply collecting material. They must explain the subject they have researched. They face two tasks: *describing* the nature of the subject and *explaining* why it was that way. The first, which involves telling the "what" and "how" of their subject, is relatively easy. It is explaining "why" and "to what effect" that presents the real challenge.

Meaningful explanation requires much of the historian. S/he must clearly grasp the purpose behind the investigation: what is the essential question that s/he is trying to examine? The historian must be familiar with the historiography of the subject and with the explanations that other historians have given. S/he must avoid bias and present-mindedness. S/he must understand his/her own point of view. In communication history, the danger of making judgments based on the professional standards of today is ever-present, a lurking form of bias and present-mindedness. Providing insightful explanation requires mature, critical judgment, for the historian cannot rely on simple formulas. Drawing conclusions in history is not as simple as in, for example, math, where the mathematician works with formulas and laws. The historian must recognize that life in the past — just like life today — was complex and hardly ever admits of a simple explanation. Simple explanations usually are simplistic explanations. Historians thus should be cautious about suggesting causation from a single cause. Rarely is an individual motivated by just one factor. That is why good historians shy away from monolithic explanations such as economics or politics or gender. Explanation usually is concerned with multiple, rather than single, causation. And, obviously, there must be supporting evidence for any statement of causation.

Likewise, we should never make the mistake of assuming that "Explanation in history is based mainly on the historian's opinion." It is not. *It must be based on facts!* Since historical research is concerned mainly with a search for truth about the past, explanation *cannot* be merely opinion. It must rely on thorough primary sources. In fact, explanation can come only from primary sources. Even when primary sources are abundant, the historian must be cautious about assuming too much. Explanation must originate in the sources themselves. For example, if one were examining the design of advertising in the late 1800s, describing the design would be possible simply by looking at ads. However, if the ads were the only sources the historian examined, s/he could make only guesses at *why* the ads were designed as they were. For the explanation of why, the historian would need explanations offered by people of the time.

Finally, conclusions must always be tentative rather than final. We can never be certain we have the complete evidence or the final answer. Tomorrow, another historian may uncover sources never before seen or use an improved technique for analyzing evidence. Our understanding of the past can always change — and that is why historical research continues to fascinate so many people.

Barzun, Jacques, and Henry F. Graff. *The Modern Researcher*, 6th ed. Belmont, Calif.: Thomson/Wadsworth, 2004.

Godfrey, Donald. *Methods of Historical Analysis in Electronic Media*. Mahwah, N.J.: Erlbaum, 2006.

Gottschalk, Louis. *Understanding History: A Primer of Historical Method*, 2nd ed. New York: Alfred A. Knopf, 1969.

Howell, Martha, and Walter Prevenier. *From Reliable Sources: An Introduction to Historical Methods*. Ithaca, N. Y.: Cornell University Press, 2001.

Mindich, David T.Z., Elliot King, Barbara Straus Reed, and David Abrahamson. "The Jhistorian Online." *American Journalism* 14:2 (1997): 209-22.

Mott, Frank Luther. "Evidence of Reliability in Newspapers and Periodicals in Historical Studies." *Journalism Quarterly* 21 (1944): 304-10.

Sloan, Wm. David, and Michael Stamm. *Historical Methods in Communication*, 3d ed. Northport, Ala.: Vision Press, 2010.

Smith, Paul. *The Historian and Film*. Cambridge: Cambridge University Press, 1976.

Trinkle, Dennis A., and Scott A. Merriman. *The History Highway: A 21st Century Guide to Internet Resources*, 4th ed. Armonk, N.Y.: M. E. Sharpe, 2006.

TO LEARN MORE

16 Field Observations and Case Studies

This chapter will provide you with guidelines for using field observation and case studies. We'll begin with field observations, as that method is actually one of the tools utilized in the case study approach.

Field observations, participant and nonparticipant, involve extended observation of behavior in natural settings. In *participant observation*, the field researcher is an active participant in the event or setting. In *nonparticipant observation*, s/he is not.

The case study may utilize field observation as a data collection method, but it may also rely upon document analysis, interviews and physical artifacts. (Interviews are covered in chapter 18 of this book.)

Field observations and case studies are qualitative research techniques. They are appropriate when the researcher needs to generate hypotheses; consider possible theoretical perspectives; gather exploratory, descriptive data; and explain phenomena (as opposed to measuring and quantifying phenomena). Observation and case studies are valuable tools for understanding events and behavioral phenomena or for deconstructing the reasons for an outcome from a complex situation.

FIELD OBSERVATION

Field observation literally means *observing the behavior associated with a specific phenomenon and unit of study*. For instance, if one is studying how consumers respond to guerilla marketing techniques like branded street performances, field observation enables the observation of those exposed to the performance, their reactions, and their subsequent behaviors. The unit of study may be an individual, a family, a group of friends, or some other unit. Observation can vary according to the degree of researcher participation in the behavior under investigation and in terms of the degree of concealment.

Consequently, there are four categories of field observation research: (1) overt observation, (2) overt participation, (3) covert observation, and (4) covert partici-

By Tracy L. Tuten
East Carolina University

pation. Here are the fundamentals of each one:

1. *Overt observation* is non-concealed observation with no researcher participation. For example, a research project studying an online community such as members of a forum on iVillage would disclose to the group the intent to study some aspect of the group's behavior, but the researcher would not actively participate in the group.

2. *Overt participation* is non-concealed observation with researcher participation in the activity of interest. The researcher not only informs the parties involved of the study, s/he also serves as one of the group participants. For instance, someone studying shopping behavior in a virtual world may be an active shopper during the study and include his or her personal observations as data.

3. *Covert observation* is concealed observation with no researcher participation.

4. *Covert participation* is concealed observation combined with researcher participation.

Covert observation and participation are both concealed forms of field observation varying only by the degree of researcher involvement in the group being studied. For example, one could observe unobtrusively the patterns of consumers exposed to outdoor advertising in populated areas such as Times Square as a form of covert observation. Covert participation might involve embedding the researcher in a sub-culture to get a more thorough glimpse of behavior among a group.

The choice of approach is dependent upon the research question, the degree of cooperation available from the units of interest, the potential impact of known observation on the phenomenon itself, and the ethical considerations of deception during the observation process. The researcher must assess whether concealment is necessary to study the behavior of interest without undue influence on that behavior. S/he must determine whether the subjects of study would cooperate openly in a study if they were aware they were being observed. S/he must determine whether covert observations are ethical given the nature of the concealment and the potential risk to the subjects.

ADVANTAGES AND DISADVANTAGES OF FIELD OBSERVATON

There are several advantages to field observation for communication research. It is useful for framing hypotheses, identifying independent and dependent variables, and defining background information associated with a phenomenon of interest. For example, if one is interested in studying the effects of celebrity endorsements on brand preferences, observation could be used to assess the responses to various endorsements. Because data are gathered by the researcher, they are not dependent upon participant willingness to report and are not subject to participant biases such as social-desirability responding. This technique can be useful for providing access to groups that would be otherwise difficult to reach. It may be possible, for instance, to identify several subjects who meet specific criteria for study but difficult to identify a group large enough to survey. Its costs are typically low, though costs depend upon the size and nature of the specific project. Among these various advantages, the most notable one is the access to information collected from a natural setting.

Despite the strengths of field observation, it does have some disadvantages.

The main one is its lack of generalizability to the larger population. Since observations are of a small, nonprobability sample, there is nothing to suggest that what is observed is typical or representative for a larger population of interest. Further, field research relies heavily on the interpretations of the researcher. This disadvantage can be dealt with, at least in part, by cross-validating with multiple observers. In addition, field observations may suffer from reactivity, that is, the bias created when behavior changes due to the influence of observers.

EXECUTING A FIELD OBSERVATON STUDY

There are several stages of planning necessary for field observation studies (after the point of specifying the research question and determining that field observation is an appropriate tool). These stages include (1) identifying the unit of interest, (2) choosing a research site, (3) arranging access, (4) sampling, (5) collecting data, and (6) analyzing and reporting. Let's examine each one.

Unit of Interest

1. The unit of interest should follow from the research question. Does the research question focus on the behavior or outcome of an individual, a family, a group of friends, an organization, or some other unit? The appropriate unit should be selected. For example, in a study of responsiveness to banner ads online, individuals represent the unit of interest.

Research Site

2. Once the unit of analysis is identified, the research site can be determined. In what setting does the behavior or phenomenon occur? It is this setting that will become the site for data collection. The setting will dictate to some extent the method for recording observations (e.g., note taking, video recording, or audio recording). Ideally, sites will be permanent enough to permit data collection over a period of time. For instance, if one is observing behavior in a mall, the location can probably be used over several days.

Access and Permission

3. In addition to identifying a site, the researcher must be granted access to the site and permission (when necessary) to record observations. Public sites have the advantage of not requiring permissions and can be suitable for observing common public behaviors such as shopping or participation in an event. The more private the behavior in question, the more difficult it will be to gain access. It can also be more challenging to gain access when the unit of analysis is an organization, such as a newsroom. In such situations, there may be legal implications for the organization to consider prior to allowing access for the researcher. Gaining access may require persistence and skill at persuasion. The researcher should identify benefits to the units of interest and the site so that they might welcome the opportunity to assist the study. When requesting permission, one will need to decide how much to disclose and what guarantees can be made in terms of confidentiality and publication intentions.

Sampling

4. The fourth stage of field observation research is sampling. Sampling refers to identifying which and how many units (individuals, groups, or organizations) to observe. For instance, if the topic is social support evidenced in newsrooms, how many newsrooms should be observed? If the topic is

sales of branded refreshments at events sponsored by the brand, how many events should be included? Because field observation is generally categorized as a qualitative technique, achieving a sample size that might permit generalizability is typically not a goal. However, there is value in utilizing more than one unit. A related issue is specifying exactly what behaviors or behavior segments to include. For instance, if shopper interactions with in-store advertising is the behavior of interest, which interactions are to be included in the study? Field observers typically utilize purposive sampling. That is, the observers will rely upon their own best judgment to determine what behaviors and events are relevant to the study and should be recorded and included.

5. Data collection means recording the behaviors and events that occur at the research site. It may require nothing more than a notebook and pencil but may also involve other instruments such as video and audio recorders, eye tracking devices, and other measurement tools. Recordings have the advantage of ensuring accurate records of what happened but also require transcription and cataloguing. Even if only a notepad is used, the observer may wish to make only mental notes during the observation session and record detailed notes afterwards. Making mental notes or automated recordings maximizes the time spent observing (rather than recording) and also minimizes the distractions that might be caused by the act of recording.

Data Collection

Field notes include not only what was said and what happened, but also the observer's thoughts and insights at the moment. Personal opinions are identified in the notes typically by enclosed brackets. How much should be recorded? It is best to err on the side of gathering too much detail than too little. Other data besides observer-generated recordings of behavior can also be collected. These might include diaries, photographic essays, unobtrusive measures of residual behavior (such as the radio station pre-sets of cars being serviced at service stations in a geographic region), and document analysis (such as receipts, checks, to-do lists, etc.). Documents that may be used include public documents such as police reports, news stories, data archives, chat room transcripts, message board posts, and so on or private documents like letters, telephone logs, appointment calendars, and text message logs. Depending upon the documents selected, the researcher may acquire the documents from public sources or by solicitation.

6. In field observation, the data must be organized properly prior to its analysis. The organization process requires that the data be filed according to meaningful labels. Once the data are assigned to files, a content analysis is conducted. Like other qualitative data, data generated by field observation studies are mined using content analysis to arrive at insights about the phenomenon of interest.

Data Organization and Analysis

The *case study* method is valuable for using several forms of data to investigate behavior, processes, and outcomes of individuals, groups, events, and organizations. For instance, a case study of the effectiveness of a campaign to reduce smoking on a college campus would examine the delivery of communication over a specified period of time at this one location along

CASE STUDIES

with behavioral indicators of effectiveness. Yin (1984) defines the case study research method as an *empirical inquiry that investigates a contemporary phenomenon within its real-life context* when the boundaries between the phenomenon and context are not clearly evident and that uses multiple sources of evidence (p. 23). Case studies rely in part upon observations as well as other sources of data. A key benefit of the case study approach is the degree of context that is provided by a thorough review of relevant history and current events and people shaping the phenomenon of interest. Case studies can focus on a single unit or on multiple units. For instance, we might study the process by which a creative team devises a new strategy and rely upon the work of a single team (for example, the book *Where the Suckers Moon*, by Randall Rothenberg, which provides an in-depth look at the advertising process from the perspective of Suburu's advertising agency); or we might investigate the processes utilized by several teams from one or more advertising agencies.

Merriam (1988) identified the four characteristics that represent the essence of case study research as the following: (1) particularistic, (2) descriptive, (3) heuristic, and (4) inductive. Case studies are particular to specific situations, which makes them a good choice for studying practical problems. They can also provide detailed descriptions in context for the topic of interest. They provide problem-solving value by offering perspective and insight into a situation. Lastly, the case study approach relies upon *inductive reasoning* — that is, it relies upon observation of details to discover insights about the phenomenon of interest.

ADVANTAGES AND DISADVANTAGES OF CASE STUDIES

The case study is a good approach when the researcher wishes to collect deep information about a specific situation. It is commonly used for exploratory research because of the rich detail that can be collected, and it is also used to gather descriptive and explanatory data as well. Case studies may focus on a single case or utilize a multiple case approach. Because many forms of data can be included in case studies ranging from observation, document analysis, historical materials, and even interview and survey data, they afford the opportunity for multiple perspectives on the phenomenon.

Despite these advantages, there are drawbacks to the case study method. Case studies are *time consuming* in terms of the process of data collection and the time necessary for data analysis. Because of the intense level of labor, case studies can be *expensive*. Another drawback is that of *limited ability to generalize* results. The researcher may draw many implications about an organization's processes and outcomes, for instance, but find herself unable to apply those same implications to other organizations, even those operating in the same industry. Even the *reliability* of the conclusions drawn for a case study is questionable given the small number of cases (sometimes only a single case). Finally, a case study is subject to researcher *bias* just as observation is. Researchers can become intensely involved in the context of a case and struggle to maintain objectivity.

EXECUTING A CASE STUDY

Case studies, given their use in exploratory research, may sometimes follow a more organic, developmental approach to design and execution compared to other research methods like survey work. In other words, case study methods can evolve during the data collection process. Still, the following stages are necessary in carrying out a case study project: (1) design and case selection, (2) protocol development and testing, (3) data collection, and (4) analysis and reporting. Let's examine each one of these stages.

1. In the first stage, design and case selection, the researcher establishes the questions to be studied as well as what the case is that is to be analyzed. What constitutes a *case*? The case may be an individual, a group or family, an organization, or even an event. The design must specify the definition of a case and what the researcher seeks to learn about the case. The general approach to use in selecting single or multiple real-life cases to examine and which instruments and data gathering approaches to use will be identified in this stage.

Design and Case Selection

In selecting cases, the researcher must choose carefully to ensure that exemplary cases are included. The researcher must determine whether to study cases that are unique in some way or cases that are considered typical. It may be desirable to select cases that represent different characteristics such as geography, size, or other such factors. In making these decisions, the researcher should refer to the study's purpose. Doing so will help to ensure that the best decisions for case inclusion are made. For example, a study of how companies can use virtual worlds as communication and engagement tools might include coverage of small businesses as well as major conglomerates and companies that market convenience goods and services.

The design should also specify what variety of data will be gathered for analysis. Data may be gathered using observations, documents, interviews, surveys, and physical artifacts (such as tangible items that are indicative of some variable).

2. In stage two, protocol is developed and tested. The *study protocol* is a document containing the procedures for data collection. It details the process of selecting cases to examine. It addresses the procedures for access to locations, individuals, and records. It establishes a schedule for data collection. It also anticipates potential logistical problems that could occur during the study, with stated methods for dealing with these problems in a standardized fashion. The protocol will identify the types of data to be collected and the details necessary for execution. For instance, if interviews are to be used, an interview guide will be developed as part of the protocol.

Protocol Development and Testing

3. Data collection takes place in stage three of the process. As data are collected, they should be systematically organized and stored using the protocol established. While the researcher should stick to protocol when possible, case study is also meant to be a flexible approach, and changes can be made as long as they are documented systematically. In addition to documents, observations, physical evidence, and interviews, the researcher should take field notes as to any perceptions and interpretations that occur during data collection. These notes can be invaluable later when interpreting data and constructing a report.

Data Collection

Analysis and Reporting

4. The final stage involves analyzing the data and reporting on the findings. It is at this stage that the researcher will review all of the data collected and seek to interpret patterns, trends, events, comments, and so on as reflected in the data. This stage may involve content analysis of the material contained in any documents, narrative comments about interviews, and descriptions of events and phenomena observed but may also include tabulations and quantitative data. Throughout, the researcher should remain open to new insights and attempt to provide evidence from multiple sources for any conclusions drawn. Multiple analysts may review the data to provide a form of interrater reliability for the interpretations drawn.

Analysis of data might be based on pattern matching, explanation building, and time-series analysis (Yin, 1989). *Pattern matching* means that the analyst compares predicted patterns with the patterns in the data set to identify whether the actual patterns match the predicted patterns. The *explanation building* approach means that the researcher constructs possible reasons for what occurred and then identifies evidence for and against the explanation in the data set. The *time-series analysis* approach compares the data to some theoretical trend predicted prior to the research.

When the analysis is complete, the findings are used to develop a report that portrays the complex problem in a way that conveys the context and phenomenon. Case study reports may follow the traditional report format, including the research problem, presentation of the methodological design, findings, and discussion and recommendations; or it might follow a nontraditional format, such as being framed as a story.

TO LEARN MORE

Angrosino, M. (2008). *Doing ethnographic and observational research*. Newbury Park, CA: Sage Publications.

Jorgensen, D. (1989). *Participant observation*. Newbury Park, CA: Sage Publications.

Kozinets, R.V. (2010). *Netnography: Doing Ethnographic Research Online*. Los Angeles, CA: Sage.

Merriam, S.B. (1988). *Case Study Research in Education*. San Francisco: Jossey-Bass.

Yin, R. (2008). *Case Study Research*, 3d ed. Newbury Park, CA: Sage Publications.

17

Oral History

Biographer Samuel Johnson once argued that the best way to document the 1745 Jacobite Rebellion in the British Isles was by collecting stories from witnesses who were still alive. "You are to consider, all history was at first oral," he said.[1]

Oral history is defined as the collection of memories and personal stories of historical significance through firsthand interviews with participants. Sometimes referred to as personal narrative, oral history is history told by the people who were there. Many people record their private memories in journals, in Web logs, or on video or audio tape; and these "diaries" can become valuable historical documents. But oral history takes place when there is an interviewer present asking specific questions of an interviewee and recording the answers verbatim.

In their *Oral History Manual*, Barbara W. Sommer and Mary Kay Quinlan define the field this way: "An oral history is created in a recorded interview setting, using a structured and well-researched interview outline, with a witness to or a participant in a historical event. Its aim is to collect and preserve the person's firsthand information and make it available to researchers."[2]

The practice of oral history has been around for generations. Many battles and wars have been documented through first-person narratives of soldiers granting interviews to historians and journalists, including the French Revolution and the American Civil War. Additionally, the lives of coal miners, mill workers, musicians, union members, sports stars, presidents, and numerous others have been preserved for future generations through the effective use of oral history.

A distinguishing feature of oral history from the early twentieth century forward is the fact that voices and images could be recorded for subsequent listening and viewing. Audio and visual archives have been amassed that allow us not only to read transcripts of interviews from the past, but actually to hear the voices and

---

[1]Paul Thompson, "The Development of Oral History in Britain," in *Oral History: An Interdisciplinary Anthology*, ed. David K. Dunaway and Willa K. Baum, 351-362 (Walnut Creek, Calif.: AltaMira Press, 1996).

[2]Barbara W. Sommer and Mary Kay Quinlan, *The Oral History Manual* (Walnut Creek, Calif.: AltaMira Press, 2002), 1.

By Anthony Hatcher
Elon University

see the faces and gestures of those long gone. Thomas Edison invented a working phonograph in 1877, and wax cylinders were used as early as the 1890s by the U.S. Bureau of Ethnography to record the songs and stories of Native Americans.[3]

The Federal Writers' Project (FWP), a branch of the Works Project Administration, was created during the Depression in 1935 to utilize unemployed writers. The massive FWP body of work includes 48 state guides, assorted community histories, and various oral histories. Among the valuable contributions by these writers were interviews conducted with more than 2,000 aging former slaves, at that time in their 80s and 90s. Some 10,000 typewritten pages of former slave interviews were archived by the Library of Congress.[4] Other such written, audio, and visual archives in the Library of Congress and elsewhere will be discussed later.

Before oral history interviews can be archived, they must be collected and preserved on tape or in digital form. It's also useful for future historians to have a transcript of a conversation or an interview. This chapter will focus on the systematic gathering, recording, storage, transcription, and uses of oral history interviews. It will also provide a brief history of and a working definition for this multi-disciplinary field.

CREATING AND CONDUCTING AN ORAL HISTORY PROJECT

Is there something you want to learn more about? Your family history? Segregation in your community before and during the Civil Rights era? What life was like for your uncle who traveled with the carnival? Oral history will help you learn such things.

Capturing oral history on tape and in transcripts requires preparation in the form of background research, but there is a technical aspect as well. Recording equipment and archiving of your interviews are necessary for preservation and future use.

All good oral history projects have the following elements in common:

1. An *interviewer*, sometimes called a *fieldworker* since the interviewer frequently travels to talk to his or her interview subjects
2. An *interviewee*, sometimes called a narrator, informant, respondent, or oral author[5] (For simplicity, this chapter will use the terms "interviewer" and "interviewee" throughout, unless quoting another source.)
3. Background research and preparation
4. Structured interview questions
5. Audio and/or video recording of an interview
6. Release forms and other documentation
7. Preservation and archiving of an interview

In order to execute a successful oral history project, clear goals need to be set, and proper planning is necessary. As oral historian Willa Baum observed, there are four broad phases in oral history. They are the following:
1. Creating
2. Processing

---

[3]Donald A. Ritchie, *Doing Oral History: A Practical Guide*, 2nd ed. (London: Oxford University Press, 2003), 21.

[4]Belinda Hurmence, ed., *My Folks Don't Want Me to Talk About Slavery* (Winston-Salem, N.C.: John F. Blair, 1984), xi.

[5]Ritchie, *Doing Oral History*, 30.

3. Curating

4. Using

In the following sections, you will learn the basics of planning, conducting, and archiving an oral history interview.

PLANNING There are many decisions to be made once you have determined what your oral history project is going to be. Whom should you interview? How many interviews should you do? Where will you do the interviews to minimize background noise on recordings and make your interviewees comfortable? What kind of recording equipment should you use? Will you use only audio recording or video? Will you have to travel to conduct the interviews? Should you make a transcript of your verbal interviews? Who will do the transcribing: students, amateurs, or professionals? Should you edit out "uhms" and "ahms" from a person's speech pattern? Who will do parallel research and fact-checking to verify the assertions put forth in each interview? What is the ultimate value of this project? Who is going to use this material, and how should it be stored and accessed? In what format?

And one big question: Who is going to pay for all of this?

As indicated earlier, setting up an oral history project means having clear goals or objectives. These goals may change as the project gets underway, but there are practical steps that will smooth the way.

PREPARATION Before an interview, you should do as much background research on your interview subject as possible. Research should include knowledge of the era and events you plan to ask your interviewee about. For example, say you decide to attend a convention of Disabled American Veterans (DAV) and conduct oral history interviews with vets from World War II, the Korean War, the Vietnam War, the Persian Gulf War, and the Iraq War. Prior to attending the convention, your research should, at a minimum, include the following:

1. The years each of these wars was fought

2. Reasons cited then and now for fighting these wars

3. Significant battles and outcomes

4. Issues involved in veteran care, veterans hospitals, and various types of war injuries and conditions, including post traumatic stress syndrome, or PTSD

5. Major issues addressed by the DAV group in your state

You could also prepare for interviewing veterans by reading published sources about various wars. Track down family histories, scrapbooks, and newspaper clippings of specific veterans that you would like to interview. Museums, universities, and libraries have repositories and archives that could prove valuable. Talk to relatives and friends of the interviewees, if possible. "Interviewers first get acquainted with the outline of interviewees' lives and then allow them to fill in the details," according to Donald Ritchie, associate historian in the U.S. Senate Historical Office.[6]

[6]Ibid., 85.

"Simply put," Ritchie says, "oral history collects memories and personal commentaries of historical significance through recorded interviews. An oral history interview generally consists of a well-prepared interviewer questioning an interviewee and recording their exchange in audio or video format."[7]

THE INTERVIEW

Before conducting an interview, consider the basic journalistic questions: Who, What, Where, When, Why, and How. John Tisdale has noted the similarities of covering a current news story as a reporter and collecting oral memories as a historian. Both journalism and oral history, he writes, "are concerned with recording information, both are concerned with accuracy, and both rely on the interview as the primary source of information and credibility."[8]

The main difference is the time element. Reporters work on short deadlines, often reporting events on the same day of an interview. Oral historians work in a longer, more relaxed time frame. Follow-up may include allowing the interviewee to review the tape and the transcripts days later to look for errors, a practice that is often impractical in daily journalism. Although reporters strive for accuracy, oral historians have the luxury of time that journalists often lack.

Former reporter Mark Feldstein has called journalism and oral history "kissing cousins." In an insightful essay, he delineated the *differences*, though, between the two, particularly when it comes to interview technique. Reporters can be aggressive, even rude, in their interrogations of interview subjects, he writes. Some journalists think such an attitude is a necessity because of time constraints or the unwillingness of a source to be forthcoming. News is often generated because of the relentless probing by a reporter, and periods of silence during an interview are to be avoided, particularly by broadcast reporters for whom silence is simply "dead air."

Oral historians by contrast are taught to be gentle, to rely on an indirect style of asking questions, even offering empathetic comments to elicit a response. Reporters are taught to be objective and straightforward. "Indeed, while oral historians rarely try to push unwilling subjects into interviews, some journalists simply do not take no for an answer," Feldstein says.[9] Oral history interviewers should strive to put their subjects at ease, making sure the interview setting is as comfortable as possible.

Donald Ritchie reminds us that there are fundamentals for oral history interviews that should not be ignored: "do your homework; be prepared; construct meaningful but open-ended questions; do not interrupt responses; follow up on what you have heard; know your equipment thoroughly; promptly process your recordings; and always keep in mind the practice and ethics of interviewing."[10]

"Oral history is an art, not an exact science," according to Willa Baum.[11] This is especially true when it comes to interviewing. The interviewer may elicit all sorts of truths and tales from the interviewee when a certain tone of voice or de-

[7]Ibid., 19.

[8]John R. Tisdale, "Observational Reporting as Oral History: How Journalists Interpreted the Death and Destruction of Hurricane Audrey," *Oral History Review* 27/2 (Summer/Fall 2000): 44.

[9]Mark Feldstein, "Kissing Cousins: Journalism and Oral History," *Oral History Review* 31:1 (September 2004) http://www.historycooperative.org/journals/ohr/31.1/feldstein.html (27 Jul. 2007).

[10]Ritchie, *Doing Oral History*, 84.

[11]Willa K. Baum, *Transcribing and Editing Oral History* (Walnut Creek, Calif.: AltaMira Press, 1991), 5.

Principles and Standards of the Oral History Association

The Oral History Association promotes oral history as a method of gathering and preserving historical information through recorded interviews with participants in past events and ways of life. It encourages those who produce and use oral history to recognize certain principles, rights, technical standards, and obligations for the creation and preservation of source material that is authentic, useful, and reliable. These include obligations to the interviewee, to the profession, and to the public, as well as mutual obligations between sponsoring organizations and interviewers.

People with a range of affiliations and sponsors conduct oral history interviews for a variety of purposes: to create archival records, for individual research, for community and institutional projects, and for publications and media productions. While these principles and standards provide a general framework for guiding professional conduct, their application may vary according to the nature of specific oral history projects. Regardless of the purpose of the interviews, oral history should be conducted in the spirit of critical inquiry and social responsibility and with a recognition of the interactive and subjective nature of the enterprise.

Responsibility to Interviewees:

1. Interviewees should be informed of the purposes and procedures of oral history in general and of the aims and anticipated uses of the particular projects to which they are making their contributions.

2. Interviewees should be informed of the mutual rights in the oral history process, such as editing, access restrictions, copyrights, prior use, royalties, and the expected disposition and dissemination of all forms of the record, including the potential for electronic distribution.

3. Interviewees should be informed that they will be asked to sign a legal release. Interviews should remain confidential until interviewees have given permission for their use.

4. Interviewers should guard against making promises to interviewees that the interviewers may not be able to fulfill, such as guarantees of publication and control over the use of interviews after they have been made public. In all future uses, however, good faith efforts should be made to honor the spirit of the interviewee's agreement.

5. Interviews should be conducted in accord with any prior agreements made with the interviewee, and such agreements should be documented for the record.

6. Interviewers should work to achieve a balance between the objectives of the project and the perspectives of the interviewees. They should be sensitive to the diversity of social and cultural experiences and to the implications of race, gender, class, ethnicity, age, religion, and sexual orientation. They should encourage interviewees to respond in their own style and language and to address issues that reflect their concerns. Interviewers should fully explore all appropriate areas of inquiry with the interviewee and not be satisfied with superficial responses.

7. Interviewers should guard against possible exploitation of interviewees and be sensitive to the ways in which their interviews might be used. Interviewers must respect the rights of interviewees to refuse to discuss certain subjects, to restrict access to the interview, or, under extreme circumstances, even to choose anonymity. Interviewers should clearly explain these options to all interviewees.

8. Interviewers should use the best recording equipment within their means to accurately reproduce the interviewee's voice and, if appropriate, other sounds as well as visual images.

9. Given the rapid development of new technologies, interviewees should be informed of the wide range of potential uses of their interviews.

10. Good faith efforts should be made to ensure that the uses of recordings and transcripts comply with both the letter and spirit of the interviewee's agreement.

meanor is present. The abilities to follow up on an unexpected conversational thread and to be a sensitive listener are important. Even the ability to flip a tape over to the other side in the recorder without interrupting conversational flow is a skill that can keep an interview on track.

An early "how-to" book on oral history methods for students by historian James Hoopes stresses that "oral history research is also a test of ourselves, of our ability to deserve and win the confidence of other people, of our ability to deal sympathetically but honestly and imaginatively with their memories, and of our ability to deal honestly with ourselves."[12]

There are assorted ways of beginning an interview, but as Hoopes notes, "the opening question should state the main purpose of the interview and require more than a short answer."[13] Let's expand on the disabled veterans example. After getting the name, age, rank, and branch of service of your interviewee, you could begin the actual probe with a direct, open-ended question such as this:

Will you tell me about your years of service and particularly about your wartime experience?

Hoopes offers this example for an interview opener with a hometown social worker about life in 1930s America:

Before we get into social work during the depression, will you tell me a little about your early life and, in particular, what brought you to this town?[14]

LISTENING

Once the question has been asked, the interviewer has a responsibility to listen closely so appropriate follow-up questions may be asked. Kathryn Anderson and Dana C. Jack have written about the importance of listening, particularly to women's perspectives on their lives, in order to be sensitive to what the interviewee has experienced. Interviewing a farm wife who worked with her husband in the fields, but who had sole responsibility for the home, Anderson recorded this exchange (with Anderson's questions in italics):

This is what was so hard, you know. You'd both be out working together, and he'd come in and sit down, and I would have to hustle a meal together, you know. And that's typical.

How did you manage?

Well, sometimes you didn't get to bed till midnight or after, and you were up at five. Sometimes when I think back to the early days, though, we'd take a day off, we'd get chores done, and we'd go take off and go visiting.

Was that typical? Neighbors going to visit each other after the chores were done?

Anderson's first question — *"How did you manage?"* — showed real interest in the hardships this woman faced. The farm wife then expressed how difficult it was to go to bed late and rise early, and how she longed for time off for visiting as in the early days of her marriage. Instead of following up on that wistful comment, Anderson asked a follow-up question about visiting her neighbors, which led the conversation away from the woman's exhausting schedule. Anderson notes her error here after the fact. "The two questions in succession," Anderson writes, "have a double message: 'Tell me about your experience, but don't tell me too much.'"[15]

[12]James Hoopes, *Oral History: An Introduction for Students* (Chapel Hill: University of North Carolina Press, 1979), 5.
[13]Ibid., 97.
[14]Ibid.
[15]Kathryn Anderson and Dana C. Jack, "Learning to Listen: Interview Techniques and Analyses," reprinted in Robert Perks and Alistair Thomson, *The Oral History Reader* 2nd ed. (New York: Routledge, 2006), 133.

Listening is essential in the spontaneous interview. Have a set of questions prepared that will get you where you want to go, but don't let your agenda blind you to good stories, interesting information, and genuine expressions of feeling. Your interviewee may hint at something that won't come out unless you specifically ask about it. Many interview subjects will be forthcoming, while others may need coaxing.

In terms of time limits, most oral history interview sessions last about an hour to an hour and a half. If there are to be multiple interviews, limiting each session to this amount of time keeps your interviewee from becoming overtired, particularly if he or she is elderly.

Interviewing Tips

The Southern Oral History Program of the University of North Carolina at Chapel Hill offers these *Ten Tips for Oral History Interviewers* on its Website (http://www.sohp.org/):

1. Ask one question at a time.
2. State your questions as directly as possible.
3. Ask open-ended questions-questions that begin with "why, how, where, what kind of," etc. Avoid "yes or no" questions.
4. Start with non-controversial questions. One good place to begin, for instance, is with the interviewee's childhood memories.
5. Don't let periods of silence fluster you.
6. Avoid interrupting the interviewee.
7. If the interviewee strays away from the topic in which you are interested, don't panic. Sometimes the best parts of the interview come about this way. If you feel the digression has drifted too far afield, gently steer the interviewee back to the topic with your next question.
8. Be respectful of the interviewee. Use body language to show you are interested in what he or she has to say. Remember, the interviewee is giving you the gift of his or her memories and experiences.
9. After the interview, thank the interviewee for sharing his or her experiences. Also send a written thank-you note.
10. Don't use the interview to show off your knowledge, charm, or other attributes. Remember, "good interviewers never shine – only their interviews do."

Used with permission of the Southern Oral History Program

EQUIPMENT Before you begin the interview, practice with the recording equipment you plan to use. Does it work properly? Can you set the sound level and leave it alone so you can focus on the interviewee?

This section addresses types of audio equipment used most often in field recordings for oral history. Some oral historians make a video recording. However, video recording has several drawbacks. One is that it sometimes inhibits the interviewee more than oral recording does. Furthermore, it costs more than oral recording. There is also concern about the uncertainty of being able to preserve video recordings over many years at reasonable costs.

Considering the disadvantages of video recording, most oral history is based on audio recording. Thus, the focus here will be on audio recording.

Recording has changed vastly since the large and primitive machines available for use in the early twentieth century. Sophisticated — and expensive — digital audio recorders are available for programs and individuals who can afford high-end equipment. There are affordable options for nearly every budget, whether your oral history project is a community-based effort, part of a university department, or an individual class assignment.

Portable recorders that record directly onto a compact disk have pros and cons. The pro is that you have a tangible product — a CD disk — at the end of your recording session. Recording via this method results in a portable compact disk that can be listened to easily for transcription and passed on to other audiences. The drawbacks are the following:

• Many CD recorders must remain stationary during interview sessions.
• Recording is limited to 74 minutes on most disks.
• CDs themselves are rapidly becoming old technology, giving way to mp3 and other digital recording methods.

For a simple, home-based project, you could get an inexpensive microphone and record directly to an mp3 device; and consumer grade video cameras are getting cheaper and more durable.

Despite the rapid improvements in digital recording, tape recorders are still in widespread use. "Although its use is in sharp decline," notes Andy Kolovos of the Vermont Folklife Center, "analog audiocassette is still a standard medium for folklore and oral history field recording."[16] Tape deteriorates over time, however, and with repeated use. Handheld digital recorders made by Marantz and other manufacturers are the preferred tools of most professional oral historians and ethnographers. They are durable in the field, and their quality audio can be uploaded to Web sites and burned onto CDs. Prices are constantly changing, but many of the better models are in the $500 range. The Southern Oral History Program (SOHP) at the University of North Carolina at Chapel Hill, for example, uses Marantz recorders with Shure lavalier and unidirectional microphones.

Regardless of the recorder, an external microphone is a must for the best recording. "Built-in microphones complicate recording by requiring one to place the machine as close to the speaker as possible, they limit the amount of monitoring one can do to the recording because any contact with the machine while recording is underway will be picked up by the mic, and internal mics pick up an enormous amount of machine noise from the recorder itself," according to Kolovos.[17]

CATALOGUING RECORDINGS

However you decide to record your subjects, cataloguing is an important step that cannot be overlooked. Prepare a tape log of the contents of the recordings as soon as possible after the interview. Here is an example of labeling an interview conducted with state Representative Dan Blue by Joseph Mosnier from the University of North Carolina at Chapel Hill:

Southern Oral History Program
Series: "North Carolina Politics Project"

Interview of Rep. Daniel T. Blue, Jr.

[16]Andy Kolovos, "Audio Field Recording Equipment Guide," The Vermont Folklife Center, October 22, 2007. http://www.vermontfolklifecenter.org/res_audioequip.htm.
[17]Ibid.

Raleigh, NC; January 19, 1996
Int. by Joseph Mosnier

Tape # 1.19.96-DB
Cassette 1 of 1 (approx. total length 70 mins)
Transcript and Field Notes are available.[18]

Willa Baum gives the following example of labeling in her book on tape transcription:

Regional Oral History Office
Narrator: *Abe Carlin*
Date: *17 May 1973*
Place: *Oakland, Calif.*
Interviewer: *Mary Fontenrose*
Project Title: *Earl Warren Era Series*
Interview Session: *1*
Length: *1 hour, 15 minutes*[19]

Less formal labeling can be used, of course. If you recorded your grandmother's memories of the Depression on two double-sided tapes, the tapes could be labeled, "side 1 of 4," "side 2 of 4," and so on. Include her name, the date, the interviewer's name, and the topics covered.

What is the best way to preserve your interview after recording it? The WAV format is a digital standard, and any audio editing or playback program should be able to open this type of file. That capability is useful for preserving your recordings over the long term. Digital storage, either in mp3 format on a hard drive or a server or on a CD, can be complex. Many researchers like the portability of a CD, but the ability to download a digital file for listening is often just as user-friendly. Server space and physical space often dictate the format for data storage.

TRANSCRIBING ORAL HISTORIES

Having an accurate written transcript of a recorded interview is extremely valuable to future generations.

"During the interview session, the interviewer should keep a running list of names, dates, words or phrases that may be hard to hear, old-fashioned, technical or otherwise difficult for the transcriber," advises Willa Baum.[20] The SOHP notes that while a transcription machine is efficient for producing transcripts of analog audiotapes, digital audio transcription is best done with digital transcription foot pedals and software. You may be asking yourself at this point, Why should I bother to transcribe at all? Why would I want to read a transcript of Grandma's story when I could hear her voice on the recording?

Baum offers three reasons:

1. Transcriptions are easier for researchers to use than audio recordings.

[18]Southern Oral History Project, "Tape label (example)." http://sohp.unc.edu/howto/guide/howto_111d.html.
[19]Baum, *Transcribing and Editing Oral History*, 9.
[20]Ibid., 8.

2. Interviewees can review a transcription to check for misstatements and inaccuracies, thereby creating a more complete record for posterity.

3. Bound transcripts of interviews can be useful for a community or archive and could form the basis for future funding of other oral history projects.[21]

Even for those doing family histories with no academic purpose, a bound copy of transcripts may be used by family members more often that the recordings themselves.

But how does one reproduce speech on the printed page, particularly if it is filled with "uhms" and "ahs" and "ehs"? "The first version of a transcript should be verbatim," according to Valerie Yow. "Stay as close as possible to the sound you actually hear. You may be writing down 'goin' and 'havin' many times, as well as 'ain't' and bad grammar…. If that was what was said, write it."[22] Yow maintains that enough repetitive words and phrases such as "like" and "you know" should be left in a transcript to give the reader the flavor of the interviewee's speech pattern.

Baum, Yow, and others have acknowledged the debate in oral history circles concerning transcripts — Should a transcript be an unedited, verbatim record, like a court document? Or is the verbatim transcript simply a framework from which to begin editing for clarity and historical accuracy? Baum writes that providing a complete transcribed interview "may require editorially adding further information such as names and dates, asking the narrator to explain, clarify, or amplify some statements, calling the narrator's attention to statements that seem to be in error."[23]

The question, then, becomes: Is an oral history a tape or a transcript? As Louis Starr, former director of Oral History Research at Columbia University, noted in a prescient 1977 essay, "A consensus emerges: tapes are more suitable for some purposes, transcripts for others; but so far as possible both should be preserved, allowing researchers to choose for themselves. Future generations may prove more aurally oriented."[24]

USES OF ORAL HISTORY

There are many uses for oral history. Valerie Yow cites the use of narratives by medical practitioners for use in the healing process; by a psychologist who studied storytelling among members of Alcoholics Anonymous; by a researcher who interviewed Southern farm families to better understand economic and social changes in more personal terms; and by many others.[25] Historians can use the personal narrative to understand how individuals were affected by sweeping historical events.

Yet, that strength may also be a limitation since, often, personal narratives are just that — personal. Studs Terkel is a sterling interviewer who has recorded thousands of hours of interviews over several decades with people from all walks of life. His books include *Working* and *Hard Times: An Oral History of the Great De-*

---

[21]Ibid., 14-15.

[22]Valerie Yow, *Recording Oral History: A Guide for the Humanities and Social Sciences* 2nd ed. (Lanham, Md.: AltaMira Press, 2005), 317.

[23]Baum, *Transcribing and Editing Oral History*, 40.

[24]Louis Starr, "Oral History," in *Oral History: An Interdisciplinary Anthology*, Dunaway and Baum, 43.

[25]Yow, *Recording Oral History*, 17.

pression. The former is a record of how people feel about their jobs, and the latter is a compendium of life in Depression-era America. Yow feels the detailed intimate portraits Terkel evokes do not reveal the big picture. In *Hard Times,* "[t]he informants talked about how they survived the Depression, rather than," she argues, "about the failure of capitalism to provide the necessities of life for most of the people."[26]

Still, world events are lived by humans, and reviewing the recordings and transcripts of the subjective experiences of humans who lived through a flood, a fire, a war, or hard economic times presents history in a more personal form. Through oral history, the past becomes real to us, something tangible that relates to our own experience.

THE EVOLUTION OF ORAL HSITORY

How do oral historians define oral history, and how did the field evolve into the multidisciplinary communication practice it is today?

"Oral history is primary source material obtained by recording the spoken words — generally by means of planned, tape-recorded interviews — of persons deemed to harbor hitherto unavailable information worth preserving," according to Louis Starr, who was director of the Oral History Research Office at Columbia University for 24 years.[27] He was the successor to Pulitzer Prize-winner Allan Nevins, an American history professor who created the country's first oral history project at Columbia in 1948. Together, Nevins and Starr are considered by many to be the founders of the oral history movement in the United States.

David K. Dunaway and Willa K. Baum have identified four generations of oral historians springing from that first center at Columbia. Nevins and Starr represent the first generation of practitioners, who envisioned oral history as a way of collecting the "unwritten recollections of prominent individuals for future historians, for research, and as a tool for orally based biography."[28] A second generation, coming of age in the 1960s and 1970s, expanded the scope of interview subjects beyond what they referred to as "elite" interviewees, mostly white men in important positions. Oral history in many areas became a grassroots effort to record the memories of the illiterate, the disenfranchised, and the underrepresented. Local, community, and regional groups set up oral history projects, involving social activists, feminists, and ethnic constituencies.[29]

A third generation arising in the 1980s had more technology at their disposal, including computers and smaller, more portable recording devices. Oral history came into its own as an academic discipline, and more field workers had received formal professional training. Divisions arose between "professional" and "amateur" oral historians, and theoretically inclined researchers emerged. Museums, libraries, and schools incorporated oral archives into their collections. The debate was on as to the purpose of oral history: "[W]as it intended," Dunaway asked, "to be (1) a set of primary source documents or (2) a process for construct-

[26]Ibid., 17.

[27]Starr, "Oral History," 40.

[28]David K. Dunaway, "The Interdisciplinarity of Oral History," in *Oral History: An Interdisciplinary Anthology,* Dunaway and Baum, 7-22.

[29]Ibid., 8.

[30]Ibid., 9.

ing history from oral sources?"[30]

Today, Dunaway writes, oral history is characterized by interdisciplinarity. It is incorporated into the practice of various other disciplines, such as folklore, ethnography, anthropology, and gender studies. Graduate study in oral history is also expanding.[31]

Robert Perks of the British Library Sound Archive and Alistair Thomson of the University of Sussex in England trace the generational chronology of oral history by referring to "four paradigm shifts in oral history theory and practice."[32] These four paradigm shifts were the following:

The post-war renaissance of memory as a source for "people's history"; the development, from the late 1970s, of "post-positivist" approaches to memory and subjectivity; a transformation in perceptions about the role of the oral historian as interviewer and analyst from the late 1980s; and the digital revolution of the late 1990s and early 2000s.[33]

A desire for a "people's history" of World War II motivated historians to conduct interviews about wartime experiences in the first era. Home front experiences were recorded along with soldiers' recollections. The oral historians of the second epoch defended the idea of subjectivity, arguing that "the so-called unreliability of memory was also its strength." In this view, the perceptions and feelings of an individual about a particular event are as important and valuable to subsequent historians as collective memory and documentary evidence.[34]

Subjective historical accounts are valued around the globe. In the introduction to their book, *African Words, African Voices: Critical Practices in Oral History*, Luise White, Stephan F. Miescher, and David William Cohen note that African history has become a burgeoning field since the mid-twentieth century. The rapid rise of African historiography has seen "the development of a central position for *the oral source* and *oral history* within the programs of recovering the African past," according to the authors. "Far from melting in the face of the historical profession's codes of *objectivity*, African oral history has been opening important inquiries into the very nature of African *subjectivity*."[35]

Valerie Yow has addressed the issue from the third era of the 1980s about the objectivity and the proper role of the interviewer in oral histories. "[L]iking or not liking," she says, "feeling repelled by difference in ideology or attracted by a shared world-view, sensing difference in gender or age or social class or ethnicity, all influence the ways we ask questions and respond to narrators and interpret and evaluate what they say."[36]

The current era has seen an explosion of technology that makes it easier than ever to record and archive first-person narratives. For example, since director Steven Spielberg founded the Shoah Foundation in 1994 after directing the World War II film *Schindler's List*, some 52,000 testimonies from the Holocaust have been recorded. The recordings are housed at the University of Southern California; and

[31]Ibid., 9-19.
[32]Perks and Thomson, *The Oral History*, 1.
[33]Ibid., 1.
[34]Ibid., 3.
[35]Luise White, Stephan F. Miescher, and David William Cohen, *African Words, African Voices: Critical Practices in Oral History* (Bloomington: Indiana University Press, 2001), 1-2.
[36]Valerie Yow, "'Do I Like Them Too Much?' Effects of the Oral History Interview on the Interviewer and Vice-Versa," *Oral History Review* 24:1 (1997): 55-79; reprinted in Perks and Thomson, *The Oral History Reader*, 67.

the archive is available at other sites such as Duke University, Freie Universität Berlin, and the United States Holocaust Memorial Museum in Washington, D.C. Visual History Archives can be accessed online through Internet2, a high capacity digital network. Segments of interviews are available via the Shoah Web site.[37]

ORAL HISTORY AS HISTORICAL METHOD

Oral history has come to be respected by historians, journalists, ethnographers, anthropologists, and others who deal with human history precisely because such narratives offer personal perspective on events often painted with a broad brush. It is one thing to read a procedural account of a hurricane or a holocaust, and quite another to hear a survivor tell you what it was like for him or her as an individual.

James Hoopes legitimizes the use of oral history, taking into account the real world factors that make up historical research. He writes:

> Things that have survived from the past, called documents, are the basis of historical knowledge. Most historians rely on written documents, such as books, letters, diaries, deeds, census and tax records, church registers, bills of lading, and so on. But houses, coins, tools, gravestones, furniture, and folklore or legends handed down from generation to generation are also documents and can tell us much about the people who created them. This last sort of document, folklore or legend, differs from the others in that it has its origins in speech. Oral history is based on documents that are spoken, and folklore and legend are only one kind of spoken document.[38]

Willa Baum was a respected pioneer in oral history methodology and interview techniques, and head of the Regional Oral History Office at the University of California at Berkeley, the second such project after the center at Columbia. Baum, who died in 2006, was a founding member of the Oral History Association in 1967. In her book about interview transcription, she states, "Oral history is a modern research technique for preserving knowledge of historical events *as recounted by participants* [emphasis added]."[39]

Italian scholar Alessandro Portelli supports Baum's assertion that the focus of oral history should be on interviewee recollection of personal experience. "Oral sources," he explains, "are credible but with a *different* credibility ... the diversity of oral history consists in the fact that 'wrong' statements are still psychologically 'true' and that this truth may be equally as important as factually reliable accounts."[40]

ORAL HISTORY PROJECTS AND ARCHIVES

Once oral histories are completed, they are often archived and maintained by museums, universities, institutions, libraries, and communities for use by the public, as well as amateur and professional historians. For example, many universities house interviews with surviv-

[37]For more information on the Shoah Foundation Institute, see http://college.usc.edu/vhi/instituteataglance .php.

[38]Hoopes, *Oral History: An Introduction for Students*, 5.

[39]Baum, *Transcribing and Editing Oral History*, 5.

[40]Alessandro Portelli, "What Makes Oral History Different," *The Death of Luigi Trastulli and Other Stories: Form and Meaning in Oral History* (New York: State University of New York Press, 1991), reprinted in Perks and Thomson, *The Oral History Reader*, 37.

ors of the terrorist attacks of September 11, 2001, as well as those who suffered in Hurricane Katrina in 2005. Some examples of established archives and projects are the following:

• The Veterans History Project of the Library of Congress relies on volunteers to send audio and video interviews with wartime veterans from World War I through present American conflicts. The U.S. Congress created the project in 2000. It also welcomes recorded first-person interviews with civilian workers with the USO, war industry plant workers, medical volunteers, and other nonmilitary personnel involved in war efforts.

• The Southern Oral History Project at the University of North Carolina at Chapel Hill, founded in 1973, "seeks to foster a critical yet democratic understanding of the South — its history, culture, problems, and prospects."[41] The SOHP archives contain some 4,000 interviews documenting the experiences of people from all walks of life in the American South.

• The Seattle Civil Rights and Labor History Project is based at the University of Washington. It documents the civil rights movement in the Pacific Northwest. According to the Project's Web site,

> Civil rights movements in Seattle started well before the celebrated struggles in the South in the 1950s and 1960s, and they relied not just on African American activists but also on Filipino Americans, Japanese Americans, Chinese Americans, Jews, Latinos, and Native Americans. They also depended upon the support of some elements of the region's labor movement.[42]

• One of the most personal and widespread oral history projects in the United States is called StoryCorps. It was launched in 2003 as a nonprofit organization "whose mission is to honor and celebrate one another's lives through listening."[43] Many of its audio recordings are heard periodically on National Public Radio, and all are archived in the Library of Congress. StoryCorps allows families and friends to enter a sound booth, conduct an interview on any subject, and leave with an audio CD of the interview. The first permanent recording booth was located in New York City's Grand Central terminal, and at least three more have been added across the nation. StoryCorps also has mobile booths inside trailers that travel about the country to various communities.

In conclusion, we may say that oral history, to be done properly, must employ *systematic* gathering, recording, storage, and transcription of interviews. Oral history, though, is not objective history. It is subjective narrative, collected by informed interviewers, from participants and observers of large and small moments in history who relate these experiences as *they* lived them. There is much "truth" in oral history, although historical facts such as dates, spelling of names, and specific occurrences need to be verified through additional research.

Recently there has been a resurgence of the personal narrative in journalism.[44]

[41]Southern Oral History Program, "Mission of the SOHP." http://sohp.unc.edu/mission/index.html.
[42]Seattle Civil Rights and Labor History Project. http://depts.washington.edu/civilr/.
[43]StoryCorps, "About Us." http://www.storycorps.net/about.
[44]*Columbia Journalism Review* (July/August, 2006), 28-32.

Sometimes called "bottom-up history," this focus on personal narrative by so many journalists, particularly those writing online and for public radio, is testament to the power of the human voice and the human experience — and the value of the individual story in the world's historical record.

With proper planning and the right equipment, organizing an oral history project for a class project, your community, or for yourself, is very feasible. Future historians — or family members — will be able to use your properly archived interviews to gain special and specific insights about the past.

TO LEARN MORE

Baum, Willa K. *Transcribing and Editing Oral History.* Walnut Creek, Calif.: AltaMira Press, 1991.

Charlton, Thomas L., Lois E. Myers, and Rebecca Sharpless. *History of Oral History: Foundations and Methodology.* Lanham, Md.: AltaMira Press, 2007.

Dunaway, David, and Willa K. Baum, eds. *Oral History: An Interdisciplinary Anthology.* Walnut Creek, Calif.: AltaMira Press, 1996.

Feldstein, Mark. "Kissing Cousins: Journalism and Oral History." *Oral History Review* 31:1 (September 2004).

Hoopes, James. *Oral History: An Introduction for Students.* Chapel Hill: University of North Carolina Press, 1979.

Lanman, Barry A., and Laura M. Wendling. *Preparing the Next Generation of Oral Historians: An Anthology of Oral History Education.* Lanham, Md.: AltaMira Press, 2006.

Perks, Robert, and Alistair Thomson, eds. *The Oral History Reader.* 2nd ed. New York: Routledge, 2006.

Ritchie, Donald A. *Doing Oral History: A Practical Guide.* 2nd ed. London: Oxford University Press, 2003.

Schneider, William. *So They Understand: Cultural Issues in Oral History.* Logan: Utah State University Press, 2002.

Sommer, Barbara W., and Mary Kay Quinlan. *The Oral History Manual,* 2nd ed. Walnut Creek, Calif.: AltaMira Press, 2009.

Thompson, Paul. *Voice of the Past, The: Oral History,* 3rd ed. New York: Oxford University Press, 2003.

Tisdale, John R. "Observational Reporting as Oral History: How Journalists Interpreted the Death and Destruction of Hurricane Audrey." *Oral History Review* 27:2 (Summer/Fall 2000).

Vansina, Jan. *Oral Tradition: A Study in Historical Methodology.* Trans. H.M. Wright. New Brunswick, N.J.: Transaction Publishers, 2006.

Vansina, Jan. *Oral Tradition As History.* Madison: University of Wisconsin Press, 1985.

White, Luise, Stephan F. Miescher, and David William Cohen, eds. *African Words, African Voices: Critical Practices in Oral History.* Bloomington: Indiana University Press, 2001.

Yow, Valerie. "'Do I Like Them Too Much?' Effects of the Oral History Interview on the Interviewer and Vice-Versa." *Oral History Review* 24:1 (1997).

Yow, Valerie. *Recording Oral History: A Guide for the Humanities and Social Sciences.* 2nd ed. Lanham, Md.: AltaMira Press, 2005.

18 Focus Groups and Intensive Interviews

This chapter will provide you with the tools needed for using two interview methods: focus groups and intensive interviews. Focus group and interview research might stand alone for a project that seeks to develop rich insight into a sample of individuals. They are also frequently used alongside quantitative studies to prepare researchers prior to a project, to assist them in understanding unexpected or unclear results after it, or to offer a deeper picture of the phenomenon of interest. These qualitative techniques help researchers to understand participants on their own terms and in their own words. They enable researchers to uncover unanticipated emotions, reactions, and relationships.

Focus group and intensive interviews are the "workhorses" of much qualitative data collection. More than 50% of exploratory studies rely on focus groups and 8% on intensives (Research Industry Trends report).

With both forms of interview (focus groups and intensives), researchers use open-ended questions and other materials to probe participants' thoughts, motivations, and opinions. The responses become textual data that can then be mined using content analysis. (For a discussion of content analysis, you may wish to read Chapter 9 of this book.) Samples are relatively small and collected in a short period of time. Both methods utilize semi-structured sets of questions and probing techniques to elicit detailed information.

The *intensive interview*, also referred to as an in-depth interview or IDI, is a one-on-one interview that follows a semi-structured series of questions. It is most commonly conducted in a face-to-face setting. Hybrid techniques are also possible that combine email interviews, telephone interviews, and interviews using chat room technology.

Focus groups bring together a group of people for an interactive discussion. They are often held in person but may be conducted online using chat technology or virtual environments.

We'll cover the steps for planning and conducting both intensive interviews

By Tracy L. Tuten
East Carolina University

and focus groups. But first, let's start with a list of questions for determining whether focus groups or interviews are right for the project.

To know whether interviews are a desirable approach, consider the following questions:

ARE INTERVIEWS THE RIGHT APPROACH?

• Are you looking for rich insights filled with descriptions of participant thoughts and behaviors?
  • Is it desirable that data collection be completed quickly?
  • Do you have access to trained interviewers and observers?
  • Is it acceptable, given the nature of the project, to use a small sample?
  • Will you have sufficient access to qualified participants?
  • Must the data be generalizable to the population of interest?
  • Must you estimate the magnitude of the phenomenon you are studying?
  • Must data be objective rather than subjective?

If you've answered yes to the first five and no to the final three questions, interviews are an appropriate method.

THE VALUE OF INTERVIEWS

Focus groups and intensive interviews share several objectives and characteristics. Both are useful for identifying data needed to define or explore a problem. Each can reveal attitudes, motives, and behaviors — sometimes even those that might be hidden from the participants themselves. They generate ideas and provide data to explain consumer responses in the marketplace. They generally last about 1-3 hours and follow a semi-structured guide. Participants may be offered an incentive as a token of appreciation.

However, there are also differences that must be considered when choosing between the two. The probing technique, for instance, is more effective when used with in-depth interviewing because it can elicit more detail. The interviewer responds to answers with additional questions, creating an opportunity for more detailed discussion of the topic. The more the participant talks, the more likely s/he is to reveal underlying attitudes, motives, emotions, and behaviors.

Because IDIs focus on one person at a time, while focus groups may include 6-12 people, participant comments can be explored more deeply in IDIs. There is a lower likelihood of participants responding simply in a socially desirable manner because the social influence is limited to the researcher. In addition, the conversation tends to be more on topic because there is no "cross talk" with other participants.

Focus groups, too, offer specific benefits to researchers over intensive interviews. Ideas can spark from the discussion, with participants "piggy backing" on the ideas of others. The interactions and body language of the group can be observed and assessed as well as the verbal responses. Particularly when the topic is relevant to group decision-making and influence, interviewing in a group context can be valuable.

Interview Characteristics and Process

Projects using either method basically follow a three-step process of

(1) planning, (2) conducting the interviews, and (3) analyzing and reporting the results. In Figure 1, specific steps for conducting interviews are identified. We'll use this same process to guide our discussions for implementing focus groups and intensive interviews, in turn.

Figure 1: Steps in Conducting an Interview

Phase/Step	Description
Phase 1	Planning
Step 1	Understand the questions/problems; establish the objective
Step 2	Create a set of research questions and develop the interview guide
Step 3	Select an environment for the interview and a moderator
Step 4	Recruit prospect pool, screen prospects, and select participants
Step 5	Prepare and send any necessary materials to all participants
Phase 2	Conducting
Step 6	Greet participant, give interview guidelines, develop rapport
Step 7	Conduct the interview
Phase 3	Analysis and Reporting
Step 8	Transcribe interviews
Step 9	Analyze responses
Step 10	Write report of results

FOCUS GROUP INTERVIEWS

Focus groups refer to interactive discussions about a topic or concept among a small group of people who are led by a professional moderator. They are standard procedure for any study requiring a depth of inquiry into a topic. They are useful for generating ideas, screening new products, identifying underlying attitudes to product concepts and brands, discovering shopping intentions, evaluating creative concepts, and acquiring a depth of understanding about consumer behavior. Groups are flexible; they may disguise the study's purpose or not and vary in the extent to which they follow a structured guide. In addition, groups provide limited exposure to concepts, which can protect information from exposure to competition.

The size of a group is most commonly 6-12, although "mini-groups" of 3 may be used as well. Discussions are semi-structured (following an outline known as an "interview guide" or a "moderator's guide") and typically last 90 minutes to 2 hours. The moderator's objective is to encourage group members to talk in detail about the topics posed while the moderator draws out experiences, ideas, and emotions from the group. When members of a group have a good rapport with each other and the moderator, one person's comments can spark a memory, reaction, or idea from another, creating a synergistic effect.

Phase 1: Planning the Study

The basic stages of the process, as illustrated in Figure 1, include planning, conducting, and analyzing/writing. The planning stage is critically important to the success of the overall study. The researcher must have a clear understanding of the purpose of the study, the definition of the problem, and the data required. In the planning stage, the researcher will complete five core steps.

The first of these steps is to ensure that the research questions are *Research Questions* stated accurately and completely. The objectives of the study are clearly identified to ensure that the questions used in the group will be designed appropriately to elicit the desired data.

During Step 2, the goal is to develop a moderator's guide. The guide *The Interview Guide* is a detailed outline of the topics and questions that the moderator will use to generate active discussion. It exists not only to ensure the right questions are asked but also to stimulate the discussion, control the flow of discussion, and ensure that participants remain comfortable and engaged. Working from the objectives and research questions identified in step 1, the specific questions to be asked during the group discussions are developed. These questions are edited and refined. For instance, asking "What do you think of Yahoo!?" will elicit very different comments from asking "In your mind, what is the core difference between Yahoo! and Google?" Even the order of question topics and the flow from topic to topic are considered as the moderator's guide is developed. Guides begin with general questions and work to specifics. In a session focusing on how to reposition Yahoo's brand image, the moderator might use a question like "Which search engine do you use most often? Why?" early in the session. Later, specific perceptions of Yahoo! and its competitors can be elicited. Figure 2 categorizes the types of questions that might be present in a moderator's guide, and Figure 3 includes a sample of a guide used in a study of stereotypes found in advertising.

Figure 2. Types of Questions Used in Moderators' Guides

• Opening questions are asked at the beginning of sessions. They are designed to be answered quickly and to allow members to identify with each other. They establish a comfort zone.

• Introductory questions introduce each specific topic of discussion.

• Transition questions are used to direct the participants from one core topic to the next. They provide a segue to and from each section of the guide.

• Critical questions are the heart of the study. These are the primary questions to which the researcher seeks answers.

• Ending questions are designed to bring about closure to a discussion.

Step 3 involves making decisions about the desired interview environ- *The Interview* ment and the moderator(s) to be used. Focus groups can be held in a va- *Environment* riety of locations such as a conference room, a meeting room in a church *and Moderator* or civic organization, an office, a hotel meeting room, or even the moderator's home. While all of these sites may be appropriate, professional focus groups commonly meet in a focus group facility equipped with a conference table and comfortable seating, an observer viewing area and one-way mirror, and built-in audio/visual recording equipment.

Although this is the industry standard, use your judgment in deciding where

Figure 3: Sample Interview Guide

<u>Introduction/Welcome</u>

- Moderator introduction
- Basic guidelines for the group
- Information sheets completed
- Introductions of participants

<u>Warm-up/basic brand associations</u>

Mod: "We're here today to talk about brand attitudes and how consumers respond to the choice of humor that brands use in their advertising. I'd like to start by asking you to think about a few specific brands and sharing attributes you associate with those brands. Okay?"

√ *TJ Maxx*
Mod: "Is everyone familiar with the brand TJ Maxx?"
Mod: "What comes to mind when you think of the brand TJ Maxx?" (probe)
Mod: "Would you say your attitude toward the brand is generally positive or negative? Why is that? What has influenced your perception of the brand?"

Mod: "Let's move on to another brand."

√ *Salon Selectives*
Mod: "Is everyone familiar with the brand Salon Selectives?"
Mod: "What comes to mind when you think of the brand Salon Selectives?" (probe)
Mod: "Would you say your attitude toward the brand is generally positive or negative? Why is that? What has influenced your perception of the brand?"

<u>Use of humor</u>

Mod: "Many brands use humor in their advertising. Advertisers hope that, by using humor, consumers will be entertained by the ad, better like the brand, recall the ad, and maybe even buy that brand the next time they shop. Given your own reactions to humor in advertising, does it sound like a good strategy? Is humor in advertising effective in reaching you as a consumer?" (probe on what works or what doesn't work and why)

<u>View ads</u>

Mod: "I've got a couple clips to show you – examples of humor in advertising – and I'd like your reactions to the ads. Let's start with one from TJ Maxx."
Mod: Show ad
Mod: "What are your initial reactions to the ad?" (probe)
Mod: Probe on emotional response (entertaining, funny, insulting, discomfort, attempt to gauge range of emotions generated by viewing)
Mod: "Now that you've seen this ad, what do you think of the brand TJ Maxx?" (Probe on any responses that are different from initial brand image.) "What is it about the ad that affects what you think about the brand?" (probe)
Mod: "What about future purchases? Are you more or less likely to shop at TJ Maxx having seen this ad?"

Mod: "The next one is from Salon Selectives."
Mod: Show ad

Continued on next page

Figure 3: Sample Interview Guide

Continued from previous page

<u>Mod</u>: "What are your initial reactions to the ad?" (probe)

<u>Mod</u>: Probe on emotional response (entertaining, funny, insulting, discomfort, attempt to gauge range of emotions generated by viewing)

<u>Mod</u>: "Now that you've seen this ad, what do you think of the brand, Salon Selectives?" (Probe on any responses that are different from initial brand image.) "What is it about the ad that affects what you think about the brand?" (probe)

<u>Mod</u>: "What about future purchases? Are you more or less likely to buy a Salon Selectives product having seen this ad?"

Stereotyping

<u>Mod</u>: (If participants have not already shifted to a discussion of stereotyping, introduce it here.) "Would you say these ads have something in common?" (probe)

<u>Mod</u>: "Stereotyping, making fun of perceptions of others with specific characteristics, is one way brands can approach humor. Did it work?" (Probe on perceived funniness of the ads overall.)

<u>Mod</u>: Recap responses to ads above.

<u>Mod</u>: "There are lots of stereotypes that have been used in advertising: ditzy blondes, angry large black women, nerdy men ... just to name a few. Would you react to "humorous" ads that use stereotypes like these?" (probe)

Messages to brands

<u>Mod</u>: "You've given some really thoughtful comments – thank you. Before we wrap this up, let's think about this from one other angle. Imagine that TJ Maxx (or SS) had asked you to view this commercial prior to its broadcast. The brands want your advice – based on your opinion of the ad – on whether to select this ad to run.... What would you tell them?" (probe)

Final thoughts

<u>Mod</u>: "We've covered a lot here today...." (Recap highlights). "Is there anything else you want to share? Anything you wish to expand on?" (probe)

<u>Mod</u>: Emphasize importance of participation/Thanks

---

to host a focus group session. Jon Steele, in *Truth, Lies, and Advertising*, advocates holding sessions in the home of one of the participants. A living room setting elicits an entirely different set of expectations for the participants than a formal research setting might do. Consider the following issues. Should participants feel as if they are "professionals" planning communications strategy? What would that lead to? Would participants think they should give the "right" answers or respond as they truly feel? The living room setting has a distinct advantage for making people feel comfortable and welcome. However, not all focus groups should be conducted in informal settings. The researcher should consider carefully what setting is the best one given the participants and the topic being discussed.

Another component of step 3 is the selection of a moderator. Moderators have a very difficult job. They must develop rapport with the participants, remember participant names, move seamlessly from topic to topic, listen to responses, develop probing questions to elicit greater detail, and manage the flow of conversation. Not everyone can be a good moderator. These are the characteristics commonly associated with effective moderators: 1) great communicators, 2) professional, 3) friendly, 4) good memory, 5) ability to make people feel at ease, 6) ability to exercise mild control over discussion, 7) reasonably familiar with topic background, 8) well-trained in probing and follow-up questioning, 9) experienced, 10) quick-witted, and 11) flexible.

Participants   Step 4 involves making several decisions relative to the focus group participants and beginning to set the stage for actually conducting the group. We begin this step by answering the following questions:

> Who should be included as participants?
> How many groups should be conducted?
> How will prospects be recruited?
> How should prospects be screened (qualified)?

Who should be included? To decide, the researcher must consider the purpose of the study and who best can provide the necessary information. The first aspect is to consider all of the types of participants that should be represented in the study. This might mean considering demographic variables like age, gender, and socio-economic indicators as well as purchase and usage behavior.

Consider, for instance, a focus group study on reactions to a series of commercials for a frozen breakfast food designed to entertain the audience with a humor appeal based on stereotypical attributes of heavy, black women. The brand in question has decided to assess pre-launch whether the commercial entertains or offends its target market. In this example, the target market is mothers — the primary shoppers for family groceries. What characteristics should we seek in our focus group participants? Clearly, we'd like mostly mothers, with some inclusion of fathers with heavy responsibility for family shopping. We'd also want to include a mix of racial groups and, given that the brand in question is a relatively inexpensive food product, a range of income groups. The product is sold nationally; so we might also want to have representation from participants living in several regions of the United States.

How many groups should be conducted? The number of groups conducted usually increases with the number of participant variables. In the example above, this means that we may need to have a group in major markets in the north, south, southwest, midwest, northwest, and southwest. Within each group, the participant mix might include 80% mothers and 20% fathers with shopping responsibility for the home. It would have a range of income levels represented. The racial identities represented in each group might include 4 whites, 4 blacks, 1 Asian, and 1 Latino. It is important to remember that there is no right answer as to how many groups to hold. One group discussion may lend sufficient insight to the problem at hand. Or several discussions might reveal that new insights occur with each one. The researcher should assess the variables of interest and select a number accordingly.

How will prospects be recruited? Prospect recruitment is one of the most difficult tasks in focus group research. It may involve a variety of methods, such as using established lists of willing participants, advertising for participants, or even telephone recruiting. Focus group researchers frequently use a technique known as *snowballing* to recruit participants. Snowballing relies upon referrals from other qualified candidates. Candidates, once qualified, are asked to suggest others whom they know with similar attributes who might be willing to participate. Research organizations with large focus group projects may conduct ongoing and frequent recruitment campaigns, maintaining lists that can be mined for participants. However, snowballing is a valuable recruitment tool also for small-scale and independent projects. In any case, it is important to remember that small samples are inherently unrepresentative. Probability sampling does not make sense for focus groups, but researchers thus must accept the limitations of non-probability samples.

How should prospects be screened? The screening questionnaire is used to ensure that the prospects recruited are actually qualified for participation in the study. It is designed to screen out the participants who do not meet the description identified in the first segment of this step. For instance, in the breakfast foods example used above, our screening guide might assess answers to the following questions:

1. Is the prospect male or female?
2. Is the prospect a parent?
3. What percentage of responsibility for grocery shopping is assigned to the prospect?
4. In what region of the country does the prospect reside?
5. What race is the prospect?
6. What is the prospect's household income level?

The responses to these questions would tell us whether the prospect meets our definition of the desired participant as well as which categories of characteristics the prospect can represent if selected.

Once we assess who the participants should be, how many groups are needed, and how to recruit and qualify prospects, we shift to implementation. The recruitment plan has been followed, prospects are screened, and qualified prospects selected for invitation to the group.

Pre-Session Materials In the final step of phase 1, any materials required are sent to the final set of participants for each group that will be held. Once participants are qualified, they are invited to attend the session and provided details on the date, time, and place. Directions to the facility and, if needed, parking passes are provided. Participants may be asked to complete an assignment (such as viewing a video, visiting a store, keeping a diary, etc.) or questionnaire prior to arrival at the actual session. Participants should confirm plans to attend, but the researcher should always assume that many will not confirm or will confirm but not show. If the goal is to secure a group of 12, 20 qualified participants should be invited. If too many actually show for the session, the "extras" can be dismissed (though they should still be offered the agreed-upon incentive).

Phase 2: Conducting the Discussions

Prior to the arrival of participants, the facility must be arranged and checked. Is the recording equipment functioning correctly? Are any props or discussion materials to be used (if any) ready and available? Refreshments and name tags should be prepared and set out for participants. Depending upon the location, signs may need to be installed to direct participants to the precise location. Just prior to the session but before participants arrive, any observers should be directed to the viewing area so as not to influence the opinions offered by participants.

Beginning the Session   As participants arrive, they should be greeted warmly and invited to partake of the refreshments available. Socialization among participants is encouraged because it will positively influence the group's rapport during the actual discussion. The moderator will briefly discuss the ground rules for the session. Common ground rules include 1) only one person should speak at a time, 2) there is no right or wrong answer, and 3) everyone's opinion is valued. The moderator will remind participants that the session will be recorded but also reassure them that their identities will not be disclosed. If the study is subject to and has been reviewed and approved by an Institutional Review Board (IRB), participants may be informed briefly of the concept of informed consent, provided contact information, and asked to indicate by signature their agreement to the ground rules of the session. The moderator may disclose the purpose and sponsor of the study unless, if it is best in order to maintain an unbiased opinion, the study is disguised.

Main Session   Using the moderator's guide, the first topic is introduced. It should be something that is interesting and easy to talk about. The first topic ensures that everyone feels confident about his or her ability to contribute in a meaningful way. The moderator will continue working through the guide, covering each topic and transitioning between topics. This will not simply be a Q&A session. In a good group, participants will react to the comments of others. The conversation will be interactive. It may be a challenge for the moderator to keep the conversation on track and ensure that depth is possible while ensuring that all topics are discussed.

Session Close   Once the pre-specified topics have been covered, the moderator will summarize what the participants have said during the session. At this point, participants should be asked a closing question that will enable them to clarify any misconceptions held by the moderator and to offer any additional ideas or opinions that were not expressed earlier. The moderator might ask, "Have we missed anything?" or "Is that a good assessment of how you felt today?" Once this conversation has tapered off, the participants are thanked for their attendance and provided any promised incentive.

Phase 3: Analyzing and Reporting Results

The final phase begins with a debriefing of any observers and an initial "debriefing analysis," which gives the researcher an opportunity to assess what happened during the session. The impressions of any observers are compared to those of the moderator, and differences are discussed. Notes are kept on the debriefing analysis for use later in analysis and reporting.

The tapes of the session must be transcribed. The transcripts will be used to analyze the data gathered during the sessions. Insight and meaning are derived from the content analysis, enabling the researcher to answer the research questions that led to the study and to draw conclusions. In the report, sample comments from participants can be used to add flavor and interest to the presentation of results. This same approach is used for analyzing the data produced from intensive interviews and is discussed in Chapter 16 in this book. Results are developed into a research report that explains the purpose of the study, any literature or secondary data used to guide the study, an explanation of the methods used to study the topic, the results, and the implications.

ONLINE FOCUS GROUPS

So far, we've focused on focus groups conducted in-person. An in-person mode of contact is still the norm in focus group research although online groups are becoming more common.

Advantages

Online focus groups offer the benefits of traditional focus groups as well as other benefits not commonly associated with in-person groups. The benefits include the following.

1. Costs may be lower because travel expenses, facility rentals, and transcription services (because a transcript is generated during the session) can be eliminated.

2. Using an online group may enhance access to low incidence populations (that is, groups with an unusual characteristic or that are difficult to identify) by allowing more geographically diverse samples to be drawn and by making participation easier for markets that are typically hard to recruit.

3. Online focus groups are convenient to participants because there is no travel to a physical site required or hassles with parking.

4. Even the data generated may be of higher quality given that socially desirable responding may be less prevalent in a virtual environment than in a face-to-face setting.

5. Online groups are useful for dealing with sensitive topics.

6. There appears to be less inhibition and editing of thoughts among participants in online groups.

7. Unrelated chatting and extensive input from one or a few participants is less common.

8. Consequently, one might imagine that rapport is difficult to establish in an online venue. On the contrary, those skilled in online relationships will recognize that personalities and attitudes can easily be relayed online; and relationships do develop among participants. Many who are willing to participate in online focus groups have previously participated in chat rooms and on message boards.

Prima facie, then, it might seem that online focus groups should be preferred by researchers as they resolve many of the problems associated with traditional groups.

Disadvantages

Despite these benefits, adoption of this online approach has been somewhat slow. In large part, the slow rate of adoption is due to the disadvantages of online focus group research, including the following:

1. Body language cannot be assessed. So the value of nonverbal cues is lost.

2. Generally, participants relay comments by typing, which can make for a more stilted, less interactive conversation.

3. Participants with poor keyboarding skills can limit the amount of information shared and the ability for the conversation to flow easily. Some prospects may feel uncomfortable with the technology or setting (given that online focus groups operate like a chat room).

4. And, of course, as with any technological innovation, there is the potential for functional difficulties.

Critics like Greenbaum (2000) point out the difficulty in establishing authority in online groups, the lack of security (particularly given the inability to confirm identities of participants), the minimal client involvement, and the inability to use tangible stimuli. The bottom line is that some research problems will lend themselves to online groups while others will not.

Still, given the advantages of online focus groups and the prevalence of focus groups for communications research, researchers anticipate a growth in this application.

Conducting an Online Focus Group

Online focus groups can be conducted asynchronously using an online message board format or synchronously using a virtual facility and chat software. Respondents see all of the moderator's questions and the comments of other participants as they are submitted into the dialogue stream. Identities are protected by the use of pseudonyms. Clients observing the session can submit notes to the moderator, but respondents cannot see these entries.

The basic stages of the research process for online groups mirror those for offline groups: setting objectives, recruiting and screening participants, preparing the facility (that is, the online site for the group discussion) and materials, developing discussion guides, moderating, and conducting data analysis. Just as with offline groups, recruitment may involve a variety of methods, from using established lists, advertising for participants, or even telephone recruiting. The following guidelines are important considerations for managing the nuances of conducting online focus groups:

1. Develop screeners that can disqualify respondents without divulging the reasons for dismissal.

2. Use blocks on email addresses of disqualified potential respondents to discourage them from trying again.

3. Provide invitations with passwords, instructions, dates, and times to those who are qualified for participation.

4. Ask participants to visit the site in advance of the group to ensure that technology is compatible.

5. Provide technical support contact information for all participants.

Just as in the case of offline groups, the show rates for those recruited vary from situation to situation; generally, it is wise to recruit 50-100% more than what is desired in attendance. Though weather and traffic, two constant concerns for focus group participation offline, are not concerns online, other factors remain, including lack of commitment on the part of those recruited, unfamiliarity with the online venue, and other personal issues that can inhibit attendance. As recruits join the virtual room, rescreening should take place. During the rescreening, participant identities can be confirmed (to the extent possible); and if too many are available for participation, the moderator can select those who will remain.

The moderator and preparation of the guide are of utmost importance in an online venue. The questions must be prepared in advance and should even be entered into the system ahead of time for easy submission when needed. Because the moderator must read responses, assess how to reply, develop and administer probes, and determine when to administer the next question (and what that question should be), s/he should minimize the amount of typing necessary. For synchronous groups, the typical time span is 90 minutes, with approximately 40-45 questions used during the discussion. Question dialogs online typically run about two minutes per question. Asynchronous groups vary in length depending on the number of days the group will last and the nature of the questions. Participants consider and respond to a new set of questions each morning. An advantage of asynchronous groups is that participants can spend more time responding to questions and reading comment threads than is possible for participants in a synchronous group.

INTENSIVE INTERVIEWS

Intensive interviews (or IDIs) involve a single interviewer asking a participant (alone) a set of semistructured questions followed by probing questions. The steps, though when executed vary slightly, are made up of the same set of decisions and actions as those used in focus groups. The primary difference lies in the numbers involved in each discussion. While a focus group is a discussion of many, the interview is made of a dyad — the interviewer and the interviewee.

Phase 1: Planning the Interview

The basic stages of the process, as illustrated in Figure 1 earlier in this chapter, include planning, conducting, and analyzing/writing. The planning stage involves ensuring that the researcher is clear on the purpose of the study, the problem definition, and the data required.

Creating the Questions

In the first step, the research questions are specified and stated. The objectives are clarified and used to generate specific data requirements.

The Interview Guide

During Step 2, the goal is to develop the interview guide. The guide provides the interviewer with the order and wording of specific questions and may even offer sample probing questions and comments. It shifts from general questions to specific questions, from easy questions to more difficult (and perhaps, sensitive) ones.

The Environment and Interviewer

Step 3 requires that an environment be selected. What is the best location for an interview given the characteristics of the participant and the nature of the topic? Like focus groups, IDIs can take place in a variety of locations so long as the interviewer and interviewee feel they have sufficient privacy, space, and comfort. Interviews may take place in an office, a home, a meeting space, the lobby of an airport, or any number of places. The key is to find a place that is comfortable and appropriate. The researcher must anticipate how context (the location) could affect the interviewee's responses.

Also part of step 3 is the selection of an interviewer. The role of interviewer is highly relevant, as interviewers can influence responses and create bias in the data. Like moderators, they must develop rapport with each individual interviewee. Rapport is critical for encouraging participants to open up and share personal thoughts and experiences. Interviewers should be capable of establishing a sense of trust in the relationship. They must listen closely to each response in order to formulate well-stated probing questions but not jump to assumptions about what the interviewee has to share. Even more than moderators, one-on-one interviewers can affect the response content and quality offered by the interviewee. Training is important to ensure that interviewer effects and other biases are minimized throughout the data collection process. Common interviewer errors arise from poor listening, faulty or sloppy recordings, and fatigue.

Participants In Step 4, the researcher addresses questions concerning who should be interviewed, how many interviews to conduct, how to recruit prospects, and how to examine the prospects to ensure that those selected for interviewing have the desired characteristics.

Who should be included? To decide, the researcher must consider the purpose of the study and who best can provide the necessary information. The first aspect is to consider all of the types of participants who should be represented in the study. Consider this example: Trinity Washington University recently changed its focus from single-sex education to a co-educational setting. It must redesign all its marketing communications to deliver a message that is relevant to both female and male college-bound high school students. Its past messages emphasized the benefits of an all-female learning environment. Consequently, they can no longer serve as the basis of the school's positioning strategy. What messages might appeal to men considering a small, liberal arts college with a history of serving only women? To explore this question, in-depth interviews could be conducted of college-bound high school males with a declared interest in small, private schools and who live within a 2-hour radius of the College.

How many interviews should be conducted? The number of interviews conducted is typically small. It would be unusual to conduct more than 25 interviews for an exploratory study, and the number might be fewer. The rule of thumb is to continue interviews as long as new insights are being generated. When repetition occurs on the main themes identified, additional interviews are unnecessary.

How will prospects be recruited? Just as with focus groups, prospect recruitment is a challenge. Recruitment can be accomplished by working from lists, advertising for participants, telephone recruiting, and snowballing.

How should prospects be screened? Prospects must be screened to ensure that they are qualified for participation in the study. For instance, in the Trinity Washington example used above, the screener might assess answers to the following questions:

1. Is the prospect male or female?
2. Is the prospect in high school?
3. Does s/he intend to go to college in the fall immediately following high school graduation?
4. Is s/he interested in attending a small, private, liberal arts college?
5. Does s/he live within 2 hours of Washington, D.C.? The responses to these questions would reveal whether the prospect meets the definition of the desired participant.

Pre-Session Materials. Qualified prospects are then invited to participate in an interview. The time, date, and location of the interview are arranged. If there are assignments the participant must complete prior to the interview session, instructions are provided.

Phase 2: Conducting the Interview

Shortly Before the Session

Prior to the arrival of participants, the location must be arranged to be conducive to a one-on-one conversation. Such questions as the following need to be answered:

Is the recording equipment functioning?
Is the area suitably quiet and private?
Are the necessary consent forms ready?
Are any props or discussion materials to be used (if any) ready?

Beginning the Session

As the interviewee arrives, s/he should be greeted warmly. The interviewer will spend a few moments chatting and establishing rapport with the participant prior to explaining consent forms, demographic questionnaires, and the use of recording equipment. If the research topic is undisguised, the interviewer may also disclose some information about the study's purpose and sponsor.

Main Session

Like the moderator's guide, an interview guide begins with broad topics and works to specific topics. The first topic should be one that is easy to address and makes the respondent feel comfortable speaking with the interviewer. Throughout, the interviewer strives to uncover connections by probing for detail. Interviewers might use the laddering technique to shift from broad to specific questions. Laddering, also known as means-end chaining or benefit chaining, follows a semi-structured pattern but relies upon the participant's previous answers to reach the core information. For example, an interview that seeks to understand the underlying appeal of energy drinks might look like the following. Note that all interviewees are consumers of energy drinks; this would be established by the screener.

Interviewer: What brand of energy drink to you drink?
Interviewee: Monster Energy, usually.

Interviewer: Why do you drink Monster Energy?

Interviewee: It gives a strong hit of caffeine but in a juice drink.

Interviewer: What's good about caffeine in juice? How's that different from other energy drinks?

Interviewee: It keeps me awake, but I feel healthy too. I know that I'm mostly getting fruit juice. Not coffee or soda like most other energy drinks. Monster has vitamins, minerals, fruit.... I'd drink juice but I need the caffeine hit. This way I get both.

Interviewer: What happens when you get both — juice and energy?

Interviewee: I get more work done. I'm productive. Balanced between work and taking care of myself. I feel like I can do more than anyone else working with me.

Interviewer: And what's good about that?

Interviewee: I feel good about myself. I found a way to work smarter. It makes me feel like a winner.

Though the interviewer must interact and converse with the interviewee, the bulk of the conversation must be provided by the interviewee. The interviewer should aim for an 80/20 talk ratio — that is, the interviewee is talking 80% of the time while the interviewer speaks only 20% of the time. Analysis of the interview tapes reveals whether the interviewer is talking too much. In addition, the interviewer must refrain from sharing his or her own ideas and experiences or offering statements that could be perceived as validating or judging. It is not the role of the interviewer to reassure, confirm, or condemn a participant for his or her opinions, ideas, and experiences. The interviewer is there only to elicit and record information.

Session Close   Once the pre-specified questions have been covered, the interviewer will ask if the interviewee has more to say on what they've been discussing. Once the participant is finished, the recorder can be stopped. But the interviewer shouldn't rush at this stage of the interview. Some people will open up at the end of the interview, just when the interviewer thinks things are wrapping up. The interviewer should thank the participant and offer contact information in case s/he remembers something else to share. The interviewer also should ask for permission to follow up if necessary.

Once the interviewee has left, the interviewer should record his or her impressions of the session. Did anything stand out? How did the interview go? Were there issues with rapport development? What comments seemed especially relevant? The interviewer may also record his or her own impressions and feelings. Did the interviewee say something that shocked or offended the interviewer? Were there any interviewee characteristics that triggered biases in the interviewer? How did the interviewer handle these feelings during the session? Notes like these can be very useful in the analysis stage and also serve to better prepare interviewers for future projects.

Phase 3: Analyzing and Reporting the Results   The final phase for interview analysis begins once the tapes from the interviews have been transcribed. The transcripts should be checked against the tapes to ensure that the transcriptions are accurate. Ideally, two or more people should read and code the transcripts. Doing so will enable the researcher to assess interrater reliability and lend credibility to the insights drawn from analysis. The readers should go through all of the transcripts and note the relationships that seem to exist. They should mark the transcripts as they conduct a content analysis. As with focus groups, the results will become part of a research report that explains the study and the findings.

Greenbaum, T. (2000 February 14). Focus groups vs. online. *Advertising Age*, 71 (7), 34. **TO LEARN MORE**

Johnson (2006 July 17). Forget phone and mail: Online's the best place to administer surveys. *Advertising Age*, 77 (29), 23.

Kozinets, R. (1999). E-tribalized marketing? The strategic implications of virtual communities of consumption. *European Management Journal, 17* (3), 252-64.

Kozinets, R. (2002). The field behind the screen: Using netnography for marketing research in online communities. *Journal of Marketing Research, 39* (1), 61-72.

Krueger, R. A. & Casey, M. A. (2000). *Focus groups: A practical guide for applied research.* Thousand Oaks, CA: Sage Publications.

McCracken, G. (1988). *The long interview*. Newbury Park, CA: Sage.

19

Cultural and Critical Studies

Cultural and critical studies employ a wide array of research methods to investigate social phenomena. There is not a specific method of analysis. Rather, there are multiple modes of investigation.

The terms "cultural" and "critical" studies essentially refer to the same group of methods. The word "critical" is often used with "theory" when discussing the theoretical aspects of cultural studies.

Commonalities do exist within the various methodologies. First, culture is primary to the analysis. *Culture* is seen as a shared set of values, beliefs, and norms that exist in a society and that assist in the everyday functioning of that society. Think of culture as the glue that holds a society together. It is the communal social meanings that are generated from everyday life occurrences and media content that are formally and informally taught to members of a society. In essence, it is a complex collection of theories, ideas, and propositions that assist the way researchers understand society and social events.

Second, cultural and critical research tends to focus on the power that the researchers believe is embedded in media content, with messages viewed to be agents of social control that have a significant impact on people and culture itself. In this sense, cultural and critical research tends to be ideological.

Third, research tends to use content analysis as an investigative tool. However, it is important to keep in mind that the method used in critical and cultural studies is considerably different from the empirical content analysis that is discussed in Chapter 9 of this book. In critical and cultural studies, the method of content analysis is also known as *textual analysis*. The terms are interchangeable, but in this chapter we will use the term "textual analysis" — mainly so that the method will not be confused with empirical content analysis. Whereas empirical content analysis is based in statistical methods, critical and cultural analysis is more subjective in the topics that are researched, in methodological approaches, and in the knowledge that is generated from the analysis. In short, critical and cul-

By Sean Baker
Central Michigan University

tural studies rely much more on *interpretation*. Interpretative research focuses on how researchers analyze the meanings about messages that they believe the audiences themselves create. Thus, researchers tend to be more engaged personally in the content by focusing on the social and cultural meaning within content.

The Ideological Assumptions of Cultural and Critical Studies

To understand research in cultural and critical studies, one needs to recognize the field's ideological foundations. The roots of cultural and critical studies are diverse and stem from sociology, psychology, and political science, among other theoretical perspectives.

Much of critical and cultural studies research investigates the "big picture" – the social, political, and cultural implications of mediated messages. The beginning assumptions relate to ideological dominance, political economy, structuralism, poststructuralism, psychoanalysis, feminism, and postmodernism.

The ideological framework assumes that dominant social ideas and beliefs are manifested in content and that these messages support the status quo. These messages, according to critical theory, have tremendous impact on audiences.

Political economy is rooted in Marxist theory and is a critique of capitalism and economic power. The main idea is that political and economic elites control media messages, thus producing a consensus in audiences that acts to keep elites in power.

Structuralist analysis breaks communication down to basic elements and considers how these elements relate to each other. It assumes that there are fundamental rules about language use that impact how receivers understand messages.

Poststructuralism rejects the stability of structuralism by asserting that language is instable and that multiple meanings are associated with communication.

Psychoanalysis was developed by Sigmund Freud and claims that media messages represent unconscious desires and that people are interested in experiencing these desires vicariously through content.

Feminist research is designed to demonstrate how communication oppresses women or how it can liberate them.

Postmodern critiques argue that reality and truth are mere social constructions and that culture and society are made up of endless communications that have no true meaning in the real world.

There are many genres of critical and cultural studies research. The most common methods are discourse, narrative, rhetorical, semiotic, auteur, and generic. Here are the essential characteristics of each one:

Discourse analysis focuses on naturally occurring language usages, both verbal and written. Language is seen as a social practice, and studies focus on its formal aspects (e.g., grammar and phonics) and the actions that are produced from the spoken and written word.

Narrative analysis focuses on the storylines, characters, plots, conflicts, action, and the values and morals that make up media content.

Rhetorical analysis is grounded in the traditions of Greek philosophy and examines the power of content by studying the strength the text has to influence audiences.

Semiotic analysis views texts as a series of signs where there is a separation between the *signifier* (a physical object) and the *signified* (the meaning associated with the object).

Auteur analysis examines texts that are created by a single person or media corporation by looking at how the creators' personal signature and values are entrenched in content.

Generic analysis focuses on broad categories of similar texts. For example, magazines are organized into a variety of genres — news, general interest, sports, entertainment, etc. — and generic analysis examines the properties and associated meanings within a specific genre.

CRITICAL AND CULTURAL TEXTUAL ANALYSIS

Research in all six of those genres involves *textual analysis*. Thus, this chapter will focus mostly on the application of such analysis by critical and cultural studies researchers. The essence of such analysis involves an examination of media content with a focus on how ideas about our social world are represented in the media. Content is seen as one mechanism that helps people understand our social world. During analysis, content is commonly called a "text." A *text* is any form of mediated message. Some examples include a television program, newspaper article, presidential speech, and MySpace page. The goal of textual analysis is to determine the *meaning* of the messages that are embedded in text.

Researchers in critical and cultural studies do both quantitative and qualitative textual analysis. Let's examine each of them.

Quantitative Analysis

Some cultural studies researchers employ quantitative analysis techniques, often in combination with qualitative ones. Whereas some use pure quantitative techniques, the topic of investigation and the researcher's perspective make cultural research distinctive. For example, one may study the representation of African-American characters in television by quantifying individual characters, their roles, social status, personal characteristics, and so forth. Cultural and critical researchers, though, might go beyond quantitative analysis of the data by commenting on the social and cultural ramifications and the power embedded in the content.

Selecting a Topic

The first step in research is to decide upon a topic. Some researchers pick an area that is interesting as a basis of inquiry while others start with a theoretical perspective and find content to analyze that addresses theory. Regardless of where one starts, critical and cultural research (and all research for that matter) needs to justify why that particular content is important to study. To do so, a researcher must spend time searching for academic journals and books that address similar topics. This examination of previous literature allows an understanding of the topic better and substantiates any claims about the relevance of the study. Conducting a literature review is explained in Chapter 6 of this book. Reading other studies often assists in refining a research topic. Then a formal research question (or questions) must be developed.

Locating Materials

The next step is to locate and define the materials to be analyzed. Locating content is generally easy. There are numerous outlets for finding content, such as bookstores for printed materials, media, and entertainment stores for television programs, films, music, and so on. Many on-line databases such as Lexis/Nexis and ProQuest have access to full-text newspaper stories, magazine articles, and television transcripts. The Internet and libraries are other places that archive a wealth of content.

In addition to simply locating materials, it is necessary to choose how much content to analyze. There are numerous factors to consider when making this decision. How much time and money can be allocated to the project? What is the project's scope? In short, the selected content should be large enough to be representative yet small enough to be manageable.

The size of the project raises another issue, that of *sampling*. Critical **Sampling** and cultural studies researchers often sample in unique ways. Frequently, content is chosen with a judgment or purposeful sample. Both of these sampling techniques pick elements to be in a study because they possess a characteristic of interest to the researcher and address the research question. For example, consider a project that focuses on television programs. Rather than randomly selecting episodes from all prime-time programs, a critical and cultural studies researcher may choose the most popular television programs since those are being watched by most people. Or shows that focus on family relationships may be purposefully selected if the topic of study is the representation of family dynamics on television. However, truly random samples are sometimes utilized as well.

Once the content is chosen, a researcher uses two processes — called **Conceptualization and** *conceptualization* and *operationalization* — to create tools to extract **Operationalization** meaning from the content.

Conceptualization is defining the key ideas, themes, patterns, etc., that will be looked for in the content. A good way to start is to look back at the previous research that has been done on the type of content that is being examined. Remember to keep your research question(s) in mind when defining the key concepts. Another way to start is to look at some of the content that was chosen. By conducting an initial analysis, it is possible to be inspired to find new things to measure and to determine if the list of identified concepts is complete.

Operationalization is a much more specific description of what is being measured. Think of operationalization as a clear statement about the "how" of measurement. There are multiple ways to measure concepts. Thus, it is important to utilize multiple variables when measuring a single concept. For example, if a study were to measure the concept "violence in cartoons," it would be appropriate to ask questions such as these: How much violence was there? What was the result of the violence? How violent was the cartoon? Were there any alternatives to violence? Also, definitions of the analysis categories need to be provided. For example: What is meant by "violence"? Is a jesting slap on the forehead — as in V8 juice commercials — violent, or does the receiver of the act need to be hurt?

Once these definitions are provided and variables are created, it is **The Codebook** necessary to create a codebook to be used during the data collection phase. A *codebook* is list of all the variables, measures, and categories that will be used to extract data from the content. For the violence example above, the codebook might look like this:

How much violence was there?
record the number of violent acts ____
What was the result of the violence?
minor injury ____ *major injury* ____ *death* ____ *other (list)* _____

How violent was the cartoon?
very violent ____ *somewhat violent* ____ *a little violent* ____
Were there any alternatives to violence?
yes ____ *no* ____

The format is up to the researcher.

It is important, though, that the codebook be easily understood because there are often multiple people who do the actual coding.

Pretesting   Once the codebook is created, a **pretest** of it needs to be performed. Here the researcher collects data on a small portion (usually about 10 percent) of the content to see if there are any problems with the codebook.

If there are multiple people coding the content, training sessions are required. Training is important because there are often subjective measures within a codebook. For example, individual perceptions of the difference between minor injury and major injury vary. Yet it is necessary for all of the coders to apply the codebook in the same way. If they do not, their bias would be introduced into the results of the study. During training, coders must be instructed in all definitions and how the codebook should be applied. Also the analysis shoud be performed as a group to see if the coders have any questions.

Next is the data-collection phase. In this step, the coders, following the criteria that the codebook has established, mine data out of the content.

Assuring Coder   Once the data is collected, an initial analysis is conducted to see if
Reliability   there are any problems that need correcting and to provide summary information. If multiple coders were used, an **inter-coder reliability** analysis should be conducted. This involves comparing how much coders agree on their application of individual variables. Thus, a researcher requires that all the people code about 15 percent of the same texts in order to see how much they agree. At minimum they should agree 80 percent of the time. If the agreement is lower than 80 percent, the researcher should determine what the problem was and retrain the coders to correct it. Problems that occur tend to lie in discrepancies in the application of the codebook. Often, one coder will incorrectly extract the data from the content, creating a reliability problem.

The solution is simple. Once the problem areas are identified, the researcher needs to retrain that coder with the correct application and ask the coder to identify content correctly. Depending on one's skills, the inter-coder reliability may be calculated either by hand or with a statistical software application such as SPSS.

Performing the Analysis   Then the analysis is performed. In this step, the researcher focuses on results and findings that address the research question. It is best to start with descriptive information about the data. This gives the researcher an idea about the distribution of information across the variables. Critical and cultural studies research often relies solely on descriptive analysis. However, more complex data assessments are also sometimes needed. By doing a complex assessment, a researcher can gain a better understanding of the content that is being analyzed. It is important for the researcher to stay directed by performing tests that address the research question. Yet, it is acceptable to explore unforeseen results. Often during data analysis, unexpected and interesting results are found.

Next, the researcher interprets the data by focusing on how it relates *Interpreting the Data* to the research question. If a hypothesis was used, the researcher must ask whether the findings support or reject the hypothesis. It is okay if the findings are contrary to what was expected. That means that the initial speculation was not correct. If it was not, then the researcher should think about what the data indicates. What do the results signify about the content being examined? The researcher should consider the social, political, cultural, and other implications of the evidence that was found.

The final step is writing the research report. It is important that the re- *Writing the Report* searcher be objective while writing. The report normally has two main sections: the analysis and the conclusion. The analysis section is where the data are presented and summarized. The conclusion section is where the answer to the research question is provided. Conclusions should focus on the social meaning of the results and highlight the most important knowledge that was gained from the study. The conclusions should relate back to previous literature. If the findings are consistent, the researcher should state that fact. If they are contrary, that fact should be stated as well. For the latter, reasons for this new information should be presented.

Along with quantitative analysis, critical and cultural studies re- **Qualitative Analysis** searchers also do qualitative investigations. The major difference between quantitative and qualitative lies in how data are collected. Qualitative analysis, a favorite of critical and cultural studies researchers, is a more in-depth study of a smaller amount of content. A codebook is not used, and only the researcher performs the analysis.

The goal is to "deconstruct" media messages by performing what is often referred to as a "read." To *deconstruct* or *read* content, an investigator should conduct a thoughtful analysis of content with the goal of looking for meaning and insights as to how audiences may interpret the message.

Audience members themselves are not asked how they interpret the message. The main reason that audience interpretations are ignored, according to cultural theorists, lies in the complexity of content. By performing a read, investigators believe they can discover hidden and deep meaning that may not be apparent to audiences. This model relies on Dow's (1996) claim that social researchers are more astute than audience members. "[B]y virtue of training and expertise," she argues, researchers are more qualified "to analyze and explain the strategies and implications of television that are often invisible to the ordinary viewer" (p. xiii).

The process requires time and normally takes many reads to be completed. To perform a read, a researcher must be ready to take a lot of notes when analyzing the content. As content is viewed, the researcher writes down the important characteristics, patterns, and themes that address the research question. It is like exploring the content to see what is meaningful within it. The idea is to find central consistencies that are apparent in most of the items being analyzed. Specifically, in the early reads the researcher attempts to condense the content into a series of preliminary categories and themes.

During the middle stage, the researcher focuses on the themes that were found in the first reads, paying particular attention to how the themes are manifested. An example of a theme in the television program *Survivor* is that dishonest and deceitful actions are usually rewarded while in everyday life a person is usually punished for those behaviors. Often, themes can be divided or combined at this stage. Another objective is to see if categories overlap or if they are dependent on each other. For example, does theme A only occur near theme B? If relationships between themes and categories are found, the researcher takes notice of them because they can develop into new patterns themselves.

In the final stage, the researcher focuses on finding examples of the themes and patterns from the middle stage, particularly looking for examples that illustrate what was found. The researcher should not pick extreme or radical examples, as they are not representative. The examples are used as "data" while writing the results section of the research report.

A brief read of the television program *The Cosby Show* will illustrate how critical and cultural studies researchers read content. Here is how Jhally and Lewis (1992) interpreted the show. At face, *The Cosby Show* was a program that highlighted the successes of an upper-middle class African-American family. In fact, that was one of the intentions of the show's creator, Bill Cosby. However, a deeper reading of the program reveals, according to Jhally and Lewis, that a conservative ideology was present in the content. Cliff and Claire Huxtable, the main adult characters in the program, were African American and were professionally successful. (Cliff was a doctor, and Claire was a lawyer.) Their achievements were based on their own merits, and the program was free of any indications of racism in American society. This, in effect, presented a worldview that racism no longer existed and that race-based economic barriers to professional success had been eliminated. However, in real life, according to Jhally and Lewis, racial barriers are still present in American society.

TEXTUAL APPROACHES At face, *text* seems to be a simple concept: any form of mediated communication. However, cultural theorists argue, texts are much more complex and vague in nature. The following points are particularly important:

• Texts are constructed by people. So in a sense a text is an action or a process. This process becomes more complicated when considering the multitude of individuals who are potential receivers of the message. Thus, there are ample opportunities for confusion about the meaning within a text. An example is a feature-length film. Audiences often have very diverse opinions about simple things such as the main point of the same film.

• Texts are comprised of a series of communicative acts that can be understood by people. The understanding is often constrained by cultural norms and values. For example, an image of an American flag can produce very different feelings from an armed services veteran and an anti-war protester.

• Texts are inherently ambiguous and open to multiple meanings within one individual as well.

• Texts are part of a system of representation with predictable patterns where cultural norms assist in the meaning. A *representation* is how a person, place, or thing is portrayed in media content. Television commercials are a good example of the systematic nature of representation. American television viewers know that commercials are not part of the program they are watching and generally know the length and frequency of commercials while watching television.

Discourse Analysis

Cultural studies analysis tends to focus on the power embedded in communication and how this power tends to guide audience interpretations of messages. Two concepts — ideology and hegemony — are important in the approach that researchers use. *Ideology* is a construction of norms, values, and customs that define and organize social reality. Ideologies are prevailing views of the social organization that justifies and maintains dominant control over society. This dominance is called *hegemony*. These views are presented as commonsensical truths about reality that have no alternatives. Critical and cultural analysis focuses on how these views are represented in the media and how audiences internalize them. In other words, critical and cultural analysis seeks to understand how the hegemonic process functions. One key mechanism in examining the process is discourse analysis.

Discourse analysis examines verbal and written words as a basis of media criticism. It sees communication as a mechanism where meaning about society is cast onto the general public. Fiske (1987) defines *discourse* as "language or a system of representation that has developed socially in order to make and circulate a coherent set of meanings about an important topic area" (p.14). These meanings are self-serving to those who created the texts. Hence, the process of culture creation involves the circulation of discourse and text that results in defining and re-defining society. The result is the construction of a social reality that assists in our understanding of the world in a way that is congruent with the interests of social elites.

Some questions that researchers include when conducting a discourse analysis are the following: "How are the discourses produced? Which discourses are privileged over others? Which social and economic interests are served by these discourses? How do the discourses of the text relate to the discourses of the viewer?" (Butler, 2007, p. 450). To begin, researchers look for patterns and themes in content and then seek to discover the ideological importance of the themes. Then, researchers examine the ideological representation by comparing it to the social stories that audiences may use to interpret the message. They consider the following points:

> Whose/what point of view, feelings, and experiences are viewers invited to identify with in this text by virtue of editing, narrative structure, and conclusion (i.e., in what subject positions do the discursive and dramatic narrative elements place the viewer)?
>
> Who is the ideal viewer; who is hailed or addressed by the text?
>
> What does the text invite the ideal viewer to regard as normal, natural, and/or enjoyable?
>
> Through what formal and technical strategies and codes is the point of

view conveyed?

Do the roles, values, actions, images, and words in the text maintain, deconstruct, or reconstruct dominant cultural discourses on this topic? (Vande Berg, Wenner & Gronbeck, 1998, p. 243).

Narrative Analysis

A majority of media content is essentially storytelling. Stories are a sequence of events that are communicated in a specific order, and the sum of these communications creates a coherent view of the world. *Narrative analysis* focuses on how stories are communicated. Stories are often fictional, but even nonfictional news content can be investigated with narrative analysis. This form of analysis tends to focus on summarizing and criticizing key points or elements in a story by focusing on the themes and structures embedded in a story. Specifically, researchers look at the main themes, key events, conflicts and resolutions, characters, and plots. Silverman (2006) lists the following questions to ask when conducting a narrative analysis:

What is the content of the story you are examining?
Who are the principle agents?
How is the story told? What purposes does the story serve?
In what place or setting is the story told?
Does the story have a clear culmination with a moral, as in a fairytale, or does it follow a different pattern? (p. 166)

Narrative research tends to look at the elements and functions in stories. Investigations often discuss the importance of events under analysis. Let's consider a news story about university campus safety as an example. A researcher would examine what is being said in the story, how important safety is, who is affected by the story, who the principal sources are, and what the potential effects on students are. In short, what does the story tell the campus community about safety? The specific steps in narrative analysis are the following:

Write out the skeleton of the plot as it happens in the text. Pay attention to the characters and the order of events as they are told.

Using the plot outline, write down the story as it happens chronologically.

Identify the "equilibrium" at the beginning and the end of the text. If there has been a change in the equilibrium [that is, what is normal in the story], list the ways in which the world has changed before and after the story. What is given as the agent of change?

Define characters according to their function in the plot (Stokes, 2003, p.70).

Rhetorical Analysis

Rhetorical criticism focuses on the power and influence of communication. How the text potentially changes audiences is a key facet of this area of research. The assumption is that texts are commanding and can alter receivers' attitudes, beliefs, opinions, and behaviors. The creator of the message is seen as a key player who creatively assembles arguments and propositions that are designed to change audiences. Researchers examine both the structure and content of the message.

Aristotle described three ways to examine the power embedded in text: logos, pathos, and ethos. *Logos* is the appeal to reason, scientific competency, and logic. That is, audience members evaluate the message according to objective standards of judgment. *Pathos* is the appeal to an emotional connection and is often value laden. That is, audiences are emotionally moved by the message. *Ethos* is the appeal of the character of the communicator. That is, audiences interpret messages according to the credibility and charisma of the sender.

It is important to note that Aristotle (and rhetorical researchers) considered logos, pathos, and ethos to act in conjunction with each other. Consider, as an example, a magazine advertisement for a skin care product picturing an attractive famous actress with the tag line "It worked for me so it can work for you." The advertisement appeals on all three levels. The text appeals to logic (logos): i.e., if a product works for the person in the ad, it may work for the reader as well. The fame of a movie star appeals to an emotional (pathos) connection that the reader may have with a celebrity. At the same time, as a social elite a celebrity's opinion is more likely to impart credibility (ethos) to the message.

Rhetorical analysis also focuses on the physical properties of the text itself. Production elements are often examined to determine the effectiveness of the messages. Thus, rhetoricians examine the quality of messages; the use of sound, color, visuals, and other special effects; consistency of arguments; aesthetics; and properties of the medium itself.

There are an abundant number of sources on how to conduct a rhetorical analysis. Burton (1997) has published one of the best. He lists the following nine basic questions to consider during analysis:

1. *What is the rhetorical situation?*
The researcher asks what event occurred to require persuasion.
2. *Who is the author/speaker?*
The researcher examines credibility, knowledge, logos, pathos, and ethos issues.
3. *What is his/her intention in speaking?*
4. *Who makes up the audience?*
The researcher focuses on who the audience members are at whom the message is directed and what their values, attitudes, lifestyles, demographics, etc., are.
5. *What is the content of the message?*
The researcher pays attention to the topics, themes, arguments, and appeals that are present in the message.
6. *What is the form in which it is conveyed?*
The researcher asks how grammar, structure, style, figures of speech, and other literary components influence the message.
7. *How do form and content correspond?*
8. *Does the message/speech/text succeed in fulfilling the author's or speaker's intentions?*
9. *What does the nature of the communication reveal about the culture that produced it?*

Semiotic Analysis

Semiotics is the study of meaning based on a system of signs. According to semiotics theory, meaning is produced by the specific structure of texts. A *sign* is composed of three elements: *signifier* (the sign or the object itself), *signified* (the meaning associated with the signifier), and the *code* (a set of signs that are recognizable or associated together in a way that assists in the understanding of the sign). Take, for example, a traffic light as a sign. A yellow light is the signifier, and the signified is "caution — be prepared to stop." The code is the rules of traffic that people follow in order to avoid chaos while driving.

According to Saussure (1960), the structure of signs can be examined in two ways: as syntagms and as paradigms. *Syntagms* are the linear sequence of signs. That is, signs are ordered, adding to their meaning. Traffic lights, for example, turn from green to yellow to red. *Paradigmatic analysis* examines the connections between signs and how the connections create coherent meaning. *Paradigms* are families of signs that relate to each other. For example, there are numerous traffic signs: stop signs, flashing lights on a bus, painted lines on pavement. Taken together, they create the code for driving.

There are cases where signifier and signified are disconnected and often have multiple different meanings. For many drivers, it seems, a yellow light indicates that they should speed up rather than use caution. When signs have multiple meanings they are called *polysemic signs* (Barthes, 1972). With such signs, meaning requires active involvement by the receiver of the messages. Analysis often focuses on how social and cultural norms tend to fix meaning in alignment with preexisting ideas. Even further, Hall (1996) argues that signs tend to be dialectal in nature and that meaning is derived from opposition. Thus, I am male only because I am not female.

Semiotic analysis studies the signification process and the potential meaning that may be derived from signs. It looks at how meaning is made from the signification process. A semiotician separates signs into individual elements and analyzes how each element creates meaning. Consider a news headline, "Mother and daughter in fatal car accident." Semiotics examines the relationships between the elements in the headline. Mother and daughter are connected by their spatial (in the same car) and implicit familial relationship. The mother/daughter represents the code of family that adds meaning to the headline. The tragedy of a mother and daughter in an accident is more powerful than if the headline read, "Adult and minor in fatal car accident." Semiotics also examines the syntagmic relationship of the text. The order of the words implies that both the mother and daughter were killed in the accident, thus adding meaning to the headline. Thus, semiotics studies the specific nature of texts in order to extract meaning from it.

Stokes (2003) lists the following guidelines for conducting semiotic analysis:

> Interpret the text…. Here you are considering the connotations of the texts. What is the relationship between the linguistic signs and the images? How do the two codes of signification work in relation to each other? Does reading the words give you a different interpretation of the images than just looking at the images alone, or are the words reinforcing the images? Draw out the cultural codes. What kinds of cultural knowledge do you need to know to understand the text? How are the images drawing on your cultural knowledge to help us create particular kinds of meaning? Are the cultural codes those one would expect from readers of this particular publication? (pp. 74-75).

Finally, semiotic analysis looks for patterns in the texts that are being analyzed. The goal is to determine if the patterns present a specific view of the world and discuss how these patterns create meaning for audiences.

Auteur Analysis

The basic principle behind *auteur criticism* is that a single individual creates texts according to predictable and measurable patterns. Quentin Tarantino's films are obvious examples with their consistent intense action, immense conflicts, and violent resolutions. Auteurs are treated as artists, and the analysis focuses on their complete body of work. A wide variety of people can be analyzed, including writers, directors, producers, journalists, actors, special effects personnel, and others.

In general, there are two ways to conduct an auteur analysis. The first is to examine the narratives; themes; production elements such as light, sound, and visual effects; storylines; and other stylistic elements in texts — essentially focusing on the creative presence of the creator. Also, any political or ideological patterns can be highlighted. The second is to investigate how specific bodies of work fit into an auteur's career. Similar to biographical or historical analysis, this perspective tracks the creative works over time and discusses how each assists or detracts from an auteur's collection of content.

To conduct an auteur analysis, a researcher should first select an auteur and create a list of all of his or her works. The next step is to collect as many of these works as possible. The goal is to analyze an entire collection. For prolific auteurs (e.g., the television producer Aaron Spelling) it is acceptable to sample a portion of the content. During analysis researchers should look for consistent themes, storylines, and stylistic elements within the content. It is important to look for patterns that highlight the auteur's "voice." It is necessary to demonstrate that the common characteristics stem from the auteur rather than a production company, publisher, or other media company. One productive goal is to create a link between the auteur's psyche and the content. Consequently, it is important to look at biographical information about the auteur in order to understand the context from which he or she is creating content.

Generic Analysis

Genres are large groups of texts that have similar elements. The most common way to describe a genre is in terms of a receiver's response to the text. Situation comedies are humorous, news informs, romance novels invoke passion, and so forth.

A second way to organize a genre is according to the stylistic elements of the text. Here common production techniques are the basis of the definition of the genre. For example, there are many types of televised reality programs that share common characteristics, such as non-professional "actors," a cinema verité format of filming, mundane activities, etc. Yet, the content of reality programming can be very diverse, including comedic, dramatic, musical, and action.

Lastly, genres can be organized according to the subject matter within the text. Here, common themes and narrative structures are the organizational tools. An investigator can examine a variety of texts across media with this technique. Consider murder mysteries. There are communities within this genre: Murder, suspense, mystery, plot twists, double-crossing, and character dishonesty are some themes. Each community — such as the murder mystery — is created in many formats: books, television programs, films, among others.

Vande Berg, Wenner and Gronbeck (1998) list useful patterns to examine while conducting a generic analysis about television programs. They are the following:

> Metagenres: how many different types of programs are there?
>
> Generic evolution: how have sitcoms changed from the 1950s to the present?
>
> Generic hybrids: what are the defining characteristics of the prime-time soap opera of the docudramas?
>
> History of genres: why did the Western peak in the late 1950s and early 1960s and then all but disappear from television? (pp. 102-103)

When conducting a generic analysis, the researcher looks for themes within the selected content. The analysis pays special attention to the setting and locations, stylistic elements of characters (e.g., clothing styles, lifestyles, etc.), subject matter, relationships between characters, plot structure, production techniques (sound, light, etc.), the use of language, and any other consistent patterns that emerge.

Some studies explore how current content fits into an existing genre. Does, for example, *The Sopranos* fit into the mafia/gangster genre? Others discuss whether or not a new genre is developing. Is *Survivor* a reality television program or a game show or a completely new genre?

Either quantitative or qualitative textual analysis methods can be used in generic analysis.

AUDIENCE ANALYSIS Commonly, critical and cultural audience research considers the process of encoding-decoding, which is how meaning is derived from media content when studying audiences (Hall, 1997; Hall, 2001).

Encoding refers to the processes used during message creation. Content producers create messages within their personal frameworks and institutional objectives, thereby attaching specific meanings to them. However, audiences *decode* messages according to their own specific norms, values, backgrounds, and contexts. Audiences are seen as "active" and create their own meanings from media messages. Thus, meaning is situated somewhere between the producers and audience and is constructed by both.

Messages can be decoded in terms of dominant positions, negotiated positions, and oppositional positions. *Dominant* means that an audience member agrees with the ideological perspective that was encoded. *Negotiation* occurs when an audience member agrees with the general social beliefs within the encoding but disagrees with specific aspects of the communication. *Opposition* takes place when an audience member disagrees with the encoded message on an ideological level.

A typical news story that depicts a suspect in handcuffs who is taken into custody by police exemplifies this process. The encoding is that a crime occurred and the police adequately responded to it, but the decoding may vary in the following manner:

In the dominant position, decoding can be *identical* to the encoding within the dominant ideology: "The police did a good job catching the criminal."

In the negotiated position, decoding can be *counter* to the encoding but still within the dominant ideology: "The police made a mistake, but the criminal justice system is legitimate."

In the oppositional position, decoding can *reject* the encoding altogether: "The police made a mistake, and the criminal justice system is corrupt."

Ethnography

Ethnography is derived from anthropology and focuses on describing a culture as it exists in the real world. It is considered field research since data is collected in natural areas. Thus, ethnographers analyze audiences in the settings where people actually experience content (e.g., a movie theater). The object is to provide **thick descriptions** that include "all the details of a social setting in an extremely detailed description and convey an intimate feel for the setting and the inner lives of the people in it" (Neuman, 2006, p. 382). Ethnographers focus on how texts are understood and interpreted. The social context of exposure to content is often examined. Critical and cultural researchers have expanded the uses of ethnography to include other methods such as focus groups and interviews. See Chapter 18 in this book for an explanation of these methods.

Specifically, in ethnography there are three modes of observation: descriptive, focused, and selective (Schroder, Drotner, Kline, & Murray, 2003). **Descriptive observation** involves examining general questions about the overall patterns that are seen. Consider, for example, television viewing habits. Descriptive observations would seek to understand the general behaviors of viewers while watching television. In **focused observation**, an investigator asks specific questions about observed patterns. For example, a researcher may inquire about why a person changes channels while watching television. **Selective observation** involves analysis of the things and social relations that are being watched. For example, an investigator may observe that television viewers tend to change channels during a lengthy scene in a program. The researcher would evaluate the conditions under which the channel was changed.

Field work requires a great deal of materials. A good list includes the following:

Written field notes:
  accounts of what is going on
  descriptions of dialogues or exchanges between informants
Visual material:
  photographs of settings and peoples
  videotapes of informants' mediated receptions and/or production practices
Audio material:
  taped conversations with or among informants (to be transcribed and hence become print material)
  recordings of the "aural tapestry" of settings
Media material used by informants (e.g., film, TV programs, screen dumps from computers)

Your research diary (e.g., reflections, comments, ideas for each day)
Sources about the field (e.g., maps, artifacts, press clippings) (Schroder, et. al., 2003, p. 93).

Reception Studies

Reception studies attempt to determine how audiences interpret messages and how decoding occurs. The goal is to determine whether an audience used a dominant, negotiated, or oppositional framework. Some defining characteristics of reception research are that it "explores the encounter of active audiences with media meanings, [and] regards meaning as a joint product of text and reader, the situational and social contexts of reading, and effect of the meanings" (Schroder, et. al., 2003, p. 124).

In reception studies, the researcher first chooses a text for examination and then performs a textual analysis on it to discover dominant meanings. In conducting the analysis, the researcher considers the audience and examines such questions as these: Who is the audience? How is the content viewed? What is the purpose for which it is viewed? How does the content relate to audiences? These questions assist in understanding the potential ideological values that the message represents.

Next, the researcher theorizes the audience. Here an attempt is made to determine how the audience would react to the content and what social norms and values could be produced from it.

Then, audiences are interviewed to gauge reactions to the content. The interviews are loosely structured to allow participants to describe what meanings they gained from exposure and how they gained them. This data is compared to the thick descriptions of content to determine from which position audiences are relating to the messages. The most common method of investigation is qualitative interviewing. See Chapter 18 of this book for an explanation of such interviewing. The style of the interview is relaxed with minimal structure. Interview questions should be written in a conversational tone, and the interview should feel like a naturally occurring conversation. Interviewees should be allowed to focus on topics about the content that they feel are important. Yet, the researcher should keep them on track with the research question. One approach is to ask the interviewees to summarize the main points of the text and tell the researcher what they found to be meaningful within it. In short, the objective is to get the subjects to reconstruct what meaning was derived from the content and how it was derived.

In summary, we may say that critical and cultural studies research is very diverse and utilizes many different methods of analysis. Keep in mind that research looks at the power in media messages and how this power influences audiences. Many research studies use more than one of the techniques discussed in this chapter. The key is that each method is guided by unique perspectives about how our social world is organized. Critical and cultural research is difficult and involves researchers in looking at large social structures that exist in society. Thus it is important to keep in mind the "big picture" about social life while conducting research.

TO LEARN MORE Allen, R. (1992). *Channels of discourse, reassembled*. Chapel Hill, NC: University of North Carolina Press.

Barker, C. (2000). *Cultural Studies: Theory and practice*. Thousand Oaks, CA: Sage.

Barker, C & Galasinski. (2001). *Cultural studies and discourse analysis: A dialogue on language and identity*. Thousand Oaks, CA: Sage.

Deacon, D., Pickering, M., Golding, P. & Murdock, G. (1999). *Researching communications: A practical guide to methods in media and cultural studies*. London: Arnold.

di Lenardo, Micaela. (2006). Mixed and rigorous cultural studies methodology — an Oxymoron? In M. White & J. Schwoch (Eds.), *Questions of method in cultural studies*. (pp. 268-285), Indianapolis, IN: Wiley.

Entman, R. (1993). Framing: Toward clarification of a fractured paradigm. *Journal of Communication*, 43:51-58.

Hesse-Biber, S., Gilmartin, C., & Lydenberg, R. (1999). *Feminist approaches to theory and methodology: An interdisciplinary reader*. New York: Oxford.

Neuendorf, K. (2002). *The content analysis guidebook*. Thousand Oaks, CA: Sage.

Orlik, P. (2001). *Electronic media criticism: Applied perspectives*. Mahwah, NJ: Lawrence Erlbaum.

Saukki, P. (2003). *Doing research in cultural studies: An introduction to classical and new methodological approaches*. Thousand Oaks, CA: Sage.

Scheurich, J. (1997). *Research method in the postmodern*. London: Falmer.

Tedlock, B. (2000) Ethnography and ethnographic representation. In N. Denzin & Y. Lincoln (Eds.), *Handbook of qualitative research* (pp. 455-486). Thousand Oaks, CA: Sage.

REFERENCES

Barthes, R. (1972). *Mythologies*. London: Cape.

Burton, G. (1997). *Silva rhetorcae*. Retreived December 9, 2007, from http://rhetoric.byu.edu/.

Butler, J. (2007). *Television: Critical methods and applications*. Mahwah, NJ: Lawrence Erlbaum.

Dow, B. (1996). *Prime-time feminism: Television, media culture and the women's movement since 1970*. Philadelphia: University of Pennsylvania Press.

Fiske, J. (1987). *Television culture*. New York: Methuen.

Hall, S. (1996). Introduction: Who needs identity? In S. Hall & P. Du Gay (Eds.), *Questions of cultural identity*. (pp. 1-17). Thousand Oaks, CA: Sage.

Hall, S. (1997). *Representation and the media*. Northampton, MA: Media Education Foundation.

Hall, S. (2001). Encoding, decoding. In M. Durham & D. Kellner (Eds.), *Media and cultural studies: Key works*. (pp.166-176), Malden, MA: Blackwell.

Jhally, S. & Lewis, J. (1992). *Enlightened racism: "The Cosby Show," audiences and the myth of the American Dream*. Boulder, CO: Westview.

Neuman, L. (2006). *Social research methods: Quantitative and qualitative approaches*. Boston: Pearson.

Saussure, F. (1960). *Course in general linguistics*. London: Peter Owen.

Schroder, K., Drotner, K., Kline, S., & Murray, C. (2003). *Researching audiences*. London: Arnold.

Silverman, D. (2006). *Interpreting qualitative data*. Thousand Oaks, CA: Sage.

Stokes, J. (2003). *How to do media & cultural studies*. Thousand Oaks, CA: Sage.

Vande Berg, L., Wenner, L. & Gronbeck, B. (1998). *Critical approaches to television*. Boston: Houghton Mifflin.

IV

Using Methods
in the Real World

Remember the discussion in Chapter 1 on the types of knowledge? There are three kinds: propositional knowledge, acquaintance knowledge, and how-to knowledge. The first three sections of this book have informed you of a myriad of ideas and methods to arm you with propositional knowledge. Now, you may want to see how these methods are used in the real world so that your knowledge can move to the next level.

Section IV is designed to do that. Often, when we learn something, that something remains passive in our brain, until we are ready to use it. For example, when we pick up a new word, we may recognize it the next time we see it, but it is still part of our passive vocabulary — words we recognize but don't use. The moment we use that word in our own writing signifies that we have made it part of our active vocabulary. We want to do the same with research methods: make your knowledge of them active. This section will move you toward that goal.

We arrange this section broadly to include print research, radio and television research, public relations research, advertising research, and new technology research. Don't limit yourselves to these areas, though. There are many ways you can categorize domains of research. This classification is for convenience and organization. The only advantage of such an arrangement is to allow us to introduce research or research services that pertain to a particular medium or area.

In Chapter 20, "Print Research," Prof. Judith Sylvester of Louisiana State University first categorizes basic and applied research in the print media. By using the important concept of *circulation*, she demonstrates how researchers approach the concept through readership studies, demographics analysis, and visual appeal studies with a host of research methods: focus group, in-depth analysis, survey, and many others. You will learn about companies that conduct print research and the kinds of research they deem important.

In Chapter 21, "Radio and Television Research," Prof. Louisa Ha of Bowling Green State University offers a set of concepts relevant to broadcast audience research. She provides a comprehensive picture of the methods used by Nielsen and Arbitron to collect TV and radio audience data, which the industries use as guides for programming and advertising. The knowledge you glean from this chapter will help you make informed decisions about the validity and reliability of these widely used indicators.

In Chapter 22, "Public Relations Research," Prof. Dennis Kinsey of Syracuse University discusses research that informs public relations practitioners to help them better communicate with, reach, and build relationships with "publics." In addition to explaining how the common methods such as focus group and survey are used, he introduces Q methodology and illustrates its application in public relations with a "winning slogan" example. You will also find the concepts of symmetrical and asymmetrical communication particularly important in this area of research.

In Chapter 23, "Advertising Research," Prof. Cliff Shaluta of Western Kentucky University gives an overview of the landscape and discusses the issues that interest academic and industry researchers in advertising. Because advertisers are interested in selling, research enthusiasm in this area is unlikely to fade. Prof. Shaluta introduces a number of companies that have established themselves in advertising research and discusses the methods they use to advance their enterprise.

In Chapter 24, "New Technology Research," Prof. Ran Wei of the University of South Carolina presents an exciting array of methodological opportunities and challenges in this burgeoning area of research. He explains how various methods are used to answer questions about mobile phones, the Internet, and other new communication technology. He also discusses new concepts — such as convergence and multitasking — and new research tools that have the potential to study the dissemination, adoption, and impact of new technologies.

Many people are satisfied just to learn something new every day. But using what you learn is just as exciting. It is our hope that this section will get you thinking about the practical applications of research. Ultimately, we hope you will make the plunge into the *fascinating real world of research*.

20 Print Research

Starting in the 1800s, both formal and informal research methods developed to gauge the influence of the printed word. The great newspaper barons of the penny press era learned that sensational headlines and newsboys yelling out the latest news on street corners sold newspapers. In the early 20th century, the *Literary Digest* led the industry toward more scientific polling techniques. In the 1936 presidential election, though, the magazine's poll declared that Alf Landon, the Republican governor of Kansas, would be the overwhelming winner. However, President Franklin D. Roosevelt carried 44 of the then 46 states. This *faux pas* led to the magazine's demise in 1938 but gave rise to a more scientific polling system, as George Gallup's American Institute of Public Opinion had correctly predicted the result of the election using a smaller sample than the *Digest* poll.[1]

As competition from the broadcast media developed, newspapers had to focus more on content and credibility, learning that if they were no longer the first to provide breaking news, they would have to be the most in-depth and comprehensive if they wanted to retain their readers. Magazines, on the other hand, had to find a niche and then develop content as the audience's preferences and demographics evolved. From the beginning, the print media needed research to convince advertisers that advertising in a print medium was effective in creating brand awareness and selling products. These goals required research.

CATEGORIZING PRINT MEDIA RESEARCH

Today, even defining what is meant by "print media" is difficult. Traditionally, the term refers to newspapers, magazines and books. But what about newsletters and Internet content such as blogs and online news sites? While this chapter will focus on the traditional print media, the research methods can be applied to any printed communication and Internet content.

Print media research first can be categorized as either *basic* (theoretic) *re-*

[1]Peverill Squire, "Why the 1936 Literary Digest Poll Failed," *Public Opinion Quarterly* 52 (1988): 125-133.

By Judith Sylvester
Louisiana State University

search or *applied* (practical) *research*.

Basic Research

Basic research, often conducted by the academy, focuses on communication theory as it applies to the print media. For example, *Agenda Setting* and *Uses and Gratification* theories both developed from print media influence studies and then later were expanded to include the broadcast media. *Content analysis* studies also are easily carried out on print media, especially now that Lexis/Nexis, an online research tool, makes it easy to collect and analyze printed news content. Databases and archives of newspapers and magazines across the country make historical research a fertile area for scholarship. *Cognitive studies* that focus on how people read and comprehend the written word have been applied to newspapers and led to many "newspaper in the classroom" programs across the country. Eye movement tracking technology has been adapted to study how people read newspapers and magazines.

The *Newspaper Research Journal* and the *Journal of Magazine and New Media Research*, produced respectively by the Newspaper Division and the Magazine Division of the Association for Education in Journalism and Mass Communication, publish many academic studies that focus on print media content, as well as the reporting and editing process. These two journals are the research publications that are most closely tied to academic research.

Applied Research

Applied research dominates the print media industry. Academics, media organizations and media companies all engage in it. The goals of applied print research are broadly these three:

1. To determine who reads print products
2. To determine how people scan or read print products
3. To evaluate the impact that design has on readership and readability

Of course, most of this research has as its objective increasing revenue through subscriptions and advertising sales for the publication.

IMPORTANCE OF CIRCULATION AND DEMOGRAPHICS

Assessing who is reading print products usually involves an audit of circulation and a readership study.

Circulation usually refers to the number of copies that are sold either through subscription or over-the-counter. Of course, the circulation figure cannot exceed the number of printed copies. So it is somewhat limited in determining the rates that can be charged for advertising.

Consequently, publications can improve their bottom line by determining audience *readership*, which usually exceeds the actual number of printed copies. Consider for a moment how many readers there are for just one copy of a magazine placed in a medical or dental waiting room. The Audit Bureau of Circulations (ABC) provides the auditing service for most publications. ABC verifies how many copies are printed and then determines how many of those copies are sold through subscription and over-the-counter. ABC also determines the average paid circulation of a newspaper by dividing the total paid circulation of all the issues during a specified period by the total number of issues.[2]

The pass-along rate generally shows that two or more persons per household read each issue of the newspaper that is delivered to the home. ABC may also determine which sections of the newspaper are most popular and if subscribers are satisfied with their delivery service.

Demographics are important both for providing content and for attracting advertisers. Researchers ask such questions as these: What is the average age of the typical newspaper reader? Are there different readership patterns between men and women? Is the typical reader a commuter who is employed full time or a work-at-home mom? These are questions that are useful to editors and publishers. A full description of ABC's telephone research verification standards can be accessed at http://www.accessabc.com/pdfs/telephonestandards.pdf.

Table 1: Example of a demographic analysis

Analysis from The Media Audit reveals that Sunday ad inserts are the second most read section of a daily newspaper, behind the front page section. Sunday ad inserts are regularly read by nearly 45 million consumers across The Media Audit's 80 measured markets. Consumers in the Midwest states (North and South Dakota, Nebraska, Kansas, Minnesota, Wisconsin, Missouri and Iowa) are the mostly likely to regularly read daily newspaper ad inserts published on Sunday when compared with other regions. Surveys were conducted across 80 U.S. cities between January 2009 and March 2010.

Among consumers least likely to read Sunday ad inserts are those who live in the Pacific (Washington, Oregon and California) and Mountain (Idaho, Montana, Wyoming, Nevada, Utah, Colorado, New Mexico, and Arizona) Census Divisions. Among those who live in the Pacific Division, 24.7% regularly read Sunday ad inserts, while 25.6% of those living in the Mountain Census Division regularly read ad inserts.

Seventy-five percent of those who read ad inserts are between the ages of 25 and 64, and 61.9% are female. Furthermore, one in five regular readers of Sunday ad inserts has a household income of more than $100,000, while one in four readers has a college degree.

The Media Audit provides readership data for thirteen different newspaper sections, in addition to classified, employment and automotive sections that can be read online.

Source: The Media Audit, July 2010

Magazines may have even narrower demographic and psychographic profiles. While *demographic* characteristics are descriptive of the person's physical characteristics (such as age and gender), *psychographic* characteristics have more to do with a person's values and lifestyle. A magazine could be designed, for example, just or for girls, 13 to 18 years old who are interested in makeup, prom dresses and dating or just for men between the ages of 35 and 65 who like to hunt. Magazines have to deliver both key demographics and psychographics to advertisers.

Uses and Gratification

Much applied print research relies on *Uses and Gratification* as a theoretic underpinning, especially when bringing values and psychographics into the mix. This theory assumes that the audience is active, that people seek information that will somehow benefit them.

For example, you might pick up the campus newspaper when a specific front page story attracts your attention or when you want to know who won last night's

---

[2]Audit Bureau of Circulations, "Glossary" at http://www.accessabc.com/bylaws/bylaw244.htm#C

basketball game. You may additionally be motivated to read the stories you seek because you know everyone in your next class will be talking about the game or the breaking news story on the front page. When you are able to join in the conversation with your fellow classmates, you receive gratification from the knowledge you have gained, your social status may rise and your self-esteem could increase. Because you are rewarded for your media consumption, you are likely to repeat this behavior and form the habit of checking out the student newspaper on a regular basis.

How you and others read publications can be studied. For example, in-depth interviews or surveys can be used to ask students where they pick up a copy of the campus newspaper, where they read it, how many other people read their copy and what content they read most consistently. Where and when they pick it up probably depends on the proximity of the distribution point to their classrooms or where they work or study. The chances are, though, that they will pick it up from the same one or two locations most of the time. In other words, picking up the newspaper becomes a habit. Most students then start to read the paper by scanning the photographs and headlines on the front page. But some go straight to the sports pages, while others start with the personal ads. In short, students have formed habits about how they read the paper, and they receive gratification from these habits.

Focus groups and in-depth interviews can be useful in assessing the gratification students might receive from reading the paper. Researchers might ask such questions as these: Do students save money by taking advantage of advertised sales or promotions? Have they found roommates or found the perfect used bike in the classifieds? Do they derive social benefits from keeping up with local bands and sports teams?

Uses and Gratification Theory also acknowledges that the media have competition for students' time and attention. Consequently, assessments (interviews or surveys) often include questions about other activities that might reduce the amount of time spent reading the campus newspaper. Students may spend more time, for example, finding a parking place or playing video games than reading the newspaper.

The elements of Uses and Gratifications research methods are just as useful and important to the local daily or weekly newspaper. Editors know that if they redesign their pages, moving the obituaries from A5 to B3, for example, or change the font, they are going to get calls from disgruntled readers who now must cope with a change in their set pattern of reading. Any change, even an improvement in the product, is likely to be met with resistance just because every reader has to adjust to the changes and form new reading habits. Woe to any editor who decides to drop a regular feature such as a bridge column or a comic strip. Readers often react by canceling subscriptions or sending angry emails to the editor. The size of the protest will determine whether the editor or the readers win that battle.

Magazines may be even more entrenched in design and content because readers expect certain things from their magazines — whether it is the *Cosmo* girl who reveals her assets or the quarterback who launches a football on the cover of *Sports Illustrated* (not to mention that swimsuit issue). People read magazines that fit their lifestyles and their fantasies. Financially secure retirees, for example, may devour travel magazines, while the 30-something mother of three may be much more interested in parenting magazines.

Gratifications are ephemeral because every reader derives his or her own pleasures from the printed page. For example, a magazine might provide tasty recipes and crafts for home-made gifts that allow the reader to be creative and to feel useful to family and friends. The long-running feature "Can This Marriage Be Saved" in *Ladies' Home Journal* attests to readers' interest in relationships and may make them feel more secure in their own marriages. People read newspapers to feel informed and to be able to discuss a controversial issue with friends and co-workers.

A third type of research involves the *visual appeal* and *readership levels* of publications. Researchers explore practical questions such as these:

How do different typefaces affect readability?

Should color photos completely replace black and white photos?

Does packaging articles horizontally improve readability?

What type of headline is more likely to attract readers to a story, and what will encourage complete readership of an article?

COMPANIES THAT CONDUCT PRINT MEDIA RESEARCH

A number of companies are engaged in collecting research about print media. While the bread and butter of print research is readership (who is reading, what they are reading and why they are reading), there are a variety of important trends in print research. Companies are, for example, expanding research on the Hispanic market and tracking readership of Hispanic publications and Websites. Uses and Gratifications-related research also is being expanded to look at both the cognitive and emotional aspects of print advertising and what types of behavior result. Concern for declining readership of print publications and advertisers' concerns about effectiveness lead to research that digs deep into the psyche of consumers to deepen the connection between the publication and the audience.

Media Ratings Council

In the early 1960s a U.S. Congressional Committee held hearings (commonly referred to as the Harris Committee Hearings on Broadcast Ratings) concerning the purpose and accuracy of audience research and considered regulation related to the television and radio industries. The hearings resulted in the formation of an industry-funded organization to review and accredit audience rating services called the Broadcast Rating Council, now referred to as the *Media Ratings Council* (MRC). Membership on the Council is open to any media organization that relies on or uses media research, and each member company is entitled to a seat on the MRC Board of Directors. Organizations (such as Nielsen or Arbitron) that provide media ratings may not be members.

There are approximately 95 Board members in total representing television and radio broadcasting; and now cable, print, Internet and advertising agency organizations as well as advertisers and trade associations are included. The MRC also maintains formal liaison relationships with the American Association of Advertising Agencies (AAAA), the Advertising Research Foundation (ARF) and the Association of National Advertisers (ANA).

The activities of the MRC include the establishment and administration of Minimum Standards for rating operations; the accreditation of rating services on the basis of information submitted by the services; and auditing, through independent CPA firms, of the activities of the rating services.

Several companies conduct or summarize studies that benefit the industry. Newspapers, magazines and other publishers conduct research to benefit their publication or company. The majority rely on research companies, some accredited by the MRC, to conduct these studies. Some of the best-known originators of research are described below.

Belden Associates

Belden Associates provides customized newspaper research and consulting for North American newspapers. As newspapers have developed online news sites, moving from the traditional printed page to the interactive Web page, research methods also have evolved and adapted. Traditional telephone surveys to assess readership of the printed product are being supplemented or replaced by interactive assessments of online newspaper sites.

Greg Harmon, director of the interactive division, says that in most cases 500 to 1,000 surveys are collected over the course of 20 to 28 days during the course of a single study. The actual sample size is determined by the average number of hits the target newspaper Website receives. In the course of evaluating 100 Websites, the company will collect 80,000 responses online.

Newspaper clients use the results of these surveys to develop content for on-line publications and increase revenue (http://www.beldenassociates.com/success.htm). "Online surveys are remarkably effective and useful tools and provide a superb way to describe our Web audience," Harmon says. "However, online surveys are less effective for describing the print product audience and much less effective in describing the market as a whole. Our interactive studies do not reach the lower quintile of the socio-economic status (SES)."

While online surveys may be overtaking telephone surveys, a substantial segment of the audience cannot be reached through this method. People in the lower quintile tend to be less educated and to have lower per capita incomes, making them the least likely segment to have (or want) regular computer access. People who prefer to get their news from an online newspaper may also read a printed newspaper, but they may differ demographically and psychographically from those who prefer the printed newspaper.

To encourage participation in the interactive surveys, Belden offers participants a chance to win $1,000. Harmon says that more males than females respond (60 percent compared with 40 percent) while the 25 to 29 age group is the best represented in most of Belden's Web surveys.

Typical questions include the following:
• How many times have you visited this site in the last seven days or in the last month?
• Which site do you visit for news? For sports? (Or other sections?)
• Do you have a paid subscription to a daily or Sunday newspaper?

Harmon says a typical questionnaire also includes shopping questions, psychographic/lifestyle questions and demographics.

GfK MRI *GfK MRI,* formerly Mediamark Research & Intelligence, promotes itself as "the leading provider of magazine audience ratings, multimedia research data and penetrating insights into consumer behavior and motivations." It has conducted the Survey of the American Consumer since 1979 and uses this vast database of media usage, demographics, psychographics and consumer behavior as "a powerful resource for penetrating insight into the actions and motivations of adult American consumers."

The company conducts approximately 26,000 in-home, face-to-face interviews with American consumers. It chooses this research method because the interview can go longer than the average 20-minute telephone interview, visual aids (such as magazine logos) can be used, and face-to-face interviewers can obtain more accurate and meaningful responses.

Minnesota Opinion Research *MORI (Minnesota Opinion Research Inc.)* is a media research and consulting firm that frequently works with clients on specific problems. Consequently, most of MORI's work is *proprietary,* meaning that the client owns the right to any data collected, which can be published only with the client's permission. MORI's Website provides general information about a few of its projects, including one that tackled ways to increase young people's newspaper readership. The company assisted the client in creating a special section and then filling it with content (including advertising) that MORI found appeals most to this target group.

MORI has conducted research for newspaper, magazine, television and Internet media clients in more than 250 markets throughout North America and Great Britain. Clients range from the largest media organizations in the world to those serving small or specialized markets.

Scarborough *Scarborough Research,* a joint partnership with the Nielsen Company and Arbitron, Inc., measures the lifestyles, shopping patterns, media behaviors and demographics of American consumers locally, regionally and nationally. Scarborough consumer insights are used by marketers and media professionals to develop successful programs that maximize return on marketing and sales investments.

The Scarborough Newspaper Audience Ratings Report highlights readership statistics for 135 newspapers across 74 local markets. Reports combine readership information for the printed and online newspaper, resulting in the Integrated Newspaper Audience ratings. Scarborough measures Website use for the past 30 days, the prior seven days and yesterday, allowing a newspaper client to put together the past week's readership for both the printed newspaper and the Website to determine how many people in total are reached.

An MRC accredited service, Scarborough Research is a major source for consumer shopping insights. The company measures the shopping patterns, lifestyles and media habits of consumers locally, regionally and nationally.

It also offers specialized services including Ciudad Hispana de Scarborough, a suite of Hispanic marketing research services, and Custom Analytics, a service that enables marketers to get the most out of their customer data and develop more effective customer relationship management programs. The company has more than 3,500 clients spanning local and national media, advertising agencies, sports teams and leagues, major advertisers and outdoor companies.

Gary A. Meo, senior vice president of print and digital media services for Scarborough, says the company does consumer surveys in 81 markets, using a two-phase method. Telephone random digit dialing (RDD) samples are used, and selected participants are asked about their newspaper readership, radio listenership and Internet usage. Demographic information is also collected. The data calculate the average newspaper readership overall and the cumulative readership for a full week and four Sundays.

The second stage of the research process involves mailing a 32-page questionnaire booklet that includes shopping and retail behavior, travel and ownership of various products. The minimum sample size for telephone surveys is 2,000 and can go much higher in markets such as New York City and Chicago. At least 1,000 questionnaires will be mailed depending on the market size and expected response rate.

Experian

Experian is the leading authority on the behavior of American consumers. Its research focuses mostly on advertising, which is discussed in more detail in Chapter 23 in this book, but much of its research applies to publications. Its National Multi-Media Engagement Study, released in fall 2009, is a measurement system utilizing a national audience, which provides ratings of the cognitive, behavioral and emotional involvement consumers have with television, the Internet and magazines. While newspaper consumption in local markets may be a future component of this ongoing study, currently only magazines are included.

John Fetto, of Experian Marketing Services, says that 90 percent of data collection for this ongoing study occurs online. Survey participants first identify the magazines they have read in the previous six months, provide demographic information and then answer 40 questions about how engaged they are with the magazines.

The following six characteristics are assessed:
Inspirational (uplifting)
Trustworthy (source is credible)
Life enhancing (learning new things)
Social interaction (talking with friends and family)
Personal time out (time just for me to kick back and unwind)
Engagement with advertising (attraction to ads, purchase intentions, etc.)
Simmons is developing this measure of engagement to help marketers meaningfully communicate with the consumer. In announcing the engagement study in 2006, Chris Wilson, president and COO of Simmons Research, said, "Advertisers are looking for meaningful and quantifiable information that will help them understand whether they are truly making a connection with the consumer. Traditional metrics of 'counting eyeballs' is no longer good enough as simple media exposure does not equate to how a person thinks and feels about programming and commercial content."[3]

[3]Simmon's Press release: "Simmons Research Unveils Landmark Multi-Media Engagement Study." May 01, 2006 (http://www.directionsmag.com/press.releases/index.php?duty=Show&id=14171&trv=1

INDUSTRY RESEARCH ASSOCIATIONS In addition to companies that make a profit from conducting research for newspaper and magazine clients, several industry associations conduct research that benefits their members. These nonprofit associations are mainly supported by membership fees and generally fund limited numbers of studies that focus on common industry challenges. Most of these associations also compile secondary data (information collected by the government or research companies) that provide a current profile of the newspaper or magazine industry.

Newspaper Association of America The *Newspaper Association of America* keeps track of daily and Sunday newspaper readership and other industry statistics, such as the number of American newspapers publishing, the newspapers involved in joint operating agreements (JOAs) and the average cost of newsprint. NAA also tracks industry trends, such as the growth of online newspapers, group ownership and financial indicators, as well as government action and laws that might affect how newspapers do business. Although some of NAA's research involves surveying members, it mainly relies on secondary data collection for its reports.

National Newspaper Publishers Assoc. The *National Newspaper Publishers Association* is the umbrella organization for the African-American newspaper industry. It provides a news service for members and keeps track of industry information that contributes to the ability of the publishers to attract advertisers. NNPA makes available to its members an "audit" of Black newspaper readers, compiled by International Demographics, that details their education, income, age, home ownership and buying habits.

Magazine Publishers of America The *Magazine Publishers of America* serves as a clearing house for research that affects the magazine industry. MPA also summarizes advertising, magazine readership, circulation, diversity and financial research for its member publications. This research comes from a variety of sources, such as Monster.com, the Aspen Institute and the Audit Bureau of Circulations. One of its typical studies focuses on "accountability" and examines consumers' purchase decision-making process (referred to as "the purchase funnel"). This research examines how both printed and online magazines stimulate brand awareness and purchase intention and concludes that magazines perform the most consistently through all stages of the purchase funnel. Those stages include the following:

Advertising/Total Brand Awareness: Consumer has been introduced to or reminded about the brand

Brand Familiarity: Consumer recognizes specific brand names

Brand Imagery: Consumer agrees with positive attributes specific to individual brands

Purchase Intent: Consumer intends to purchase the brand[4]

The study concludes that magazines most consistently drive Web traffic and

[4]Comparing Media Contribution Throughout the Purchase Funnel http://www.magazine.org/ASSETS/7FF4463
1435140149D24542527F6DED8/MEFullStudy2006.pdf

searches and that they are the most effective medium in driving purchase intent. However, the study acknowledges that media synergy (combining different media) gets the best purchase decision results.

MPA emphasizes that "circulation" and "audience" reflect different measures. "Circulation" reports information about magazine copies distributed. MPA points out that "audience" reports information about readers, as measured by readership studies and/or subscriber studies that provide information such as demographic characteristics and product usage data. The total "audience" formula is

Circulation (Average # of Copies) x Readers-per-Copy = Audience[5]

Readership or audience analysis, therefore, may be compared to the audiences of broadcast media, which use consumer-based measures, while circulation cannot.

The *Poynter Institute*, founded in 1975 by Nelson Poynter, chairman of **Poynter Institute** the *St. Petersburg Times* and its Washington affiliate, *Congressional Quarterly*, describes itself as "a school for journalists, future journalists and teachers of journalism." Its mission is to promote "excellence and integrity in the practice of craft and in the practical leadership of successful businesses. It stands for a journalism that informs citizens and enlightens public discourse. It carries forward Nelson Poynter's belief in the value of independent journalism in the public interest."[6]

As part of its teaching mission, the Poynter Institute conducts a number of projects intended to improve journalism. For example, in 2007 it began a large study to understand how people read. To conduct the EyeTrack07 research project, Poynter partnered with four news organizations — the tabloid newspaper *Philadelphia Daily News*, two broadsheets (the *St. Petersburg Times* and the *Minneapolis-St. Paul Star Tribune*) and two news Websites (sptmes.com and startribune.com).

These partners were selected because they shared comparable reputations for producing quality journalism, represented diversity in ownership and geographic location and were willing to host the study and recruit and pay participants. According to Poynter, this is the largest eyetracking effort anyone has undertaken. The 582 reading session recordings yielded more than 102,000 eye stops to be coded and analyzed. For an explanation of how the research was conducted, see Table 2.

Among the key findings of this research project are the following: Online participants read an average of 77 percent of story text they chose to read. This is substantially higher than the amount of story text participants read in broadsheets and tabloids. Broadsheet participants read an average of 62 percent of stories they selected. Tabloid participants read an average of 57 percent. Sixty-three percent of story text chosen by online participants was read to completion. Reading in the two print formats was considerably lower. Forty percent of stories selected were read all the way through in broadsheets and 36 percent in tabloids.

---

[5]Magazine Publishers of America, "Understanding Magazine Circulation, A Guide for Advertising Buyers and Sellers," 2006, p. 4. http://www.magazine.org/research/Understanding_Magazine_Circulation.pdf
[6]http://www.poynter.org/content/content_view.asp?id=8090

Table 2: EyeTrack07 Methodology

Two people at a time were brought into two eyetracking stations where technicians placed the eyetracking equipment on the participant's head and calibrated it for each person. The participant was either handed a fresh copy of that day's newspaper folded and covered by a sheet of paper or was asked to turn to a computer and click a button to start reading the newspaper's home page.

Trying to duplicate as closely as possible real-world reading patterns, participants were told to read as they normally would, for as long as they normally would, or until they were asked to stop – whichever came first. Participants were stopped after 15 minutes of reading the newspaper or Website. Participants were encouraged to sit comfortably and read as they normally would. Each subject sat in an identical chair; the room lighting was the same from city to city. The mobility of the eyetracking equipment allowed participants to move freely, to sit back in their chairs and to raise or lower the newspaper. Participants were allowed to read whatever they liked, in whatever sequence they chose, with the exception of classified ads that were not the focus of this study.

The Mobile Eye, developed by Applied Sciences Laboratories in Bedford, Massachusetts, was used in the study. Two small cameras were mounted above the subject's right eye on the optics. One recorded the position of the eye as it was reflected in a small monocle at 60 frames per second. The other camera recorded what the subject was viewing, also at 60 frames per second. These two images were married to create a video that superimposed a crosshair over the newspaper or monitor that the subject was reading. The crosshair is a mathematical representation of the cornea's position. As the participant read, the crosshair followed his or her gaze with accuracy to about a quarter-inch. Technicians monitored the exact position of the pupil throughout the reading period, while a magnified image of the participant's eye was shown on a monitor. The optics connected to a portable mini DVCR. The reading session was recorded onto a mini-DVD or directly to a digital video file on a computer.

For the second phase of the study, each participant was given one of three printed or one of three online prototypes developed for this study. The same story was presented in a different way in each prototype. Participants were asked to read the story, and then they were given questionnaires to test their recall of the information. When data collection was completed, researchers and students from the University of Florida watched each video and recorded where people looked as they made their way through the news. They counted the number of times the eyes stopped on each coded element. Mediamark Research Inc. analyzed the data and collaborated in the design of the study.

Source: Poynter Online EyeTrack micro-site:
http://eyetrack.poynter.org/
Used with permission

The Poynter Institute study has not been without its critics, who complained that too much effort was put into the research method while not enough was put into determining what content attracted readers the most.

American Press Institute

The *American Press Institute*, founded and supported by the newspaper industry for sixty years, has undertaken research that it hopes will save newspapers by creating new business models. The Newspaper Next study, launched in 2006, researches and tests viable new business models for the newspaper industry. Both a consulting firm, Innosight LLC, and a task force of opinion leaders collaborate with API to find innovative ways to connect newspapers and readers. According to API, "The threats [to newspapers] come from many directions but are manifesting themselves in the form of declining circulation, rising costs and downward revenue pressure. The industry's very survival is dependent on its ability to reframe completely the way it does business, and find new ways to attract and keep customers…"[7] To that end, The Newspaper Next (N2) Game Plan focuses on a "strategic framework for diversification."[8]

The Pew Research Center for the People and the Press is an independent opinion research group that studies attitudes toward the press, politics and public policy issues. It is "best known for regular national surveys that measure public attentiveness to major news stories, and for our polling that charts trends in values and fundamental political and social attitudes." Data sets dating back to 1997 and current studies are available for free downloading at http://people-press.org. Focusing on public opinion research, Pew focuses on seven main projects:

Pew Research Center

The Pew Research Center for the People & the Press — studies attitudes toward the press, politics and public policy issues.

Project for Excellence in Journalism — uses empirical methods to evaluate and study the performance of the press.

Pew Internet & American Life Project — explores the impact of the Internet on children, families, communities, the work place, schools, health care and civic/political life.

The Pew Forum on Religion & Public Life — seeks to promote a deeper understanding of issues at the intersection of religion and public affairs.

Pew Hispanic Center — improves understanding of the U.S. Hispanic population and chronicles Latinos' growing impact on the nation.

Pew Global Attitudes Project — conducts a series of worldwide public opinion surveys on an array of subjects, including people's assessments of their own lives, the current state of the world and important issues of the day.

Social & Demographic Trends — studies behaviors and attitudes of Americans in key realms of their lives, including family, community, health, finance, work and leisure.

Topics range from the political (such as the Obama presidency and coverage of health care reform) to societal issues (such as social media and race). Of course, many of the studies also assess the public perception of the news media, tracking the declining readership of American newspapers, the rise of online news sites, and trends in new media use, including the use of cell phones, blogs and Twitter.

The Center relies on stratified, random-digit dialing telephone samples selected from telephone exchanges in the continental United States. Typical selection and callback strategies are used to contact the randomly selected households. According to the Center's description of the selection process, "In each contacted household, interviewers ask to speak with 'the youngest male, 18 years of age or older, who is now at home.' If there is no eligible man at home, interviewers ask to speak with 'the youngest female, 18 years of age or older, who is now at home.' This systematic respondent selection technique has been shown empirically to

---

[7]The American Press Institute, "What is Newspaper Next?" (http://www.newspapernext.org/2006/08/what_is_newspaper_next_1.htm)

[8]The American Press Institute, "Blueprint for Transformation," (http://www.newspapernext.org/N2%2520 report%25202-07%25202.pdf)

produce samples that closely mirror the population in terms of age and gender."

IN-HOUSE RESEARCH   Although there are many commercial and primary sources of data on the print media industry, some publications do their own in-house research to supplement data that may be collected for them from one of the professional research companies. Typical of this approach are the efforts of the *Austin* (Tex.) *American-Statesman* newspaper (part of the Cox Newspaper Group).

Don Vail, the research manager at the *American-Statesman*, says the newspaper has used several sources for analysis of the market and readers. "In 1999, 2001, 2003 and 2005," he explains, "we employed the Gallup Organization to perform random-sample surveys of adults in our metro area. These have concentrated on shopping activity and media choices and have been actively used by Marketing and Advertising to present our position in the market. We have also used syndicated surveys by Scarborough Research."

For content analysis and media preferences for news and information, the *American-Statesman* has contracted with Urban & Associates, a research and consulting firm in Massachusetts that specializes in newspaper research. The most recent survey by Urban in Austin was in 2006.

"The *Statesman* only rarely utilizes local vendors for phone or mail-based surveys," Vail says. "We have fielded some surveys locally but don't feel that we get the same level of consulting services and quality control that we can get with a national firm." The newspaper is doing more surveys now using Web-based methods, he adds, "with the realization that this does not give us the broad and representative look at our market that we get from phone surveys. Even so we can get relatively quick feedback on our Web offerings. These are developed and analyzed within our research department."

While the Cox Newspaper Group allows its four larger metros located in Austin, Atlanta, Dayton and West Palm Beach to obtain research that is appropriate for their diverse markets and newspapers, Vail says, "Cox does assist with online research that tests the usability of new Websites and features. It is fairly often that Austin takes the lead on this since we are a very active market online."

We may conclude that, clearly, a variety of research methods are being used to track print media. Commercial research companies are using telephone surveys, online surveys and face-to-face surveys to collect volumes of information about the American consumer and readership patterns for most newspapers and magazines. The goal is to produce publications that appeal to readers and that are viable advertising vehicles. Competition is stiff both among the commercial research companies and the media that serve the public.

Associations and organizations such as the Poynter Institute and the Pew Research Center often are concerned with the societal aspects of the print media. Increasingly, studies are concerned with cognitive processes and value judgments about the content the print media provide.

Will readership and consumer research preserve the printed page and keep newspapers and magazines commercially viable? Publishers are betting that it will.

American Press Institute: http://www.americanpressinstitute.org/ **WEBSITES**
Audit Bureau of Circulations: http://www.accessabc.com/
Belden Associates: http://www.nacorp.com/NAC2/adv/mktg/belden.html
Experian Simmons: http://www.smrb.com/web/guest/home
GfK MRI (Mediamark): http://www.gfkmri.com/
Lexis/Nexis: http://global.lexisnexis.com/us
Magazine Publishers of America: http://www.magazine.org/
Media Audit: http://www.themediaaudit.com/
Mediamark Research and Intelligence: http://www.mediamark.com
MORI: http://www.moriresearch.com/
National Newspaper Publishers Association: http://www.nnpa.org/
Newspaper Association of America: http://www.naa.org/
Pew Research Center for the People and the Press: http://people-press.org/
Poynter Institute: http://www.poynter.org
Poynter Online EyeTrack micro-site: http://eyetrack.poynter.org/
Scarborough Research: http://www.scarborough.com/
Simmons Market Research Bureau: http://www.smrb.com/web/guest/home

21 Radio and Television Research

In this chapter, you will be introduced to the most common types of methods used to conduct research for the television and radio industry and the academic research on radio and television. At the end of the chapter, you will find a list of companies that offer research services so that you can understand them better — and perhaps find a job if you are interested in a career in television and radio research. The list includes the companies' website addresses.

There are two types of television and radio research. One is the commercial research that the TV and radio industry uses to gauge audience behavior and size. Its primary purpose is administrative: to serve as a basis to set advertising rates and increase audience size. Many research companies offer consulting services to provide solutions and suggestions to media companies. The other type is the academic research that scholars use to understand the industry and audience behavior. Its purpose is to build theories that explain the TV and radio industry and audience and to assess the media's impact on society. The research methods that the television and radio industry uses the most are among those that have been discussed in other chapters in this book, but there are some unique methods used in the industry that will be explained in detail in this chapter.

SYNDICATED AND CUSTOM COMMERCIAL RESEARCH

Commercial research can be divided into syndicated and proprietary/custom research. *Syndicated research* is made available to a number of clients. *Proprietary research* is conducted for a specific client. Audience ratings research is the most commonly used research in the TV and radio industry; and because it can be so costly, it usually is done on a syndication basis. Because of the great importance that audience ratings have for the income of the TV and radio industry, a large sample audience that represents the population is necessary. The cost is high to conduct such research, and so multiple firms — such as TV stations and advertisers — subscribe to research services in order to share the cost. The best known companies

By Louisa Ha
Bowling Green State University

that specialize in audience research and ratings are Nielsen and Arbitron. Table 1 shows the differences between syndicated research and proprietary research.

Table 1. Syndicated Research vs. Proprietary Research

	Syndicated Research	**Proprietary/custom research**
Research Questions/Results	Standardized	Customized to the client
Number of Clients	Multiple subscribers	Usually one
Examples	Nielsen ratings, Arbitron ratings	Radio auditorium tests, callout research, survey of a TV station
Advantages	Low cost to each user (shared cost)	Tailored, customized to the needs of the station
	Objective	Valuable to the user only, and only applicable to the user
	Standardized format easy to use and compare	
	Official numbers to do business transactions (Currency to use)	
	Large sample and conducted on a continuous basis	
	Accessible to public/subscribers	
Clients	Established TV and radio stations/networks	Cable and new broadcast TV and radio stations, strategic needs of established TV and radio stations/networks

Audience rating is the number of audience members tuned to a TV or radio program or a station/network as a whole. Nielsen Media Research is the only company in the United States to provide national and local TV audience ratings on a regular basis. It uses two methods to determine how many people watch a TV show. One is the *diary method*. It is used in most local markets. For 56 selected markets, the *people meter* is used to record how many television sets are tuned to a TV channel. Participants allow Nielsen to install the meter on their television sets, and it sends data automatically to Nielsen. The data are compiled by computer, and audience ratings are generated on an overnight, daily basis.

EVOLUTION OF AUDIENCE RATINGS RESEARCH

Audience ratings research developed in conjunction with recording measurement technologies. It evolved from mail to diary to telephone and then to passive people meter and portable meter services. When radio became a popular medium and needed to estimate its audience size for advertisers, the old primitive method of counting mail from listeners could not be used anymore. Cooperative Analysis of Broadcast was the first company to offer audience surveys for radio stations. Since then, companies such as Birch Radio have sprung up to offer radio research services. Through a series of mergers and acquisitions, the United States was left with two companies that offer regular rating services: Nielsen Media Research for national and local television ratings and Arbitron Inc. for local radio ratings.

Nielsen is owned by VNU, a Dutch research conglomerate. It began as a division of ACNielsen, which began its business in radio ratings research in 1947 with its Nielsen Radio Index using the audiometer in sample households. The Nielsen TV Ratings have been produced since the 1950s. They statistically measure which programs are watched by different segments of the population.

The best known portion of Nielsen's research is the "diary." During the four sweeps months of February, May, July and November, Nielsen interviewers in Dunedin, Florida, and Radcliff, Kentucky, call randomly selected households in all 210 Designated Market Areas (DMAs) to fill out a diary of the programs watched in their home for a one-week period. Figure 1 is an excerpt of Nielsen's diary book instructions.

Figure 1. Instruction Page of Nielsen's TV diary

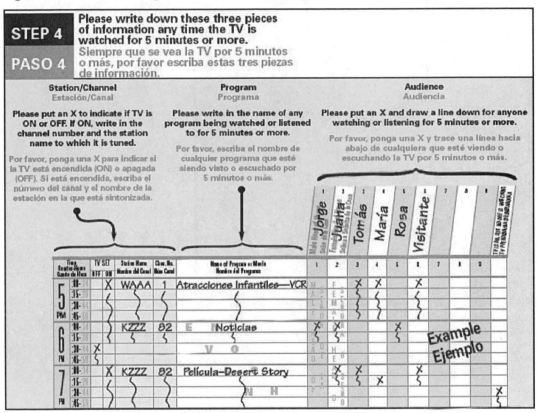

Copyright © Nielsen Media Research. Reprinted by Permission.

Market Definition To understand Nielsen's TV ratings, first it is important to know how Nielsen defines markets. A *Designated Market Area* (DMA) is a trademarked term of Nielsen Media Research and refers to a group of counties that form an exclusive geographic area in which the home market television stations hold a dominance of total hours viewed. There are 210 DMAs, covering the entire continental United States, Hawaii and parts of Alaska. Each county is assigned to only one DMA. But one DMA can consist of multiple counties. It usually is based on TV signal coverage and not on political geographical boundaries. The DMA map of Cincinnati in Figure 2 shows the difference between the Metro Area and the local DMA. The DMA is larger than the metro area. It not only includes the metro area but also encompasses counties in three states. A metro survey area is defined by the U.S. Office of Management and Budget. For Nielsen's purposes, it generally includes the town, the county or some other designated areas closest to

TV stations' transmitters. The TSA ("total survey area"), which includes the metro and additional counties, is usually used to determine a station's the maximum reach. Nielsen's NSI ("Nielsen Station Index") area is equivalent to the TSA.

Figure 2. DMA illustration – Cincinnati, Ohio

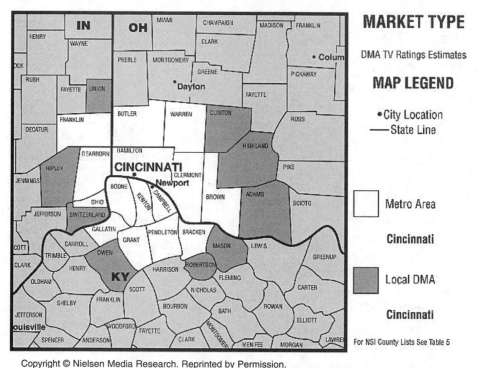

Metered markets are local markets where Nielsen uses set-tuning meters, which report set usage; or People Meters, which report both set usage and information about the individuals who were viewing. For metered markets, the local ratings from 56 television markets are usually available the following morning. The National People Meter data are available at approximately 11:00 a.m. Eastern Time. For this reason, the early ratings estimates are usually called "metered market overnights" or "preliminary" estimates. When reporting all 56 metered markets, the ratings are weighted by the size of a market, with each rating point representing approximately 1% of 76,156,430 households. Nationally, each rating point represents 1% of the 109,600,000 households. The Nielsen Media metered markets that constitute overnight ratings are listed in Table 2.

Sampling in Ratings

Television and radio ratings demonstrate the importance of obtaining a representative sample for the national or local market. With about 110 million households in the United States, it is impossible to ask everyone about viewership or listenership of programs. Yet stations and networks need to know how many people are viewing, or listening to, every program so that they can determine how much to charge advertisers for commercial time.

In upfront TV advertising purchases, networks will promise to deliver a cer-

Table 2. Nielsen Metered Markets

Rank	Designated Market Area (DMA)	TV Homes	Rank	Designated Market Area (DMA)	TV Homes
1	New York	7,391,940	30	Nashville	966,170
2	Los Angeles	5,647,440	31	Kansas City	927,060
3	Chicago	3,469,110	32	Columbus, Oh.	905,690
4	Philadelphia	2,939,950	33	Cincinnati	904,340
5	Dallas-Ft. Worth	2,435,600	34	Milwaukee	891,010
6	San Francisco-Oakland-San Jose	2,419,440	35	Salt Lake City	874,650
7	Boston (Manchester)	2,393,960	36	Greenville-Spart-Ashevll-And	838,270
8	Atlanta	2,310,490	37	San Antonio	792,440
9	Washington, DC (Hagerstown)	2,308,290	38	West Palm Beach-Ft. Pierce	775,340
10	Houston	2,050,550	40	Birmingham (Anniston, Tuscaloosa)	730,430
11	Detroit	1,925,460	42	Norfolk-Portsmouth-Newpt Nws	717,440
12	Phoenix (Prescott)	1,802,550	43	Las Vegas	707,470
13	Tampa-St. Pete (Sarasota)	1,783,910	44	Albuquerque-Santa Fe	677,740
14	Seattle-Tacoma	1,782,040	45	Oklahoma City	676,850
15	Minneapolis-St. Paul	1,706,740	46	Greensboro-H.Point-W.Salem	671,980
16	Miami-Ft. Lauderdale	1,536,020	47	Memphis	667,890
17	Cleveland-Akron (Canton)	1,533,710	48	Louisville	657,180
18	Denver	1,477,280	49	Jacksonville	655,470
19	Orlando-Daytona Bch-Melbrn	1,434,050	50	Buffalo	636,700
20	Sacramneto-Stockton-Modesto	1,391,790	51	Austin	635,860
21	St. Louis	1,244,370	52	Providence-New Bedford	626,800
22	Pittsburgh	1,158,210	53	New Orleans	600,150
23	Portland, Ore.	1,150,320	58	Knoxville	534,410
24	Baltimore	1,095,490	59	Richmond-Petersburg	526,760
25	Charlotte	1,085,640	60	Tulsa	519,820
26	Indianapolis	1,072,090	62	Dayton	511,220
27	San Diego	1,051,210	63	Ft. Myers-Naples	491,760
28	Raleigh-Durham (Fayetteville)	1,039,890		Total	76,156,430
29	Hartford & New Haven	1,007,490			

tain number of rating points for the prime-time periods advertisers commit to buy for the following TV season. If a TV program fails to deliver the promised number of rating points based on Nielsen's ratings, the network will provide additional air time to the advertisers to make up for the under-delivery of audience (i.e., ratings). This is what is called *make-good* in network TV advertising.

A cost-efficient way to determine audience size is to have an authoritative research company representing all the stations and the advertisers to select a probability sample that will have minimal errors and to conduct a study regularly to provide a basis for comparison and trend analysis.

Nielsen employs a multi-stage probability cluster sampling to ensure that the sample reflects the actual population distribution. That way, the data can be projected to the entire market population. Nielsen's sampling involves four stages: (1) selection of counties in the country, (2) selection of block groups within the counties, (3) selection of certain blocks within the county, and (4) selection of individual households within blocks. Nielsen selects households through one of two different methods: (1) geographic selection (cluster or area probability sampling) in the national sample and larger markets and (2) randomly generated telephone numbers (in a process it calls "Total Telephone Frame") in smaller markets. It replaces 20% of the metered market each year.

The national metered sample in 2010 consisted of 9,000 households and 18,000 people. The size of the sample in each of the 56 local metered markets is determined by the size of the market. For example, the Cincinnati market, which is the seventeenth largest in the nation, has a sample size of 369 households. The local metered market samples are integrated into the national metered sample.

Sample Recruitment Procedures

The procedure that Nielsen uses to set up its ratings research is a sophisticated one. The Nielsen field team is comprised of field representatives and membership representatives. They are responsible for establishing ongoing relationships with sample households, and they possess technical expertise that is essential to the meter installation process.

Here's the way Nielsen's procedure works.

Designated households are initially contacted by an introductory letter in the mail, which includes a questionnaire with a request to provide Nielsen with basic demographic information. Nielsen will select some of the households that respond to be part of the sample. The families receive a follow-up letter from Nielsen's membership representatives, inviting them to participate and notifying them of a forthcoming home visit. When the membership representative visits the sample home, s/he will explain how Nielsen Media Research works and the rules of being on the panel. The rules require, for example, that families not discuss their participation with others. Participants usually are enthusiastic about being involved. The representative ensures that the household understands the technical process. After the family agrees to the terms, the representative schedules an appointment for installation of the meter.

The meter method is an unobtrusive observation method that collects data automatically from viewers' TV sets, transmitting it to Nielsen's central computer. Nielsen's National Television Index (NTI) uses the national metered sample to provide ratings. Television set-tuning meters indicate only two things: (1) whether the television set is on or off and (2) the channel to which the set is tuned. They provide no data about who is watching — unless the participants provide additional input. Such information used to be obtained by pooling TV meter data with diaries submitted by the participating household. People Meters attempt to simplify the process by requiring each person in the household, as well as all visitors, to push a specific button on a device that records the viewing. Each person in the home is assigned a button on the meter. The meter then can record how many people in the households are watching the show and the identity of each viewer.

Although Nielsen emphasizes its metered service, more than two-thirds of the DMAs are still covered only by viewer dairies. During the sweeps periods, participants in all 210 DMAs are sent diaries to report the channels they watch, the time periods, and the number of people viewing each program or during each segment of the day, along with demographic information about them.

Criticisms of Nielsen's Ratings Methods

Diaries as a method have serious limitations. Participants are asked to provide information for one week only and to write down the shows all family members watch. This procedure easily leads to over-reporting of stations that the participant is familiar with and under-reporting of stations that s/he seldom uses. The accuracy of reporting is also a major concern since people are involved in various activities during the day and sometimes forget to write down TV viewing that lasts only a short period of time. They may not be able to report accurately other household members' TV use, especially in a multi-TV set household.

Meters relieve participants of the burden of writing station information in the diaries. However, meters can be unreliable too, especially when households have many children who don't want to press the buttons. "Button fatigue" is also a problem because participants must push the button every time they watch television. Furthermore, the procedure requires all household members to cooperate, but frequently some participants in a household forget to press the button. As a result, people meter ratings are lower than are ratings from diaries and set-tuning meters installed on the TV set.

Another problem with Nielsen's ratings is the small sample size it uses for local markets. With only a few hundred households comprising a sample, the number of viewers is low during daytime. Thus, the sampling error in local market ratings will be magnified because the size of sampling error depends on sample size. The margin of error is higher in a small sample than a large sample. The industry convention is that a TV station must have a 3-point or higher rating in order to get advertising. When the sampling error is large, many stations may not achieve that 3-point threshold and thus not receive adequate advertising support.

Despite the concerns with Nielsen's method, the industry still uses it because it has been the standard practice for years, and thus it is convenient for tracking data from year to year.

Arbitron's Radio Ratings Methods

Unlike Nielsen's panel, Arbitron uses a tracking method, that is, different samples for each survey. Diaries are the principal data collection method. The Personal People Meter (PPM) is used in fifty markets. PPM is a pager-like portable meter that participants wear to automatically record the programs they listen to. Data is reported on a monthly basis. Diary participants, on the other hand, fill out a 7-day diary of radio programs they have listened to. Each participant reports only his or her listening habits, not those of family members, as does Nielsen's.

Arbitron uses very specific procedures to collect data. Every survey week begins on a Thursday and ends on the following Wednesday. Arbitron divides the United States into 302 markets and four types: Continuous Measurement Markets, Standard Measurement Markets, Condensed Markets and PPM markets. Markets are differentiated by the frequency of data collection, type of method and sample size. The following list indicates the characteristics of each one.

1. The Continuous Measurement Market collects diary data year round, not just during four periods.

2. The Standard Measurement Market collects data once every quarter.

3. The Condensed Market has smaller sample objectives for the Metro and TSA and contains fewer "dayparts" and demographics than the Standard market.

4. PPM markets collect data via PPM rather than diaries.

Public and noncommercial radio stations are reported in Arbitron's special services and in the special public radio service marketed by the Radio Research Consortium (RRC). Noncommercial stations are also reported in Arbitron's national radio ratings services such as Nationwide and the National/Regional Database (NRD).

Arbitron provides free online training modules on its website at http://arbitron.colearn.com/.

Many audience size measurement metrics are used in the radio and TV industry. Ratings and shares are the most common ones. Let's examine how they are reported in the trade press. We'll use the example of a TV rating report in *Television Week* (Figure 3). Ratings are always reported with a decimal, and shares are always in whole numbers. Ratings usually precede share. Hence in Figure 3, *Two and a Half Men* on Monday has an overall rating of 6.2%, a share of 10%, and a 2.9% rating in the 18-49 age group.

Audience Size Measurement Metrics

Figure 3. Television Week's Rating Report

Copyright © Television Week. Reprinted by Permission.

To examine the meaning of such metrics, let's use a simplified version of the TV universe. Suppose there are only three broadcast TV networks in a market with a total of 10 households and the viewership breaks down the following way:

	Number Households
Watch ABC	3
Watch CBS	2
Watch NBC	3
Not watching TV	2
Total HH	10

Ratings: An audience rating is the percentage of people or households in a population tuning to a specific radio or TV program, station or network. The rating is determined by dividing the number of viewing people (or households) by the total number of people (or households) in the total population (or households) in the market:

$$\text{Rating} = \frac{\text{People or Households watching the network}}{\text{People/HH Population in the market}}$$

Thus, in our example, the rating of ABC is 3/10 =30%. Accordingly, CBS's rating is 20%, and NBC's is 30%.

The percentage of households using television (HUT) is the combined ratings of households watching ABC, CBS and NBC. That is,
HUT=30%+20%+30%=80%.

Shares: An audience share is the percentage of Households (HUT) or Persons Using Radio (PUR) out of the total number who are tuned to a specific program (or station or network) at any one time. Share is based on the number of radio or TV sets turned on at the time, not on the entire population. Hence, the share number is always larger than the rating number. Here is the formula for determining shares:

$$\text{Share} = \frac{\text{Number of People/HH watching the network}}{\text{PUR or HUT}}$$

Thus, in our example, the share of ABC is 30/80 = 37.5% (~38% share). NBC's share is also 38% (that is, 30/80), and CBS's is 25% (that is, 20/80).

The sum of shares of all stations in the market should equal 100%. Thus, ABC's, CBS's and NBC's shares =37.5%+37.5%+25%=100%.

In addition to shares and ratings, there are other metrics that deal with more specific measurements of viewer and listenership. Let's briefly look at these six: (1) average quarter-hour persons, (2) gross impressions, (3) gross rating points, (4) cumulative audience, (5) reach, and (6) frequency.

Average quarter-hour (AQH) persons: the estimated *average* number of persons who listened to or watched a station for a minimum of five minutes within a selected daypart. The estimate is the average of the reported listening or watching for the total quarter-hours the station was on the air during the selected daypart. It is expressed in hundreds (00) in Arbitron and thousands (000) in Nielsen.

Gross Impressions (GIs): the number of "impressions" a TV or radio advertising schedule will deliver. As the name implies, Gross Impressions represent the *total number of times* a spot is heard or watched — not the number of persons who heard or watched it. It is a *duplicated measure*, meaning that it does not exclude audience duplication. An advertising schedule is a combination of TV or radio spots during a four-week period that covers many programs. GIs are computed by multiplying the AQH Persons estimate for the particular daypart by the number of spots to be run in the daypart. The GIs for the individual dayparts are then summed to obtain the total number of GIs a schedule will deliver. Thus, if an advertiser advertises in a hypothetical market with two spots in ABC (with each having 100,000 audience exposures) and one spot in NBC (each with 150,000 audience exposures), the GI will be (2 x 100,000) + 150,000 = 350,000. Usually the number of GIs for national TV networks is huge, running into millions.

Gross rating points (GRPs): GRPs are used in a similar way as Gross Impressions to measure the weight of an advertising schedule. However, instead of the sum of exposures as in GI, GRP is the sum of rating points. Hence the GRP of the above example will be the following:

GRPs = 2 x ABC rating + NBC rating = 2 x 30 rating points + 30 ratings points = 90.

Cumulative audience (CUME): the size of the total unduplicated audience for a station over a period of time (typically four weeks). When the CUME is expressed as a percentage of the market population, it is referred to as the "cume rating" or "reach."

Reach: the percentage of the population who watched or listened to a program or was exposed to an advertising schedule over a period of time (typically four weeks), excluding any duplication. If the program is shown only one time, then the one-time rating is the same as reach.

Frequency: the average number of times an individual is exposed to an advertising spot.

Advertising Cost-efficiency Measurement

In addition to audience-size and advertising-exposure metrics, the advertising industry and the media industry sell and buy advertising based on some cost-efficiency measurements. Such measurements compare the costs of advertising on different TV or radio programs. The most commonly used ones are "cost per thousand" and "cost per point."

Cost per thousand (CPM): The "M" in CPM is the Roman numeral for 1,000. CPM is the cost the advertiser pays to reach 1,000 viewers or listeners. For example, if ABC charges $100,000 for its 30-second TV spot at 8 p.m. and it has 10,000,000 viewers, and if NBC charges $80,000 for its 30-second TV spot at the same time and it has 6,000,000 viewers, to compare the cost efficiency, we compute the CPM for each network. To do that, we divide the cost of each spot by the total audience number and then multiply by 1000. The formula is this:

$$\text{Cost per thousand} = \frac{\text{Cost of Advertising Spot}}{\text{Total number of audience}} \times 1000$$

Thus, the CPM for ABC = ($100,000/10,000,000) x 1000 = $10; and the CPM for NBC = ($80,000/6,000,000) x 1000 = $13.3.

So if ABC and NBC deliver the same type of audience, then the advertiser will choose ABC because — even though the absolute cost of ABC's $100,000 is higher than NBC's $80,000 — ABC's CPM is lower.

Cost per point (CPP): a cost-efficiency measure to compare the cost the advertiser pays for each rating point. Note that the number of audience members that each rating point represents varies by market. Thus, advertisers can only use CPP in comparing stations in the same market. Cost per point is particularly used in comparing TV and radio media because ratings — rather than raw audience numbers — are often employed as the currency of transactions and audience goals. The CPP is calculated by dividing *the cost of an advertising spot* by the *audience rating of a program or network*. Using the same example above — where the rating of ABC is 10 and the rating of NBC is 6 — the CPP is computed this way:

$$\text{Cost per point} = \frac{\text{Cost of Advertising Spot}}{\text{Audience Rating of the program/network}}$$

Thus, the CPP for ABC = $100,000/10 = $10,000; and the CPP for NBC = $80,000/6 = $13,333. Note that the result is the same using either CPP or CPM. Thus, in this example, on either measure ABC is more cost-efficient than NBC.

The Use of Ratings and Shares

Many students are confused why ratings and shares are both used in estimating audience size. Why not just use one measure only? The reason is that ratings and shares measure different things. Ratings tell the audience size, and shares tell the relative strength of a program compared to competitors.

Shares are particularly useful as a metric of success during daytime TV programs and for radio stations (because the number of households or individuals using radio or daytime television is comparatively low). When an audience is small, shares can be a good indicator of the performance of a program or network. So even if a program has only a 1 point rating, it can have a 50 percent share showing that it is doing much better than competitors at the same time slot. Hence, if a station wants to achieve a dominant position within a time slot, then it examines how high its audience share is rather than how high its rating is.

Deciphering the Ratings Books

Reading the rating books can seem a daunting task because they contain many rows of numbers and many columns and use abbreviations. Once one understands the conventions of the tables, though, they become fairly simple to use. Let's look at how the Nielsen Station Index and Arbitron Ratings Books work.

Nielsen's Station Index (NSI) is the most commonly used report for local market TV ratings. It is divided into 6 sections: (1) Daypart summary, (2) program averages, (3) time period, (4) person shares, (5) household and persons trends and (6) program index. Let's examine each section.

1. *Daypart summary.* Figure 4 on the next page is an example of a daypart summary. On the left column are the metro household ratings and shares. The local and cable network channels are listed under each daypart time (such as Mondays-Fridays 7-9 a.m.). Then the DMA household rating and share information are shown with a share trend in the past four sweeps period (November, July, May and February). After household information, DMA ratings are broken down into segments: (1) persons by age groups, (2) women by age groups, (3) men by age groups, (4) teens (12-17) and (5) children (2-11 and 6-11). Then percent distribution and TV Household ratings in adjacent DMAs are shown. The figures are all listed as percentages. The complete daypart summary (not included in Figure 4) will also include the average weekly CUME (the non-duplicated cumulative ratings for the week) for all weeks for the DMA households. The total number of households is listed in thousands. The summary also will list the total number of households and audience segments by audience size for persons 2+, 18+, 12-24, and women, men, teens and children.

Using the example of WABC, an ABC affiliate (see the "A" on its right) at M-S 8:00-11:00 p.m., we can see that it received a 4% rating and a 6% share. Its viewership has improved over the past four sweeps period, including last February's 11% share. In the complete summary (not shown in Figure 5), we would find that a total of 265,000 TV households tuned to WABC during that time period, representing 347,000 viewers two years of age or older. The "daypart summary" does

Figure 4. Nielsen's Daypart Summary Sample Page

NEW YORK, NY

DAYPART SUMMARY	METRO HH RTG	SHR	DAYPART TIME(ETZ) / STATION	DMA HH RTG	SHR	IN MKT SHR	MAY '07	FEB '07	NOV '06	MAY '06	PERSONS 2+	12-24	12-34	18-34	18-49	21-49	25-54	35+	35-64	50+	WOMEN 18+	12-24	18-34	18-49	25-49	25-54	WKG	MEN 18+	18-34	18-49	21-49	25-49	25-54	TNS 12-17	CHILD 2-11	6-11
	1	2		7	8	9	10	11	12	13	15	17	18	19	20	21	22	23	24	25	26	27	28	29	31	32	34	35	36	37	38	39	40	41	42	43
			MON.-SAT. 8:00P-10:00P & SUN. 7:00P-10:00P (CON'T)																																	
	1	1	AMC	1	1		1	1	1	1																										
	<<		APL	<<																																
	1	1	BET	1	1			1	1	1		1	1									1	1											1		
	1	1	BRVO	1	1				1	1																			1							
	1	1	CMD	1	1		1	1	1	1		1																								
	<<		CNB	<<																																
	1	2	CNN	1	2		1	1	1	1								1		1	1	1														
	<<		CRT	1	1		1	1	1	1																										
	1	1	DISC	1	1		1	1	1	1																	1				1	1	1			
	2	3	DSNY	2	3		3	3	4	3	1	1	1									2	1	1	1									2	4	5
	<<		ENT	<<			1																													
	1	2	ESPN	1	2		2	1	3	2	1		1	1	1	1	1	1	1	1							1	1	1	1	1	1			
	<<		ESP2	<<																																
	1	1	FAM	1	1		1	1	1	1		1									1													1		1
	1	1	FOOD	1	1		1	1	1	1									1															1		
	1	1	FX	1	1		1	1	1	1																								1		
	1	2	FXNC	1	2		2	2	2	1	1							1	1	2						1		1								
	2	3	HBOM	2	3		3	1	2	4	1		1	1	1	1	1	1	1	1		1	1	1	1	1	1	1	1	1	1	1	1			
	1	1	HGTV	1	1		1	1	1	1									1							1										
	1	1	HIST	1	1		1	1	1	1									1																	
	<<		HLN	<<				NR	NR																											
	1	2	LIF	1	2		1	1	1	2								1		1	1	1				1	1									
	1	1	MNBC	1	1		1	1	1	1										1																
	1	1	MTV	1	1		1	1	1	1		1	1	1								1	1											1		
	<<		MTV2	<<																																
	<<		NAN	1	1			1	1																									1	1
	<<		NGC	<<					NR																											
	1	2	NICK	2	3		2	2	2	NR	1	1	1								1	1												2	4	5
	<<		NOGT	<<					NR											1														1		
	1	1	SPI	1	1		1	1	1	1								1								1	1	1	1					
	2	3	SNY	2	3		2	NR	NR	2	1	1	1	1	1	1	1	1	1	2	1			1	1	1	2	1	1	1	1	1	1			
	1	1	SPK	1	1		1	1	1	1																	1									
	<<		STEP	<<																																
	2	3	TBSC	2	3		1	2	2	2	1	1	1	1	1	1	1	1	1	1	1		1	1	1	1	1	1	1	1	1	1	1		
	1	1	TCM	1	1		1	NR	1	1								1		1																
	1	1	TLC	1	1		1	1	1	1																										
	2	3	TNT	2	3		3	3	3	3	1	1	1	1	1	1	1	1	1	1	1		1	1	1	1	1	1	1	1	1	1	1		
	1	2	TOON	1	2		2	2	2	3	1	1																							1	2	3
	<<		TRAV	<<																																
	<<		TVL	<<				NR		1																										
	<<		TWC	<<																																
	2	3	USA	2	3		2	3	3	3	1	1	1	1	1	1	1	1	1	1	1		1	1	1	1	1	1	1	1	1	1	1		
	<<		VH1	<<			1	1	1																											
	<<		WE	<<																																
	2	3	YES	2	3		3	NR	NR	4	1				1	1	1	1	1	2	1					1	1	2	1	1	1	1	1			
	60		H/P/T.*	59		24	64	66	65	65	36	25	28	28	32	32	35	42	38	47	39	24	29	33	37	37	38	37	27	30	30	31	33	28	28	31
			MON.-SAT. 8:00P-11:00P & SUN. 7:00P-11:00P																																	
	<<		LNNT	<<																																
	<<		NWNJ	<<																																
	4	6	WABC A	4	6	15	12	12	13	11	2	1	1	1	2	2	2	2	2	2	2	1	1	2	2	2	2	2	1	2	2	2	2	1	1	1
	5	8	WCBS C	5	8	20	10	13	12	11	2		1	1	2	2	4	3	5	3		1	2	2	2	3	2	1	1	2	2	2			
	1	1	WFUT+ TF	1	1	3	1	1	1	1																			1		1	1			
	<<		WLIW P	<<			1	1																											
	1	1	WLNY I	1	2		1	2																											
	<<		WMBC I	<<																																
	4	6	WNBC N	4	6	16	8	9	11	10	2	1	2	2	2	2	3	2	3	3	1	2	3	2	3	2	2	1	2	2	2	1	1	1
	1	2	WNET P	1	2		2	2	2	2	1							1	1	1	1														
	<<		WNJN+ P	<<																																
	2	3	WNJU T	2	3	7	3	3	3	3	1	1	1	1	1	1	1	1	1	1	1	1	2	2	1	1	1	1	1	1	1	1	1	1
	<<		WNYE P	<<																																
	4	7	WNYW F	4	7	16	10	11	6	10	2	1	2	2	2	2	2	3	2	3	3	1	2	3	3	3	2	2	2	2	2	2	1	1	1
	2	3	WPIX Y	2	3	8	4	4	4	4	1	1	1	1	1	1	1	1	1	1	1	1	1	1	1	1	1	1	1	1	1	1	1	1	1
	<<		WPXN X	<<			1	1																											
	2	3	WWOR M	2	3	7	3	2	2	4	1		1	1	1	1	1	1	1	1	1		1	1	1	1	1	1	1	1	1	1	1	1	1
	3	5	WXTV U	3	5	11	5	5	5	5	2	1	2	2	2	2	2	2	2	2	2	2	2	2	2	2	1	2	1	2	2	2	1	1	1
	<<		2NY1	<<																																
	<<		2TWC	<<																																
	<<		ADSM	<<																																
	1	1	AEN	1	1		1	1	1	1									1	1																
	1	1	AMC	1	1		1	1	1	1																										
	<<		APL	<<																																
	1	1	BET	1	1			1	1	1		1	1									1	1											1		
	1	1	BRVO	1	1			1	1	1									1											1						
	1	1	CMD	1	1		1	1	1	1		1	1	1																		1	1			
	<<		CNB	<<																																
	1	1	CNN	1	2		1	1	1	1								1		1	1															
	1	1	CRT	1	1		1	1	1	1																										
	1	1	DISC	1	1		1	1	1	1																			1	1	1	1	1	1			
			CON'T...																																	
	1	2		7	8	9	10	11	12	13	15	17	18	19	20	21	22	23	24	25	26	27	28	29	31	32	34	35	36	37	38	39	40	41	42	43

Figure 5. Nielsen's Program Averages Sample

NEW YORK, NY — WK1 5/31-6/06 WK2 6/07-6/13 WK3 6/14-6/20 WK4 6/21-6/2

METRO HH	STATION DAY PROGRAM	DMA HOUSEHOLD RATINGS / MULTI-WEEK AVG / HUT	DMA RATINGS — PERSONS / WOMEN / MEN / CHILD
R/T/G · S/H/R		WEEKS 1 2 3 4 · RTG/SHR · HUT	(demographic columns)

9:00AM

WABC M-F REGIS&KELLY (Metro 5/19) — 5 5 5 4 5 18 27 ...
SAT EMPRS-SCHL-ABC (1/4) — 1 1 2 2 1 4 32 ...
SUN EYEBOWS SU 9AM (2/6) — 2 3 1 2 2 6 34 ...

WCBS M-F INSIDER (1/4) — 1 1 1 1 1 3 27 ...
SAT CBS2NWS SAT 9A (1/4) — 1 2 1 2 1 4 32 ...
SUN SUNDAY MRN-CBS (4/11) — 4 4 4 3 4 11 34 ...

WFUT+M-F MUJR-PANTLN-TF (<<) — << << ... << 26
M-F VIUDA-TF (<<) — 27
SAT PLZ SESM SA-TF (<<) — << << << << << 32
SUN PLZ SESM SU-TF (<<) — << << << << << 33

WLIW M-F SESAME STREET (<<) — << << << << 27
SAT JAKERS-P WINKS (<<) — << << 32
SAT RICK-R KITSAKI (<<) — << 33
SUN GET BUSY-NULL (<<) — << 36
SUN JAKERS-P WINKS (<<) — << << 32
SUN MY-POP LEGENDS (<<) — << 35

WLNY MON WILD AMRCA-SYN (<<) — << << << << << 28
TUE REAL LIFE 101 (<<) — << << << << << 26
WED ULTIMTE CHOICE (<<) — << << << << << 27
THU J HANNA-ADV (<<) — << << << << << 27
FRI ANIMAL RESCUE (<<) — << << << << << 27
SAT COVER 3.1 (<<) — << << 32
SAT DRAMA WAND (<<) — << << 32
SUN SUNDAY MASS (<<) — << << << << << 33

WNBC M-F TODAY SHR2-NBC (2/7) — 2 2 2 2 2 8 27 ...
SAT FRENCH-SAT-NBC (2/5) — 2 2 5 33 ...
SAT TODY-NY WKD 9A (3/9) — 3 3 4 3 10 32 ...

Copyright © Nielsen Media Research. Reprinted by Permission.

not show specific programs.

2. *Program averages*. Since the daypart summary does not include specific programs, you have to turn to the "program averages" section. An example is shown in Figure 5. (For purposes of illustrations, we are including the figures for only one hour. The complete summary would include all stations in the market.) The programs are listed under the station name with the time period. The programs of WABC at 9 a.m. on different days have different ratings. On weekdays, for example, WABC aired *Regis and Kelly*. That program's multi-week average rating is 5%, and its share is 18%. The HUT level is 27% at the 9 a.m. time period. You can further explore the demographic segment ratings and see that the program's rating is much higher among people 50+ (5% rating) than people 21-49 (1% rating).

3. *Time period*. If you want to compare the programs shown on the same day and time period, you need to look at the "time period" section for data — because programs are listed under time period. The HUT total is listed under each time period.

4. *Person shares*. The "person shares" section breaks down time period by each demographic group, including a share trend comparison for each group.

5. *Household and persons trends*. The "household and persons trends" section shows five-year data of the four sweeps periods by day and time period for households and specific demographic groups. The section has no station and program specific information.

6. *Program index*. The "program index" lists the programs in alphabetical order. It includes station names and schedules. So if you are interested in a specific program's performance week-by-week and the average quarter-hour viewing

data, you should refer to this section.

Arbitron Ratings Books are structured differently than Nielsen's index. After introducing the station information in the market at the beginning of a book, Arbitron provides a profile about the metro market reported in the book. The profile includes household income, house value, household size, education, occupation, car ownership, and so forth. It provides area lifestyle information using the PRIZM groups (geodemographic groups that define consumers by the neighborhood in which they live), retail sales data, the top 10 employer industries, other competitive media information such as the circulation of magazines and local newspapers, and general radio listenership (such as the time spent listening to radio in general by age and gender groups).

Arbitron's ratings books have seven sections: (1) target listener trends, (2) target listener estimates, (3) listening locations, (4) time spent listening, (5) CUME duplication, (6) ethnic composition, and (7) TSA target listeners and DMA target listeners.

Both target listener trends and target listener estimates report the same demographic groups, the AQH in raw numbers, the CUME in raw numbers, the AQH rating and the AQH share; but they differ in the time periods reported. For example, *target listener trends* report persons age 12-24, list the results of the past four survey periods and the current survey period, and break down the dayparts into Monday-Friday 6 a.m.-10 a.m., 10 a.m.-3 p.m., 3-7 p.m., and 7 p.m. to midnight. But in *target listener estimates*, Monday-Friday is reported from 6 a.m. to 7 p.m. with no breakdown of dayparts, and the current ratings are compared with the four-book average ratings (i.e., the average of the current and previous three periods). The example shown in Figure 6 is for the Toledo, Ohio, metro market (rank 81).

The Arbitron report has several pieces of key information. *Listening location* is a unique feature in radio ratings. Arbitron asks listeners if they listen to the radio at home, in the car, at work or in another location. The difference in settings helps advertisers determine the program with the best setting for their products. *Time spent listening* reports total listeners, indicating men and women by age groups in the total amount of time listening to a station within a week. The *CUME duplication percent* shows the overlap between stations in terms of listener coverage. Advertisers may choose the degree of overlap in audiences among stations to place their advertisements. Advertisers interested in customers of adjacent areas to the metro market will find the TSA ("total survey area") listener report more useful than the DMA ("designated market area") report.

Future of Ratings Research

New technology is affecting the research that both Nielsen and Arbitron are doing. With the proliferation of new technologies such as digital video recorders (DVRs), digital television, high-definition TV, and mobile video. Nielsen is poised to provide additional methods to measure households with these technologies. Arbitron began its satellite radio reporting in 2007. As audiences become more and more fragmented with many media choices, the need for good recording devices is called for to capture the audience use of TV and radio. Cable and satellite TV's set-top boxes and DVRs contain a wealth of audience data that research companies may mine in the future

Figure 6. Arbitron Target Listeners Rating Sample Page

Target Listener Trends
Persons 12+

© 2006 Arbitron Inc.

	Monday-Sunday 6AM-MID				Monday-Friday 6AM-10AM				Monday-Friday 10AM-3PM				Monday-Friday 3PM-7PM				Monday-Friday 7PM-MID			
	AQH (00)	Cume (00)	AQH Rtg	AQH Shr	AQH (00)	Cume (00)	AQH Rtg	AQH Shr	AQH (00)	Cume (00)	AQH Rtg	AQH Shr	AQH (00)	Cume (00)	AQH Rtg	AQH Shr	AQH (00)	Cume (00)	AQH Rtg	AQH Shr
WCWA-AM																				
SU '06	5	172	.1	.7	2	24		.2	3	29	.1	.3	3	41	.1	.3	8	56	.2	2.2
SP '06	4	126	.1	.6	6	21	.1	.6	3	38	.1	.3	4	49	.1	.5	4	23	.1	1.2
WI '06	3	125	.1	.4	1	9		.1	3	24	.1	.3	3	36	.1	.4	2	27		.7
FA '05	3	131	.1	.4	1	16		.1	3	24	.1	.3	5	31	.1	.6	3	39	.1	.8
4-Book	4	139	.1	.5	3	18		.3	3	29	.1	.3	4	39	.1	.5	4	36	.1	1.2
SU '05	3	167	.1	.4	2	39		.2	4	44	.1	.4	2	26		.2	4	49	.1	1.2
WDMN-AM																				
SU '06	*3	43	.1	.4	*3	13	.1	.3	3	24	.1	.3	2	15		.2	*1	4		.3
SP '06	**	**	**	**	**	**	**	**	**	**	**	**	**	**	**	**	**	**	**	**
WI '06	**	**	**	**	**	**	**	**	**	**	**	**	**	**	**	**	**	**	**	**
FA '05	**	**	**	**	**	**	**	**	**	**	**	**	**	**	**	**	**	**	**	**
4-Book	**	**	**	**	**	**	**	**	**	**	**	**	**	**	**	**	**	**	**	**
SU '05	**	**	**	**	**	**	**	**	**	**	**	**	**	**	**	**	**	**	**	**
WIMX-FM																				
SU '06	34	379	.7	5.0	61	208	1.2	7.0	40	225	.8	4.0	42	230	.8	4.9	12	121	.2	3.4
SP '06	42	300	.8	6.0	71	268	1.4	7.4	51	199	1.0	5.0	52	254	1.0	5.9	17	143	.3	5.3
WI '06	28	364	.5	4.1	43	207	.8	4.4	31	196	.6	3.1	38	187	.7	4.5	12	103	.2	3.9
FA '05	24	298	.5	3.5	34	183	.7	3.8	28	149	.5	2.9	37	174	.7	4.2	11	94	.2	2.9
4-Book	32	359	.6	4.7	52	217	1.0	5.7	38	192	.7	3.8	42	211	.8	4.9	13	115	.2	3.9
SU '05	20	283	.4	3.0	35	153	.7	3.9	21	136	.4	2.1	14	110	.3	1.7	12	101	.2	3.5
WIOT-FM																				
SU '06	45	874	.9	6.6	78	443	1.5	9.0	60	406	1.2	6.0	52	473	1.0	6.0	24	265	.5	6.7
SP '06	42	822	.8	6.0	77	431	1.5	8.0	51	341	1.0	5.0	49	434	.9	5.6	23	234	.4	7.1
WI '06	43	839	.8	6.4	90	524	1.7	9.3	59	352	1.1	5.8	47	424	.9	5.6	19	229	.4	6.2
FA '05	48	831	.9	7.0	86	439	1.7	9.6	71	345	1.4	7.4	57	397	1.1	6.5	23	206	.4	6.1
4-Book	45	842	.9	6.5	83	459	1.6	9.0	60	361	1.2	6.1	51	432	1.0	5.9	22	234	.4	6.5
SU '05	40	844	.8	5.9	78	427	1.5	8.8	49	349	.0	4.0	45	395	.9	5.5	23	222	.4	6.7
WJUC-FM																				
SU '06	26	463	.5	3.8	18	199	.3	2.1	35	243	.7	3.5	42	294	.8	4.9	21	164	.4	5.9
SP '06	21	433	.4	3.0	24	179	.5	2.5	28	211	.5	2.8	29	239	.6	3.3	14	170	.3	4.3
WI '06	22	490	.4	3.2	20	187	.4	2.1	20	198	.4	2.0	31	265	.6	3.7	19	202	.4	6.2
FA '05	25	445	.5	3.6	20	176	.4	2.2	24	185	.5	2.5	37	280	.7	4.2	24	201	.5	6.3
4-Book	24	458	.5	3.4	21	185	.4	2.2	27	209	.5	2.7	35	270	.7	4.0	20	184	.4	5.7
SU '05	22	444	.4	3.3	21	172	.4	2.4	24	173	.5	2.4	27	241	.5	3.3	19	188	.4	5.5

** Station(s) not reported this survey.   * Listener estimates adjusted for reported broadcast schedule.   + Station(s) changed call letters – see "Special Notices."   4-Book: Avg. of current and previous 3 surveys.   2-Book: Avg. of most recent 2 surveys.

The estimates and data contained in this printed report have been obtained from Arbitron's electronic Radio Market Report ("Arbitron eBook") and are for the exclusive use of Arbitron subscribers pursuant to a written license agreement. See the Arbitron eBook for further information on limitations and restrictions on use.

ARBITRON

Listener Estimates, LE-1 of 198

to provide more detailed audience information.

TVQ: Television Quotient

TVQ — which stands for "television quotient" — is a non-ratings syndicated research service that the TV and radio industry uses. Instead of measuring audience size, it measures how much an audience *likes* individual programs. TVQ measures familiarity and appeal of performers, characters, sports and sports personalities, broadcast and cable programs as well as company and brand names. Among other things, TVQ helps stations choose the right host or anchor for a newscast or program.

Based on its "One of My Favorites" concept, Marketing Evaluations, Inc., offers Q Scores services, which summarize the various perceptions and feelings that consumers have in a single "likability" measurement. The company, headquartered in Manaset, New York, interviews people by telephone. A positive Q Score is the number of respondents who say a program is "One of My Favorites," expressed as a percentage of the number of respondents who are familiar with the program. A negative Q Score is the number of respondents who say a program is "poor or fair," expressed as a percentage of the number of respondents who are familiar with the program. When an individual or program has both high positive and high negative Q scores, then it is controversial. Figure 7 is an example of a ranking report of Performer Q.

There are eight types of Q scores reports: Performer Q, TVQ, Cable Q, Cartoon Q, Sports Q, Brand Attachment Q, Kids Product Q and the Dead Q. Let's look briefly at each one.

Performer Q assesses the familiarity and appeal score of 1,700 TV personalities using a nationally representative survey sample of 1,800 people twice a year.

Figure 7. Performer Q Ranking Report Sample Page

MARKETING EVALUATIONS, INC.
PERFORMER Q STUDY

Q SCORE RANKING FOR TARGET DEMO

PERSONALITY NAMES	ONE OF MY FAVORITES	VERY GOOD	GOOD	FAIR/ POOR	TOTAL FAMILIAR	POSITIVE Q SCORE	NEGATIVE Q SCORE
CUBA GOODING, JR.	24	24	20	6	75	33	8
MICHAEL JORDAN	29	24	22	13	88	33	14
SAM WATERSTON	15	12	14	5	46	33	10
JENNIFER ANISTON	26	22	21	11	81	32	14
DICK VAN DYKE	26	23	20	10	80	32	13
DORIEN WILSON	5	4	4	3	16	32	20
DAVID JAMES ELLIOTT	13	10	12	5	40	32	12
WHOOPI GOLDBERG	28	22	20	17	88	32	20
JAMES GARNER	21	19	18	8	66	32	11
JOHN WALSH	22	18	22	8	70	32	12
RAY ROMANO	26	20	19	15	80	32	19
MEGAN MULLALLY	16	11	15	8	50	32	15
BENJAMIN MCKENZIE	6	4	5	3	19	32	18
WILMER VALDERRAMA	12	8	12	5	38	31	13
JOHNNY DEPP	26	21	22	15	83	31	18
BILL MURRAY	26	26	23	8	83	31	10
MIKE MYERS	24	19	19	14	76	31	19
TOM WELLING	9	6	10	5	30	31	15
DAMON WAYANS	19	15	18	9	60	31	15
OPRAH WINFREY	28	19	20	24	90	31	26
HENRY WINKLER	23	23	22	7	75	30	9
TIGER WOODS	27	22	22	18	89	30	20
MAURA TIERNEY	12	11	11	5	39	30	12
KURT RUSSELL	24	22	24	10	81	30	12
MO'NIQUE	7	5	7	6	24	30	24
TONY SHALHOUB	14	11	13	9	46	30	20
PATRICIA HEATON	18	18	16	9	62	30	14
SHIA LABEOUF	8	5	8	5	25	30	20
TY PENNINGTON	10	9	9	6	35	30	19
TIM ALLEN	27	29	25	11	93	30	12
MATTHEW PERRY	21	18	21	11	71	29	16
MATT LEBLANC	20	17	19	12	67	29	18
ADAM RODRIGUEZ	11	12	12	3	39	29	8
EMERIL LAGASSE	17	14	16	10	57	29	18
DOLLY PARTON	26	21	24	17	87	29	19
GORAN VISNJIC	11	9	11	6	36	29	15
GEORGE CLOONEY	24	27	22	10	83	29	12
GEORGE STRAIT	20	15	20	13	68	29	19
JACKIE CHAN	25	22	24	15	86	29	17
TINA TURNER	24	17	24	18	83	29	22
VINCENT D'ONOFRIO	11	10	12	5	39	29	14
LAURA PREPON	11	9	12	5	37	29	13

Figure 8. TVQ Ranking Report Sample Page

MARKETING EVALUATIONS, INC.
TVQ PROGRAM RATINGS

Q SCORE RANKING AMONG TARGET DEMO

BROADCAST PROGRAMS	NETWORK	ONE OF MY FAVORITES	VERY GOOD	GOOD	FAIR/ POOR	TOTAL FAMILIAR	POSITIVE Q SCORE	NEGATIVE Q SCORE	MATCHED 1+ EPISODES PAST FOUR WEEKS POSITIVE Q SCORE	NEGATIVE Q SCORE
MEDIUM	NBC	9	7	10	4	31	30	16	48	5
COLD CASE	CBS	17	18	16	4	56	30	10	40	3
K-VILLE	FOX	5	4	3	2	15	30	19	31	15
FAMILY GUY	FOX	16	9	12	10	52	30	30	46	9
SATURDAY NIGHT COLLEGE FOOTBALL ON ABC	ABC	8	7	9	3	27	30	11	36	6
TWO AND A HALF MEN	CBS	15	12	15	8	52	29	19	40	9
SHARK	CBS	8	8	6	3	27	29	16	37	7
JERICHO	CBS	7	6	8	4	23	29	20	34	14
FOOTBALL NIGHT IN AMERICA ON NBC	NBC	8	10	8	2	27	28	8	33	5
THE OFFICE	NBC	8	6	9	5	30	28	24	48	9
PRISON BREAK	FOX	8	7	9	4	29	28	17	39	7
SMALLVILLE	CW	9	9	10	5	35	27	19	45	7
AMERICA'S MOST WANTED: AMERICA FIGHTS BACK	FOX	13	14	16	5	49	27	12	42	5
PRIVATE PRACTICE	ABC	4	5	4	2	16	26	12	28	12
LIFE	NBC	3	5	2	2	12	26	19	28	10
MEN IN TREES	ABC	5	4	6	3	18	26	20	39	11
ER	NBC	14	15	18	7	56	26	16	48	4
DANCING WITH THE STARS	ABC	14	12	15	11	55	25	26	37	11
SCRUBS	NBC	11	10	12	8	45	25	26	40	7
BOSTON LEGAL	ABC	8	9	7	5	30	25	20	39	10
MY NAME IS EARL	NBC	10	8	12	6	39	25	22	43	10
AMERICA'S NEXT TOP MODEL 9	CW	6	6	6	4	22	25	23	33	13
EXTREME MAKEOVER: HOME EDITION	ABC	15	16	17	12	63	24	24	37	7
JUST FOR LAUGHS	ABC	4	4	5	2	16	23	18	26	16
THE BIGGEST LOSER 4	NBC	6	5	9	5	26	23	23	31	10
LAS VEGAS	NBC	8	10	10	4	33	23	17	34	7
DEAL OR NO DEAL	NBC	15	17	19	11	66	23	21	37	8
ACCORDING TO JIM	ABC	10	12	14	7	44	23	19	34	9
EVERYBODY HATES CHRIS	CW	6	7	9	3	26	22	18	01	6
THE SIMPSONS	FOX	15	14	13	14	72	21	33	37	9
30 ROCK	NBC	4	6	5	2	18	20	19	28	4
COPS	FOX	12	15	21	11	62	20	21	32	6
AMERICA'S FUNNIEST HOME VIDEOS	ABC	14	18	24	12	72	20	22	32	8
BEAUTY AND THE GEEK 4	CW	4	5	4	4	18	19	28	19	12
20/20	ABC	12	13	11	7	63	19	13	33	4
ARE YOU SMARTER THAN A 5TH. GRADER?	FOX	10	16	16	9	54	19	21	26	10
1 VS. 100	NBC	6	9	11	5	32	17	19	24	9
HOW I MET YOUR MOTHER	CBS	5	9	10	6	32	17	25	25	10
KING OF THE HILL	FOX	9	12	16	11	57	17	33	30	9
60 MINUTES	CBS	11	23	23	12	71	16	20	27	8
WIFE SWAP	ABC	8	6	12	13	44	13	45	27	20
THE BACHELOR	ABC	4	4	8	16	33	13	51	27	17

The audience rankings provide a rank order list of personalities for different target audience groups.

TVQ measures the familiarity and appeal of all regularly scheduled broadcast programs, in all scheduled dayparts, to determine targeted audience attraction. TVQs are conducted nine times each TV season using a nationally representative sample of 1,600 people. Figure 8 is an example of a TVQ ranking report by program.

Cable Q measures the familiarity and appeal of all major cable networks and regularly scheduled cable programs, in all scheduled dayparts, to determine their attraction to the targeted audience. In Cable Q, a national sample of 2,600 cable or satellite TV households is surveyed six times a year. Figure 9 on the next page is an example of a Cable Q report.

Cartoon Q measures the familiarity and appeal of cartoon characters among kids, teens and adults. Studies with a national sample of 1,800 are conducted twice a year, in May and November, and cover more than 600 characters.

Sports Q measures the familiarity and appeal of about 500 personalities in a variety of sports categories. It is conducted once a year.

Brand Attachment Q (Product Q) measures consumer feelings about brand and company names, using their logos to elicit responses. Both broadcast network

Figure 9. Cable Q Ranking Report Sample Page

MARKETING EVALUATIONS, INC.
CABLE Q PROGRAM RATINGS

Q SCORE RANKING AMONG TARGET DEMO

CABLE PROGRAMS	NETWORK	ONE OF MY FAVORITES	VERY GOOD	GOOD	FAIR/ POOR	TOTAL FAMILIAR	POSITIVE Q SCORE	NEGATIVE Q SCORE
UNWRAPPED	FOOD	12	14	15	4	45	27	8
WITHOUT A TRACE ON TNT	TNT	12	13	15	4	43	27	9
MEDIUM ON LIFETIME	LIF	6	6	7	2	22	27	12
ROME	HBO	9	8	10	4	31	27	15
REBA ON LIFETIME	LIF	11	9	13	5	40	27	16
TNA WRESTLING: IMPACT!	SPK	5	5	6	2	19	27	16
GOOD EATS	FOOD	13	14	18	4	49	26	9
ENTOURAGE	HBO	7	6	10	3	27	26	15
SOUTH PARK	CON	16	13	18	9	63	26	26
COLD CASE ON TNT	TNT	11	15	14	3	43	25	8
DEADLIEST CATCH	DSC	11	13	14	4	43	25	12
NBA ON TNT	TNT	7	7	10	3	27	25	13
DIRTY JOBS	DSC	17	19	21	7	66	25	14
THE WIRE ON BET	BET	5	6	7	2	21	25	16
THE 4400	USA	6	6	8	4	25	25	17
STARGATE SG-1	SCI	10	9	14	6	40	25	18
REAL TIME WITH BILL MAHER	HBO	7	7	9	5	31	25	22
INSIDE THE NFL	HBO	9	13	12	4	39	24	11
NFL LIVE	ESPN	12	14	19	5	51	24	11
COPS ON G4	G4	8	10	13	3	35	23	10
COLD CASE FILES	A&E	14	20	22	6	64	23	11
HBO BOXING	HBO	9	11	14	3	38	23	12
FRIENDS ON TBS	TBS	11	13	18	6	49	23	13
NBA ON ESPN	ESPN	8	9	14	5	36	23	14
THE COLBERT REPORT	CON	7	9	10	4	31	23	15
SPORTSCENTER	ESPN	12	14	19	8	54	23	16
DA ALI G SHOW	HBO	5	6	6	3	20	23	19
I LOVE NEW YORK	VH1	7	7	9	5	31	23	28
NBA COAST TO COAST	ESP2	5	6	9	1	22	22	8
BODY OF EVIDENCE	CRT	7	11	11	3	32	22	9
THE HILLS	MTV	6	5	8	4	25	22	24
THE INVESTIGATORS	CRT	7	10	13	2	32	21	8
COPS ON COURT TV	CRT	11	15	19	7	53	21	14
THE DEAD ZONE	USA	6	9	10	4	30	21	15
BEST WEEK EVER	VH1	6	7	10	4	28	21	18
THE O'REILLY FACTOR	FNC	9	11	14	7	42	21	22
WHAT NOT TO WEAR	TLC	8	9	13	7	39	21	23
THE L WORD	SHO	5	5	6	5	22	21	28
THE FIRST 48	A&E	7	12	12	3	34	20	10
FLIP THAT HOUSE	TLC	9	12	18	6	46	20	14
INSIDE THE ACTORS STUDIO	BRV	6	9	10	4	30	20	15
CURB YOUR ENTHUSIASM	HBO	6	8	9	5	30	20	23

and cable network brands are included.

Kids Product Q examines overall brand or company appeal and imagery among children 6-11 and teens 12-17, as well as users of specific brands.

Dead Q measures the current familiarity and appeal of deceased personalities in a variety of categories to determine their attraction among targeted audiences.

Proprietary Research

When syndicated research cannot meet the specific needs of an individual media company or advertiser, proprietary research will be conducted. Proprietary research is important for new TV or radio stations — for they will not be reported or will be severely under-reported in syndicated research, whose methodology inherently favors established media companies. To provide data for advertisers, new stations need to conduct research for their own use. Established media companies may also use proprietary research that can be customized to their own needs if they plan to make changes in what they are doing.

The research questions in proprietary research are company specific and may not apply to the whole industry. The cost for each proprietary research project is usually much more than for syndicated research because the lone client bears the entrie cost, whereas multiple clients share the cost of syndicated research. Some proprietary research is conducted in-house by the research departments of a station, but most stations will outsource the research.

Some examples of commonly used proprietary research are (1) program and commercial testing and (2) hook testing in callout research and auditorium tests. Let's look at each of them.

Program and Commercial Testing

Program testing is conducted during the development phase of a TV or radio program before it is shown on air. Tests can be on the program concept or the pilot episode (either as a rough cut or a finished product). Usually program tests are conducted for prime-time series that are costly to produce, since the financial stakes are high for the networks.

Here's how the testing procedure works. The program concept usually is described to a group of audiences either in a survey or a focus group. Participants are asked if they would like to watch or listen to the show. If their responses are positive, then the producer will continue production of the work. The preliminary production will result in a rough cut that contains video or audio to demonstrate how the program concept is executed. Respondents will be recruited to examine the rough cut and identify areas they like or dislike so that the producers can make modifications.

The pilot episode is a sample program of a series that will be pitched to a network in the hope it will commit to finance the show. There are several ways that the pilot episode is tested. It can be tested in a theater by recruiting subjects to view it in a typical theater building or even in a mobile van with a large TV set for a group of viewers. Split cable or telephone tests may also be used for television programs and radio programs, respectively. In a split cable test, the networks or production companies pre-recruit subscribers of a cable system locally to participate. The cable system will show the pilot to selected participants. Afterwards, telephone surveys will be conducted with the participants, or they will receive self-administered questionnaire booklets for their comments on the pilot episode. In telephone tests, short segments of a radio program will be played over the phone after consumers agree to be participants. They will be asked for comments.

Commercial testing goes through the same process as program testing. Many commercials are tested because advertisers spend millions of dollars not only on producing the commercials but also on placing them on stations and networks.

Hook Testing in Auditorium and Callout Research

Music is the program content for many radio stations. The songs that a station plays can affect the station's audience ratings. To test the popularity of individual songs, research is conducted for a station's program director or music director to determine which songs its listeners like or dislike. *Hooks* are short segments of songs usually lasting 5-15 seconds representing the song.

Here's how hook testing works. Hooks are usually used to test songs that respondents are already familiar with. Respondents are asked to identify the song from the hook to test for familiarity or rate the song on some type of evaluation scale. Hooks are used two ways in music research. The first is in *auditorium tests*, which are designed to evaluate recurrents (recently popular songs) and oldies. The second way is in *callout research*, which a station uses to test music that is currently playing on air. For the last 10 years, callout — along with national charts and single sales — has become the norm for determining hit songs. The biggest radio stations in the United States in current-oriented formats use it.

Program and Scheduling Diagnosis

Some research companies such as Marketing Evaluations offer program diagnosis services. *Program diagnostics* include evaluations of program elements, characters and storylines for improving the viewer appeal of future episodes. The research attempts to uncover the reasons for program attraction and rejection. Diagnostic research also can evaluate scheduling strategies to measure a program's appeal in various time periods in order to maximize its competitive strength.

Format Studies

Because the world of radio is segmented by station formats, it is important to determine which stations provide the best service in a variety of areas such as news, traffic reports and specific music genres. Radio format studies enable programming consultants and stations' advertising sales departments to measure the success of the format a station is using. Katz Media, a large media sales representative company, for example, provides national radio format studies for stations to use as reference.

ACADEMIC RESEARCH

Along with commercial research, many academic researchers are interested in studying television and radio as important mass media affecting society. The Broadcast Education Association (BEA) publishes two scholarly journals dealing with television and radio: *Journal of Broadcasting and Electronic Media* and *Journal of Radio and Audio Media*. Other academic journals also publish research on television and radio. Some of the topics — such as business models, consumer and audience behavior, and media content — can be of practical value to industry practitioners. Some of the research mainly assesses the media's impact on society and poses criticisms and suggestions to public policy makers and the media industry.

The main difference between academic and commercial research is that the former emphasizes the development and application of theories, while commercial research emphasizes the practical use of the results to solve immediate problems or generate profits for the media. Surveys, content analysis and experiments, which are three major research methods discussed in other chapters of this book, are applied to radio and television in different types of academic research. Let's look at some of the kinds of theoretical research that scholars are conducting.

Audience Surveys: Interests and Opinions

Some academic research may seem to resemble commercial research, but it is actually theoretical in nature. For example, like commercial researchers, some academic researchers conduct surveys of the audience's program preferences in TV and radio programs. One stream of this type of research is to assess the audience selection of programs within uses and gratifications theory. Katz, Blumler and Gurevitch's (1973) review on uses and gratifications research shows the different typologies of audience uses of media. Academic researchers have also examined audiences in their commercial-skipping behavior and their use of technologies accompanying television such as the remote control, VCRs, DVD players and digital video recorders (e.g., Van Den Bulck, 1999). Another stream of audience research is to ask audience members to evaluate the content of television and radio programs and their perceptions of it. An example of such research is Clifford, Gunter & McAleer's (1995) study examining how children evaluate and comprehend television programs.

Content Analysis of Programming

Instead of focusing on the audience, content analysis provides a good measure of television and radio programming. By analyzing the content of television using a representative sample, researchers can examine such matters as how violent or sexually explicit the media content is and how a certain gender or race is portrayed. For example, Mastro and Greenberg's (2000) study on racial minorities in prime-time television showed Latinos and Asian-Americans being under-represented and African Americans being slightly over-represented.

Many researchers conduct longitudinal analysis of TV and radio programming to assess the increase or decrease of certain types of content. Two major studies that documented the violence in prime-time broadcast network television were the National Commission on the Causes and Prevention of Violence in 1967-68 and the Surgeon General's Scientific Advisory Committee on Television and Social Behavior in 1972. George Gerbner and his research team (Gerbner et al., 1982) showed that violence in television was much more exaggerated than in real life. Violence on TV occurred at least 10 times more often than in the real world, with an average of five to six acts of overt physical violence per hour. In his meta analysis of 25 sexual content studies on American primetime network programming between 1975 and 2004, Hetsroni (2007) showed that the frequency of sexual acts consistently decreased over the years.

Experiments: Responses to Format, Content and Commercials

To assess the impact of media content such as TV violence and sex on the audience, many researchers conduct experiments on children and adults to examine the short term or long term impact of such content. Longitudinal studies, especially those from the perspective of cultivation theory, discuss the cumulative effect of media (Gerbner, 1990).

Along with the study of controversial media content, researchers use experiments to test consumer response to new TV and radio program formats. For example, Goldberg and Gorn (1987) showed how sad and happy TV programs affect viewers' responses to commercials. Advertisers test the effectiveness of TV and radio commercials and specific execution elements by comparing audience members who are exposed, and those who are not exposed, in terms of their attitude toward a brand and purchase intention after the experiment. Experiments are designed to help advertisers determine how effective commercials are.

Economic Analysis

Finally, many scholars and policymakers are interested in television and radio as parts of the industry sector, and they conduct economic analyses of the media market. One type of economic analysis assesses the degree of market concentration and diversity in the media industry, as Bates' (1993) study of the local TV industry did. Researchers collect data regarding ownership from various published and proprietary sources and perform economic statistical models and analysis of the media industry. Such data can be used to make inferences about the impact of ownership on media content diversity (e.g., Litman, 1979). The Federal Communications Commission (FCC) uses this method to determine the owner-ship limits of media companies. Another type of economic analysis assesses the trade imbalance of TV and radio program imports and exports between the United States and other countries. Such research has had significant implications on the quota systems employed by countries in limiting foreign media product imports (e.g., Hoskins, Mirus & Rozeboom, 1989).

RESEARCH COMPANIES

Arbitron Inc.: http://www.arbitron.com/
Bullseye Marketing Research Inc: http://www.bullsi.com/
Comquest Callout: http://www.callout.com/
Edison Media Research: http://www.edisonresearch.com/
GfK MRI: http://www.gfkmri.com
Harker Research: http://www.harkerresearch.com/
HitPredictor: http://www.hitpredictor.com/
Katz Media: http://www.katz-media.com/
Marketing Evaluations/TVQ Inc. : http://www.qscores.com/
Nielsen Media Research: http://www.nielsenmedia.com/
Radio Research Consortium: http://www.rrconline.org/
Scarborough Research: http://www.scarborough.com/media.php
Steve Casey Research: http://www.upyourratings.com/index.html

RESEARCH RESOURCES

Cable Advertising Bureau (CAB) Research: http://www.thecab.tv/
Media Rating Council: http://www.mediaratingcouncil.org/
National Association of Broadcasters Research: http://www.nab.org
     /resources/research.asp
Radio Advertising Bureau Research: http://www.rab.com/radioChannel.cfm
Radio Research Consortium: http://www.rrconline.org/
Television Advertising Bureau (TVB) Research: http://www.tvb.org/nav/build_
     frameset.asp?url=/rcentral/index.asp
TV By the Numbers: http://tvbythenumbers.com/

TO LEARN MORE

Balone, R. E. (1995). *New rules of the radio ratings game.* Washington, DC: National Association of Broadcasters.

Beville, H. M. (1998). *Audience ratings: radio, television, cable* (Rev. ed.). Hillsdale, NJ: Lawrence Erlbaum.

Buzzard, K. (1992). *Electronic media ratings: Turning audiences into dollars and sense.* NY: Focal Press.

Dominowski, P. (1997). *Audience ratings: A primer for non-commercial radio stations.* Olney, MD: Radio Research Consortium.

Marx, S. A. and Bouvard, P. (1992). *Radio advertising's missing ingredient: The optimum effective scheduling system.* Washington, DC: National Association of Broadcasters.

Pecora, N., Murray, J. P. & Wartella, E. (2006 Ed.). *Children and television: 50 years of research*. Mahwah, NJ: Lawrence Erlbaum.

United States Government (1997). *Television ratings system: Hearing before the Committee on Commerce, Science and Transportation*, United States Senate, One Hundred Fifth Congress, first session, February 27, 1997.

Webster, J. G., Phalen, P. & Lichty, L. W. (2006). *Ratings analysis. The theory and practice of audience research* (3d Ed.). Mahwah, NJ: Lawrence Erlbaum.

Zapoleon, G. (2002). *R&R interview on callout research*. Available: http://www.zapoleon.com /zms/kbase.asp?article_id=41

REFERENCES

Bates, B. J. (1993). Concentration in local television markets. *Journal of Media Economics* 6(1), 3-22.

Clifford, B. R., Gunter, B., & McAleer, J. (1995). *Television and children: Program evaluation, comprehension, and impact*. Mahwah, NJ, : Erlbaum.

Gerbner, G. (1990). Epilogue: Advancing on the path of righteousness (maybe). In N. Sinoreilli and M. Morgan (Eds.). *Cultivation analysis: New directions in media effects research*. Newbury Park, CA: Sage.

Gerbner, George, Larry Gross, Michael Morgan, & Nancy Signorielli (1980). The "Mainstreaming" of America: Violence Profile No. 11. *Journal of Communication*, 30(3), 10-29.

Goldberg, M.E. & Gorn, G. J. (1987). *Happy and sad TV programs: How they affect reactions to commercials. The Journal of Consumer Research*, 14(3), 387-403.

Hestroni, Amir (2007). Four decades of violent content on prime-time network programming: a longitudinal meta-analytic review. *Journal of Communication*, 57(4), 759–784.

Hoskins, C., Mirus, R., & Rozeboom, W. (1989, Spring). U.S. television programs in the international market: Unfair pricing? *Journal of Communication*, 39(2), 55-75.

Katz, E., Blumler, J. G., & Gurevitch, M. (1973). Uses and gratifications research. *Public Opinion Quarterly*, 37(4), 509-523.

Litman, B. R. (1979). The television networks, competition and program diversity. *Journal of Broadcasting*, 23, 393-410.

Mastro, D. E. & Greenberg, B. S. (2000). The portrayal of racial minorities on prime-time television. *Journal of Broadcasting and Electronic Media*, 44(4), 690-703.

Van den Bulck, J. (1999). VCR-use and patterns of time shifting and selectivity. *Journal of Broadcasting & Electronic Media*, 43 (3), 316-326.

22 Public Relations Research

Public relations is the process of building and maintaining positive relationships, mutual understanding and open communication between an organization and its publics.

The term *publics* is used in public relations to refer to the various constituents, customers and stakeholders that have a connection to or potential relationship with the organization. Publics can be external (e.g., customers, clients, media, suppliers, people who live in proximity to the factory, et al.) or internal (e.g., employees, volunteers, advisory boards, et al.).

Research on publics will typically focus on three areas: (1) knowledge, (2) predisposition and (3) behavior. The goal is to better communicate with publics and to reach and build relationships with them.

Research on *knowledge* may involve questions directed at how much the public knows about the organization, specifics about what the organization does, details about its services, the kind of community activities with which it has been involved, new plans or policies, etc.

Research on *predispositions* might include an assessment of how well the public likes the organization, believes it is doing a good job, supports organizational initiatives, approves or disapproves of new plans or policies, etc.

Research on *behavior* might include things such as how frequently people visit the organization's website, donate to causes, volunteer in the community, talk about the organization with others, read the organization's newsletter, etc.

THE IMPORTANCE OF RESEARCH

The only reliable way for public relations practitioners to know the public's level of knowledge, predispositions and behaviors is to conduct research. Successful public relations is research driven. Research is essential to the public relations process.

Three Research Models

An indication of the importance of research can be found in the prior-

By Dennis F. Kinsey
Syracuse University

361

ity given to it in the following popular public relations models:

RACE — Research, Action, Communication and Evaluation (Marsdon, 1963)
ROPE — Research, Objectives, Programming and Evaluation (Hendrix and Hayes, 2007)
ROSTE — Research, Objectives, Strategies, Tactics and Evaluation (Parkinson and Ekachai, 2006)

All three of these models start with research. Research is essential to planning and implementing a public relations program and eventually to evaluating the effectiveness of the public relations efforts.

The RACE model is popular in public relations education and for understanding that public relations is a process. The "R" in the acronym RACE stands for research. Research is needed at the very beginning to fully understand the public relations problem, to explore it, to define it, to determine the boundaries of the problem.

For example, let's say you are the director of communication for a company. While walking through your company's cafeteria, you overhear the following conversation coming from people at one of the tables: "Nobody tells us what is going on around here … we are the last to know anything. I have to find out about my own company by reading the newspaper. They don't tell us a thing." Perhaps you have an internal communications problem. Maybe you do not. Perhaps the people you overheard talking about lack of communication from their company are workers from the hospital across the street. They like the food at your cafeteria better than their own. So they are eating at your place. But maybe you do have an internal communications problem. You've caught wind of a possible public relations problem. Now you need to conduct research to see if the problem exists, how extensive it is, who thinks it is a problem and why, and how to address it.

This research will then guide the strategic planning in the public relations process. The "A" in RACE stands for action, as in planning and programming. Research results will guide the strategic thinking about the PR problem, developing the appropriate objectives, tactics, messages, etc.

The "C" in the RACE model stands for communicating or executing the public relations program — the implementation step. Research can be used to track the progress of your campaign to see that you are "moving the needle" on knowledge, predispositions or behavior as the campaign moves forward. Tracking polling will allow you to adjust your strategy, tactics or messages before the end.

The "E" in RACE stands for evaluation. Research is used to determine if your program was successful. Did you achieve your objectives?

The ROPE and ROSTE models are variations of RACE. Sometimes "objectives" are highlighted more, or objectives, strategies and tactics are distinguished and emphasized. What doesn't vary is the prominence of research in all these models.

All research methods are appropriate for use in public relations. That is, there is not one method that is specific to public relations research. Every research method discussed in this book can be used in the pub-

METHODS USED IN PUBLIC RELATIONS

lic relations process. Methods are selected based on their appropriateness for a specific problem. That is, the research questions and information needs will dictate the methodology used. As we have seen in earlier chapters, no method is perfect. Every method has strengths and weaknesses. Public relations researchers select the method most appropriate based on the strength of that method at addressing the particular public relations need.

The methods used in public relations research are the same as those used in academic research. The public relations practitioner needs reliable and valid information. This means that public relations must rely on rigorous, scientifically valid empirical research. The difference between academic research and public relations research is in the types of data collected and the use of those data. Academic research is focused on advancing knowledge, and often knowledge for knowledge's sake. Public relations research is more applied. It is less interested in testing hypotheses than providing direction for campaign planning or evaluation. It uses data differently. Public relations needs "actionable" data — data that can be used to make decisions for applied purposes.

Survey Research

Public relations utilizes both quantitative and qualitative research. The two "bread and butter" methods are survey research and focus group research.

Publics of interest are often large. Survey research is the best method available for describing a public that is too large for direct observation. That is, with the random sampling methods used in survey research, one can accurately describe the knowledge, predispositions and behavior of a large population (within a certain margin of error). If you need a refresher on survey research, you may wish to reread Prof. Luther's treatment of it in chapter 10 of this book.

Survey research is a wonderful method for public relations. With it, the public relations practitioner can identify the publics, including how best to reach them. A survey will also determine levels of knowledge, predisposition and behavior.

Surveys are often used to determine the starting point, or the benchmark, to be used later in evaluating the success of a campaign and the tactics or activities that were used. For example, a public relations campaign or "outcome" objective might be to "increase the number of employees who say the organization does an 'excellent' job of keeping them informed from 50% to 75% by March 24." The initial survey might find that 50% of the employees think the organization does an excellent job of keeping them informed. This 50% is the benchmark. It is what exists now. Activities geared at increasing that predisposition from 50% to 75% would be implemented — e.g., increasing the frequency of the company newsletter, sending e-mail notices about company news that occurs between newsletters, starting a blog focusing on employee concerns or encouraging interactive posts to the organization's blog. On March 24, a follow-up survey would check employee attitudes toward the organization's internal communications by asking the same question asked in the benchmark survey. If 75% say the organization is doing an "excellent job" of keeping them informed, then the organization achieved its objective.

The other frequently used research method in public relations is the focus group. If you need a refresher on this method, you may wish to reread Prof. Tuten's discussion in chapter 18 of this book.

Focus Groups

Focus groups can be used as stand-alone research methods or in conjunction with other methods. For example, a public relations researcher might use focus groups prior to conducting a survey in order to improve the quality of the questions asked.

That is, focus group data can help public relations researchers understand how people are thinking and talking about an issue, the words and phrases they use, the arguments they construct, etc. This type of information can be incorporated into the survey questions. With the insight gained from the focus groups, the public relations researcher will be better able to write questions that are on point with how the public is thinking.

Focus groups also can be conducted after a survey is completed and thus, for example, help clarify confusing findings. Suppose you conducted a survey of the residents in the community where one of your company's factories is located. You ask respondents to rate your company on a number of issues. The information you get back is generally positive and indicates that the company is being a pretty good "corporate citizen." However, the youngest participants in the survey give the company a low rating on being socially responsible. The survey results are unable to shed light on why this is the case. Focus group research with young participants will allow you to explore this issue in more detail and perhaps understand what your company is doing wrong in the eyes of this particular public as well as how to correct the situation.

In an attempt to understand publics, public relations practitioners find focus group research very helpful. Of course, one cannot generalize from a small sample to a larger population with any degree of statistical accuracy. However, focus group results allow the public relations practitioner to dig deeper into the factors that influence the knowledge, predispositions and behaviors of the publics of interest. Focus groups also allow access to the comments and language used by these publics that might be missed with survey research or with other methods.

Q METHODOLOGY

Q methodology is the most powerful research tool available to the public relations practitioner. Q measures holistic attitudes, not the bits and pieces of attitudes that survey research typically measures. Q methodology also overcomes the inarticulateness frequently observed in focus groups or in-depth interviews.

Q methodology is a method for the scientific study of subjectivity. The study of subjectivity seems strange given that we live in an "objective science" world. Q methodology does not fit neatly into the qualitative or the quantitative camps. It is best viewed as a bridge between quantitative and qualitative research.

Q methodology was invented by British physicist and psychologist William Stephenson (1953) and initially was used mostly in psychology. Q was then picked up in other academic fields and in the practice of journalism, political science, advertising, marketing, political consulting and others. Lately, this method has migrated to public relations.

Q methodology is important for public relations because it provides insight into the subjective and holistic views of publics. By knowing the subjectivity of people with whom you want to communicate, your communication will reflect your understanding of them. This leads to more successful public relations. Given the desire of public relations to build and maintain positive relationships, mutual understanding and open communication between an organization and its publics, having this type of information about people with whom you need to communicate is invaluable.

Fundamentally, Q methodology is a *rank-ordering procedure*. Participants rank-order various statements of opinion (known as the "Q sample") according to some "condition of instruction" (e.g., from "most agree" to "most disagree"). The resulting "Q sorts" are then correlated and factor analyzed. People who have sorted the statements in a similar fashion will cluster together on a factor. A factor represents a point of view or attitude of those "loaded" (that is, clustered) on the factor. Other participants who sort the statements similarly to each other, but differently than those on the first factor, will cluster together on a different factor. This other factor represents a different point of view or attitude. For a detailed description of Q methodology, see Brown (1980, 1986) and McKeown and Thomas (1988).

Once the computer has determined the factor structure, the researcher must "interpret" what points of view or attitudes are held by the people on each factor.

Let's look at an example that will illustrate the power, yet simplicity, of Q methodology. It comes from a public relations campaign in which the author of this chapter was involved.

A CASE STUDY:
Selecting a
Winning Slogan

Several years ago, I conducted research to guide an issue campaign in the Midwest. A local community college (which I'll refer to here as CC) placed an issue on the ballot, requesting voters to increase their property tax. The increased tax revenues would go to the CC for improvements to its infrastructure, facilities, new equipment, etc.

A big question on the minds of the campaign committee was "What is our perceived role in the community?" That is, is CC a traditional college, where a high school graduate might go for the first couple years of a college education and then transfer to a larger four-year degree granting institution? Or, is CC more of a training and retraining facility — a place where a laid-off autoworker, for example, might go to be retrained in some other job skill?

We started our research, as is typical, with a large-sample (n = 600) benchmark survey in the county to examine our public's (voters in this case) knowledge, predispositions and behaviors regarding CC. On the key question of CC's role, one-third said it should be traditional education. Another third said it should be one of training and retraining. The final third refused to choose and volunteered that CC should do both.

CC needed to do both (training and traditional education) and to stress both during the campaign. To emphasize one over the other would run the risk of alienating a significant portion of the electorate. But how does one pick a slogan or theme for a campaign that must appeal to apparently two diverse groups of voters?

The ad agency, campaign committee and researchers pulled together, for assessment during a focus group, 33 possible slogans to give to voters. The focus group participants sorted the 33 slogans from "most appealing" to "most unappealing." The resulting Q sorts were correlated and factor analyzed. Two factors emerged — a "training factor" and a "traditional education factor."

Participants associated with the training factor found most appealing the following slogans:

"CC: Training For Today," ""CC: A Real Education For The Real World," and "Help Yourself."

Participants associated with the traditional-education factor found most appealing these slogans:

"CC: On Course For The Future," "CC: The Community's College," and "CC: Learning More For Less."

Applying Q Methodology

To pick a powerful slogan for the campaign, we needed to examine the consensus items from the Q results. Consensus items were items that both groups of participants scored the same. Consensus items can be positive, negative or neutral. In this case, we needed a positive consensus slogan, a slogan that appealed to both groups. The positive consensus slogan that we selected was "CC: Where Futures Begin."

It is easy to see how this slogan might appeal to each perspective. Let's say, I'm a laid-off autoworker thinking, "Now what am I going to do? I'm going to go to CC. That's where my future will begin." Or let's say I'm a recent graduate of high school. "Now what? CC, that's where my future begins."

"CC: Where Futures Begin" became the slogan and theme for the campaign. It was used as the tag on the radio and television spots. It was prominently featured on all printed campaign material. The campaign won by a greater margin than polls had originally predicted. "CC: Where Futures Begin" was viewed as a major contributor to the success of the campaign.

As this example suggests, Q methodology can be useful in speech writing, message construction, audience segmentation, and other ways. By having access to the public's subjectivity, the public relations practitioner will be better equipped to understand, communicate and build lasting relationships.

TWO-WAY COMMUNICATION

Successful public relations is characterized by two-way communication. Two-way communication can be either *asymmetrical* or *symmetrical*. By utilizing research, public relations can practice both of them.

Asymmetrical Communication

Two-way *asymmetrical* communication uses research to acquire reliable insight into the public's level of knowledge, predispositions and behaviors, in order to create more powerful messages targeted at the public. Its aim is to figure out how to persuade publics to behave as an organization wants them to do. For example, the American Heart Association might use data from public relations research to develop messages to convince people that part of managing type 2 diabetes is maintaining a heart-healthy diet and making smart food choices.

Symmetrical Communication

Two-way *symmetrical* communication also involves research. However, it seeks to promote mutual understanding, develop ongoing communication and manage long lasting relationships. The goals of two-way symmetrical research are successful negotiation, compromise and "win-win" solutions for the public and the organization. An organization that practices two-way symmetrical communication will be characterized by senior management changing views and policies based on its understanding of what the public wants.

Two-way symmetrical communication is viewed as the most effective and efficient form of public relations, and it is also seen as the most ethical form. The idea is for organizations to understand the point of view of their publics and for the publics to understand the organizations' point of view. By accurately understanding each side's point of view, better communication can take place, leading eventually to positive relationships.

COORIENTATION

A Research Model for
Two-Way Symmetrical
Communication

To successfully practice two-way symmetrical communication, a *coorientational model* can provide the structure and direction needed to design and collect the most appropriate research data. "In the two-way symmetric model," note Grunig and Hunt (1984), "... public relations people do not change only the orientation of publics. They try to change the way the organization and its publics jointly orient to each other and the common parts of their environments" (p. 127). From this perspective, communication attitudinal effects are best defined as *coorientational effects*.

Coorientational models were first advanced by interpersonal communication scholars attempting to define communication. Newcomb's (1953) A-to-B-re-X model of communication, for example, simply indicates that person A talks to person B about any topic X. That is, A and B co-orient on a topic.

The analysis model in public relations follows Chaffee and McLeod's (1968) coorientational methodology. The basic idea is to analyze an organization and one of its publics as a social unit, not as unrelated entities. For example, for the organization, two measures are taken: first, the organization's own view of itself; and, second, its perception of the public's view of the organization. Similarly for the public, two measures are taken: the public's own view of the organization; and, second, the public's perception of how the organization views itself.

Agreement,
Accuracy and
Congruency

Cross comparisons are then made to determine *agreement* and *accuracy*, important concepts in communication between an organization and its publics. The *level of agreement* is calculated by looking at the organization's view of itself and the public's view of the organization. *Accuracy* can be calculated for both the organization and the public. That is, how accurate is each in estimating the other's point of view? The organization's accuracy is determined by comparing the organization's perception of how the public views the organization and the public's actual view. The public's accuracy is determined by examining the public's perception of how the organization views itself and the organization's actual view.

One additional coorientational variable can be calculated from the data con-*gruency* (i.e., perceived agreement). Congruency does not describe the relationship between the organization and its public. It describes how one side views the relationship and provides insights on the extent to which the organization or the public thinks the other's views are similar to its own.

Using such a coorientational model, both the organization and a public can be described as being *cognitive* of what each thinks of the organization's characteristics, its issues, its reputation and so on. Each is further able to evaluate that cognition and form an attitude/orientation on the value of the subject at hand. Finally, coorientation assumes that both the organization and the public have a perception of each other's views, ideas and evaluation on that same subject. Grunig and Hunt explain that in considering if perceptions coincide, "The parts of the coorientation model that help us to define symmetric communication effects are the relationships between the [actual] ideas and evaluations and the perceived ideas and evaluations" (1984, p. 128).

Reputation

Reputation is an important concept in a coorientation model. To reduce the possibility of misperceiving reputation, it is important to define and assess the concept accurately. A coorientational agreement approach allows for an intensive and holistic diagnostic of how an organization and a public perceive or coorientate on the idea of reputation. Through this process, reputation can be modeled and audited, relationships can be assessed and reputation benchmarks can be set. Coorientational outcomes and findings can then be used in setting reputation management goals and objectives based on achieved symmetry of communication whether for agreement or accuracy.

A COORIENTATION CASE STUDY: Reputation Management

To illustrate the coorientation model, let's examine an actual study in detail. It is one in which Christiane Pagé and I used a coorientation model to examine the reputation of a long-distance learning program (Pagé and Kinsey, 1997). The organization was an independent study degree program (ISDP) affiliated with a private university in the northeastern United States.

For the coorientational purposes of the study, the views of faculty and administrators represent the organization's views, while the views of current and recent students represent the public's view.

A 36-item questionnaire was sent to the organization's representatives (faculty and administration) and to the public (the students). Questions were based on the *Fortune* magazine reputation criteria for most admired corporations. *Fortune* annually lists the most admired corporations. Its ranking is made up of eight items: quality of management; quality of products or services; innovativeness; value as long-term investment; financial soundness; ability to attract, develop and keep talented people; community and environmental responsibility; and use of corporate assets.

Respondents to our questionnaire about the long-distance learning program were asked to answer each of the 36 questions twice — once to represent their view and again to represent how they thought the other side would answer.

Indices of Reputation and Symmetrical Communication

We developed nine indices from the 36 question items — eight indices to represent the *Fortune* magazine reputation criteria and one to represent symmetrical communication. The items were structured in the following manner:

1. *Quality of Management* was an index consisting of four question items. An index is a new variable created by adding the results of separate questions together. We asked all respondents to indicate, on a scale of 1 to 7 where 1 means *strongly disagree* and 7 means *strongly agree*, how much they agreed or disagreed with each of the following items:

"The management of the program is of the highest quality."

"Business planning is a big part of the program's success."

"Management policies, values and behaviors are consistent with the vision and goals of the program."

"Students are seen as partners in the management of the program's reputation; their opinions are sought and respected."

(Scale mean = 20.26; SD = 3.82; Cronbach's alpha = .79)

2. *Quality of Products and Services* was an index consisting of the following four items scored on the same 1 to 7 scale:

"The program is the industry leader."

"There is consistency in the excellence of the teaching and curriculum."

"The program delivers value and stands behind its products and services."

"[The university's] 'student centered' values are apparent in the quality and level or professionalism of the administration of the program."

(Scale mean = 21.13; SD = 3.72; Cronbach's alpha = .83)

3. *Financial Soundness* was an index consisting of the following four items scored on the same 1 to 7 scale:

"The program has the support and financial backing of [the university]."

"[The university] and ISDP planned for this start-up program understanding that there are high costs associated to developing, launching and sustaining such a program in its introduction and growth phases."

"The program believes in crisis prevention and crisis communications planning."

"The program is managed efficiently; its efficiency is measurable (demonstrable, provable, quantifiable)."

(Scale mean = 20.70; SD = 3.81; Cronbach's alpha = .67)

4. *Ability to Attract and Keep Talented People* was an index consisting of the following four items scored on the same 1 to 7 scale:

"The program attracts and keeps quality students."

"The program attracts and keeps quality faculty."

"The faculty and the students trust that the program has their best interests in mind."

"Entry requirements are high and are used effectively to help attract the best students."

(Scale mean = 23.48; SD = 2.48; Cronbach's alpha = .71)

5. *Innovativeness* was an index consisting of the following four items scored on the same 1 to 7 scale:

"The program is not risk averse. It sees getting to the top as a constant challenge. It is not complacent and continues to take risks that will help get it there."

Continued on next page

"The program is innovative and growth oriented."

"The program provides students the autonomy to make decisions and discretion to control projects and assignments."

"[The university] is considered a national pioneer in developing independent study degree programs that make independent learning marketable — generating responsible, highly motivated, highly organized and strategically inclined graduates."

(Scale mean = 21.52; SD = 3.81; Cronbach's alpha = .69)

6. *Long-Term Investment Value* was an index consisting of the following four items scored on the same 1 to 7 scale:

"The program gives public relations practitioners the managerial skills they need to grow professionally."

"This program fills a competitive void and its formula affords it a sustainable advantage."
"There is value in the longevity of the program that impacts the long-term value of the diploma."

"The program offers value in condensing education and professional development in a cost-and-time-effective formula that has lifetime benefits."

(Scale mean = 23.39; SD = 2.39; Cronbach's alpha = .46)

7. *Community Responsibility* was an index consisting of the following four items scored on the same 1 to 7 scale:

"The program believes it has a responsibility to help each student have a successful educational experience."

"The program recognizes the value of the human systems and the interpersonal networks it generates and, although it keeps a close eye on efficiency, it does not put management efficiency and quantification of financial results ahead or its human systems at all costs."

"The program is involved in and cares about the public relations and communications management professional community."

"The program can expand and can afford to try some new activities because of its reputation."

(Scale mean = 23.39; SD = 2.72; Cronbach's alpha = .50)

8. *Use of Corporate Assets* was an index consisting of the following four items scored on the same 1 to 7 scale:

"[The school] has a good reputation in the business community."

"The program has a good reputation in the business community."

"The fact that the program is fully accredited by [the state] creates reputational equity."

"The fact that the program's advisory board is made up of opinion leaders and leaders in the field is used as reputational capital for the program."

(Scale mean = 21.22; SD = 3.13; Cronbach's alpha = .51)

9. *Symmetrical Communication* was an index consisting of the following four items scored on the same 1 to 7 scale:

"The program listens to the students, respects what they have to say/contribute in terms of innovative ideas, and adjusts quickly to match expectations and needs."

"The program holds an open dialogue with and seeks feed-back from participating faculty and

Continued on next page

administrators."

"The program effectively negotiates for faculty from a variety of [the university] schools and manages its relationships to increase the value of the program."

"Conflict resolution is used in this program as an ethical and effective means to work out problems and improve information flow between its constituencies."

(Scale mean = 20.09; SD = 4.34; Cronbach's alpha = .81)

Results

We ran a series of t-tests to compare similarities and differences between the organization and its public for the coorientation measures of accuracy and agreement. The coorientation measure of congruency was examined within each party.

Measures of Agreement for Reputation Indices

On eight of the nine reputation indices, there was no significant difference between the organization's rating of itself and the public's rating of the organization. That is, there was considerable agreement on the rating of the organization on "Quality of Products and Services," "Financial Soundness," "Ability to Attract and Keep Talented People," "Innovativeness," "Long-Term Investment Value," "Community Responsibility," "Use of Corporate Assets" and "Symmetrical Communication." On all eight of these indices, the organization's view of itself was slightly higher, though not significantly so, than was the public's view of the organization.

However, the organization rated "Quality of Management" significantly higher than the public did. Further analysis revealed that the difference in views was pronounced in two of the four question items that made up this index: "Students are seen as partners in the management of the program's reputation; their opinions are sought and respected" ($t = 3.69$, $p < .001$), and "Business planning is a big part of the program's success" ($t = 2.82$, $p < .01$). On the other two items in the "Quality of Management" index — "The management of the program is of the highest quality" and "Management policies, values and behaviors are consistent with the vision and goals of the program" — there was no difference in rating ($t = 1.26$, n.s., and $t = .99$, n.s.).

Measures of Accuracy: Examining Each Other's Views

In examining the results of the study, we found that there were no significant differences between the organization's perception of the public's view of the organization and the public's actual view. That is, the organization was fairly accurate in estimating how the public saw it. It is interesting to note, however, that on seven out of nine indices the organization overestimated the public's view. This was especially prevalent on "Quality of Management" and "Symmetrical Communication."

There were no significant differences between the public's perception of the organization's view of the organization and the organization's actual view. That is, the public was fairly accurate in estimating how the organization saw itself. However, it is interesting to note that on eight out of nine indices the public overestimated the organization's view. This was especially prevalent on "Symmetrical Communication."

Measures of Congruency

The organization's views were quite congruent. That is, the organization's own view and the organization's perception of the public's view were not significantly different on eight out of nine indices. The only significant difference was on "Financial Soundness." Further analysis revealed that the significant lack of congruency was manifest in two of the four question items that made up this index: "The program is managed efficiently; its efficiency is measurable (demonstrable, provable, quantifiable)" (t= 3.86, p < .01), and "The program has the support and financial backing of [the university]" (t = 2.55, p < .05).

In both cases, the organization's own view was significantly higher than its perception of the public's view. There was no difference in congruency on "The program believes in crisis prevention and crisis communications planning" (t = 1.00, n.s.), and "[The university] and ISDP planned for this start-up program understanding that there are high costs associated to developing, launching and sustaining such a program in its introduction and growth phases" (t = 2.16, n.s.).

However, there was little congruency in the public's view. That is, the public's view of the organization and the public's perception of the organization's view were significantly different on all nine indices. In each case, the public's estimate of the organization's view was significantly higher than the public's own view of the organization.

The value of coorientation research to public relations can be seen in this example. The results revealed no explicit or immediate reputation problem for the ISDP program. In fact, the results showed high agreement and high accuracy between the views of the organization and the public. That is, the public and the organization actually agreed on the reputation of the program and that agreement was accurately perceived. *What the Case Study Discovered*

The most significant findings were in the area of congruency or perceived agreement measures from the public side. Where most of the coorientational outcomes consistently converged on consensus where agreement was concerned, a significant disconnect occurred at the level of the public's estimation of the organization's view. That the public systematically rated the organization's view of itself as higher than its own view of the organization was of concern. "Perceived agreement" was a significant indicator of how the public might look at its relationship with an organization. It could indicate future behavior and enactment of this public or of other similar publics such as subsequent new classes enrolling in the program. Perceived agreement, as noted earlier, does not describe the relationship that a public has with an organization. What it does highlight is what a public thinks of the relationship. In this case it seemed to denote, in the mind of the public, a sense of perceived imbalance in the relationship.

In conclusion, we can observe that this particular reputation case study of the ISDP program exemplifies the flexibility and vast diagnostic capabilities of the coorientational model for public relations research.

THE EXCELLENCE STUDY

The most influential and important public relations research project conducted in the last few decades was the "Excellence Study." It was commissioned and funded by the International Association of Business Communicators (IABC) Research Foundation. It was one of the largest public relations studies ever conducted. The results have greatly influenced the focus and direction of academic and applied public relations research.

The study focused on two fundamental research questions: (1) What are the characteristics of an excellent communication department, and (2) How does excellent communication management and public relations make an organization more effective, and how much is that contribution worth economically?

To answer these questions, the researchers surveyed the CEOs, top communicators and employees in 148 corporations, 58 not-for-profit organizations, 71 government agencies and 44 professional-trade associations in Canada, the United Kingdom and the United States.

The findings highlight the importance of the knowledge base of an organization's communication department, the shared expectations of top communicators and senior managers about the function and role of communication, and the importance of an organization's culture either to nurture or impede communication excellence. CEOs in organizations that practiced excellent public relations estimated a greater return of investment for communication expenditures than did CEOs with least-excellent programs.

THE FUTURE OF PR RESEARCH

Research is essential to the public relations process. Research has played an important role in public relations for generations. All research methods, qualitative and quantitative, can be used in public relations as appropriate. The most important methods have been survey research and focus group research. Those methods, along with Q methodology, probably will become even more important in the future.

TO LEARN MORE

Aldoory, L. (1998). The language of leadership for female public relations professionals. *Journal of Public Relations Research, 10,* 73-101.

Alessandri, S. W., Yang, S-U., & Kinsey, D.F. (2006). An integrative approach to university visual identity and reputation. *Corporate Reputation Review, 9,* 258-270.

Cameron, G. T., Cropp, F., & Reber, B. H. (2001). Getting past platitudes: Factors limiting accommodation in public relations. *Journal of Communication Management, 5,* 242-261.

Cutlip, S. M., Center, A. H., & Broom, G. M. (2006). *Effective Public Relations.* Englewood Cliffs, NJ: Prentice-Hall.

Downes, E. J. (1998). Hacks, flacks and spin doctors meet the media: An examination of the congressional press secretary as a (potential) public relations professional. *Journal of Public Relations Research, 19,* 263-286.

Dozier, D. M., Grunig, L. A., & Grunig, J. E. (1995). *Manager's guide to excellence in public relations and communication management.* Mahwah, NJ: Lawrence Erlbaum Associates.

Evatt, D. S., Ruiz, C., & Triplett, J. F. (2005). *Thinking big, staying small: Communication practices of small organizations.* San Francisco, CA: International Association of Business Communicators.

Grunig, J. E. (Ed.). (1992). *Excellence in public relations and communication management.* Hillsdale, NJ: Lawrence Erlbaum Associates.

Grunig, J. E., Grunig, L. A., & Dozier, D. M. (2002). *Excellent public relations and effective organizations: A study of communication management in three counties.* Mahwah, NJ: Lawrence Erlbaum Associates.

Grunig, L. A. (1992). Matching public relations research to the problem: Conducting a special focus group. *Journal of Public Relations Research, 4,* 21-43.

Grunig, L. A. (1993). Image and symbolic leadership: Using focus group research to bridge the gaps. *Journal of Public Relations Research, 5,* 95-125.

Krueger, R. A. & Casey, M. A. (2000). *Focus groups: A practical guide for applied research.* Thousand Oaks, CA: Sage Publications.

Lyon, L. & Cameron, G. T. (2004). A relational approach examining the interplay of prior reputation and immediate response to a crisis. *Journal of Public Relations Research, 16,* 213-241.

Stacks, D. W. (2002). *Primer of public relations research.* New York: The Guilford Press.

Yang, S-U. (2007). An integrated model for organization-public relational outcomes, organizational reputation and their Antecedents. *Journal of Public Relations Research 19,* 91-121.

REFERENCES

Brown, S. R. (1980). *Political subjectivity: Applications of Q methodology in political science.* New Haven, CT: Yale University Press.

Brown, S. R. (1986). Q technique and method: Principles and procedures. In W. D. Berry & M. S. Lewis-Beck (Eds.) *New tools for social scientists: Advances and applications in research methods* (pp. 57-76). Beverly Hills, CA: Sage Publications.

Chaffee, S. H., & McLeod, J. M. (1968). Sensitization in panel design: A coorientation experiment. *Journalism Quarterly, 45,* 661-669.

Grunig, J. E., & Hunt, T. (1984). *Managing Public Relations.* New York: Holt, Rinehart and Winston.

Hendrix, J. A. & Hayes, D. C. (2007). *Public relations cases (7th Edition).* Belmont, CA: Thomson Wadsworth.

Kinsey, D. F. (1991). Selecting a winning campaign slogan. *Operant Subjectivity, 15,* 1-10.

Marston, J. A. (1963). *The nature of public relations.* New York: McGraw Hill.

McKeown, B. & Thomas, D. (1988). *Q Methodology.* Newbury Park, CA: Sage Publications.

Newcomb, T. M. (1953). An approach to the study of communicative acts. *Psychological Review, 60,* 393-404.

Pagé, C., & Kinsey, D. F. (1997). *A coorientational model for reputation management.* Paper presented to the Annual Conference of the International Association of Business Communicators, Los Angeles, California.

Parkinson, M. G. & Ekachai, D. (2006). *International and intercultural public relations: A campaign case approach.* Boston, MA: Pearson Education, Inc.

Stephenson, W. (1953). *The study of behavior: Q-technique and its methodology.* Chicago: University of Chicago Press.

23 Advertising Research

Research is essential to effective advertising. It's used to shape the messages that advertisers deliver to target audiences. It also helps advertisers determine how to reinforce or change consumer attitudes to impact behavior in some measurable fashion. Advertising is not about just being clear. It's about delivering a carefully crafted message, being persuasive and presenting a company or brand in the best possible light. Business and consumer markets are very fluid. What was hot last week may be long forgotten this week. Advertising research plays a huge role in determining this dynamic.

RESEARCH KNOWLEDGE IS POWER! Research directly impacts advertising strategy development and ultimately creative execution. Research insight is more important than ever. There are five major trends contributing to the need for advertising research today. They are the following:

1. Competition
2. The Internet
3. More parity products
4. Explosion of media choices
5. Changing consumer markets

Let's look briefly at each one.

Competition
Business today is increasingly competitive. Managers are trying to position their businesses to thrive among myriad changes, and technology is accelerating this dynamic. In *The World is Flat*, Thomas Friedman describes how technology is being used to provide a competitive edge to businesses around the world. India has become a hub of customer service call centers for many large multi-national companies, and the Internet infrastructure in other parts of the

By Cliff Shaluta
Western Kentucky University

world has made it easy for their citizens to compete in a global economy. The relative ease of entry for online ventures and general competitive pressures demand that the marketing and advertising efforts for any business must produce results. There is tremendous pressure on businesses to improve. Regular research can create a strategic advantage.

The Internet

Consumer use of the Internet is exploding. According to the *Pew Internet & American Life Project* website (updated January of 2010), "74% of American adults (ages 18 and older) use the internet." The Internet provides the infrastructure necessary for businesses to operate in new and innovative ways. But the Internet also means that consumers have a wealth of data available as they make purchase decisions. Websites like http://www.nextag.com rank products based on prices. Information based on competitive data clearly makes selling online more challenging than selling through traditional retail channels. The Internet can assist managers by providing tremendous behavioral research through *web analytics*. This relatively young area in advertising research measures and evaluates consumer use of specific websites. The objective of web analytics is to better understand overall website traffic as well as the performance of specific pages within the website.

More Parity Products

A quick tour of any American supermarket will demonstrate the sheer number of products available to consumers. Angela Lee of Northwestern University and Aparna Labroo of the University of Chicago report on the Association for Consumer Research website that marketers and advertisers "are on the constant lookout for ad copy strategies that can break through the clutter, change consumer perception, develop preference, and foster brand loyalty." Building a strong brand identity requires creative insight, time and money. But brands dominate in a world of other great products. Brands allow goods to rise above parity products — items that are essentially alike — in the marketplace. Consumers often perceive name brand products to be better, whether they really are or not. Differentiation is the key to success, and successful brands are made distinctive. Consumer research can lead to effective advertising that shapes brand image.

Explosion of Media Choices

The 500+ TV channel universe that was beyond belief just a few years ago now seems somewhat dated. Consumer media choices today are truly staggering. From broadcast television to viral videos, the media landscape is undergoing an unprecedented transformation. Back in the 1960s, it would have been relatively easy to reach 80% or more of the U.S. viewing audience with ads on one or two of the broadcast networks. That is nearly impossible today using only broadcast television. Advertising on the Internet almost caught up with radio in 2008, and researchers predict Internet advertising will continue to grow while advertising money spent on other media may stagnate over the near future. Research is more important than ever to understand the media consumption patterns of consumers. Insights into consumer behavior can impact the development of media content as well as advertising decisions.

Changing Consumer Markets

Aging populations and the emergence of powerful ethnic markets are just two illustrations of the need to conduct regular population audits. Baby boomers — those born between 1945 and 1964 — have transformed many social institutions and continue to do so as they retire. The segment is generally much better off financially than previous generations. Understanding the mindset of boomers is crucial to advertisers, and research provides that insight. Advertising agency Saatchi & Saatchi's use of Dennis Hopper to promote Ameriprise retirement planning services is strategically sound based on today's demographics. According to an online press release by Ameriprise (2006), the use of Hopper and retirement "dreams" in the advertisements will appeal to boomers. The emergence of the Hispanic market is also attracting advertisers of all types. According to the Pew Hispanic Center (2008), "The Latino population, already the nation's largest minority group, will triple in size and will account for most of the nation's population growth from 2005 through 2050." Research not only helps advertisers understand the size of emerging markets, but it also provides a look into the mindset of these markets.

IS ADVERTISING RESEARCH DIFFERENT?

Advertising research uses many of the same methodologies that are used in other fields, but the purpose or intent of the work is likely to be different.

Applied, Basic and Methodological Research

Much of the research used to develop advertising strategies and creative executions is *applied research*.

Applied research focuses on a specific situation at a specific point in time. It can rarely be generalized from one situation to another situation. Thus, the shelf life of applied research is relatively short when compared to basic or methodological research.

Basic research studies advertising issues with the intent to share ideas and information to enhance the general field of advertising. It is often conducted by academicians, think tanks or foundations. It is shared freely through journals, such as the *Journal of Advertising Research*.

The intent of *methodological research* is to provide discussion and insight about research methods. The primary goal is to help develop more accurate data collection methods. Methodological research is also more likely to be conducted by academicians or theorists than agency employees.

Exploratory or Predictive Research

Another way to categorize the intent of advertising research is to look at its specific purpose or range. There are times when research is used at the beginning of a campaign to gain insight into the thoughts of consumers on an issue, product or service. The intent of *exploratory research* is to brainstorm with consumers to generate campaign ideas or to validate as quickly as possible survey instruments such as lists of focus-group questions. Exploratory research is not generally meant to provide statistically useful information. It is limited in scope and application. *Predictive research* attempts to test a hypothesis. A direct marketer may use predictive research methods to determine, for example, which of two catalogs will generate more orders. For a review of research categorization, you may wish to reread Prof. Zhou's Chapter 1 in this book.

The methods that advertising researchers use are commonly organized by *secondary* or *primary data collection.*

Secondary researchers use existing published resources to develop a basic understanding of a particular industry, company or consumer market. This information is used to help complete a *situation analysis* or *SWOT (strengths, weaknesses, opportunities or threats).* The situation analysis provides the foundation needed to develop strategic advertising decisions. Secondary research also provides benchmarks to draw comparisons and can create a basis for more comprehensive research projects later.

Advertising makes full use of the *primary* research tools described throughout this book, including mail surveys, telephone interviews, personal intercepts and Internet surveys to collect quantitative data. Advertising researchers also make liberal use of qualitative research, such as in-depth interviews, focus groups and ethnographic studies to uncover consumer insight that will, they hope, lead to creative advertising.

Given the range of potential options for researchers, it is useful to understand how these tools are used in (1) developing, (2) monitoring and (3) evaluating advertising campaigns. Let's look at each of these three stages in research.

THE PURPOSE OF ADVERTISING RESEARCH

RESEARCH USED TO DEVELOP AD CAMPAIGNS

Research is often used to develop advertising campaign strategies or to test creative executions before launch of the plan. Time spent testing ideas before the rollout of a campaign can be a great investment for advertisers. Advertisers who must change aspects of a campaign after roll out certainly waste valuable time and money. There are five typical ways that research can be used in advertising campaign development. They are the following:

1. Consumer research
2. Media audience research
3. Competitive activity research
4. Positioning research
5. Creative testing

Let's look at how each one works.

Consumer Research

Advertisers are interested in reaching the right audience in the right place at the right time. Understanding the *demographics* and *psychographics* of key consumers is a competitive imperative. Knowledge of consumers is essential to develop a strategy to reach and motivate them with a message that resonates.

Audience Research

Researchers seek to measure the audience size and composition of various media outlets. Media planners can't make intelligent decisions without this information. Measuring media audiences is huge business. Key research companies include Nielsen for TV and Arbitron for radio audiences. Nielsen and Arbitron are involved in developing media usage numbers for the Internet as well. They rely on web analytics and sampling representative user groups to project audience figures to the larger population.

Competitive Activity Research

The purpose of competitive activity research is to learn how much money competitors spend on advertising and what media they are buying. Competitive research may also be concerned with the creative plans of competitors, such as new campaigns or promotions. All of this information helps form the basis of strategy development. Advertisers may choose to copy a competitor or proceed in a completely different manner. Key sources for researchers are *Leading National Advertisers (LNA)* and *Broadcast Advertiser Reports (BAR)*.

Positioning Research

Positioning is the view or perception that consumers have of a business, product or brand. Advertisers can easily capitalize on a favorable position, while an unfavorable position is problematic for the advertiser. Since position can change, it is important for advertisers to monitor consumer perceptions over time.

Creative Testing

Creative testing attempts to quantify the ability of test ads to deliver a specific message or leave the consumer with a certain impression. As Jack Meyers (2006) explains, there has "always been debate about how effective creative testing is in identifying effective ads." The debate generally centers on whether it is really possible to measure creativity. Researchers in this area of advertising research counter that they are measuring the effectiveness of a test ad to deliver a specific message, not the perception of the ad's creativity.

SYNDICATED RESEARCH

Secondary research can provide a general overview of the business climate, competitive situation and overall consumer trends. But there are also several *syndicated research* sources that advertisers commonly use to help develop more specific information on consumer demographics, psychographics, usage patterns and possible media options. Let's look at the major ones.

GfK Mediamark Research & Intelligence

GfK MRI, formerly Mediamark Research and Intelligence, has been gathering consumer information since 1978. Its *Survey of the American Consumer* is very popular with marketers. According to its website, the massive annual survey includes "consumer product usage, demographic/psychographic information and media habits from face-to-face interviews with over 26,000 American consumers." GfK MRI reports that its "data set includes information on 6,000+ brands in 550 different categories."

The use of personal interviews makes GfK MRI unique, as most syndicated research companies rely on mail or telephone interviews to gather information, according to the company. GfK MRI sends a letter of introduction to a random sample of potential respondents spanning a cross-section of consumer groups. Once the respondents agree to participate, a GfK MRI representative visits them to conduct the survey and leave a written questionnaire. The representative returns later to pick up the completed questionnaire.

Since 1954, Simmons Market Research Bureau has been conducting interviews each year for its reports on consumer buying habits and magazine readership. Today, as part of Experian Marketing Solutions, **Simmons Market Research Bureau** the company offers clients an extensive list of research services. According to the SMRB website, the Simmons' National Consumer Study collects over 60,000 data variables from 25,000 American consumers. The research is conducted in two phases. Phase 1 consists of a telephone interview to recruit subjects. Phase 2 is the mailing of a self-administered survey booklet to each participant. The result is a "comprehensive data set including 450+ product categories and 8,000+ brands." The study includes extensive demographic and psychographic information that researchers can use to develop a consumer analysis and a rough strategy.

According to the its website, VALS was originally developed by "futurist Arnold Mitchell in the 1970's." SRI International formally **VALS** adopted it in 1978. The VALS system categorizes individuals into eight groups based on their answers to a number of attitude and demographic questions. It further organizes individuals into "primary motivations" and "resources." Primary motivations include those individuals who are "ideals motivated," "achievement motivated" or "self-expression motivated." Individuals who are more ideals-motivated are driven by what they believe to be right rather than by raw emotions. Achievement-motivated individuals want products or services that help them reach their goals or be more efficient. Individuals motivated by self-expression are looking for variety and risk taking. The VALS system also factors various resources into its typology. Resources include income, education and willingness to take risks.

In 1974, Jonathan Robbin cross-referenced United States postal ZIP codes with census data and consumer surveys to create the first "consumer clusters" (Weiss 1988). According to the PRIZM website, Claritas (now owned by Nielsen) uses the PRIZM (Potential Rating Index for ZIP Markets) system to rank more than 66 clusters for its clients. According to the company, PRIZM can be used to determine the "best retail site locations as well as the consumer groups with the most sales potential for specific products." The 66 PRIZM segments, outlined on its website, are divided into 14 "Social Groups," based on "urbanization and socioeconomic rank." These groups range from "U1 - Urban Uptown to T4 - Rustic Living." PRIZM also clusters consumers using 11 "LifeStage Groups organized by age, children in the home and socioeconomic rank." Life-Stage groups include Y3-Striving Singles to M1-Affluent Empty Nests. The field of consumer mapping is exploding because of the "growth of databases containing millions of transactions and population trends" (Weiss 1988).

Tapestry, an innovation of ESRI Business Information Solutions, grew out of Claritas' PRIZM ZIP code system. According to the company's **Community Tapestry** website, Tapestry uses "cluster analysis to organize neighborhoods into 65 segments based on over 60 attributes, such as income, housing, employment, home value and education." As with PRIZM, retailers can use Tapestry to locate new stores or to help decide which products to offer in specific locations.

According to ESRI's Community Tapestry's Handbook, advertisers can use consumer profiles to "analyze and rank markets based on segmentation profiles or demographics targeted by age, income, lifestyle, and lifestage."

Nielsen Media Research

Nielsen Media Research is a subsidiary of ACNielsen and is located in Northbrook, Ill. VNU purchased the company in 2001. It specializes in collecting television ratings from a variety of sources, including national and regional broadcast and cable networks as well as local TV stations. It uses people meters to collect national viewership information. Researchers use a combination of meters and printed diaries to collect viewership data in the 210 local *Designated Market Areas (DMA's)* in the U.S. (Fletcher and Bowers 1987: 245). The data collection periods are called *sweeps* and occur at least four times a year. The resulting *ratings* represent a percentage of viewers watching a particular program out of the total households or population in a market. Nielsen also uses *audience share* numbers to represent the number of TV program viewers out of all TV sets turned on in a particular market. Audience share numbers reflect the viewing share that a program has out of all TV viewing in a market.

Arbitron

Arbitron, Inc., is headquartered in New York, with field offices around the U.S. It specializes in network and local radio audience research, but it also collects audience data on online radio and other media. Its national radio audience research is called RADAR. For local radio audiences, Arbitron surveys more than 250 radio markets during 12-week bursts. The largest markets are sampled four times a year. Smaller markets may only be sampled once a year. While Arbitron is leading the industry with the development of "portable people meters," printed diaries are currently the primary data collection instrument. Diaries are sent to "every person 12 and older in each cooperating household" (Fletcher and Bowers 1987:241). After follow-up phone calls by Arbitron, respondents are asked to record their radio listening habits for one week. At the end of the week, they return the diary to Arbitron in a postage-paid envelope. Surveys from each *Area of Dominant Influence* (ADI) are used to produce the actual Arbitron ratings book. It contains ADI ratings for radio stations in each market. As with television ratings, ADI ratings are segmented by different ages to help advertisers reach the right audience with their message.

Nielsen//NetRatings

Nielsen//NetRatings is a service of the Nielsen Company. It includes the Nielsen//NetRatings and BuzzMetrics brands. According to the company's website, Nielsen//NetRatings "offers a range of proprietary research tools and services to help [clients] meet [their] business challenges in a highly competitive market." Services include software to track consumer online behavior as well as consumer panels to gather in-depth usage patterns for clients.

PRIMARY RESEARCH

Syndicated research provides valuable information to help shape the advertising campaign, but primary research may be needed for more specific data collection. Primary research is collected through original means. While there are a variety of primary research methods, they are usually divided into *quantitative* and *qualitative* methods. *Quantitative re-*

search relies on sampling a representative group and using statistical analysis to generalize findings to the larger population under study. *Qualitative research* tends to utilize smaller sample sizes to develop unique insight into the consumer's mindset.

Quantitative Methods

A number of quantitative research methods are available. Among them, surveys are the most commonly used. For a review of the survey methodology and its uses, you may wish to reread Prof. Luther's Chapter 10 in this book. In addition to mail surveys, telephone surveys and face-to-face interviews, an emerging method that is particularly pertinent to advertising research is the online survey.

Online surveys are written surveys that are created using Internet services, such as http://www.surveymonkey.com/ or http://www.zoomerang.com/. These two websites, like many others, have grown over the past few years as more consumers have gone online.

While the interfaces and procedures may differ, the basic approach of online survey companies is generally the same. The services provide an easy-to-use system to post and administer surveys using the Internet. Once the survey is created, the system generates a web address that can be pasted into an e-mail cover letter or on a website. Some online survey companies also provide a pool of potential respondents. To meet pre-determined criteria, the survey companies categorize these potential respondents. For example, it's possible to draw a sample from a pool of registered users who have downloaded music in the past week or those who have made a purchase from Amazon.com in the past month.

Qualitative Methods

Qualitative research methods rely on a more personal exploration of consumer attitudes than quantitative methods do. Quantitative research can easily provide data on consumer preferences, but qualitative research has the better potential to uncover the reasons why consumers think about products in a certain way. This *behind the scenes* approach can unlock consumer insight that is often neglected in other types of research. As with quantitative research, there are several specific qualitative research methods used in advertising. Let's look at four of them.

In-depth Interviews

In-depth interviews provide a longer opportunity to interview target respondents than is usually possible with intercept research. In-depth interviews can last as long as necessary to discuss the desired questions. Personal interviews of several hours are not uncommon.

Focus Groups

Focus groups are led by a moderator who guides a group of 8 to 10 participants through a series of open-ended discussion questions pertaining to the topic under study. The objectives of focus group research are varied, and the technique can be used at almost any stage of an advertising campaign. But focus groups are particularly useful at the beginning of the advertising process. They provide unique insight into the perceptions that consumers have of a product or brand and can also be used to help generate ideas for campaigns. At the very least, focus groups can help researchers develop topics or questions that can be statistically validated later with quantitative research.

Online Focus Groups   Technology is now in place to conduct *online focus groups.* The research includes text, audio or video chat sessions with respondents.
The research company typically draws from a pool of potential participants. Online focus groups are led by a moderator and take place in a private chat room.

According to the market research firm Greenfield Online (2007), online focus
groups offer several advantages. They are efficient to administer and convenient
for participants. Groups can be organized in as little as "three days and the logis-
tics are simple as no travel or special facilities are required for the session." Group
members can participate from the comfort of their own home or office. Online
focus groups can be conducted for about "half the cost of more traditional focus
groups," according to the company. Another big advantage is that it's possible for
the researcher to utilize hybrid designs. For example, an online survey could be
administered to a pool of respondents meeting certain criteria. From that pool, a
smaller group of respondents could be pulled for an online focus group. The combination of online focus groups with other research methodologies certainly
makes this technique worth considering.

Online focus groups do, however, present several disadvantages. Greenfield
Online has found that the best groups "have 6-8 members working for no more
than 90 minutes." These limits keep the number of discussion threads to a manageable level and reduce screen fatigue. Online focus groups are ideally suited for
"straightforward topics and less suited for emotionally charged issues."

Ethnography   *Ethnography* is a type of cultural anthropology. Researchers utilize
personal observation, photo and video diaries, and in-depth inter-
views to obtain information about consumers' product and brand experiences. In
ethnography, researchers may actually dine with those they are surveying at the
restaurant under study, or play video games with consumers to capture their reactions to a specific product. Thus, ethnography is becoming popular in advertising
research because it can uncover consumer insights that are more difficult or impossible to collect with other, more quantitative research techniques. Advertising
agencies such as Goodby and BBDO Worldwide have developed special departments to collect and analyze ethnographic research. Nate Cavalieri (2005) discusses Goodby's efforts in *Real to Reel,* and *Businessweek's* Diane Brady (2007) examines
BBDO's efforts in *Daily Rituals of the World.* (The reference list at the end of this
chapter includes the URLs.)

Creative Testing   *Creative testing* attempts to help advertisers decide which ads will
deliver stated objectives before the ads actually run. Creative testing
of advertisements was formalized with the *PACT (Positioning Advertising Copy
Testing)* statement in 1981. Several prominent agencies worked together to develop a set of principles of good creative testing. The principles still apply today.

The PACT report made it clear that researchers should have specific goals
when doing creative research. These goals should relate to the objectives of the ad.
Research developers should agree on the goals of the research and how the findings will be used. For example, if an ad encourages consumers to try a product,

trials should be a part of the testing and evaluation. The advertiser and the researcher should agree on what constitutes a successful ad well before the research takes place.

The PACT group recommended that researchers should always use a *representative sample* of participants who reflect the composition of the target audience. The creative testing should then be done in such a way to ensure that the research is a valid measurement of creative impact and that the findings can be repeated under the same conditions again and again. The ability to replicate findings is a critical element in any research project. If you need a refresher on reliability, you may wish to reread Prof. Doyle's chapter 7 on measurement in this book.

The *validity* of creative testing will always be a concern for advertisers. The PACT group made several recommendations to address validity. The report suggested that *multiple measurements* be used in creative testing, so that a spectrum of persuasion can be evaluated.

Using a variety of measurements means that different types of ads can be tested, but it also enables researchers to analyze the impact of repeat exposure. It's possible that consumers may need more than one exposure to really comprehend the message of an ad.

The PACT group also acknowledged that advertisements move through production from the initial concept to rough work leading to a completed ad. It recommended that test ads be at the same stage of production so that one ad would not appear to be "better" because it looked more complete than the others. Testing ads at the same level of production also helps to ensure validity. (PACT: Positioning Advertising Copy Testing report from the *Journal of Advertising* [1982]).

Creative Testing Companies

A number of companies provide testing services for print and broadcast advertisements. The services that test print ads have a much longer history and are better known than those that test broadcast ads. The testing of a print advertisement is also easier to manage due to the nature of the test. But Amertest has been able to create an affordable and reasonably simple testing system for broadcast ads using mail survey kits. Let's look at four companies that offer services.

Gallop & Robinson

According to the Gallop & Robinson website, the company has been testing advertisements for more than 50 years. Its *Magazine Impact Research Service (MIRS)* uses a sample of 150 adults in 10 major markets across the United States. To qualify, participants must have read two of the last four issues of the test magazine or magazines of a similar genre. Participants are mailed the test magazine and are asked to read it that day. A telephone interview is conducted the next day. Interviewers read a list of ads appearing in the test magazine and the participants are asked which ads they remember. Participants are then asked a series of "impact" questions to determine the effectiveness of the test ads. Impact scores help determine three key measurements. According to the company's website, the "measurements include *intrusiveness,* which is the percentage of respondents who can describe the ad the next day; *idea communication,* which is an accurate description of the advertisement's pitch; and *persuasion,* which attempts to assess purchase interest." The client receives its test scores along with its advertisement as well as the norms of ads tested in the same category.

Readex Reader   Readex Research is located in Stillwater, Minn. It was founded in
Interest Studies   1947. Readex is widely known for its publication research. It relies on mail surveys to collect readership data.

According to its website, Readex offers "four standard ad readership studies which can vary in scope and customization depending on the needs of the client." Its Message Impact service asks respondents to rate ads 1-5 to reflect the "stopping power" of the ads. Respondents are asked to consider the ads' attention-getting ability, believability and information value. Respondents are also asked for verbatim comments about the "feeling" they got from the test ads. The Readex On Target service looks more specifically at the effectiveness of advertisements. Respondents are asked to evaluate the visual appeal of the ads as well as what respondents think could be done differently in the ads to communicate better with them. Readex Red Sticker measures the recall of ads and editorial content. This study asks three questions: (1) Did you see it? (2) Did you read it? (3) Did you find it interesting? Readex also offers the Ad Perception service. It looks at the attention-getting power of the test ads, the believability of the ads and how informative they are.

According to the company, Readex can provide a lower project cost by using mail surveys when compared to other message research companies. Mail surveys also allow for large, "more geographically diverse" samples.

Roper Starch   Based in New York, Roper Starch Worldwide, Inc., has been conduct-
Worldwide   ing a variety of consumer research for over 25 years. It uses *"recognition testing"* to measure the readership of ads. Personal interviews are conducted with respondents to determine if they have actually read a test publication. Respondents are then read a list of ads in the publication. Respondents are asked more specific questions to determine the depth of recognition for ads they recall.

These interviews are then analyzed to produce three levels of ad recall. A *"noted"* score means that respondents remembered seeing the test ads, but they can't recall the product or advertiser. An *"advertiser associated"* score recalled an ad and can also recall the product and/or advertiser. The *"read most"* score means that respondents recall 50% or more of the ad's content (Burton and Purvis 2006).

Amertest   Amertest is based in Albuquerque, N.M., with an additional office in Tokyo, Japan. It has developed testing systems for print and television ads utilizing mail, online and in-person data collection methods. According to the Amertest website, "90% of their clients are household names."

The company utilizes "clutter reel" for television ads and a "clutter book" for print ads. The clutter reel is a collection of five television ads that are mailed to 100-150 survey participants. One of the ads is the test ad, and the other ads are distracters. Depending on a client's needs, some of the distracters may be ads for competing products. Survey participants watch the video and are then asked questions to determine "attention" and "brand linkage." Participants then watch the test ad by itself and are asked a series of questions to measure communication. Finally, participants are asked to review "Picture Sorts" to uncover the emotional impact of the test ad. *"Picture Sorts"* is a proprietary system that asks survey participants to organize a series of still frames from the TV ad in response to certain questions. The "Picture Sorts technique attempts to understand the non-verbal response to the ad," according to the company.

The end result of the testing for TV or print ads is a summary of performance on three levels. The *"Performance Summary"* provides a general assessment of attention, brand linkage and motivation of the test ad. *"Brand linkage or brand perception* scores measure the participant's view of the brand after seeing the test ads." These scores are compared to benchmark scores that the company has for other brands for a relative ranking. Finally, Amertest provides diagnostics of the ad using the "Picture Sorts" technique.

RESEARCH USED TO MONITOR AD CAMPAIGNS

Research is often used to evaluate an advertising campaign in progress. Such endeavors can be challenging, as advertisers can't really be sure of a final outcome of their efforts. But defining clear objectives or *Key Performance Indicators* early in the advertising planning process can make evaluation much more productive.

Key performance indicators, or KPI's, are measurement metrics built into business plans of all types. For example, a company may want to know its customer service KPI's to see how it can improve its service. In advertising, KPI's are assessed at different intervals to evaluate campaign success. Advertising KPI's focus on sales, brand preference, market share, website traffic, coupon redemption, request for information via the web or 800 numbers, advertising recall scores or dozens of other measurements related to the impact of advertising.

Mike Toten, a consultant who writes about human resources, outlines on www.workplaceinfo.com the *SMARTA* method for developing KPI's. The Key Performance Indicators, he says, include the following six points:

* *Specific*. KPI's need to be clearly defined at the beginning of the planning process. Those responsible must understand how they contribute to achieving the goals.

* *Measurable*. KPI's must be *"quantifiable."* That is, performance should be observable and documented.

* *Agreed To*. KPI's should be the result of a "two-way communication process." Top management should not set KPI's without the input of all involved in meeting the KPI.

* *Realistic*. KPI's should be based on past performance models to ensure they are realistic.

* *Timely*. KPI's should have a way to be monitored, and they should have a specified time period for measurement.

* *Aligned*. KPI's should be reflective of overall organizational goals. In other words, advertising goals should be in support of overall business goals.

The purpose of monitoring the advertising campaign through KPI's is to uncover any problems that need to be corrected in flight. For example, evaluation during an advertising campaign may show that certain markets are selling more products than other markets. By moving quickly during the campaign, funds may be channeled to targeted areas to increase sales. Monitoring during a campaign again illustrates the dynamic nature of advertising and underscores the need for research.

POST-CAMPAIGN ANALYSIS　Recognizing problems during an ad campaign is always preferable to finding out about problems at the end. Still, all advertising campaigns are subject to a rigorous post-analysis.

Post-analysis can refer to a general analysis of campaign goals/results or a more specific media evaluation. For example, most ad agencies compare the media schedules that were ordered for the campaign to what ran on the media outlets. The purpose is generally to make sure that advertisements actually ran during specific times or programs.

But many ad agencies also look for changes in ratings or audience delivery. For example, if an ad agency buys a television program with a 10 rating, a post-buy analysis will ensure that a 10 rating was actually delivered by looking at the most recent ratings information. Should media outlets deliver a smaller audience than was agreed to in the original buy, the outlets will offer make-goods or cash rebates as compensation to the client. These make-goods or rebates can mean thousands of dollars to the agency and client.

Post-buy analysis is critical in understanding what went right or wrong with the campaign. This knowledge will help in developing future campaigns and KPI measurements.

FUTURE TRENDS　Technology is revolutionizing all aspects of media and advertising as consumers and advertisers use digital media in ever increasing numbers. Given its rapid growth, Internet advertising may ultimately displace traditional media in audience size and revenues.

The Internet not only provides an amazing technology to reach consumers in unique ways, but it also allows the real-time tracking of the results of campaign efforts. The nature of the Internet and its infrastructure permits precise measurement of the impact of offline and online advertising. Let's briefly look at two future trends.

Web Analytics　*Web analytics* has grown from simply recording hits and clickthroughs to actually looking at consumer behavior on websites. According to Avinash Kaushik in *Web Analytics: An Hour a Day*, today's web analytics "mean that we have a significantly enhanced ability to listen to our website customers."

In practice, web analytics uses a variety of tools to better understand consumer preferences while at a website. For example, it's possible to set up several versions of a particular website. The different versions may have graphics or buttons in different places or completely different content areas. As users visit the website, they see one of the various versions of the website. Web analytics can be used to track the movement of the user through the site, thereby identifying the style of the content area that leads to a desired outcome or KPI. So, if sales is a key purpose of the website, then website traffic can be used to determine what consumers actually respond to. The critical aspect to keep in mind is that this research is real-time and based on actual site traffic.

Web analytics has developed into a unique skill set, one that is growing, as the web becomes a key factor in advertising campaigns.

Another aspect of web analytics is the ability to target consumers based on general search patterns and provide relevant advertisements based on their searches. Google has built its entire business model on delivering relevant text ads in search results. While this seems fairly routine today, Google was the first company to generate huge profits from online searches.

Behavioral Targeting Online

The next step in the evolution of online advertising is to actually identify consumers who are looking at specific websites. As Esther Dyson (2008) explains in "The Coming Ad Revolution" in the *Wall Street Journal*, "New companies are pitching tools to Internet service providers (ISP's) that will enable them to track users and show them relevant ads." With the use of cookies, ISP's can track consumers through their entire online session to build a profile of their web visits. "Take user number 12345, who was searching for cars yesterday," Dyson explains, "and show him a Porsche advertisement." Keep in mind that cookies only identify the IP address of the computer being used, not the actual name of the user. But the idea that individual consumer movements can be monitored with the result being more targeted advertisements is both amazing to some and alarming to others. As Dyson suggests, "the line between privacy and helpfulness has yet to be determined."

We may conclude that advertising would not exist in the way we know it today without research. It would be nearly impossible to develop strategic plans or produce creative advertisements without the research tools advertisers are using today. From the shaping and testing of the message to media placement and campaign evaluation, research is essential to the advertising process.

The future looks bright for advertising researchers. While new methods are still being developed to measure conventional media audiences, web research may soon be at the forefront, highlighting the impact of the Internet in advertising campaigns.

Fletcher, Alan D., and Thomas A. Bowers. *Fundamentals of Advertising Research,* 4th ed., Bellmont, CA: Wadsworth, 1999.

TO LEARN MORE

Parente, Donald E., *Advertising Campaign Strategy: A Guide To Marketing Communication Plans,* 4th ed., Mason, OH: South-Western College Publishing, 2006.

Wells, William, Nancy Mitchell, and Sandra Moriarty, *Advertising Principles & Practice,* 8th ed., Upper Saddle River, NJ: Pearson Prentice Hall, 2009.

Ahrens, Frank. (2006, December 4). *A newspaper chain sees its future, and it's online and hyper-local.* Washingtonpost.com. Retrieved January 2, 2008, from http://www.washingtonpost.com/wpdyn/content/article/2006/12/03/AR2006 120301037.html

REFERENCES

Ameriprise Financial. (2006, August 7). *New evolution of ameriprise financial advertising emphasizes "dreams don't retire."* Retrieved March 31, 2008, from http://www.ameriprise.com/amp/global/press-center/press-release-80.asp

Amertest. *Our products and services.* Retrieved February 21, 2008, from http://www.ameritest.net/products/tv.php

Brady, Diane. (2007, May 10). *Daily rituals of the world*. Retrieved March 14, 2008, from http://businessweek.com/bwdaily/dnflash/content/may2007/db20070510_522420.htm

Burns, Enid. (2007, December 4). *Online ad spending to continue growth through 2010*. The ClickZ Network. Retrieved March 31, 2008, from http://www.clickz.com/showPage.html?Page=3627767

Burton, Philip W. and Scott C. Purvis. *Which Ad Pulled Best?*, 9th ed. New York, NY: McGraw-Hill, 2002.

Cavalieri, Nate. (2005, March 16). *Real to reel*. Retrieved March 13, 2008, from http://www.sfweekly.com/2005-03-16/news/real-to-reel/1

Claritas. *Claritas service solutions*. Retrieved December 22, 2007, from http://www.claritas.com/claritas/Default.jsp?ci=3&si=3

Dillman, Donald A. *Mail and Internet Surveys: The Tailored Design Method*, 2nd ed. New York, NY: Wiley Publishing, 2000.

Dyson, Esther. (2008, February 2). The coming ad revolution. *The Wall Street Journal*, pp. A16.

ESRI Business Information solutions. *Community Tapestry Handbook*, 1st ed. 2004.

Fletcher, Alan D., and Thomas A. Bowers. *Fundamentals of Advertising Research*, 3rd ed. Belmont, CA: Wadsworth, 1988.

Friedman, Thomas L. *The World is Flat: A Brief History of the Twenty-First Century*, 1st ed. New York, NY: Farrar, Straus and Giroux, 2005.

Gallop & Robinson. *Copy Testing: The Gallop & Robinson impact system*. Retrieved February 5, 2008, from http://gallup-robinson.com/copytesting.html

Greenfield Online. *Who we are*. Retrieved December 22, 2007, from http://www.green field-group.com/onlinegroups.asp

Kaushik, Avinash. *Web Analytics An Hour a Day*, 1st ed. Indianapolis, IN: Wiley Publishing Inc., 2007.

Lee, Angela Y. and Aparna Labroo. *Conceptual and Perceptual Fluency for Marketers*. Retrieved August 4, 2008, http://www.acrwebsite.org/topic.asp?artid=77

Link, Michael W., Michael P. Pattaglia and Martin Frankel. (2007). Reaching the U.S. cell phone generation: Comparison of cell phone survey results with an ongoing landline telephone survey. *Public Opinion Quarterly*, 71, 814-839. Retrieved February 21, 2008, from http://poq.oxfordjournals.org/cgi/content/full/71/5/814

Mediamark. *Research and intelligence*. Retrieved December 22, 2007, from http://www.mediamark.com/showcontent.aspx?content=~/The_Survey_of_the_American_Consumer/002_Survey_Methodology/002_Data_Collection.xhtml

Meyers, Jack. (2006, November 2). *DDB's Lee Garfinkel speaks out on being media inventive, creative testing, and agency fees*. MediaVillage.com. Retrieved March 14, 2008, from http://www.mediavillage.com/jmlunch/2006/11/02/lam-11-02-06/index_print.html

Nielsen//NetRatings. *Product offerings*. Retrieved February 22, 2008, from http://www.nielsen-netratings.com/products.jsp

PACT: Positioning Advertising Copy Testing. *Journal of Advertising*, 11 (4), 3-29 (1982). Retrieved February 2, 2008, from Business Source Premier database.

Parente, Donald E. *Advertising Campaign Strategy: A Guide To Marketing Communication Plans*, 4th ed. Mason, OH: South-Western Publishing, 2006.

Pew Hispanic Center. (2008, February 11). *U.S. Population Projections 2005-2050*. Retrieved April 2, 2008, from http://pewhispanic.org/reports/report.php?ReportID=85

Pew Internet & American Life Project (updated February 15, 2008). *Demographics of Internet users*. Retrieved April 2, 2008, from http://www.pewinternet.org/trends/User_Demo_2.15.08.htm

Simmons Market Research Bureau. *National consumer study*. Retrieved December 22, 2007,

from http://www.smrb.com/aspx/content.aspxpid=5&sid=21&page=Methodology
_The_Simmons_Methodology

Toten, Mike. (2005, March 17). The importance of being smart. Workplaceinfo Publishing. Retrieved March 18, 2008, from http://www.workplaceinfo.com.au/nocookie/alert/2005/050317135.htm

University of Pennsylvania. *Methods: What is ethnography?* Retrieved February 21, 2008, from http://www.sas.upenn.edu/anthro/CPIA/METHODS/Ethnography.html

VALS. *Welcome to VALS.* Retrieved December 23, 2007, from http://sric-bi.com/VALS/

Weiss, Michael J. *Clustering of America,* 1st ed. New York, NY: Harpercollins, 1988.

Wells, William, Nancy Mitchell, and Sandra Moriarty. *Advertising Principles & Practice,* 8th ed., Upper Saddle River, NJ: Pearson Prentice Hall, 2009.

Zikmund, William G. *Business Research Methods,* 7th ed. Mason, OH: South-Western Publishing, 2003.

24 New Media Research

A growing area of importance in mass communication is research of communication technologies. They have given rise to new media such as the Internet, digital TV, satellite radio, wireless telephone, podcasts, blogs, and search engines, to name a few. Broadly, the term "new media" refers to channels and outlets for disseminating information and entertainment that rely on digital communication technologies, with the computer at the core.

Compared to traditional media such as newspapers and terrestrial broadcast radio and TV, new media are digital and interactive and "typically involv[e] computer capabilities" (Rice et al., 1984. p. 35). *Digital* is a binary system that presents information as either 1 or 0. Digitization refers to the process of converting information, no matter whether it is text, graphics, image, music, voice, video, or data, into a series of zeroes and ones. *Interactivity* refers to two-way communications or feedback between users and source. Three forms of interactivity exist: user-to-user, user-to-document, and user-to-system (McMillan, 2002). Computers, which run on microprocessors, are at the core of new media because computers are a networked communication technology — without which there would be no Internet.

As Table 1 on the next page shows, communication technologies are complex and diverse. They involve systems, networks, distribution technologies, end-user terminal devices, and applications. Each has a wide range of technologies of its own.

METHODOLOGICAL OPPORTUNITIES AND CHALLENGES

In the 1980s, when the computer became personal and the Internet first appeared on American campuses, scholars pointed out that research on new media "does not necessarily reflect new methods" (Williams, Rice, & Rogers, 1988, p. xi). Conventional research methods such as focus groups, content analysis, surveys, or experiments can be applied to the study of new media because newly emerged online research methods are not, in principle, much different from offline methods.

By Ran Wei
University of South Carolina

Table 1. The Trajectory of Communication Technologies

Systems	Networks	End-user Devices	Applications
Telecommunications/ DSL & Cellular	LAN (local area networks)	PCs, Tablets, PDAs, Kindle	E-mail, BBS chatroom, WWW, blogs, IM, social networking
Cable (fiber optics)	WLAN (wireless LAN)	Digital TV sets	Digital broadcasting, HDTV, Video-conferencing, VoIP
Satellite	Wi-Fi & Wi-Max	iPod, MP3 Players, MP4 Players, iPad	Podcasting
	Intranet	Mobile Phone	Wireless e-mail, SMS, mobile Internet, mobile TV

Table 2 on the next page compares the most commonly used methods in Internet research as reported in three thematic meta-analyses (Tomasello, 2001; Kim & Weaver, 2002; Cho & Khang, 2006). The table uses a study of mass communication research trends from 1980 to 1999 by Kamhawi and Weaver (2003) as a baseline. The figures from their research are shown in the 2nd column in the table. As Cho and Khang (2006) reported, methods that were used for online data collection (41.1%) in communication and marketing journals published during 1994-2003 were outnumbered by offline methods (58.9%). Furthermore, it is clear that quantitative research methods were more common than qualitative methods. This methodological trend persisted across the three trend analyses of publications focused on Internet research. The top three most used quantitative research methods in published Internet-focused articles in leading communication journals were survey, content analysis, and experiments.

New and interactive communication technologies, particularly the Internet, offer opportunities to apply conventional research methods in new contexts and with newly developed tools. For example, content — Websites, blogs, e-mail, and BBS — that appears on the World Wide Web is increasing and provides a vast mine for data collection. E-mail surveys are an example of new approaches to assess public opinion. In addition, Web-based software offers tools for recruiting subjects, data collection, and analyses. Because of such opportunities, in 2008, *online* research accounted for 20% of research-industry revenues and was projected to total $4 billion for the year (Neff, 2008).

This chapter will provide an overview of the cutting-edge methods for communication technology research. We'll look at the application of both conventional and new methods in new media research. We'll also examine important theoretical and methodological issues in communication technology and approaches to deal with them.

METHODS AND TECHNOLOGY

Conventional research methods dominate the research of communication technology. One reason is that they can be easily adapted to the online environment because the Internet allows the application of these methods in new contexts. However, research via computer-

Table 2. Most Used Methods in Mass Communication vs. Internet Research

Method(s) Used	Mass Communication Research (Kamhawi & Weaver, 2003)	Internet Research (Tomasello, 2001)	Internet Research (Kim & Weaver, 2002)	Internet Research (Cho & Khang, 2006)
Time Period	1980-1999	1994-1999	1996-2000	1994-2003
Online vs. Offline Methods	N/A	N/A	N/A	41.1% vs. 58.9%
Survey	33.3%	11.0%	10.5%	19.3%
Content Analysis	30.0%	27.0%	7.0%	16.0%
Experiment	13.3%	11.0%	3.6%	10.3%
Secondary analysis			3.6%	5.5%
Quantitative Methods Combined	3.1%		2.0%	
Historical	4.7%		8.0%	
Policy study/ Legal		8.0%	4.6%	4.0%
Interview/case study		8.0%		6.3%
Other qualitative (essays/critique) Analysis of issues/ problems	7.1%	27.0%	49.2%	30.8%
Discourse/textual analysis			2.1%	
Cultural analysis			2.1%	
Observation/Focus Groups			2.0%	
Qualitative Methods Combined	4.2%		26.7%	
Combined Q&Q	2.4%	8.0%	72.9%	
Total	100%	100%	100%	100%

mediated networks and interface also has the promise to encourage new methodologies. The Internet and World Wide Web are having an impact on each of the major research methods. Let's look at some of the major methods, highlighting unique methodological considerations of conducting research in cyberspace.

Case Studies

Case studies provide detailed accounts from various data sources of an individual, organization, or any other social unit. Rather than using large samples, the case study method involves an in-depth, longitudinal examination of a single instance or event known as a *case*, from which to draw some generalizable principles. For a discussion of case study methodology, you may wish to reread Prof. Tuten's Chapter 16 in this book.

The method is highly applicable to communication technology research because early adopters of new media technologies are always few in number. Studies of the early adopters may lead to theoretical insights about the motivations and social status of people who adopt technology in its early stages. However, this method is not widely used in studies of online media. As Table 2 shows, case studies (the 3rd and 5th columns) accounted for only 8% and 6.3% of the publications examined respectively in the 1994-1999 and 1994-2003 periods.

New communication technologies facilitate case studies. *Digitalized archives*, which are searchable online and indexed in databases, provide researchers with greater than ever access to documents, policies, newspaper clippings, and other files. Also, *e-mail* can be used as a research medium for in-depth interviewing. E-mail interviewing can be an alternative to face-to-face and telephone interviewing.

Other communication technologies such as IM (instant messaging), teleconferencing, and mobile video conferencing also enable the researcher to conduct interviews in real time, making it possible to do case analyses in a *synchronous* environment, that is, interviews are conducted at the same time at various sites via simultaneous interaction. Participants in this process are also said to be "co-present," that is, they have a sense of being together short of being physically face to face (Stieger & Göritz, 2006).

Focus Groups

Focus group is a research method for conducting simultaneous face-to-face interviews among a small group of 6 to 12 individuals who are recruited based on certain criteria to discuss an issue, a product, or a service. For a discussion of focus group methodology, you may wish to reread Prof. Tuten's Chapter 18 in this book. A moderator is used to guide the discussion. Focus groups work well for gathering a wealth of depth data about participants' attitudes and opinions on issues under investigation.

The focus group is a valuable research method for communication technology research because social dynamics is a key factor influencing the diffusion and use of technologies. The insights generated from focus groups are helpful to understand the process of social influence.

However, focus group is an infrequently used method in research of online media. Kim and Weaver found that it was used in only 2% of research projects (2002).

An advantage of online focus group research is the *availability of participants*. One of the difficulties in conducting face-to-face focus groups is recruiting participants. Geographic dispersion, physical conditions (e.g., patients at home), and time zone differences are some constraints. With the Internet and computer-mediated settings, however, hard-to-recruit participants can be approached via e-mail. Millions of online communities provide a pool of participants who may not be available offline.

More importantly, the group *interview can be conducted entirely online* where video-conferencing facilities are accessible or by use of synchronous online chat. The online environment and Web technologies give new meaning to the focus group methodology (Stewart & Williams, 2005). Online focus groups, e-focus groups, or virtual focus groups have emerged. E-focus groups take the interview and moderation entirely online. The interviews are recorded as digital data.

Because of the increasing possibilities for online focus groups, technological support for e-focus groups has appeared. For instance, the group support system

(GSS) supports focus groups with two forms of anonymous interviews: same time/same place (synchronous groups) and same time/different place (asynchronous groups) (Klein, Tellefsen, & Herskovitz, 2007).

Content Analysis

Content analysis is defined as a technique for the objective and systematic description of various characteristics of communication and artifacts, that is, a method of quantitatively analyzing messages. If you need a refresher about the method, you may wish to reread Profs. Stroud and Higgins' explanation of content analysis in Chapter 9 of this book. Content analysis is used extensively in communication research (30%) and research of communication technology (ranging from 7% to 17%).

The World Wide Web and computer-mediated communication do present challenges for content analysis. New technologies profoundly affect key steps in content analysis, from the content, to the coding instrument, to analysis. Media content is much broader than it was before the Internet. It includes all forms of online communication, such as e-mail, chat, Websites (personal, business, and social groups), blogs, and microblogs (such as Twitter).

For data analysis, there are textual *software tools* to simplify and even automate the analysis of coded content. There are three groups of software: (1) dictionary-based programs, which do word counting, sorting, and simple statistical analysis; (2) development environments programs designed to automate the construction of dictionaries, grammars, and other text analysis tools; and (3) annotation programs for automatic content analysis (Lowe, 2008).

Surveys

Surveys involve collecting self-reported information on individuals, households, or organizations by asking standardized questions. For a discussion of survey methodology, you may wish to reread Prof. Luther's Chapter 10 in this book. As Table 2 shows, survey is the most used research method in both mass communication research and communication technology research.

New communication technology has affected survey research by making available e-mail surveys and Web surveys. *E-mail surveys* allow for the recruitment of participants, distribution of questionnaires, and collection of responses by e-mail. *Web surveys* invite respondents to visit a Website to fill out a questionnaire. Both methods are rapidly becoming popular.

One of the advantages is *low cost*. Recruiting respondents via the Internet is less expensive and time-consuming than traditional methods. A user who has an html code generator can conduct online surveys at his or her Website. There are a wide range of Web survey *software* and free Web-based *services* (such as Survey Monkey, for example) for creating, administering, and analyzing surveys. Speed is also an advantage of online surveys. The cycle of data collection is shorter than telephone and mail surveys.

Methodologically, Web surveys and e-mail surveys involve the same three components as traditional surveys: (1) a standardized questionnaire, (2) sampling, and (3) self-reported data.

However, sampling and the mode of data collection online differ from traditional surveys. In terms of *sampling*, most online surveys rely on volunteer participants using non-probability samples. In terms of *data collection*, survey software assists the collection of responses through Web page drag and drop.

Despite their advantages, online surveys have opened a door for new problems as well. A major concern is *quality control*. Regarding sampling, a study found that 0.25% of respondents account for 30% of online surveys, whereas 20% account for 80% of traditional surveys (Neff, 2008). Hence, sample representativeness and result generalizability are concerns. Moreover, to increase the response rate of online surveys, which ranges from 1% to 30% for academic research, it is possible for researchers to cheat by using software bots to automate the data collection process. An industry study found that about 14% of respondents across 20 online panels were fraudulent (Neff, 2008).

Experiments

The *experiment method*, with its control and deliberate manipulation of variables, is particularly suited for studies of cause and effect. It is considered to be the most scientific of all methods. For a discussion of the methodology, you may wish to reread Prof. Bradley's Chapter 11 in this book. Experimental methods are used mainly in communication research to test the effects of design, presentation, and format of various print, broadcast, and multimedia content on audiences. In both mass communication research and communication technology research, the experiment is the third most used quantitative method, behind survey and content analysis.

The Internet has emerged as a laboratory to observe human behavior. Web-based experiments use the Internet to recruit participants, administer stimuli, and collect data.

An advantage they have over traditional experiments is that Web labs provide worldwide *access to subjects*, some of whom may be otherwise hard to reach.

But there are *ethical and validity concerns* about Web experiments. To correct for problems, Reips (2002) proposed five do's and five don'ts in conducting Internet-based psychological experiments. The *do's* are the following:

1. Utilize dropout (subjects who decide not to continue participation) as a dependent variable.

2. Use dropouts to detect motivational confounding. (Since subjects can drop out of a Web experiment easily, dropouts can be turned into a tool for detecting their motivation for participation.)

3. Place questions for personal information at the beginning, not the end of the study.

4. Use a collection of techniques developed for data collection on the Internet such as using multiple sites and single-use passwords.

5. Use Internet-based tools such as software for Internet surveys.

The *don'ts* are the following:

1. Do not allow unauthorized access to participant data.

2. Do not show access to confidential participant data through URLs (Uniform Resource Locator).

3. Do not reveal the experiment's setup and procedures.

4. Do not ignore the differences in Internet technologies such as use of different Web browsers, connection methods, and types of computers.

5. Do not collect biased data due to improper programming of data collection.

**KEY ISSUES —
AND HOW TO
DEAL WITH THEM**

The most significant development in communication technology over the past few years has been the convergence of traditional and new media. *Convergence* refers to the merging of traditional media with new, interactive media for the production, presentation, and dissemination of news, information, entertainment, and data. Technically, the term means that digitized text, audio, video, and databases are connected by hyper-links (Baldwin et al., 1996). From the users' end, media convergence means that communication technologies, which offer a variety of multifunctional digital media devices (e.g., PC tablets, PDAs, iPod, MP4 Players, Kindle, and smart phones, such as iPhones), enable them to access, download, and view media content anywhere anytime.

Examples of convergent media include Websites as newspapers, the iPod as radio, the mobile phone as radio, the computer as a platform to view TV shows, the Web as telephone, and the home TV set as a device to watch Web TV. As an illustration of a convergent medium with a unified platform, consider the smart mobile phone. It was invented for voice communications but has evolved into a device for both interpersonal and mass communication (Leung & Wei, 2000; Wei, 2008) with added functions such as text messaging, radio receiving, viewing made-for-mobile-phone TV, sending and receiving e-mail, connecting to the Internet, and portable video conferencing. Thousands of apps are available for iPhone.

Convergence causes a paradigm shift in mass communication (1) from passively receiving media content to actively using it; (2) from mass, generic programming to personalizable content; (3) from a single-function reading or viewing medium to convergent cross-media platforms (which may be TV, the Web, the mobile phone, or even game consoles); (4) from using media with a fixed schedule to time-shifting, making it possible to use media 24/7; and (5) from using personalized media content at a fixed location to mobility thanks to space-shifting (e.g., viewing downloaded media content on a digital device). Thus media use is possible almost anywhere.

Let's look at some approaches used to research media convergence and to deal with theoretical and methodological issues arising from convergence.

Adoption of Convergent Media

The most commonly applied theoretical approach of researching consumer response to convergent media is *diffusion of innovations* (Rogers, 1995), a theory that attempts to explain the adoption of an innovation in society. Adoption research provides insights that can help assess the market demand for a convergent medium and predict its diffusion pattern.

Adoption of Digital TV

Rogers (1986) defined *adoption* as a "process through which an individual passes from first knowledge of an innovation, to forming an attitude toward the innovation, to a decision to adopt or reject, to implementation of the idea, and to conformation of this decision" (p. 163).

Several studies have examined the *adoption patterns of digital TV*. Digital TV is more than just television. It combines the technological capacities of broadcast television, cable TV, computing, and telephony. It provides broadband Internet access, multimedia data, games, and e-commerce. Interactive applications of digital TV include VOD (Video on Demand), PPV (Pay per View), and DVR (Digital

Video Recording) using an interface device known as EPG (Electronic Program Guide).

In the first study on digital TV, Leung and Wei (1998) found that the awareness of and interest in digital TV were high. More than 60% of TV viewers indicated a willingness to adopt it. Young, better educated male viewers with a higher income had a higher intention to subscribe to digital TV services than did the general population. In addition, the more digital TV was perceived to be superior in providing information, entertainment, utility, and self-paced educational services, the stronger the intention to adopt it.

In examining predictors of Americans' interest in digital TV, Atkin, Neuendorf, Jeffres, and Skalski (2003) found that knowledge about digital TV was low, with only one-third of respondents knowing something about it. The eagerness to adopt digital TV was found low as well. Young males were more knowledgeable about and more interested in adopting it than was the average person. Atkin et al. (2003) further explored the influence of motivational factors on the adoption intention for digital TV applications. Affective sensation — that is, seeking humor uniquely from digital TV programming — was found a significant predictor.

Internet TV, or IPTV (Internet Protocol Television), is an emerging TV   *Adoption of Webcasting*
viewing platform thanks to the convergence of television, telecommunications, and the Internet (Gerbarg & Noam, 2004). The migration of traditional TV to the Web is underway. TV programming can be delivered to users with a broadband connection, wired or wireless. Internet users are able to view TV broadcast on computers (the so-called "second screen") over the Internet network or a smart phone (the so-called "third screen") anytime anywhere (Gerbarg & Noam, 2004). Technically, IPTV involves broadcast video streaming on the Internet. As such, it is also known as *Webcasting*.

In exploring who the early adopters of Webcasting were, the reasons why they adopted it, and the potential factors that predict Webcasting adoption, Lin (2004) surveyed 454 Internet users. She found younger users had a great interest in accessing Webcasting. In addition, the adoption of Webcasting was predicted by perceived Internet technology fluidity. In another study to assess Internet users' needs for IPTV, Carey (2004) found that age and TV hardware were influential variables. Younger users who did not own high-end home theatre TV sets were more interested in viewing television on the Internet. Yang and Kong (2006) also explored factors influencing adoption of IPTV among Internet users. Their study showed that gender and income were significant predictors. Moreover, Internet users' perceptions of IPTV played an important role in predicting their intention to adopt. The more they believed in the programming quality of Internet TV and expected greater media impact caused by Internet TV, and the less they were concerned about harmful contents, the more likely they were to adopt IPTV.

According to the International Telecommunication Union (ITU), the   *Adoption of*
number of mobile phone users worldwide reached nearly 5 billion in   *Mobile Phones*
2010, more than twice as many as the number of Internet users of 1.97 billion. The mobile phone was viewed as the most successful new communication technology in the history of technology diffusion. Thus, mobile phone adoption

research focused on people who did not own a mobile phone and explored motives for owning one. Leung and Wei (1999a) examined the demographic profile of what they called "mobile telephone have-nots" in Hong Kong at a time when the mobile phone diffusion rate reached 50% (p. 209). The have-nots tended to be older women with lower education and income. Instead of having a mobile phone, they had pagers as an alternative. In a follow-up study, Wei (2001) probed the question of who remained a mobile phone have-not when the mobile phone had gone from luxury to utility. His longitudinal analysis revealed that one-third of mobile phone non-adopters had converted to adopters in a period of 25 months. He characterized those who did not convert as "laggards" (p. 715).

For millions of mobile phone adopters, a question is, Do they view a mobile phone as just an update of the fixed telephone, or do they assign it special values? In a study that focused on communication technology as a symbolic tool and physical extension of the human body, Katz and Sugiyama (2006) found that fashion attentiveness had played a significant role in the acquisition and replacement of the mobile phone among American and Japanese youth. They concluded that mobile phones are fashion statements. For adult mobile phone adopters, Wei (2006) explored the influence of various lifestyles on the adoption status of the mobile phone in China. Mobile phone users were identified as yuppies. Further, yuppies were found to have integrated the mobile phone into their conspicuous, westernized, and socially active lifestyle. Adopting a mobile phone was found to be a way to achieve social differentiation and identity among this lifestyle segment in China.

For late adopters, owning the mobile phone itself was found to have special meaning. Exploring the relationship among motives of mobile phone use, patterns of use, and psychological variables such as loneliness, Wei and Lo (2006) found that late adopters, as compared to early adopters, used the mobile phone less on a daily basis and less for social purposes. Wei and Lo argued that late adopters probably sought to use the mobile phone *not* as a means to express affection, but as a technology with symbolic value. They concluded that as the mobile phone saturates a society, it represents a symbolic community. It confers a unique advantage to those who are not socially well connected by offering a trendy fashion accessory — a mobile phone strapped around one's neck or on one's belt — and, through its display, one instantly becomes a member of a large community, whether he or she actually uses the phone or not.

As more convergent media debut, more adoption research will be needed because convergent media are by definition interactive as compared to traditional media. Future adoption research of convergent media can explore social influences on the adoption of interactive convergent media. Methodologically, traditional research relied mostly on surveys offline (telephone surveys). Only two studies used online survey. As convergent media have social and symbolic meanings, future adoption research can consider more in-depth qualitative research methods such as an ethnographic approach in seeking a better understanding of the motives of adoption.

Use of Convergent Media

Use of convergent media refers to the use of a medium in a way that is broader than the function for which the medium was originally invented. Some examples of such new functions are getting news on search engine sites, viewing TV shows on computers, listening to radio on the mobile phone, and watching TV on the mobile phone.

The use of convergent media is increasing. More than 50 million Americans read their favorite newspaper on the Internet; for early adopters of broadband at home, the Internet is their primary news source (Horrigan, 2006). Nearly one out of four American Internet users visit the local TV Websites; and 40% are regularly visitors to these sites (Bachman, 2007). According to the Pew Internet & American Life Project, 57% of online adults have used the Internet to watch or download video, and as high as 74% of broadband users watch or download video (Madden, 2007) on their computers (the second screen). About half a million people watch TV on the mobile phone (the third screen).

As the use of convergent media has been increasing, research about *Use of Pagers* them has also been on the rise. Pagers and the mobile phone provide examples. The pager is a mass-media-like electronic medium from which users can obtain information and entertainment services such as stock updates, sports, horoscopes, cinema schedules, weather and traffic reports, and news headlines. Prior to the global popularity of the mobile phone in the late 1990s, the pager was the king of the hill in personal communication technology. More than 34 million Americans used pagers in 1996. There were 11 million users in Japan in 1995. The pager penetration rate was as high as 70% among college students in Hong Kong.

In examining use of the pager beyond sending and receiving text messages, Leung and Wei (1999b) found that it was the second major channel, after television, to learn about breaking news. As one might expect, prior exposure to news via the pager was a positive predictor of future news-seeking from it. Two psychological factors — the motive of owning a pager for information-seeking and the view of the pager as an information instrumentality — were also significant predictors. The more pager users perceived that news via the pager had the values of being useful, interesting, important, and timely, the more likely they were to use it as a news medium.

Since the late 1990s, millions of people worldwide have embraced the *Use of Mobile Phones* mobile phone. Researching why people turned to it to get news and entertainment, and investigating the relationship between voice-based use and non-voice use of the mobile phone, Wei (2008) found that the most popular non-voice use was playing games (51.4%), followed by surfing the Internet (26.4%), and news-seeking (13.5%). Instrumental use motives drove the use of the mobile phone for news-seeking and Web-surfing. Furthermore, he found that the more intensively people used the mobile phone for voice calls, the more likely they were to use mobile data services.

In addition to functional use, how teens and adolescents use the mobile phone represents a cultural phenomenon. Personalizing the mobile phone with ring tones, faceplates, carrying cases, and other accessories has become a pastime among youth. To examine use, sense-making, and reinvention of the mobile phone among adolescents, Wei (2007) focused on *pursuing a mobile phone-based identity* from a media dependency perspective. He found that the key to understand this pursuit is the extent to which teen mobile phone users put their personal touches on phones. That is, the more teens were dependent on the mobile phone as a means to express themselves, the more they personalized their phone from ringtone to accessories. Broadly speaking, findings of this study shed light on the question of how the mobile phone is used as a social technology. For adolescents, the mobile phone reflects who the owner is, it is an integral part of the self, and it is a technology that is used to define oneself. Personalizing the shape, color, or ring tone of the mobile phone makes a statement about oneself.

Methodologically, studies of the mobile phone used mostly telephones surveys. None of them used the mobile phone. However, the total of American households with only a mobile phone (25%), however, now outnumbers the total of households with only a fixed line (15%) (Blumberg, 2010). Hence, future research needs to use the mobile phone and the Internet (as most new phones have Internet connection) as modes of data collection. Otherwise, 15% of Americans will not be represented in any national samples.

NEW RESEARCH OPPORTUNITIES

Behind the buzz of convergence is the paradigm shift of mass media from a single-function platform to all-in-one platforms (no matter whether it is TV, the Internet, mobile phones, or game consoles). With the new technology, the use of media is changing from one-way single-purpose, passive use to active, simultaneous use of several media. The impact of convergent media on people's media consumption patterns needs to be systematically studied. Let's look at some research opportunities for assessing the impact of convergent media on traditional media.

New Approaches in Convergence Research

The rise of a new medium always affects existing media. Research on the relationship between new and traditional media is informed by the theoretical perspective of *media displacement*, which states that existing media will be displaced by new media. One aspect of displacement is the reduced time audience members spend with the original medium.

Displacement Effects

Time displacement effect research, which frames the relationship between new and traditional media as competitive, has a long history. It started in the 1940s when radio was the newest mass medium. Lazarsfeld (1940) did the earliest displacement study and examined radio's impact on newspapers. When television gained popularity over radio and newspapers, how it affected radio was the focus of displacement research in the 1940s and 1950s (Lasswell, 1948; Belson, 1961). As the popularity of the Internet and World Wide Web has increased, a growing number of studies have examined the changing patterns of media use and assessed if, and how, the Internet and the Web displaced television and newspapers as a functional alternative (Stempel, Hargrove, & Bernt, 2000).

However, mixed results have been found about the relationship between Internet use and use of traditional media. The displacement effect of the Internet on reading newspapers and watching television was less than conclusive (Bucy, Gantz, & Wang, 2007). Why? There are two major problems with media displacement effects research in this era of convergence.

First, displacement effect research assumes that use of a given medium is exclusive and that use of one medium is at the expense of the other. The media competitive view may have been valid in the era of the one-way, one-to-many paradigm of communication with very limited choice in content in only a few media. However, this view is no longer useful to capture media use patterns in our era of media convergence. Traditional media are converging with new, interactive media. It no longer makes sense in research to pit the use of one medium against the other. For example, when people watch TV on the Internet (e.g., *YouTube*), which medium was displaced: TV or the Web? The answer is neither.

Second, displacement effect research takes a "winners take all" or "zero-sum game" approach. In the era of media convergence, this approach is problematic. People use more than one medium at the same time. The term "media multitasking" is a common part of today's vocabulary. Pilotta and Shultz (2005) reported that simultaneous media use was as high as 40% to 65%. This phenomenon is particularly common among teenagers, and it is described as a kind of "teen media juggling act" (Foehr, 2006).

Thus, to examine the impact of convergence on media use, researchers *Multitasking* need to go beyond the paradigm of passive, single-function, and mechanical use of the media. To capture the rapidly changing patterns of convergent use — which are characteristically interactive, diverse, and multifunctional — the concept of media multitasking holds some promise to advance media displacement research.

Foehr (2006) operationally defined media *multitasking* as engaging in more than one media activity over any specific half hour. Others (Jeong & Fishbein, 2007) define it as an audience behavior that combines media use with another non-media activity. Both definitions are useful, but they fail to conceptually differentiate activities that are media non-exclusive (such as talking and viewing TV) and those that are media-exclusive (such as viewing TV and reading newspapers). To explicate the concept of media multitasking, we need a typology of multitasking.

As Figure 1 illustrates, along the dimensions of single-multitasking and activities that involve and that don't involve media use, four types of media multitasking can be developed: (1) a single activity without the use of media (e.g., eating); (2) multitasking mixing media use with other non-media activities (e.g., watching TV and eating, or using the mobile phone while driving); (3) multitasking mixing the use of one medium with another (e.g., watching TV and surfing the Internet, or using the mobile phone to text while viewing TV); and (4) a single activity involving media use (e.g., watching TV, reading newspapers, or

Figure 1. Typology of Multitasking

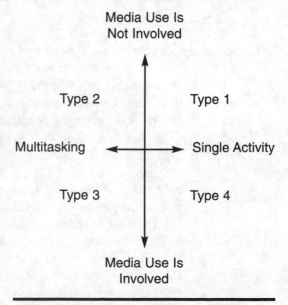

surfing the Internet).

Whereas past media displacement effect research focused narrowly on Type 4, new research opportunities exist in Types 2 and 3. The new approach of media multitasking promises to advance communication technology research because it emphasizes media use beyond exposure, frequency, and attention. That is, the approach to *media use needs to be changed from a passive, mechanical view to one that emphasizes active, participatory use.* The new approach will be broader in scope, emphasizing user experiences with convergent media, which include access, contact, perceptions, allocation of sensory resources, and emotions.

The new approach will also open up new avenues in methodology. For example, Website log files can be useful for multitasking research, and e-diaries can be an instrument of data collection.

A NEW RESEARCH AGENDA Developments in media convergence call for a new research agenda in communication technology. The agenda includes the following challenges in theoretical approaches. With each one, we'll note some questions as examples of those that researchers may confront.

1. Examine the influence of circumstances and locality of media use.

Because the use of traditional media was confined to the living room, past research ignored the circumstances and location of media use. The ubiquitous access to media via portable devices expands media use from fixed locations to broader contexts. Circumstance, locality, and motion have become key variables of media use. For example, a recent study (Wei & Huang, 2008) of using the mobile phone to view television suggests that mobile television was viewed the most under circumstances in which the user was physically in a mobile environment such as buses or taxis. Such audience practices raise questions about how circumstances and locality affect the use of convergent media.

2. Pay attention to the impact of social networking Websites on the use of convergent media.

The growth of social networking sites has been phenomenal in the last few years. Online social network sites are destinations especially favored by young people. They are the newest media platforms for communication. *Facebook*, for example, lets people discover connections among themselves and their friends. For researchers, networking sites raise such questions as these: Do social networking sites mean a new era in peer-to-peer communication? What is the impact of social networking sites on users' social relationships?

Moreover, with the notion of a one-stop site that caters to the interests of various groups, social networking sites will offer multimedia for content distribution and sharing of videos, photos, chatrooms, and blogs. What will be the impact of this trend on overall media use patterns? Will there be a time when *Facebook* takes over e-mailing?

Although membership-based social networking Websites are highly popular, some are more popular than others. A program of research can be pursued to examine the growth of such sites from a critical mass perspective. Adoption research will be enriched by examining the process of how each additional user adds value to a network site.

3. Evaluate the impact of convergence.

The impact of convergent media on individuals, media industries, and society in general will be enormous. For example, social networking sites such as *MySpace* and *Bebo* are popular with music fans. Research shows that two out of five social Website users embed music in their profile as a way to express themselves. Musicians as well use these sites extensively to market themselves and reach out to their fans. Thus, researchers may ask such questions as "Will musicians bypass big record companies?" and "How does it affect listeners if musicians use personal sites to market themselves?" Also, with new interactive media platforms such as DMB (Digital Multimedia Broadcasting), the access to media is ubiquitous, further eroding the boundaries of public and private space. Thus, researchers may wish to examine such issues as how to protect the privacy of users in ubiquitous media consumption.

4. Explore Web 2.0 and the popularity of UGC.

User generated content (UGC) is enormously successful thanks to Web 2.0 technologies, which provide a platform for producing and distributing Do-it-Yourself content. Users now have much more control than ever over the production and consumption of media content. From a user perspective, do people use UGC sites the same way as they use regular media? How do UGC sites affect the relationships between journalists, audiences, and advertisers? Recently, UGC Websites like *Youtube* have come into the mainstream. For example, *Youtube* was used to distribute 2008 presidential debates. Will this trend continue? Will the Internet and Web 2.0 give people a universal platform?

Castells, M. (2006). *Rise of the network society*. NY: Wiley.   **TO LEARN MORE**

Cho, C., & Khang, H. (2006). The state of Internet-related research in communications, marketing, and advertising: 1994-2003. *Journal of Advertising*, 35(3), 143-163.

Grant, A., & Meadows, J. (Eds.) (2010). *Communication technology update and fundamentals*. NY: Focal Press.

Katz, J. (Ed.) (2008). *Handbook of mobile communication studies*. Cambridge, MA: MIT Press.

Kim, S., & Weaver, D. (2002). Communication research about the Internet: A thematic meta-analysis. *New Media & Society*, 4(4), 518-538.

Lievrouw, L., & Livingstone, S. (Eds.) (2002). *The handbook of new media*. Thousand Oaks, CA: Sage.

Lin, C., & Atkin, D. (Eds.) (2007). *Communication technology and social change: Theory and implications*. Mahwah, NJ: Lawrence Erlbaum.

Lo, V., & Wei, R. (2010). New media and political communication in Asia: A critical assessment of research on media and politics, 1988-2008. *Asian Journal of Communication*, 20(2), 265-276.

Noam, E., Groebel, J., & Gerberg, D. (Eds.) (2004). *Internet television*. Mahwah, N.J.: Lawrence Erlbaum.

Tomasello, T., Lee, Y., & Baer, A. (2010). New media research publication trends 1990–2006. *New Media & Society*, 12(4), 531-548.

Wei, R. (2008). The convergent mobile telephone: An emerging bridging medium. In *Mobile telephones: Networks, applications, and performance*. NY: Nova Publishing.

Wei, R., & Hao, X. (2010). Effects of government regulations on spam: Lessons from Singapore in regulating mobile advertising. *Asian Communication Research*, 7(3), 77-101.

REFERENCES   Atkin, D., Neuendorf, K., Jeffres, L., & Skalski, P. (2003). Predictors of audience interest in adopting digital television. *Journal of Media Economics*, 16(3), 159-173.

Bachman, K. (2007). Media audit: Local TV sites paying off. Retrieved January 26, 2008, from http://www.adweek.com/mw/news/media_agencies/article_display.jsp?vnu _content_id=1003635244

Baldwin, T., McVoy, D., & Steinfield, C. (1996). *Convergence: Integrating media, information and communication*. Thousand Oaks, CA: Sage.

Belson, W. (1961). The effects of television on buying and reading of newspapers and magazines. *Public Opinion Quarterly, 25*, 366-381.

Blumberg, S. (2010). Center for Disease Control, National Health Interview Survey.

Bucy, E., Gantz, W., & Wang, Z. (2007). Media technology and the 24 hour news cycle. In C. Lin & D. Atkin (Eds.), *Communication technology and social change: Theory and implications* (pp. 143-163). Mahwah, NJ: Lawrence Erlbaum.

Carey, J. (2004). Content models: Will IPTV be more of the same or different?" In E. Noam, J. Groebel, & D. Gerberg (Eds.), *Internet television*. Mahwah, N.J.: Lawrence Erlbaum.

Cho, C., & Khang, H. (2006). The state of Internet-related research in communications, marketing, and advertising: 1994-2003. *Journal of Advertising, 35*(3), 143-163.

Foehr, U. (2006). Media multitasking among American youth: Prevalence, predictors and pairings. Retrieved December 6, 2007, from http://www.slideshare.net/Frankwatching /media-multitasking-among-american-youth.

Gerbarg, D., & Noam, E. (2004). Internet television: Definition and prospects. In E. Norm, J. Groebel, & D. Gergerg (Eds.), *Internet television*. Mahwah, NJ: Lawrence Erlbaum.

Horrigan, J. (2006). Online news. Retrieved January 10, 2008, from http://www.pewinter net.org/pdfs/PIP_News.and.Broadband.pdf

http://www.nytimes.com/2007/08/27/technology/27drill.html

Jeong, S., & Fishbein, M. (2007). Predictors of multitasking with media: Media factors and audience factors. *Media Psychology, 10*, 364-384.

Kamhawi, R. & Weaver, D. (2003) Mass communication research trends from 1980 to 1999. *Journalism & Mass Communication Quarterly*, 80(1), 7-27.

Katz, J., & Sugiyama, S. (2006). Mobile phones as fashion statements: Evidence from student surveys in the U.S. and Japan. *New Media & Society*, 8(2), 321-337.

Kim, S. T., & Weaver, D. (2002). Communication research about the Internet: A thematic meta-analysis. *New Media & Society*, 4, 518-538.

Klein, E., Tellefsen, T., & Herskovitz, P. (2007). The use of group support systems in focus groups: Information technology meets qualitative research. *Computers in Human Behavior, 23*, 2113-2132.

Lasswell, H. (1948). The structure and function of communication in society. In L. Burson (Ed.), *The communication of ideas* (pp. 37-51). NY: Harper.

Lazarsfeld, P.F. (1940). *Radio and the printed page: An introduction to the study of radio and its role in the communication of ideas*. New York: Duell, Sloan and Pearce.

Leung, L., & Wei., R. (1998). Exploring factors of interactive TV adoption in Hong Kong: Implications for advertising. *Asian Journal of Communication*, 8(2), 124-147.

Leung, L., & Wei, R. (1999a). Who are the mobile phone have-nots? Influences and consequences. *New Media and Society*, 1(2), 209-226.

Leung, L., & Wei, R. (1999b). Seeking news via the pager: A value-expectancy study. *Journal of Broadcasting & Electronic Media*, 43(3), 299-315.

Leung, L., & Wei, R. (2000). More than just talk on the move: A use-and-gratification study of the cellular phone. *Journalism & Mass Communication Quarterly*, 77(2), 308-320.

Lin, C. (2004). Webcasting adoption: Technology fluidity, user's innovativeness and media substitution. *Journal of Broadcasting & Electronic Media*, 48, 446-465.

Lowe, W. (2008). Software for content analysis: A review. Retrieved April 8, 2008, from http://people.iq.harvard.edu/~wlowe/Publications/rev.pdf

Madden, M. (2007): Online video. Retrieved January 10, 2008, from http://www.pewinternet.org/pdfs/PIP_Online_Video_2007.pdf

McMillan, S. (2002). Exploring models of interactivity from multiple research traditions: Users, documents, and systems. In L. Lievrouw & S. Livingstone (Eds.), *The handbook of new media* (pp. 163-182). Thousand Oaks, CA: Sage.

Mindlin, A. (2007, August 27). Cellphone-only homes hit a milestone. *New York Times*. Retrieved April 14, 2008, from http://www.nytimes.com/2007/08/27/technology/27drill.html

Neff, J. (2008, March 31). Chasing the cheaters who undermine online research. *Advertising Age*. Retrieved April 14, 2008, from http://adage.com/digital/article?article_id=125978

Pilotta, J., & Shultz, D. (2005). Simultaneous media experience and synesthesia. *Journal of Advertising Research*, 45, 19-26.

Reips. U. (2002). Internet-based psychological experimenting: Five dos and five don'ts. *Social Science Computer Review*, 20, 241-249.

Rice, R., & Associates. (1984). *The new media: Communication, research and technology*. Beverly Hills, CA: Sage.

Rogers, E. (1995). *Diffusion of innovations* (4th ed.). NY: Free Press.

Stempel, G., Hargrove, T. & Bernt, J. P. (2000). Relation of growth of use of the Internet to changes in media use from 1995 to 1999. *Journalism & Mass Communication Quarterly*, 77(1), 71-79.

Stewart, K., & Williams, M. (2005). Researching online populations: The use of online focus groups for social research. *Qualitative Research*, 5, 395-416.

Stieger, S., & Göritz, A. S. (2006). Using instant messaging for Internet-based interviews. *CyberPsychology & Behavior*, 9, 552-559.

Tomasello, T. (2001). The status of Internet-based research in five leading communication journals, 1994-1999. *Journalism & Mass Communication Quarterly*, 78(4), 659-674.

Wei, R. (2001). From luxury to utility: A longitudinal analysis of cell phone laggards. *Journalism & Mass Communication Quarterly*, 78(4), 702-719.

Wei, R. (2006). Lifestyles and new media: Adoption and use of wireless communication technology in China. *New Media & Society*, 8(6), 991-1008.

Wei, R. (2007). The high-tech cell phone as self phone: Social identity and goal attainment in individual cell phone dependency. *Asian Communication Research*, 3(1), 5-24.

Wei, R. (2008). Motivations for use of the cell phone for mass communications and entertainment. *Telematics & Informatics*, 25(1), 36-46.

Wei, R., & Huang, J. (2008, April 16-19). Profiling user responses to mobile TV: Effects of individual differences, mobility and technology cluster on critical mass. Paper presented at the 53rd Convention of Broadcast Education Association, Las Vegas, NV.

Wei, R., & Lo, V. (2006). Staying connected while on the move: Cell phone use and social connectedness. *New Media & Society*, 8(1), 53-77.

Yang, K., & Kong, Y. (2006). Exploring factors influencing Internet users' adoption of Internet television in Taiwan. *First Monday*, 11(3). Retrieved April 18, 2008, from http://www.uic.edu/htbin/cgiwrap/bin/ojs/index.php/fm/article/view/1319?.(2003).

EDITORS

SHUHUA ZHOU is a professor of telecommunication and film at the University of Alabama, where he serves as the dean of graduate studies in the College of Communication and Information Sciences. His primary research area is human cognition of mediated messages. His research concentrates on three areas: the representation, utilization, and manipulation of information; the basic processes of cognition, including perception, attention and memory; and individual and situational differences in cognition. He has published numerous articles in journals, including *Media Psychology*, *Communication Research*, *Journal of Broadcasting & Electronic Media*, *Journalism & Mass Communication Quarterly*, *Journal of Advertising*, and *Mass Communication & Society*. He is the co-editor of a bilingual book, *Continuity and change: Perspectives on journalism and mass communication education*, and has written many book chapters. Before going into teaching, he worked in television news. In 2007 the Guangdong TV Artists' Association recognized him as one of the 100 Best TV Hosts for his work as anchor and director of the English News program at Guangdong TV Station in Guangzhou, P. R. China, from 1988 to1993. He received his Ph.D. in mass communication from Indiana University.

WM. DAVID SLOAN is a professor of journalism at the University of Alabama. He is the founder of the Southeast Journalism Conference, a student-oriented organization of sixty university journalism departments, and the American Journalism Historians Association. He has published more than thirty other books, among them *Historical Methods in Mass Communication* and *The Media in America*, the leading textbook in communication history. He is co-editor of the seven-volume series "History of American Journalism." He has also served a five-year term as editor of the journal *American Journalism*. He has written more than eighty articles and papers and has been recognized with research awards for several of them. He has received two *Choice* awards for outstanding academic books, and his book *American Journalism History* won an Amercan Library Association "Best Bibliographies in History" award. In 1998 he received the AJHA's Kobre Award for lifetime achievement. The AJHA also recognizes him with its annual "Sloan Outstanding Faculty Research Paper" award. He is profiled in the book *Mass Communication Education*, edited by Michael Murray and Roy Moore, as one of nineteen national "leaders in mass communication education," and in 2010 the AJHA gave him its National Award for Teaching Excellence. He has served as national president of both the AJHA and Kappa Tau Alpha, the mass communication honor society. On its ninetieth anniversary, KTA selected him as one of the five most important members in its history. He received his Ph.D. in mass communication and United States history from the University of Texas.

AUTHORS

SEAN BAKER is a professor of journalism at Central Michigan University. He has also taught at the University of Kentucky and Towson University. He is a former data analyst for numerous public opinion research firms. His academic research focuses on visual communication, crime and the media, new media theory, and race, class, and gender. He received his Ph.D. in communication from the University of Washington.

SAMUEL D. BRADLEY is an assistant professor of advertising at Texas Tech University. A former reporter and editor for the *Las Cruces Sun-News*, *Modesto Bee*, and *Albuquerque Journal*, he also worked as an advertising research analyst. His research — which focuses on the cognitive processing of media and psychophysiology — has been published in the *Journal of Advertising*, *Media Psychology*, *Communication Methods and Measures*, and *Human Communication Research*. He received his Ph.D. in mass communications and cognitive science from Indiana University.

LARRY L. BURRISS is a professor of journalism at Middle Tennessee State University. A former lieutenant colonel in the United States Air Force, he is particularly interested in issues of media and national security. He is the author of two books, *Newscraft* and *Controversies of the Music Industry*, and has written chapters for five others. He has published in *Journalism Quarterly*, *Journalism Educator*, *Visual Communication Quarterly*, *Journal of Visual Literacy*, *Popular Culture Review*, *Journal of Research in Childhood Education*, *Academic Leader*, *School Administrator*, *Temp Digest*, and *Scott Stamp Monthly*. He received his Ph.D. from Ohio University and J.D. from Concord Law School.

DAVID R. DAVIES is a professor of journalism and dean of the Honors College at the University of Southern Mississippi. A former reporter for the *Arkansas Gazette*, he specializes in the history of American newspapers since World War II and media coverage of the civil rights movement. He has written two books, *The Press and Race: Mississippi Journalists Confront the Movement* and *The Postwar Decline of American Newspapers, 1945-1965*. He received his Ph.D. in media history from the University of Alabama.

DENNIS DAVIS is a professor of communications at Pennsylvania State University. He has held faculty and administrative positions at Cleveland State, Southern Illinois, North Dakota, and Otago University in New Zealand. He was editor of the *Journal of Broadcasting and Electronic Media* and a Fulbright Senior Lecturer (Netherlands/Belgium). He has coauthored books including *The Effects of Mass Communication on Political Behavior* (with Sidney Kraus) and *Mass Communication Theory: Foundations, Ferment and Future* (with Stanley Baran). His research interests include global media, new media, political communication and media theory. He received his Ph.D. in mass communication from the University of Minnesota.

KENNETH O. DOYLE is an associate professor of journalism and mass communication and director of the Communications Research Division, School of Journalism and Mass Communication, University of Minnesota-Twin Cities. He specializes in research methods, differential psychology, and financial psychology. In addition to refereed journal articles, he is author/editor of the book *The Social Meanings of Money and Property: In search of a talisman* and of "The Meanings of Money," "Ethnicity and Money," "Psychology and the New Media," and "Psychology and the New Media, Volume 2," all special issues of *American Behavioral Scientist*. He is founding president of the Association for Financial Psychology, web co-editor for Transformative Consumer Research, and president of the Minnesota Association of Scholars. He received his Ph.D. in psychology from the University of Minnesota.

LOUISA HA is a professor and Acting Chair of the Department of Telecommunications at Bowling Green State University. She is Associate Editor of *Journalism & Mass Communication Quarterly*. A former Research Director at the Gallup Organization and Media Manager at Leo Bur-

nett China, she specializes in media convergence and media management, media business models, international advertising, online advertising, and audience research. Her edited book, *Webcasting Worldwide: Business Models of an Emerging Global Medium*, won the 2007 AEJMC Robert Picard Award for Books and Monographs in Media Management and Economics. She has also received the AEJMC Barry Sherman Teaching Award for Innovation and Excellence in Media and Management. She received her Ph.D. in mass media from Michigan State University.

ANTHONY HATCHER is an associate professor of communications at Elon University. A former newspaper reporter who covered the religion beat, he specializes in religion, media, and popular culture. He also teaches public speaking and interviewing. He is the coauthor (with David Copeland) of the book *Mass Communication in the Global Age*, now in its second edition. He received his Ph.D. in mass communication research from the University of North Carolina at Chapel Hill.

VANESSA DE MACEDO HIGGINS JOYCE is an assistant professor in the Journalism Division at Southern Methodist University in Dallas. Her research has been published in *Journalism, Brazilian Journalism Research, Media Tenor Forschungsbericht* and the book Women, Men, and *News: Divided and Disconnected in the News Media Landscape*. She has worked as an analyst for two major public opinion research companies analyzing local, national, and international studies. She received her Ph.D. in journalism from the University of Texas at Austin in 2009.

DENNIS F. KINSEY is Director of Public Diplomacy and an associate professor of public relations at Syracuse University. A former vice president of a Cleveland-based public opinion research firm, he directed policy and planning studies in the public sector, communication and marketing studies for corporate and institutional clients, projects for educational institutions, ballot issues, and political candidate campaigns. He has published in *Corporate Reputation Review,* the *Journal of Advertising Research*, *Journalism Educator*, *Political Communication*, *Political Psychology*, and *Operant Subjectivity*. He received his Ph.D. in communication from Stanford University.

CATHERINE A. LUTHER is an associate professor in the School of Journalism and Electronic Media at the University of Tennessee. She is the author of the book *Press Images, National Identity, and Foreign Policy: A Case Study of U.S.-Japan Relations from 1955-1995*, and has published in such journals as *Journalism & Mass Communication Quarterly* and *Journal of Communication*. In 2007, she was awarded a Fulbright grant to conduct research on media coverage of anti-terrorism legislation and public opinion in Japan. She received her Ph.D. from the University of Minnesota.

GILBERT D. MARTINEZ is an assistant professor of journalism and mass communication at Texas State University-San Marcos. He is a former reporter with *The Jersey Journal* in Jersey City, N.J. His research areas include shield laws, reporter's privilege, and journalism ethics. He received his J.D. from Fordham University.

BRIAN PARKER is an assistant professor of advertising and public relations at Florida State University. He has extensive field experience as an advertising research analyst and media relations coordinator. His research interests are in consumer behavior, branding, and statistical analysis; and he has most recently published in *The Journal of Consumer Marketing*. He received his Ph.D. in mass communication from the University of Florida.

KATE PEIRCE is a professor of journalism and mass communication at Texas State University-San Marcos, where she teaches undergraduate and graduate courses in research methods. Before going into teaching, she worked as a newspaper reporter and public relations practitioner in Florida. Her primary research area is gender and media; and she was the first to research teen magazines, which then became a popular topic among media researchers. She has published in journals such as *Sex Roles*, *Journalism & Mass Communication Quarterly*, and *Journalism and Mass Communication Educator*. She received her Ph.D. from the University of Texas.

JAMES POKRYWCZYNSKI is an associate professor at Marquette University. He teaches undergraduate and graduate courses in advertising planning and research. He has published research articles in journals covering advertising, marketing, promotion, and communication on subjects such as couponing, irritating commercials, job satisfaction among advertising practitioners, sports and event marketing, and product placement in movies and television. He has spoken to more than a dozen marketing trade organizations on sports sponsorship and product placement. He received his Ph. D. from the University of Georgia.

MICHAEL RYAN is a professor of communication at the University of Houston. Before going into teaching, he worked as a reporter for the San Angelo, Texas, *Standard-Times* and Long News Service, an Austin news bureau. His specialty is communication ethics and writing, and he has published (with James W. Tankard) two books, *Basic News Reporting* and *Writing for Print and Digital Media*. His articles have appeared in *Journalism & Mass Communication Quarterly*, *Journalism & Mass Communication Educator*, *Journal of Mass Media Ethics*, *Journalism & Mass Communication Monographs*, and other scholarly and professional journals. He received his Ph.D. from Southern Illinois University.

MEGHAN S. SANDERS is an assistant professor of mass communication at Louisiana State University. She has conducted experimental and survey research specializing in cognitive processing of and emotional responses to entertainment media; and she has published chapters in two books, *The Horror Film* and *Psychology of Entertainment*. She received her Ph.D. in mass communication from Pennsylvania State University.

CLIFF SHALUTA is an associate professor and coordinator of the advertising and public relations programs at Western Kentucky University. He has written for various publications on the topics of advertising and marketing. He was awarded an Advertising Educational Foundation (AEF) fellowship in 2007 to work two weeks with the Young & Rubicam advertising agency in New York City and with VML, an interactive advertising agency that is part of the WPP Group in Kansas City. His research interests are in the field of social media. He received his M.A. in marketing communications from Marshall University.

NATALIE (TALIA) JOMINI STROUD is an assistant professor of communication studies at the University of Texas at Austin and Assistant Director of the Annette Strauss Institute for Civic Participation. Her research has appeared in *Political Communication*, *Public Opinion Quarterly*, and the *Journal of Communication*. She is the author of the book *Niche News*. She received her Ph.D. in communication from the University of Pennsylvania.

JUDITH SYLVESTER is an associate professor of mass communication at Louisiana State University. She is the author of the books *The Media and Hurricanes Katrina and Rita: Lost and Found* and *Directing Health Care Messages toward African Americans, Attitudes toward Health Care and the Mass Media*, and coauthor of *Women Journalists at Ground Zero: Covering Crisis* and *Reporting from the Front: The Media and The Military*. She has been named an LSU Rainmaker for being among the top researchers at LSU. She received her Ph.D. in journalism from the University of Missouri.

TRACY TUTEN is an associate professor of marketing at East Carolina University. She is the author of the book *Advertising 2.0: Social Media Marketing in a Web 2.0 World*; and her research has appeared in such journals as *Psychology & Marketing, The Journal of Business Research,* and *Social Science Computer Review,* among others. During her tenure teaching at Virginia Commonwealth University, she won VCU's Excellence in Scholarship award. She has twice served as a Fulbright Scholar (in Korea in 2001 and in Argentina in 2007). She has won two national awards for teaching excellence as well as a university-wide award. She received her Ph.D. in business administration from VCU.

GEORGE WATSON is an emeritus Parents Association professor of political science in the School of Journalism and Telecommunication at Arizona State University. His books include *Empirical Political Inquiry, Statistical Inquiry,* and *Shaping America: The Politics of Supreme Court Appointments*. He is a past president of the International Society for Exploring Teaching and Learning, the founding director of Arizona's Wakonse teaching fellowship, and a charter member of ASU's Distinguished Teaching Academy. He received his Ph.D. from Duke University.

RAN WEI is the Gonzales Brothers Professor of Journalism at the University of South Carolina. A recognized scholar in the emerging field of mobile communication, he specializes in adoption, use, and impact of new media technology. His publications include forty refereed journal articles and book chapters and one co-authored book, *The Chinese Journalist in Transition*. He is on the editorial boards of four journals in mass communication. A former TV reporter, he serves as a media consultant. He received his Ph.D. in mass communication from Indiana University.

Index of People

Index of Topics

Glossary of Terms

Acquaintance knowledge — Information acquired through actual contact

Administrative rules — Rules and regulations promulgated by administrative agencies

Agenda setting theory — Media audience generally perceives the items on the media agenda to be more important than issues receiving less media attention

Alternative hypothesis — A statement that predicts either differences between groups or a relationship between variables; represented by H_a

American Association of Advertising Agencies — Founded in 1917, the national trade association representing the advertising agency business in the United States

American Jurisprudence (Am. Jur. 2d) — A legal encyclopedia detailing about 400 legal topics

American Law Reports (A.L.R.) — Publication that contains leading cases on particular topics as well as descriptions from various jurisdictions of those cases

American Press Institute — Founded by newspaper publishers in 1946 and devoted to the training and development of journalism professionals and educators

Amertest — Research firm specializing in creative testing of print and television advertisements

Analog audio — A representation of an object, sound or other information in intensity and / or frequency

Analysis of Variance (ANOVA) — A statistical technique that compares differences in mean scores of a dependent variable for more than two groups

Analytical survey — A survey designed to explain and/or predict attitudes, opinions, beliefs, or phenomena

Annotated bibliography — A list of the printed materials on a topic area that includes brief summaries of each article, book, or other items included

Appellate Court — Court to which a lower court decision is appealed

Applied research — Research conducted to solve real-world problems

Arbitrary assignment — In experiments, assignment of participants to one of two or more groups without any apparent purpose or pattern

Arbitron — Research firm that collects radio listener data; similar to Nielsen for television viewership

Archives — A repository of unpublished primary sources and other records

Association of National Advertisers — An association leading the marketing community by providing its members insights, collaboration and advocacy

Asymmetrical communication — Targeted communication designed according to the audience's levels of knowledge, predispositions and behaviors

Attitude scales — Survey based techniques used to provide quantitative measurements of peoples' predispositions to act in specific ways

Attribute — A characteristic of a variable. Attributes of sex, for example, are male and female

Attribution of meaning — The process of constructing meaning

Audience — Consumers of media

Audimeter — An electronic device developed by the A.C. Nielsen Company in 1942 to measure radio audiences

Audit Bureau of Circulations — Non-profit association of advertisers, ad agencies, and publishers

Auditorium test — Music tests held in an auditorium in which participants are asked to evaluate recurrents (recently popular songs) and oldies

Auteur analysis — Research that examines texts that are created by a single person or media corporation by looking at how the creators' personal signature and values are entrenched in content

Autonomy — The right of a potential research subject not to participate in a research study

Average — In statistics, any measure of central tendency; often used imprecisely to refer to the arithmetic mean

Average Quarter Hour (AQH) — The average number of persons or households tuned in to a specific station for at least 5 minutes during a 15-minute time segment

Basic research — Research conducted to generate general knowledge

Behavioral targeting — A method of media placement using surfing history along with other consumer research to place web ads at optimal locations

Belden Associates circulation — The average number of copies of a publication (newspaper or magazine) that is printed for distribution

Biasing effect — Within the context of questionnaire design, the effect of prompting respondents to answer in a particular manner

Bibliography — A list of the printed materials (books, articles, etc.) on a given topic or subject area

Blue Book — Legal stylebook published by *Harvard Law Review*. Considered the standard for creating legal citations

Boolean logic — A symbolic logic system of operators that act like floodgates, allowing and inhibiting record retrieval in a database search

Brand attachment Q (Product Q) — Measurement of consumer feelings about brand and company names

Bricks & mortar library — A building that houses traditional library materials such as books, newspapers, magazines as well as contemporary information sources like digitally accessible materials

Broadcast Advertiser Reports (BAR) — Research organization monitoring broadcast advertising expenditures and the placement of ads

Cable Q — Measurement of the familiarity and appeal of all major cable networks and programs

Callout research — Test for music that is currently playing on the air

Cartoon Q — Measurement of the familiarity and appeal of cartoon characters

Case — In legal terms, a judicial proceeding; in content analysis, one of whatever the unit of analysis is. If the unit of analysis is people, a case is a person.

Categorical data — Another term for nominal data

Census — In sampling, a census takes all members of a population

Central limit theorem — The distribution of an average tends to be normal, if enough samples of such an average is taken

Central tendency — In statistics, the most typical or representative attribute of a particular variable within a set of cases

Central tendency error — The tendency to avoid the extremes of a rating scale, that is, to concentrate on the middle of the scale

Closed-ended questions — Survey questions that require respondents to choose from a listed selection of responses

Cluster sampling — Initially sampling natural groups or groups with similar features before again sampling members from each group

Code — A set of rules that assists in understanding a sign

Code of Federal Regulations (C.F.R.) — A compilation of federal agency rules and regulations

Codebook — A document with formally written instructions (codes) for how coders should systematically evaluate each coding unit in a content analysis

Coding categories — The options connected with each code in a content analysis

Coding unit — The segment of a message chosen to be categorized individually in a content analysis

Common law — Judge-made law. Law as determined by the court

Community tapestry — Profiling system using various consumer research and zip codes to map concentrations of consumer groups. Similar to PRIZM

Competitive activity research — Media spending estimates organized by key industries and major brands

Computer-assisted reporting (CAR) — The journalistic practice of using computers to search databases to create original news stories

Concealment — A practice used by experimenters to shield the purpose of a study without using deception

Concept — An abstract idea

Conceptual definition — Abstract definition of a variable

Conceptualization — Definitions of key ideas, themes, patterns, etc., that will be looked for in a research study

Concurrent validation — Meaning attributed to one measure by contemporaneous connection with another

Concurring opinion — A written opinion supporting a court decision

Confederate — A person posing as a participant in a study who is, in fact, an associate of the experimenter

Confounding variable — An item that may affect the results of an experiment, which is not taken into account by the experimenter

Consistency — Agreement pattern in a body of data; reproducibility

Constitution — The supreme law in a jurisdiction, generally a country or state

Construct — An abstract idea too big to be directly observable

Construct validation — Process by which meaning is attributed to hypothetical constructs

Constructivism — Philosophical approach that emphasizes personal perception over empirical evidence

Consumer research — Used to help create an accurate profile of a target market

Content analysis — A method of scholarship that involves studying material that has already been published or broadcast

Content validation — Meaning attributed to a measure by the opinions and judgments of experts

Contingency table — A distribution of cases across the attributes of two or more variables at a time

Continuous variable — A variable that can take any value

Contrast effect — The tendency to let one's memories of a person exert undue influence on one's perception of a stimulus person

Control — The ability (or responsibility) of an experimenter to eliminate or hold constant confounding variables in an experiment

Control group — The group that does not receive the experimental manipulation

Convenience sample — A purposive sample of people easily accessible to the researcher

Convergence — The merging of traditional media with new, interactive media

Corpus Juris Secundum (C.J.S.) — A legal encyclopedia that attempts to link all reported United States cases to a series of encyclopedia-like topics

Covert observation — Concealed observation with no researcher participation

Covert participation — Concealed observation conducted by a researcher who participates in the activity of interest

CPM — Advertising cost-efficiency metric that computes the cost the advertiser pays to reach 1,000 viewers or listeners

CPP — An advertising cost-efficiency measure to compare the cost the advertiser pays for each rating point

Criterion-oriented validation — Meaning attributed by association with a known measure

Critical value — A value that represents the portion of a distribution that corresponds to the significance level

Cronbach's alpha — A measure of internal consistency reliability

Crosstabs table — See **contingency table**

Cultural studies — A broad category of research that examines social relations through the lens of culture

Culture — A shared set of values, beliefs, and norms that exist in a society

CUME — The total number of different people who tuned to a particular broadcast for at least 5 minutes during a given daypart over a period time

Cumulative nature of science — An aspect of science in which knowledge is achieved by replication and validation

Data mining — A research technique that utilizes statistical and proprietary software programs to discover hidden patterns

Database — An electronic collection of information

that provides a logical system for data retrieval and management

Database query — An act of requesting information from a database

Dead Q — A measurement of current familiarity and appeal of deceased personalities

Debriefing — Telling participants the purpose of a concealed study after the study is complete

Deception — A practice used by experimenters to mask the true purpose of a study

Decoding — Meaning that audiences derive from messages

Deconstruction — An analysis of content with the goal of looking for meaning and insights as to how audiences may interpret the message

Deductive research — Research conducted to test theory

Defendant — The person who is sued or against whom a lawsuit is begun

Degrees of freedom — A statistical term that represents the number of scores in a statistical test that can possibly vary in value

Demographics — Individual or audience characteristics such as gender, age, and education level

Deontology — An approach to making ethical decisions in strict terms of right and wrong

Dependent variable — The item that is measured in an experiment

Descriptive survey — An exploratory survey designed to describe and/or estimate current attitudes, opinions, beliefs, or phenomena

Designated Market Area (DMA) — A trademarked term used by Nielsen to mean an exclusive geographic area in which the home market television stations hold a dominance of total hours viewed

Diary method — A data collection method in which participants write down the names of the shows and channels that they watched or listened to in a specific time period

Dicta/Dictum — Language in an opinion that is not necessary to that opinion

Digital audio — The representation of information in binary form

Digitalized archives — Archives that are searchable online and indexed in databases

Digitization — The process of converting information ranging from text, graphics, image, music, voice, video to data into a series of zeroes and ones

Directional hypothesis — A hypothesis that states the nature of difference between groups or relationships between variables

Discourse analysis — Research examining verbal and written language usages

Discrete variable — A variable that can only take finite number of values

Dissenting opinion — A written opinion opposed to a court decision

Dominant position — When an audience member decodes the message in accordance with the encoding of the message

Double negatives — The use of two negatives within a single statement

Double-barreled question — In a survey, asking two questions in one questionnaire item

EBSCOhost — An online database that links to many other specialized databases

Effect size — A statistical term that describes the magnitude to which variables are interdependent or associated with one another

E-focus groups — See **Online focus group**

Electronic database — A collection of digitized information organized for ease of use and rapid retrieval via a computer

Elements — In survey, the individual members of a population

E-mail interviewing — Interviewing of sources via e-mail for collection of in-depth data

E-mail surveys — The recruitment of participants, distribution of questionnaires, and collection of response questionnaires via e-mail

Empirical methods — Methods that use observations of the social world to measure attributes of objects

Empirical nature of science — An aspect of science, in which only observable phenomena are studied

Empiricism (or **scientism**) — A strategy for doing social science research that favors the use of quantitative data and observations

Encoding — Meaning that content producers put into messages

Error — In statistics, factors that inhibit the clear and meaningful understanding of a variable

Ethnography — The use of field work in order to study human societies

Ethos — The appeal of a communication based on the character and charisma of the communicator

Experimental demand — The likelihood that a participant will anticipate the purpose of a study and respond accordingly

Explanatory research — Research aiming to find answers to the why question

Exploratory research — Preliminary research to find out patterns and underlying themes

External criticism — In history, a process aimed at determining the authenticity of a record, that is, whether a document is what it appears to be

External validity — The extent to which the results of a study relate to the real world

EyeTrack07 — A cognitive study conducted by the Poynter Institute to gain insight into how readers scan both printed and online newspaper content

Factorial analysis of variance (ANOVA) — A form of analysis of variance that examines between-group and within-group variability of more than one independent variable on a dependent variable

Factorial design — An experiment that uses two or more independent variables, or factors

Federal reporter — Publication that contains appellate court decisions

Federal Supplement — Contains selected decisions by federal district courts

Feministism — A theory on how communication oppresses or liberates women

Field — In a relational database, a field represents a single piece of information

Field experiment — An experimental study that occurs in a natural location

Field observation — Observation of the behavior associated with a specific phenomenon

File — In a relational database, a file, also called a table, is a complete set of records

Finding aid — Part of a legal publication that references cases used in that publication

Focus groups — Small group discussions conducted by a trained interviewer for the purpose of exploring a research topic

Footnote style — In research reports, citations that are placed as footnotes rather than in the body of the text

Format studies — Research conducted for radio stations to determine the success of programming format

Frequency — In audience research, the number of times a program or a commercial is being exposed to the audience

F-statistic — Test statistic for analysis of variance that represents the ratio of between-group variability to within-group variability

Gallop & Robinson — Research firm specializing in consumer testing of print advertisements

Generalizability theory — Cronbach and colleagues' general statement of consistency across all dimensions

Generic analysis — Research that focuses on broad categories of related media content

Goodness-of-fit test — A statistical procedure that compares the observed distribution of a variable or variables with some hypothesized or expected distribution

Gross impressions — The total number of audience

exposures to a program or a commercial for two or more time periods

Gross rating points — The total of audience ratings of a program or a commercial for two or more time periods

Halo/Discrepancy effect — The tendency to focus on the overall stimulus versus its discrete parts

Headnote — In legal research, explanatory material located before a court decision

Hegemony — The process by which dominant classes gain consent to rule over subordinate classes in a society

Historiography — The study of history; also, the body of works written about history; also, the interpretations (or explanations) of history

History — In experiments, the events affecting participants that occur between observations during an experiment

Hits — The number of records retrieved from a database

Hooks — Short segments of songs usually lasting 5-15 seconds and representing a song in radio or music research

Household Using Television (HUT) — The percentage of TV households who are tuned to any TV station at a time period

How-to knowledge — Procedural knowledge

Hypothesis — A tentative explanation of a phenomenon or a supposition about associations that might exist between two or more concepts

Hypothesis testing — Statistical procedure designed to test a claim through analyzing and interpreting collected data

Ideological research — Research conducted to support (or to attack) predetermined political, social, or cultural values and attitudes

Ideology — A construction of norms, values, and customs that define and organize social reality

Implicit theory — Assumptions that particular traits and behaviors go together

Independent sample t-test — A form of t-test that compares differences in means between two sample groups representing nominal-level attributes of an independent variable

Independent variable — The item that is manipulated in an experiment in order to produce a change in the dependent variable

Indexes — Research materials (articles, books) consolidated from multiple sources and sorted based on subject matter

Indicator — A looser word for "measure," less frequently used, emphasizing the uncertainty of measurement

Inductive research — Research conducted to build theory

Informed consent — The right of a research subject to know enough about a study to make a reasonable decision to participate or not

In-house research — Studies that a particular organization plans and executes internally without reliance on outside research organizations or businesses

Injunction — A court order that either requires someone to do something, or prohibits the person from doing something

Instrument — Another word for "measure," used especially with regard to tests and questionnaires

Intensive interviews — One-on-one discussions conducted by a trained interviewer

Interaction effect — An effect on a dependent variable that is produced by multiple independent variables working together

Interactivity — Two-way communications or feedback between users and source

Inter-coder reliability — Measurement of the extent to which coders agree in their coding in a content analysis

Interlibrary loan — A department of university libraries that borrows materials from other university libraries for its patrons

Internal criticism — In history, a process aimed at determining if a record is trustworthy

Internal validity — The extent to which an experiment measures what it is designed to actually measure

Internet2 — A networking consortium based in Michigan for the purpose of education and high-speed data transfer

Interpretative research — Research that focuses on how meanings are created by audiences

Interval data — Data that name and order, with *equal intervals* between scale points

Intervals — Distance between points on a scale

Interview — A conversation, conducted by a questioner, in which facts or statements are elicited from another

In-text style — A citation style in which references are placed in the body of the text. Used in legal briefs and court decisions

Journalistic questions — Who, what, when, where, why, and how, often referred to as the 5Ws and 1H

J-STOR — An online database of communication journals and publications

Judgment sample — A sampling technique that picks elements because they possess a characteristic of interest to the researcher

Key Performance Indicator (KPI) — Benchmark measurement used to evaluate the performance of a plan or project

KeyCite — A series of links between cases and concepts used in legal publications by the West company

Keywords — Specific words related to a subject of interest

Kids Product Q — Measurement of overall brand or company appeal among children 6-11 and teens 12-17

Laboratory experiment — An experimental study that occurs in a laboratory

Laddering — An interviewing technique that involves building subsequent questions on the answers to the previous questions

Law review — A legal periodical usually published quarterly, providing in-depth treatment of legal issues and cases

Lawyers Edition (L.Ed. 2d) — An unofficial series of Supreme Court reports

Leading National Advertisers, Inc. (LNA) — Research organization that provides competitive advertising spending reports to paid subscribers

Leading question — A question that suggests a certain response

Legal citation — The title and reference to a case, statute, law review, etc.

Legal encyclopedia — A publication that gives brief overviews of legal topics

Legislative history — A record of committee hearings, debates, and votes relating to a particular law

Leniency/Stringency effect — The tendency to be too gentle/harsh in rating a stimulus

Level — In experimental studies, the number of manipulations within an independent variable

Leveling/Sharpening — A predecessor term for halo/discrepancy effect

Levels of measurement — Classification that says what information numbers contain and what operations may properly be carried out on them

Lexis/Nexis — An online database with searchable documents from more than 32,000 legal, news, and business sources

Likert scale — A questionnaire format that allows uniformity in the responses to questions by providing standardized response categories

Literature review — A summary and interpretation of the published materials on a topic

Logical error — A predecessor term for "implicit theories"

Logical positivism — A school of philosophy advocating a strict form of positivism in which modern forms of logic were combined with empirical observation to provide a foundation for all forms of science

Logos — The appeal of a communication to reason, scientific competency, and logic

Magazine Impact Research Service (MIRS) — Research firm specializing in reader measurement studies

Magazine Publishers of America — An industry association for consumer magazines (established in 1919)

Main effect — An effect on a dependent variable that is produced by one independent

Manuscript — In history, a document in the handwriting of its author

Maturation — Changes that take place among participants over a period of time between observations in an experimental study

Mean — The arithmetic average; total score divided by the number of elements

Means-end chaining — An interview technique that explores the connections individuals have with issues, objects, behaviors, and attitudes

Measure — Device for attaching numbers to constructs so they can be analyzed and understood

Measures of maximum performance — Measures that test how many answers you can get right

Measures of typical performance — Measures that tap into your usual thoughts, feelings, and behaviors

Media multitasking — The behavior of engaging in more than one media activity

Media Ratings Council — An industry-funded organization reviewing and accrediting audience rating services

Mediamark Research & Intelligence — A research firm studying American consumers

Median — Point below which half the elements occur

Metered markets — Local TV markets where Nielsen uses set-tuning meters or people meters to record TV viewership

Method of authority — Learning through the assumed expertise of another person

Method of intuition — Accepting information based on instinct and hunches or psycho-logic means

Method of personal experience — Learning through the five senses

Method of tenacity — Learning through knowledge passed from history

Method of tradition — See **the method of tenacity**

Methodological research — Conducted to generate discussion and insight into various research methods

Minnesota Opinion Research — A media research

and consulting firm

Mode — The highest-frequency element; the most "popular" number

MP3 - A sound file that has been compressed through MP3 encoding, making the files smaller and easier to send across the Internet

MRI MediaMark Research — A firm specializing in consumer and media research

Narrative analysis — Research that focuses on the storylines, characters, plots, conflicts, action, and the values and morals that make up media content

National Newspaper Publishers Association — An umbrella organization for African-American newspaper publishers

Negotiated position — Decoding of a message agrees in general with the encoding of the message, but may disagree with specific points of the message

Nelson Media Research — A research company owned by VNU, a Dutch research conglomerate, providing national and local TV ratings

New media — Channels and outlets for disseminating information and entertainment that rely on digital communication technologies with the computer at its core

Newspaper Association of America — A nonprofit organization of the newspaper industry in America

Nielsen Station Index (NSI) — The most commonly used report for local TV market ratings supplied by Nielsen Media company

Nielsen/Net Ratings — A service of the Nielsen Company that monitors consumer behavior online for clients

Nominal data — Data that name or categorize

Non-directional hypothesis — A kind of alternative hypothesis that does not state the nature of either difference between groups or relationships between variables

Nonprobability sample — A sample that is not selected based on probability theory

Nonprobability sampling — Various methods of sampling in which each member of a population does not have the same chance of being selected for a sample

Null hypothesis — An implied statement or claim that alludes to either no difference or change between groups, or no relationship between variables; represented by H_0

Objective nature of science, the — Science should be conducted without the interference of personal bias

Objectivity — The condition of being untainted by actions of the mind or free of subjective influence

Observation — A measurement of the dependent variable within a study

Offline methods — Conventional research methods such as focus groups, content analysis, surveys or experiments

Online focus group — Group interview conducted online involving video-conferencing facilities

Online research — Research via computer-mediated networks and Web-based interface in virtual environment

Online research methods — Applying conventional research methods to collect data on the Internet using specially developed Web-based software

Open-ended questions — Survey questions that require respondents to fill in answers using their own words

Operational definition — Concrete, measurable definition of a variable

Operationalization — A specific description of what is being measured in a study

Operationalize — To specify a set of steps that will permit the observation or measurement of a construct

Opinion/Court opinion — A ruling by a court in a legal case

Oppositional position — Decoding of the message is in conflict with the encoding of the message

Oral history — The systematic collection of memories and personal stories of historical significance through firsthand interviews with participants

Ordinal data — Data that name and order

Original source — In history, an original document (as opposed to a reproduced one); an unpublished primary source

Overt observation — A non-concealed observation with no researcher participation

Overt participation — Non-concealed observation with researcher participation in the activity of interest

Paired sample t-test — A form of t-test that compares two related groups or the same group twice, on a dependent measure

Paradigmatic analysis — Examination of the connections between signs and how the connections create coherent meaning

Parallel citation — In legal research, a citation format that includes multiple reporters

Pass-along rates — The number of readers for each copy of a newspaper or magazine

Pathos — The appeal of a communication to an emotional connection that is often value laden

Peer review — The evaluation of the quality of a researcher's book, article or grant proposal by fellow researchers

People Meter — A recording device used by Nielsen Research that reports both a TV set's channel usage and information about the individuals who were viewing the TV show

Performer Q — A measure of familiarity and appeal of TV personalities

Personal narrative — Firsthand experiences recorded on audio, video, or in print

Personal People Meter (PPM) — A pager-like portable meter that participants wear to automatically record the programs they listened to

Pew Research Center for the People and the Press — An independent opinion research group that studies attitudes toward the press, politics, and public policy issues

Placebo — A fake treatment given to a group whose members believe they are receiving the same treatment as the experimental group

Plagiarism — Using ideas without proper attribution to the original source

Plaintiff — The person bringing a lawsuit

Poll — A survey of people on how they feel about a particular topic

Polysemic sign — A sign that has many meanings

Population — In sampling, everyone or everything that can be studied in a research project

Positioning — The perception consumers have of a particular company or brand

Positioning Advertising Copy Testing (PACT) — Guidelines for creative testing of advertisements developed in 1981 by representatives from various advertising agencies

Positivism — Philosophical approach that emphasizes empirical, observable evidence over personal perception

Postmodernism — A theory arguing that reality and truth are mere social constructions and that culture and society are made up of endless communications that have no true meaning in the real world

Post-positivism — The belief that conjecture and subjectivity can lead to human knowledge, as opposed to strict scientific method and empiricism

Poststructuralism — A theory that states that language is unstable and there are multiple meanings associated with communication

Poynter Institute — A school for journalists, future journalists, and teachers of journalists

Precedent — A court decision that is used as an example in similar cases

Predictive research — Testing a hypothesis that predicts what is going to happen

Predictive validation — Meaning attributed to a new measure by connection with an existing measure

Predictor variable — In survey research, a variable that affects an outcome variable

Present-mindedness — The error of judging the past by views of the present. (Sometimes called "presentism")

Primary material — In legal research, documents containing what the law actually says

Primary research — Original research conducted to address a research question

Primary sampling unit — When sampling more than once, the first sample drawn

Primary source — In history, a document or other source made by an eyewitness or a contemporary to the fact the source records; a contemporaneous record or a record in close proximity to some past occurrence

Principal concepts — The main words and/or phrases that comprise a research topic

Print media — An umbrella term including newspapers, magazines, and books, but may also include newsletters and Internet content

PRIZM — Profiling system that uses various consumer research studies along with ZIP codes to map concentrations of consumer groups

Probability sample — A sample that is drawn in a manner in which every member of a particular population has an equal chance of being included in the sample

Probability sampling — Various methods of sampling in which each member of a population has an equal chance of being selected for a sample

Professional obfuscators — Communication specialists who use bogus research results to confuse an issue to such an extent that no action is taken

Program diagnostics — Evaluations of program elements, characters, storylines for improving the viewer appeal of future episodes, and scheduling strategies

Propositional knowledge — Awareness of certain information

Proprietary research — Research that is sponsored by a single client or a company

Proximity operator — Commands in search queries that instruct databases to find keywords with distance thresholds in a record

Psychographics — Attributes relating to personality, values, attitudes, interests, or lifestyles

Psychological discomfort — An uneasy feeling when one lives in uncertainty

Psyshoanalysis — A psychological theory of communication stating that media messages represent unconscious desires

Public nature of science — An aspect of science in which scientists are obligated to share all data and methodologies so others can evaluate the validity of the study

Public relations — The process of building and maintaining positive relationships, mutual understanding, and open communication between an organization and its publics

Publics — In public relations, the various constituents, customers, and stakeholders that have a connection to, or potential relationship with, the organization

Purposive sample — A nonprobability sample in which participants are chosen because they contain a characteristic of interest to the researcher

P-value — See **significance level**

Q methodology — A method for the study of subjectivity that has participants rank-order various statements of opinion

Q sample — Statements of opinion used in a Q-methodology study

Q scores — Quotient scores of audience likings of programs reported in Marketing Evaluations Inc.'s TVQ studies, expressed as a percentage of the number of respondents who are familiar with the program

Q sort — A rank-ordered Q sample

Qualitative research — Research using non-numbers in analysis

Quantitative research — Research using numbers in analysis

Quasi-experimental design — A study using a design similar to an experiment, without, however, maintaining the control of an experiment

Quasi-interval data — Data that are not quite interval data but close enough to use interval-level statistics

Quota sample — A nonprobability sample in which the researcher surveys a certain number of elements of a group

RACE — An acronym for a public relations process model: short for Research, Action, Communication, and Evaluation

Random assignment — In experiments, assignment to one of two or more groups in which all participants have an equal chance of selection

Random chance hypothesis — A statement of conjecture that typically asserts that any observed relationship between two or more variables or difference between two or more groups is due to chance

Random digit dialing — A simple random sampling technique in which a computer generates random telephone numbers of respondents

Random error — Error that is not patterned

Range — The highest score minus the lowest score; the distance between highest and lowest points

Ranking — Ordering, e.g., from most to least, best to worse (or vice versa)

Rater error — Traits and behaviors of the rater that inhibit his or her reliable and valid description of a stimulus

Rating — In audience research, the percentage of people or households in a population that are tuned to a specific channel at a specific time period

Ratio data — Data that name and order, with equal intervals and a true zero point

Reach — In audience research, the total number or percentage of people or households exposed to a program or a commercial during a specific time period

Readership — The total audience for a print publication

Readex — Research firm specializing in print readership studies

Reception studies — Research that focuses on how audiences interpret messages and how decoding occurs

Record — In a relational database, a complete set of single fields

Relational database — A database using a model structure to organize information

Relevancy sorting — A database system feature that sorts retrieved records by relevance to query information

Reliability coefficient — Quantitative index of consistency in a body of data

Reliability of measurements — The extent to which empirical measurements of objects are consistent, stable, and dependable

Repeated-measures — An experimental design wherein measures are repeatedly drawn from the same participant in order to counteract individual differences

Reporter — In legal research, a published series of court decisions

Research — A systematic process to seek answers to questions and understanding of phenomena

Response bias — Skewed data resulting from certain members of a sample being more willing to complete the survey or respond to the items in a particular way than other members of the sample

Response rate — The number of surveys actually completed by sample members divided by the total number of members in the sample

Restatement — In legal research, a publication designed to provide interpretations and explanations of court rulings

Restraining order — Similar to an injunction, but issued *ex parte*, that is, on the request of one party, without the opposing party having an opportunity to be heard

Rhetorical analysis — Research that examines the power of content by studying the strength the text has to influence audiences

ROPE — An acronym for a public relations process model: short for Research, Objectives, Programming, and Evaluation

Roper Starch Worldwide — Research firm specializing in print readership studies

ROSTE — An acronym for a public relations process model: short for Research, Objectives, Strategies, Tactics, and Evaluation

Sample — A subset of a population; a small portion of all possible people or things to be studied in a research project, usually selected to represent the population of all possible people or things

Sampling — Drawing a portion of elements from a universe of elements (with a representative portion preferred)

Sampling error — Error in sampling due to one or more of the following: chance, sampling techniques, the measuring instrument, the participants, and reporting error

Sampling frame — A list of all the elements, or individual members, in a population

Scarborough Research — A research firm measuring shopping patterns, lifestyles, and media habits of consumers

Scatterplot — A format for displaying a bivariate (two-variable) distribution along a Cartesian two-dimensional coordinate system in which each dot represents the scores of a single case on the two variables

Scientific method — The acquisition of knowledge through systematic and objective means

Scientism — See **empiricism**.

Secondary material — In legal research, explanations of what the law says or does not say

Secondary research — Studies conducted by utilizing previously published resources

Secondary sampling unit — When sampling more than once, the second sample drawn

Secondary source — In history, a document or other source that was not made by an eyewitness or someone contemporaneous to the fact the source records; a source based on primary sources but published later

Segmentation — Categorizing consumers into groups to maximize marketing impact and efficiency

Semiotic analysis — Research that studies individual components of messages and the meanings that are created from them

Share — The percentage of households or persons tuned to a program out of all who are watching TV or listening to radio at the time period

Shepardizing — A process based on Shepard's Citation Service that searches for updated case law to determine whether a case or statute is still "good law"

Sign — The most basic element of communication practices. A sign is composed of a signifier, signified, and code.

Significance level — The probability that results reflect random chance; equivalent to the probability of Type I error

Signified — The meaning that is connected to a signifier

Signifier — An object or word with which meaning is associated

Simmons Market Research Bureau (SMRB) — Organization specializing in consumer and media audience research

Simple random sampling — A process in which each member of a sampling frame is given an equal chance of being included in a sample by selecting a random sample starting point and identifying a sampling interval

Snowball sample — A sample consisting of participants who were recruited for a survey through introductions (in which each participant, beginning with the first, introduces the researcher to another potential participant)

Social desirability — The likelihood that a participant in a study will respond to stimuli in a socially acceptable manner

Special collections — Materials of a unique or special significance that often are stored in a special area of the library

Split-half reliability — Consistency measured by correlating two parts of the same measure

Sports Q — A measurement of the familiarity and appeal of sports personalities

Standard deviation — Interval-level measure of variation; the square root of the variance

Standard error — The standard deviation of means representing an entire sampling distribution

Standardization — The effort to make measuring conditions consistent in order to make for a "level playing field"

Statute — Law emanating from a legislative body ranging from Congress to city councils

Steps of research — The procedures a researcher follows to conduct research

Stimulus material — In research, whatever is presented to a participant in order to generate an attitudinal, behavioral, or physiological reaction

Stratified random sampling — A type of random

sampling in which a population is divided into homogeneous subgroups from which random samples are selected

Structuralism — A theory of communication that focuses on basic elements of communication and how these elements relate to each other

Structured observation — The use of standard, pre-planned measurement techniques to collect data for all observations in a study

Structured Query Language (SQL) — SQL is a common computer language used in relational data-bases for data storage, management, and retrieval

Summary judgment — Judgment issued by a court without a trial

Supreme Court Reports — Unofficial reporter issued by West Publishing

Survey — A research method to poll respondents for their opinions, attitudes, and behaviors

SWOT — An acronym for a marketing evaluation designed to access Strengths, Weaknesses, Opportunities, or Threats for a given product or situation

Syllabus — In legal research, a brief summary of the court's decision prepared by the Reporter of Decisions

Symmetrical communication — In public relations, a two-way process aimed at helping organizations understand the point of view of their publics and helping publics understand the organizations' point of view

Syndicated research — Research conducted with the intent to make the findings available for a fee

Syntagm — A linear sequence of signs

Systematic empirical observation — Repeated use of the same measurement techniques with the goal of obtaining reliable measurements

Systematic Error — Error that is patterned

Systematic nature of science — An aspect of science in which research is conducted following a set of predetermined procedures

Systematic random sampling — A variation of simple random sampling that requires a list of the population, in which each subject is numbered and a mathematical process is used to select participants

Target market — In marketing, a group of consumers designated as key prospects for a specific campaign

Teleology (or **utilitarianism**) — An approach to making ethical decisions in which individuals predict the consequences of different actions and then do what is best for the greatest number of people

Television Quotient (TVQ) — A measurement of the extent an audience likes individual programs

Test statistic — A number that represents the relationship between research variables of interest and how they are expected or presumed to be in reality

Testing effects — The results of participants' experience with the measures of a study between observations

Test-retest reliability — Consistency measured by repeated administration of the same measure

Text — In cultural and critical studies, any form of mediated communication

Textual analysis — A type of content analysis that is used by cultural studies researchers

Textual analysis software — Computer applications that simplify and automate the analysis of digitally coded content

Thick descriptions — Detailed field notes taken during an ethnographic study

Title field searching — A search that restricts a query to specific records in a database

Trade publications — Materials geared specifically to an audience in a particular industry

Transcript — The printed or written record of an oral conversation

Treatise — A publication that contains an in-depth treatment of a particular topic

Treaty — An agreement between two nations

Trial court — A court of original jurisdiction where evidence is introduced

T-test — A statistical test used to determine if the means of two groups are statistically different from each other

Type I error — A kind of error committed when the researcher incorrectly rejects the null hypothesis and accepts the alternative hypothesis; a false positive; also known as alpha error because the chances of committing this kind of error are equal to the significance level

Type II error — A kind of error committed when the researcher incorrectly accepts the null hypothesis and rejects the alternative hypothesis; a false negative; also known as beta error

U.S. Reports — The official version of Supreme Court decisions

UGC (user generated content) — Content produced and distributed on the Internet by users

Unit of analysis — The most basic unit of communication to be observed or analyzed in a content analysis

United States Code (U.S.C.) — The official version of laws passed by Congress

Use of convergent media — Use of a medium broader than the function for which the medium was originally invented

Uses and gratification theory — A theory that assumes that audience members are active and seek information that will somehow benefit them

Utilitarianism (or **teleology**) — See **teleology**

Validity — The property of a measure that truly measures what it purports to measure, that the measure reflects reality

VALS — Psychographic research categorizing consumers on the basis of their values, attitudes, and lifestyles

Variable — A concept that can vary

Variance — Sum of the squared differences from the mean; the total amount of variation in a set of data

Variation — In statistics, the dispersion of a property's various attributes among the cases

Virtual focus groups — See **online focus group**

Volunteer sample — A nonprobability sample in which participants for a research project select themselves for participation

Ways of knowing — Various means of obtaining information or acquiring knowledge

Web 2.0 — Web technologies that facilitate the creation, sharing, and storing of personal and public media content on the Internet, including blogs, RSS, tags, and Wiki

Web analytics — The measurement and evaluation of website traffic to increase usage or to enhance usability

Web surveys — Surveys that invite respondents to visit a website to fill out a digitized questionnaire

Web-based experiments — Use of the Internet to recruit participants, administer stimuli, and collect data

West/Westlaw — In legal research, one of two major publishers (the other being LexisNexis) of court decisions and numerous legal books in both print and electronic form

Within-subjects experiment — An experimental design wherein participants receive all experimental treatments, instead of receiving only particular treatments pertaining to which group they are assigned